AF251390

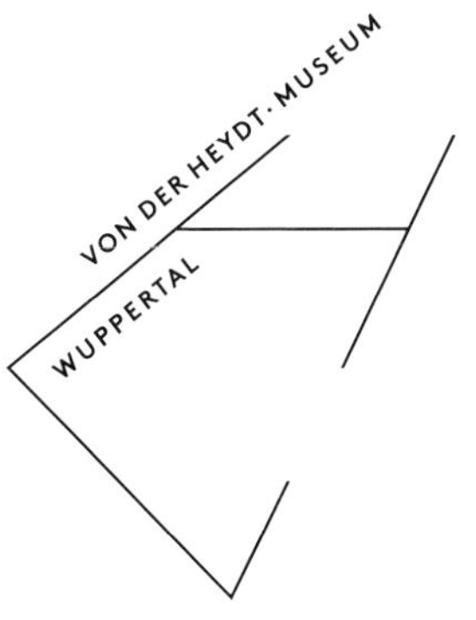

MUSEUM BARBERINI

POTSDAM

A New Art

Photography and Impressionism

Edited by
Ortrud Westheider
Michael Philipp
and Daniel Zamani

Exhibition and catalog:
Ulrich Pohlmann
with Helene von Saldern

Exhibition curator, Wuppertal:
Anna Baumberger

With contributions by
Monika Faber
Dominique de Font-Réaulx
Matthias Krüger
Miriam Leimer
Ulrich Pohlmann
Christine Rottmeier-Keß
Esther Ruelfs
Bernd Stiegler
Daniel Zamani

PRESTEL Munich · London · New York

Lenders

Céline, Aeneas, Heiner Bastian
Kicken Berlin
Staatliche Museen zu Berlin, Kunstbibliothek
Universität der Künste Berlin, Universitätsarchiv
Kupferstich-Kabinett, Staatliche Kunstsammlungen Dresden
Museum Folkwang, Essen
Museum für Kunst und Gewerbe Hamburg
Auer Photo Foundation, Hermance
Universitätsbibliothek Marburg—Dr. Rolf H. Krauss-Forschungsbibliothek /
    Deutsches Dokumentationszentrum für Kunstgeschichte—Bildarchiv
    Foto Marburg
Bibliothèque de l'École nationale des Ponts et Chaussées, Marne-la-Vallée
Münchner Stadtmuseum, Munich
Dietmar Siegert Collection
The Metropolitan Museum of Art, New York
Beaux-Arts de Paris
Bibliothèque historique de la Ville de Paris
Collection Serge Kakou, Paris
Musée des Arts Décoratifs, Paris
Musée d'Orsay, Paris
Musée d'Orsay, Dépôt de la Fondation Dosne-Thiers, Paris
Musée d'Orsay, Dépôt du Mobilier National, Paris
Société française de photographie, Paris
Mayer Collection, Stuttgart
Staatsgalerie Stuttgart
Musée des Beaux-Arts de Troyes
Albertina, Vienna
Photoinstitut Bonartes, Vienna
Österreichische Nationalbibliothek, Vienna

Contents

Foreword

In the West, the nineteenth century marked the beginning of the modern age: rail transport, electrification, and telegraphy had created a dynamic that in turn engendered economic and communicative globalism. The new medium of photography was both linked to the industrial revolution and the increasing dissemination of knowledge, and it was introduced to an international audience at the world's fairs. Photographic exposure and reproduction techniques served the panoramic view specific to the age as well as the encyclopedic desire to document: the possibility of creating collections on any conceivable topic through the medium of photography corresponded to the new need to make knowledge accessible and archivable. Similar to the way that the city centers of Paris, London, Vienna, Budapest, and Munich were transformed by historicizing architecture, the new medium fused tradition and modernity. Museums, libraries, and archives were created. Travelogues, surveys, and maps shaped the era. At the same time as sociology became a subject, social reportage in photography emerged alongside the social novel of literary realism. The rapidly developing natural science reflected the present: what could be more obvious than to put the precision of photography at its service?

Was this a new form of art? Was the new medium, interwoven with the progress of the applied and the useful, to become more than simply an auxiliary science of painting? In 1859 Charles Baudelaire wrote a scathing critique of the first Paris Salon to include photographs. In a fictional argument he had a photographer say, "I want to represent things as they are, or rather as they would be, supposing that I did not exist." Against this, Baudelaire set the answer of a painter from his favored faction of "imaginatives": "I want to illuminate things with my mind, and to project their reflection upon other minds." In this way Baudelaire, a visionary and friend of the Impressionists, established the antagonism between machine and spirit that would continue for decades to come. Even Walter Benjamin's 1936 reflections on the loss of the aura of the work of art in the age of its mechanical reproduction still return to this distinction. And yet the mass reproduction of Impressionist works may very well have been more than welcome to the artists, collectors, and art critics who had been opposed to monopolized exhibitions in the Salon since the 1860s. They had to engage in new distribution channels. Having made their own perception the center of interest, they were closer to the natural sciences and their new publication and information channels than to the academic art establishment.

Sur place: at the beginning of modernism in painting was the commitment to geographical references. No one sold more artworks to the United States than Claude Monet, and yet he declined all invitations to study the American landscape. He felt that he had to be intimately familiar with a landscape to paint it. Monet, just like Berthe Morisot, Camille Pissarro, and Pierre-Auguste Renoir, worked *en plein air* in order to broach the issue of the new relationship between humankind and nature. The result was a painting of pure presence that made individual reactions to changing light and weather phenomena its subject. The Impressionists dedicated their painting to the fleeting moment. This made them natural allies of the photographers. They held their first group exhibition in the former studio of the photographer Nadar on boulevard des Capucines in Paris in 1874. Actors, composers, politicians, and writers—including Baudelaire—were already familiar with the venue because they had been photographed there.

From its early days photography was associated with artistic education. Landscape photographs took the place of drawn *aides-mémoires*. The early photographers had often studied art. The 1981 exhibition *Before Photography: Painting and the Invention of Photography* at the Museum of Modern Art in New York made it clear that instead of emerging from a scientific context, photography was derived from the landscape painting of artists such as John Constable and Camille Corot. The exploration of the medium's perspectival and subjective nature has been the focus ever since, making possible pivotal exhibitions such as *Gustave Caillebotte: An Impressionist and Photography* (Frankfurt am Main and The Hague, 2012–13) and *The Impressionists and Photography* (Madrid, 2019). Nevertheless, the interplay between photography and Impressionism deserves to be explored in more depth.

Similar to cast iron as a new material within the field of architecture, the new medium was versatile. Beyond that, it also offered freedoms that led to its emancipation as an artistic medium in competition with painting. Photographers chose the same motifs as the Impressionists: the forest of Fontainebleau, the cliffs of Étretat, and the modern metropolis of Paris. They too studied the changing light situations, seasons, and meteorological conditions. From the beginning they pursued their artistic ambitions by experimenting with composition and perspective, using different techniques and materials, and employing blurring, dramatization, and montage. Even those who were rooted in local culture were able to capture fleeting moments of universal validity in photographs. Light—the basis of photography—was, like vision itself, a shared theme of painting and photography. The exhibition *A New Art: Photography and Impressionism* at the Museum Barberini and the Von der Heydt-Museum illuminates the artistic emancipation of the new medium from the 1850s through to around 1900, when it became an autonomous art form.

This is the first photography exhibition to be presented at the Museum Barberini since it opened in 2017. The point of departure is the collection of Impressionist and Post-Impressionist paintings by museum founder Hasso Plattner—including works by Gustave Caillebotte, Claude Monet, and Berthe Morisot—which has been on permanent display since September 2020. The Von der Heydt-Museum is one of the few institutions that began to collect Impressionist art early on, setting an example in both Germany and Europe overall. It houses a civic collection in the classical sense. Many top-tier paintings by artists such as Gustave Courbet, Edgar Degas, Édouard Manet, Claude Monet, and Alfred Sisley had already entered its holdings before World War I or were owned by citizens of Wuppertal. We thank our guest curator Ulrich Pohlmann for his dialogical concept tailored to our collections. Our heartfelt thanks go to cocurator Helene von Saldern as well. At the Von der Heydt-Museum the exhibition was curated by Anna Baumberger.

An international symposium held at the Museum Barberini on September 1, 2021, set the stage for this exhibition catalog. In addition to Michael Philipp and Daniel Zamani, the catalog's coeditors, we would like to thank Ulrich Pohlmann, Monika Faber, Dominique de Font-Réaulx, Matthias Krüger, Esther Ruelfs, and Bernd Stiegler for their research, which is now available in printed form in this catalog. We would also like to thank Miriam Leimer for compiling the biographies, Christine Rottmeier-Keß for the glossary entries, and Helene von Saldern and Marie-Louise Monrad Møller for their careful editing.

We would especially like to extend our thanks to those who lent us works for the exhibition. Three institutions were particularly engaged: the Münchner Stadtmuseum in Munich, the Société française de photographie in Paris, and the Photoinstitut Bonartes in Vienna. We are grateful to Ulrich Pohlmann, Vincent Guyot, and Monika Faber for their belief in our project. For their generous loans of iconic photographs, we would also like to thank private collectors Céline, Heiner, and Aeneas Bastian; Serge Kakou; Rolf Mayer; and Dietmar Siegert. We are indebted to numerous other lenders from Austria, France, Germany, Switzerland, and the United States. The exhibition *A New Art: Photography and Impressionism* was made possible at the Von der Heydt-Museum by the support of the Dr. Werner Jackstädt Foundation, Wuppertal. We would like to express our sincere thanks to the foundation board for the benevolence with which it continuously accompanies the museum's development and its program.

We wish our visitors many surprising impressions and insights as they discover a new facet of nineteenth-century art.

<table>
<tr><td>Ortrud Westheider
Director,
Museum Barberini, Potsdam</td><td>Roland Mönig
Director,
Von der Heydt-Museum, Wuppertal</td></tr>
</table>

Ulrich Pohlmann

Rivalry and Emancipation

Photography and the Traditional Fine Arts in the Nineteenth Century

Photography and the fine arts were engaged in productive competition in the nineteenth century. The history of their intertwined development could also be described as a mutual process of emancipation in which photography was to gain temporary acceptance as an artistic form of representation while painting was pushed to redefine its forms of expression.

Although photography had artistic ambitions from the very beginning, nineteenth-century viewers regarded it as a hybrid of science, technology, industry, and art. In addition to painters, scientists were involved in the invention and development of photographic processes. Photographs were also used in various fields such as astronomy, medicine, botany, zoology, archaeology, and criminology. The question of the extent to which photography is an art form has been debated since the mid-nineteenth century. This essay examines the quest to establish photography as an art form on par with painting.

A Powerful Rival

As soon as the invention of the daguerreotype was announced at the Institut de France in Paris on August 19, 1839, the new medium of photography entered into competition with existing image forms. The economic and aesthetic rivalry between the traditional arts and photography is exemplified by Théodore Maurisset's caricature *Daguerreotypomania* (fig. 1). Published in *La Caricature* in December 1839, the drawing reflects the impact of the new invention on the established system of the arts. In this caricature, photography, a symbol of technical progress and modern civilization par excellence, is associated with steam power, railroads, and aeronautics, and situated between fairground amusement and prosperous industry. The consequences for the arts are indicated in a scene depicting engravers hanging from gallows that are for rent and a protester bearing a banner that reads "Down with aquatint." The existential hardships of etchers, lithographers, engravers, and painters of portraits and miniatures that the spread of photographic art reproduction and portraiture had triggered are indicative of the profound changes in existing hierarchies within the visual arts.[1] The profession of painting, as later caricatures also conveyed, was engaged in a grave crisis and cast in the shadow of its powerful new rival: photography. Competition between portrait painters and photographers seemed to escalate around 1860 with the mass distribution of cartes de visite. In Carl Tetzel's 1865 wood engraving *Photography and Portrait Painting,* wealthy portrait photographers are contrasted with an impoverished, neglected painter-proletariat (fig. 3). While successful photographers resided in spacious attic studios, many painters had to live in gloomy garrets similar to the one in Carl Spitzweg's painting *The Poor Poet* (1839, Neue Pinakothek, Munich).

A Recognized Aid

Over the course of the advancing industrialization of portrait production in the 1860s, two photography-based image processes became popular that competed with painting and sculpture. Both *photosculpture* and *photopeinture* enjoyed a vogue beginning in 1865. The latter was based on the enlargement of a negative or slide that was projected onto photographic paper or onto a canvas prepared with light-sensitive emulsion using a solar camera.[2] In France the photographer André Adolphe Eugène Disdéri acquired the patent for the process. Painters employed by Disdéri traced the contours of the projected image on the screen and copied them with "mathematical precision," as a report in *Le Figaro* put it. Their work apparently turned out so convincingly that Disdéri was soon successfully marketing portraits of celebrities such as Prince Jérôme Napoléon, a nephew of Emperor Napoléon, or the composer Gioachino Rossini. The technique of *photopeinture* was considered inexpensive and efficient, as it significantly reduced the duration of portrait sessions. This practice is evidenced by a caricature by Cham (Amédée de Noé) that shows Disdéri at work in his Paris studio on boulevard des Italiens (fig. 2).[3] In addition to portraits, the process was used for replicas of paintings[4] and depictions of genre scenes, and later for landscapes and other motifs as well.[5] Examples were on display at the Paris world's fairs of 1867 and 1878. *Photopeinture* was apparently a common practice in many painters' studios at the time. In 1884 the journal *La Nature* reported that "in this way photography will still render considerable service to the painter but will leave him the freest latitude as regards the free development of his, as it were, poetic ideas."[6]

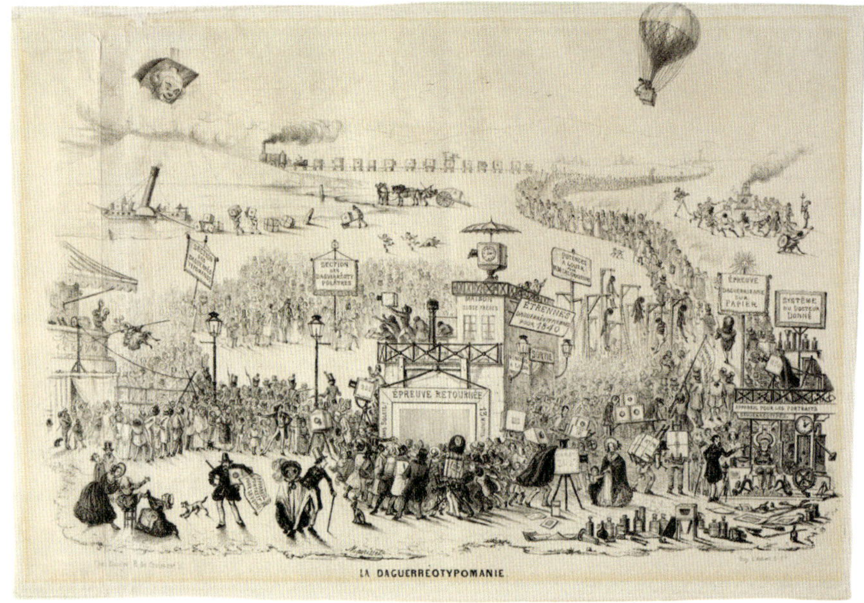

1

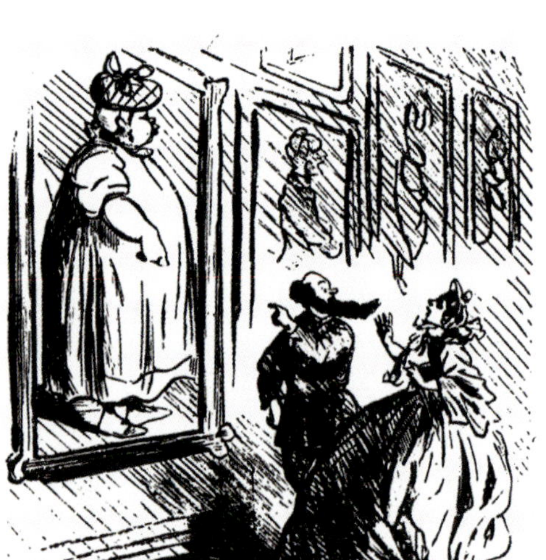

2

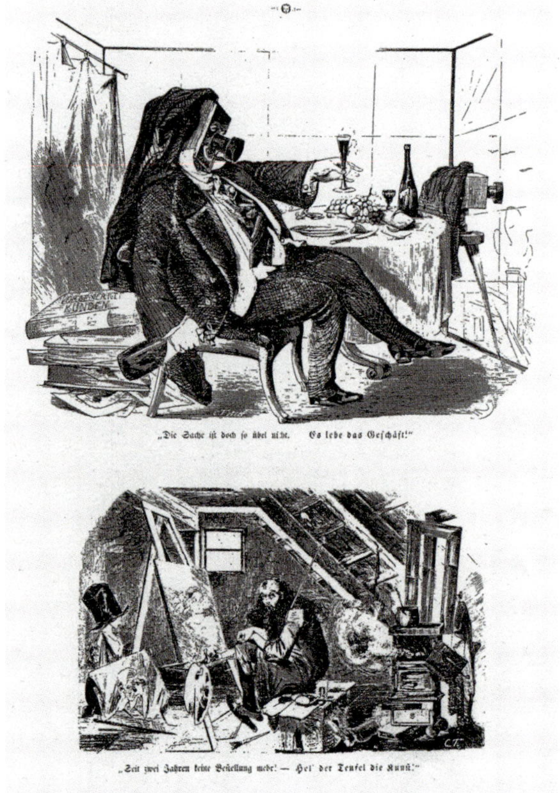

1 Théodore Maurisset,
Daguerreotypomania, Paris 1839,
in *La Caricature* (December 8, 1839)

2 Cham [Amédée de Noé],
*Caricature of the Portrait "Grandeur Nature"
by Disdéri,* 1861,
in Cham, *Choses et autres,* Paris 1861, n.p.

3 Carl Tetzel,
Photography and Portrait Painting, 1865,
Münchner Stadtmuseum, Munich,
Sammlung Fotografie

3

The French writer and caricaturist Albert Robida, author of several science fiction novels in which he imagined the effects of scientific and technological progress on everyday life in a dystopian vision, saw the coming development of modern painting as dependent on the latest photographic processes. In his futuristic novel of 1883, *Le Vingtième Siècle,* he described a visit to the Musée du Louvre. Along with painters, *photopeintres* were on hand to create perfect copies of the paintings with their cameras (fig. 5). As the culmination of mechanistic image production, a mechanical rendering of photography serviceable for the artistic work process, *photopeinture* produced hardly any innovative results and by no means created a new form of painting. Its acceptance, however, was an indication of the legitimacy of an artistic practice in which the medium of photography was taken for granted in terms of its use as an aid. Many painters and sculptors had followed the recommendation of French history painter Paul Delaroche in 1839 that they should create archives of photographic originals. This found resonance both in the studios of independent artists and in the European training centers for the arts and crafts.

The extensive photographic holdings of the École des beaux-arts in Paris and of the art academies in Berlin, Frankfurt am Main, Vienna, Budapest, and Saint Petersburg, where thousands and thousands of photographs were used in teaching, bear witness to this today. The medium was used in history painting classes as well as in portraits, landscapes, animal portraits, nude studies, and architectural drawings. The *études d'après nature* (studies from nature) were particularly valued as models. They were "taken from life," as was often indicated on the mount, and provided an "incalculable advantage . . . to the painter and sculptor, where it is necessary to make time-consuming studies from nature!"[7] Compositions in the style of *paysage intime* or a Romantic *Erdlebenbild* (earth-life painting) were among them, as were tree and plant studies, all patterns that served painters as inspiration and corrective. According to prevailing opinion, these photographs represented an authentic rendition of nature due to their attention to detail. Nevertheless, the photographs were rarely perceived as works of art in and of themselves. This was also evident in contemporary inventories of artist estate auctions, in which photographs are listed without detailed descriptions and declared to be of little value.

Inspirational Rivalry

In view of the public status and disposition of photographers in the nineteenth century, it should be noted that those who had an artistic education represented a small minority. Only about twenty percent had a corresponding record to show for it.[8] The situation was different for the leading photographers in France and the United Kingdom, where the public perception of photography as an art was more pronounced than on the rest of the continent. Analogous to the *artiste peintre,* there was talk of the *artiste photographe,* the *photographe amateur,* and even the *peintre photographe* in the 1850s. The latter designation referred to both artistic training and the simultaneous practice of both painting and photography.[9]

Among the most successful photographers whose works were discussed in the context of art in the French daily and weekly press were contrasting personalities such as Gustave Le Gray and André Eugène Adolphe Disdéri. Their studios were considered tourist attractions and were meeting places for a wealthy clientele of bourgeoisie and high nobility who, as the social elite of the Second Empire, could feel at home in such spaces. Views of their establishments circulated in the picture press. A comparison with Parisian artist studios, which were also published as wood engravings in *L'Illustration,* reveals considerable differences. In addition to their function as production facilities, the studios of famous artists functioned as publicly accessible showrooms that, at certain times, were open to visitors. In the case of Eugène Delacroix's Paris studio, the artist is visible in the foreground while visitors or assistants pursue various activities in the spacious artist's workshop. The room, filled with plaster casts, paintings, and drawings, is presented as a place of creative production and erudition. Various paintings on easels—Delacroix was busy at the time producing paintings for the Palais Bourbon, the seat of the French parliament—emphasize busy activity (fig. 4). A similar situation reigned in Rosa Bonheur's studio, which notoriously featured the painter's live animal model at home among her props. The photo salons of Le Gray and Disdéri on the other hand, were markedly different. Instead of a productive workshop atmosphere, the interiors reflected the social advancement and social status of their owners, legitimized by attributes of art. The laboratory had "succeeded the workshop," as the art critic Paulin wrote in 1856; the studio had become a salon "and even, as in the case of M. Legray, a highly curious cabinet, of which the anteroom already gives a foretaste."[10]

In Le Gray's studio a valuable Rococo work by the Neapolitan painter Francesco de Mura adorned the staircase (fig. 6), and in the salon there were chinoiseries, furniture, and paintings in the style of French court art. Le Gray's salon on boulevard des Capucines housed Nadar's studio from 1860, after the photographer had moved out, and the Impressionists mounted their first exhibition in its rooms in 1874. Disdéri's salons on boulevard des Italiens were hardly less luxuriously furnished, and *L'Illustration* enthusiastically reported on them in detail in 1860.[11]

Under Pressure for Legitimacy

Despite its socially established status, photography came under pressure to legitimize itself as it entered the sphere of fine art and as a result of the competition with painting and graphic art in the press. The initial enthusiasm for the new image process gave way to skepticism about its specific properties. The accuracy with which photography captured representational reality, without differentiating between "important" and less important picture elements, and its ability to depict more than the human eye could perceive earned photography the reproach of being a soulless technique that was unable to compose and invent. Unlike painting, it was incapable of creativity and only provided a reproduction of physical reality. Théophile Thoré, art historian and patron of Édouard Manet, Claude Monet, and Pierre-Auguste Renoir, described this unease with the medium in 1845 as follows: "The artist is not simply an eye like the daguerreotype, a fatal and passive mirror that physically reproduces the image presented to him; he is a moving and creative soul that in turn fertilizes the external creation."[12]

The stigma of a mechanical *techné* accompanied public discussion about the artistic value of photography until the turn of the century. The widespread accusation was that the photographer only let his camera and light do the work in order to disqualify photography as a "stupid and blind light machine."[13] The expediency of the process as an aid to the arts was never questioned, but many critics missed a subjective hand in photography and lamented its lack of artistic imagination.[14]

This discussion also unfolded in connection with the reproduction and duplication of works of fine art. Photographic facsimiles of original drawings by Raphael or prints by Rembrandt or Albrecht Dürer were considered artistic achievements that, although they were reproductions, were appreciated as works of art in their own right. And yet, since photographs only had limited legal protection as artistic works until the twentieth century, a central concern of photographers was to protect themselves against the unauthorized reproduction of their images.[15] Photographers such as Julia Margaret Cameron (fig. 7), Gustave Le Gray, and Gustav Völkerling signed their photographs by hand, either on the print or on the cardboard mount to claim authorship. Due to the lack of legal protection, however, numerous photographs remained unpublished.[16] In the 1860s the unauthorized reproduction of photographs sparked a debate about the artistic value of photography, which was fought out in numerous legal suits. Photographers and publishers such as Mayer et Pierson, Joseph Albert, or Piloty und Löhle sued in Paris, Munich, and Vienna against the unauthorized reproduction of their works in order to enforce the recognition of photography as art in court, albeit with varying degrees of success. As far as the law was concerned, photography was a minor art form.

The Struggle for Recognition

According to the French, British, and German art critics of the time, within the hierarchy of the arts photography occupied the position of an *art industriel* comparable to works on paper, with which photographs occasionally shared the same spaces in exhibitions. The lively exhibition scene in Europe is an important indicator of the medium's position in the system of the arts. Shortly after the first photographic processes were announced, photographs also found their way into art spaces. In addition to pharmacies and polytechnical institutes, it was the art shops that were responsible for the display and distribution of daguerreotypes and talbotypes in photography's first decade. In the smaller states of the German Confederation, the regional art associations also took on this task. There it was customary to present photographs with gouaches, engravings, lithographs, or paintings for a period of a few weeks. The fact that cameras and technical equipment were occasionally exhibited alongside the photographs indicates how closely linked the technological and artistic developments of the medium were. In the exhibitions of the photographic societies and at the trade and industrial shows,

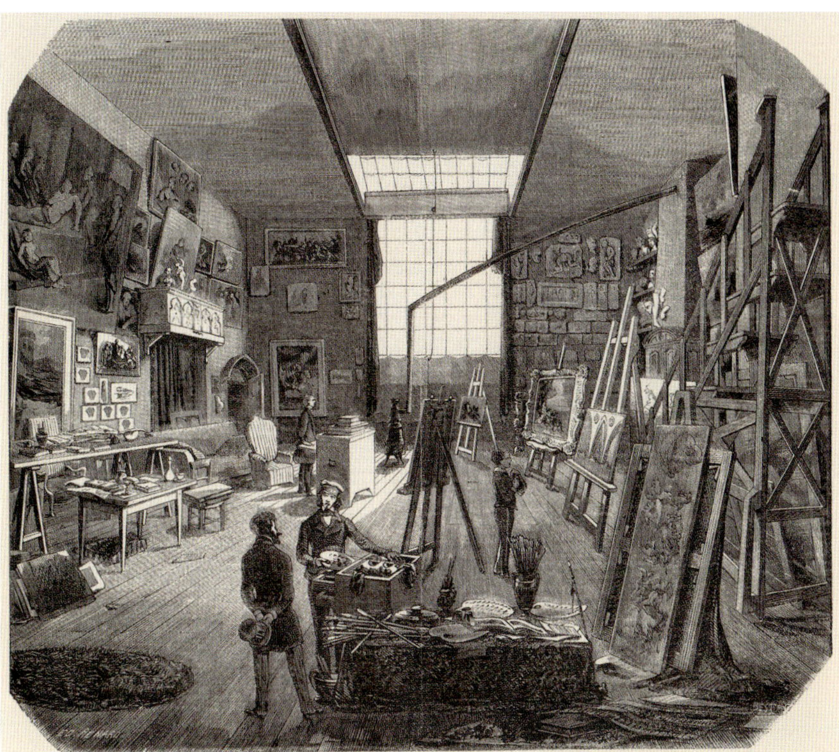

Atelier d'Eugène Delacroix.

4

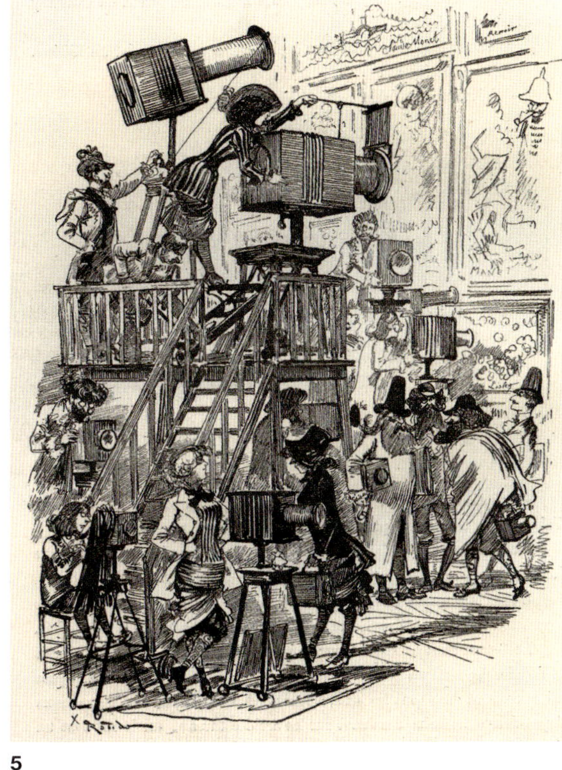

5

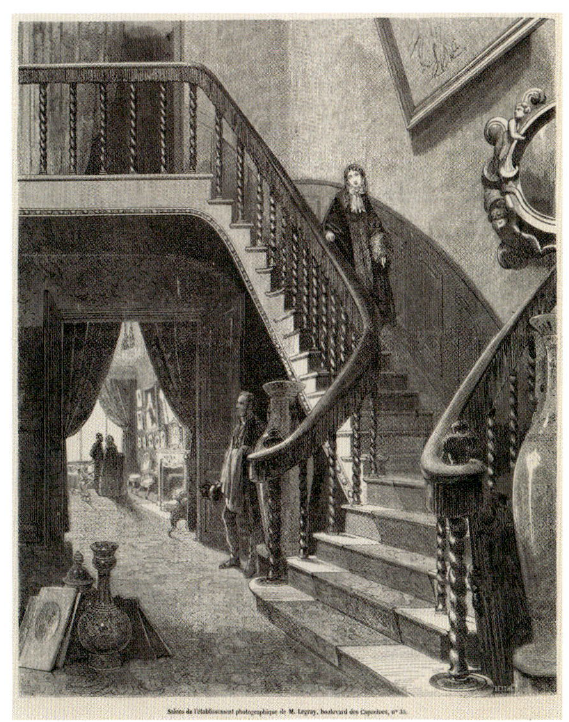

Salons de l'Établissement photographique de M. Legray, boulevard des Capucines, n° 35.

6

4 *Interior View of the Studio of*
Eugène Delacroix, Rue Notre-Dame-de-Lorette,
Paris, 1852, in *L'Illustration* (1852), 205

5 Albert Robida,
Les Photopeintres au Louvre,
in Albert Robidas, *Le Vingtième Siècle,*
Paris 1883, 52

6 *Interior View of the Studio of*
Gustave Le Gray, Boulevard des Capucines 35,
Paris, in *L'Illustration* (1856), 240

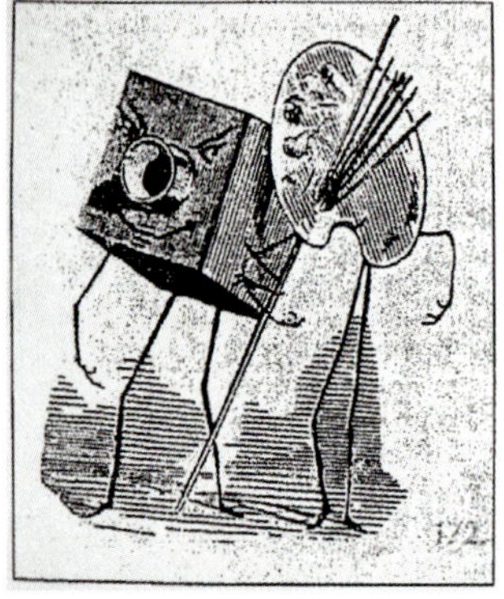

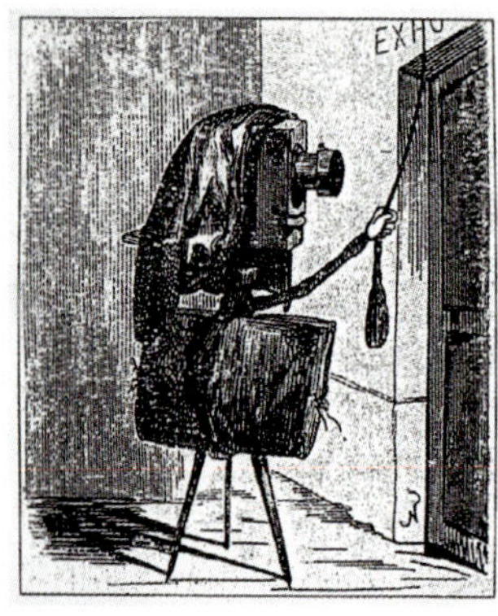

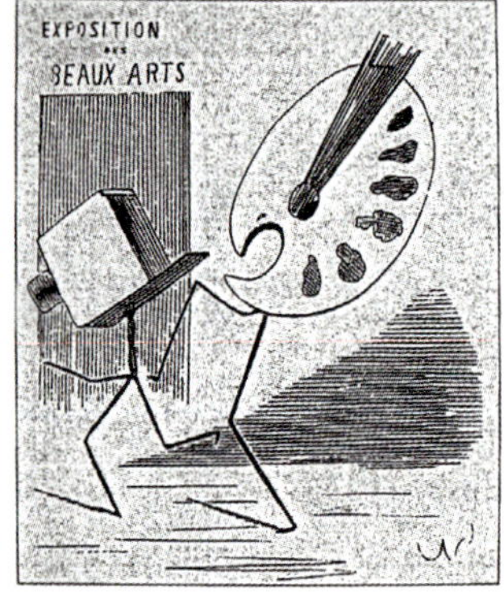

8

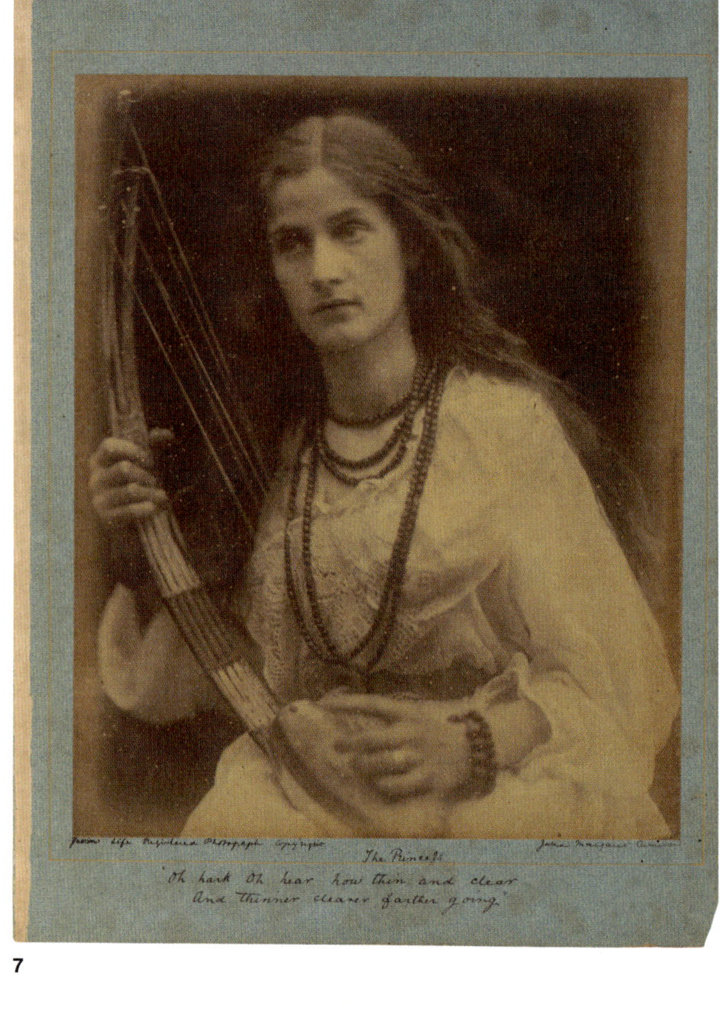

7

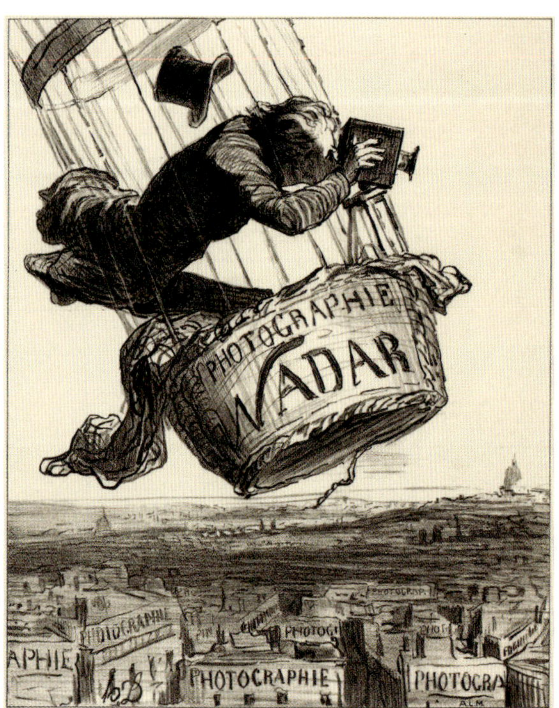

9

7 Julia Margaret Cameron,
The Princess: "Oh hark oh hear how thin and cle
and thinner clearer farther going,"
in Alfred Tennyson, *The Idylls of the King,* 1874–
Münchner Stadtmuseum, Munich,
Sammlung Fotografie

8 Nadar, *Three Caricatures.* Top: *Photography ,*
for a Tiny Place in the Art Exhibition, 1857;
center: *The Ingratitude of Painting, Which Denie*
Photography the Smallest Place in Its Exhibition
Though It Owes It So Much, 1857; bottom:
The Union of Photography and Painting, 1859,
Münchner Stadtmuseum, Munich,
Sammlung Fotografie

9 Honoré Daumier,
Nadar Elevates Photography to the Level of Art,
1862, Münchner Stadtmuseum, Munich,
Sammlung Fotografie

photographers and entrepreneurs were also shown as equals with their products. The general atmosphere of art exhibitions and museums, however, remained largely off-limits to photographers until the end of the nineteenth century, as the example of Gustave Le Gray illustrates. The photographer, a student of Paul Delaroche's, had submitted nine works—landscapes, portraits, and reproductions of paintings—as *dessins* for the Paris Salon of 1850, none of which were ultimately selected following heated discussion. The debate had obviously divided the jury members. While some classified the photographs as works of art, others saw them as products of science.[17]

A series of Nadar's caricatures illustrates the difficulties photographers had in gaining access to the Parisian painting salon. When photography, in the guise of a camera on a tripod with its pictures under its arm, knocked in vain at the door of the *Exposition des beaux-arts* in 1857, it was chased away with a kick by painting in the form of a palette, even though painting owed so much to photography.[18] It was not until 1859 that painting and photography found themselves united arm in arm, but the photography exhibition was only accessible through an entrance separate from the painting salon. This backhanded compliment makes it clear that there could be no question of the medium being given equal rights as art (fig. 8).

Nevertheless, the go-getting Nadar—bohemian, draftsman, inventor, and aeronaut—also enjoyed a special status as a photographer in the Parisian art world. Honoré Daumier, whose drawings usually exposed the artistic pretensions of photographers to ridicule, gave his friend Nadar a more favorable report card. His caricature, laced with irony, reflects the balloonist as *primus inter pares,* but without ascribing photography any artistic status (fig. 9). Daumier brusquely rejected photography, as Charles Blanc, founder of the *Gazette des beaux-arts,* reported: "Photography imitates everything and expresses nothing. It is blind in the world of the spirit."[19]

In the German-speaking countries photographs were admitted to art exhibitions in a similar fashion that was strictly regulated. Photographs were only permitted "insofar as they can contribute to supplementing the art-historical side of the exhibition," as the regulations of the Second General German and Historical Art Exhibition in Cologne in 1861 stated.[20] For these reasons, the regional trade and national industrial exhibitions as well as the international world exhibitions (described by Walter Benjamin as "places of pilgrimage to the commodity fetish")[21] were among the most productive and popular platforms for photography. At the same time, the events and all exhibits shown at it were committed to the primacy of technological progress and economic utilitarianism. Stimulating "harmony between art and industry" and "nourishing the sense of beauty amongst the people" was the guiding idea of the first world's fair in London, which attracted more than six million visitors in 1851 and proclaimed free trade between nations in the age of the first industrial revolution. Photography had not been accorded artistic status in London; rather, it had been placed in the "Philosophical, Musical, Horological, and Surgical Instruments" class in the "Manufacturing Machines and Tools" section. About seven hundred different photographic exhibits were placed in the immediate vicinity of telescopes, barometers, electric telegraphs, globes, and astronomical instruments, far removed from the paintings, sculptures, drawings, and prints.[22]

This pattern was to be repeated at the world's fairs to come. In Paris in 1855 international photography was presented in the Palais de l'industrie instead of at the Palais des beaux-arts, exhibited with other printed works as *dessins industriels*. Seven years later, in London, although the participants were granted their own section, "Photography and Photographic Apparatus," it was housed in the exhibition's industrial complex (fig. 10). This classification was met with protest from English photographers' associations, who demanded equal status at least with drawing and graphic art.[23] Four hundred exhibitors took part in the London world's fair with two thousand photographs, a number that was to be increased by more than half in Paris in 1867. The architecture of the exhibition building there, an oval spiral-shaped structure, made it possible for visitors to experience all the exhibits of the photography department across national borders at once.

At the following world's fair, held in Vienna in 1873 at the height of an international economic crisis, photography was assigned to the "Graphic Arts and Industrial Drawing" section. This classification took into account the use of the medium in teaching at art academies and arts-and-crafts schools. A further enhancement of the status of photography occurred at the world's fair in Philadelphia in 1876 where photographs were presented in their own building on the fairgrounds near the Pavilion of Arts, in conjunction with the exhibitions of the "Department of Art." For the first time in the history of world exhibitions a generously dimensioned exhibition hall divided into numerous cabinets enabled a comprehensive overview and international comparison of a total of 322 exhibitors with 2,833 photographs.

At the following world's fairs in Paris in 1878 and 1889, amateurs whose photographs were perceived as artistic in comparison to the photographic trade participated alongside professional photographers. The final report, published in 1890 by Émile Monod, advocated the future establishment of special departments for artistic photography. While the Chicago world's fair of 1893 did not yet follow this recommendation, the Paris world's fair of 1900 made the first separation between artistic and commercial photography. The Palais de l'Enseignement featured works by the Vienna Camera-Club and the Photo-Club de Paris, but the North American, Belgian, and German Pictorialists boycotted the event because the organizers had not given photography a place alongside painting, sculpture, and graphic art in the Palais du Trocadéro. Alfred Stieglitz, responsible for organizing the North American section, refused to participate in industrial and trade shows unless a spatial and substantive division was made between photography as art and as trade.[24]

This marked an abrupt break in exhibition history, for amateur artistic photographers had for the first time succeeded in having their works be perceived as tableaux in their own right. With reference to the centuries-old tradition of painting, they demanded that their photographs be presented as autonomous pictorial art (fig. 11). In this way, a development took place at the fin de siècle that was repeated about a century later, when contemporary photographic artists distanced themselves from a commercially functional and narrative context of the medium in advertising, photojournalism, and so on. This process of artistic emancipation was also based on the specific characteristics of the tableau, which forgoes captions or any other sort of textual reference.[25]

A New Art

In the nineteenth century painting was forced to develop new strategies for confronting photography, as it was inferior to photography in terms of the precise reproduction of visible reality. Painting had to increasingly defend its monopoly as an art form in reaction to the prevailing concept of art that renounced photography. While mimesis was devalued, the value of personal authorship increased—an element that was categorically denied to photography. The points of criticism used against photography thus integrally shaped the concept of art.[26]

This is also evident in artistic photography from 1890 onward, which tried to free itself from the stigma of mere mimesis. While it oriented itself more strongly to the iconographic canon of painting, it also expanded its repertoire of design. In order to promote the reception of their photographs as art, the Pictorialists developed complex pictorial strategies. The use of fine-art printing processes to produce images fundamentally changed the material appearance of photographs. The smooth, often glossy surfaces of the brownish albumen and celluloid papers were replaced by supports having an inherent structure, such as canvas, watercolor paper, or textured papers whose surface was reminiscent of processes used in painting and graphic art. Manual interventions in the image process—ranging from drawing, overpainting, and incisions on the negative to subsequent processing of the positive image and experimental montage—also contributed to the altered materiality of the photographic image.[27]

Another aspect was a sophisticated approach to image sharpness. Human vision was extensively discussed in terms of the complex relation of sharpness and blur, with reference to the perceptual theories of Hermann von Helmholtz and Eugène Chevreul. The use of monocular lenses and other technical tricks created images that were blurred to different degrees in an attempt to refute the prevailing stigma of the image produced in perfect detail by the camera. These interventions emphasized the pictorial act as an expression of individual creative action and expanded the design repertoire—the choice of camera location, framing, staging of a group of people, and observation of lighting conditions. In addition, the choice of the frame and passe-partout played an important role in the aesthetic enhancement of the photographic tableau. Finally, colored pigment or gum bichromate printing, and later autochrome, made it possible to resolve the deficiencies of a black-and-white representation.

What appears to be a prominent turning point in the history of photography is put into perspective when compared with the history of the development of contemporary painting. While the avant-garde turned to the Nabis and later to Cubism, many of the Pictorialists' work continued to be

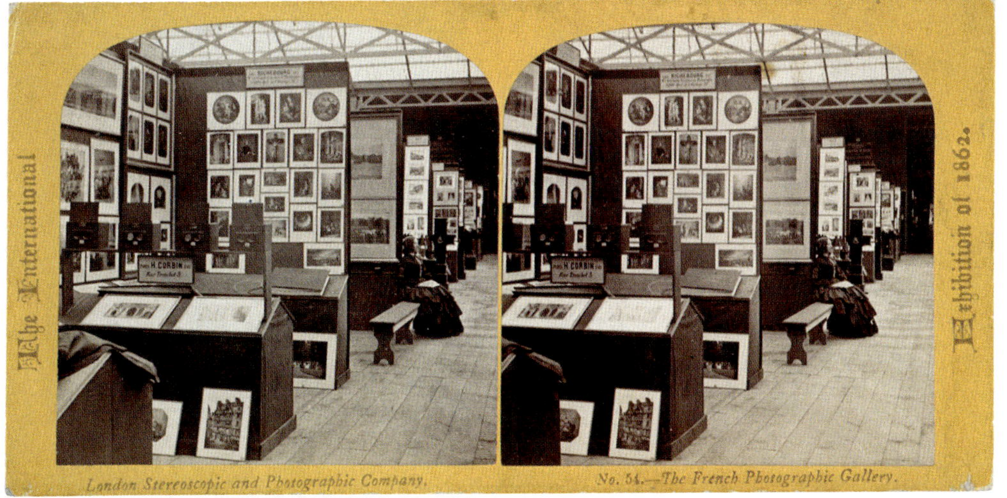

10

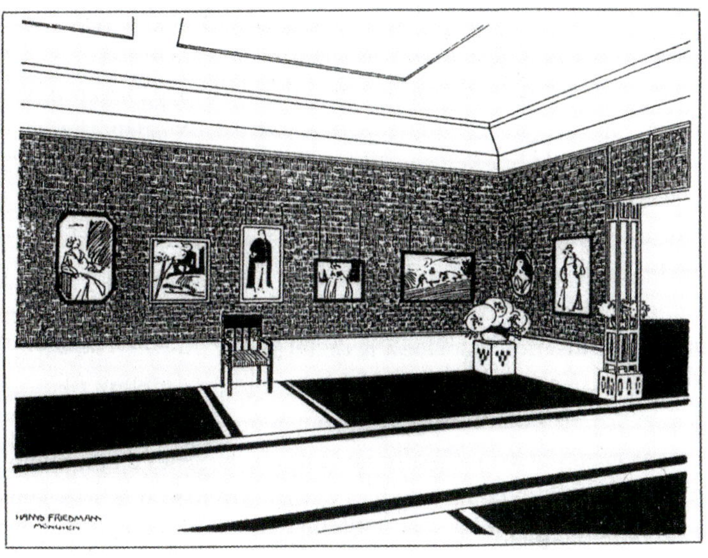

11

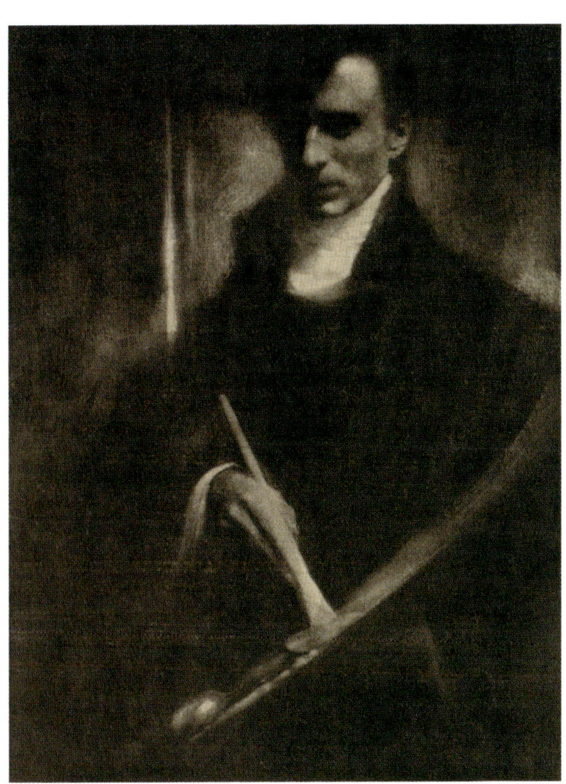

12

10 The London Stereoscopic and Photographic Company, *Interior View of the International Photography Exhibition at the World's Fair in London,* 1862, Museum Ludwig, Cologne, Acquisition Sammlung Agfa 2005

11 Hanns Friedmann (Architect), *A Modern Photographic Exhibition Space,* in *Photographische Kunst* (1905–06), 227

12 Edward Steichen, *Self-Portrait,* 1901, Los Angeles County Museum of Art

influenced by Impressionism and Symbolism. Again and again in their tableaux the art photographers reacted to Impressionist paintings, sometimes with a delay of decades, as a comparison between Claude Monet's painting *Under the Poplars* (1887, Hasso Plattner Collection) and Constant Puyo's landscape makes clear (cat. 67). At the same time as art photography the Impressionists' paintings had become known in North America and Europe through the art market and the activities of Paul Durand-Ruel. As Edward Steichen's self-portrait shows (fig. 12), the Pictorialists were aware of these traditions when they made their art.

Translated from German by Alexander Booth

1 Cf. Ulrich Pohlmann, "Die Fotografie im Visier der Karikatur," in Munich 2004, 315–22, here 316–17.

2 The photographer Jacob Wothly of Aachen had produced larger-than-life figure portraits in the format of 260 × 150 centimeters using this technique and presented them at the French Academy of Sciences in Paris in 1860.

3 The photographers Mayer et Pierson and Trinquart in Paris and Joseph Albert, court photographer to the king of Bavaria, also produced portraits using *photopeinture* at the same time.

4 *Le Figaro* mentions the reproduction of the painting *Smalah* by Horace Vernet, which is probably the monumental history painting *Capture of the Smalah of Abd El-Kader* (1845) in the Palace of Versailles.

5 Anonymous, "La Photo-peinture," in *Le Figaro* (August 10, 1865), 7. The author predicted that in the future *photopeinture* would be used to produce "a landscape, an opera decoration, a group of dancers."

6 Quoted after *Photographische Correspondenz* 21 (1884), 193; translated here by Alexander Booth.

7 *Organ für christliche Kunst* 9 (1859), 235.

8 Timm Starl, "Überwiegend Künstler? Zur beruflichen Herkunft von Daguerreotypisten," in *Fotogeschichte* 40 (1991), 38–44.

9 Cf. also Ernest Lacan, "Du photographe artiste: Esquisse physiologique," in *La Lumière* 3,2 (January 8, 1853), 7–8; and Lacan, "Du photographe amateur," in *La Lumière* 9 (February 26, 1853), 36.

10 Paulin, "Atelier photographique de M. G. Legray," in *L'Illustration* 1 (1856), 239; translated here by Alexander Booth.

11 P. D., "Les Salons de Disdéri," in *L'Illustration* 1 (1860), 351.

12 Théophile Thoré, "A Béranger," in *Le Constitutionnel* (July 16, 1845), 5; translated here by Alexander Booth.

13 Anonymous, "Kunst-Kritik: Die Akademische Kunst-Ausstellung," in *Die Dioskuren* 45 (1870), 352–54, here 352; translated here by Alexander Booth.

14 Cf. M. Sr. [Max Schasler], "Die Photographie in ihrer Beziehung zu den bildenden Künsten," in *Die Dioskuren* 26 (1865), 221–23, and 27 (1865), 229–30.

15 Anonymous, "Kunst-Industrie und Technik: Das Recht der Photographie," in *Die Dioskuren* 9 (1865), 34–36. In 1855, for example, the legal view was that "the reproduction of a replica of a work of art is not to be considered punishable"; anonymous, "Das unbefugte Nachbilden von Kunstwerken," in *Deutsches Kunstblatt* 27 (July 5, 1855), 231–33. For more detail, see Plumpe 1990, 53–95.

16 See M. Carriere, "Die Münchener Academie und das hr. Recht," in *Die Dioskuren* 47 (1864), 418.

17 Francis Wey, "De l'influence de l'héliographie sur les beaux-arts," in *La Lumière* (1851), quoted after Font-Réaulx 2012, 70.

18 This was the caption of the published caricature.

19 Quoted after Heinrich Schwarz, "Daumier, Gill and Nadar," in *La Gazette des beaux-arts* 99 (1957), 99.

20 Cf. author unnamed, "Kunst-Institute und Kunst-Vereine," in *Die Dioskuren* 2 (January 13, 1861), 18; translated here by Alexander Booth.

21 Walter Benjamin, *The Arcades Project,* trans. Howard Eiland and Kevin McLaughlin, Cambridge, MA, 1999 (1927–40), 7.

22 The reports by the juries had the following to say about photography: "Its destiny will undoubtedly be closely connected with art; but far from becoming a rival, it will prove a most useful tool by which the deserving artist's reputation and importance will be enhanced. By using photography as a means to replace the purely mechanical parts of his work, the work of the artist can be greatly facilitated." Cf. *Reports by the Juries on the Subjects in the Thirty Classes into Which the Exhibition Was Divided,* London 1852, 243–79, here 279.

23 "That photography is an entirely mechanical science, although many practice it as such, we cannot admit. That it should be elevated to the same rank as painting and sculpture, we also do not want to claim; but we believe that it will be on a par with the art of drawing as soon as its processes have become more sensitive and its instruments and methods of operation more perfect." Sir David Brewster in *Photographische Monatshefte* 1,7 (1862), 393. At the London world's fair photographic snapshots of clouds, waves, and Parisian street life were also offered as study material for artists, cf. *Österreichischer Bericht über die Internationale Ausstellung in London 1862,* ed. Joseph Avenstein, Vienna 1863, 416–21.

24 Cf. Keller 1984, 262.

25 On this aspect see Jeff Wall, "Patrick Faigenbaum," in Bottrop 2021, 206–07; see also Jean-François Chevrier, "Die Abenteuer der Tableau-Form in der Geschichte der Fotografie," in Stuttgart 1989, 9–45.

26 See Krüger 2007, 254.

27 Gustave Le Gray, Oscar Gustave Rejlander, and Henry Peach Robinson had already experimented with these image processing techniques in a different form.

Dominique de Font-Réaulx

Countryside, Seaside, City
Painting and Photography *en plein air*

Landscape painting, long considered inferior in the hierarchy of pictorial genres, enjoyed new appreciation in the early nineteenth century. Interest in the genre continued unabated throughout the century; landscapes were much admired by the public and were the most frequently represented subject at the Salon from the 1830s on. This success was not merely a popular one; as has often been observed, the new fondness for the depiction of nature also favored the great revolutions of nineteenth-century art in both painting and photography. Scorned by the academy for its submission to nature and, in contrast to history painting, its sole focus on imitation, landscape painting raised essential questions that lay at the heart of the artistic challenges of its time—for indeed, the vantage point of the artist, whom Romantic thought had elevated to the rank of a creator and even a demiurge, played a determinative role in the framing of the work.

The early part of the century was marked by the impulse to reject codified images of the landscape and instead verify one's own observations of nature *sur le vif*. Neither the idea nor the practice was new: in the seventeenth century, Claude Lorrain had frequently depicted artists working from nature, in direct proximity to the motif, in both his drawings and his paintings (fig. 1). He thus recalled his own excursions to the Roman Campagna and his concern for fidelity to nature; yet by choosing to represent the painter absorbed in his own creation, he also called attention to the process of abstraction inherent in the act of drawing. A deliberate distinction was drawn between the observation of visual stimuli and the act of recording them on canvas, and it was the landscape painter's talent that enabled him to go beyond mere imitation.[1]

Thinkers and painters in the early nineteenth century affirmed the necessity of seeking inspiration directly from nature. In 1830 the writer and statesman François-René de Chateaubriand, for example, exhorted young artists: "First, students should concern themselves with the study of nature itself: it is amidst the countryside that they must take their first lessons."[2] Pierre-Henri de Valenciennes expressed a similar point of view in his treatise *Élémens de perspective pratique à l'usage des artistes, suivis de réflexions et conseils à un élève sur la peinture, et particulièrement sur le genre du paysage* (Elements of Practical Perspective for the Use of Artists, Followed by Reflections and Advice to a Pupil on Painting, in Particular the Genre of Landscape Painting), published in 1799. He encouraged young painters to study nature *sur le vif,* as he himself had done in Rome; in his view, however, these drawn or painted observations were only studies, designed to support a final painting composed in the studio.[3]

The development of artistic practice *en plein air* was determinative for the transformation of landscape painting in the nineteenth century: it gave rise to new motifs, encouraged new modes of creation, and gave birth to a new relationship with the natural and urban landscape. The invention of photography was no stranger to this process; indeed, the new discipline played an essential role.

Landscapes without Temples

The presentation of *The Hay Wain* (fig. 2) by the English painter John Constable at the Paris Salon of 1824 constituted a major turning point for young French painters in their understanding of landscape. Constable broke with the tradition of the mythological or religious landscape and instead took his motif from observation of the countryside of Suffolk near his own home. By choosing to emphasize the changing sky and its reflections, he rejected the postulate of an eternal, immutable landscape: as he himself emphasized, "light and shadow never stand still." His painterly approach, with its clearly visible brushstrokes and intense colors, reinforced the impression of a contingent landscape captured on location.

Constable reworked his large paintings—his "six-footers"—in the studio but executed a number of preparatory studies from nature. In keeping with the Dutch tradition of which he felt himself a part, Constable's finished canvases owed much to the careful study of nature *sur le vif*.[4] This close relationship between an artist and a place intimately familiar to him, whose appearance under varying conditions of light and atmosphere offered a wealth of motifs first to observe and then to paint, had a strong appeal for the young Théodore Rousseau. Rousseau had discovered the forest of Fontainebleau in 1827 and remained one of its most loyal visitors and observers until the end of his life. As he himself said, he did not wish to paint "trees where dryads dwell, but rather the innocent oaks of Fontainebleau, honest roadside elms, the simple birches of Ville-d'Avray, and all this without any Greek temple, without Ulysses, without the tiniest Nausicaa" (fig. 3).[5]

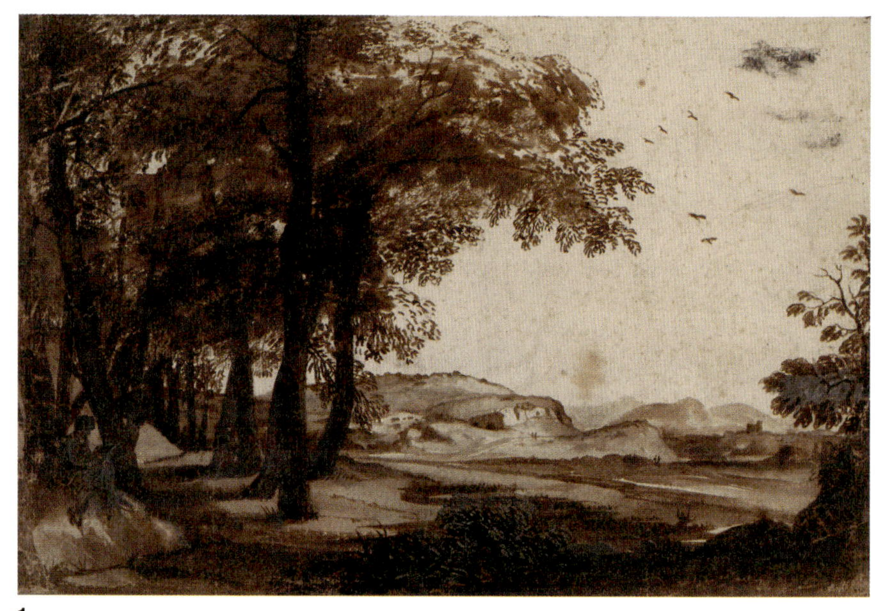

1

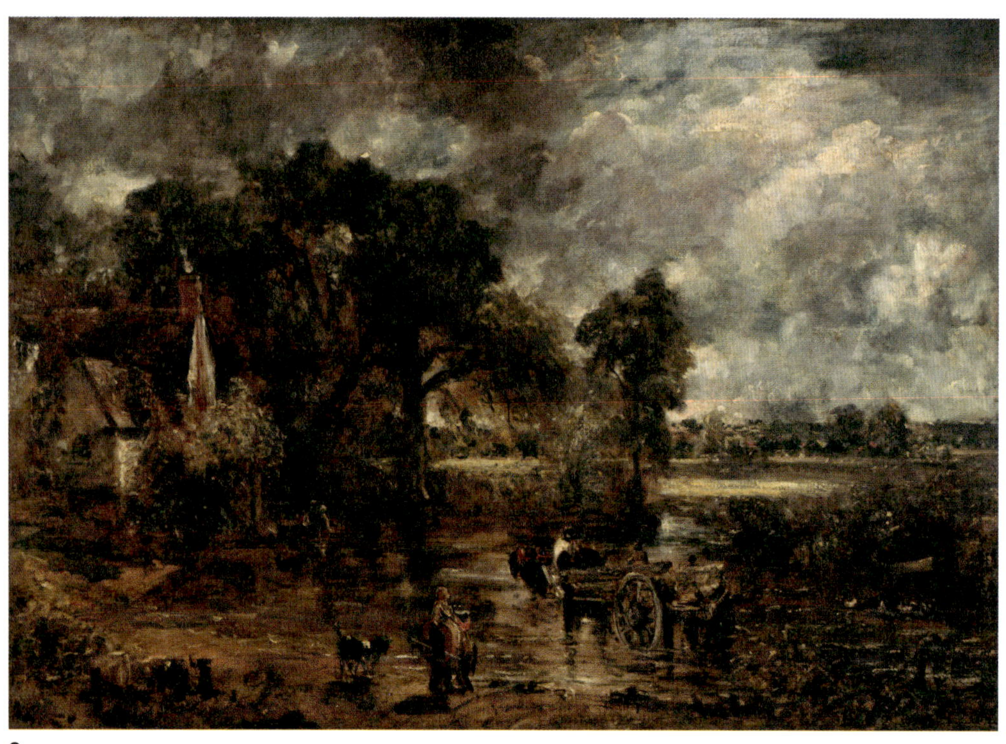

2

1 Claude Lorrain,
*Draftsman in a Landscape at the Forest
Edge with a View of the Grotta Rossa,* ca. 1640
The British Museum, London

2 John Constable,
The Hay Wain, 1821,
The National Gallery, London

Rousseau strove for a closer connection to reality and its rendering, and emphasized the essential role of the artist's unique vision in determining the motif and manner of painting. This Romantic notion informed artistic thought in the first half of the nineteenth century and exerted a lasting influence not only on painting, but also on the nascent discipline of photography.[6] The absence of academic subjects in Rousseau's oeuvre and his fidelity to the sites he painted prejudiced the jury of the annual Salon against him.

Rousseau was one of the first painters to choose the forest of Fontainebleau as his studio, and beginning in the late 1840s he was joined by numerous young painters and photographers. There, a new approach to painting and photography was born that would enjoy a long and fruitful legacy.[7] Thus the challenge of reproducing the landscape *en plein air,* directly from nature, preceded the invention of photography. It was the painters who were first confronted with the task of finding subjects for their work in the heart of nature. With characteristic irony, Honoré Daumier showcased the difficulties faced by artists when choosing a motif for their pictures. His print *The Landscape Painters* (1865) shows two artists with easels and paint boxes, seated one behind the other in a hilly landscape recognizable as Fontainebleau. The caption reads: "The landscape painters, the first copies nature, the second copies the first."[8]

Modern painters liked to be depicted outside, brush in hand, in front of their easels. Camille Corot was photographed in this way by his friend Charles Desavary (fig. 4); his paintings, however, like those of most of his contemporaries, were completed in the studio (fig. 5). New technical innovations supported the naturalistic aspiration of painting directly from the motif, and the need for artists to mix their own colors from binder and pigments gradually declined. Watercolor became more common from the 1820s on, and from the 1850s the availability of paint in tubes encouraged the practice of working in the open air.[9]

Yet even "copying nature"—a phrase hurled at landscape painters like an anathema by the proponents of academic criticism—did not preclude the need for talent. The painter had to choose his subject and moment, overcome the pitfalls of time and weather, and distinguish himself from others who had chosen to render the same motif. Photographers even more than painters had to compose their images exclusively from the natural elements to which their practice was in fact subordinated. They had to choose their motifs with discernment and anticipate their effect in order to mentally compose the *tableau* that would later assume concrete form in a photographic print. In 1860 a critic in *La Lumière,* a journal founded in 1851 by the short-lived Société héliographique, issued this imperative: "The photographer, even more than the painter, must search for and choose the correct vantage point, because unlike the latter he does not have the ability to add to or subtract from his picture. . . . Regardless of the choice of location, the photographer must still choose the moment when the landscape is best lit and the day when nature is at its most beautiful . . . ."[10] Despite the apparent simplicity touted by Louis Jacques Mandé Daguerre at the presentation of his invention in 1839, images did not make themselves in the darkroom.[11] The talent of the photographer was essential to a successful creation.

Old Inspirations, New Models

To isolate a subject for a painting or photograph in the midst of nature was not a simple matter; neither was it as fortuitous or risky as one might think. To choose a subject well, artists first had to hone both the eye and the mind. Nineteenth-century painters and photographers drew inspiration from the works of the Old Masters; a naturalistic apprehension of the landscape was inseparable from the model developed by previous visions of nature. The classic painterly approach of Nicolas Poussin or Claude Lorrain still persisted, and painters and photographers borrowed the masters' rigorous approach to composition, well-tempered play of light, differentiation of planes, and balance of forms. The influence of Dutch painting, rediscovered in the mid-nineteenth century by critics and collectors, likewise manifested itself in a renewed interest in vernacular subjects, sudden changes in the weather—a gust of wind, a ray of light—and images of the sea, coastlines, and waves. The canvases of Rousseau, Dupré, and Narcisse Díaz de la Peña, in turn, provided new models that were quickly seized upon and imitated by younger artists.

The works of the Barbizon School explored new motifs from nature with a realism tinged by lyricism and a marked empathy for the natural environment. The painter André Giroux, who had received the Prix de Rome for historical landscape in 1826 for *The Hunt of Meleager* (Paris, École des

Beaux-Arts), had studied photography in the 1840s.[12] His photographs were very similar to his painted canvases in their subjects and rendering. When he exhibited them at the world's fair in 1855, the critics were full of praise.[13] Ernest Lacan compared Giroux's photographs to the painted landscapes of Rousseau and Dupré; his rural, bucolic scenes, always devoid of human presence, recalled the Barbizon painters' ideal images of untouched nature. His photograph of *The Ponds at Optevoz* (fig. 6) in the Dauphiné in the south of France evokes the canvases of Charles-François Daubigny with its play of reflections on the water, clouds, and expanse of sky. Daubigny painted a number of landscapes in the same region in 1854–55, including *The Lock in the Valley of Optevoz* (fig. 7).

Painting or photographing *en plein air* both required and encouraged a new familiarity with nature. It suggested new vantage points—not an overall view of nature encompassed in a vast perspective, but a landscape surveyed at eye level, traversed on foot, revealing its various elements little by little in keeping with the rhythm of walking and observation. A boulder, gnarled roots, the foot of a stone embankment sprouting with ferns and herbs, the thick, rough bark of a tree trunk—all these presented themselves as new motifs. Photographers were particularly skilled at capturing them and took advantage of the opportunity to demonstrate their virtuosity in evoking the different textures of sand, grass, stone, bark, and foliage and controlling the sources of light. Thus little by little, a unique photographic aesthetic emerged and was embraced by its authors.

Gustave Le Gray fiercely defended the artistic ambition of the new discipline of photography. Trained as a painter in the studio of Paul Delaroche, he claimed that photography was guided by the same *théorie des sacrifices* that governed painting. He challenged the mechanistic view of photography as a mere technical instrument: "Its influence will be immense . . . . In my opinion, the beauty of a photographic print almost always consists in the sacrifice of certain details . . . . Thus it is really only the artist or man of taste who is sure to achieve a perfect work with an instrument capable of rendering the same object in an infinite variety of interpretations, since only he can intuit the effect that best suits the subject he is rendering." Le Gray emphasized the skill of the photographer and his ability to construct the image not only through the choice of motif, but also by "varying the focus and exposure time," thus enabling the artist to "emphasize or minimize this or that area, produce a powerful sense of light and shadow, or create a soft, very smooth effect."[14] His exceptional technical skill and artistic talent enabled him to create works of striking beauty. During his various stays in the forest of Fontainebleau, Le Gray photographed a number of large trees (fig. 8). These *portraits d'arbres* were reminiscent of earlier works by Achille-Etna Michallon. The artist also adopted a unique vantage point, in which a portion of the tree was cropped out of the image, thus intensifying the impression of its power as the frame of the picture struggled to contain it. The photographer's subtle use of light and his meticulous care in the handling of both the negative and the prints conferred new importance on bark, foliage, and undergrowth. The tree became not just a motif, but the entire focus of the picture.

Le Gray's works, exhibited multiple times, in turn served as models for painters. Gustave Courbet recalled them when he painted his masterpiece *The Oak at Flagey* (fig. 9). Here the artist, who came from the region of Franche-Comté, combined landscape, history painting, and self-portraiture in a single work and thus called attention to the depth of his own rootedness in the land, just like this oldest tree in his native region.[15] Claude Monet, as well, developed a new interpretation of Le Gray's composition in his painting *Bodmer Oak* (fig. 10), also created at Fontainebleau.

Photographic Virtuosity

The very idea of "landscape" implies its representation. By creating new illustrations, paintings, and photographs, artists contributed to the invention of new landscapes. In the mid-nineteenth century, images of the sea drew from two traditions: Dutch painting of the seventeenth century and the mid-eighteenth-century Romantic notion of the sublime, conceived by Edmund Burke and echoed by Denis Diderot in his criticism of the Paris Salon. Transformed into painting, the vision of the tempest, the fear of shipwreck, and the despair of the sailors fueled the "delicious terror" so dear to Burke. Kept at a distance through painting, the sea nonetheless retained its strength and mystery and confronted viewers with the beauty of its raging waves and the dark magnificence of its stormy skies. This conception, which persisted through the end of the nineteenth century, informed Romantic painting as well as poetry.[16] It also manifested itself in the large seascapes of Gustave Le Gray, whose photographic works recalled the maritime paintings of artists before him (cats. 5, 6, 9, 10).[17]

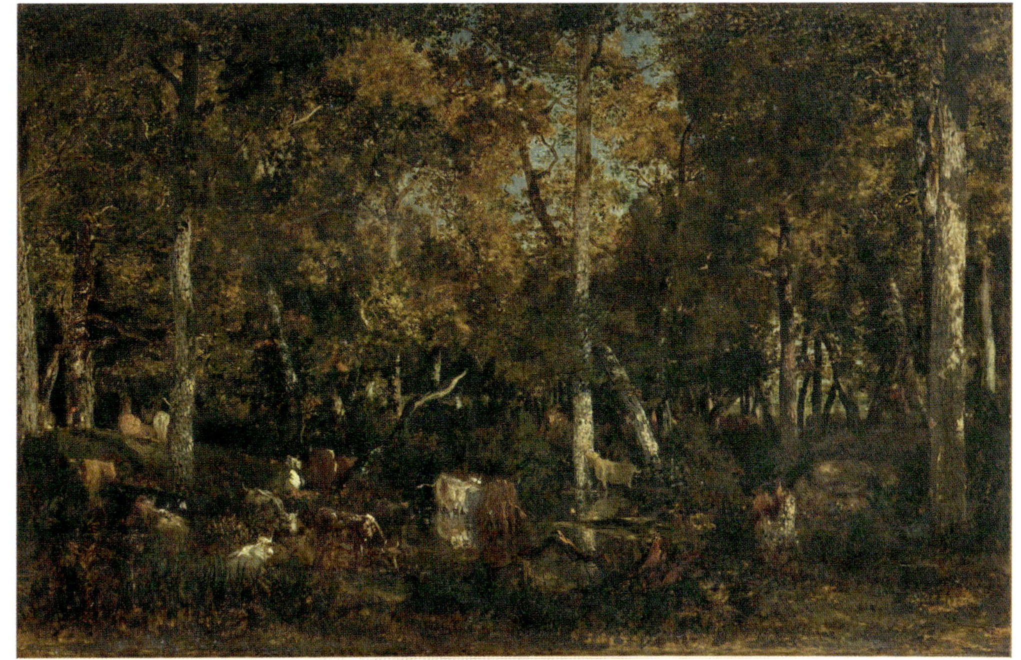

3

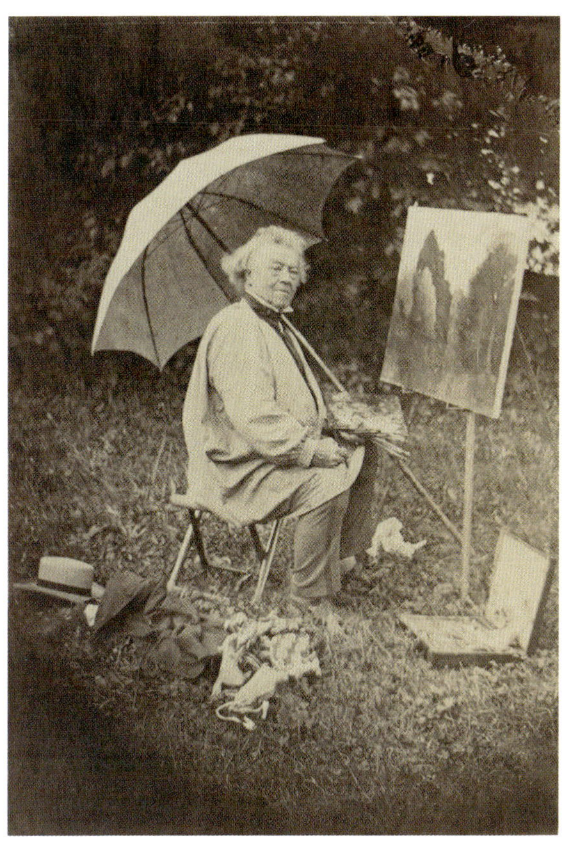

4

3 Théodore Rousseau,
In the Forest of Fontainebleau, 1855
(begun 1836),
Musée d'Orsay, Paris

4 Charles Desavary,
Camille Corot Painting en plein air, 1871–72,
Musée d'Orsay, Paris

5 Camille Corot,
At the Edge of the Forest of Fontainebleau, ca. 1850,
De Mesdag Collectie, The Hague

6 André Giroux,
The Ponds at Optevoz, 1855,
Victoria and Albert Museum, London

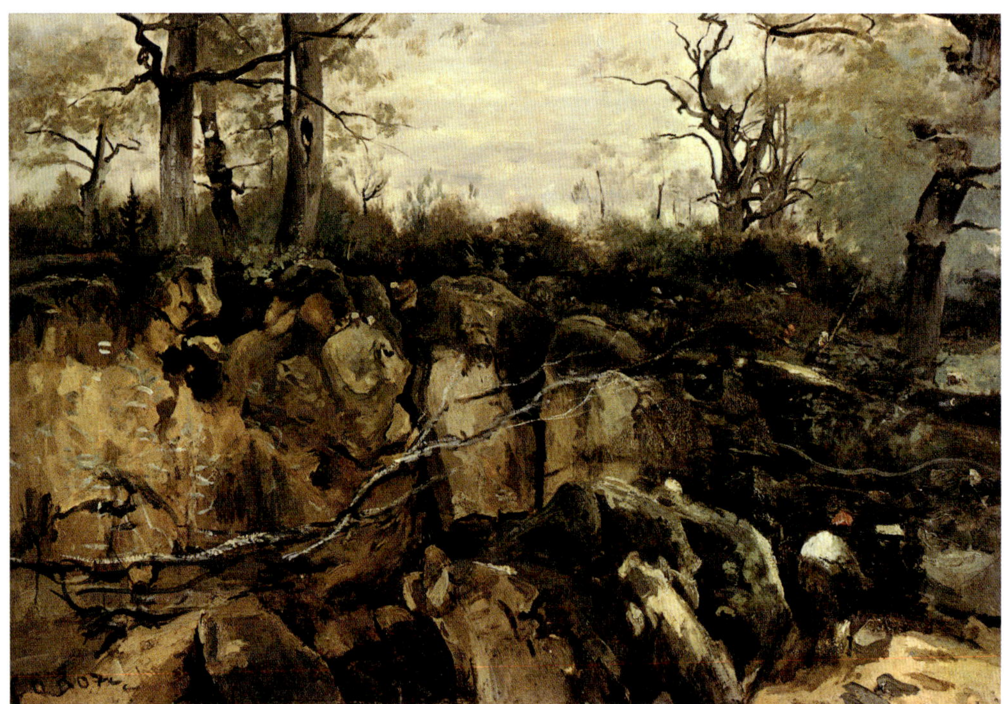

5

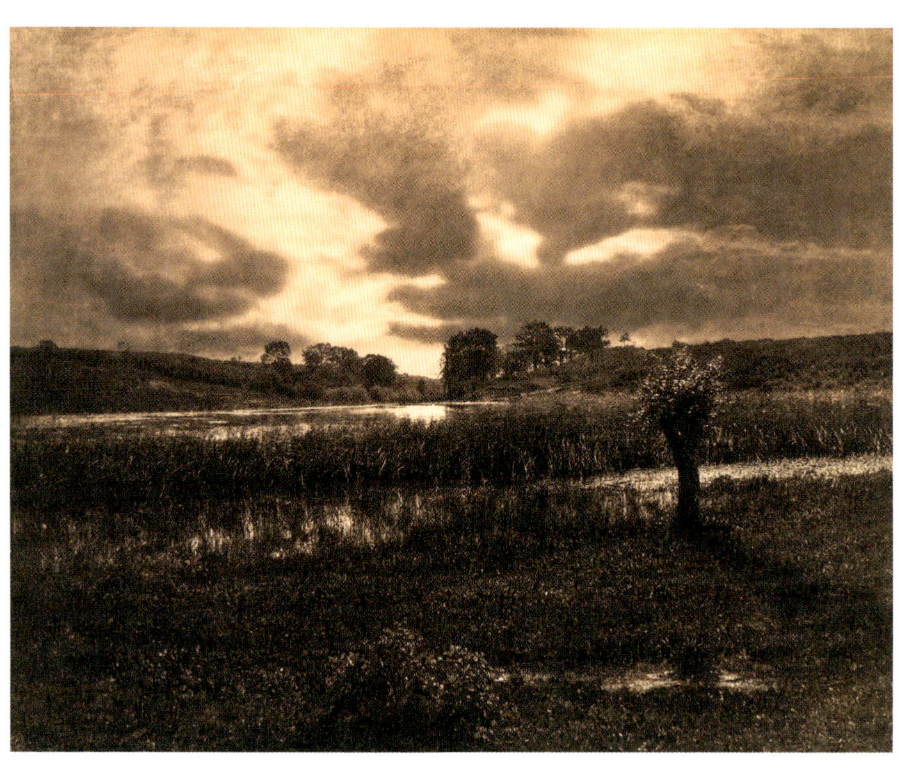

6

Le Gray played with the difficulties associated with exposure times and invented new seascapes by superimposing two negatives for the same print: one for the sky, the other for the waves, thus intensifying the definition of the horizon line. Whether photographed in Normandy or on the shores of the Mediterranean, the ocean as interpreted by Le Gray did not belong to either of those two places; triumphing over his instrument, he succeeded in evoking an eternal sea whose power was not tied to any local or anecdotal contingencies.

The quest for virtuosity that motivated photographers gave rise to another favorable and fruitful consequence. From the earliest years of Daguerre's invention, one of the great challenges his followers had faced was that of reducing exposure times. In 1839 several minutes were required; by the 1840s technical improvements had reduced the time to a few seconds. The desire to seize the moment in its very mobility was a utopian one.[18] Intrinsically, photography was not capable of preserving the motion of living beings or fluid substances such as air and water. It could, however, arrest such motion and freeze the subject, whether a portrait or a landscape, in a moment that the eye had not, or had only briefly, perceived. The photographic image thus imposed a transformation of the motif—as in *The Great Wave, Sète* (cat. 14)*,* where the perpetual motion of the waves is transfigured into a still, solid, telluric sea. And like the paintings of Constable in Suffolk or Corot in Rome, it also established a close connection between the motif and the precise moment of its depiction.

The photographer Auguste Autin, who came from Normandy, sought to represent the ocean sky as naturalistically as possible. A member of the Société française de photographie, he submitted his photograph *Sunset, October 1861 at 5 p.m.* to the society as proof of his skill (cat. 13). By noting the exact time of day and year, Autin not only demonstrated his technical mastery, but also signaled that the landscape shown here was different from the one that had existed the moment before or the moment thereafter. Photography gave rise to a new relationship to time, one that combined duration and representation and prepared the ground for the idea of the series.[19]

The young Claude Monet, who like Autin was from Le Havre, had probably seen the latter's experiments. Monet assimilated Autin's reflections; the way in which photography sequenced views of an identical landscape, while at the same time varying them in accord with the time of day or year, inspired the painter to conceive his own series of Rouen Cathedral, the grainstacks, or the water lilies. The motif observed on location was now less important than the subtle variations of light and color that would become the true subject of Monet's art. This interest in the transformation of the landscape likewise informed the work of Eugène Cuvelier in Fontainebleau from the early 1860s on. Cuvelier excelled at rendering variations of light, changes of weather, and the passage of the seasons, and knew how to wait for the moment that would transform or amplify the landscape. His talent for capturing the winter light and the white blanket of snow that shrouded rocks and softened forms was exceptional, and he combined artistic finesse with extraordinary mastery of photographic technique (cat. 64). His interest in the hourly and seasonal transformations of the landscape and the play of light on natural elements—rocks, foliage, undergrowth—recalled the approach of the young painters of his time such as Claude Monet, Camille Pissarro, and Pierre-Auguste Renoir. Cuvelier's prints were collected and used by the artists.

Urban Landscapes

The invention of photography in the first third of the nineteenth century coincided with the growing importance of cities and their transformation. By the middle of the century, the natural landscape had also become an urban one. No longer did artists turn their attention only to individual monuments, but instead sought to convey a vision of the city as a whole, emphasizing its scale. The influence of the panorama—an optical spectacle that afforded viewers a comprehensive, overall vision of the landscape—permitted the invention of expansive new images of the city. With its 180-degree view, the daguerreotype panorama invented by Friedrich von Martens (also known as Frédéric Martens) in the early 1840s added new breadth to the depiction of the urban landscape.[20] The format of the panorama even gave rise to a theatrical dimension: the city became a stage for modern life, and Paris took its place as the preferred subject for photographers.

Beginning in the early 1850s, Édouard Baldus, who was trained as a painter, conceived a series of views of Paris to be sold by consignment. Produced as large-scale prints, they showcased monuments and used manipulation of the negatives to remove the surrounding houses. The precisely focused images clearly illuminated the stone and metal of the bridge arches (cat. 29).[21] From 1854 on, Baldus documented the renovation of the Louvre, photographing the demolition and reconstruction as well as parts of the restored building. Photographers invented a new way of representing the city and created new motifs by positioning the landscape within a new frame of reference.

The Impressionist painters, most of whom were born after the invention of photography, began their work in the 1860s at a time when photographic images were already widely available thanks to the efforts of various publishers and printers. By that point the photographic vision of the 1840s and 1850s was no longer a novelty. Together with classical French painting, the Dutch masters, the art of the Barbizon School, and Gustave Courbet, the work of the earliest photographers afforded a range of models for young painters in the conception of their own landscapes and contributed to the creation of new motifs, vantage points, and compositions. The modern city of Paris with Baron Haussmann's long boulevards, bordered and overhung with continuous balconies, offered a multiplicity of new vantage points for observing the incessant movement of the crowds. Not only the old city with its monuments and remains, but the new Paris, as well, emerged as a subject for painting. The new structures that had first appeared in photographs—railway stations, industrial buildings, factories, and bridges—were now adopted as motifs by the Impressionists (cat. 47). Their subjects, taken from the everyday urban world of work and Sunday leisure on the banks of the Seine or Marne, seemed to be captured just as they appeared.

The works of the Impressionist painters were ultimately more complex: their seeming instantaneity, like that of contemporaneous photography, was constructed, and their motifs were less immediate than they might at first appear. Building on a traditional understanding of painting and enriched by exposure to other aesthetic approaches—in particular Japanese art—the Impressionists discovered a new relationship to light and duration in the art of the photographers. What the latter had experienced as a seemingly insurmountable challenge now became, once the challenge was accepted, a tremendous creative opportunity. Monet, Renoir, Pissarro, and Alfred Sisley knew how to seize this opportunity and make it their own.

Bound to its motif, the new artistic discipline of photography *en plein air* demonstrated its capacity for invention and creativity through the talent of its practitioners. Its relationship to contemporaneous painting was one of ongoing exchange, marked less by the direct subordination of one medium to the other than by encounters arising from new interpretations of the landscape—whether rural, maritime, or urban—in which first the one, and then the other took the lead. When the first color photographic process, the autochrome, which had been developed by the brothers Auguste and Louis Lumière, was finally marketed in 1907, the painter and amateur photographer Antonin Personnaz, a friend and collector of the Impressionists, created a double homage to photography and painting by combining the photographer's choice of motif and moment with the painterly juxtaposition of luminous colors, amplified in the grainy hues of the autochrome (cat. 138).[22]

Translated from German by Melissa M. Thorson

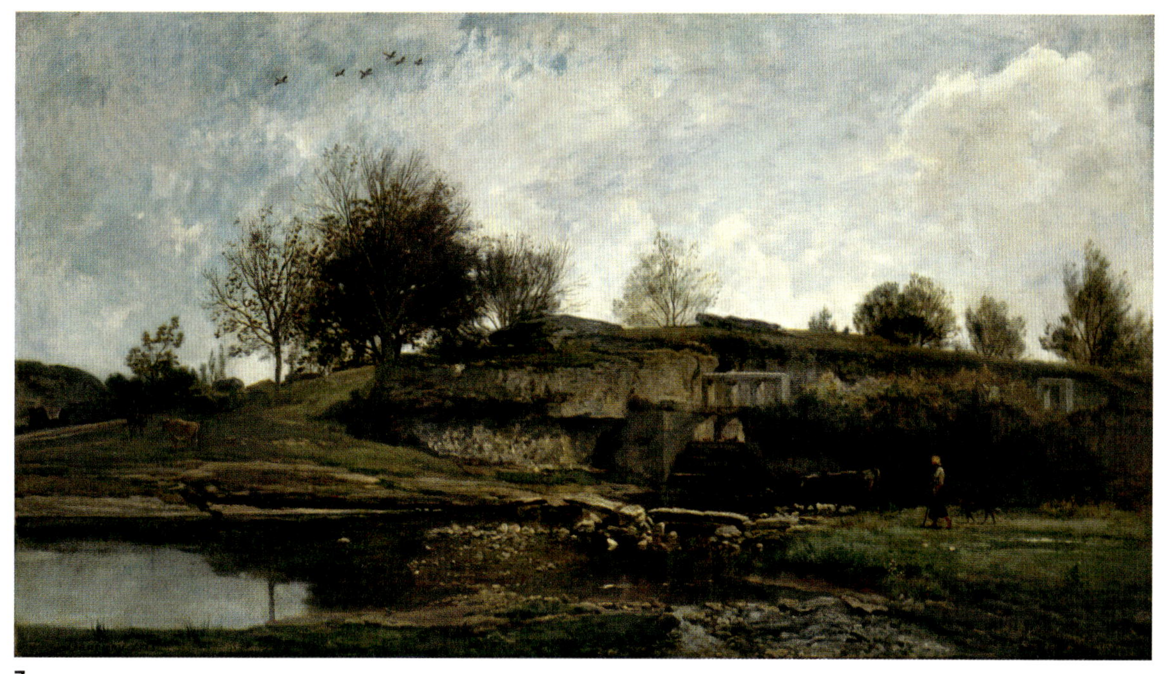

7

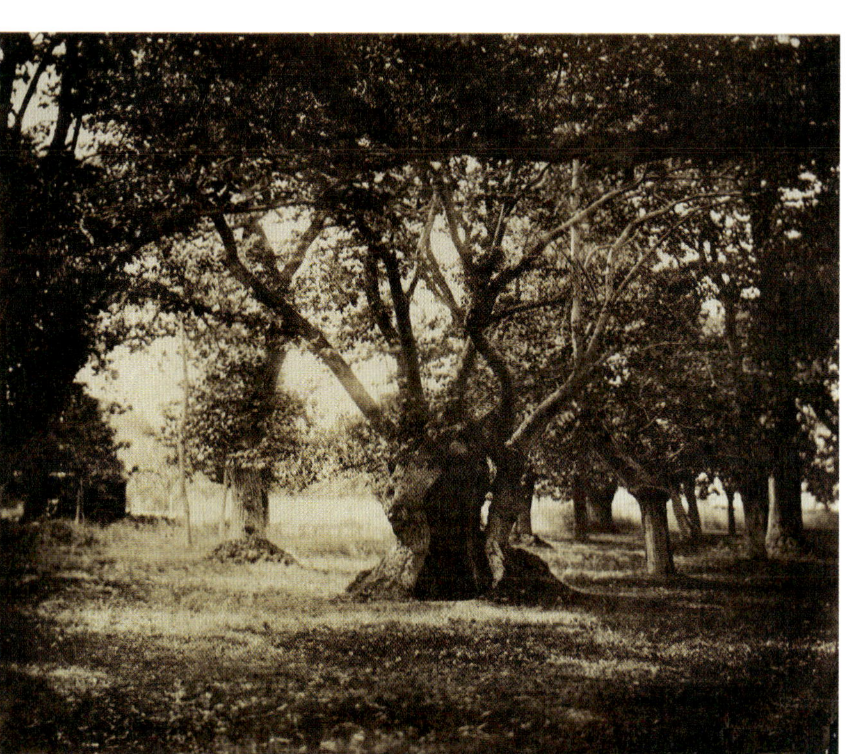

8

7 Charles-François Daubigny,
The Lock in the Valley of Optevoz, undated
(1850s), Musée des Beaux-Arts, Rouen

8 Gustave Le Gray,
Oak in the Forest of Fontainebleau, 1855–57,
Liszt Collection

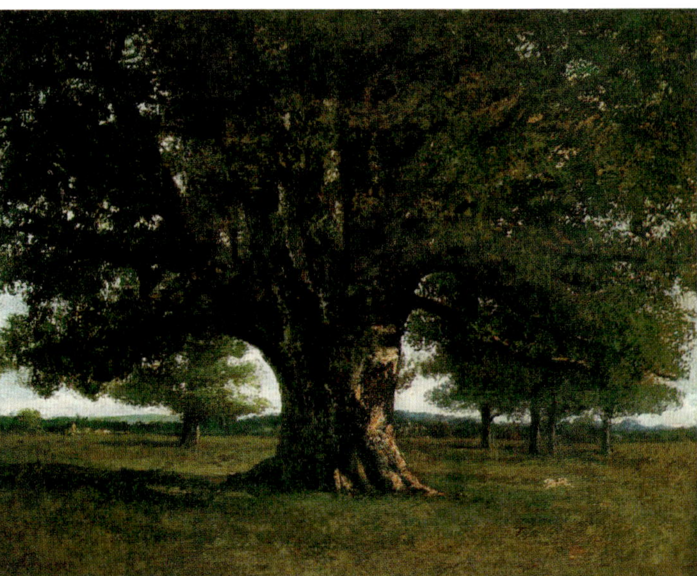

9

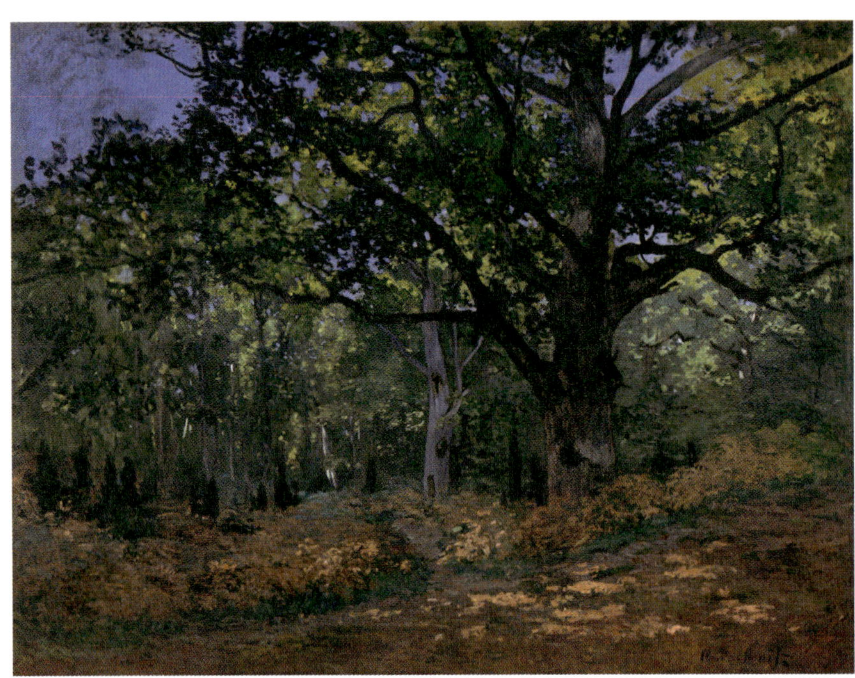

10

1   See *Dessiner en plein air,* exh. cat., Musée du Louvre, Paris 2018.

2   François-René de Chateaubriand, *Lettre sur le paysage en peinture* (1830), La Rochelle 1993, 5; translated here by Melissa M. Thorson.

3   In 1816 Valenciennes established the Grand Prix du paysage historique to be awarded to young landscape painters every four years; the prize was a sojourn in Rome at the Académie de France in the Villa Medici. The first award in 1817 went to Achille-Etna Michallon for his painting *Democritus and the Abderites* (1817, Paris, École des Beaux-Arts); the prescribed theme, taken from antiquity, called for an evocation of the Greek philosopher Democritus.

4   See *John Constable: The Great Landscapes,* exh. cat., Tate Britain, London 2006.

5   Alfred Sensier, *Souvenirs sur Théodore Rousseau*, Paris 1872, 321, translated here by Melissa M. Thorson.

6   Dominique de Font-Réaulx, "L'Invention de la photographie, avatar du romantisme," in *De l'utopie au désenchantement,* ed. Daniel Couty and Robert Kopp, Paris 2009, 325–46.

7   See *La Forêt de Fontainebleau, un atelier grandeur nature,* exh. cat., Musée d'Orsay, Paris 2006.

8   Honoré Daumier, "Les Paysagistes," in *Le Charivari* (May 12, 1865).

9   See Marie-Pierre Salé, *L'Aquarelle,* Paris 2020.

10 Anonymous, "L'Art et la photographie," in *La Lumière* (May 19, 1860), 77; translated here by Melissa M. Thorson.

11 See Quentin Bajac and Dominique de Font-Réaulx, eds., *Le Daguerréotype français, un objet photographique,* Paris 2003.

12 His father, the painter Alphonse Giroux, had been a pupil of Jacques-Louis David and ran a paper, paint, and gallery business ("Papeterie, couleurs et Galerie de tableaux") at rue du Coq-Saint-Honoré 7 (now rue de Marengo) in Paris. He supplied artists with canvases and paints and sometimes sold their paintings. In 1839 the Giroux family joined forces with Daguerre, to whom they were probably related, to market a daguerreotype camera developed by the inventor.

13 Ernest Lacan, "Exposition universelle, photographie, 4ème article," in *La Lumière* (October 6, 1855), 157. André Giroux received an honorable mention for his photographs at the Exposition universelle of 1855, accompanied by the following commentary: "To M. Giroux, in Paris, for his very picturesque landscapes, which reveal the taste of an outstanding artist." Quoted after "Extrait des rapports du jury mixte international de l'Exposition universelle," in *La Lumière* (May 2, 1857), 71.

14 Gustave Le Gray, *Nouveau traité théorique et pratique de la photographie sur papier et sur verre,* Paris 1852, 2 and 4; translated here by Melissa M. Thorson.

15 See *Gustave Courbet,* exh. cat., The Metropolitan Museum of Art, New York 2008, especially the chapter on Courbet's landscapes.

16 *Tempêtes et naufrages, de Vernet à Courbet,* exh. cat., Musée de la vie romantique, Paris 2020.

17 See Paris 2002.

18 See *La Révolution de la photographie instantanée,* exh. cat., Bibliothèque nationale de France, Paris 1998.

19 See Font-Réaulx 2012.

20 See *Paris et le daguerréotype,* exh. cat., Musée Carnavalet, Paris 1992.

21 See New York 1994.

22 A conference on color photography was organized in Cerisy (Département Manche in France) in August 2021 under the direction of Nathalie Boullouch and Gilles Désiré dit Gosset; publication of the conference proceedings is forthcoming.

Bernd Stiegler

Fleetingness

Paris, Modernity, and the Arts

The street about me roared with a deafening sound.
Tall, slender, in heavy mourning, majestic grief,
A woman passed, with a glittering hand
Raising, swinging the hem and flounces of her skirt . . .[1]

For Walter Benjamin, the sonnet "À une passante" (To a Passer-By) by Charles Baudelaire, whose opening lines are quoted here, turns an ephemeral encounter in the big city into love "at last sight" and at the same time transforms fleetingness into an aesthetic category.[2] As if in a burning glass, Baudelaire's poetic snapshot brings fleetingness into focus as the condition for the possibility of aesthetic knowledge in the nineteenth century. Due to the interaction of a number of factors, the transient would become the quality, indeed the very principle, of modernity. This essay explores these factors by examining four different, but complementary aspects. The first is the radical renovation of the city of Paris, since it formed the backdrop and horizon against which all other changes occurred. Secondly, fleetingness constituted a central element in a symbolic revolution in art that had begun with Édouard Manet and went on to inform other positions, including Impressionism. Thirdly, photography and art conquered the street and in their own way employed the principle of circulation, which was complementary to that of fleetingness. Finally, fleetingness also implicated the modern subject, whose perception and self-perception in the second half of the nineteenth century call for new descriptive categories.

A City in Transition

In the mid-nineteenth century, Paris was a city in transition. Anyone who left town for just a few weeks might return to find long-familiar neighborhoods suddenly torn down. Such persons might at times feel "like Rip Van Winkle, who woke up after a long sleep of twenty years" and found himself transported to a world that shared little with the one he had previously known.[3] But while Washington Irving's character fell asleep during the English colonial period and woke up as a free citizen in the United States of America, the changes in France involved not only politics but urban space as well.

The radical redesign of the city of Paris extended throughout the entire period of the July Monarchy (1830–48), the Second Empire (1852–70), and the Third Republic (1870–1940). The most comprehensive renovation was the "Haussmannization" of Paris, the redesign of the urban structure by Baron Haussmann. As prefect of the Seine from June 1853 to January 1870, he subjected the capital city to a dramatic modernization. His first project was the *grande croisée,* a restructuring of the city by means of new cross-shaped arteries running east-west along rue de Rivoli and rue Sainte-Anne and north-south along boulevard de Sébastopol and boulevard de Strasbourg. Already in the late 1850s, he tore down the whole area of the Île de la Cité around Notre-Dame, leaving only the Hôtel-Dieu, a barracks, and the chamber of commerce in a district that had previously consisted of numerous small alleys and houses, many of medieval origin.[4] All that remains of the demolished buildings are photographs, since Charles Marville had begun his activity as official photographer for the city of Paris in 1862. Marville documented portions of *le vieux Paris,* and more extensively the construction sites and new buildings of the city (fig. 1). During this same period, photography attracted the interest of rulers: both Prince Albert, prince consort of Queen Victoria of England, and Napoleon III, who ruled France during the Second Empire, were passionate collectors of the new medium. Indeed, photography represented a symbolic cultural element of their reign.

Under the aegis of Baron Haussmann, 165 of the 845 kilometers of street were completely torn down and rebuilt. In 1867 alone, no fewer than 2,325 buildings were demolished and 3,809 new ones erected. The world's fair that took place the same year on the Champs de Mars was both the occasion and the incentive to show the world a new, modern Paris. By 1867 the *grands travaux,* as they were called at the time, were largely completed and Paris had become a different city. By the end of the Haussmann era, 34,000 new buildings had been constructed to replace the old ones.[5] Entire neighborhoods disappeared, and for years a stroll through Paris meant a walk among ruins. Such an experience was described—with rhetorical hyperbole—by Edmond About in his essay "Dans les ruines," printed in the Paris guidebook published in 1867 in connection with the world's fair, a tome of well over a thousand pages.[6] There, he wrote: "I had undertaken a journey that was less distant, but more dangerous than a trip around the world: I went from the Passage Choiseul to the Théâtre-Français across the Butte des Moulins. Halfway there, I realized I had lost my way amidst a general demolition, but it was almost as incautious to go back as to go on or to stay. In front, behind, to the right, to the left, everywhere masonry fell with thunderous noise, clouds of dust darkened the heavens, workers shouted with long battens in their hands, cars laden with rubble plowed valleys of mud between mountains of plaster; the earth quaked, it rained rubble and bricks."[7]

About's path began at the Passage Choiseul, which—not far from the Bibliothèque nationale, which at that time was also under renovation—connects rue des Petits-Champs and rue Saint-Augustin. It then led over the now-vanished hill of the Butte des Moulins to the Théâtre-Français (better known as the Comédie-Française), located not far from the Louvre between the latter and the Palais Royal. Marville's photographs show how these interventions in the urban structure and the district mentioned by About looked to contemporaries. The demolition of the neighborhood was also captured by the printmaker and painter Félix Buhot, whose works number among the few artistic witnesses to this urbanistic upheaval (fig. 2).

Far more often, artists were drawn to the newly created *grands boulevards* and squares or the renovated parks. The *percées* or "openings" of Haussmann, intended to facilitate circulation throughout the city, were the precondition for a new kind of art that had little interest in the old Paris and instead sought to join the new movement encompassing all aspects of society. Circulation and fleetingness go together in the Paris of modernity, and the renovation of the city demonstrates that the breakthroughs of modernism were also achieved by the wrecking ball. Against this background, an interest in permanence must necessarily appear as the goal of an outdated, outmoded era.

At the same time, the arcades or *passages*—those "strange hybrids of building and street" sacred to flaneurs and prized by cultural historians since Walter Benjamin at the latest—had begun to appear on the right bank of the Seine, the Rive Droite, as early as the beginning of the nineteenth century.[8] Unlike the boulevards, they were zones of deceleration, which nonetheless were the first to make consistent use of iron architecture. These zones of tension are a part of Parisian modernity: acceleration and deceleration, *mode* and *éternité,* art and commerce are not mutually exclusive, but permeate one another. The fleeting moment, too, becomes an aesthetic principle only through this interconnection of opposing tendencies.

Baudelaire's poem "À une passante," quoted at the beginning of this essay, embodies this interconnection in the highly structured form of a sonnet. Here, the individual and the crowd, the rapid passing and pausing, moment and duration, external and internal perception go hand in hand precisely inasmuch as they conflict. Baudelaire's poem is inconceivable without the perceptual figure of the flaneur, who through him became the protagonist of modernity. To seek him only in the decelerated space of the arcades would be historically inaccurate: he was everywhere in Paris, including the boulevards and the newly created *terrains vagues* in the heart of the city.

Even before Haussmannization, efforts had begun to provide the city streets with trottoirs, thus paving the way for the flaneurs. While in 1833 only sixteen kilometers of the street network boasted sidewalks, by 1848 that number had risen to 195. Some of the *grands boulevards* had also already been built, such as the Champs-Elysées in 1838. Previously, *flânerie* would have been unthinkable; now, however, it became a fashion, indeed even an attitude, one that discovered the fleeting as an aesthetic principle.

A View of the World's Fair

Édouard Manet, too, observed the world's fair of 1867—from whose art exhibition he had been rejected—from a distance. In the area of the later Palais du Trocadéro, he built his own pavilion with a view of the grounds and there exhibited his works. In his painting *A View of the 1867 Exposition Universelle* (fig. 5), the world's fair—the outstanding attraction of its time, sought out by more than ten million visitors—appears as a background phenomenon. Nearly all the passersby have their own objects of visual curiosity. Some stare at the balloon that, it is tempting to imagine, might have been piloted by the famous photographer Félix Nadar, who at that time had almost completely abandoned his studio to pursue aviation. More likely, however, it is one of the tethered balloons that were among the attractions of the world's fair.

Other figures in Manet's painting focus their attention on their work, their dog, or their horse, or converse with one another, presumably about the latest military events. The image is dominated by the transient, ephemeral, and fleeting, and Manet makes no effort to compositionally

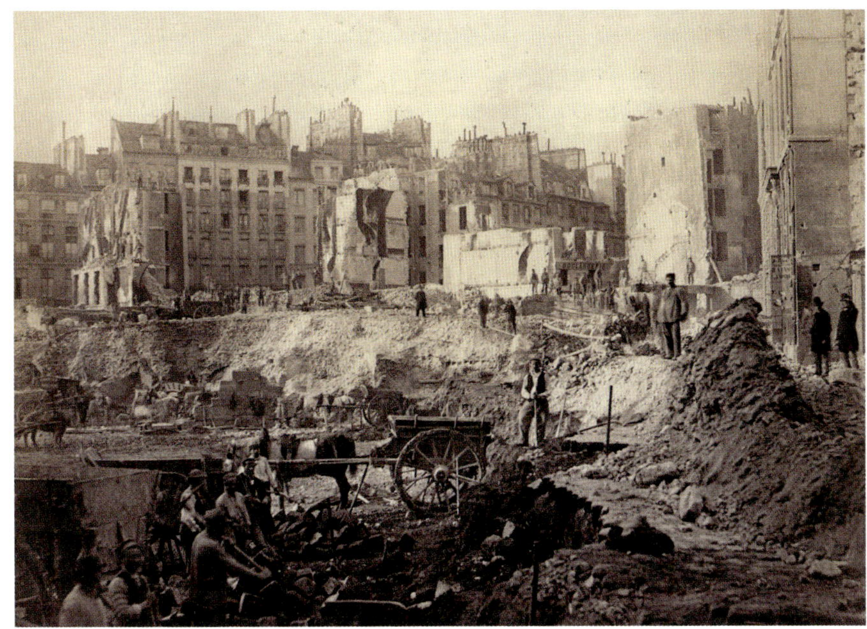

1 Charles Marville,
*Construction between Rue de l'Échelle
and Rue Saint-Augustin,* ca. 1877,
Ph. Doublet Collection

2 Félix Buhot,
*Demolition of the Butte des Moulins
for Avenue de l'Opéra,* 1878,
Musée Carnavalet, Paris

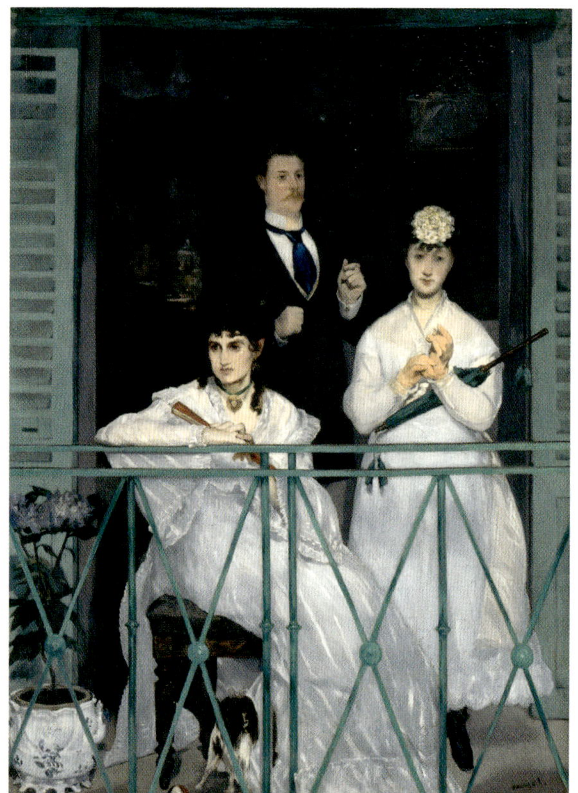

3

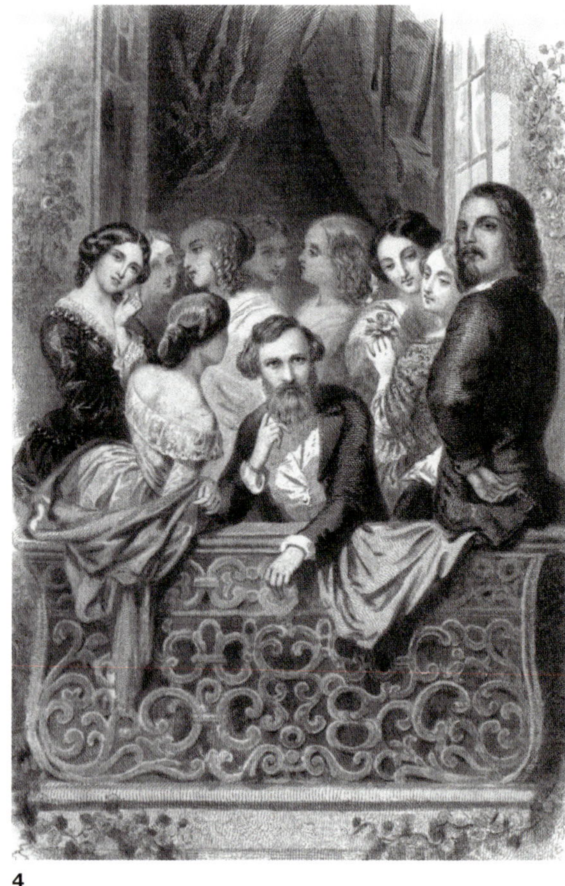

4

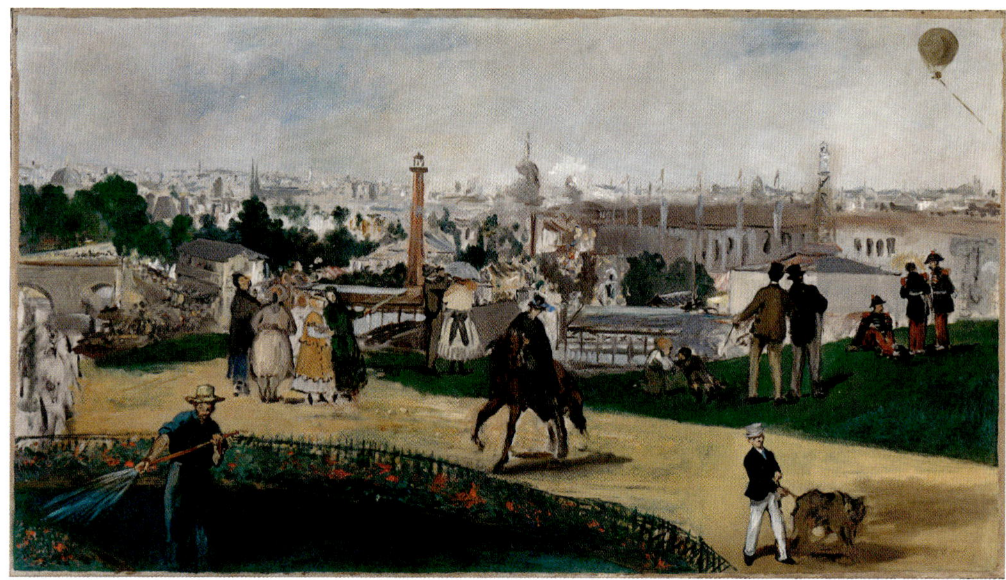

5

3 Édouard Manet,
The Balcony, 1868–69,
Musée d'Orsay, Paris

4 Arsène Houssaye,
Voyage à ma fenêtre, in Houssaye,
Voyage à ma fenêtre, Paris 1851, n.p.

5 Édouard Manet,
View of the 1867 Exposition Universelle, 1867,
Nasjonalmuseet, Oslo

unify these divergent elements, since juxtaposition and contingency were more important to him than integration into a strict order. Predetermined thematic or compositional constraints were foreign to him; with Manet, we enter a pictorial realm in which the fleeting itself has inherent value. And with him we can observe the process of departure from the dominant norms and forms of tradition.

Manet thus marks the tipping point at which a new understanding of art gradually began to assert itself. Like many of his works, his painting of the world's fair represents a new way of seeing and a pictorial conception that was unusual—and sharply criticized—in his day. But what was so provocative about Manet's pictures? For his contemporaries, their motifs were scandalous and their compositions marked by incongruities; they were much too large for their subject matter and brazen in their quotation of tradition. In Manet's paintings, the ancient, noble, and traditional collided with the contemporary and the trivial; their perspective was unclear, and they demonstrated a tendency toward formalism on the one hand and flatness and materiality on the other. Finally, Manet's contemporaries considered his works badly painted, abominably composed, and marked by a repulsive realism. Such was the harsh judgment of his critics, and they raised the stakes even further from a moral perspective: Manet's pictures overturned the established order that distinguished between the religious and sacred on the one hand and the profane on the other and that had assigned to each its specific genres and formats. Thus his works were considered morally objectionable as well, for pictorial forms are also forms of life. Manet consistently explored new pictorial forms as forms of life, a fact that made him interesting to theorists including Georges Bataille, Michel Foucault, and Pierre Bourdieu, all of whom interpreted him as a practitioner of radical change, a painter who had accomplished a symbolic revolution.[9] One of the decisive categories of this art was fleetingness.

On the other hand, what characterized the traditional world of art in which Manet worked as a painter, from which he came, and with which he broke? Unlike Manet's works, such art is now almost forgotten and is viewed as sentimental history painting. Only with the inauguration of the Musée d'Orsay in 1986, dedicated to presenting the full range of nineteenth-century art, were paintings from this period once again restored to prominence in key collections. Previously they had languished in storage and had served only as examples of an anti-modernism that had no place in museums. In France they were categorized as *l'art pompier* or, to put it in more neutral terms, Salon painting. The proponents of this style viewed painting as fundamentally didactic, since such works were intended first and foremost as a means of historical education. Classical norms, derived from antiquity, were the primary focus and formed the basis for a normative academic aesthetic that was largely uninterested in originality.

Such models were so momentous and significant that it was more important to copy and interpret them than to create distinctive pictures of one's own or to supersede or significantly alter tradition. Accordingly, copying was also an established part of artistic training. Artists spent years learning their craft from these models; in the nineteenth century, there was even a museum devoted solely and exclusively to exhibiting particularly successful copies of model works. The aesthetic quality of one's own later pictures was then measured by the standards of completeness, accuracy of detail, and the invisibility of the painting process. Brushstrokes were to be indistinguishable, and the surface of the picture was to be smooth. In this respect, Salon paintings were closer to photography than those of Manet and after him the Impressionists. They resembled illusionistic, photorealistic illustrations—albeit of subjects that were historical, mythological, or both, and whose presentation emphasized permanence. Ultimately, the picture was intended more to be read than to be looked at, and it was meant to evoke a deep connection to tradition, supported by motif and composition.

Manet was a catalyst who first called attention to traditional, unquestioned rules by breaking them. In this way he exposed—in the truest sense of the word—the normative system along with its restrictions. This rule-breaking manifested itself in such elements as the often sketch-like quality of his pictures—which at the same time constituted an ethical lapse, since it revealed carelessness and negligence—as well as the abandonment of hierarchies, the inclusion of contemporaneous elements, and an emphasis on the flatness of the picture plane. The tendency toward flatness also signified a rejection of space and the painterly illusionism typical of Salon painting.[10] Instead, Manet pursued a "flattening out of the world," achieved through the explicit inclusion of the surface, cropped compositions, and an emphasis on rectangular formats. These were the prerequisites for an art committed to fleetingness.

Photography long wrestled with fleetingness, and at the beginning of its history was described as the medium through which, as William Henry Fox Talbot stated in 1839, "the most transitory of things, a shadow, may be fixed for ever."[11] In fact, however, the long exposure times of the earliest photography caused the fleeting to either disappear or register only as shadowy entities. The boulevards famously photographed by both Talbot and Louis Jacques Mandé Daguerre seem deserted, though when the pictures were taken the streets were crowded with passersby and horse carriages. These are transformed into ghostly apparitions, leaving at most a trace of light on the images (figs. 6, 7).

Two decades later, this was no longer the case due to the availability of more light-sensitive photographic plates. The stereographs of Claude-Marie Ferrier, Jacques-Alexandre Ferrier, and Charles Soulier now showed *vues instantanées* of contemporary Paris—including the figures of couples and passersby who had previously been lost to photographic time (cats. 30–33). Photography now quickly conquered the street, and that in a double sense: first of all, photographs of the boulevards and squares of Paris were sold in mass quantities alongside images of actual tourist attractions not only as large-scale albumen prints, but also as series of cartes de visite and stereographs—proof enough that the streets had long since joined the ranks of Paris attractions. But in addition, photographers soon began roaming the boulevards—albeit incognito, with their cameras hidden. The camera became mobile, and photographs could be made while in motion. Beginning in the 1880s, the new "detective cameras," worn on a shoulder or hip strap like a pistol, made possible mobile "photographic assassinations" that remained "entirely unobserved by their surroundings."[12] Later, street photographers offered pedestrians pictures of themselves for sale. Preprinted cards with the message "You were just photographed" were pressed into the hands of potential customers in the hopes that they would later purchase prints. Tourists wanted photographs of their trips to take home with them, thus transforming the fleeting moment into a permanent image. And those who were content with pictures in which they themselves did not appear could acquire heliotypes from the series *Paris instantané,* with images of life in the metropolis (fig. 8).

Large photographic studios on the *grands boulevards* offered the entire panorama of current pictorial production. Some of them occupied multiple floors of buildings, providing yet another novel view of the urban scene from the windows of the upper stories. Claude Monet, for example, painted two views looking down on the street from Nadar's studio on boulevard des Capucines in 1873; one of these works returned to the photographer's atelier a year later, when it was shown at the so-called *Première Exposition des peintres impressionnistes* (First Exhibition of Impressionist Painters). Other painters, including Gustave Caillebotte and Camille Pissarro, captured the same angle of view, and in literature as well—beginning with E. T. A. Hoffmann's *Des Vetters Eckfenster* (My Cousin's Corner Window) of 1822—it emerged as the armchair equivalent of the mobile flaneur. In 1851—halfway between Hoffmann and Monet—Arsène Houssaye, a friend of Charles Baudelaire, wrote a travel account which, rather than venturing into the distance, stays close to home and gazes down at the life on the boulevards. Yet his Parisian retreat is not one of resignation; on the contrary, the view through the window quite literally opens up a new kind of journey, one that both integrates and alters his own gaze.[13] In any event, as the epigraph to the multivolume work on Paris by Houssaye's friend Maxime Du Camp proclaimed, "Paris is not a city, but a world."[14] Houssaye included a number of illustrations with his text, one of which resembles Manet's later painting of *The Balcony* (figs. 3, 4). The viewers of the image see those who are seeing, but do not see what they are looking at. In differing ways, their gaze goes out onto the street, which becomes the world; at the same time, the view from above—a hitherto unusual perspective—transforms the world into a different one.[15]

Two movements above all are decisive for this new way of seeing. First, the paintings of the Impressionists resemble early photographic images, since once again the activities of the street are transmuted into shadowy apparitions. The accuracy of detail so characteristic of Salon painting gives way to a view in which the line of the street and the transience of its phenomena are far more important than the precision of individual pictorial elements. Fleetingness becomes the dominant principle of the image. Secondly, the "framing" of the view looking down onto the street brings with it a change in pictorial composition. Painters were more radical than photographers, apart from figures like Nadar, who ascended in balloons to take photographs from the sky. But pictures captured from a balloon were used less for purposes of art than for those of cartography and aerial reconnaissance.

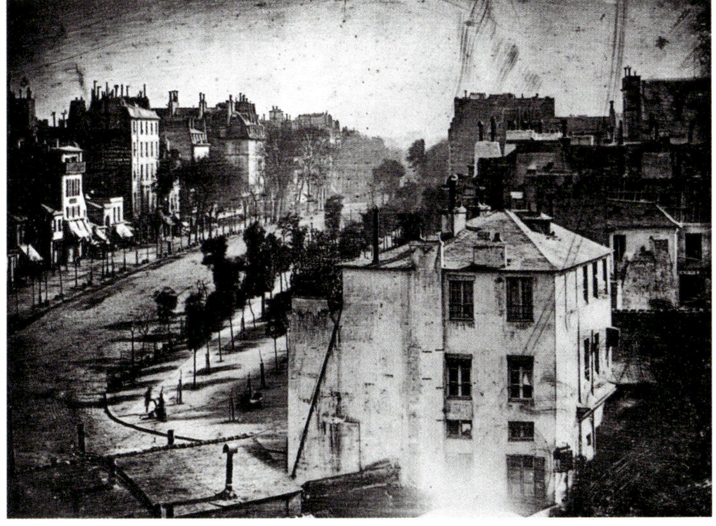

6

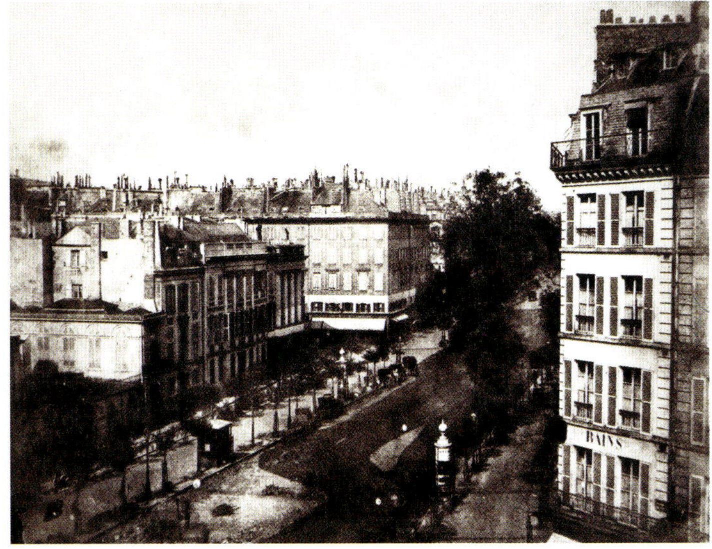

7

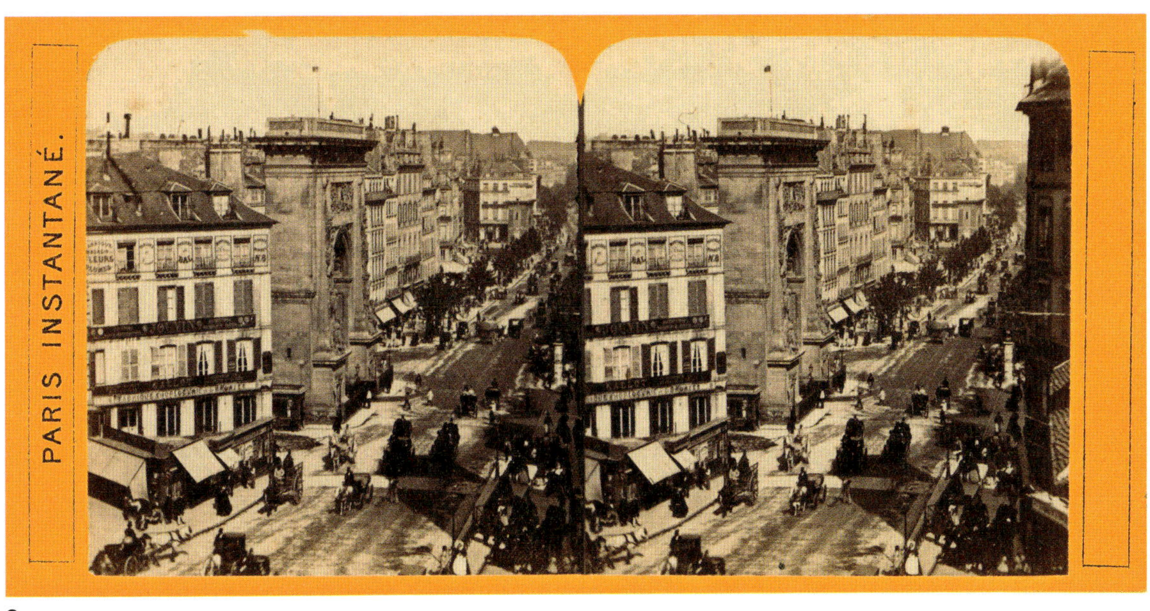

8

6 Louis Jacques Mandé Daguerre,
Boulevard du Temple, spring of 1838,
Bayerisches Nationalmuseum, Munich

7 William Henry Fox Talbot,
Boulevard in Paris, 1843,
British Library, London

8 Unknown photographer,
Boulevard Saint-Denis, Paris, undated,
Rijksmuseum, Amsterdam

Nevertheless, both photography and painting—and literature as well, in a different form—manifested a new way of seeing, which in its own manner continued and embodied the symbolic revolution that had already begun with Manet. At the same time, the principle of circulation occurs here as well, since literature, photography, and painting maintained an osmotic relationship with each other and blithely traded images. Many literary figures such as Théophile Gautier and Baudelaire, as well as photographers like Nadar, wrote book-length reviews of the Salon. Artists including Edgar Degas took up photography while others made use of photographs, and numerous magazines published images and texts, many of which sought to capture the changing contemporary world. The Paris of modernity was an empire of circulating images.

New World, New Perception

These perceptual shifts ultimately impacted the subject as well, or more precisely the way in which it was imagined. The subject, too, is now experienced and described as something fleeting—in a double sense. On the one hand, its very appearance is ephemeral, fleeting, variable; as the art critic and painter Roger Fry wrote in his 1894 essay "The Philosophy of Impressionism": "But to the Impressionist, what in common parlance we call the same human figure, is not the same inside the studio that it was outside, is not the same at 5 p.m. that it was at 2 p.m. It is in each case only a momentary group of sensations in the perpetual flux, existing in necessary relations to its surroundings and an inseparable part of them."[16] Not only things, but also people represent protean, fleeting apparitions. On the one hand the self is, as the writer Paul Bourget observes, a "bundle of phenomena continually in the process of designing and discarding"; or to follow the philosopher Hippolyte Taine, it is a "web" that constantly associates stored and perceived images.[17] The self, too, gains its fleeting and figurative reality only in the act of perception.

This creation of the world in the act of perception is frequently invoked in pictures and texts from this period. Here the self is constituted only through the flow of images; thus the subject and object of perception are not only associated in the images, but arise from them in the first place. The distinction between inner and outer worlds is thereby rendered as obsolete as that of the subject and object. On the one hand, in 1870 Taine defines the self as the ordering function of sensory impressions, which gains its contours only through perceptual and memory images: "the Ego is nothing more than the continuous web of its successive events."[18] On the other, images of the exterior world are only the conjunction of its sensory-physiological simulacra. The world and the self have both become fleeting. Yet at the same time, this change is understood not as a loss, but as the principle of a new art, a new world, and a new humanity.

Translated from German by Melissa M. Thorson

1 Charles Baudelaire, "To a Passer-By," in Baudelaire, *The Flowers of Evil / Les Fleurs du Mal* (1857), trans. William Aggeler, Fresno 1954.

2 Walter Benjamin, "The Paris of the Second Empire in Baudelaire" (1938), in *The Writer of Modern Life: Essays on Charles Baudelaire,* ed. Michael W. Jennings (Cambridge, MA, 2006), 46–133, here 77.

3 C[harles] Klary, *La Photographie nocturne,* Paris 1893, 9; translated here by Melissa M. Thorson.

4 Marie de Thézy, *Marville,* Paris 2015, 33.

5 Statistics taken from *Le Paris du baron Haussmann: Paris sous le Second Empire,* ed. Patrice de Moncan and Christian Mahout, Paris 1991, 61.

6 The guide included numerous contributions by authors such as Victor Hugo, Félix Nadar, and George Sand.

7 Edmond About, "Dans les ruines," in *Paris-guide: Par les principaux écrivains et artistes de la France,* vol. 2, Paris 1867, 915–22, here 915; translated here by Melissa M. Thorson.

8 Walter Benjamin, "Das Passagenwerk," in Benjamin, *Gesammelten Schriften,* vol. 5, Frankfurt am Main 1991, 1041; translated here by Melissa M. Thorson.

9 Georges Bataille, *Manet: Biographical and Critical Study,* trans. Austryn Wainhouse and James Emmons, New York 1955; Michel Foucault, *Manet and the Object of Painting,* trans. Matthew Barr, London 2009; Pierre Bourdieu, *Manet: A Symbolic Revolution,* trans. Peter Collier and Margaret Rigaud-Drayton, Cambridge 2017.

10 Cf. Bourdieu 2017 (see note 9), 489.

11 William Henry Fox Talbot, *Some Account of the Art of Photogenic Drawing, or The Process by Which Natural Objects May Be Made to Delineate Themselves without the Aid of the Artist's Pencil: Read before the Royal Society, January 31, 1839,* London 1839, 6.

12 Gustav Fritsch, "Über einige Apparate zur Geheimphotographie und über photographische Vergrösserungen," in *Polytechnisches Journal* 2 (1888), 177–93, here 184 and 179; translated here by Melissa M. Thorson.

13 Arsène Houssaye, *Voyage à ma fenêtre,* vol. 4 of *Œuvres de Arsène Houssaye,* Paris 1855.

14 Maxime Du Camp, *Paris: Ses organes, ses fonctions et sa vie,* vol. 1, Paris 1874, n.p.; the phrase is quoted from a letter from the French king François I to Emperor Charles V: "Paris n'est pas une ville, c'est un monde."

15 Cf. also Kemp 2006, esp. 62–67.

16 Roger Fry, "The Philosophy of Impressionism," in *A Roger Fry Reader,* ed. Christopher Reed, Chicago 1996, 12–20, here 16.

17 Paul Bourget, *Critique: Essais de psychologie contemporaine,* vol. 1 of *Œuvres complètes,* Paris 1899, 121; Hippolyte Taine, *On Intelligence,* trans. T. D. Haye, vol. 1, London 1871, 201–15.

18 Taine 1871 (see note 17), 206–07.

Matthias Krüger

Taches

Spots, Blots, and Blurs in Impressionism and Photography

With the invention of photography, painting changed as well. No painter could avoid confronting the new medium. For a group of artists like the Impressionists, who sought their subjects within contemporary reality and whose ethos included painting their canvases not in the studio but outdoors *en plein air,* this was particularly true. Claude Monet even seemed to be daringly exposing himself to the competitive pressures of photography when he set out to depict *instantaneité,* or instantaneity.[1]

The competition had already begun long before the Impressionists appeared on the scene. Early on, this involved the surface of images as well. Already in 1857 the art critic Théophile Gautier saw the painter of his time following "photography's advice" by suppressing visible brushstrokes. In this way, to make the subject of the picture stand out more clearly, painting became invisible. Accordingly, artists sought to lend the medium of painting the same transparency as that inherent in photography.[2]

At the same time, however, a countertendency can be observed: there were numerous artists who—instead of suppressing their brushwork—openly displayed it all the more (figs. 1, 2). This, too, can be understood as a reaction to photography. Photographers were often reproached for not actually acting as the authors of their works since the production of images was done by a machine—the camera. Against the background of such an accusation, the brushstroke, called *touche* in French, became more important in painting. For it is through the brushstroke that painters physically inscribe themselves into the production process of their work. The traces of the brushstrokes thus become the material proof of authorship.[3]

The Impressionists' open brushwork also provoked controversy in the press. But in debates about their painting style, the *touche* was usually overshadowed by another stylistic feature: the *tache,* the French term for "spot," "patch," or "stain." Although scholars have extensively investigated the Impressionist *tache,* it has rarely been discussed in the context of the competition between painters and photographers. It is here that this essay would like to start by raising the question of whether and in what way the *taches* in Impressionist painting were also connected to just such a competition.

The Spot as a Source of Irritation

The *tache* was considered *the* hallmark of Impressionism by contemporary critics. As a result, art criticism also labeled Impressionist painting *peinture de taches* or *peinture à la tache*—quite literally "painting by spots"[4]—and the group of artists themselves as an *école des taches,* a school of "spot-painters," whose founder was identified as Édouard Manet.[5] To the art dealer and critic Léon Gauchez in 1876 the Impressionists appeared to be a "secte de la pure tache" (a sect of the pure spot),[6] whose supreme creed was that there was only one true and pure spot, and that the Impressionists were its only true and venerable masters—"long live the pure spot!"[7] And still other critics spoke of a veritable *tachisme*[8]—a term that would have its own career in the reception of Neo-Impressionist Pointillism.

As opposed to the *touche* (brushstroke), a *tache* is frequently the result of an unintentional act. Spots usually arise by chance, unplanned; often they are the result of a mishap as well. Even where spots are created deliberately—as in the blotting process of Alexander Cozens in the eighteenth century—their shape at the very least owes a great deal to chance.[9] Generally speaking, however, spots are unintentional and perceived as a kind of flaw.[10] As such, painters attempt to avoid them—and when this is impossible, to get rid of them afterwards. Such unpleasant spots were also a topic in nineteenth-century discourse on photography. Almost every handbook of photography had something to say about them, noting how they could appear in various forms in a photograph and that their cause lay in either imperfect working materials or in faulty execution during developing.[11] At times there are entire lists of the most diverse spots, each with an explanation of where they came from and how they could be avoided.[12]

In relation to painting, *taches* were usually viewed critically. Just as in photography (fig. 3), the *taches* found in Impressionist paintings were often ascribed to accidents in the criticism of the salon[13] as well as its caricatures,[14] even if only at a polemical level. For example, a caricature by Cham (Amédée de Noé) that appeared in the magazine *Le Charivari* in 1877 under the title *The Art of Producing a Truly Impressionist Painting* shows a painter falling from a ladder along with his paint bucket. Here, the caricaturist has thus qualitatively equated the ensuant splashes of paint with an Impressionist painting.

That same year, in view of the round spots that speckle Pierre-Auguste Renoir's works *The Swing* (fig. 4) and *Dance at the Moulin de la Galette* (1876, Musée d'Orsay, Paris)*,* the critic Roger Ballu also initially assumed that the paintings had been involved in accident while on their way to the exhibition rooms. Only upon closer inspection did he realize that they were the result of the artist's intention to depict the effect of light filtering through the foliage onto people sitting beneath the trees.[15]

In addition to accidents, however, various painting processes based on chance were also put forward as fictitious explanations for the spots in Impressionism. Victor Fournel speculated in 1877 that Monet's painting of the Gare Saint-Lazare had come about thanks to the artist hurling a sponge full of paint against the canvas.[16] In 1880 the same critic speculated that the accumulation of colorful *taches* in the works of the Impressionists was due to a painting process that involved throwing paint-soaked brushes against the canvas.[17] In 1882 in relation to Alfred Sisley's works at the seventh Impressionist Exhibition the journalist Albert Wolff wrote in the conservative daily newspaper *Le Figaro* of *peinture en fusil* (painting with a gun), where the artist fired tubes of paint onto the canvas[18]—a polemic which would become a topos in the reception of Impressionism.

Still other reviewers compared the paintings of the Impressionists to a kaleidoscope because of their seemingly randomly arranged colored spots.[19] Finally, considering the style of Neo-Impressionist Pointillism, it was always joked that it was a *peinture en confetti*—a painting technique that consisted of sprinkling the canvas with bits of colored paper.

Spots in Painting

The use of the word *tache* in reference to a painting was common even before Impressionism; the term had even taken on its own meaning in the jargon of painting technique. As a specialist term, *tache* had been used since the mid-eighteenth century to refer to a portion of a work whose color did not harmonize with the adjacent parts of the picture—a meaning that was still to be found in the *Larousse* dictionary in 1875.[20] Both in salon criticism and in studio usage, however, the term had long since ceased to be employed in a pejorative sense alone. This was also known to the critic Jules Guillemot, who in his review of the third Impressionist Exhibition was enraged by the fashionable use and abuse of the word. For example, the cloak of Saint John in Peter Paul Rubens's *Deposition* in Antwerp would commonly be praised as a *tache superbe* (a magnificent patch) (fig. 5). With the Impressionists, however, a spot was only that which was commonly understood as a spot, and their painting was consequently nothing more than an indistinct series of them.[21]

The example of Rubens given by Guillemot already shows that the term *tache* can refer to a larger portion of a painting. This is also true of the *taches* that critics discovered in the paintings of the Impressionists. In 1867, for example, Émile Zola praised Manet's *Olympia* (fig. 6) as "a large pale mass against a black background,"[22] and in 1877 Gaston Vassy mocked Claude Monet's *The Turkeys* (fig. 7) as a large green patch populated by white spots with necks.[23] Nevertheless, in most cases discussions of *taches* referred to smaller units—such as the stick figures on Monet's *Boulevard des Capucines* (fig. 8). In extreme cases, a *tache* could even consist of a single dab of paint.

The *taches* of Impressionist painting are characterized by the fact that, viewed in isolation, they often elude interpretation in representational terms and only when seen together do they suggest an urban scene or landscape. For critics, *peinture à la tache* represented a radical break with the conventional painting methods practiced by the Old Masters.[24] Indeed, Impressionist spot-painting broke with traditional conventions of representation as taught at the Academy—not only with *dessin* (drawing) but also with modeling, that is, with the subtle shading that painting had employed since the Renaissance to lend a three-dimensional effect on depicted objects.[25] This is why Gustave Courbet negatively compared Manet's works to playing cards,[26] while Émile Zola, on the other hand, compared them positively to the *taches magnifiques* of Japanese woodblock prints.[27] Similarly, however, the teeming mass of countless small *taches* as found in many Impressionist paintings denies any evocation of spatial depth.[28]

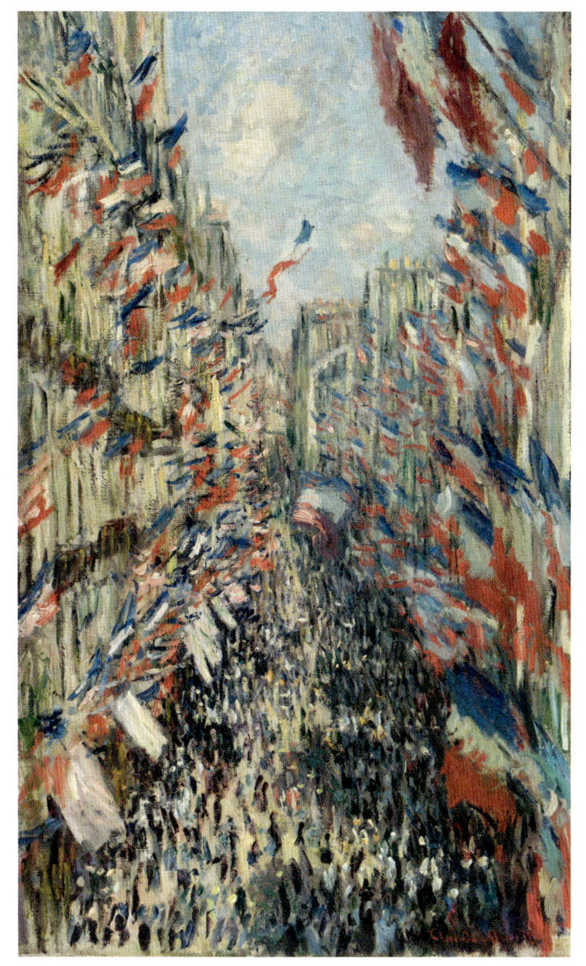

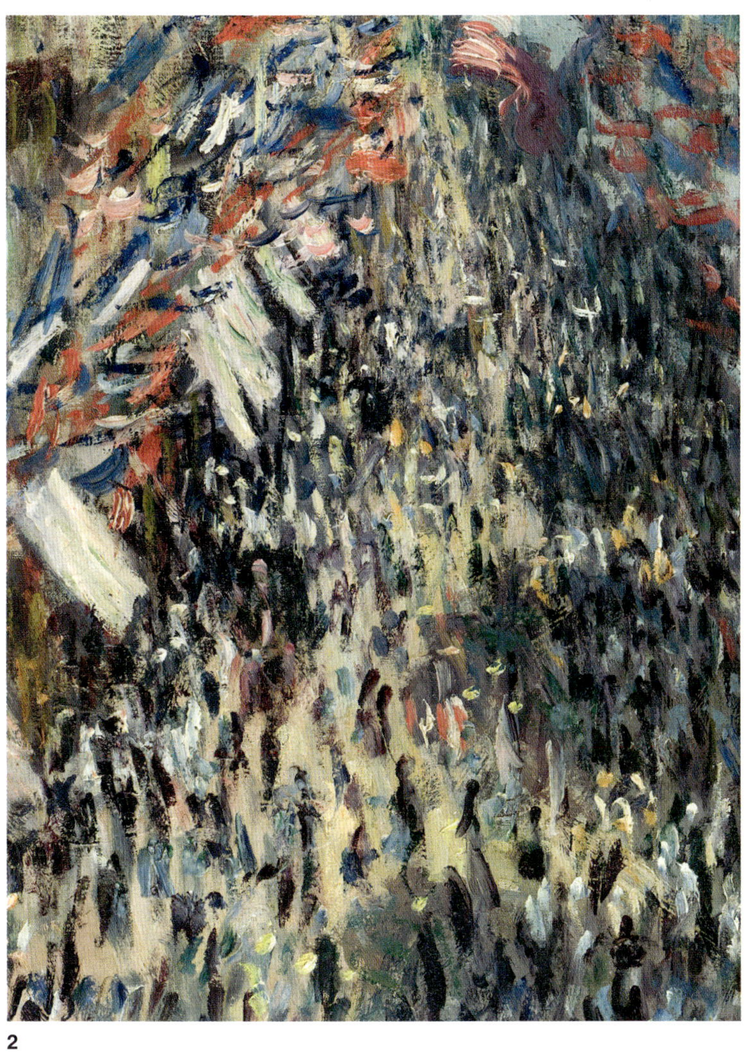

1 Claude Monet,
Rue Montorgueil in Paris:
Celebration of June 30, 1878, 1878,
Musée d'Orsay, Paris

2 Claude Monet,
Rue Montorgueil in Paris:
Celebration of June 30, 1878 (detail), 1878,
Musée d'Orsay, Paris

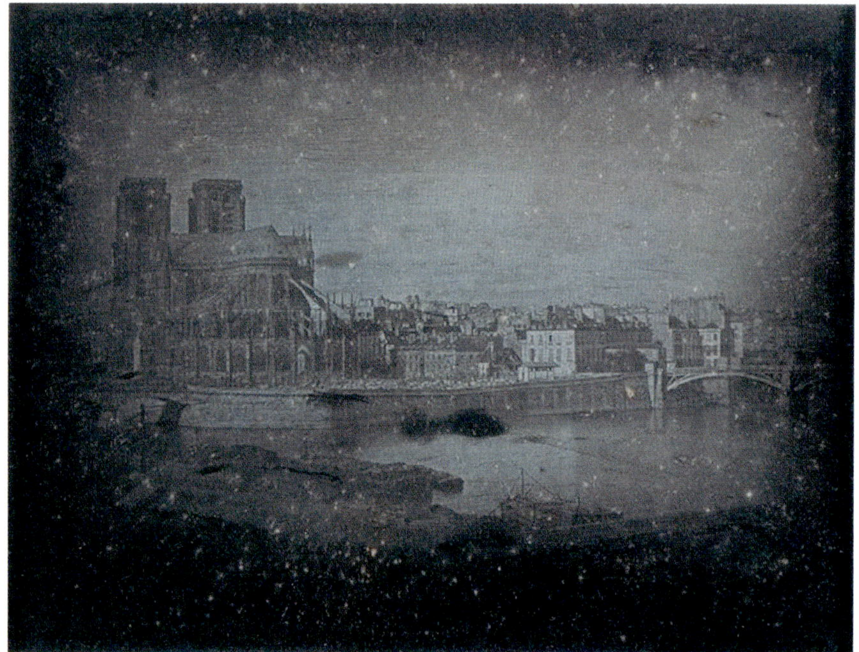

3

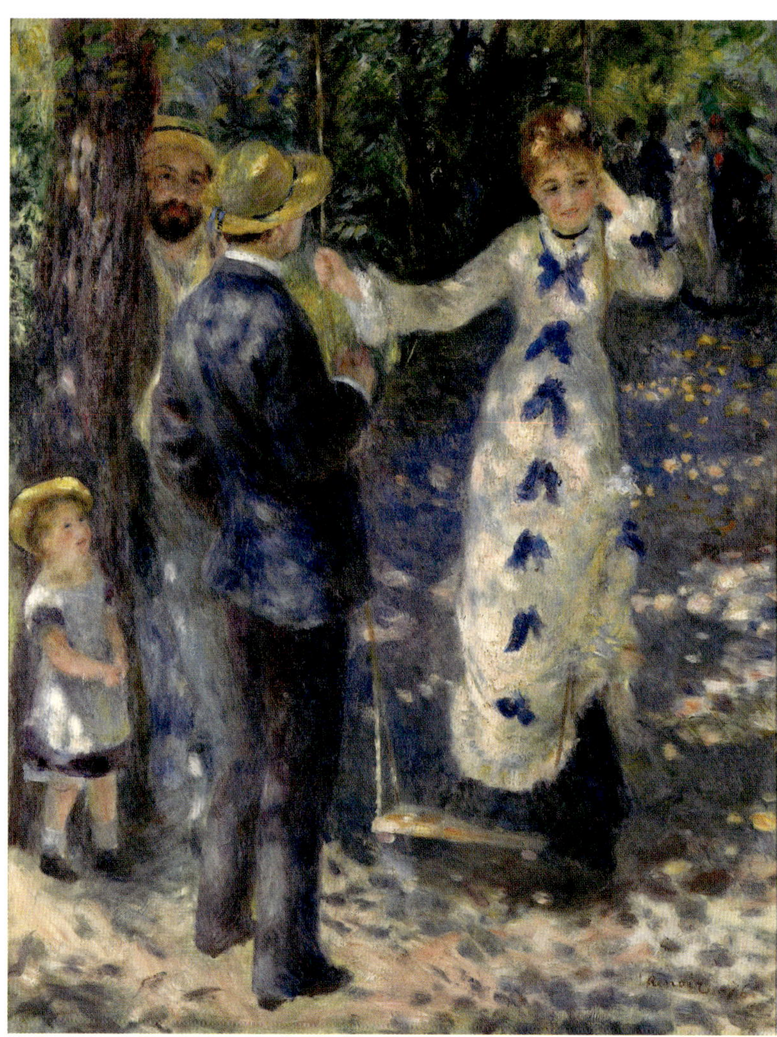

4

3 Louis Daguerre,
Notre-Dame and the Île de la Cité, Paris,
ca. 1838, Harry Ransom Center, Austin

4 Pierre-Auguste Renoir,
The Swing, 1876,
Musée d'Orsay, Paris

The two-dimensional arrangement of pictures with juxtaposed *taches* had a programmatic meaning for the Impressionists. In their paintings, they were primarily concerned with capturing not the subject as such, but the visual impression it evoked. The French term *impression* has to do with sensory physiology: *impression* refers to the stimulus received by a sensory organ. An *impression* is thus at the same time the sensory raw material of perception—it must be processed by the brain in order to become a sensation.

In visual perception, the *impression* is the image that the retina receives before it is evaluated and interpreted by the brain.[29] Each individual stimulation of the retina was imagined as a colored dot, so that the retinal image resembled a patchwork of different colored spots. In order to explain this as vividly as possible, Hippolyte Taine instructed readers of his 1870 book *De l'intelligence* (On Intelligence) to climb the Arc de Triomphe at the beginning of the first chapter. From this vantage point, a truly Impressionist panorama presents itself: "If we ascend the Arc de l'Étoile and look down on the Champs-Élysées, we see a number of black or various coloured specks stirring about on the roadway or pavements. That is all our eyes distinguish."[30]

Taine attributed the fact that these spots can be interpreted as walking people to experience: only due to experience are we able to interpret this raw sensory data. Spots in Impressionist paintings can thus be directly linked to the most current findings of contemporary perceptual physiologists, who understood that strictly speaking the Impressionist *taches* are not spots at all, but the representation of spots—the very spots that form images on the retina.[31]

Even contemporary critics repeatedly associated the paintings of the Impressionists with retinal images—though their judgments about them differed. While proponents of Impressionism considered this a reflection of a highly sensitive power of observation, skeptics only viewed it as evidence of pronounced visual impairment, if not serious eye disease.[32] There was also criticism of the importance of the eye in Impressionist paintings. French politician Amadée Descubes in 1877 warned, for example, that the Impressionist doctrine imposed the inferiority of our organs on art. He believed that the fact that a fleeting glance only affords viewers a vague impression of their environment was due to the imperfection of our eyes. He felt that this imperfection could be corrected through attentive observation, a few moments of which would turn (indecipherable) spots into (determinable) forms.[33]

Images received by the retina actually represent only the raw sensory material of visual perception—for Taine too. The fact that we do not perceive reality as a chaotic collection of colorful spots is due to the experience that constantly configures retinal images into meaningful pictures. For Taine, this is where the perception of a person who has always been able to see differs from that of someone born blind and later gifted with sight, or a newborn child who does not yet have any experience. Unable to interpret what they see, both would perceive the outside world only as a swarm of *taches* of different colors.[34] Yet Taine also believed that painters who were versed in color could reacquire such primal ways of seeing and could reduce their models to a colorful spot that was more or less differentiated.[35]

The Impressionists also seemed to believe in the possibility of freeing themselves from all traditional artistic conventions so that they could devote themselves to the direct observation of nature—thus regaining the "innocence of the eye." This myth of the "innocent eye" and the belief that there was such a thing as "pure vision"—in other words, a way of seeing that was not always simultaneously filtered by our experience and our previous knowledge—were widespread in the nineteenth century.[36]

Between Proximity and Distance

In as much as they saw themselves indebted to the natural eye the Impressionists also differentiated themselves from those painters who—as Gautier had put it—were following "photography's advice." They opposed modern mechanics with natural vision. This is remarkable because the recording medium of the camera was considered superior to the retina. For contemporaries, the camera was distinguished by the high degree of precision with which it reproduced even the most minute details—details that the human eye is incapable of registering in such abundance with a single glance. Such precision was one of the great advantages of the new medium for scientific use. At the same time, the details often exerted such great fascination on the lay public that people liked to study them under a magnifying glass, eager to extract even more information—however trivial it might be—from the image.[37]

Only in the field of art was the detail afforded by photography not considered an advantage, but a disadvantage. In 1870 *Larousse* defined detail as a "secondary and less important aspect of a work of art" in relation to literature and the fine arts—and in this regard also quoted Voltaire, according to whom details were vermin capable of killing great works of art.[38]

It was precisely this obtrusiveness of details that usurped the viewer's attention that was criticized from an art-theoretical point of view. Famous in this context are the remarks that Eugène Delacroix noted in his diary on September 1, 1859. "If the eye had the perfection of a magnifying glass," the painter mused, "photography would be unbearable: one would see every leaf on a tree, every tile on a roof, and on these tiles, mosses, insects, etc."[39]

In many respects the Impressionists' painting marked a kind of counterpole, though it hardly met the standards of academic art theory either. Unlike photography, Impressionist painting did not invite close-up observation with a magnifying glass. When viewed up close—and critics were largely unanimous on this point—it was often not even possible to determine the subject of the painting with any certainty. What imposed itself upon the viewer at such a close distance were not details, but raw color. Even a critic sympathetic to Impressionism, such as Ernest Chesneau, freely admitted that Monet's painting *Boulevard des Capucines,* for example, which one would call a masterpiece from a distance, dissolved into an indecipherable chaos of paint scraped off the palette when viewed up close (fig. 8).[40] Therefore, critics always advised looking at the paintings of the Impressionists from some distance. This opinion was expressed by both Impressionism's supporters and opponents. In the case of the latter, it always took on a polemical undertone, spurring critics to outdo themselves in specifying the exact distance that the viewer had to keep in order to be able to make out any form in an Impressionist painting at all. The more moderate among them estimated it at ten steps, the more malicious at thirty to fifty meters even. Several critics advised looking through narrowed eyes so as to preserve the impression captured in the painting[41]—that is, instead of concentrating the gaze, putting a kind of soft focus "lens" over it to merge the disparately juxtaposed *taches* into a harmonious image.

Photographic Effects in Painting

While spots in a photograph were always seen as a flaw because they impaired the transparency of the medium, they were constitutive for Impressionist painting. But it would be shortsighted to see the Impressionist *taches* only as a means of distinguishing itself from the detailed precision of photography. The facts are more complicated. For there was at least one kind of *tache* in Impressionism whose existence it owed to photography. This assertion is intended here to tie in with a thesis launched as early as 1968 by Aaron Scharf in his seminal monograph *Art and Photography,* although he did not address the controversy over Impressionist *taches* in that context. Rather, Scharf was interested in a different phenomenon, which he called the "blurred image." As a noun, *blur* refers to an out-of-focus area of an image.

Scharf argued that the imprecise execution of certain details in Impressionist paintings—as previously in those of Camille Corot—derives from the motion blur of early photography. Thus, in the soft manner Corot had used to paint foliage since the 1850s Scharf saw the reception of early landscape photography, in which the movement of the trees often showed a similar indeterminacy due to the longer exposure time still required (cat. 56).[42] Accordingly, the passersby in Monet's *Boulevard des Capucines* are not reproduced as the eye would see them, but as a camera would have recorded them—though, as the author admits, not a camera from when Monet created his painting, when it became possible to freeze the movement of pedestrians without any blur due to a shorter exposure time, but rather one from the early days of photography, when passersby could often only be captured as shadows (fig. 9).[43] According to Scharf's thesis, Monet had thus been inspired by an "imperfection" of early photography. Moreover, Scharf says, in the painterly simulation of photographic blurring of movement Monet saw a means of catching hold of the *instantaneité* that was so important to him in his pictures. Unlike instantaneous photography, he did not aim to freeze the movement, but instead to capture its fleeting nature on the canvas.[44]

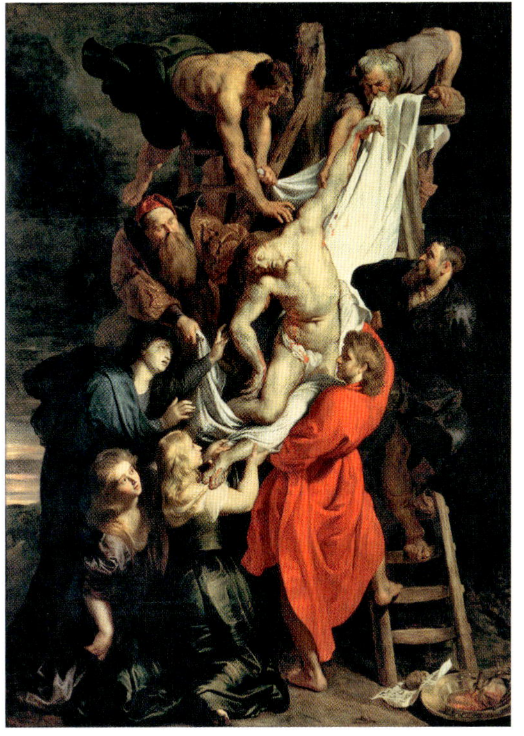

5

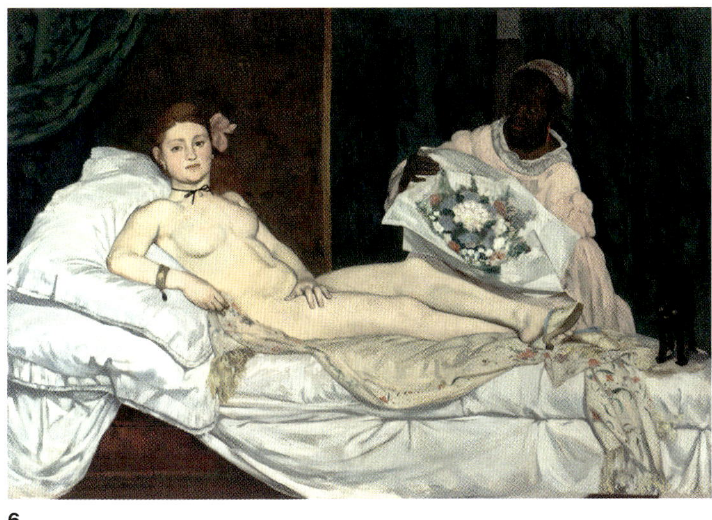

6

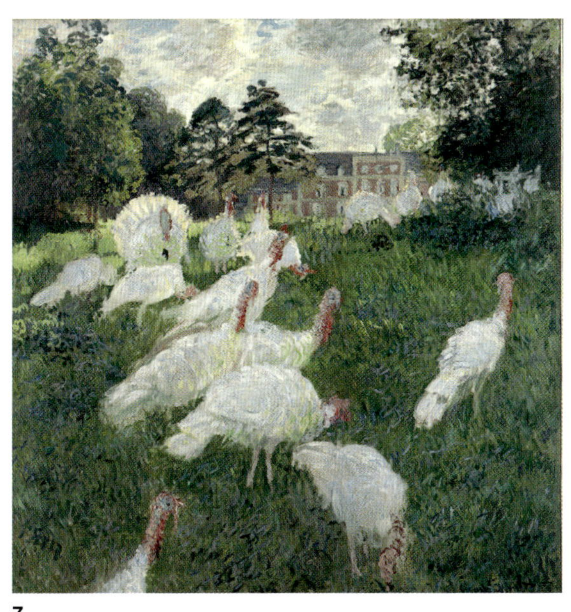

7

5 Peter Paul Rubens,
The Descent from the Cross, 1612,
Cathedral of Our Lady, Antwerp

6 Édouard Manet,
Olympia, 1863,
Musée d'Orsay, Paris

7 Claude Monet,
Turkeys, 1877,
Musée d'Orsay, Paris

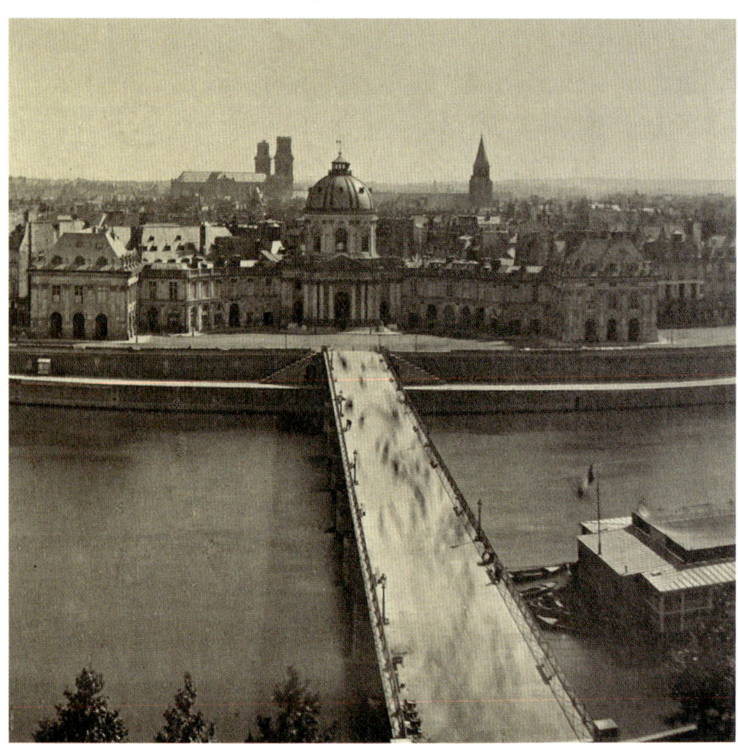

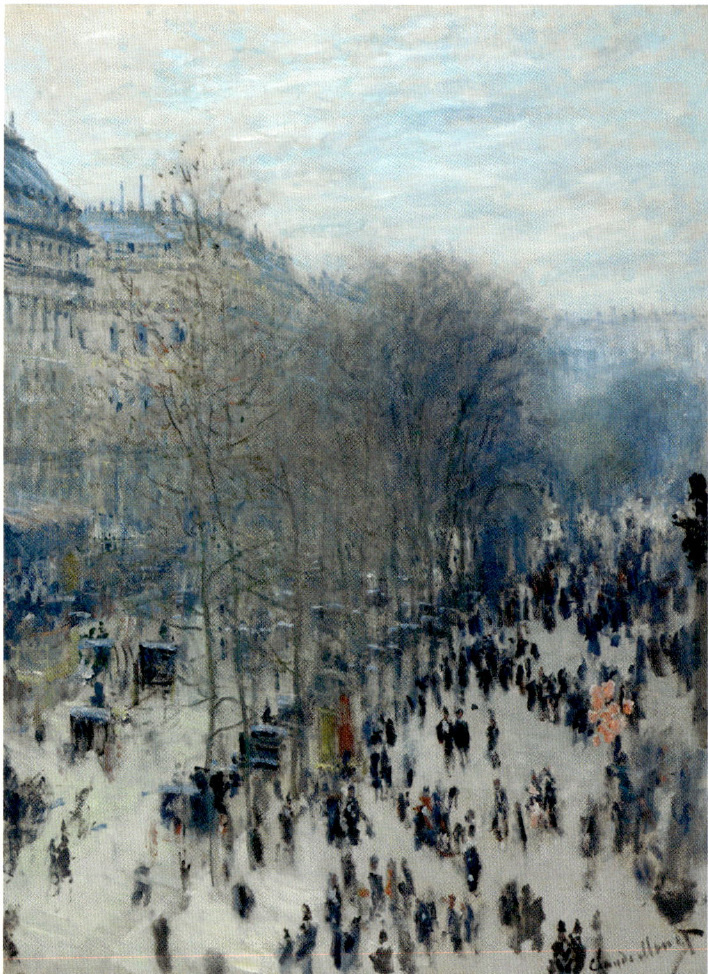

8 Claude Monet,
Boulevard des Capucines, 1873–74,
The Nelson-Atkins Museum of Art,
Kansas City

9 Adolphe Braun,
Panorama of Paris (detail), 1867,
Société française de photographie, Paris

10 Édouard Manet,
Self-Portrait with a Palette, 1879,
Steven A. Cohen Collection, Greenwich, CT

8

9

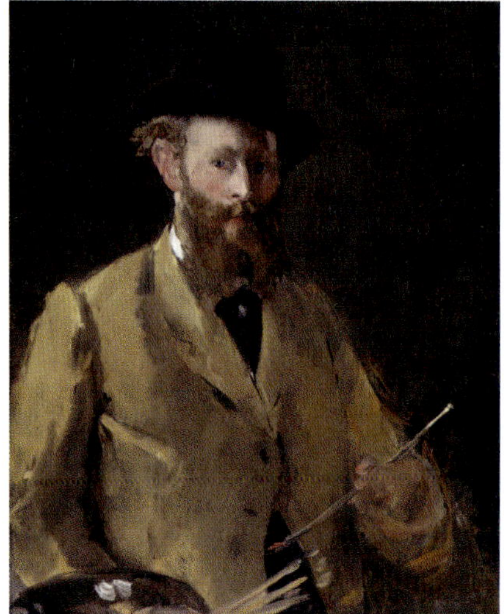

10

While not every *tache* in an Impressionist painting can be understood as an indicator of motion, Scharf's observation can be applied to many other Impressionist paintings—including numerous landscapes, such as Pierre-Auguste Renoir's painting *The Gust of Wind* (1872, Fitzwilliam Museum, Cambridge), in which the parts of the picture that have apparently been smudged using a rag are also strongly reminiscent of motion blur in photography. In Édouard Manet's work, on the contrary, it is often the hands that trigger such associations, such as the one of the gentleman holding a cigar and sitting behind the table in the painting *Luncheon in the Studio* (1868, Neue Pinakothek, Munich) or the one with the brush in *Self-Portrait with Palette* (fig. 10)—a diffuse *tache* so masterfully placed in the picture, it is as if the artist had wanted to present himself as the leader of the *école des taches* that the press had declared him to be.[45]

Translated from German by Alexander Booth

My thanks to Gustav Eckart, Franz Hefele, and
Christine Krüger for their critical reading.

1   Monet formulates this aim in a letter of October 7, 1890,
    to Gustave Geffroy, which is published in Gustave Geffroy,
    Claude Monet: Sa vie, son temps, son œuvre, Paris 1922,
    189.
2   Théophile Gautier, "Salon de 1857," in *L'Artiste,* nouvelle
    série 1 (1857), 189–92, here 191.
3   On the *touche* in the competition between painters and
    photographers see Krüger 2007, 229–86, 353–67.
4   Albert Wolff, for example, speaks of a "peinture de taches";
    see "Édouard Manet," in *Le Figaro* (May 1, 1883). The label
    "peinture de taches" is used by Pierre Véron, "Courrier
    de Paris," in *Le Monde illustré* (April 13, 1879), 22, quoted
    after Berson 1996, vol. 1, 249.
5   Marius Chaumelin, "Actualités: L'Exposition des intran-
    sigeants," in *La Gazette des étrangers* (April 8, 1876), 1–2,
    quoted after ibid., 67. Cf. also Charles Bigot, "Causerie
    artistique: L'Exposition des 'impressionnistes,'" in *La Revue
    politique et littéraire* (April 28, 1877), 1045–48, where
    the Impressionists are described as the "école de teinte
    plate"; quoted after ibid., 136.
6   Léon Mancino [Léon Gauchez], "Deuxième exposition de
    peintures, dessins, gravures, faite par un groupe
    d'artistes," in *L'Art* 5 (1876), 36–37, quoted after ibid., 98.
7   Léon Mancino [Léon Gauchez], "La Descente de la cour-
    tille," in *L'Art* 9 (1877), 68–71, quoted after ibid., 165.
8   See, for example, Richard Graul, "Pariser Ausstellungen,"
    in *Kunstchronik* 20 (1885), col. 581–88, here col. 584,
    where the expression is used in view of the works shown
    by Monet at the Salon in 1885. Cf. also Victor Fournel,
    "Les Œuvres et les hommes: Courrier du théâtre, de la
    littérature et des arts," in *Le Correspondant* (May 10, 1880),
    524, where the Impressionists are described as
    "tachistes"; quoted after Berson 1996, vol. 1, 282.
9   On the productive use of spots and blots in the art of the
    early nineteenth century see at length Friedrich Weltzien,
    *Fleck: Das Bild der Selbsttätigkeit; Justinus Kerner und
    die Klecksografie als experimentelle Bildpraxis zwischen
    Ästhetik und Naturwissenschaft,* Göttingen 2011.
10 An exception are the spots in an animal's plumage or fur,
    which were often perceived as beautiful. But at the latest
    with Charles Darwin's theory of evolution even such
    natural spots were understood as the result of countless
    coincidences. On this point see Matthias Krüger, "Der
    Begriff des *disegno* im Zeitalter der Evolutionstheorie:
    Biologische Konzepte in Charles Blancs Grammaire des
    arts du dessin," in *Die Biologie der Kreativität:
    Ein produktionsästhetisches Denkmodell in der Moderne,*
    ed. Matthias Krüger, Zurich 2013, 75–90, here 82–84.
11 On such accidents see Peter Geimer, *Bilder aus Versehen:
    Eine Geschichte fotografischer Erscheinungen,* Hamburg
    2010, 57–134.

12 This observation is based on an extensive review of the
    digital offering of photographic handbook literature
    available from the Bibliothèque nationale de France in
    Paris: gallica.bnf.fr. For reasons of space, I only cite three
    randomly selected examples here: Auguste Belloc,
    *Photographie rationelle: Traité complet théorique et pra-
    tique, applications diverses,* Paris 1862, 320–22 ("Des
    taches et de quelques difficultés"); D[esiré] v[an] Monck-
    hoven, *Traité général de photographie,* Paris 1865, 267
    ("Taches"); Alphonse Davanne, *La Photographie: Traité
    théorique et pratique,* vol. 2, Paris 1888, 80–81, 110–14. In
    contrast, the photographic handbook literature of the
    nineteenth century does not contain a single reference
    that acknowledges stains as a positive quality of a
    photograph.
13 On art criticism's reception of the *tache,* cf. Oscar Reutersvärd,
    "The Accentuated Brush Stroke of the Impressionists:
    The Debate Concerning Decomposition in Impressionism,"
    in *Journal of Aesthetics and Art Criticism* 10 (1951), 273–78.
14 On caricatures of Impressionist *peinture de taches,* cf.
    Anna Großkopf, *Die Arbeit des Künstlers in der Karikatur:
    Eine Diskursgeschichte künstlerischer Techniken in der
    Moderne,* Bielefeld 2016, 312–38.
15 Roger Ballu, "L'Exposition des peintres impressionnistes,"
    in *La Chronique des arts et de la curiosité* (April 14, 1877),
    392, quoted after Berson 1996, vol. 1, 125.
16 Bernadille [Victor Fournel], "Chronique Parisienne:
    L'Exposition des impressionistes," in *Le Français*
    (April 13, 1877), 130, quoted after ibid., 130.
17 Fournel 1880 (see note 8), quoted after ibid., vol. 1, 282.
18 Albert Wolff, "Quelques expositions," in *Le Figaro*
    (March 2, 1882), 1, quoted after ibid., 416.
19 Camille Delaville, "Chronique parisienne: Débauche
    de peinture," in *La Presse* (April 2, 1880), 1–2, quoted after
    Berson 1996, vol. 1, 276.
20 *Grand Dictionnaire universel du XIXe siècle,* ed. Pierre
    Larousse, vol. 14, Paris 1875, 1382, s.v. "tache." Cf. also
    the French expression *faire tache* for "to stand out" or
    "to disturb harmony." On the word's etymology cf.
    Dictionnaire historique de la langue française, ed. Alain Rey,
    vol. 3, Paris 2019, 3745, s.v. "tache."
21 Jules Guillemot: "Causerie artistique: L'Exposition des
    impressionnistes," in *La Nation* (April 19, 1877), 3, quoted
    after Berson 1996, vol. 1, 153–54.
22 Émile Zola, "Édouard Manet, étude biographique et
    critique" (1867), in *Écrits sur l'art,* Paris 1991, 160; English
    translation by Michael Ross in *Portrait of Manet by Himself
    and His Contemporaries,* ed. Pierre Courthion and Pierre
    Cailler, London 1960, 113–39, quoted after *Art in Theory,
    1815–1900: An Anthology of Changing Ideas,* ed.
    Charles Harrison, Paul Wood, and Jason Gaiger, Malden,
    MA, 1998, 562.
23 Anonymous [Gaston Vassy], "La Journée à Paris:
    L'Exposition des impressionnalistes," in *L'Événement*
    (April 6, 1877), 2, quoted after ibid., 145.
24 See, for example, Étienne Carjat, "L'Exposition du
    boulevard des Capucines," in *Le Patriote français*
    (April 27, 1874), 3, quoted after Berson 1996, vol. 1, 15.
25 Edmond Bazire, *Manet,* Paris 1884, 135–36. The author,
    however, recommends that his readers make up their
    own minds by looking at a photograph of a Manet to see
    that the missing "dessin" and "modelé" do not detract
    from the spatial effect of the paintings.
26 At least this is the anecdote as reported by Albert Wolff,
    among others. Wolff 1883 (see note 4).

27 Zola 1991 (see note 22), 152.

28 These qualities of Impressionist painting led the American art critic Clement Greenberg to later speak of "flatness." See Clement Greenberg, "Modernist Painting," in Greenberg, *The Collected Essays and Criticism,* ed. John O'Brian, vol. 4: *Modernism with a Vengeance, 1957–1969,* Chicago and London 1988, 85–93, here 86.

29 *Grand Dictionnaire universel du XIXe siècle,* ed. Pierre Larousse, vol. 9, Paris 1873, 605, s.v. "impression."

30 Hippolyte Taine, *De l'intelligence,* vol. 1, Paris 1870, 25; English translation by T. D. Haye published as *On Intelligence,* London 1871, 1. Here my argument follows that of Charles Stuckey, "Monet's Art and the Act of Vision," in *Aspects of Monet: A Symposium on the Artist's Life and Times,* ed. John Rewald and Frances Weitzenhofer, New York 1984, 107–21.

31 On the ambivalent status of the *tache* as "sign" and "non-sign" see particularly Øystein Sjåstad, *A Theory of the Tache in Nineteenth-Century Painting,* Farnham 2014, 19–21. Less convincing, on the other hand, is the neuroscientist reading of Impressionist brushwork in James D. Herbert, *Brushstroke and Emergence: Courbet, Impressionism, Picasso,* Chicago and London 2015, 51–74.

32 On the impact of physiology on the critical reception of Impressionism see Carla Cugini, *"Er sieht einen Fleck, er malt einen Fleck": Physiologische Optik, Impressionimus und Kunstkritik,* Basel 2006.

33 Amadée Descubes, "L'Exposition des impressionnistes," in *Gazette des lettres, des sciences et des arts* 1 (1877), 185–88, quoted after Berson 1996, vol. 1, 143. Cf. also Arthur Baignères, "Exposition de peinture par un groupe d'artistes, rue Le Peletier, 11," in *L'Echo univers* (April 13, 1876), 3, quoted after ibid., 54.

34 Taine 1870 (see note 30), vol. 2, 25–26.

35 Ibid., 120–22. John Ruskin already had committed painting to the reproduction of the patches perceived by the eye. John Ruskin, *The Elements of Drawing in Three Letters to Beginners,* London 1857, 7n. The Impressionists' approach was later described in identical terms. See, for example, Georges Guéroult, "Du rôle du mouvement des yeux dans les émotions esthétiques," in *La Gazette des beaux-arts* 24 (1881), 88n.

36 On the concept of the "innocent eye" in the reception of Impressionism cf. Annika Lamer, *Die Ästhetik des unschuldigen Auges: Merkmale impressionistischer Wahrnehmung in den Kunstkritiken von Émile Zola, Joris-Karl Huysmans und Félix Fénéon,* Würzburg 2009.

37 On the role of details in the contest between painting and photography cf. Krüger 2007, 24–251; van Brevern 2018, here 112–15.

38 *Grand Dictionnaire universel du XIXe siècle,* ed. Pierre Larousse, vol. 6, Paris 1870, s.v. "détail," 612 ("Parties secondaires et moins importantes d'un ouvrage").

39 Eugène Delacroix, *Journal: 1822–1863,* Paris 1981, 744; English translation by Walter Pach, in *The Journal of Eugène Delacroix,* London 1938, quoted after *Art in Theory, 1815–1900* (see note 22), 362.

40 Ernest Chesneau, "Avant le Salon," in *Paris-Journal* (April 2, 1874), 3, quoted after Berson 1996, vol. 1, 18. On this debate see Reutersvärd 1951 (see note 13), 275–76, and Matthias Krüger, "Ernest Meissonier und die Lupe: Fern- und Nahsicht im französischen Salon," in *Kunstgeschichte* 2 (2009), 1–40, here 1–2.

41 See, for example, Henrie Mornand, "Les Impressionnistes," in *La Revue littéraire et artistique* (May 1, 1880), 67–68, quoted after Berson 1996, vol. 1, 303; X., "Choses et autres," in *La Vie Parisienne* (May 10, 1879), 275–76, quoted after Chicago und London 1988, 252; Joris-Karl Huysmans, "L'Exposition des indépendants en 1880," in Huysmans, *L'Art moderne,* Paris 1883, 85–123, quoted after Berson 1996, vol. 1, 285.

42 Scharf 1968, 89–92.

43 Ibid., 169–72. On the state of instantaneous photography in around 1860, see ibid., 182. Cf. also Marlene Schnelle-Schneyder, *Photographie und Wahrnehmung am Beispiel der Bewegungsdarstellung im 19. Jahrhundert,* Marburg 1990.

44 Scharf 1968, 172. Regarding the blur in photography cf. Amelia Groom, "Objects Moving Are Not Impressed: Reading into the Blur," in *Time in the History of Art,* ed. Dan Karlholm and Keith Moxey, New York and London 2018, 240–48. On the blur in the competition between painters and photographers, cf. London 2000, 57. This was not, however, done by evoking photographic blur alone, but by suggesting quick execution as well. See ibid., 17. On concepts of time in Impressionist painting, cf. André Dombrowski, "Instants, Moments, Minutes: Impressionism and the Industrialisation of Time," in *Monet and the Birth of Impressionism,* exh. cat., Städel Museum, Frankfurt am Main 2015, 36–45.

45 Regarding this party cf. Diana Wiehn, "Medial Transpositions: Édouard Manet and Photography," in *Manet: Painting the Gaze,* exh. cat., Hamburger Kunsthalle 2016, 103–11, here 108–09.

Monika Faber

Color Experiments
The Vienna Camera-Club

For a long time the fact that photography could initially only depict its subjects in black-and-white seemed to be one of the medium's shortcomings. Unlike painting, for decades photography could only reproduce motifs in a limited color spectrum. At the turn of the twentieth century, however, the development of artistic color photography in Austria was to receive a decisive boost. In the circles of the Vienna Camera-Club, photographers Hugo Henneberg, Heinrich Kühn, and Hans Watzek experimented with different methods to produce color-intensive photographs. Anyone who sees one of these large, gum bichromate landscapes for the first time will hardly believe that they are looking at a photograph.[1] The unusual format of these fine art prints, their deep color, their lack of detail, and the smoothness of their surface are more reminiscent of graphic sheets, but this effect could not be achieved by means of any painterly or drawing technique. Similar to gum bichromate prints, the autochromes that had been projected on the walls of the Camera-Club in Vienna since 1907 did not fit into any particular visual tradition. Not even the manually colored diapositives that traveling amateur photographers had proudly presented at the club could hold their own against the radiance and intense colors of the new autochrome technology. This essay explores the scientific experiments leading to the realization of a dream to create a colorful photograph between photosensitive paper and prepared glass plates that would have been inconceivable without them.

While the Pictorialist work of Hugo Henneberg and Hans Watzek barely spanned a decade that lasted only until 1904, Heinrich Kühn continued to work with similar goals until his death in 1944. Late in life, he published books and articles that shed light on his working methods and those of his friends in the Camera-Club. In these writings Kühn emphasizes his passion for working in the darkroom, which is where the experiments to perfect the complex printing techniques that made each image unique took place. He strictly rejected any direct manual markings or interventions. As a result, his color experiments, ranging from gum bichromate prints to autochromes, particularly lend themselves to comparison with Impressionist paintings.

Photography's rapid technical development since its invention was announced in 1839 more or less amounted to an improvement in the precision of the image quality. This was what distinguished it from all other visual media and made it so indispensable in personal, scientific, and commercial use as a document that was purportedly objective since it was considered "authentic." Consciously distinguishing themselves from this, from about 1880 onward some amateurs began to lead the photograph out of the "lowlands" of commercial use, with the compromises this required, toward being a "free" medium with artistic pretensions.[2]

The idea had originated in England, where the journal *The Amateur Photographer* (under Alfred Horsley Hinton's direction since 1884) promoted new developments in photography. In 1887 the Club of Amateur-Photographers (later renamed Camera-Club), "which had set itself the goal of awakening an understanding of 'pictorial photography' in wide circles," was founded in Vienna.[3] What is less known is the fact that all aspects of scientific photography were examined in detail and the latest developments in this field presented first in the *Photographische Rundschau* and then in the *Wiener Photographische Blätter,* the association's own lavishly designed publications.

These scientific photographs were regarded less as true images of nature than as disembodied surrogates of the objects depicted, objects that often revealed more about themselves in the images than to the naked eye: as a result, not only was the artist's pencil regarded as deceptive, but under certain circumstances the viewer's eye as well. The term *scholar's retina* became common for photographs that captured a potential increase in image information in long exposures (for astronomy) or through extremely short shutter speeds (chronophotography).[4] When a little later it turned out that the light-sensitive layer also responded to phenomena invisible to humans, such as electric charges or X-rays, the difference between how the eye functioned and the creation of a photographic image finally became evident.

It seems quite clear that the photography-obsessed amateurs in Vienna informed themselves about these constant improvements in photography through lectures and publications. What is less obvious, however, is the fact that important protagonists of the new direction of Pictorialism such as Alfred Stieglitz in the United States, Robert Demachy in France, and Heinrich Kühn and Hugo Henneberg in Austria were themselves versed in the field of scientific photography. This and

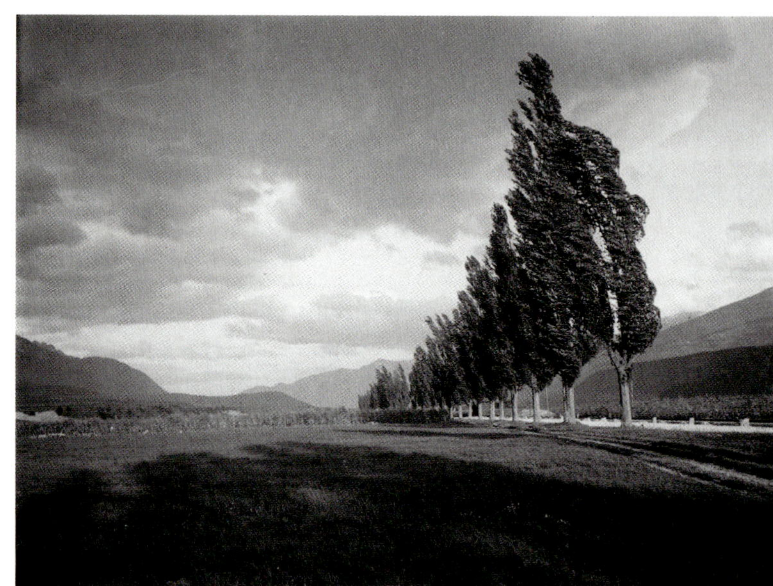

1

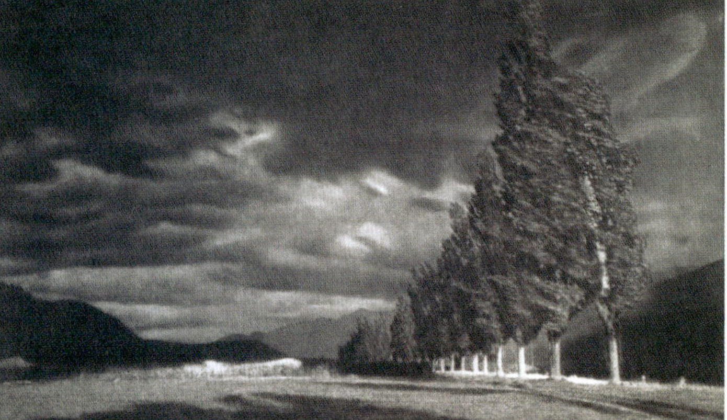

2

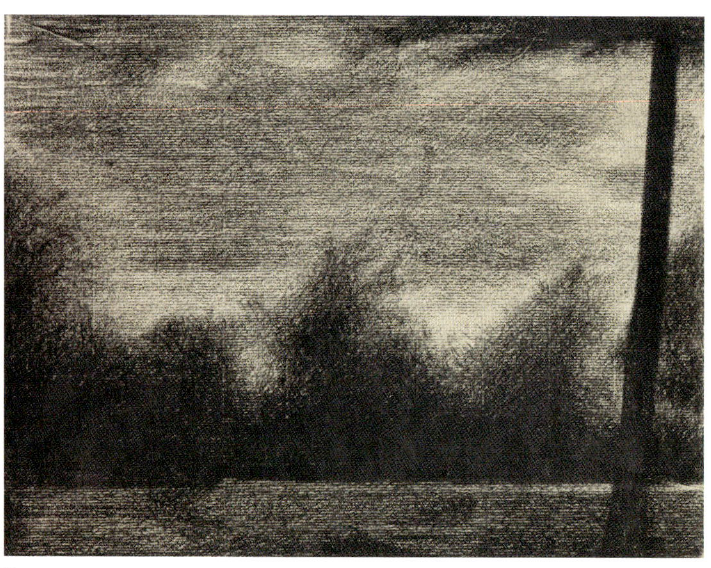

3

1 Heinrich Kühn,
Scirocco, 1898, author's archive

2 Heinrich Kühn,
Scirocco, 1899–1901,
The Metropolitan Museum of Art, New York

3 Georges Seurat,
The Edge of the Forest, ca. 1883,
Von der Heydt-Museum, Wuppertal

other scientific knowledge was indeed helpful for the success of their experiments on the way to "pictorial photography" as a kind of retina of subjective perception.

The photography amateurs are a symptom of the bourgeoisie, which in the second half of the nineteenth century enjoyed increasing levels of prosperity in the Western world that in turn allowed a larger group of people to spend time on personal interests. In contrast to their fathers' generation, some of whom had amassed large fortunes and displayed them in traditional ways, many of the sons had different values. Although these upwardly mobile citizens shared the aristocracy's resentment toward actively making money, for many of them aristocratic idleness was not the model to be imitated but rather a turn to culture, which in Germany is known as *Bildungsbürgertum*.[5] Collecting paintings, going to the theater, studying classical literature, and personal involvement in promoting cultural institutions were widespread. But it was only in photography, which many had learned to master as a result of the medium's technical simplification in the 1880s, that the wealthy attempted to be creative on a large scale themselves. What had begun as a modern, highly athletic pastime that people pursued together in clubs was "elevated to an artistic sphere."[6]

Heinrich Kühn and Hugo Henneberg are typical examples of this phenomenon. However, the drawing teacher Hans Watzek was also a welcome member of the Camera-Club, as were renowned scholars such as the physicist and Gestalt psychologist Ernst Mach. The ideal of the educated middle class was that artists and scientists could achieve a social status that blurred their economic differences to millionaires.[7] Nor should the female photographers of the aristocracy and bourgeoisie be forgotten: the Camera-Club in Vienna was the first on the continent to also admit women.

Henneberg, who became a member of the Camera-Club in 1891, was soon joined by Watzek. Kühn was to follow in 1894. The three were associated with the founding artists of the Vienna Secession that in turn recognized the artistic efforts of the "Kleeblatt" (Trifolium), as the photographing friends referred to themselves, by publishing pictures of theirs in the first volume of the magazine *Ver Sacrum* as early as 1898. In 1902 the artists' association also exhibited their photographs in Joseph Maria Olbrich's new building on Karlsplatz.

Subsequently, several important advocates of Viennese modernism were to become involved in writing about art photography.[8] They argued that photography should be considered an art form as part of the Secession's general renewal efforts, often in comparison with the similarly highly valued achievements of the applied arts. There, too, "machine" production was rejected in favor of the elaborate manual process that later became constitutive of the Wiener Werkstätte. Henneberg and Viktor Spitzer, an amateur photographer who is occasionally considered a "Kleeblatt"[9] member, participated in the project of an artists' settlement on Vienna's Hohe Warte hill and moved into the houses designed by Josef Hoffmann in 1902. Their neighbors were the painter and interior designer Koloman Moser as well as the painter and art entrepreneur Carl Moll, two founding members of the Vienna Secession.[10]

Not only had Hoffmann already provided space for the photographs of the owners in the houses on the Hohe Warte, but paintings and photographs enjoyed equal status on the walls—in Henneberg's case, for example, next to his own landscapes and Klimt's portrait of his wife Marie (1901–02, Kunstmuseum Moritzburg, Halle an der Saale). At Moll's, photographs by Henneberg and Kühn were hung adjacent to works by Paul Gauguin or Vincent van Gogh, which Moll—initially as exhibition organizer of the Vienna Secession and then as director of the avant-garde gallery Miethke—had exhibited for the first time in Vienna.

Platinum Prints: Mood Pictures

The work that Kühn retrospectively identified as his first artistic photograph has survived. A platinum print labeled *Innsbruck, December 1894,* it differs markedly from the surviving conventional landscapes of the previous period. The recognizable locations of the earlier period—a motif on Lake Garda, say, or a city view of Innsbruck—have given way to an unspectacular, focused glimpse of nature in which snow-covered grass and undergrowth extend into the depths, and the horizon is bordered by bare trees.

With this image Kühn inscribed himself into a precisely defined artistic environment that allowed for both photographic influences and connections to contemporary painting. The dating proves that it was created immediately after his first encounter with Henneberg and Watzek. For their intimate landscapes they used English photographs that had been known to them for some time as models.[11] They were familiar with Peter Henry Emerson's ideas from his influential book *Naturalistic Photography for Students of the Art* (1889), which provided a reckoning with the usual staged and retouched photographs. Following the German physiologist Hermann von Helmholtz, Emerson also distinguished between the perception of machines and humans: in order to depict human vision—which does not perceive equally sharply in the entire visual field—as faithfully as possible, photographs were not to be sharp throughout the entire image.[12] In Vienna this went so far that Ernst Mach's radical understanding of Helmholtz's visual field could serve as a frame to evoke an impression of the subjective mood during the process of seeing (fig. 8). The result represented the direct counterpart to the "scholar's retina," and could be understood as a "reproduction of the impression as seen through an artistic temperament."[13]

Stimmung, meaning "mood" or "atmosphere," is also the term that is closely linked to painting in the German-speaking world of the time, such as the landscapes of Rudolf Ribarz, Robert Russ, Emil Jakob Schindler, and Marie Egner. These artists were featured in an exhibition at the Künstlerhaus in 1894 when Kühn was in Vienna for the first time. In the reviews of these artists, the expression *Naturstimmung* (mood of nature) was used again and again, and there was talk of the "magic of tone and mood" to describe the landscapes' novel charm, which stood in contrast to academic doctrine.[14] The creators of these works were subsequently ascribed to a movement of "mood realism" or *Stimmungsimpressionismus* (Mood Impressionism).[15]

The decision to take as his models such "mood paintings" that were indebted to the ideas of Impressionism and the artist colonies in Worpswede and Dachau was the turning point in Kühn's life. His formerly pleasant pastime became the main driving force of his life. The coincidence of the change in his circumstances, from the erratic life of a student to an upper middle-class gentleman of independent means with artistic ambitions, was not a contradiction, but rather amounted to the opposite. Using motifs from the latest trends in painting, he waged a battle in another field: to make photography a subjective and individual form of expression—that is, "artistic" in the spirit of the era. These intimate landscapes, both painted and photographed, struck a chord with the zeitgeist; the urban upper middle class found an ideal counterworld in these romanticized depictions of nature.[16]

For photographers, however, the rendition of intimate landscapes shown in the changing seasons or times of day—a realm of subject matter that had been adopted from painting—presented a technical challenge. Not only did they lack the means to reproduce colors; it was impossible to characterize the sky, clouds, or reflective water surfaces in a way that approached the impression of the eye—and would have evoked the desired *Naturstimmung* celebrated by painters. The ambitious amateurs saw only distorting and mindless routine in the usual photographic process and missed the "subjective image" with its implicit "inner truth" that they were used to from painting.[17] Only by using platinum prints, which had been praised by Emerson for its allowance of more subtle gray tones than gelatin prints, along with rough paper and Watzek's uncorrected monochrome lens, was it possible to create images that satisfied the demands for a flowing blur that was produced with genuinely photographic means.

Gum Bichromate Prints: Open Color Surfaces

It was at the end of 1895, in London, that Henneberg first saw prints by Robert Demachy in the gum bichromate printing technique (cats. 109, 124).[18] The sheets, which he enthusiastically acquired and brought back to Vienna, had no resemblance to conventional photography whatsoever. The image on the positive copy was no longer produced by the trace of the silver or platinum salts blackened by exposure to light; instead, it was composed of the visible traces of color pigments that had been dissolved in a mixture of a gum arabic tincture and light-sensitive chromate salts and then fixed by exposure to light. This eliminated any of the original characteristics of photographs from the gum bichromate prints, opening up a new, desirable path for those who were interested in bringing photographs closer to what was recognized as products of artistic creation, such as drawings done in charcoal or red chalk. As a critic remarked in 1897 in the Camera-Club, it took less imagination to think of these works as gouache paintings "than it takes to imagine that these effective pieces owe their origin to purely photographic means."[19]

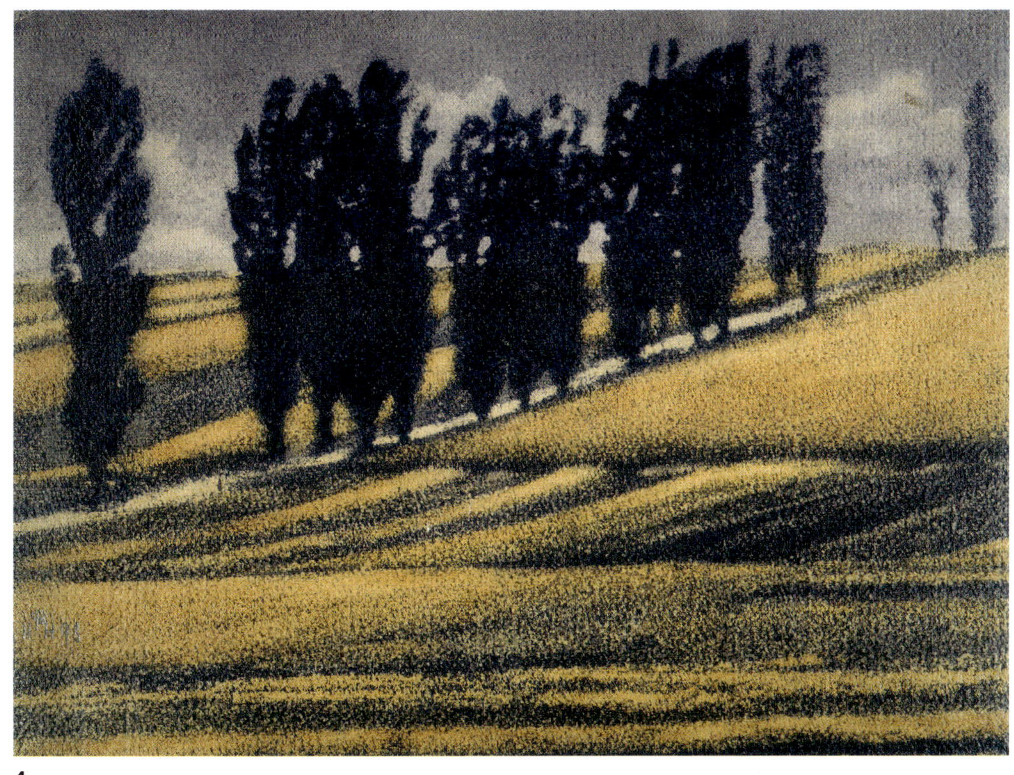

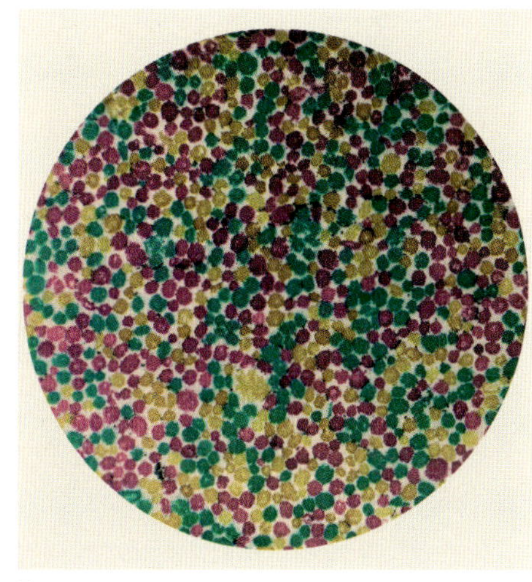

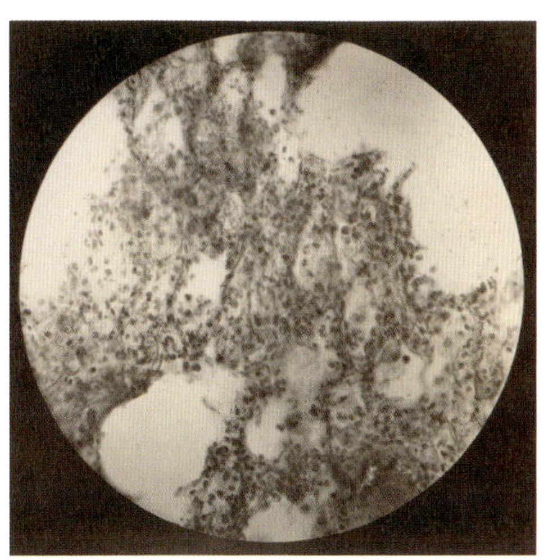

4 Hugo Henneberg,
Avenue of Poplars, 1898,
Staatliche Museen zu Berlin, Kunstbibliothek

5 Heinrich Kühn,
Micrograph of an Autochrome, 1907,
Österreichische Nationalbibliothek, Vienna

6 Heinrich Kühn,
Medical Micrograph from His Student Days,
author's archive

7 Heinrich Kühn,
Mary Warner and Hans Kühn, 1908,
Österreichische Nationalbibliothek, Vienna

8 *Sehfeld* (Visual Field), in Ernst Mach,
*Die Analyse der Empfindungen
und das Verhältnis des Physischen zum
Psychischen,* Vienna 1886, 15

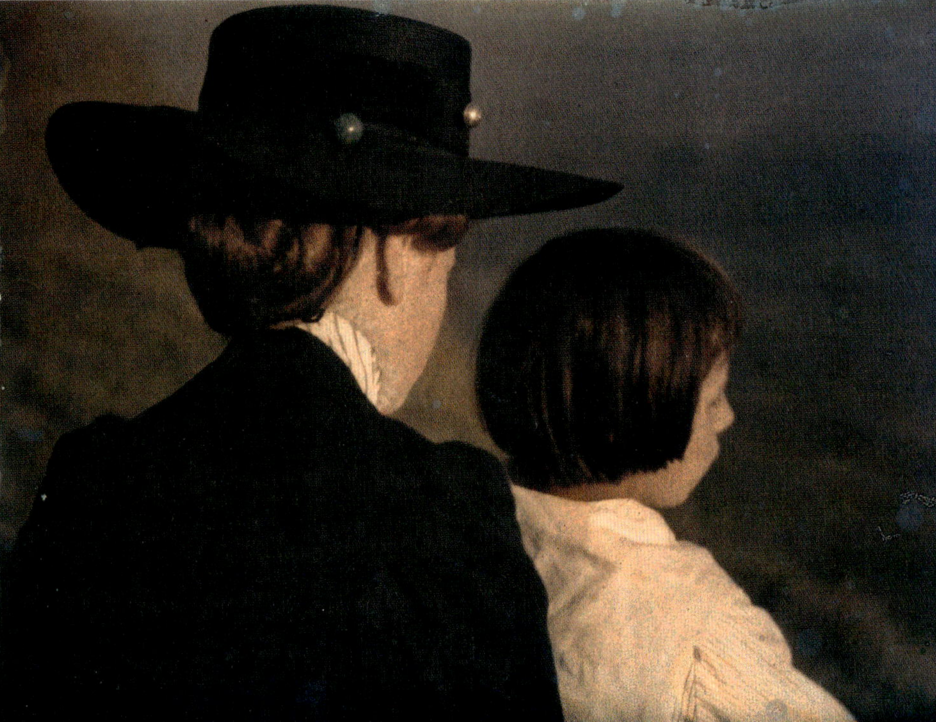

7

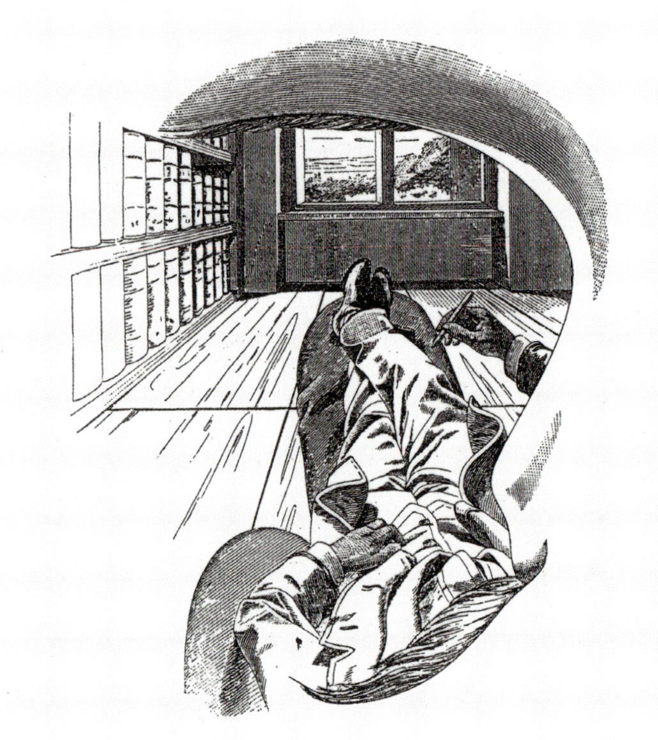

8

60

The main advantage offered by gum bichromate printing was the great range of design possibilities, which, however, could only be mastered with much practice and constant experimentation. On the one hand, there were no restrictions in the choice of colors; any pigment could be used. By repeating the copying process several times under different conditions or by changing pigments, it was possible to precisely control and influence the gradations of color and brightness within the image with the help of the wash. On the other hand, all the details registered by the camera were lost: the pigment particles bound in the photosensitive chromate salts distributed themselves according to the brightness and darkness of the image without producing any clear outlines. Moreover, in gum bichromate printing there is no "handwriting" to indicate the manually performed procedures within the copying process either. Though no imitation of painting, it lacks all the usual features of traditional photographs as well (figs. 1, 2).

Numerous attempts were made to coin terms other than *fuzzy* or *blurry* for these tonally graded pigmented surfaces. Kühn spoke of "raw" prints or "open color surfaces,"[20] and in Berlin the word *primitive* was used on the occasion of the first presentation,[21] a term which was also common for describing techniques of artists such as Paul Cézanne or Paul Gauguin. The artist and publicist Fritz Matthies-Masuren later recalled the first gum bichromate prints he had seen in Germany at the end of 1896 as an "artistic bombshell."[22] He attributed it to the bold consistency with which the technique had been used "to produce Impressionist studies in the spirit of modern art."[23] An analogy to Post-Impressionism was offered by the colored gum bichromate print: several negatives were produced in succession in the camera with the aid of differently colored filters. One after the other, different color pigments were applied to the light-sensitive background. Only the mixture of the applied colors created the desired effect in the viewer's eye and varied from print to print, even if the same negatives were used.

In addition to the free choice of color pigments, the use of a wide variety of papers as carriers for the light-sensitive layer that was applied with a brush each time allowed almost unlimited variability in the elaboration of the same photographic motif. But it was not only the color nuances of the potential image carrier that played a role. Soft papers with high absorbency produced a matte impression, while coated papers produced a glossy one. The surface structure could range from fine and smooth to coarsely grained. The latter, combined with the application of the gum arabic by means of a broad, hard brush, produced effects like those of charcoal drawings by artists such as Georges Seurat (fig. 3). Indeed, in a similar fashion to Seurat, in Kühn's *Twilight* there is almost no structural correspondence between nature and the image (cats. 116, 117). This is only partly due to the choice of color, which has no equivalent in traditional graphic art. This detachment from the pictorial motif in nature is even stronger in some of Henneberg's colored gum bichromate prints, which are dominated by an impression of flatness and abstraction (fig. 4; cats. 110, 114).

In his *Geschichte der Unschärfe* (The History of Blur) Wolfgang Ullrich compares Seurat's prints with gum bichromate prints: Seurat used coarse-grained Michallet paper on which the chalk leaves traces either only on the surface or else over the entire sheet, depending on how hard it is pressed down. This results in a play of light and dark that, up close, makes the drawing appear rather abstract, but from a distance appears as figurative schemes that shimmer into one another.[24] For both Kühn and Seurat, however, the question arose as to "when a blur still imitates the mode of intensive perception, but when it goes beyond that and rather serves the goal of alienation."[25] According to Helmholtz or Mach, stimulus selection fulfilled a selective function and, as a means of harmonization, was better suited to producing emotional and mood effects of the kind that the *Bildungsbürger* sought in their idyllic landscapes.

Autochromes: Matching Colors

Only painstaking experimentation could guarantee the effect the photographer desired. Heinrich Kühn, some of whose gum bichromate prints have survived in several variants, made use of his knowledge of the natural sciences: using photomicrographs to study the color effects on the felt side, noting details related to the composition and tempering of the chemicals or color pigments used on the backs of the prints, commenting on the results in successive studio books (figs. 5, 6).

The same applies to his experiments with autochromes: in 1907, the Lumière brothers introduced glass plates to the market, which for the first time made it possible for color photographs to be taken in a single exposure. Here, too, Kühn investigated the effect of the material in photomicrographs, which were also based on the optical mixture of individual dots of color in the human eye. Since slides were used, it was an additive rather than a subtractive procedure. Kühn was enthusiastic about the new process and created entire series of photographs that, due to their focus on the effects of different light on the same motif, can be compared to series by Impressionist painters (figs. 9–11).

Kühn used a method that he had applied to monochrome prints from 1906 onward and programmatically called "tonal value studies" (*Tonstudien*): to control the results, he had "photographic clothing" made for his children and their nanny in black, white, and various shades of gray (fig. 7; cats. 79, 139). He first determined the balance of these potentially moving spots of color in sketches. The models, accustomed to waiting patiently, had to hold still until the desired light illuminated the rooms through a window (Kühn almost never worked with artificial light) or fell as desired on meadows or slopes. For this he had also tested which shades of gray corresponded to differently colored fabrics in monochrome printing. The models—who, according to Kühn's youngest daughter, were often unenthusiastic—also received bespoke clothing for autochrome photography, whereby here, too, the desired color effect was determined before a correspondingly dyed fabric was chosen (figs. 12, 13). According to Kühn, though the "matching of tones" achieved in this way was "at the expense of objective truth," it was the autochrome plates' main appeal.[26]

Kühn was also fascinated by the phenomenon of the image in transmitted light. Two diametrically opposed possibilities were available to him: on the one hand, the small-format slide that could be held in the hand and viewed against the light, which one focused on and, as it were, blocked out all other perceptions. On the other, the autochromes that were projected at the Camera-Club—about the size of the width of the wall in the cinema hall of the Künstlerhaus in Vienna—resulting in a magical, novel color experience.

Summary

The "purely photographical,"[27] as practiced by Heinrich Kühn, was contradictory. Technique and artful surface utilization, the impression of the eye and media-specific effects, perceptual fidelity and alienation all came together to form the specifics of art photography. Kühn was intent on implementing his pictorial ideas through precise knowledge of the effects of the photographic means employed in each individual case—from the filters used during shooting to the choice of paper and pigments. Like a painter, he controlled and manipulated the distribution of certain colors on a picture surface and believed a "single, thoroughly considered picture, obtained by using the technically most advanced method as the result of a systematically continued series of experiments" was more valuable "than a dozen half-finished works that were merely sufficient in their technique."[28]

With the help of perfectly controlled technical means used in a new way every time, in their pictures the members of the Camera-Club reshaped reality as they pursued their goal of transforming reality into art. And yet viewed critically the results can also be understood as aesthetic escapism.[29] In Kühn's case this was quite literally true: his artificial paradise, his ideal counterworld was destroyed when he lost the considerable fortune that had made his intellectual and bourgeois idyll possible in the first place. Economic disillusionment, however, was unable to destroy his artistic ideals. On the contrary, Kühn reacted symptomatically to the New Vision style in his last published text: he rejected it as an emerging form of "photo-Bolshevism" that, without the carefulness of darkroom work, would inevitably lead to "homogenizing" image making.[30]

Translated from German by Alexander Booth

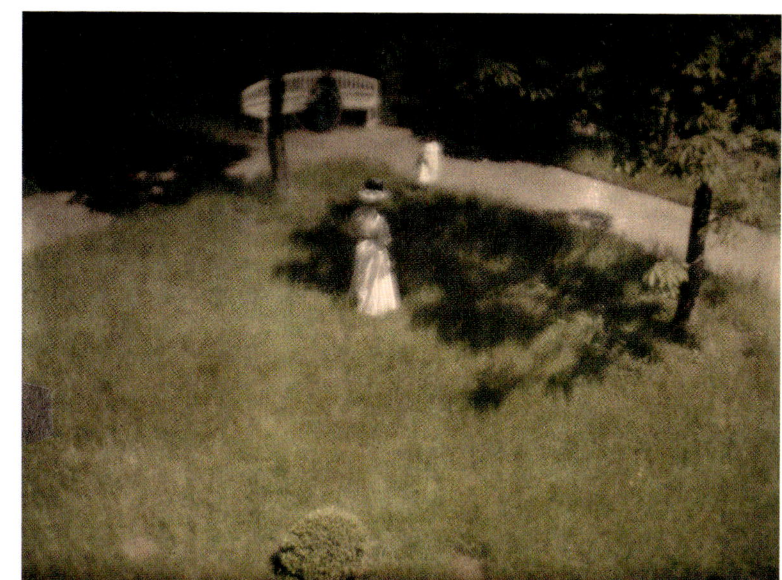

9

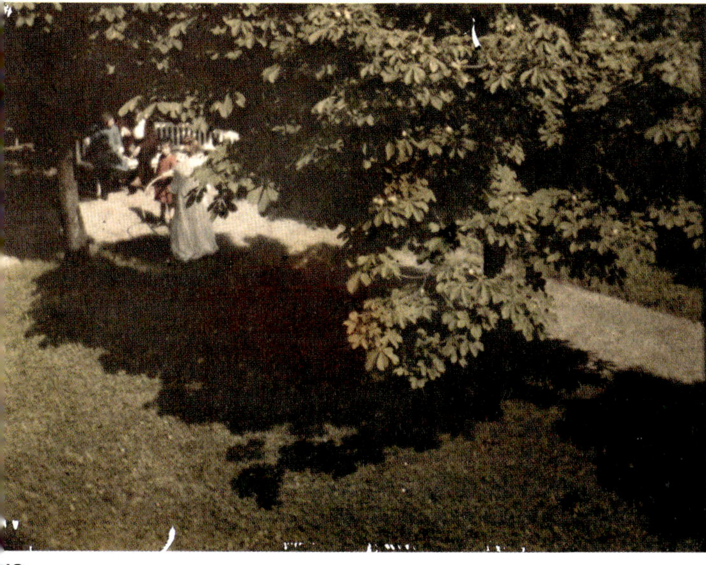

10

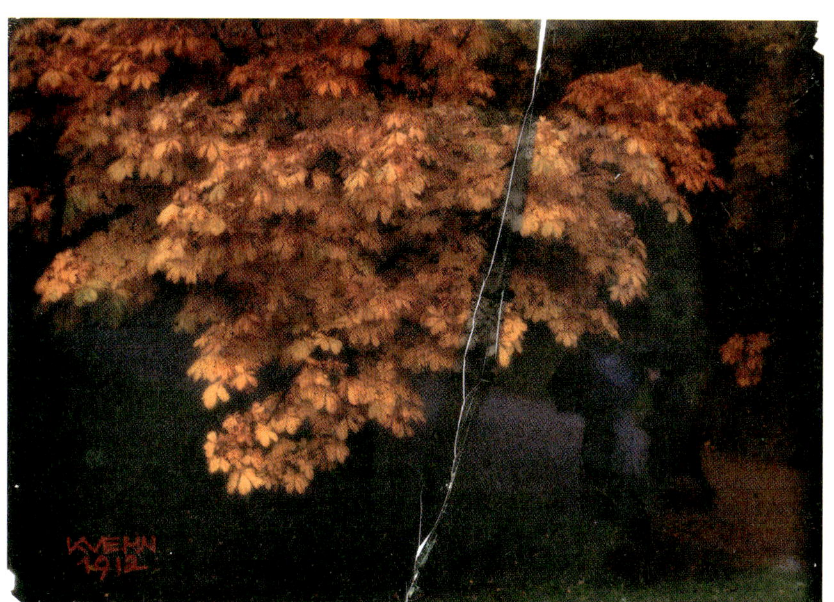

11

9 Heinrich Kühn,
Miss Mary Warner and Lotte Kühn
in the Hofgarten in Innsbruck, 1907,
Österreichische Nationalbibliothek, Vienna

10 Heinrich Kühn,
Edeltrude, Walter, and Lotte Kühn with Mary
Warner in the Garden, 1912,
Österreichische Nationalbibliothek, Vienna

11 Heinrich Kühn,
View into the Garden of the Villa Kühn, 1912,
Österreichische Nationalbibliothek, Vienna

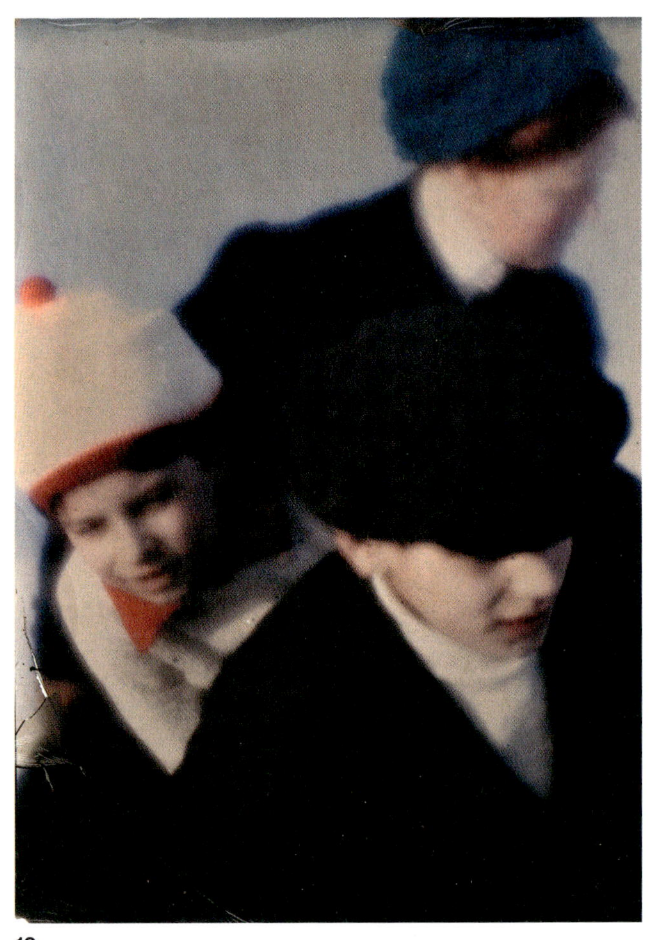

12

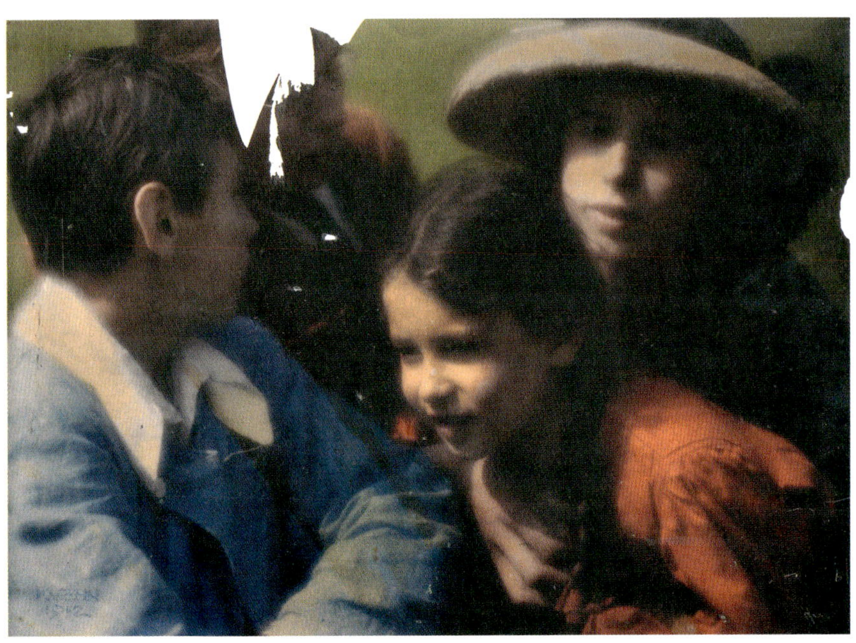

13

12 Heinrich Kühn,
Lotte and Hans Kühn, Miss Mary Warner in Winter Clothes, 1912,
Österreichische Nationalbibliothek, Vienna

13 Heinrich Kühn,
Hans, Walter, Lotte, and Edeltrude Kühn, 1912,
Österreichische Nationalbibliothek, Vienna

1 This essay is based on considerations that were first addressed and formulated by the author in the following publications: Vienna 2010 and Halle an der Saale 2018.

2 The term *amateur* was applied—not only in photography—to someone who dealt with a particular subject as a hobby and not for professional reasons.

3 *Photographische Correspondenz* 24 (1887), 226.

4 The formulation "la vraie rétine du savant" was first used by the astronomer Jules Janssen in 1888, cf. Stiegler 2001, 33. On the concept of the retina in Impressionist theory and practice, see Matthias Krüger's contribution, 42–53.

5 Cf. Lothar Gall, *Walther Rathenau: Portrait einer Epoche,* Munich 2009, 21; for a particularly illuminating overview of this phenomenon see his *Bürgertum in Deutschland,* Berlin 1989.

6 *Ver Sacrum* 4 (1898), 26.

7 Cf. Astrid Mahler, *Liebhaberei der Millionäre: Der Wiener Camera-Club um 1900,* Beiträge zur Geschichte der Fotografie in Österreich, vol. 18, Vienna and Salzburg 2019, 35–44.

8 These were, above all, Peter Altenberg, Hugo Haberfeld, Ludwig Hevesi, Joseph August Lux, and Adalbert Franz Seligmann. Information on texts by these authors can be found in Timm Starl's biobibliographical database on photography in Austria at www.albertina.at/forschung/fotografie/biobibliographie.

9 Heinrich Hugo Henneberg, Heinrich Kühn, and Hans Watzek formed the core of the "Kleeblatt" (Trifolium); Viktor Spitzer, a member of the Camera-Club and supporter of the Vienna Secession, was only added incidentally. Cf. Hugo Haberfeld, "Die Wiener Amateurphotographen," in *Die photographische Kunst* 5 (1906), 34–48, here 41.

10 The fact that many of the initiators of the Secession were closely connected to photography has only been marginally addressed by research so far. Artists used photographs as models (Josef Engelhart and Gustav Klimt, for example); took photographs themselves (Viktor Krämer, for example); or were related to the photographic trade (Carl Moll, for example, whose father August ran the largest Viennese trade in photographic supplies). Schindler had also taken photographs on his travels; cf. Vienna 2016.

11 Peter Henry Emerson's portfolio *Pictures of East Anglian Life* was exhibited for the first time in 1891 at the Camera-Club.

12 Alfred Stieglitz, "A Plea for Art Photography in America," in *Photographic Mosaics 28* (1892), 135–37, quoted after *Stieglitz on Photography: His Selected Essays and Notes,* ed. Richard Whelan, New York 2000, 30.

13 Hans Watzek, "Über das Künstlerische in der Photographie," in *Wiener Photographische Blätter* (August 1895), 161–63.

14 "Frequent visits to galleries, but especially to the first Secession exhibition in Munich, particularly stimulated me. The new expression of fine art had a determining effect on my work." Cf. [Fritz] Matthies-Masuren, *Heinrich Kühn,* in *Photographisches Centralblatt* 5,9 (1899), 161–66, here 163. Kühn mentioned the landscape views of the Munich Secessionists as well as those of Ludwig Dill and Eilif Peterssen as sources of inspiration. Cf. F[ritz] Matthies-Masuren, "Hugo Henneberg—Heinrich Kühn—Hans Watzek," in *Camera Work* 4,13 (1906), 21–41, here 28.

15 Cf. the definition of *Stimmungsimpressionismus* (Mood Impressionism) in *Stimmungsimpressionismus,* exh. cat., Österreichische Galerie Belvedere, Vienna 2004, 281–87, here 284–85.

16 Andrea Winkelbauer, *Frühling im Abendrot: Robert Russ und sein vergessenes Meisterwerk,* in ibid., 281–87, here 284–85.

17 Watzek 1895 (see note 13).

18 Josef Maria Eder, *Geschichte der Photographie,* Halle an der Saale 1932, 784–85. The process had already been mentioned on page 128 of the July 1894 issue of *Wiener Photographische Blätter.* The technique was indeed much older and merely taken up again by Demachy.

19 Alfred Buschbeck, *Rundgang durch unsere Ausstellung künstlerischer Photographien,* in *Wiener Photographische Blätter* 4 (1897), 36; translated here by Alexander Booth.

20 Heinrich Kühn, quoted after Fritz Matthies-Masuren, "Hugo Henneberg, Heinrich Kühn, Hans Watzek," in *Photographische Rundschau* (1905), 4.

21 Ibid.

22 Ibid.

23 Ibid.

24 Wolfgang Ullrich, *Geschichte der Unschärfe,* Berlin 2002.

25 Ibid.

26 Kühn 1921, 222.

27 See letter from Heinrich Kühn to Alfred Stieglitz (March 19, 1923), Beinecke Rare Book & Manuscript Library, Yale University, New Haven; translated here by Alexander Booth.

28 Ibid.

29 Cf. Ivo Kranzfelder, "Natürlicher Hang zum Künstlichen: Einige Bemerkungen zur Kunstfotografie um 1900 und ihrer 'Modernität,'" in *Fotogeschichte: Beiträge zur Geschichte und Ästhetik der Fotografie* 58 (1995), 55–62.

30 Heinrich Kühn, "Klarheit!," in *Das deutsche Lichtbild: Jahresschau 1937,* T11–T18, here T16.

Esther Ruelfs

The Path to the Museum

Early Photographic Collections in Germany

An 1860 stereograph from the Parisian photo studio Ferrier père, fils et Soulier shows the view of the bustling boulevard de Sébastopol from one of the top stories of a building (cat. 32). Eighteen years later in his painting *Rue Halévy, View from the Sixth Floor* (p. 260, fig. 2), Gustave Caillebotte offered a similar glimpse of modern Paris's traffic and pedestrian-filled pavements. Auguste Hippolyte Collard's image of the steel girders on the underside of the Pont de Grenelle was created in 1875–76 (cat. 47), whereas Caillebotte finished his painting of the similarly constructed Pont d'Argenteuil around 1883 (p. 260, fig. 5). But even if nineteenth-century painting and photography influenced each other reciprocally, there is no clear evidence in these pairs of images that one medium was lagging behind the other. Yet can it really be chance that the photographs were taken earlier than the paintings with which they have been juxtaposed?

This essay considers the perspective of the Hamburg-born museum director Alfred Lichtwark, a pioneer of photographic collections in museums, on the interplay of the media of photography and painting as expressed in his lectures on the 1893 *Internationale Ausstellung von Amateurphotographien* (International Exhibition of Amateur Photographs) in Hamburg. Further, it examines the institutionalization of the young medium based on photographic collections in the city, while also illustrating the rise of photography into the canon of art.

Painting and Art by Way of the Example of the Representation of Nature

In 1883, three years before he became director of the Hamburger Kunsthalle, Alfred Lichtwark encountered French Impressionism at Fritz Gurlitt's art salon. At the *Grosse Kunstausstellung des Kunstvereins in der Kunsthalle* in 1895 Lichtwark exhibited paintings by Mary Cassatt, Édouard Manet, Claude Monet, Berthe Morisot, Camille Pissarro, and Alfred Sisley for the first time. He followed this up in 1896 with a still life by Monet: the first acquisition of a piece of Impressionist art for the Hamburger Kunsthalle.[1] From 1893 to 1903 Lichtwark and the collector and exhibition organizer Ernst Juhl had introduced the annual exhibitions of amateur photography, which were renamed Ausstellungen zur Kunstphotographie (Exhibitions of Art Photography) in 1903.

In 1893 Alfred Lichtwark gave a lecture on the occasion of an exhibition of amateur photographs in which he explained that artists looked down on amateur photographers. One reason for this, he felt, apart from the photographers' young age, was the general disdain for dilettantism in Germany.[2] Lichtwark identified the landscape as the "training ground of amateur photography" and recommended that amateurs should not go to "areas that are considered beautiful by others" but should instead immerse themselves in the nearest surroundings "that they know and love."[3] In another lecture marking that exhibition, Lichtwark highlighted a work by an amateur photographer from Hamburg, H. Strebel, as exemplary of a new aesthetic (fig. 1).[4] He considered Strebel's pictures of the heaths a successful example of the Hamburg school, and he noted that obvious models of art were absent in Strebel's work. "For who would have painted the heath as he captures it?" Lichtwark asked rhetorically.[5]

Lichtwark placed photography in relation to contemporary painting while simultaneously distinguishing it. His lectures give the impression of a constant back and forth between distance and proximity. When photographers moved too close to painting—as, for example, Adolphe de Meyer did—Lichtwark saw "the recreation of historical costumes modeled on a [Thomas] Gainsborough, [Jacques-Louis] David, or Marcus Stone."[6] In the case of Strebel, on the other hand, he pointed out that "precisely the most artistically outstanding photographs . . . are completely independent of models in painting." He exuberantly praised the amateur photographer's choice of motifs "to which art has not yet laid a hand." Furthermore, since the northern German landscape had not been painted much at all, the amateur could "discover" things everywhere.[7]

Finally, Lichtwark saw a similarity in the way the various arts handled the landscape in terms of atmosphere. The amateur was discovering what earlier artists had discovered about the landscape.[8] In his lecture "Der Amateur-Photograph und die Natur" (The Amateur Photographer and Nature) he discussed how photography, similar to landscape painting, had devoted itself to observing atmospheric effects, mist, or haze only late in its development. He noted that this was "the same path that landscape painting had taken in art." There, too, "one began with the infinite love of the exact, perceptible detail, with the joy of narration, with the preference for the distant, the epic, with the study of things," and only "gradually advanced to the feeling for space and relationships, to the study of color, light and air."[9]

When Lichtwark wrote this in the 1890s, the discussion about the art status of photography had already been going on for thirty years in French and English art theory. The issue was invariably the possibility or impossibility of using a technical medium to produce an image characterized by the photographer's subjectivity. The discussion culminated in the question of whether photography could even be considered art. In Germany, it reached a climax relatively late with Pictorialism. By this time, the photographic representation of nature had undergone a transformation from the beginnings of photography to the end of the nineteenth century. Initially, it had been used as an aid to painting, as *études d'après nature* (studies after nature) and as teaching material for the academies.[10] Gustave Le Gray's images of clouds and seascapes (cats. 5–7, 9–10) are paradigmatic for the interplay of painting and photography, for Le Gray was quite familiar with Romanticism, which in turn also influenced his work.[11] With amateur photography, which developed first in England and France and at the latest around 1890 in Germany, nature photography finally acquired the status of art.[12]

In 1893 Lichtwark compared Strebel's nature photographs to painting, pointing out that painters would "usually [render] the heath as infinite space, as a basis for the towering cloudy sky. Strebel renounces the absolute spatial effect; he does not seek the distant horizon but places himself right up close to an unlimited piece of nature."[13] Here Lichtwark brought Strebel into contact with landscape painters such as Hamburg-born Christian Morgenstern and Valentin Ruths. Works by both entered the collection during Lichtwark's tenure, for example through a major purchase from Ruth's estate in 1905.[14] According to Lichtwark, the painters each specialized in "their own" subjects: Morgenstern created broad, dramatic landscapes, often depicting the natural forces of stormy seas or coastal scenery (fig. 2), while Ruths painted heaths and forest scenes. However, like Strebel, Ruths seemed to abandon broad perspective in his series of woodland pieces created between 1870 and 1895. Instead, he depicted unconventional details, such as a section of forest rock in close-up or a view of ferns alongside a path (fig. 3).[15] While Morgenstern's paintings confirmed Lichtwark's assertion that Strebel the photographer had a completely different approach to nature, Ruth's paintings seem similar to Strebel's photographs, if not in terms of subject matter, then at least in their narrow cropping and low horizons.

Aestheticization of the Landscape

Lichtwark did not mention the most obvious models for heath landscapes in Hamburg during the 1890s, namely, those artists working between Hamburg and Bremen in the village of Worpswede: Fritz Mackensen, Otto Modersohn, and Fritz Overbeck.[16] The heaths and moors were projection screens for their artistic ideals. In 1895 Modersohn wrote in his diary: "Wonderfully gray day; woman out in the field, against the sky—Millet. On the bridge a while, which leads across the canal, on all sides these exquisite scenes."[17] Here too his imagination seems to be directed toward other paintings, namely, works by the French Impressionists. The artists were urbanites who had come to Worpswede to flee city life. They sought depictions of nature beyond what had been considered "beautiful" up until the early nineteenth century. In a letter from Worpswede, which Overbeck published in the newspaper *Die Kunst für Alle* in 1895 on behalf of the artists Karl Vinnen and Heinrich Vogeler, with whom he had moved to the country, he wrote: "The moor stretches far into the horizon, where the blue hills of the Ge[e]st rise, intersected in a straight line by canals and dykes, which in turn are crossed at right angles by others. At equal intervals along the way stand pale birch trees whose trunks, yielding to the prevailing northeast winds, rise obliquely. And though it is lonely in the wide surroundings, traces of human activity remain. But they are not a pleasant sight. We encounter districts where the ground has been excavated meters deep, and the peat, stacked in long rows into regular pyramids or mounds, dries in the air and the sun."[18] Overbeck's text described the exploited landscape beyond the classical idea of beauty. Instead, his depictions of dramatically scripted weather phenomena present themselves as pure atmosphere, indeed showing the expanse and towering cloud formations Lichtwark believed to be typical of landscape painting (fig. 4).

While Overbeck focused on the human-driven destruction of the landscape in his letter from Worpswede, he and the other Worpswede painters—as well as the amateur photographers Oscar and Theodor Hofmeister—aestheticized the Teufelsmoor region as a seemingly pristine landscape (fig. 5). The Hofmeister brothers captured the moor in an unusual portrait format that was the size of

1 H. Strebel,
Untitled, 1893, in Alfred Lichtwark,
Die Bedeutung der Amateur-Photographie,
Halle an der Saale 1894, 60

2 Christian Ernst Bernhard Morgenstern,
Dunes on Helgoland, 1854,
Hamburger Kunsthalle

3 Valentin Ruths,
Rocky Outcropping in the Forest, ca. 1870,
Hamburger Kunsthalle

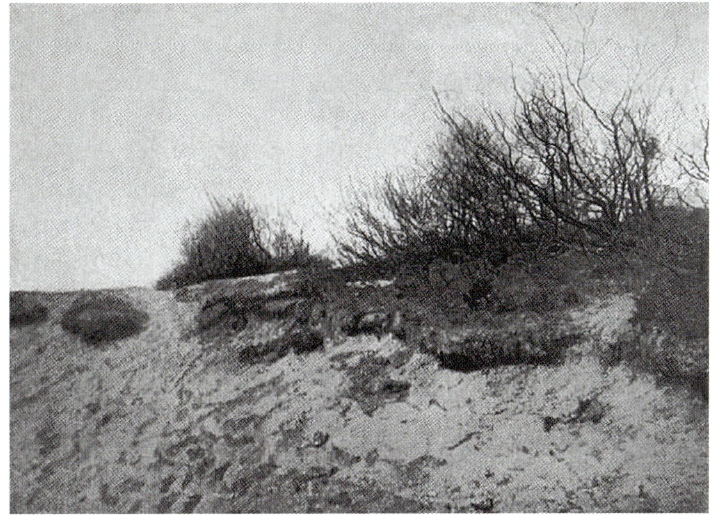

1

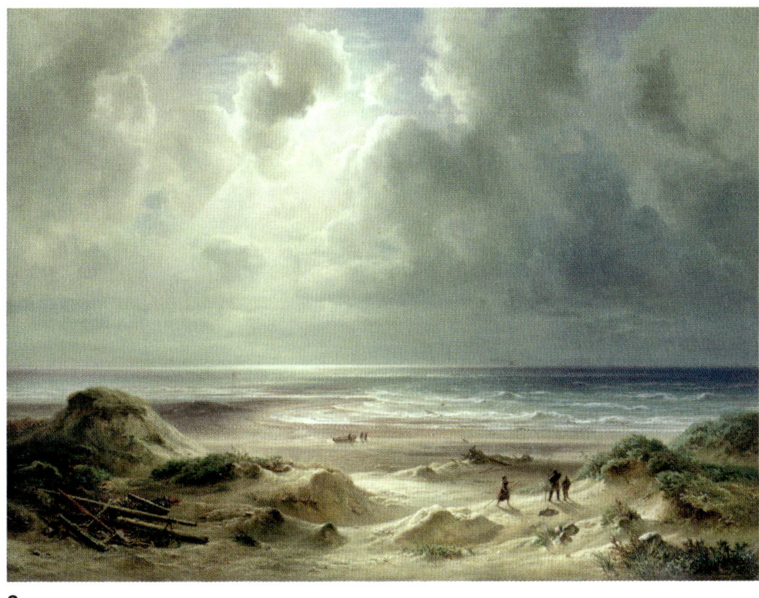
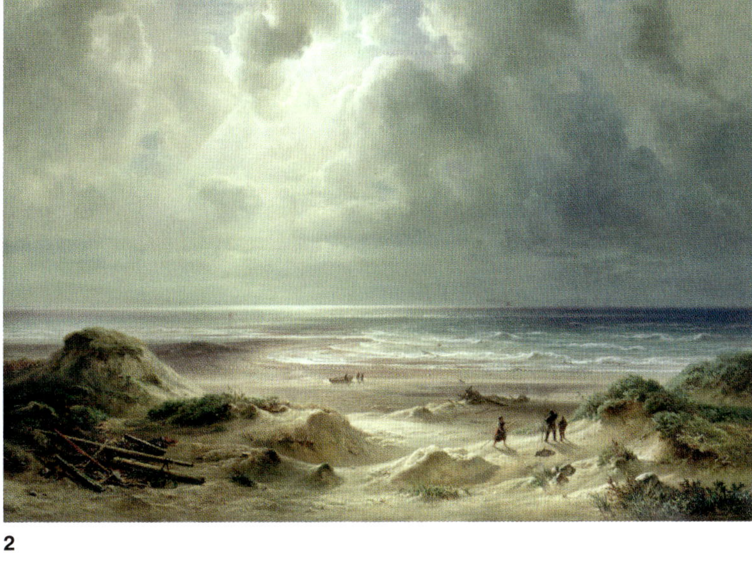

2

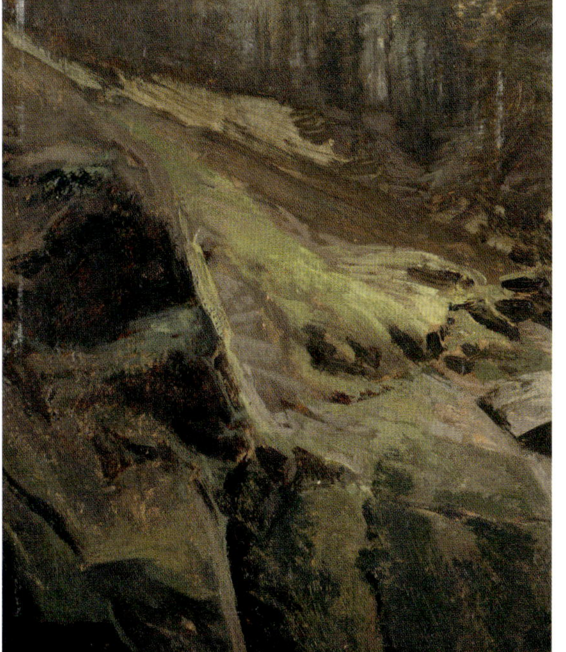

3

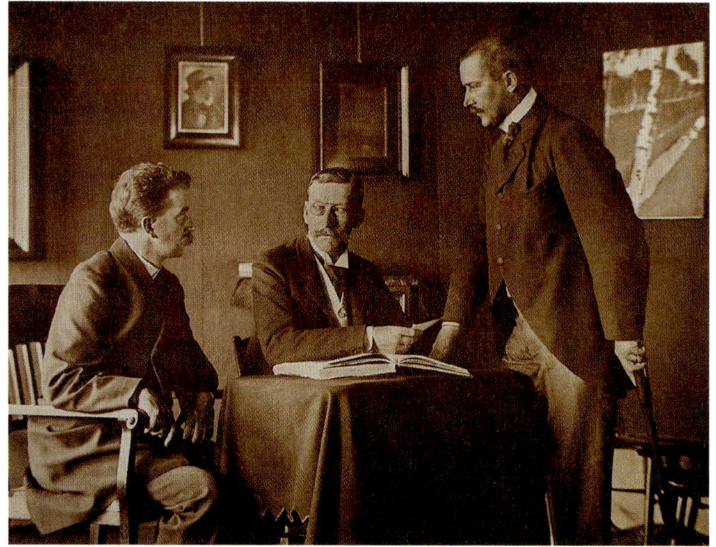

4

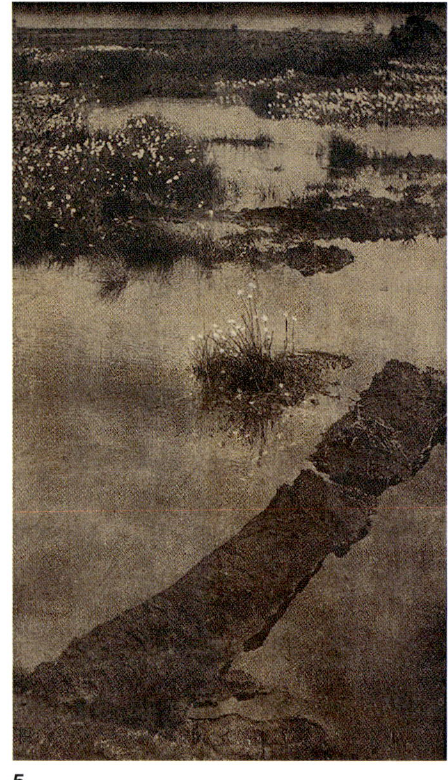

5

6

4 Fritz Overbeck,
Clouds over the Moor, ca. 1898,
Overbeck-Museum, Bremen

5 Oscar and Theodor Hofmeister,
Bog Flowers, 1897,
Museum für Kunst und Gewerbe Hamburg

6 Oscar and Theodor Hofmeister,
*The Executive Committee of the Society for the
Promotion of Amateur Photography:
Ernst Juhl, Eduard Arning,
and Walter von Ohlendorff,* 1899,
Museum für Kunst und Gewerbe Hamburg

a painting, and they mounted the gum bichromate print in a thick wooden frame. This draws attention to a section of a greater whole, in which the gum bichromate printing process lends an immaterial quality to the water surfaces and moor flowers. The discrepancy between the description of the human-modified landscape and the idealized one, which became the subject of the Hofmeisters' interaction with space and light, is obvious. In Lichtwark's argumentation their work *Bog Flowers* stood for those photographs that were oriented toward painting.

Just as escaping the city had been essential for the painters of Worpswede, Lichtwark recommended that stressed city dwellers and amateur photographers take trips to the countryside.[19] In addition to offering technical equipment, training courses, and lectures, the associations for amateur photography also organized excursions that allowed the study of nature. In the early exhibitions of amateur photographers—held in Bremen and Hamburg in 1892 and 1893, and in Vienna in 1888 and 1891—the depiction of nature was the most represented subject by far.[20]

A Club for More Elite Circles

Founded in 1891, the Gesellschaft zur Förderung der Amateur-Photographie (Society for the Promotion of Amateur Photography) was one of Hamburg's two clubs for amateur photographers—and the most influential club in the German Reich. With the support of Ernst Juhl, chairman of the society and managing director of the Hamburger Kunstverein, and Alfred Lichtwark it organized the annual *Internationale Ausstellung von Amateurphotographien* (International Exhibition of Amateur Photographs), which was shown at the Hamburger Kunsthalle from 1893 to 1903. The first show was an enormous success, with thirteen thousand visitors over the course of fifty-one days.[21] But it also led to heated debates, as the director wrote to a close colleague.[22] In a meeting of the administrative commission of the Kunsthalle in 1894, Lichtwark caustically remarked: "To the public it seemed as if a congress of natural scientists intended to use a church as a meeting hall."[23] This makes it clear just how much the worthiness of photography as an art form was still questioned at this time.

Amateur photography was part of the dilettantism movement that Lichtwark supported, and it was an essential pillar of his new understanding of the museum as an institution. Lichtwark belonged to a far-reaching museum reform movement in the period around 1900 that, in response to the popularity of the applied arts museums, wanted to open up those institutions dedicated to the fine arts to broader sections of the population.[24] Being exhibited in an art museum meant recognition of the activity of the Gesellschaft zur Förderung der Amateur-Photographie. The community consisted mainly of amateurs and dilettantes from the middle class. In Hamburg, these were representatives of the business bourgeoisie, including merchants and factory owners, and the educated bourgeoisie, including doctors and academics.[25] Its members lived in the wealthier districts and belonged to an elite circle of men, as women were not admitted as regular members until 1906. The 1899 portrait of the Hofmeister brothers from the presidium of the Gesellschaft zur Förderung der Amateur-Photographie (fig. 6) bears witness to the association's image of itself. It shows Ernst Juhl, the photographer Eduard Arnig, and Walter Heinrich von Ohlendorff, who since 1893 had been the heads of the exclusive association whose membership fees were the highest in the whole empire. Visible in the background are the gum bichromate prints of the club's members, fitted with opulent wooden frames. This cooperation with Lichtwark and the Kunsthalle represented a significant gain in prestige for the amateur photographers. Their path to the museum can also be seen as a success for the middle classes, who could now decide what art was and what would be collected in a museum.[26]

Art or Industry

The amateur photography movement played an important role in the first initiatives for establishing photographic collections in Germany in the late 1880s.[27] The collections of artistic photography were preceded by historical collections of samples that were created by professional associations with the intention of—similar to those of the museums of applied arts—stimulating the taste of artisans. The collection of the Photographischer Verein zu Berlin (Photographic Association of Berlin), for example, contained 340 photographs in 1863.[28]

In Hamburg and Dresden photography was located at two different institutions: a museum of applied arts and a collection of art. The museumization of photography also reflects the change in significance of the medium. The institutionalization of photography around 1900 took place in different groupings that are also reflected in the institutions involved: the *Heimatkunst* (homeland art) and *Heimatschutz* (homeland protection) movements upon which the idea of the documentary collection of the Museum für Hamburgische Geschichte (Museum for Hamburg History) was based; the history of technology and images, which was collected in the Hamburg Museum für Kunst und Gewerbe (Museum of Fine, Applied, and Decorative Arts); and the collections of "artistic photography," which were founded in the Kunsthalle in Hamburg and the Kupferstich-Kabinett (Collection of Prints, Drawings, and Photographs) in Dresden.[29]

Although it can be assumed that photographs had been collected at the Museum für Kunst und Gewerbe in Hamburg since its founding in 1877, they initially served as tools for scholars. For example, Japanese travel photography supported the research of the East Asia Department. Justus Brinckmann had acquired the first objects of East Asian art at the 1873 world's fair in Vienna. Brinckmann, who had never traveled to Japan, understood the documentary value of photographs. They offered a glimpse of a still unknown country that was just beginning to open up to the West. These photographs were acquired not as independent works but as part of the collection of East Asian art, and they were seen in the context of the collection, which consisted of porcelain, sword guards, and sculptures. The first photographic objects to be acquired independently for their historical value were the daguerreotypes that Wilhelm Weimar, Brinckmann's colleague, began collecting in 1900. These were valued as historical documents of a technique that at that point was already sixty years old and recommended to contemporary photographers as models.

Lichtwark's efforts at the Kunsthalle were simultaneously focused on photography and the organization of exhibitions of amateur photography with Ernst Juhl. Juhl also reported on a collection of artistic photography whose whereabouts are now unknown.[30] In 1897 Lichtwark recommended to the Hamburg Senate that a collection of documentary photographs of the city and its surroundings be created for the Museum für Hamburgische Geschichte—images of the "local landscape" and of "local life." The museum responded by selecting photographs from the Kunsthalle's annual exhibitions to "incorporate" into its collection.[31] And yet, despite Lichtwark's recommendation and even though the Kunsthalle both exhibited and collected photographs, following Juhl's death, his collection of European and American art photography went in equal parts to the Museum für Kunst und Gewerbe and to the Berlin Kunstgewerbemuseum (Museum of Decorative Arts)—but not to the Kunsthalle.

Aside from the Hamburger Kunsthalle (whose collecting activities are only documented in isolated marginal notes in Juhl's lectures), the Kupferstich-Kabinett in Dresden was the first German art institution to dedicate itself to photography as a medium to collect. Max Lehrs, the director of the Kupferstich-Kabinett, exchanged ideas with Lichtwark and began a photography collection in 1898. This collection was exhibited just one year later. Early on, the pictures came to Dresden mainly in the form of donations from the Hamburg exhibition.[32] But the change in the perception of photography is evident in the Kupferstich-Kabinett's internal inventories as well. From 1899 onward the inventory of "art reproductions" was joined by one for "artistic photographs." The acceptance of photography as art became manifest with its institutionalization in museums around 1900.

Translated from German by Alexander Booth

1 Markus Bertsch, "Paris als Taktgeber: Alfred Lichtwark und der französische Impressionismus," in *Impressionismus: Deutsch-französische Begegnungen,* exh. cat., Hamburger Kunsthalle, Hamburg 2021, 29–47.

2 Alfred Lichtwark, "Der Amateur-Photograph und die Natur" (October 22, 1893), in Lichtwark, *Die Bedeutung der Amateur-Photographie,* ed. Hamburger Amateur-Photographenverein, Halle an der Saale 1894, 1–12, here 4; translated here by Alexander Booth.

3 Ibid., 7–8.

4 Alfred Lichtwark, "Die Nationen und ihre Vertreter auf der Hamburger Ausstellung 1893," in Lichtwark 1894 (see note 2), 30–64, here 59; translated here by Alexander Booth.

5 Ibid.

6 Ibid., 46.

7 Alfred Lichtwark, "Der Amateurphotograph und die Natur," in Lichtwark 1894 (see note 2), 22.

8 Lichtwark 1893 (see note 2), 8.

9 Lichtwark n.d. (see note 7), 20.

10 Munich 2004, 172.

11 Paris 2002.

12 On periodization see Stiegler 2006a, 137.

13 Lichtwark 1893 (see note 4), 59.

14 Many of Ruths's heath landscapes and forest studies entered the collection.

15 Valentin Ruths, *Hopfen und Farn am Waldrand* (Hops and Ferns in Woodland), 1870, in *Hamburger Schule: Das 19. Jahrhundert neu entdeckt,* exh. cat., Hamburger Kunsthalle, Hamburg 2019, 285.

16 The painters exhibited for the first time at the Bremer Kunstverein in 1895 and that same year in the annual exhibition of the Münchner Künstlergenossenschaft (Munich Artists' Cooperative) at the Münchner Glaspalast; cf. *Otto Modersohn: Worpswede 1889–1907,* exh. cat., Otto Modersohn Museum, Fischerhude 1989.

17 Fritz Overbeck, "Ein Brief aus Worpswede," in *Die Kunst für Alle* 11 (1895–96), 20–24, here 22; translated here by Alexander Booth.

18 Ibid.

19 In 1891, during a trip to Paris, Lichtwark visited the village of Barbizon, located by the forest of Fontainebleau, which is considered the cradle of the Barbizon School and French plein-air painting. See Bertsch 2021 (see note 1), 31.

20 Enno Kaufhold, *Bilder des Übergangs: Zur Mediengeschichte von Fotografie und Malerei in Deutschland um 1900,* Marburg 1986, 30.

21 Jens Jäger, "Amateurphotographen-Vereine und kunstphotographische Bewegung in Hamburg 1890–1910," in *Kunstphotographie um 1900: Die Sammlung Ernst Juhl,* ed. Margret Kruse and Jens Jäger, Hamburg 1989, 33–38, here 36.

22 Letter from Alfred Lichtwark to Robert Koldewey (December 24, 1893), quoted after Henrike Junge-Gent, *Alfred Lichtwark: Zwischen den Zeiten,* Berlin and Munich 2012, 253.

23 Meeting minutes of the administrative commission of the Kunsthalle, October 2, 1894; quoted after Junge-Gent (see note 22), 274. Lichtwark used the same phrasing thirteen years later; see Alfred Lichtwark, "Vorwort," in *Künstlerische Photographie: Entwicklung und Einfluss in Deutschland,* ed. Alfred Lichtwark and Fritz Matthies-Masuren, Berlin 1907, 1–7, here 2; translated here by Alexander Booth.

24 Friedrich Deneken, the director of the Kaiser Wilhelm Museum in Krefeld, wrote that the aim was to make it "attractive as well as instructive for broader sections of the population, from industrial workers and craftsmen to wealthy citizens, from children and young people to senior citizens"; quoted after Sylvia Martin, "'Eine sich immer erneuernde Quelle der Anregung und Belehrung': Friedrich Deneken und die Lehr- und Vorbildersammlung des Kaiser Wilhelm Museums," in *Marcel Odenbach: Plötzlich konnte eins wie das andere sein,* exh. cat., Kunstmuseen Krefeld, Krefeld 2021, 45–61, here 45. This statement contrasts with the social structure of Hamburg's clubs as elaborated by Jens Jäger (Jäger 1989 [see note 21]), and Lichtwark's dilettantism movement, which was also aimed at a middle-class audience.

25 On the structure and social background of the members cf. Jäger 1989 (see note 21).

26 Ibid.

27 Ulrich Pohlmann, "Das Fotomuseum im Münchner Stadtmuseum 1961–1991: Chronik einer Institution zwischen Tradition und Neubeginn," in *Fotomuseum im Münchner Stadtmuseum; Eine Auswahl von 150 Fotografien aus der Sammlung Braus,* Heidelberg 1991, 8–26.

28 Ulrich Pohlmann, "Die vergessenen Fotomuseen: Zur Geschichte realisierter und unausgeführter Vorhaben in Deutschland," in *Fotogeschichte: Beiträge zur Geschichte und Ästhetik der Fotografie* 35 (1990), 14–21, here 14.

29 See Pohlmann 1991 (see note 27), 8.

30 ". . . with the exception of the Kunsthalle in Hamburg, the Königliches Kupferstichkabinett in Dresden, and the Kaiser Wilhelm Museum in Krefeld, art institutions have not yet decided to collect the art born of our time." Ernst Juhl, "Theodor und Oskar Hofmeister, Hamburg," in *Photographische Rundschau* 16 (1902), 65–70, here 68.

31 Alfred Lichtwark, "Die fünfte internationale Ausstellung von Amateurphotographien in Hamburg," in *Die Kunst für Alle* 13 (1897–98), 145–55, here 153.

32 Agnes Matthias, "'A Selection of the Best That Has Been Achieved in the Wide Field of Amateur Photography': On the Origin of the Photography Collection of Dresden's Kupferstich-Kabinett," lecture held on November 23, 2013, on the occasion of the conference Inspirations—Interactions: Pictorialism Reconsidered, http://piktorialismus.smb.museum/images/lecture_4.pdf?1624618755, 3 (accessed on October 7, 2021).

Majestic Expanses
Sky and Sea

Daniel Zamani

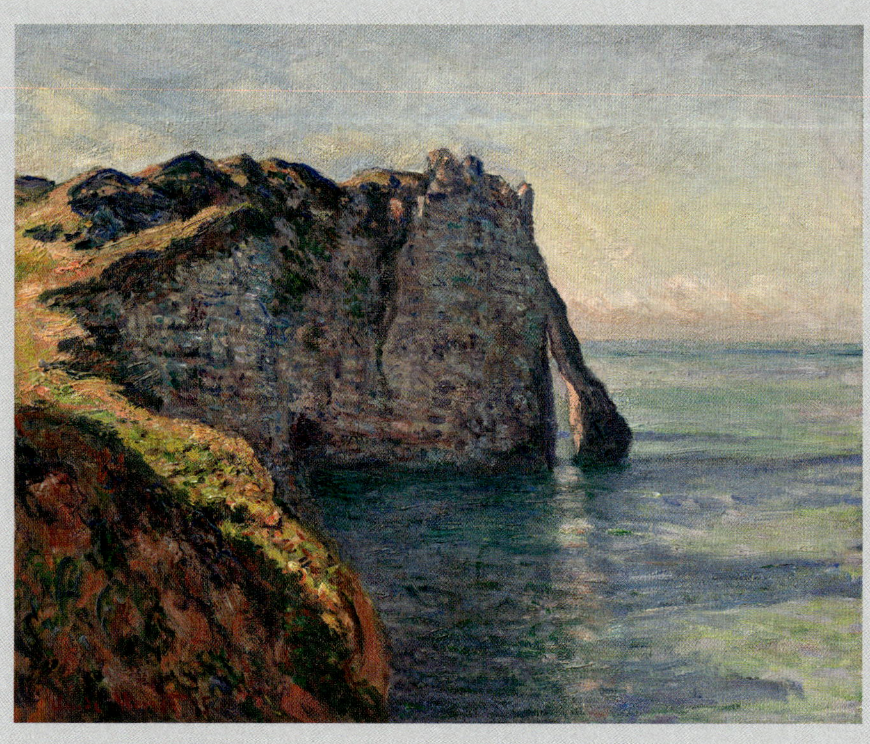

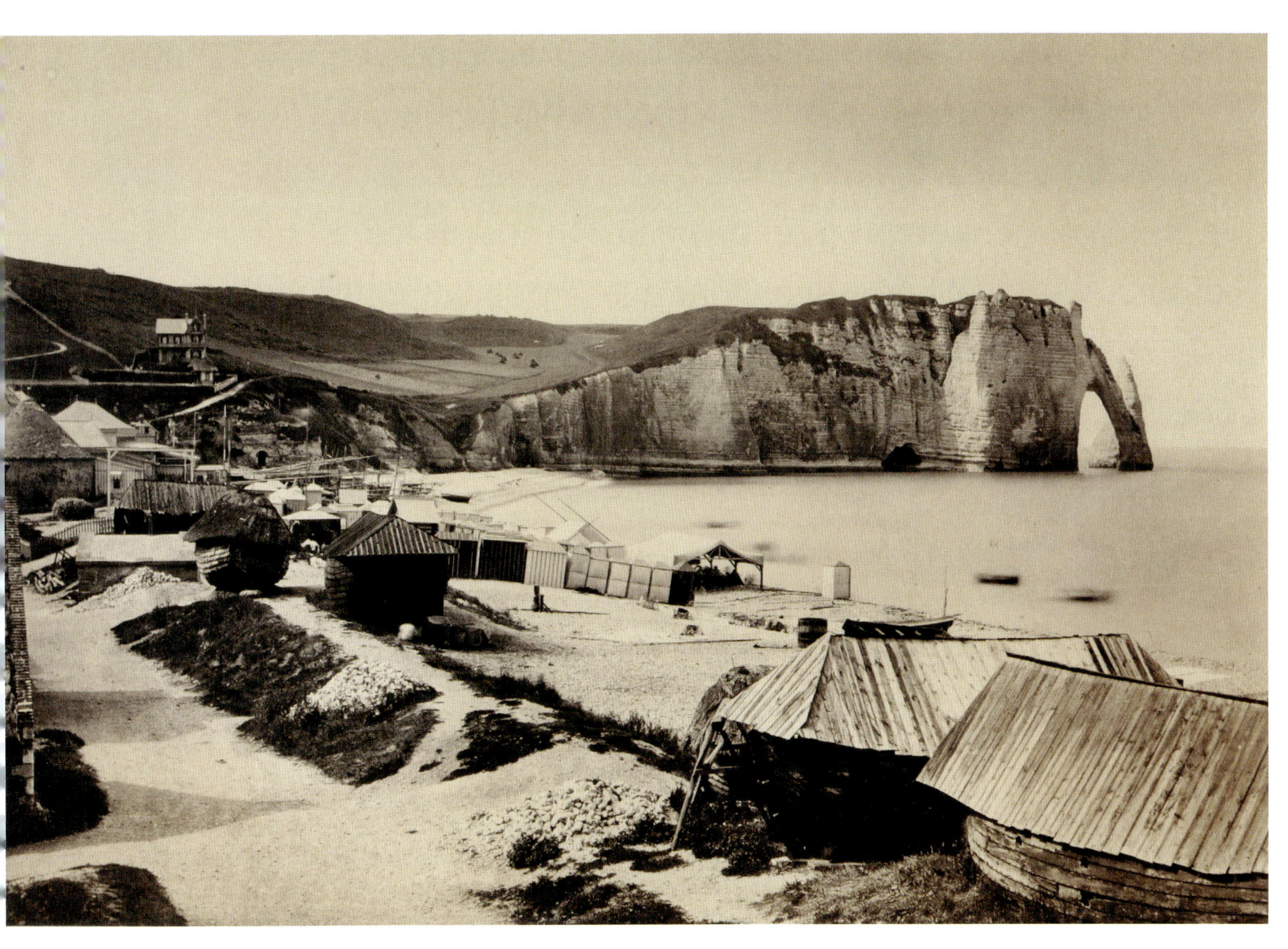

Claude Monet
The Cliff and the Porte d'Aval, 1885
Oil on canvas
Hasso Plattner Collection

1 Louis Alphonse Davanne
Étretat, Cliff to the Left, No. 2, 1864

In his influential treatise *Élémens de perspective pratique* (1799), Pierre-Henri de Valenciennes enjoined his fellow painters to carefully observe nature. He ascribed particular significance to the practice of sketching *en plein air*. Although many such oil sketches were cloud studies made in preparation for larger landscape paintings, they also were also valued as autonomous works of art.

In the second half of the nineteenth century, painted sketches were frequently replaced by photographic images created specifically to serve as prototypes for painting. As an expression of boundless expanse, both cloud pictures and seascapes were associated with the idea of the sublime—the conception of nature as a majestic, but also an indomitable and potentially terrifying elemental force. For the Impressionists, such motifs evinced a momentary quality that corresponded to their desire to capture fleeting sense impressions on the canvas as directly as possible. Yet photographers, too, intensively explored the representation of sky and sea in the second half of the nineteenth century and in so doing pursued both artistic and scientific ambitions.

One of the most important early art photographers was Gustave Le Gray. From 1856 to 1859 he produced a series of seacoast images remarkable for their sharpness of detail and high level of artistic quality. Despite the large size of his negatives, Le Gray succeeded in creating nuanced photographic renderings of dynamic elements, such as the slight rippling of the sea or the dramatic surging of the waves (cats. 6, 9, 10, 11, 14, 15).[1] Like the Impressionists in their later series of works, in his *marines* Le Gray experimented with different vantage points and recorded his motifs at differing times of day and under varying conditions of light. By aiming his camera at a layer of clouds under backlighting, he produced images that evoke the impression of a night scene and which, like Henry Stuart Wortley's *How Sweet the Moonlight Sleeps upon the Wave* (cat. 8), stand in the tradition of Romantic landscape painting. Since the realistic representation of sky and sea required different exposure times, Le Gray sometimes used a process in which he combined two negatives. Precisely because of their extreme realism, the seascapes were enthusiastically received when they were first exhibited at the Photographic Society of London in December 1856. The picture *The Brig (Brig in Moonlight)* (cat. 10) was even described by a critic as "the grandest effort ever seen in photography."[2]

In the mid-nineteenth century the effort to render weather phenomena as authentically as possible was also associated with developments in the science of meteorology, which received its impetus from the creation of numerous new research institutions. With his 1803 publication "Essay on the Modification of Clouds" the British scientist Luke Howard had laid the foundation for the systematic classification of cloud formations, an area in which photographic documentation would soon play a crucial role. Numerous meteorological societies used photographs specially prepared by professionals, as well as amateur shots, to establish comprehensive visual databanks. In 1896 the first edition of the elaborately produced *International Cloud Atlas* was published in Paris, in which most of the illustrations were based on color photographs. Images such as the photographs of lightning by the scientists Heinrich Kayser and Emil Jacobsen from the mid-1880s not only yielded new understanding of the duration and structure of spark discharges, but also led to new visual forms in landscape painting, where lightning had hitherto been depicted primarily as a simple zigzag form (cats. 24, 25).

The function of the camera as an aid to the natural sciences also informed the development of chronophotography. Beginning in the 1870s, this technique enabled complex sequences of movement to be documented by means of a series of photographs taken in rapid, almost cinematic succession. One of the pioneers of chronophotography was Albert Londe, who in 1882 developed a technique to facilitate the medical examination of muscular movements. For his photographs, Londe used a camera first with nine, then with twelve lenses, enabling him to take individual shots at intervals of a tenth of a second. Under the direction of neurologist Jean-Martin Charcot, the photographs were used at the hospital of La Salpêtrière in Paris to document phenomena including the spasms of epileptic and "hysterical" seizures. In 1887 Londe participated in the founding of the Société d'excursions des amateurs de photographie; in addition to his medical works, he also devoted himself privately to a wide range of motifs. For his photograph *The Wave* (cat. 18), created around 1890, he used a twelve-lens camera; when printed, the series appears in three rows on a single sheet. The work was reproduced in Londe's 1903 publication *Album de chronophotographies documentaires à l'usage des artistes.*[3]

While works such as Londe's chronophotographs used mechanical transfer to create cool, detached renderings of natural phenomena, the Pictorialists simultaneously pursued artistic goals that were diametrically opposed to this technical, objectifying aim. In their landscape photographs, they embraced the tradition of European painting and employed complex, fine art printing processes as well as manual manipulation of the prints to produce works that foregrounded the subjective element in the experience of nature. In many instances, the influence of Impressionism is apparent in both the choice of motif and the artificial effect of haziness and blurring. In his view of the cliffs at Étretat from 1895, Arthur Da Cunha explored a motif that had inspired Claude Monet to produce a series of ambitious paintings and also enjoyed great popularity among amateur photographers in the late nineteenth century (cats. 3, 4). The dark form of the cliff on the left side of the image stands out as a decorative silhouette against the mysterious, glowing surface of the sea. Like Robert Demachy's composition *Breaking Wave* (cat. 19), Da Cunha's photograph is marked by a lyrical permeation of the pictorial space that resonates with the traditional metaphor of the sea as a symbol of the unfathomable. The deserted scenes, devoid of human presence, suggest a confrontation with the forces of nature far removed from civilization. In this respect, they closely parallel Monet's Impressionist seascapes of the 1880s, painted on the Atlantic coast of northern France.

Translated from German by Melissa M. Thorson

[1] Christiane Stahl, "Die große Welle: Das Meer als Erfahrungsraum von Gustave Le Gray bis Otto Steinert," in Hamburg 2015, 32–43, here 32–33.

[2] *Norfolk News* (December 1857), quoted in *Photography: Discovery and Invention,* Papers Delivered at a Symposium Celebrating the Invention of Photography, J. Paul Getty Museum, January 30, 1989, Santa Monica 1990, 94.

[3] Ulrich Pohlmann, "Wellen und Wolken," in Munich 2004, 171–73, here 173.

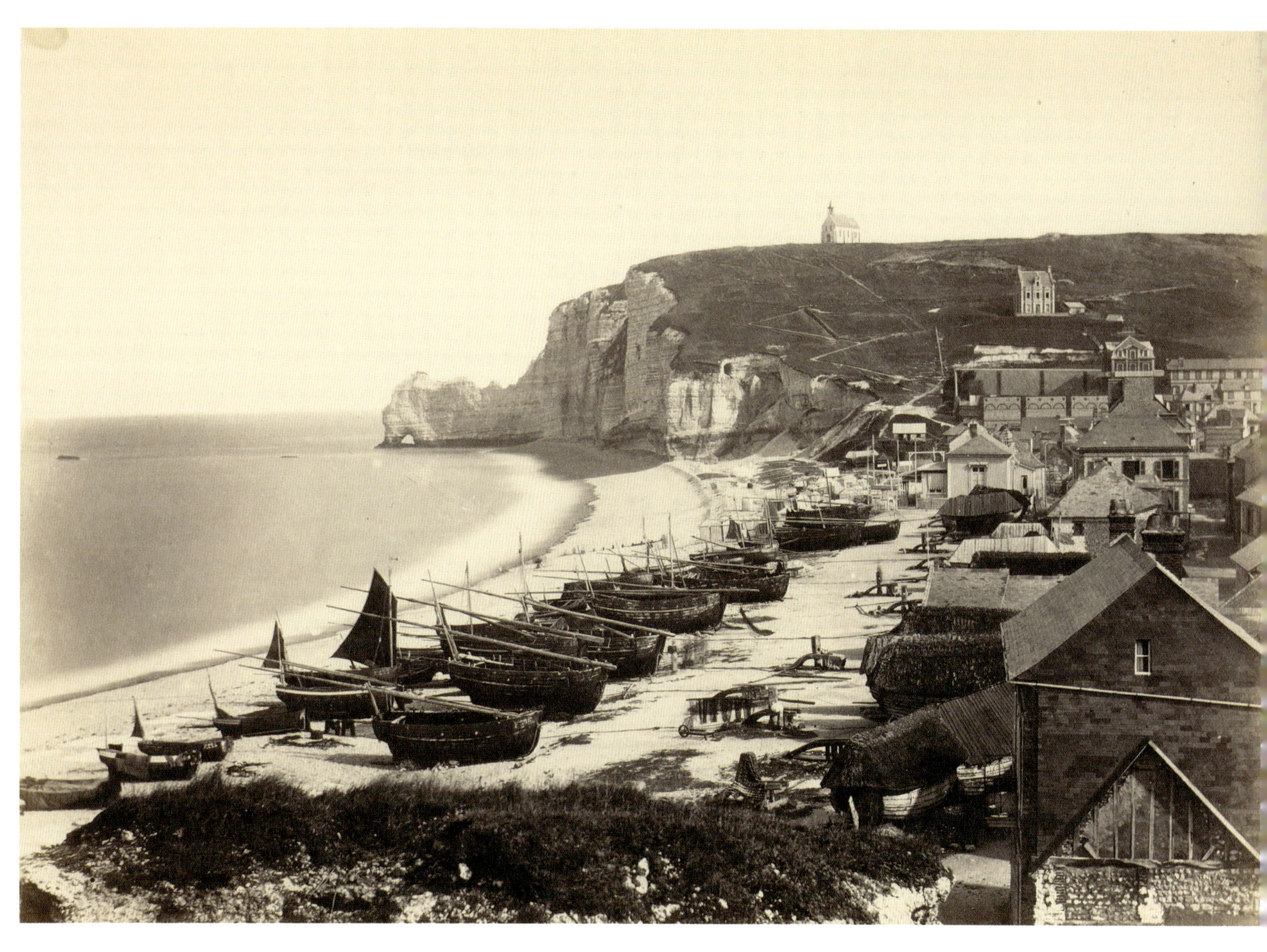

2 Louis Alphonse Davanne
Étretat, ca. 1864

3 Anonymous
Étretat, from the album *Bretagne
Normandie,* 1889

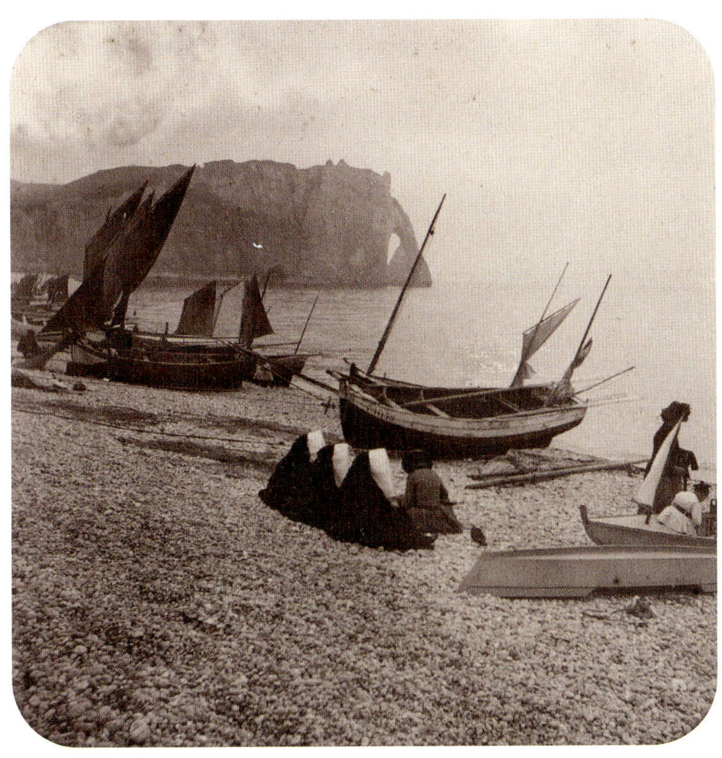

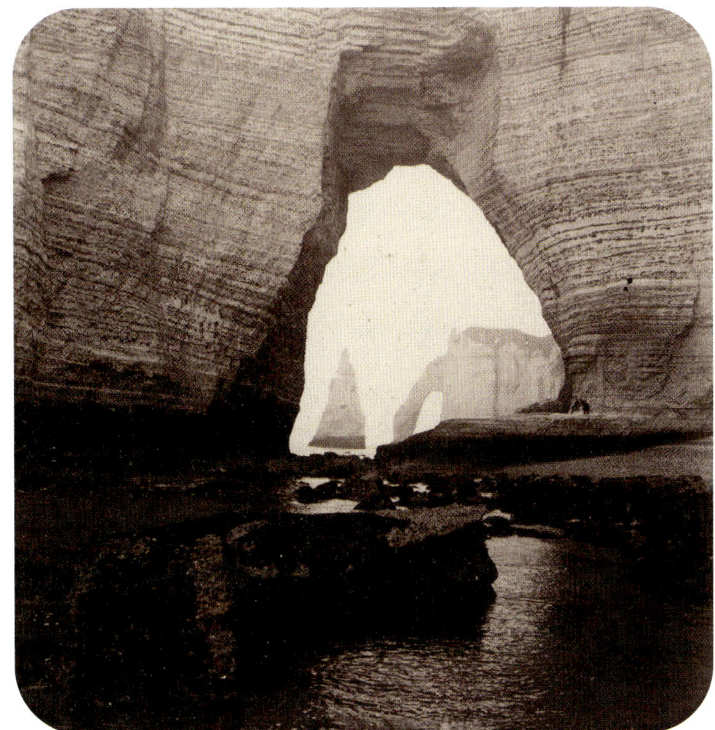

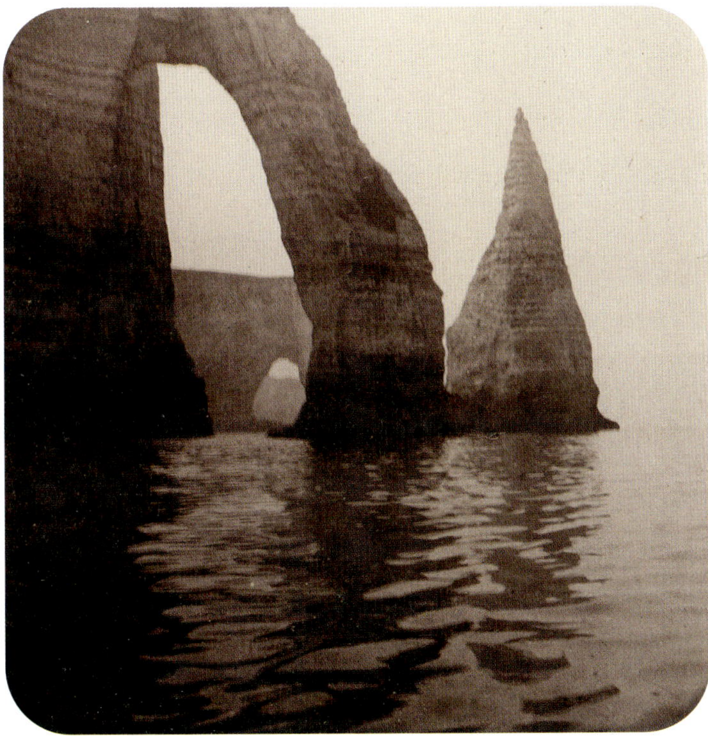

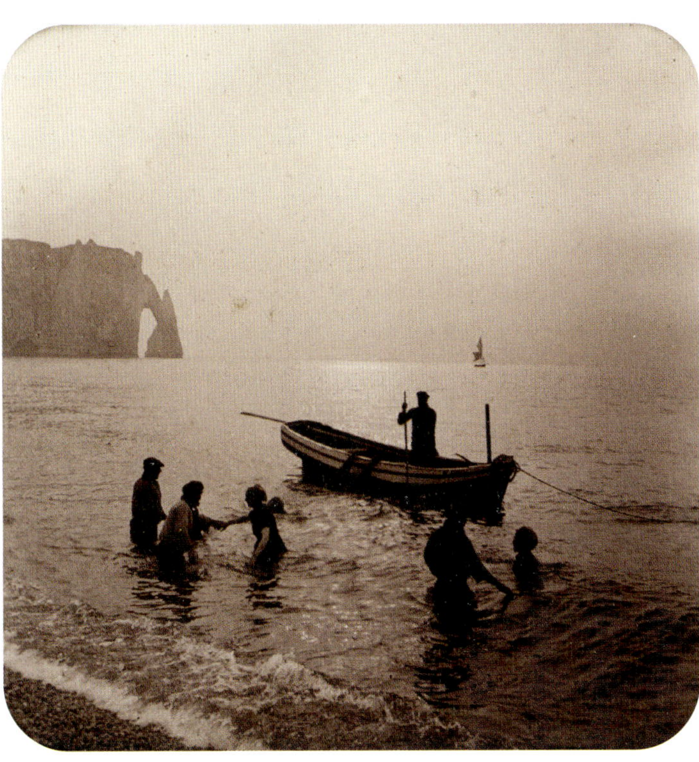

4 Arthur Da Cunha
Étretat, 1895

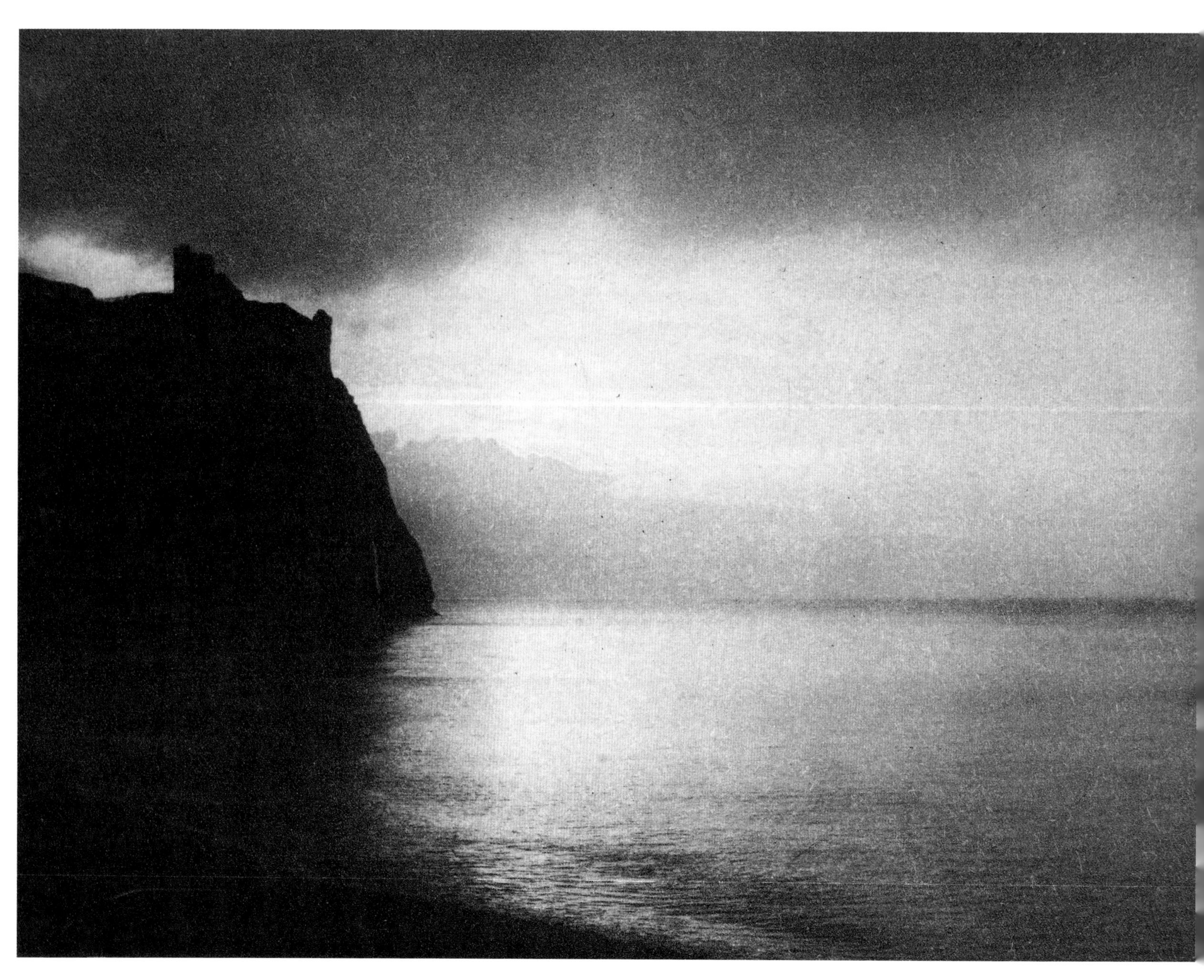

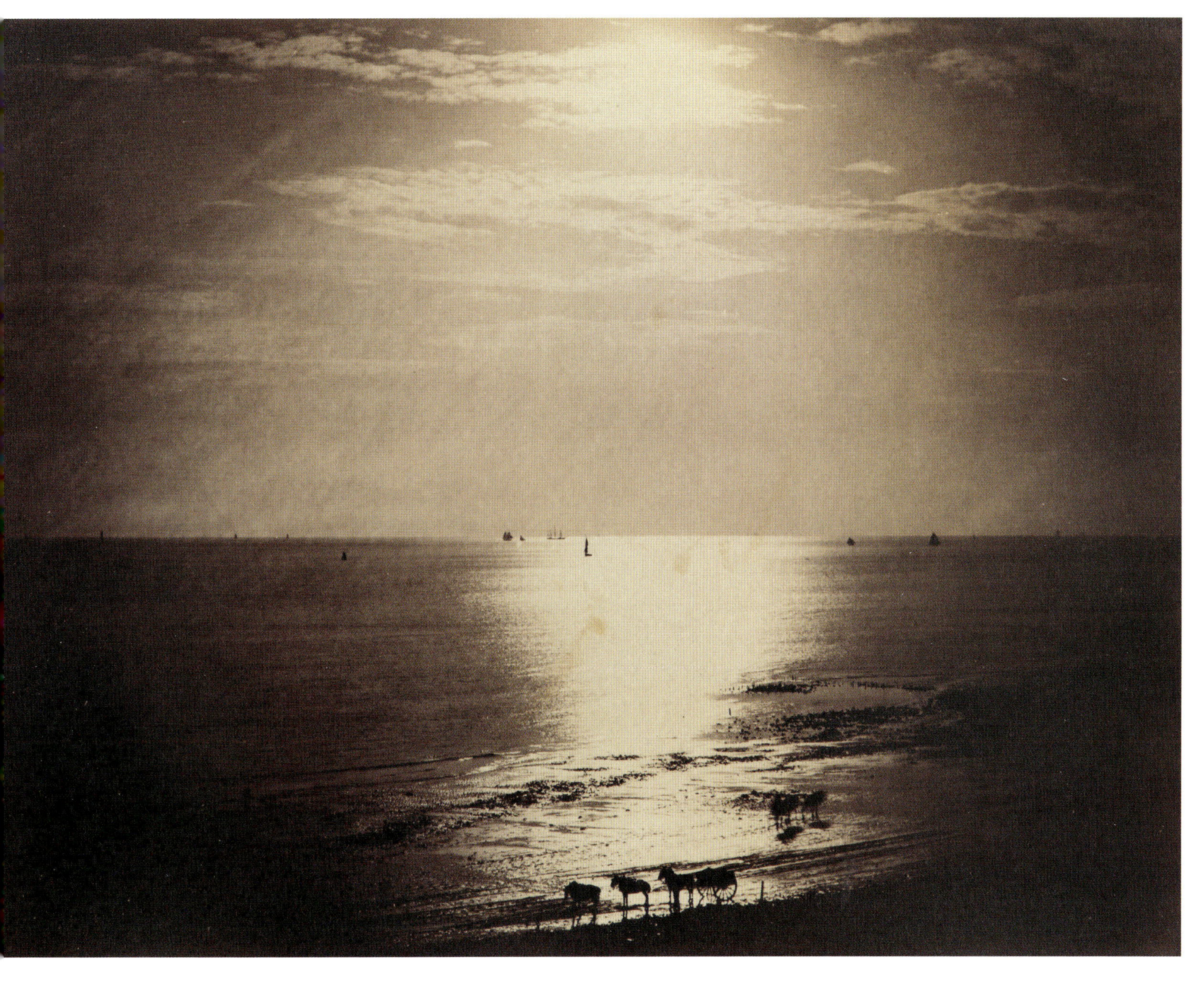

5 Gustave Le Gray
The Sun at Zenith,
Normandy, 1856–57

Sunlight in the Clouds—Ocean, 1856

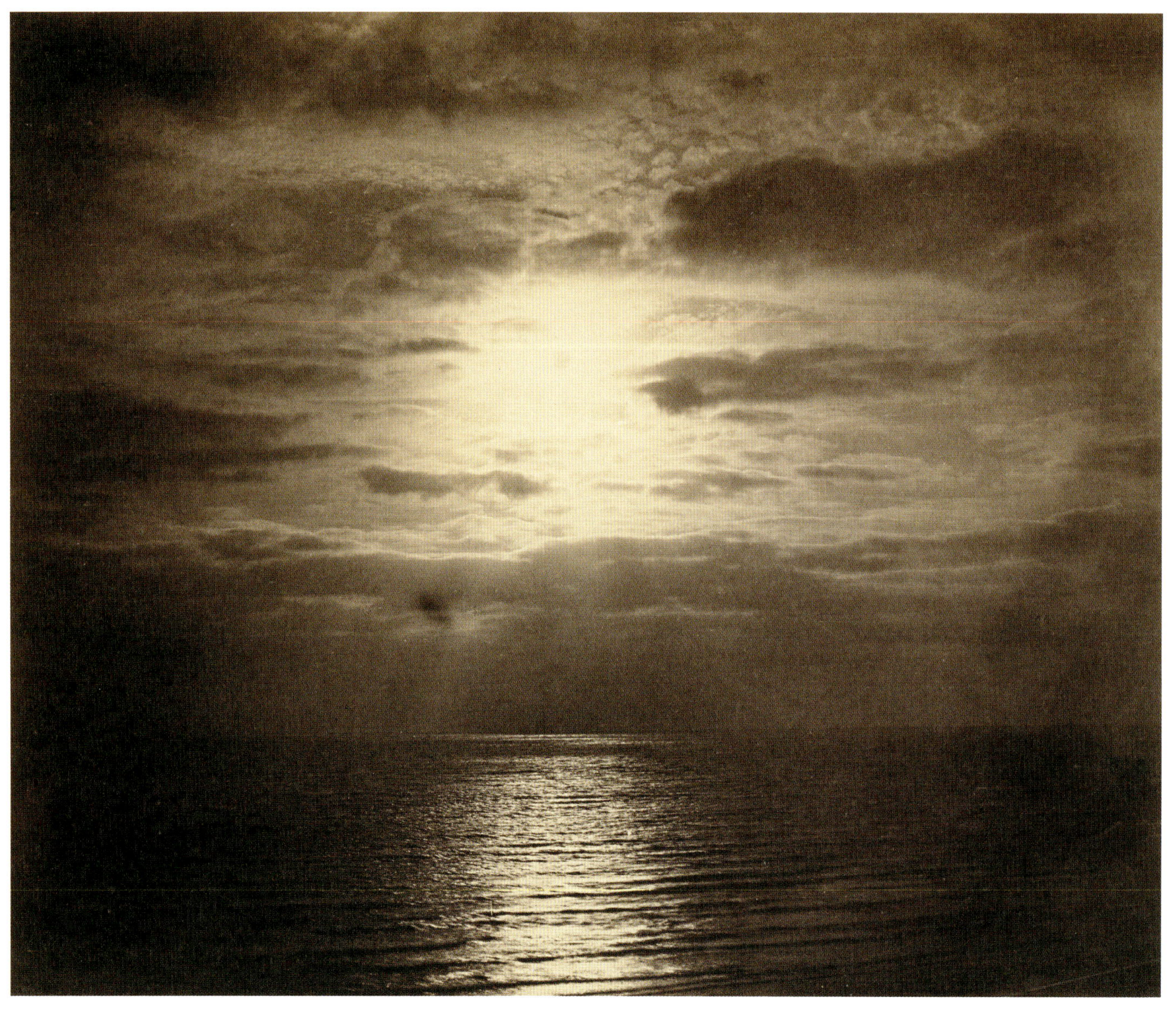

7 Gustave Le Gray
Cloud Study, Clair-obscur, 1856–57

8 Henry Stuart Wortley
*How Sweet the Moonlight Sleeps
upon the Wave*, ca. 1869

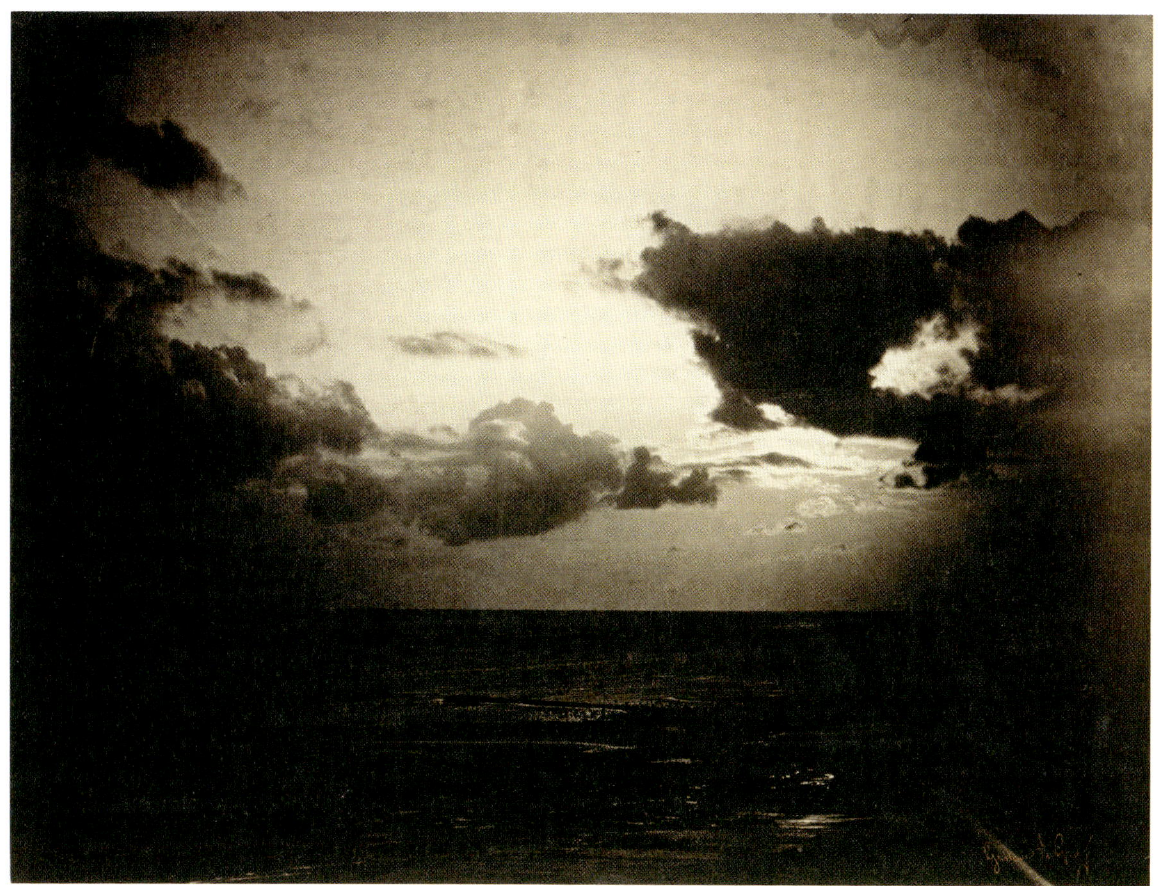

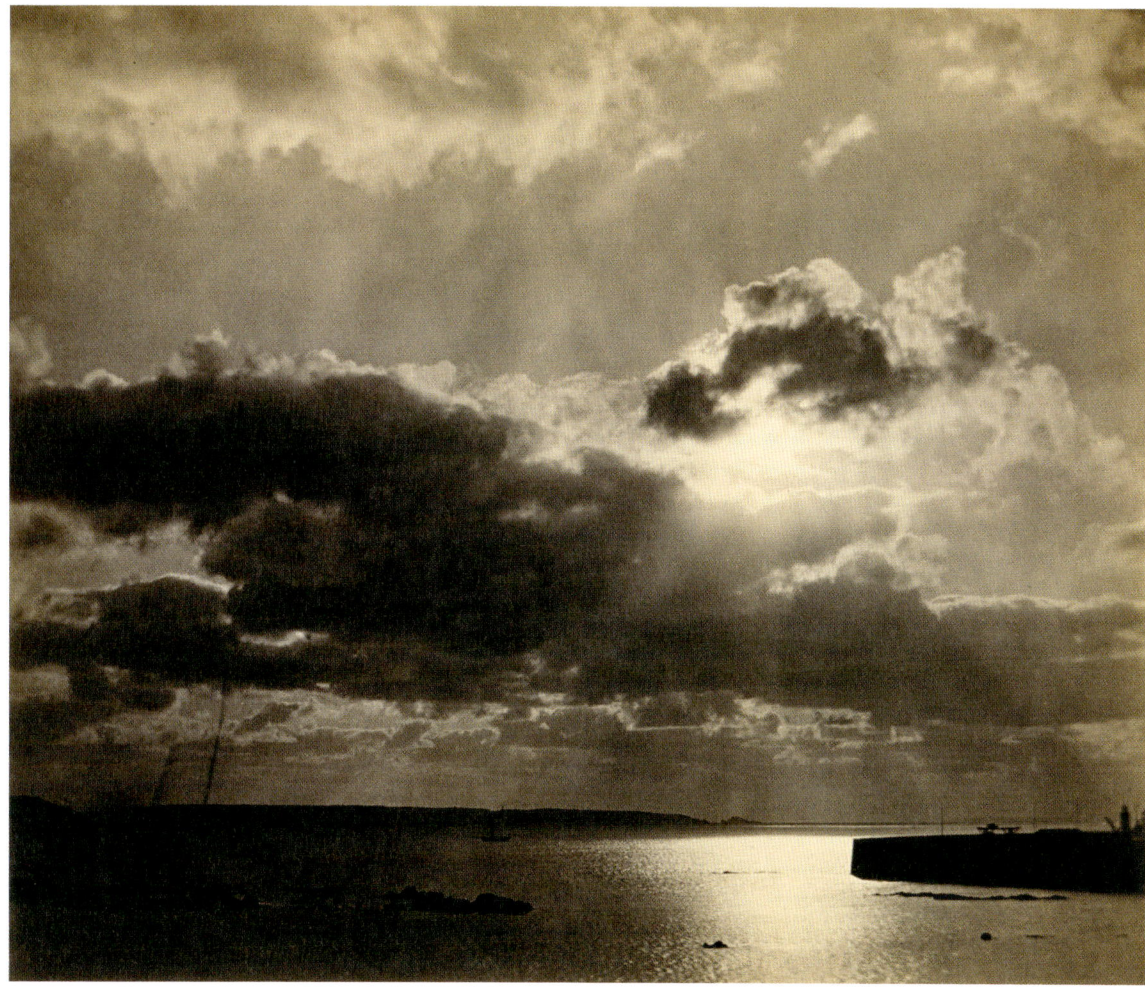

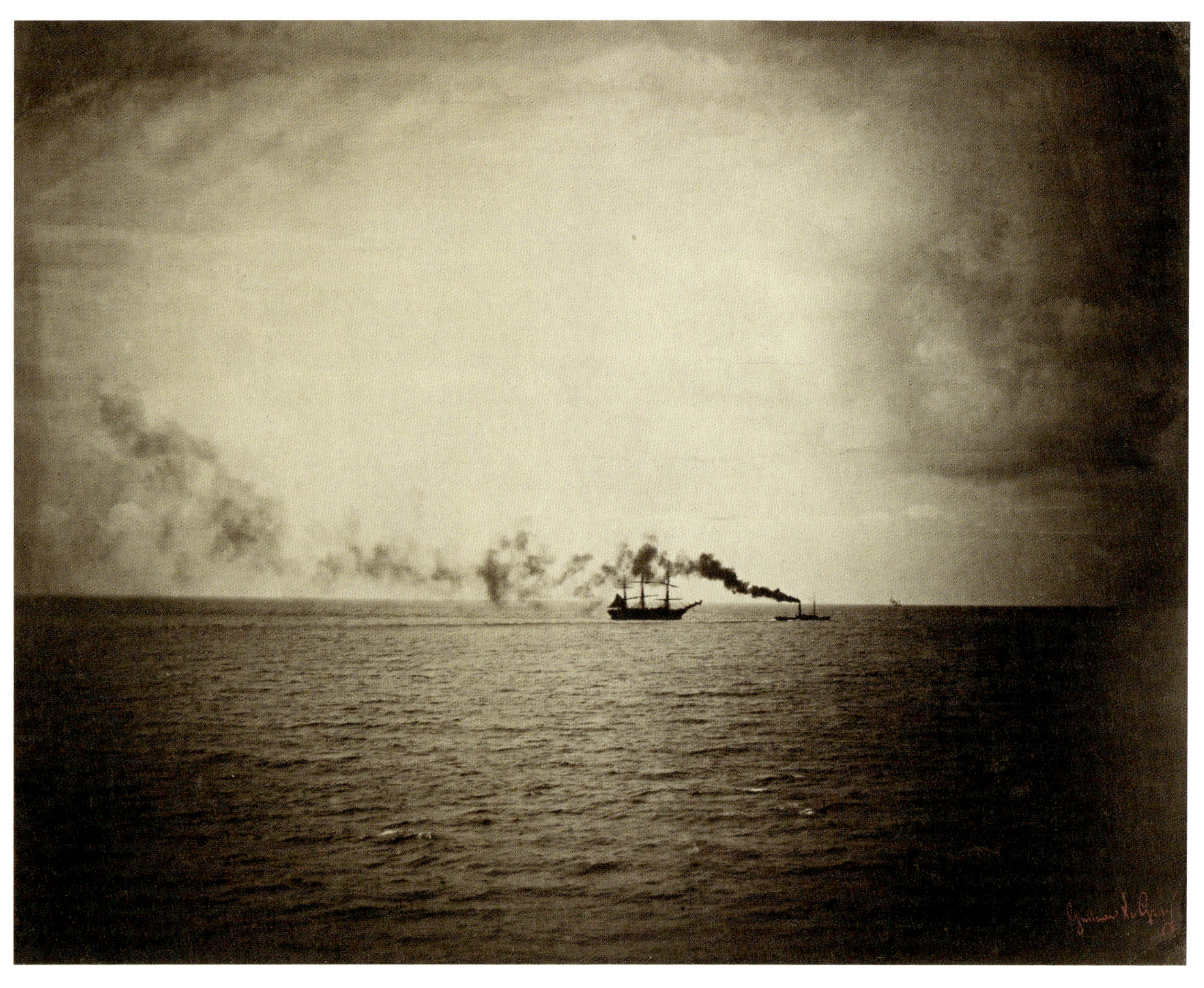

9 Gustave Le Gray
Steam, 1856

10 Gustave Le Gray
The Brig (*Brig in Moonlight*), 1856

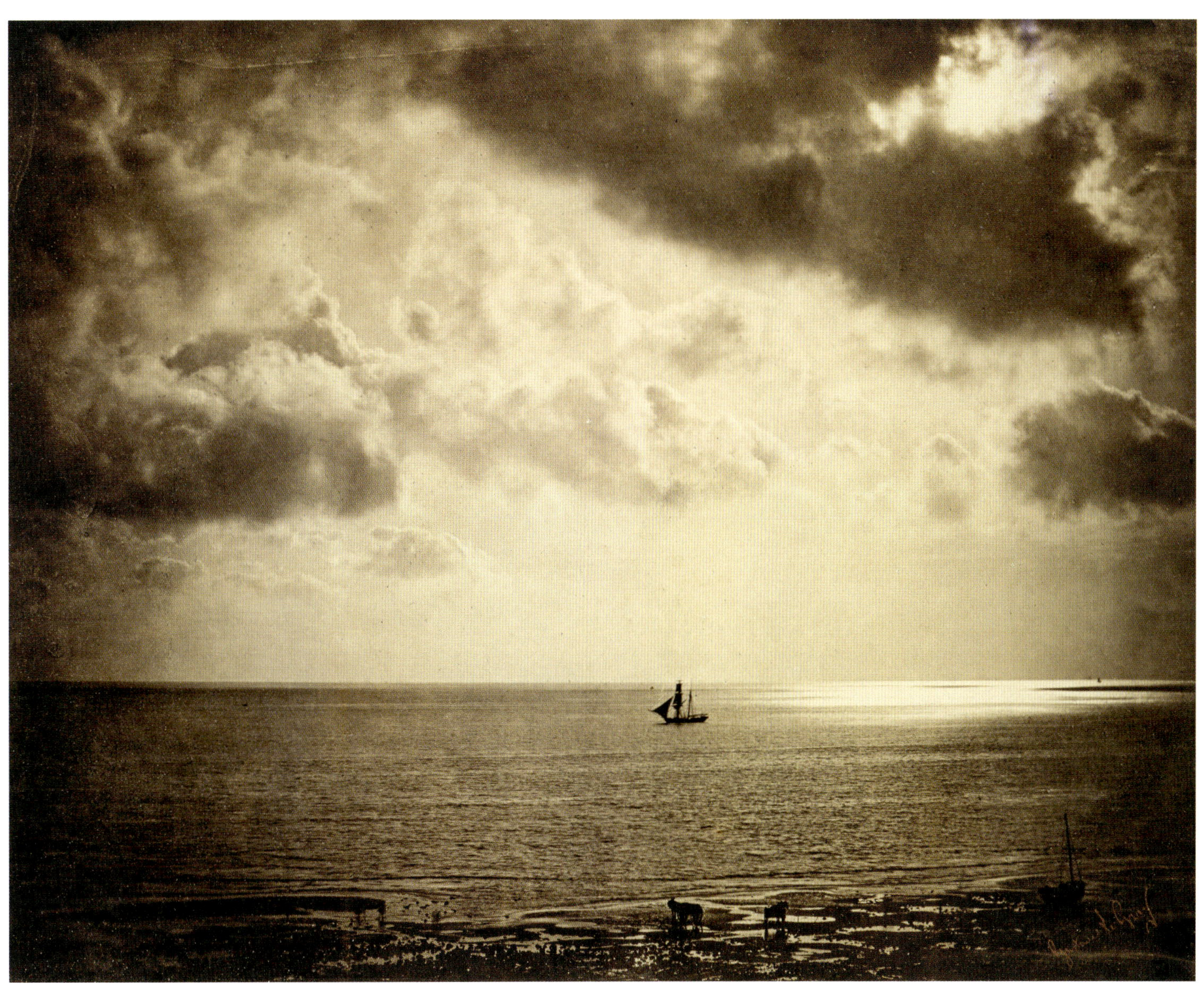

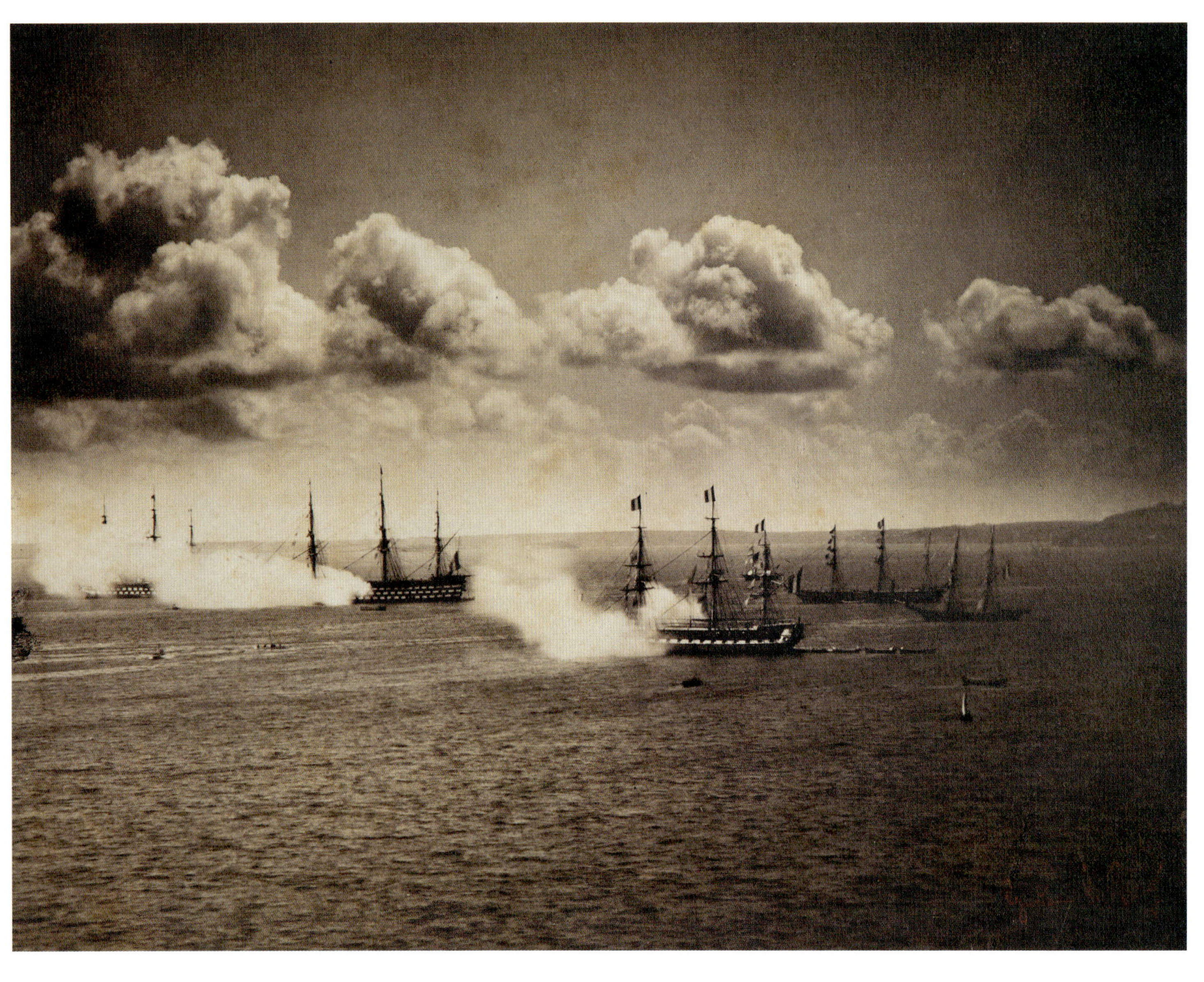

11 Gustave Le Gray
*Salute of the French Fleet off
Cherbourg,* 1858

Seascape with Ship, ca. 1865

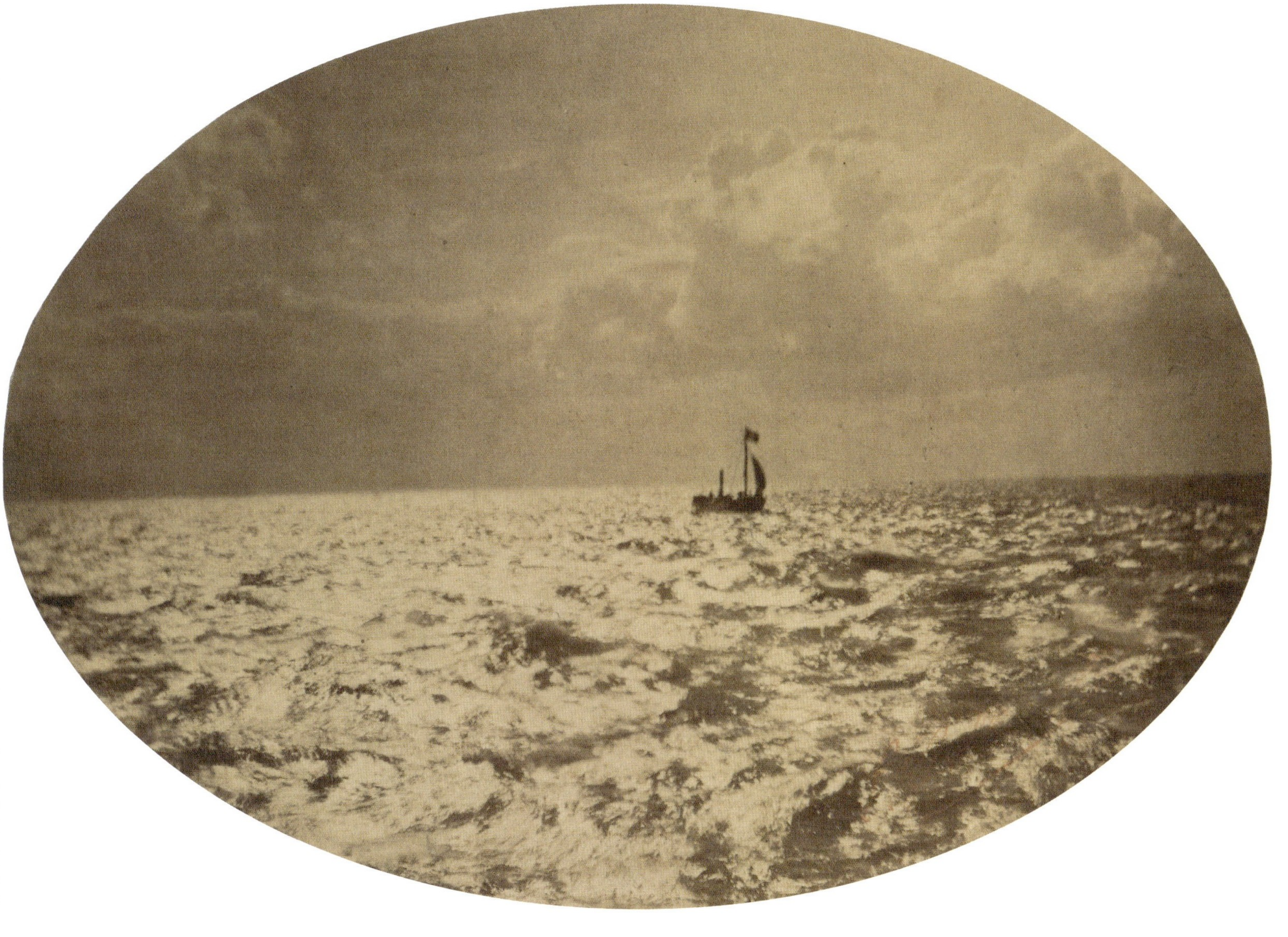

13 Auguste Autin
Sunset, October 1861 at 5 p.m., 1861

14 Gustave Le Gray
The Great Wave, Sète, 1857

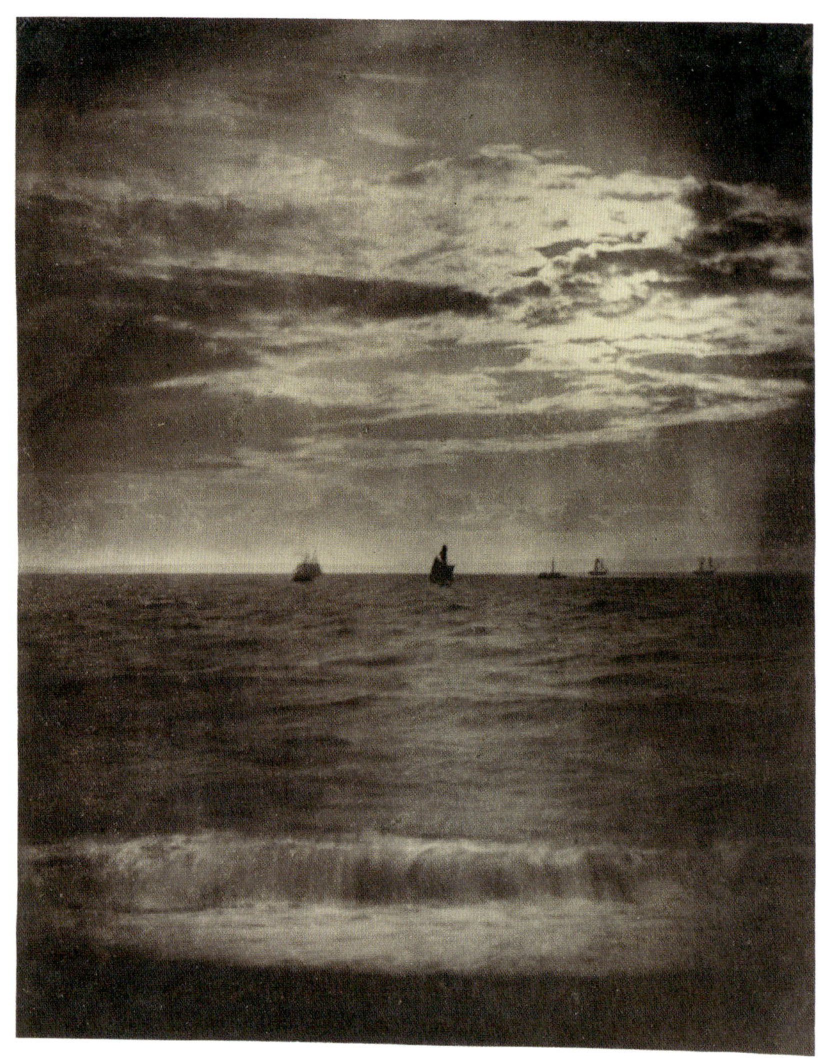

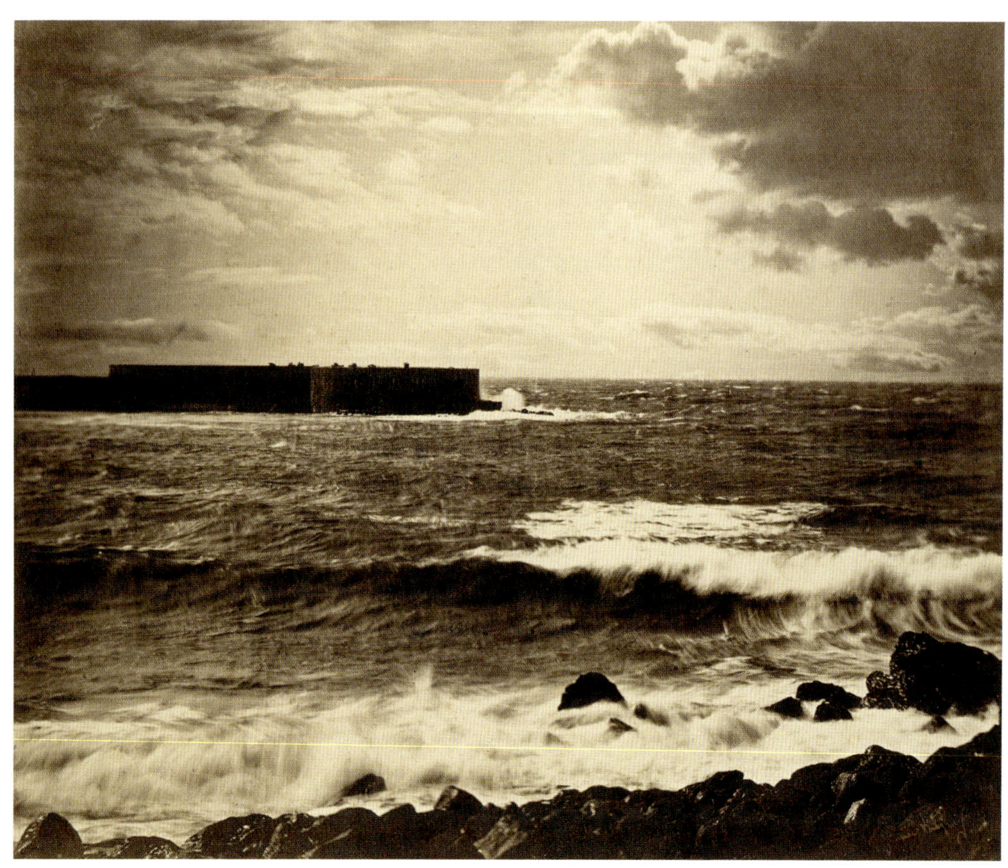

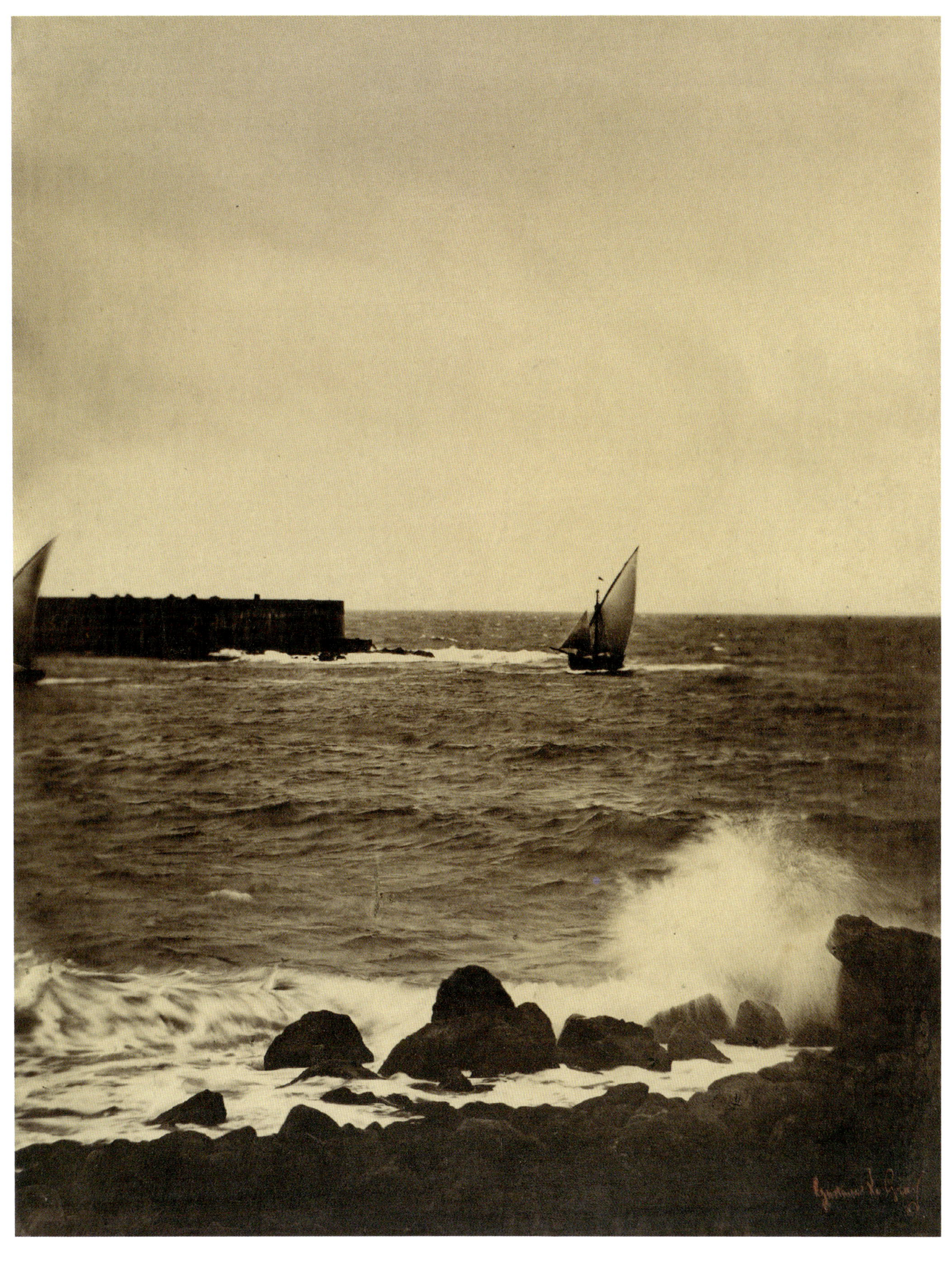

15 Gustave Le Gray
The Brig, Seascape and Clouds
Photographed Simultaneously
(Mediterranean), 1857

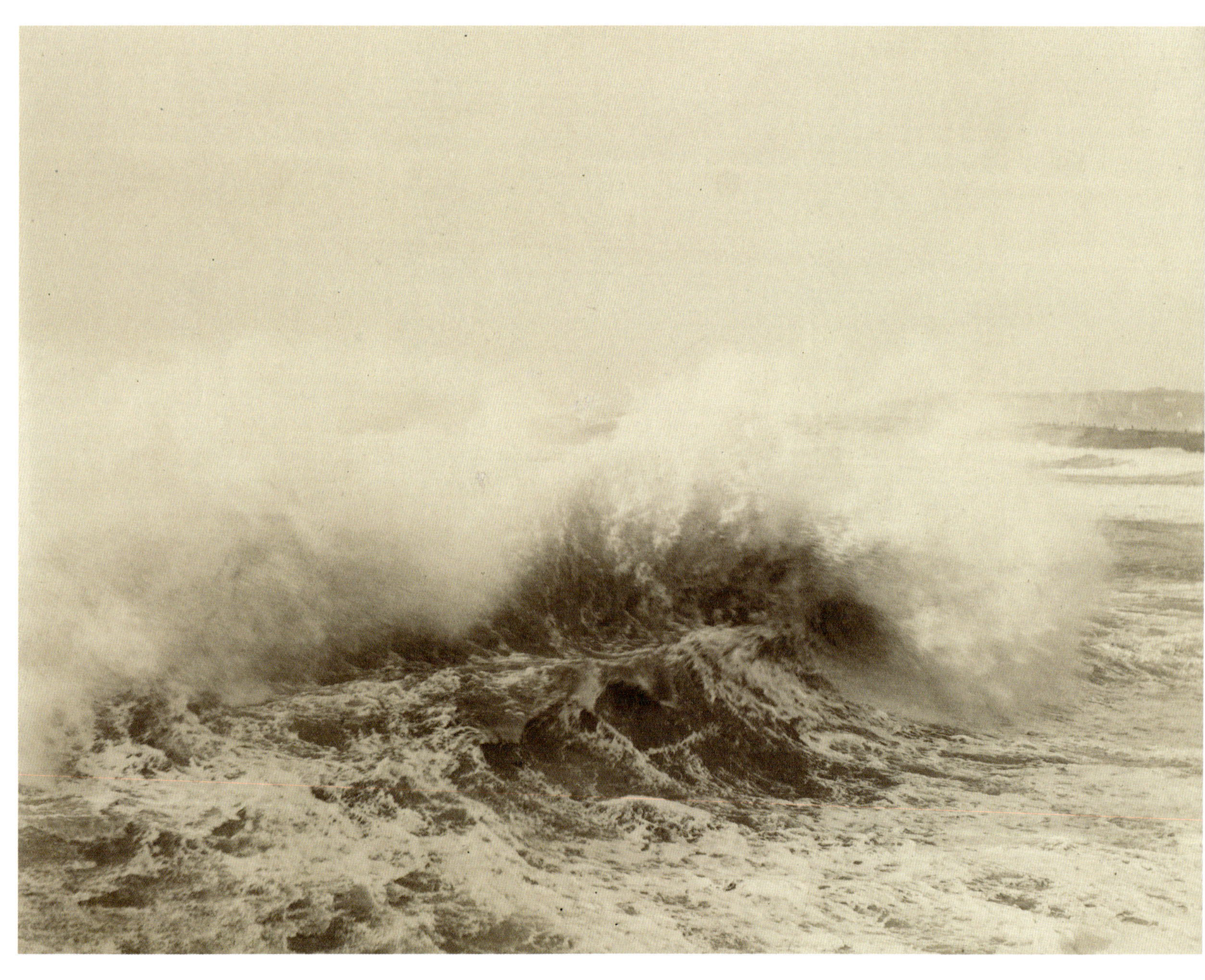

16 Charles Grassin
Breaking Waves, ca. 1882–84

17 Henry Peach Robinson
and Nelson King Cherrill
The Beached Margent of the Sea, 1870

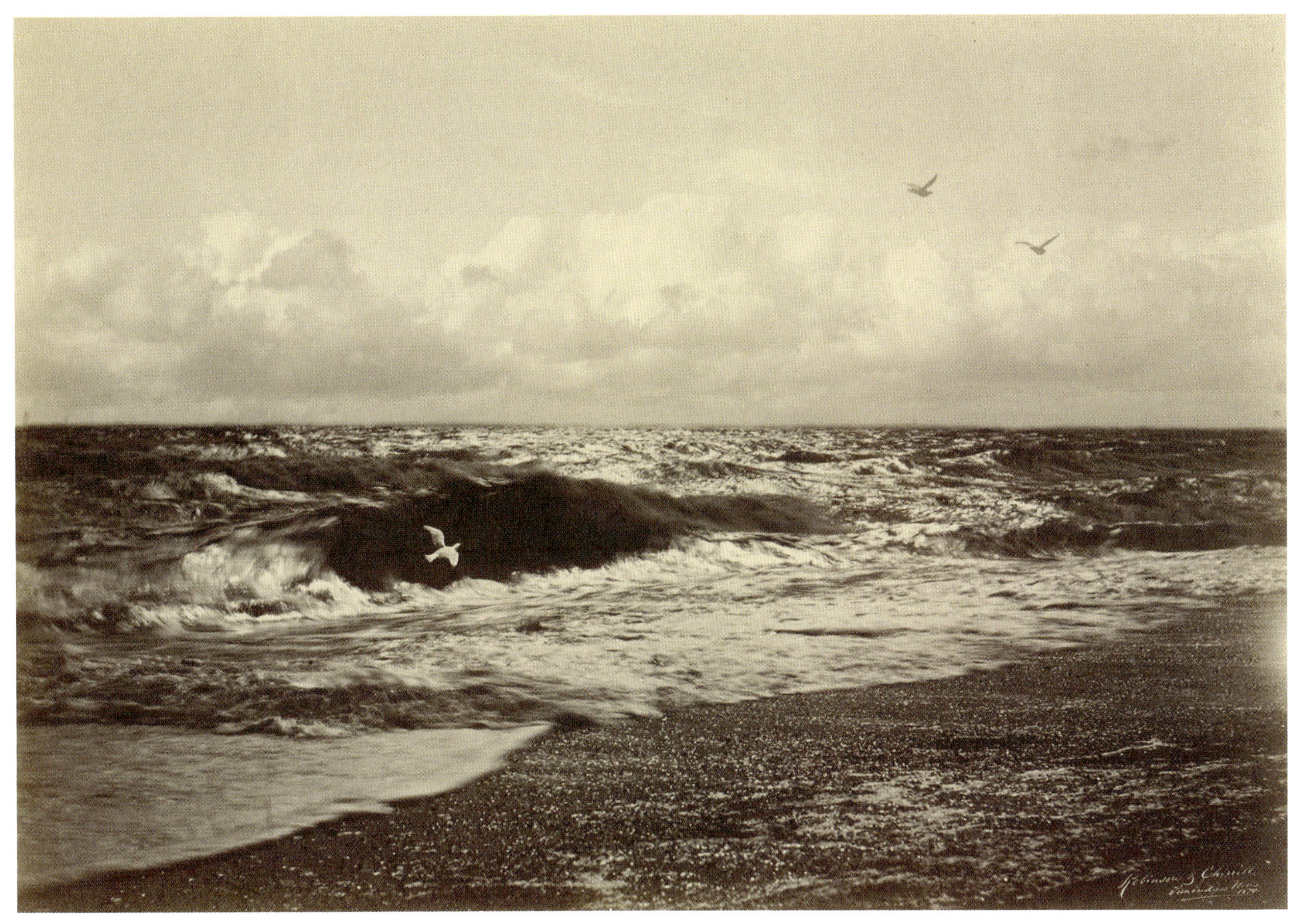

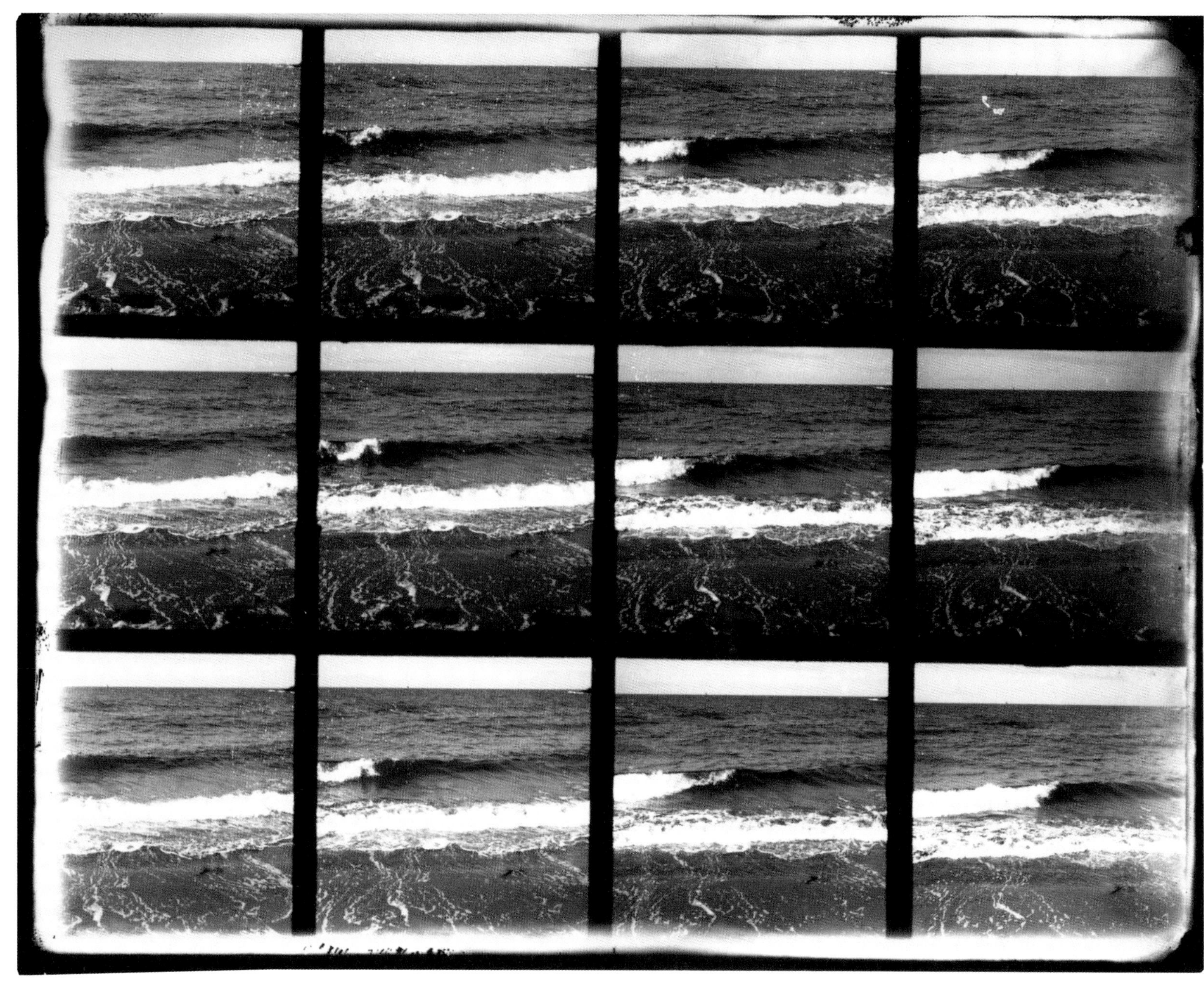

18 Albert Londe
The Wave, 1893

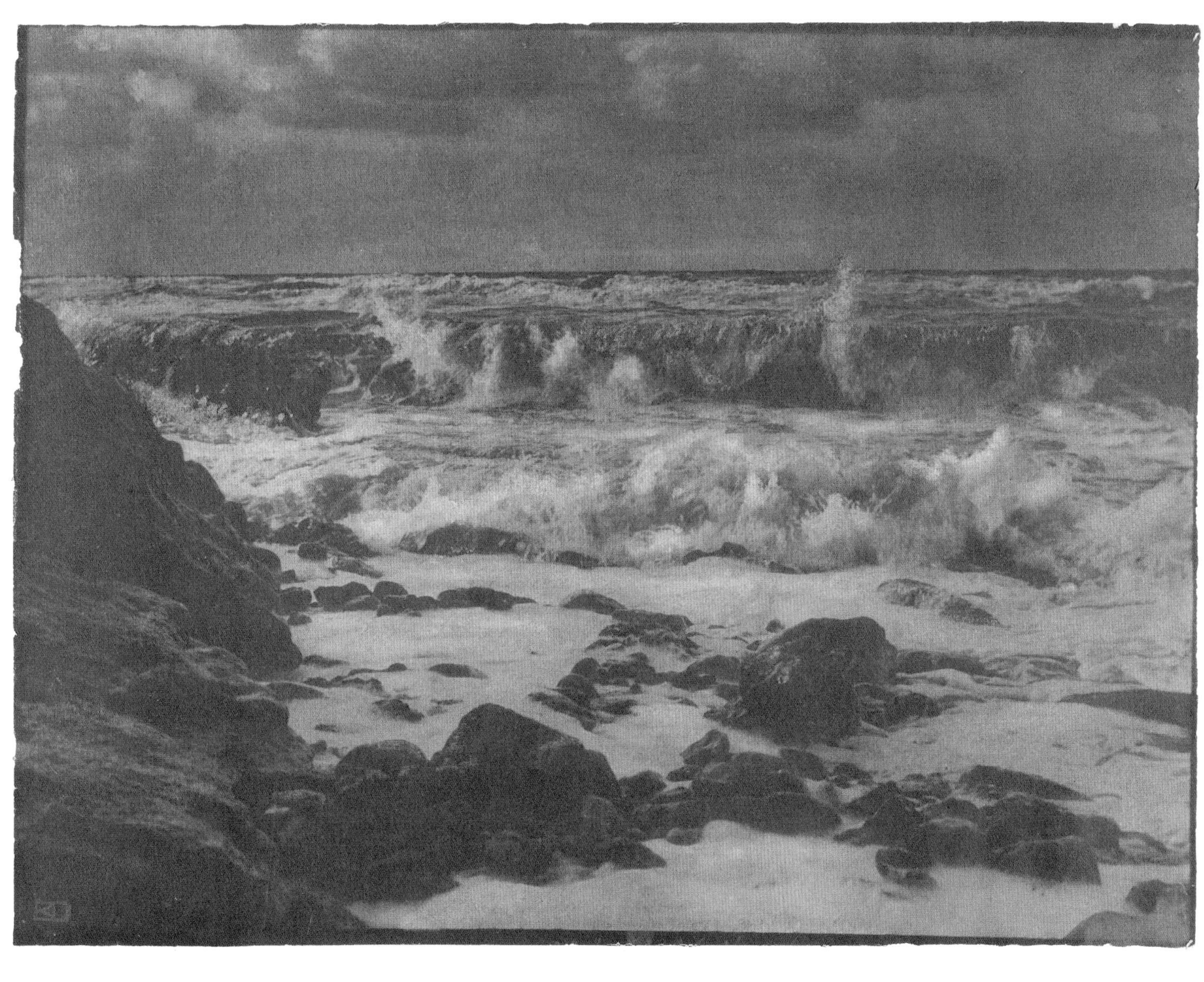

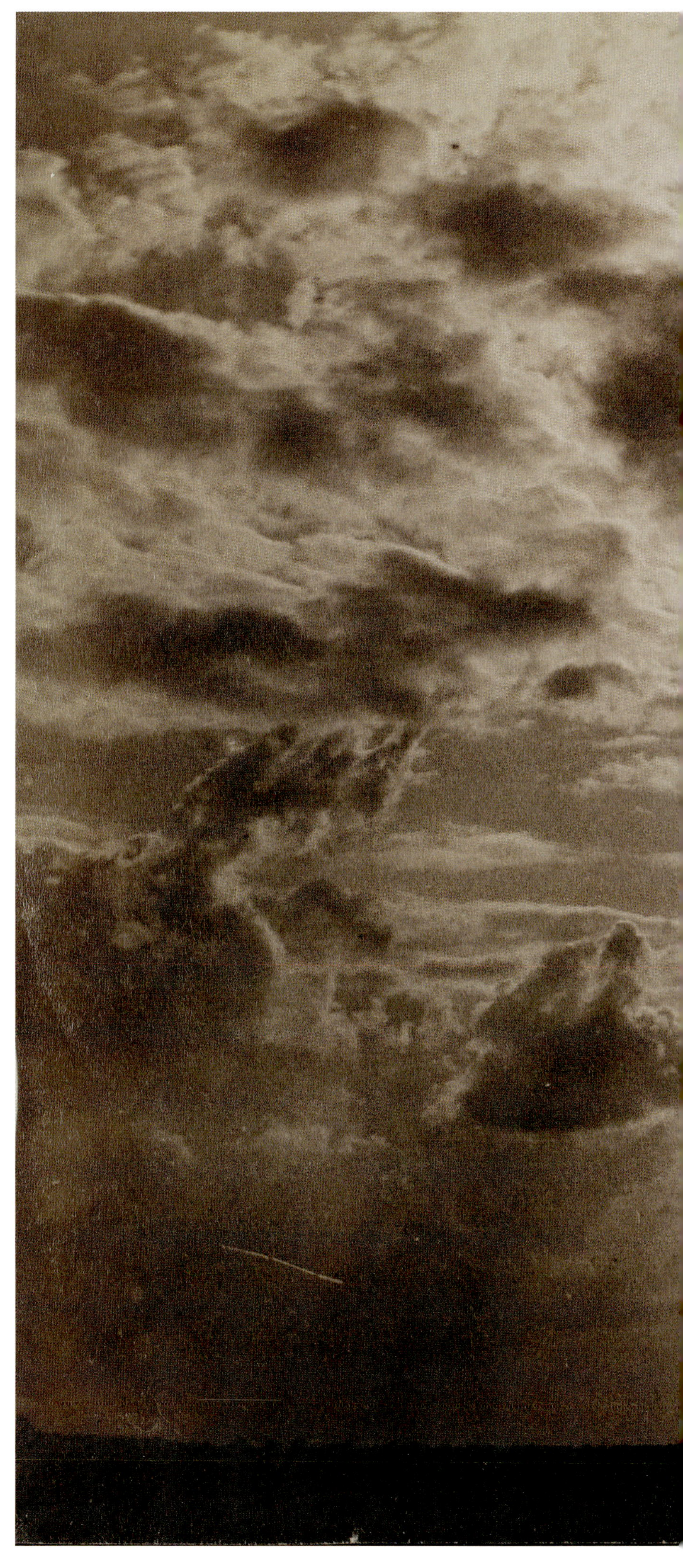

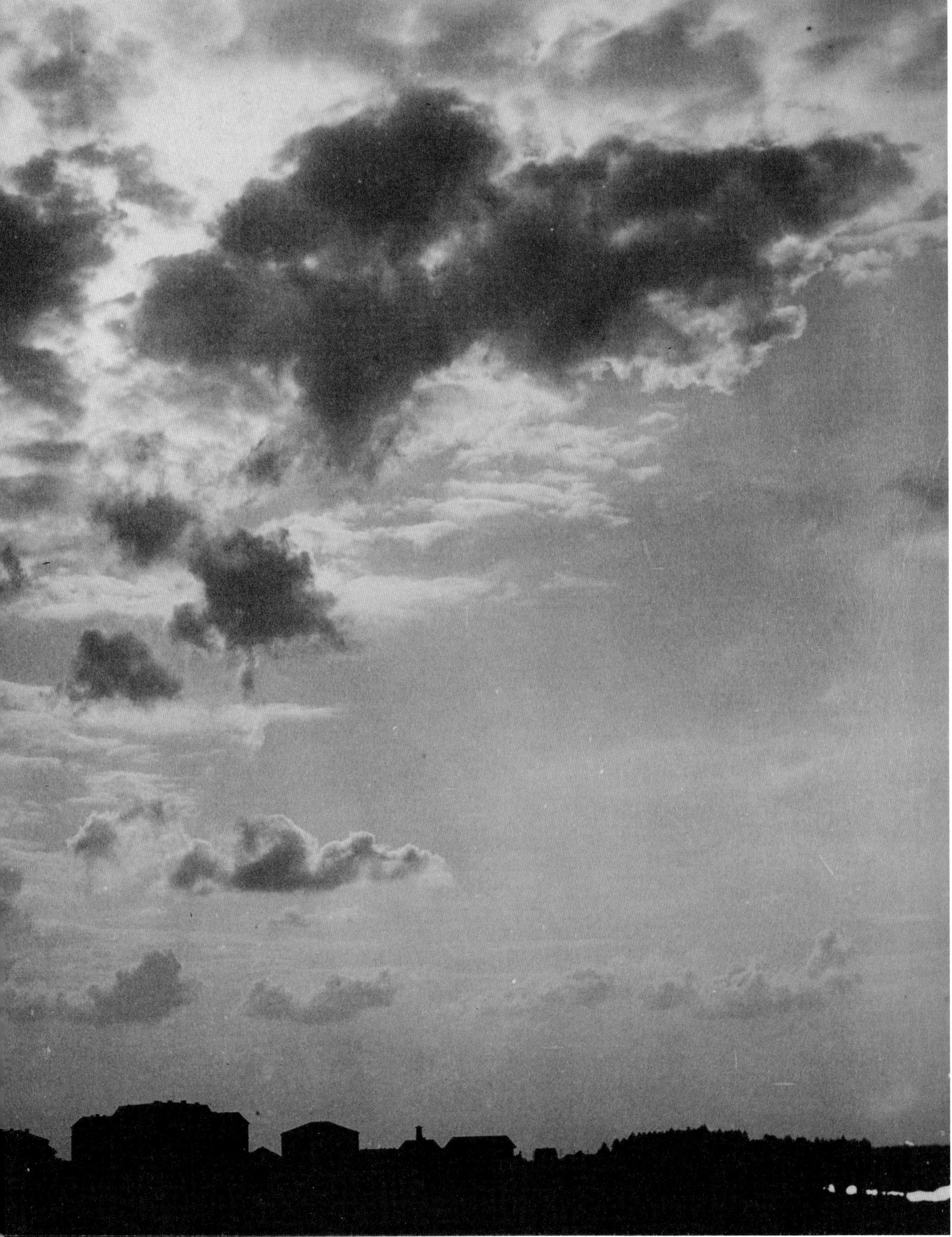

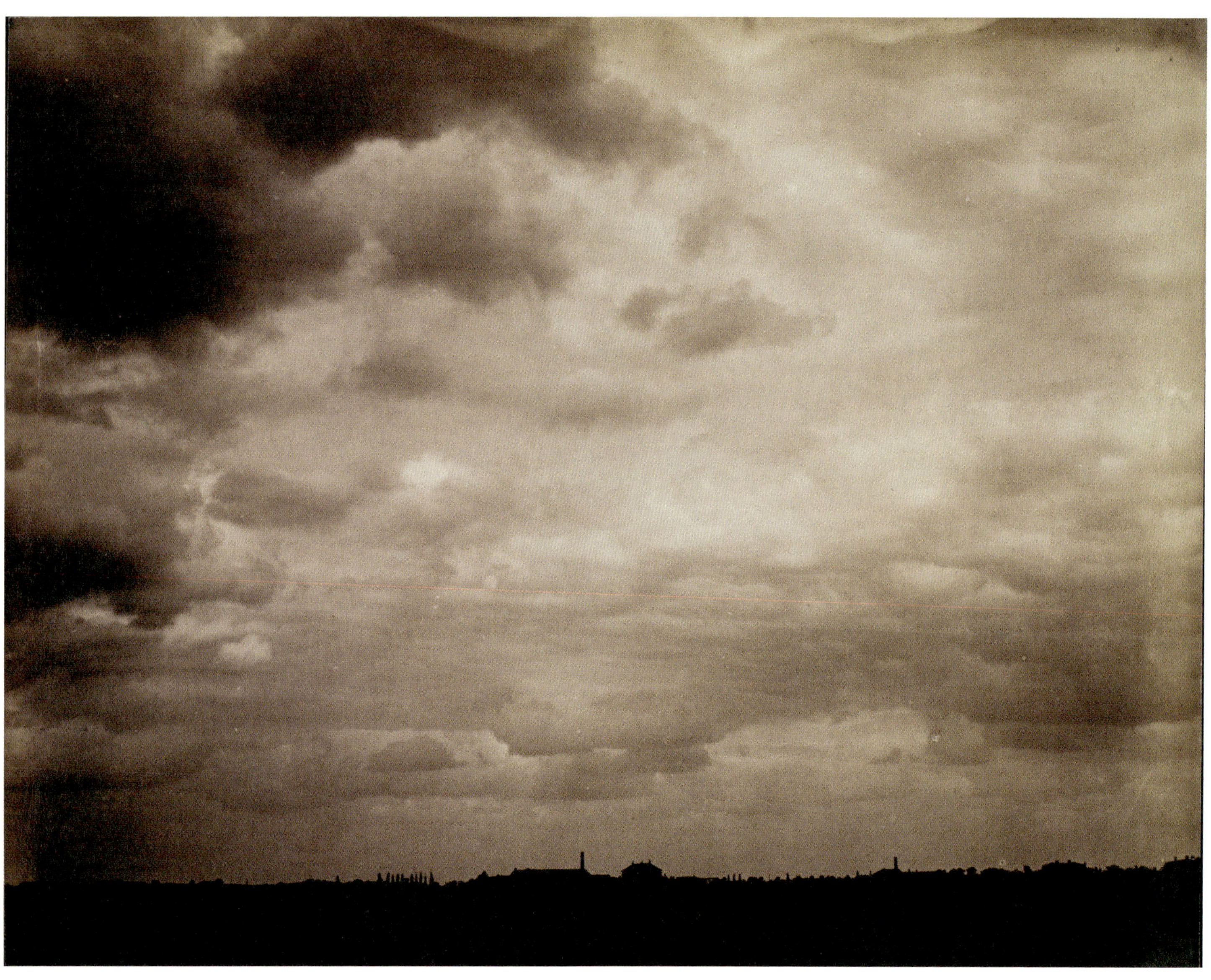

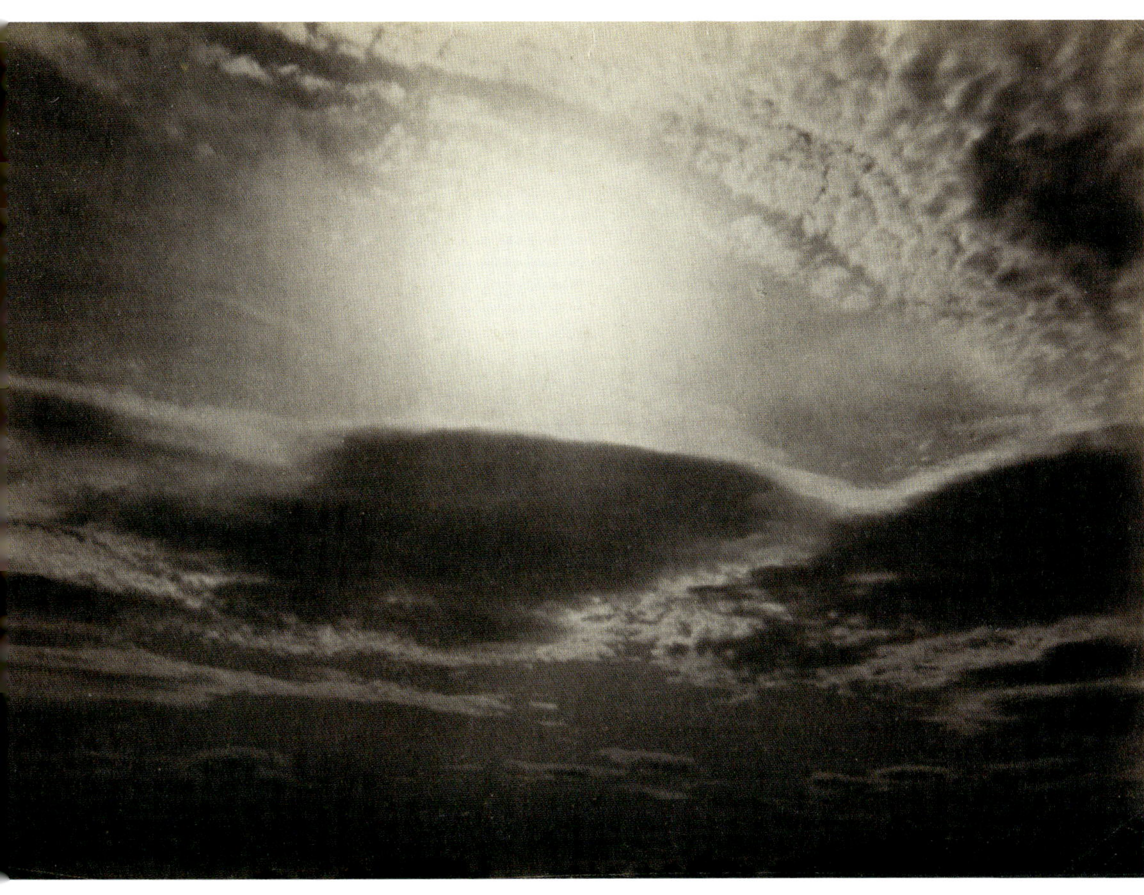

22 Robert Scholz
Cloud Study, ca. 1870

23 Léopold Louis Mercier
Cloud Study, No. 2694, 1890

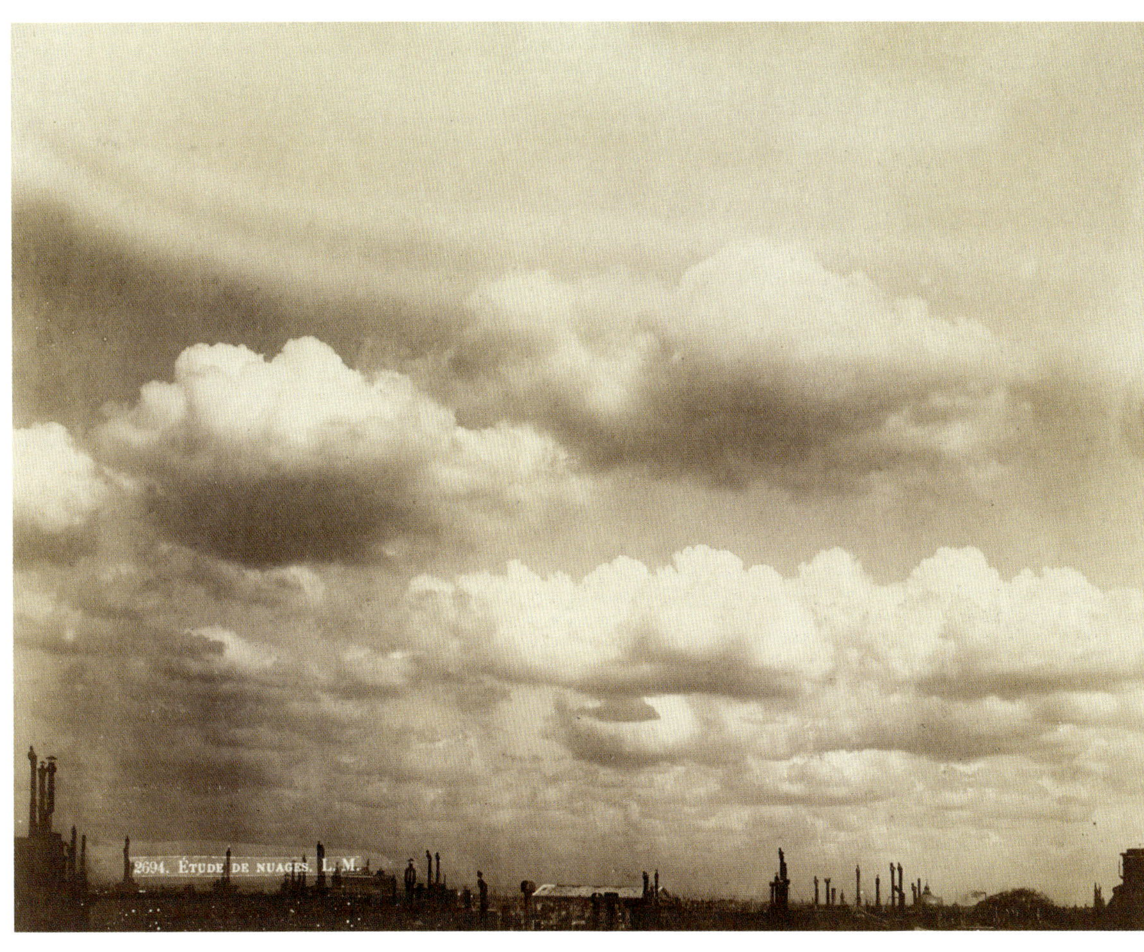

24 Heinrich Kayser
Photograph of Lightning, Enlarged
Six Times, July 16, 1884, 1884

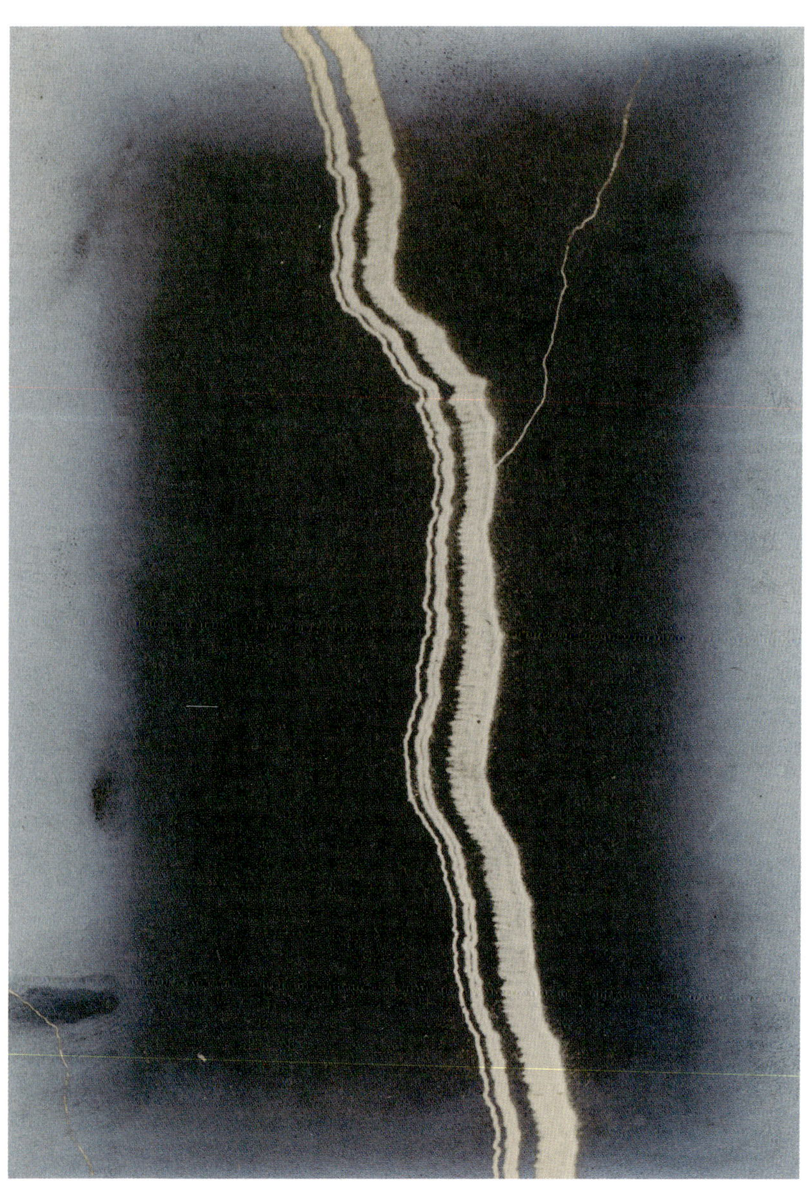

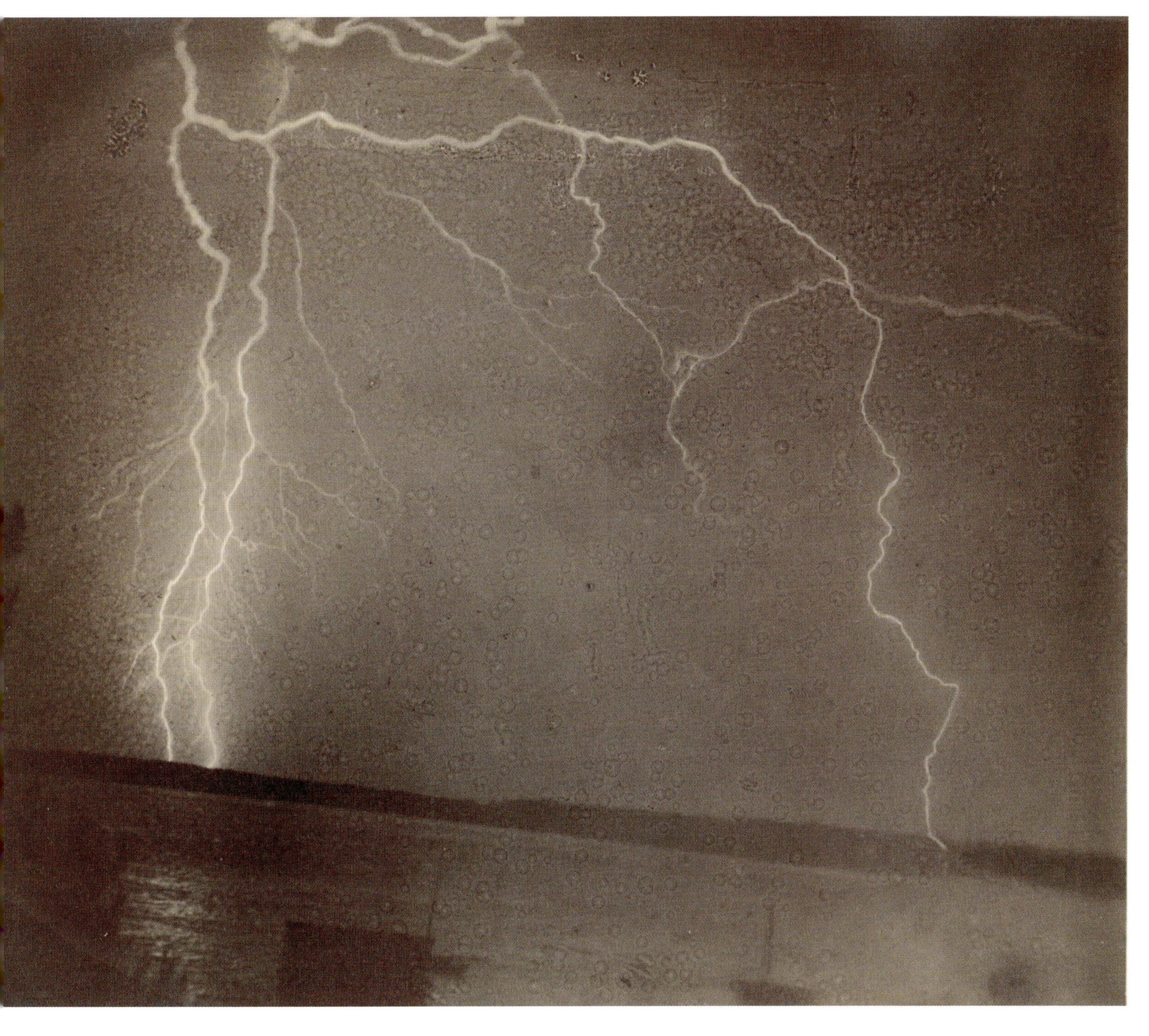

25 Emil Jacobsen
Lightning, 1885

Daniel Zamani

Center of Modernity

Paris

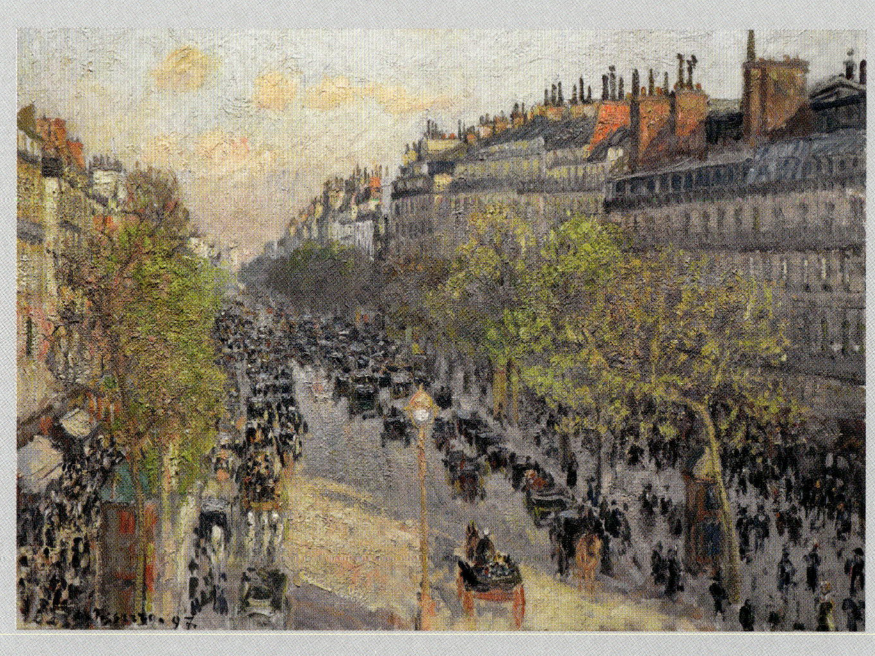

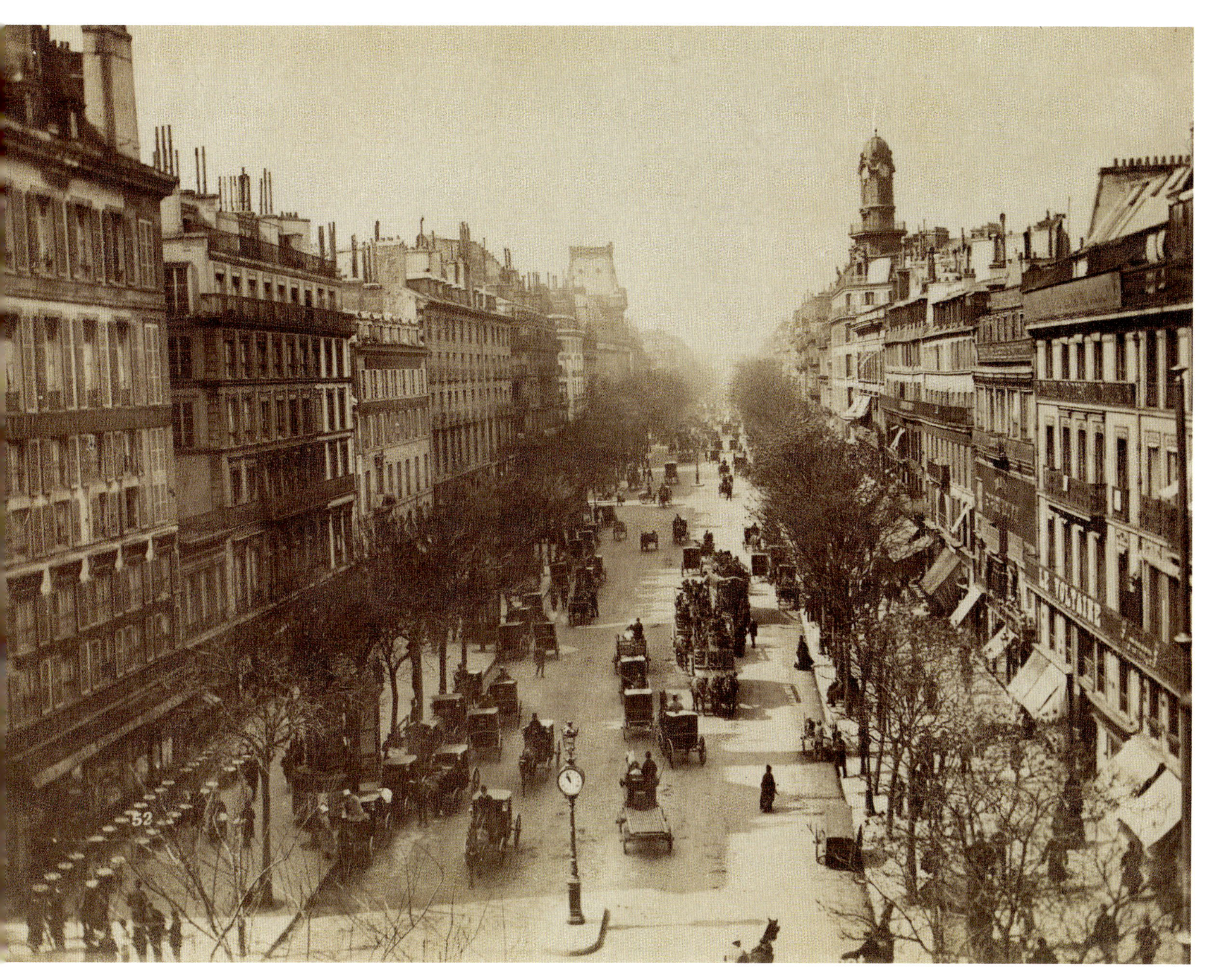

Camille Pissarro
Boulevard Montmartre,
Twilight, 1897
Oil on canvas
Hasso Plattner Collection

26 Anonymous
Grand Boulevard, Paris, ca. 1875

The renovation of Paris was one of the most ambitious projects of the Second Empire (1852–70), the reign of Emperor Napoléon III. In the early 1850s he had tasked his prefect of the Seine, Georges-Eugène Haussmann, with the comprehensive redesign of the city. Up to that point the center of Paris had consisted of a tangle of medieval alleyways and had become the focus of intense public criticism on account of its catastrophic health conditions.

In the course of this so-called Haussmannization, large portions of the old Paris were razed and replaced with ambitious new buildings in a uniform, classicizing architectural style. A rationally articulated network of wide boulevards and avenues brought air and light into the capital city and provided modern infrastructure for the rapidly increasing street traffic. The redesign and new construction of gardens, parks, and public squares, along with the elaborate renovation of historic monuments, endowed Paris with a kind of theatrical opulence.[1] By 1870 it was considered the most modern metropolis in the world.

Photography became a central medium for Haussmann's administration, both to preserve the memory of those parts of the city slated for demolition and to document the splendor of the newly reconstructed capital for purposes of public relations. Among the many artists who enthusiastically embraced this project was Édouard Baldus, who had established himself as one of the leading architectural photographers in France in the mid-1850s.[2] Some of his most famous works are his countless photographs, commissioned by the emperor, of the renovation of the Louvre. Baldus's photograph of the Hôtel de Ville shows the city hall from across the Pont d'Arcole, an arched, wrought-iron bridge eighty meters in length that had been built between 1854 and 1856 (cat. 29). For this image Baldus adopted a slightly elevated vantage point on the north side of the Île de la Cité, positioning the line of the bridge as a diagonal axis to energize the pictorial space. The finely articulated façade ornamentation of the Hôtel de Ville as well as the complex metal architecture of the Pont d'Arcole are recorded in precise detail—a trademark of the artist, who was admitted to the Legion of Honor in 1860 for his contributions to photography.

Like Baldus, the photographer Charles Marville was also known for his technical perfection and the detailed depth of field of his works (cats. 27, 28). His numerous photographs of the capital city made him one of the most important chroniclers of Haussmannization from the late 1850s on, and in 1862 he was appointed official photographer of the city of Paris.[3] For images like his view of rue de Rivoli alongside the Louvre, photographed in 1877, Marville used long exposure times to eliminate moving elements such as carriages and pedestrians (cat. 27). The deserted appearance of his street scenes gives them a still, timeless impression that further underscores the stage-set-like character of the new Paris. The low vantage point emphasizes the majestic breadth of the streets, while the accentuated recession in depth makes rue de Rivoli seem to continue on into infinity.

In addition to the Haussmannian boulevards, many photographers of the Second Empire turned their attention to the documentation of modern industrial architecture, which also found its way into Impressionism early on as a symbol of technical progress (cats. 44–47). Auguste Hippolyte Collard had begun to photographically document the Seine bridges of Paris in the late 1850s, and subsequently turned his attention to the infrastructure of the growing railway system as well, including railway bridges and train stations—motifs that would likewise capture the attention of Impressionists such as Gustave Caillebotte and Claude Monet.[4] Collard's most important patron was the Ministry of Trade, Agriculture and Public Affairs. Many of his photographs show the construction of ambitious new buildings, which he documented step by step in extensive photographic portfolios. He employed unusual visual axes and close-up views of architectural details to dramatize the presentation of his motifs (cats. 46, 47) while the formal rigor and sharp detail of his images anticipated central elements of modernist photography.

Among the most popular images of the new Paris were so-called stereoscopic photographs, snapshots whose extremely short exposure times and small negative formats made it possible to realistically depict movement and dynamism (cats. 30–33, 35). In these works, two photographs of the same motif taken from slightly different angles were printed side by side; when viewed through a special device with two lenses, the resulting image seemed three-dimensional. This invention was celebrated at the world's fair in London in 1851 and paved the way for a visual experience that went far beyond the illusionistic possibilities of painting, allowing viewers to immerse themselves in scenes with theater-like backdrops. Views of boulevards teeming with people and carriages, which evoked the hustle and bustle of Haussmann's new Paris in an astonishingly realistic manner, were especially popular (cats. 26, 34). Many of the photographs focused on broad urban canyons or showed the view from elevated vantage points such as windows or balconies, thus intensifying the effect of spatial depth. In their city scenes, the Impressionists often showed the boulevards of Paris in a similarly dramatic way.[5] In his painting *Rue Halévy, View from the Sixth Floor* (p. 260, fig. 2) Gustave Caillebotte adopted a perspective highly reminiscent of the cropped composition of a photograph, and also depicted pedestrians and carriages in the slightly blurred manner typical of moving objects in stereoscopic photographs.[6]

The focus on immediacy that characterized stereoscopic photographers and their snapshot-like images, known as *vues instantanées,* was a distinguishing feature of nineteenth-century Paris. In his 1863 essay "The Painter of Modern Life," the writer and critic Charles Baudelaire associated modernity with the experience of the fleeting and ephemeral. In his view, the contemporary artist should adopt the perspective of the flaneur, the dandy who idly wanders through the city and finds an element of the poetic and marvelous in the observation of mundane, everyday activities.[7] While Baudelaire's aesthetic position is often associated with the city scenes of the Impressionists, it also showed itself paradigmatically in the early examples of street photography, a genre in which everyday occurrences or encounters in an urban context were captured in a snapshot-like manner (cats. 37–40). Early proponents of the genre, such as the French photographers Charles Nègre and Eugène Atget, often focused on the darker side of the modern metropolis, a theme that also came to the fore in the contemporaneous milieu studies of literary Naturalism. Louis Vert's photograph *Clochard, Paris* (cat. 41) is marked by a ruthless realism tinged by social criticism, and a similarly unaffected gaze had already informed the Paris paintings of Édouard Manet in the mid-nineteenth century.

Translated from German by Melissa M. Thorson

[1] For Haussmann's Paris, see Saalman 1971, Paris 1991c, and McAuliffe 2020.

[2] Cf. New York 1994.

[3] Cf. Washington 2013 and Amsterdam 2017.

[4] On Collard's industrial photographs, see Isabelle-Cécile Le Mée, "Collard: Photographe des Ponts et Chaussées," in *Histoire de l'art* 13,11 (1991), 31–35.

[5] For the Paris of the Impressionists, see Essen 2010.

[6] On Caillebotte and photography, see Frankfurt am Main 2012a.

[7] Cf. also Bernd Stiegler's contribution, 32–41.

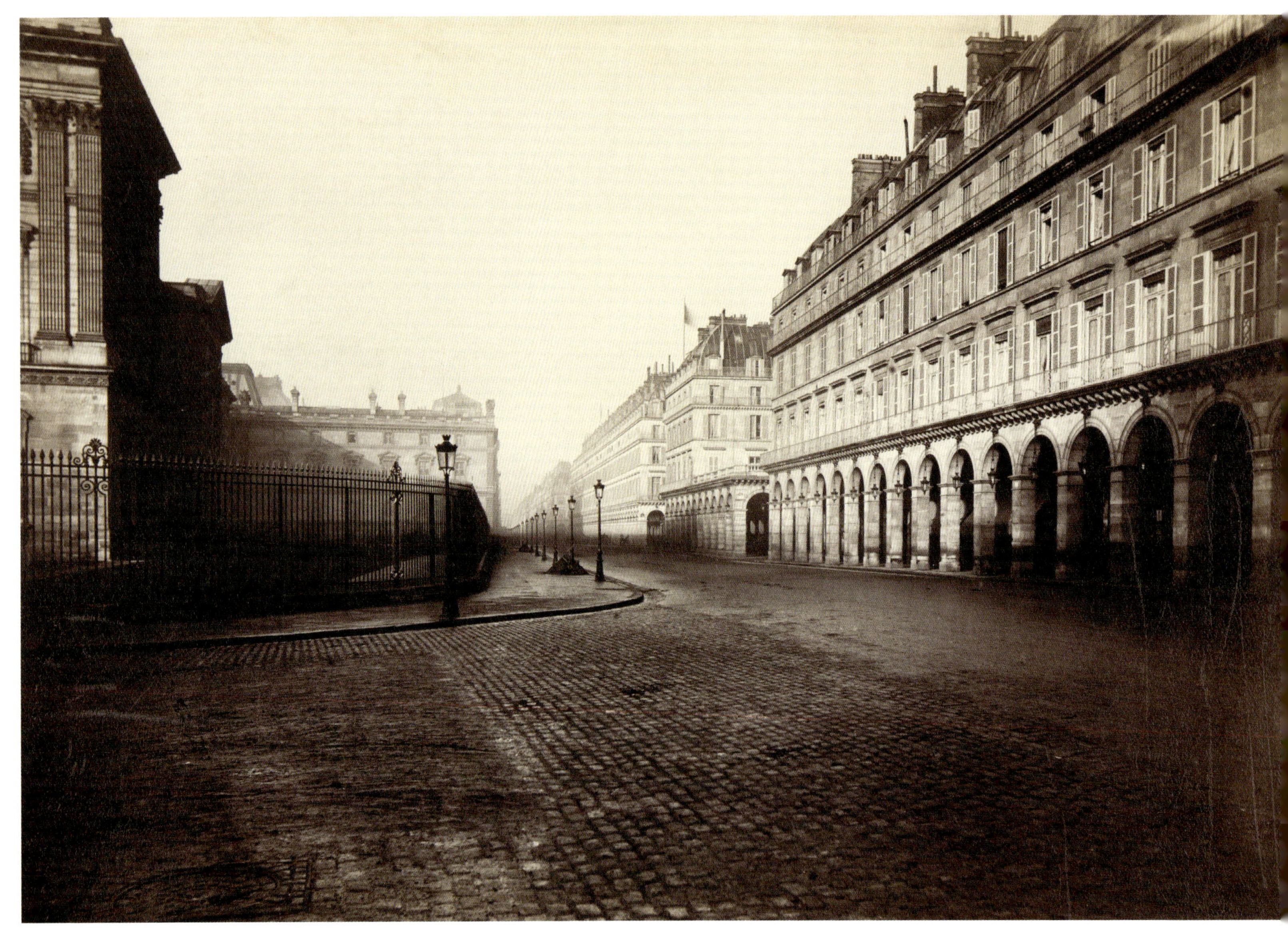

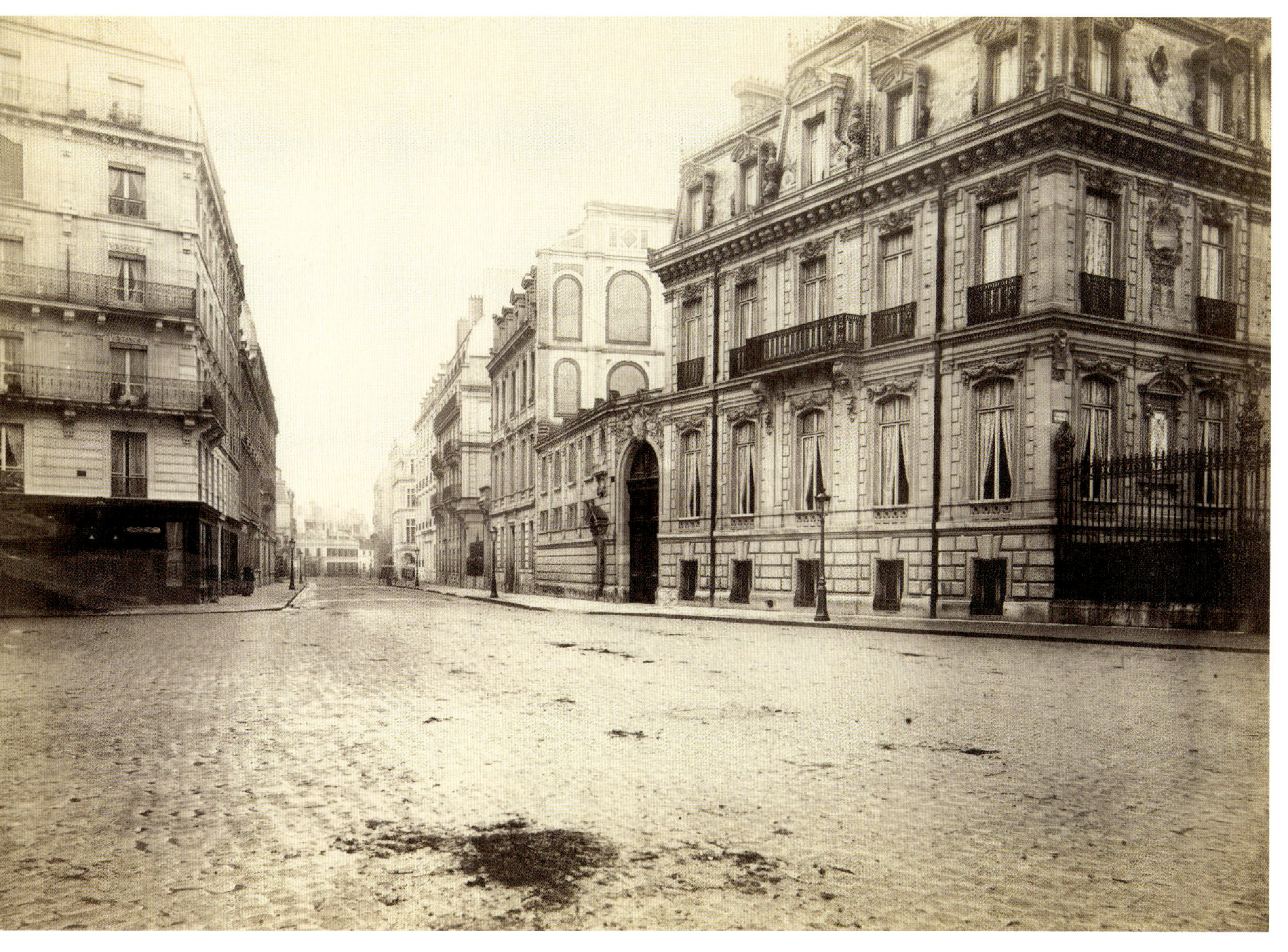

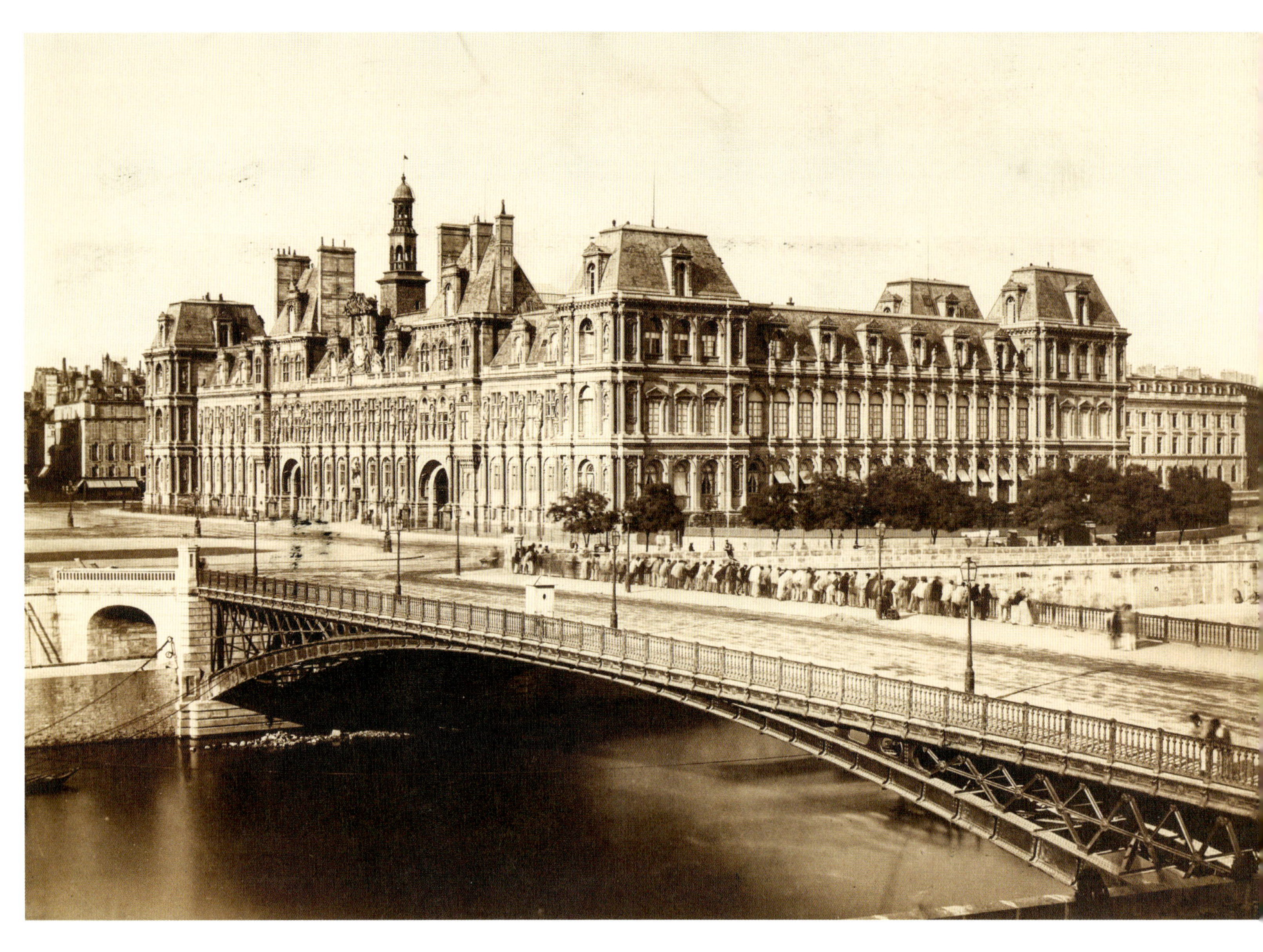

29 Édouard Baldus
Paris, View of the Pont d'Arcole and the Hôtel de Ville, ca. 1860

30 Ferrier père, fils et Soulier
The Seine and the Pont-Neuf in
Paris, 1860

31 Ferrier père, fils et Soulier
Pont des Arts, 1860, 1860

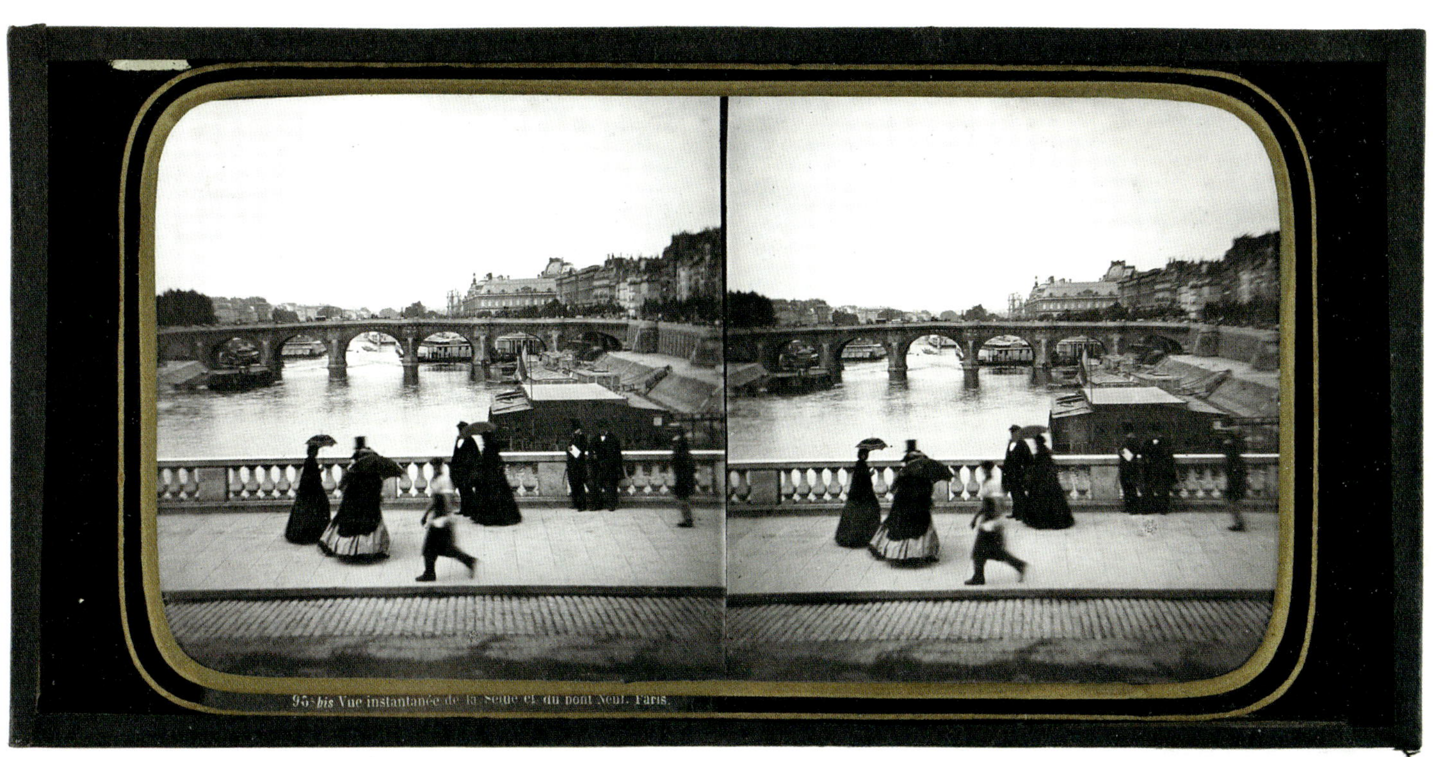

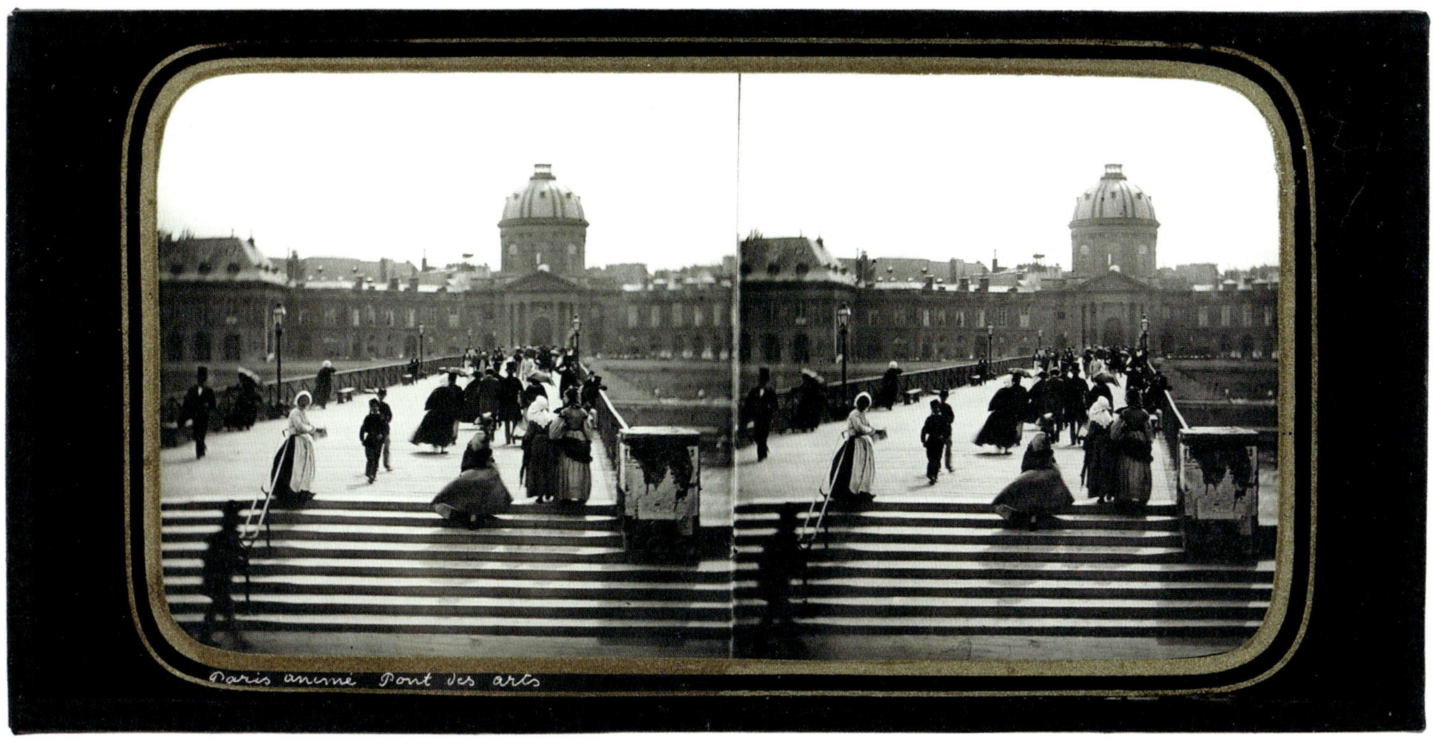

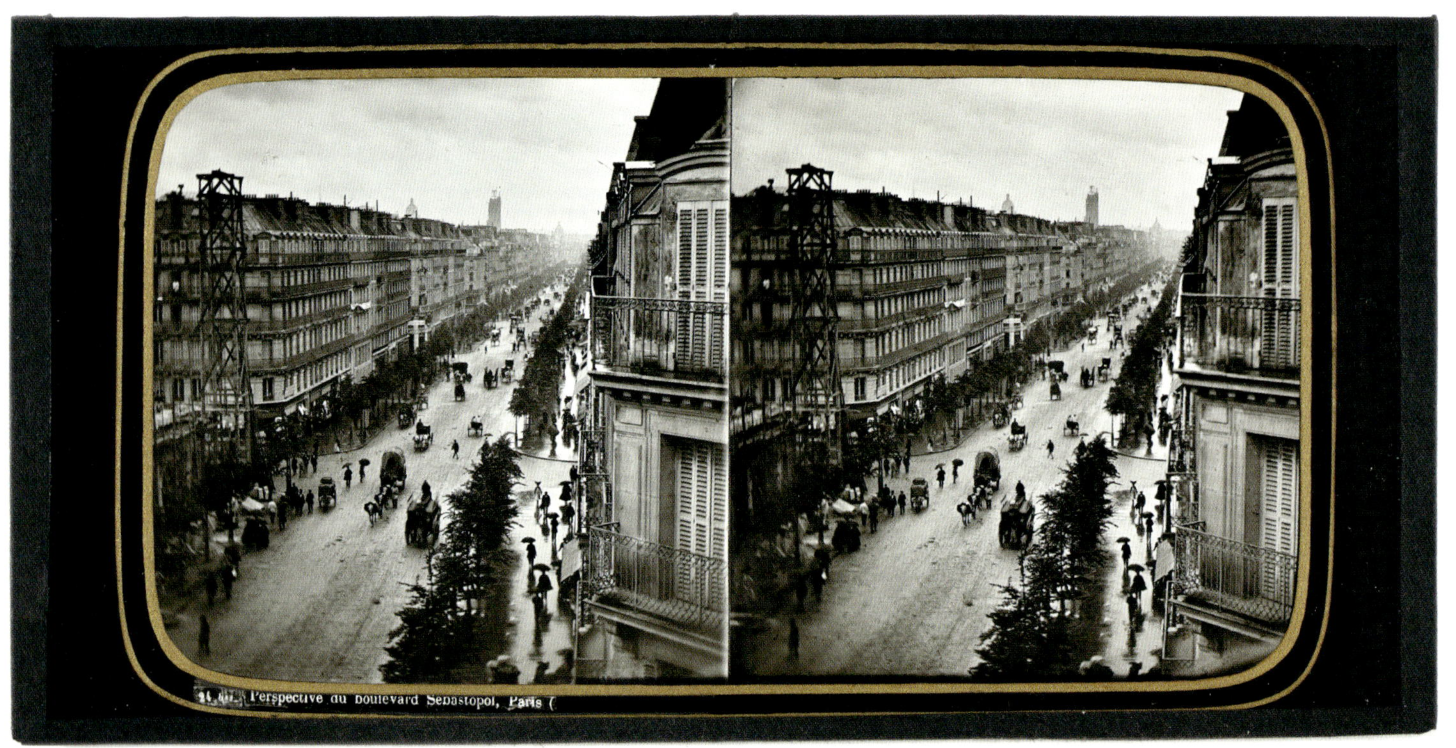

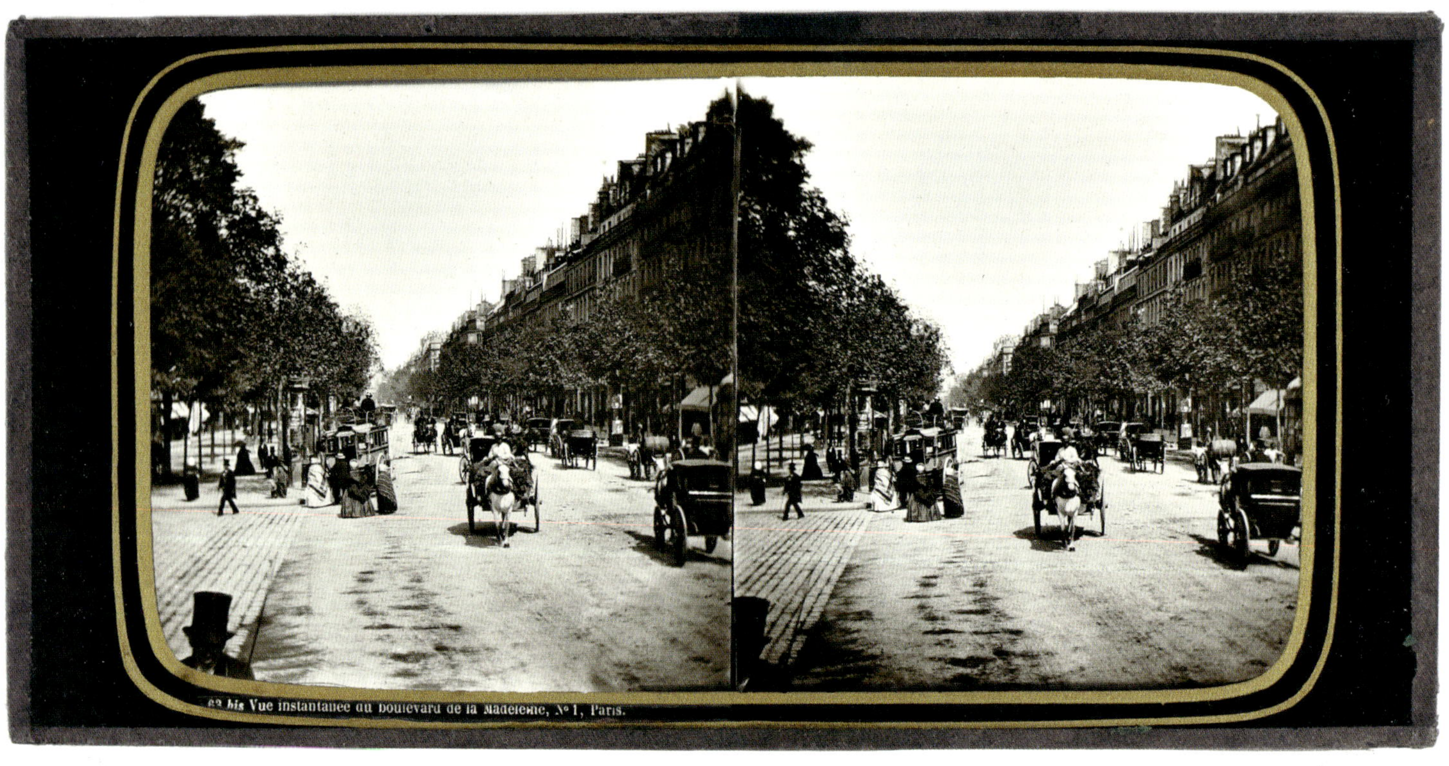

32 Ferrier père, fils et Soulier
*Boulevard de Sébastopol
(Looking East), Paris,* 1860

33 Ferrier père, fils et Soulier
*Boulevard de la Madeleine, No. 1,
Paris,* 1860

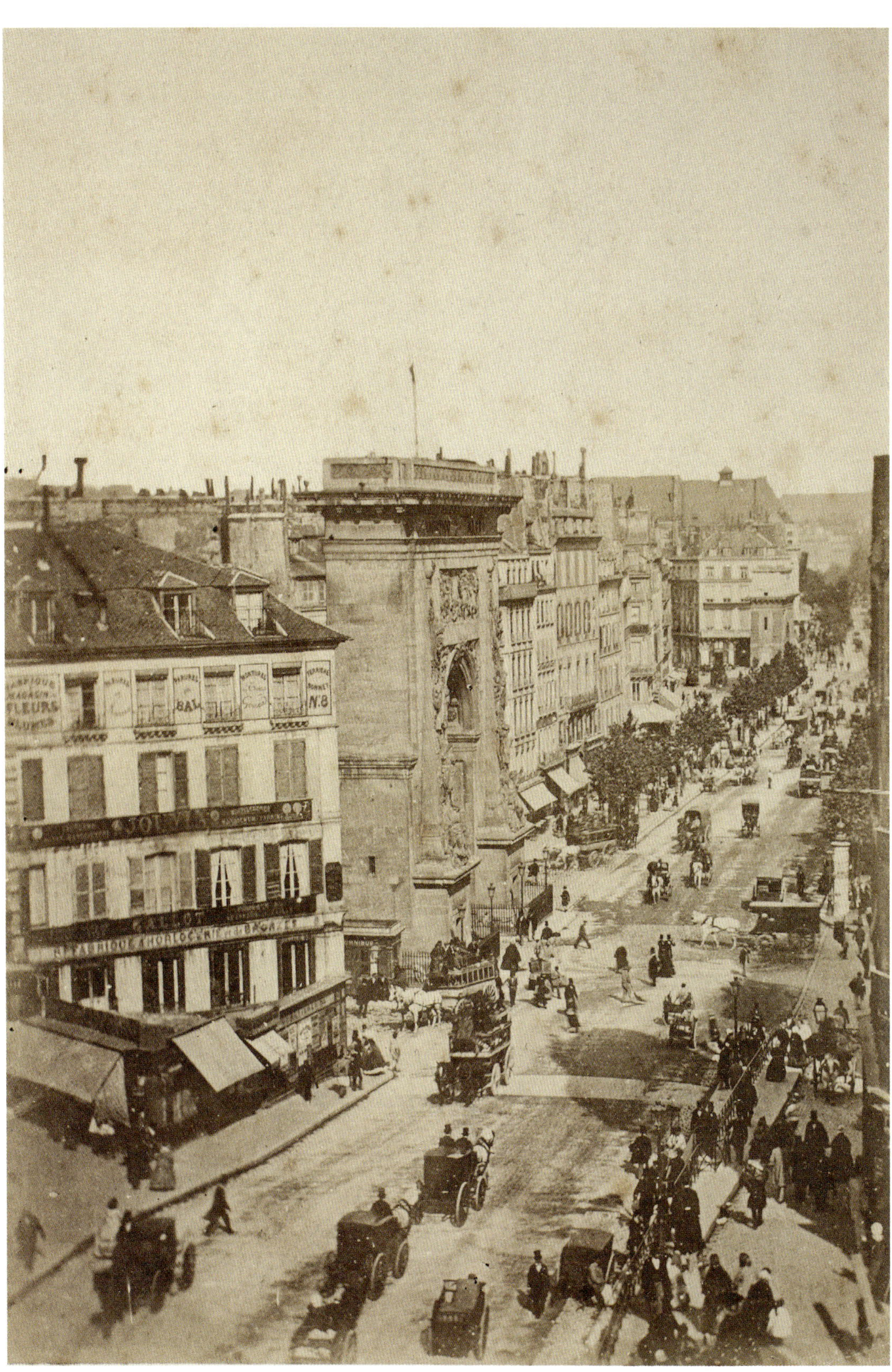

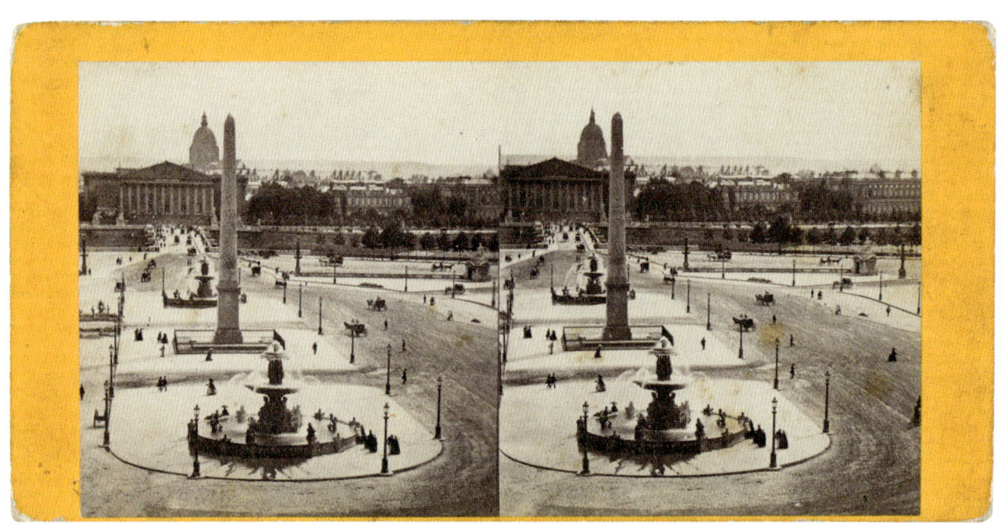

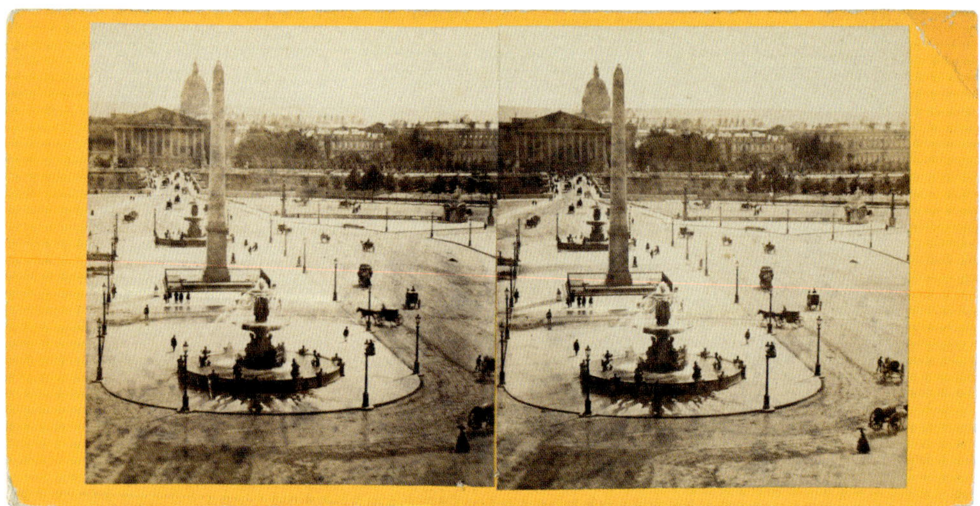

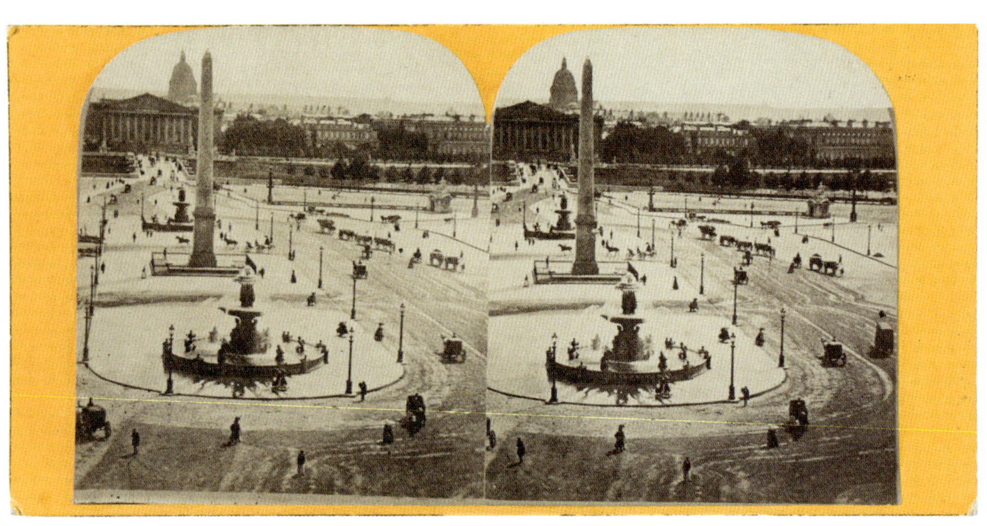

36 Louis Antonin Neurdein,
attributed
Avenue de l'Opéra and
Place de la Concorde, from the
album *Paris et ses environs,*
ca. 1885

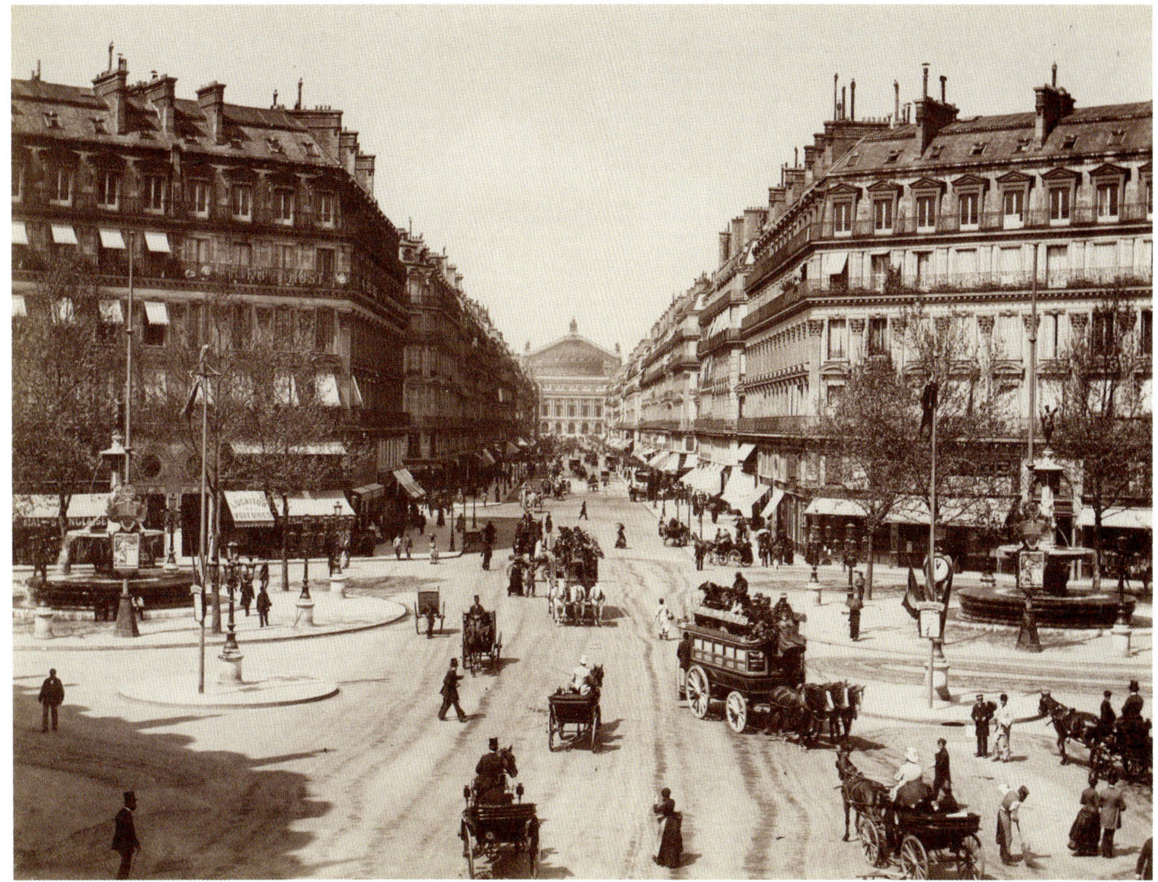

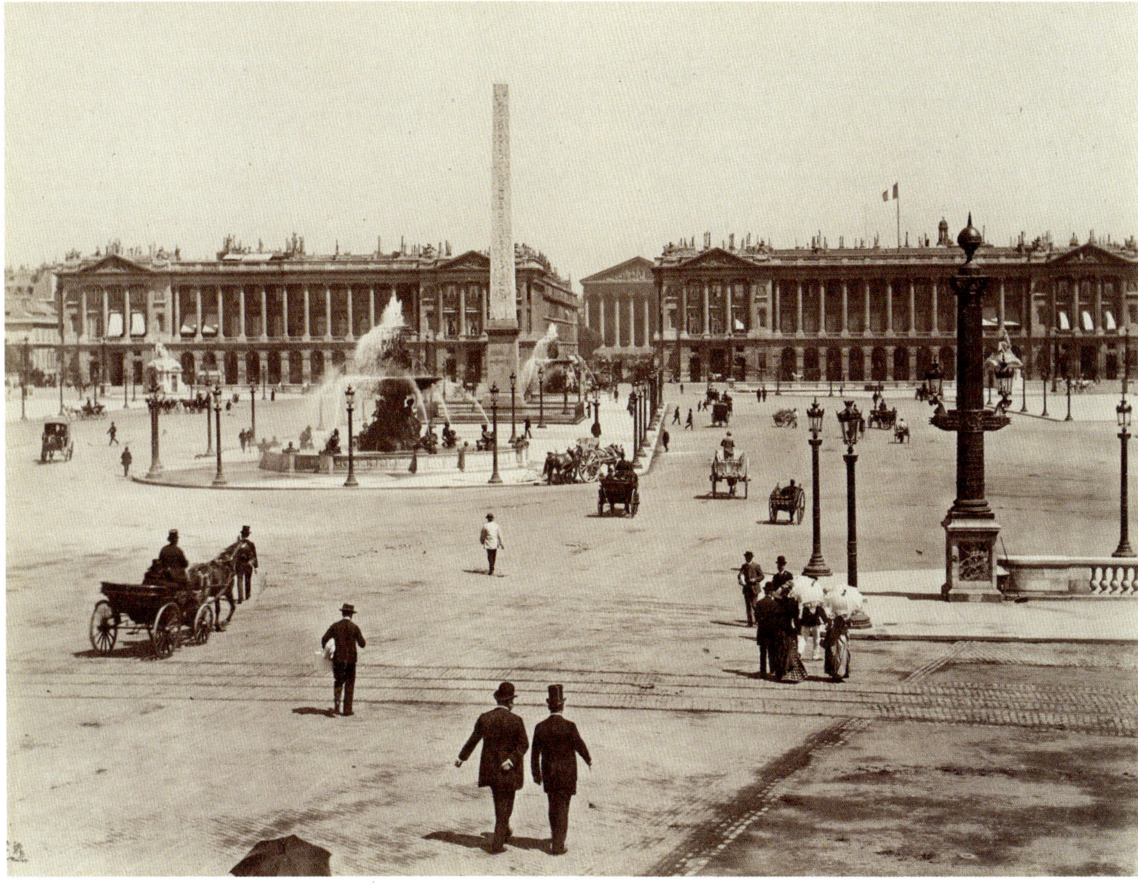

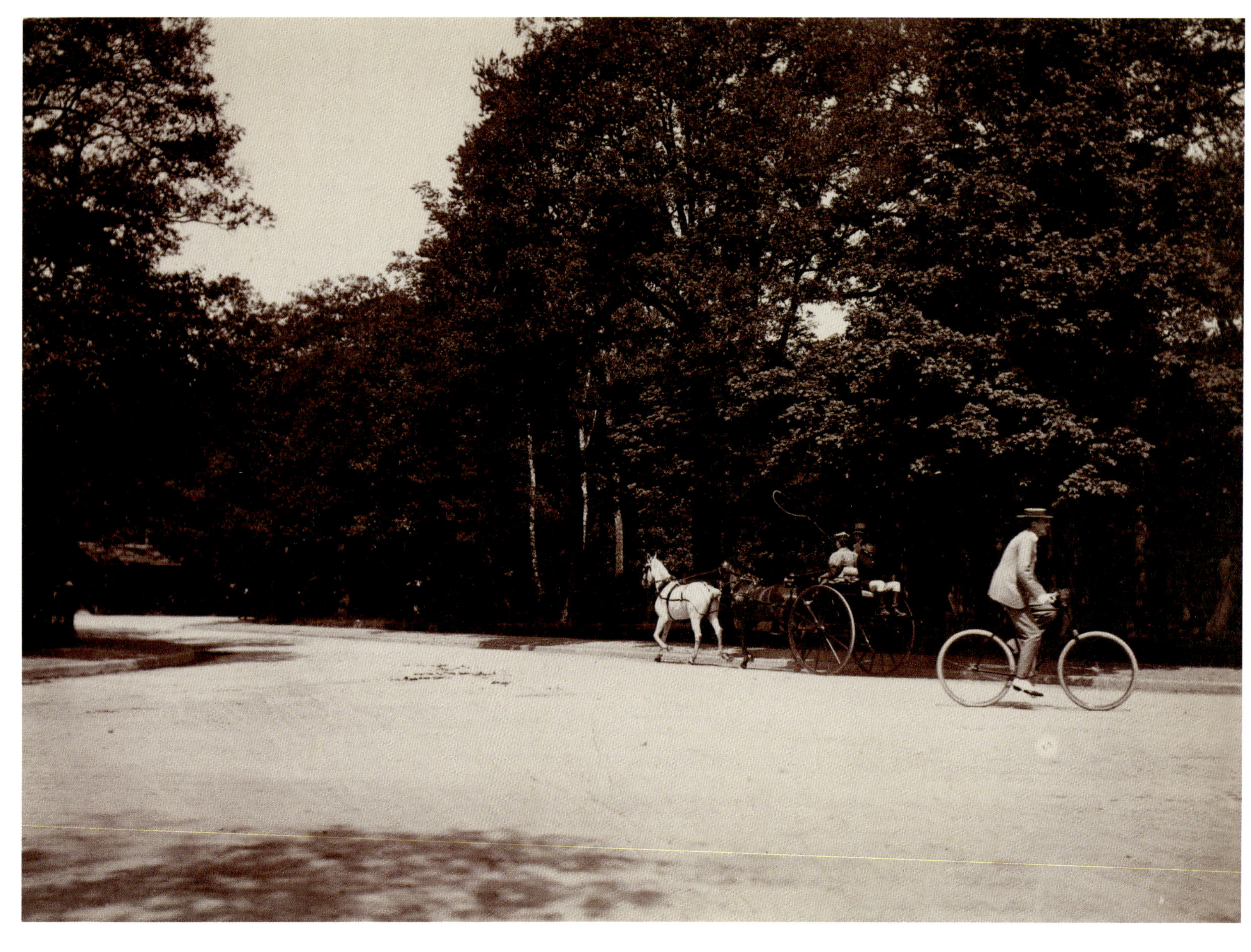

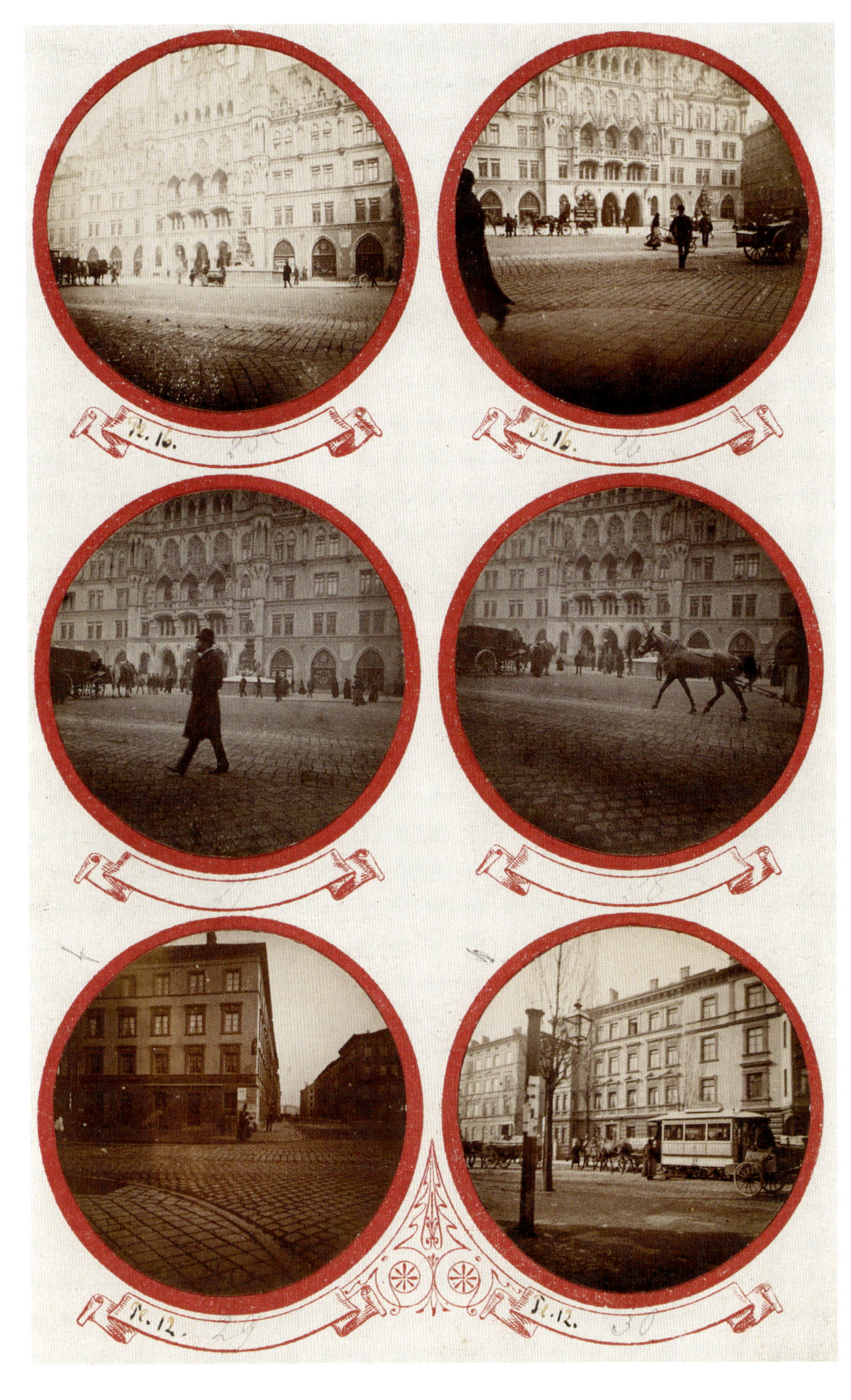

38 Anonymous
Street Scenes, Photographed with
C. P. Stirn's Secret Camera, ca. 1885

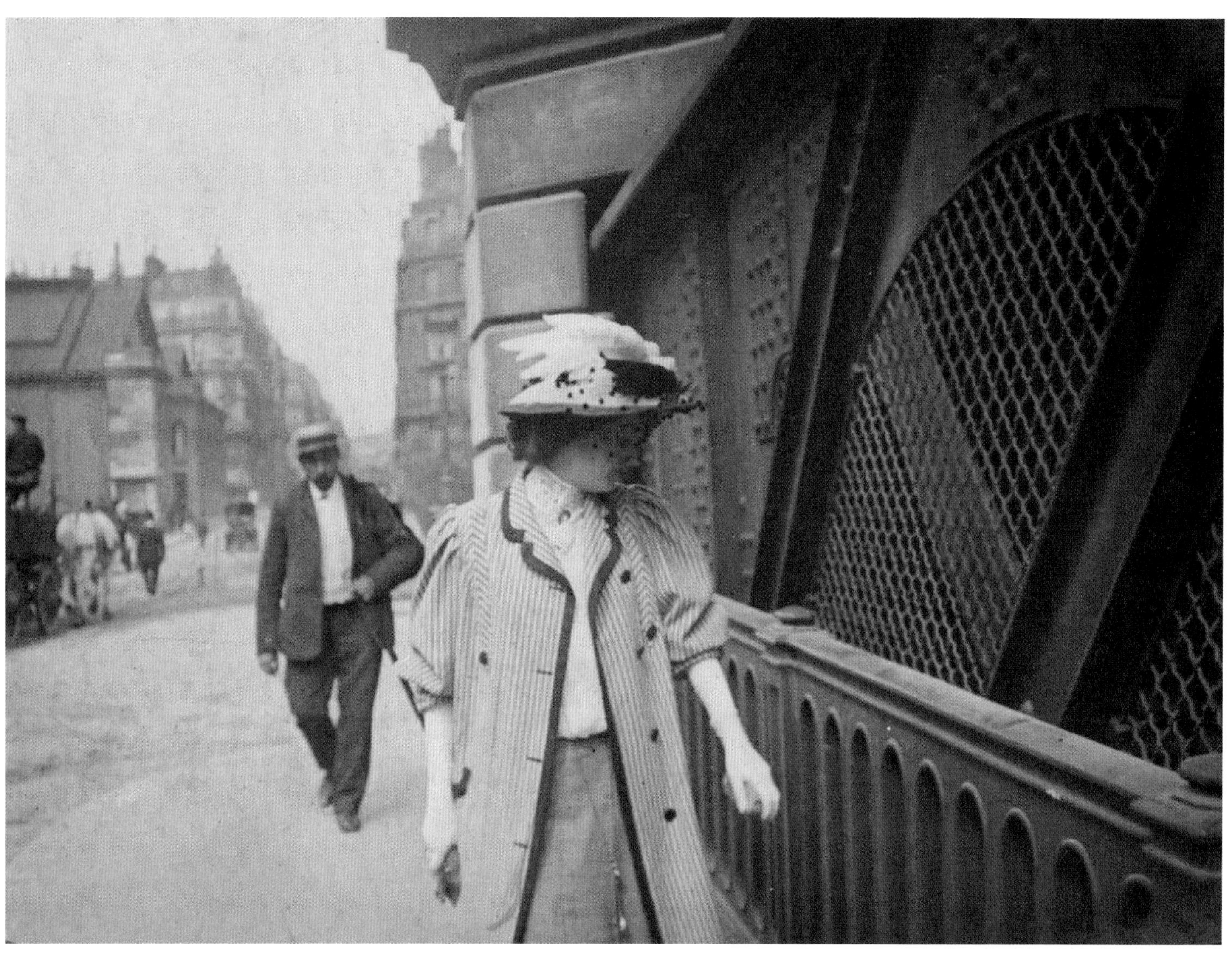

39 Anonymous
The Pretty Passersby,
Parisian Women in Hats, from the album
The Pretty Passersby, 1906–08

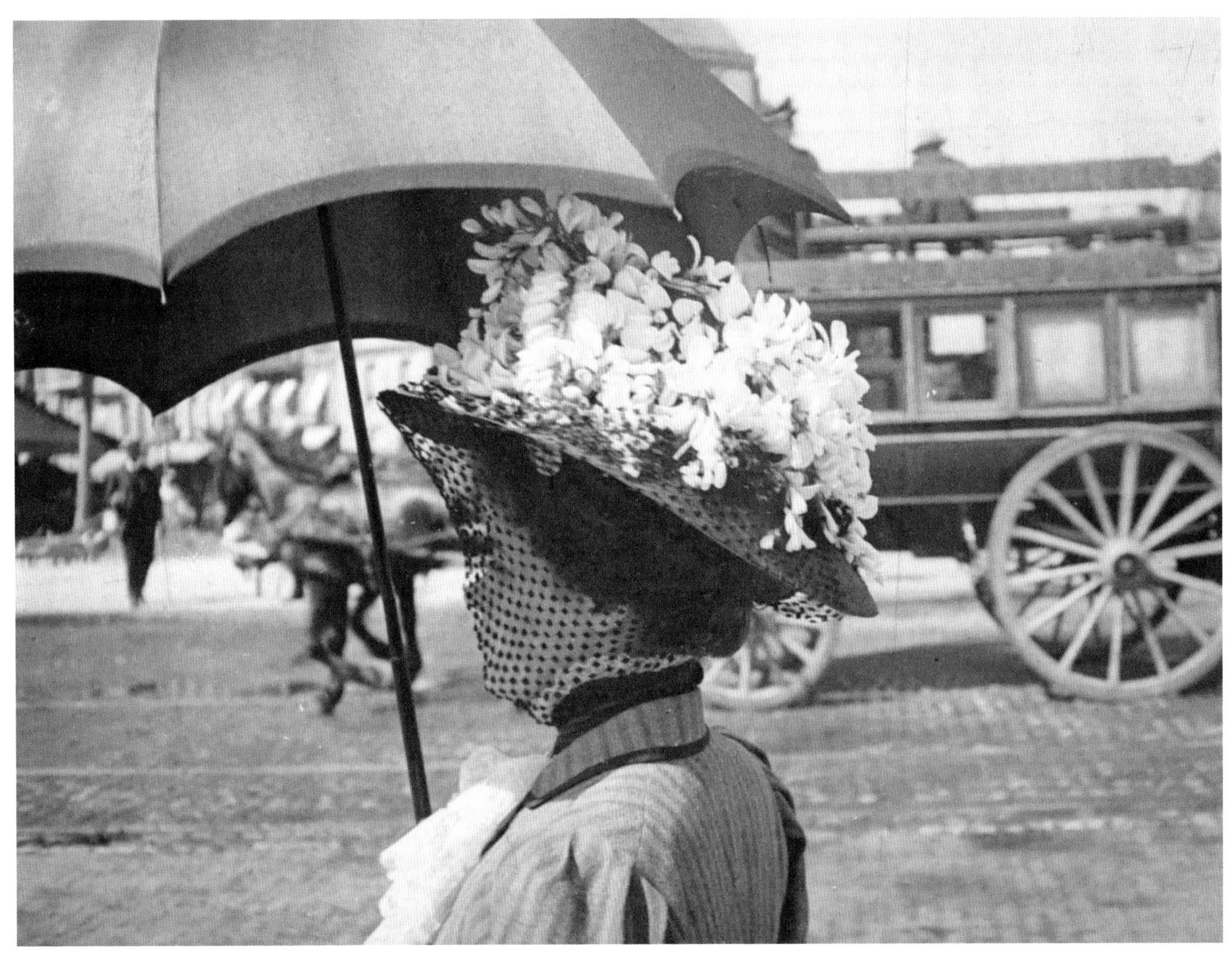

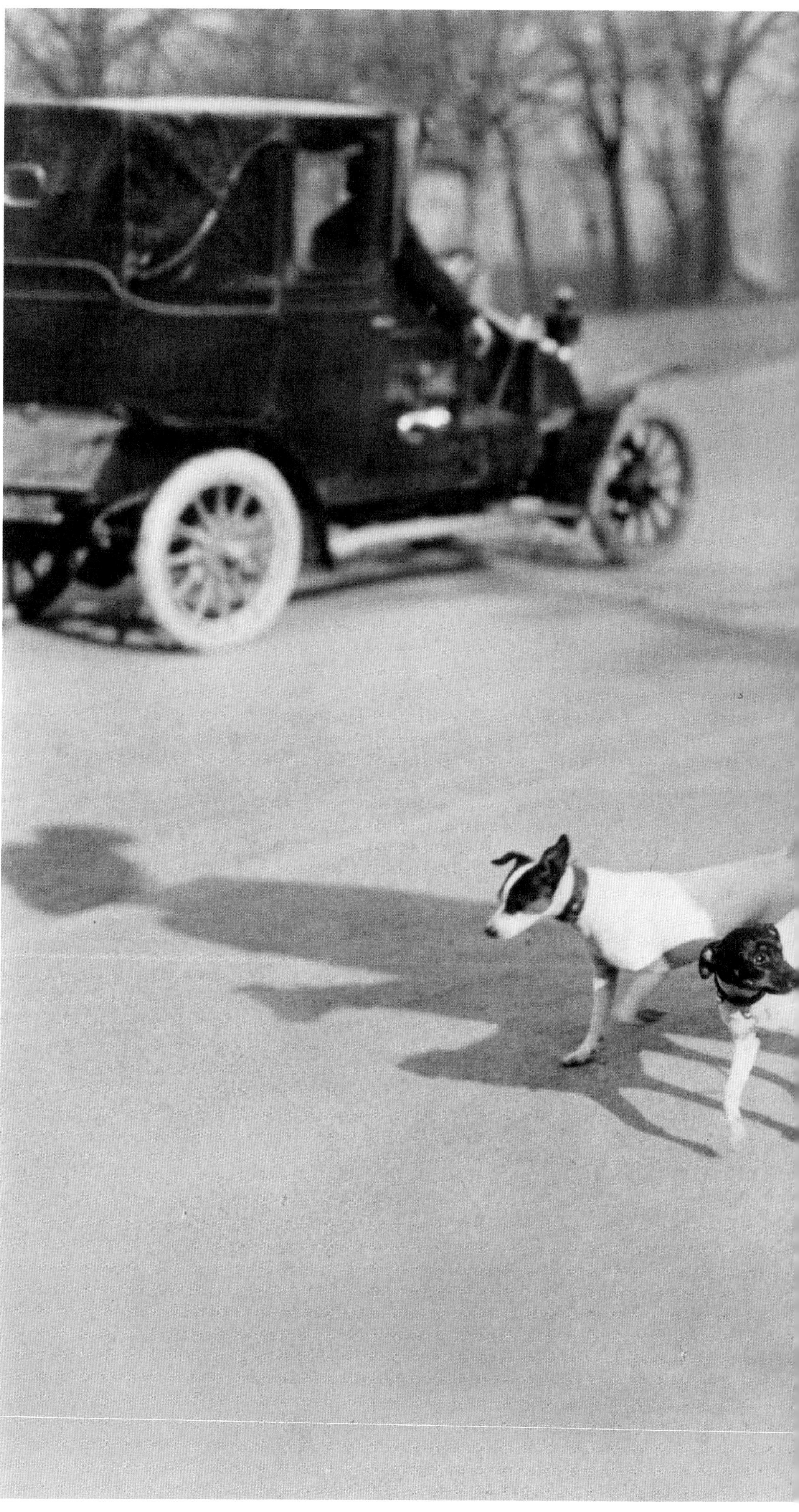

40 Jacques Henri Lartigue
Arlette Prevost, called Anna la Pradvina, Avenue du Bois de Boulogne, January 15, 1911, 1911

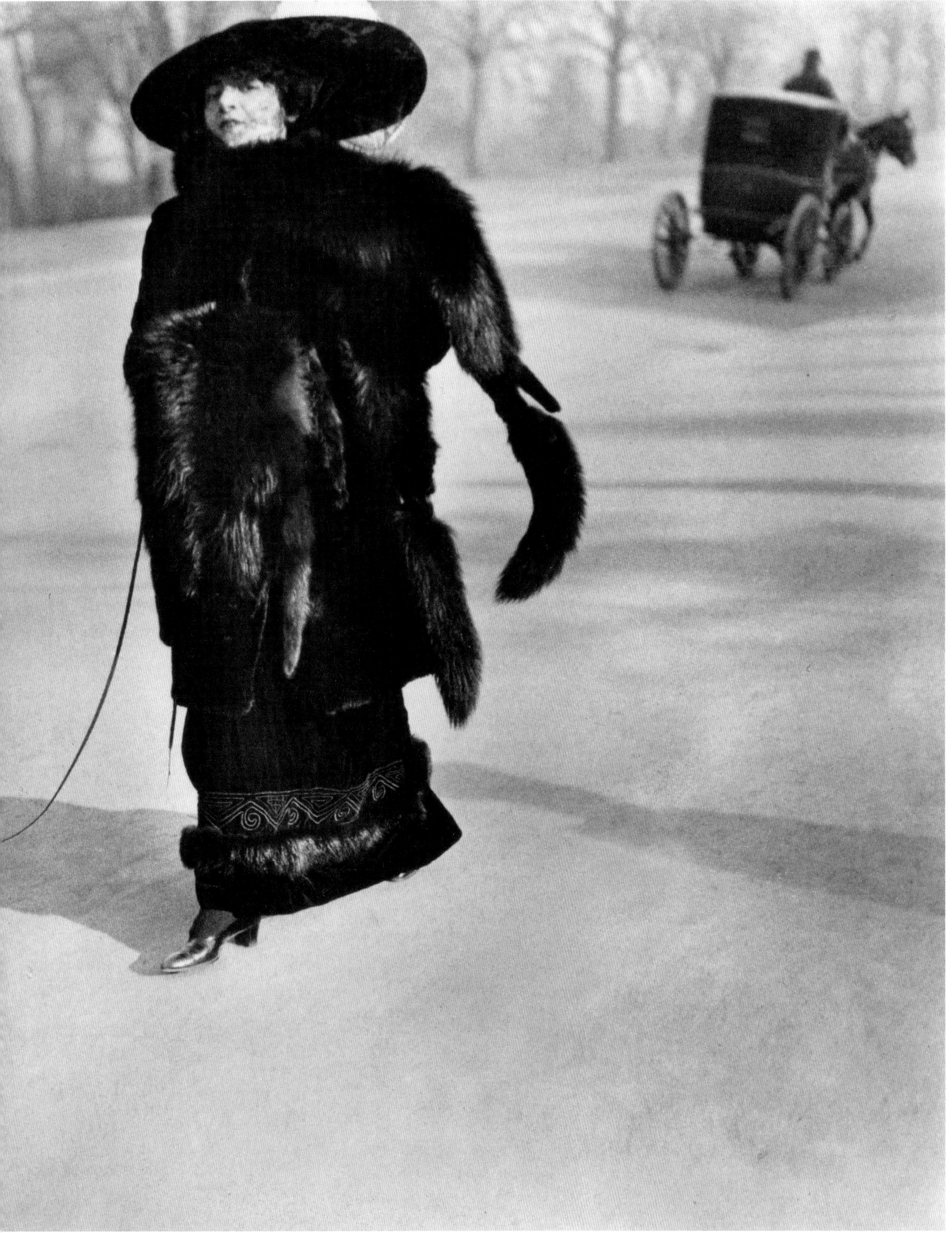

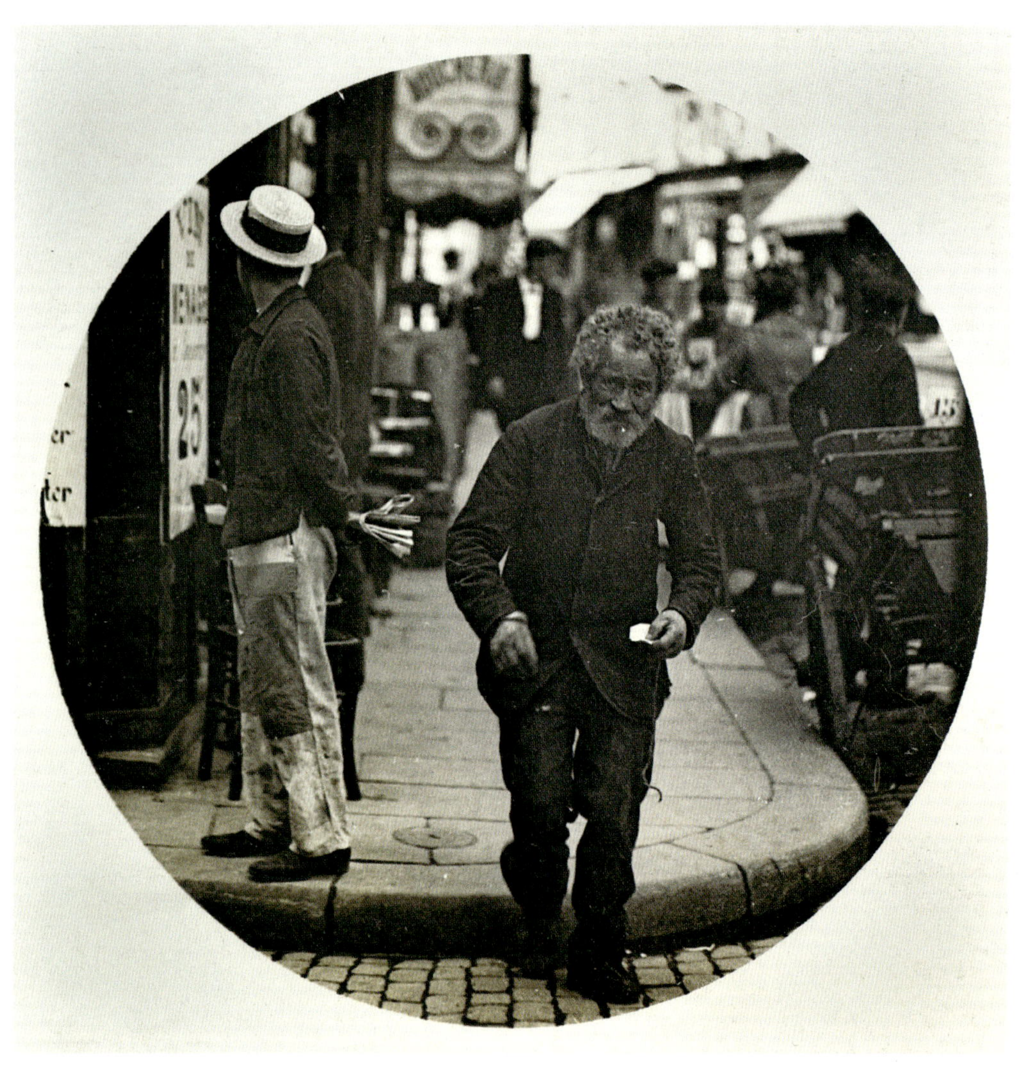

41 Louis Vert
Clochard, Paris, ca. 1900

42 Robert Demachy
Crowd, 1910

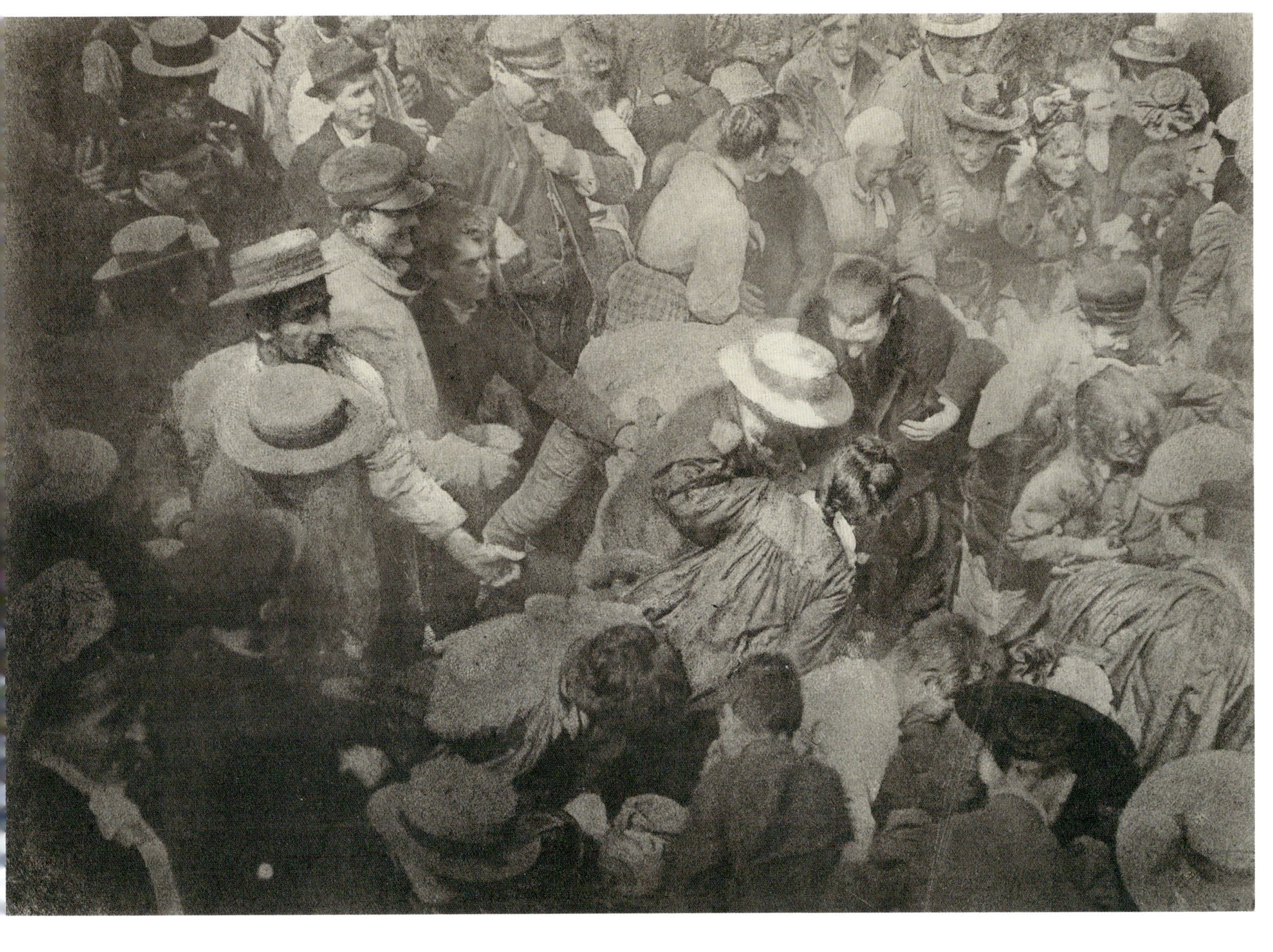

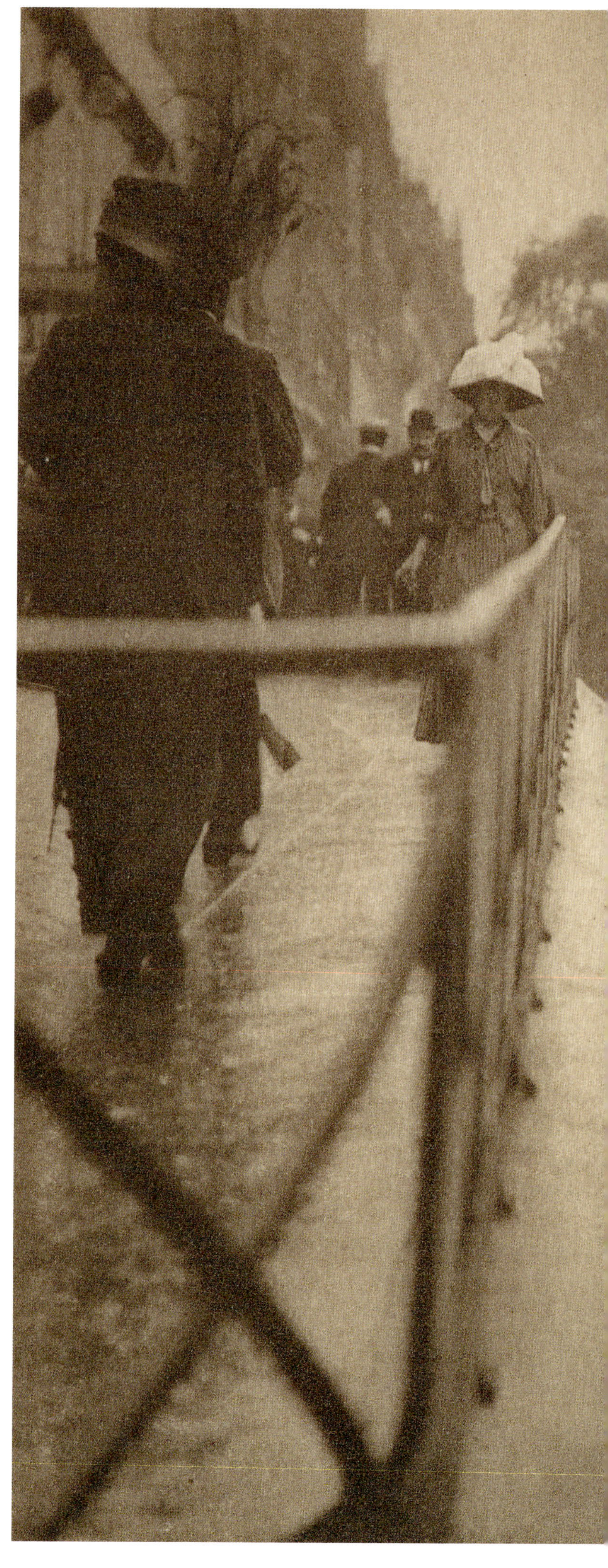

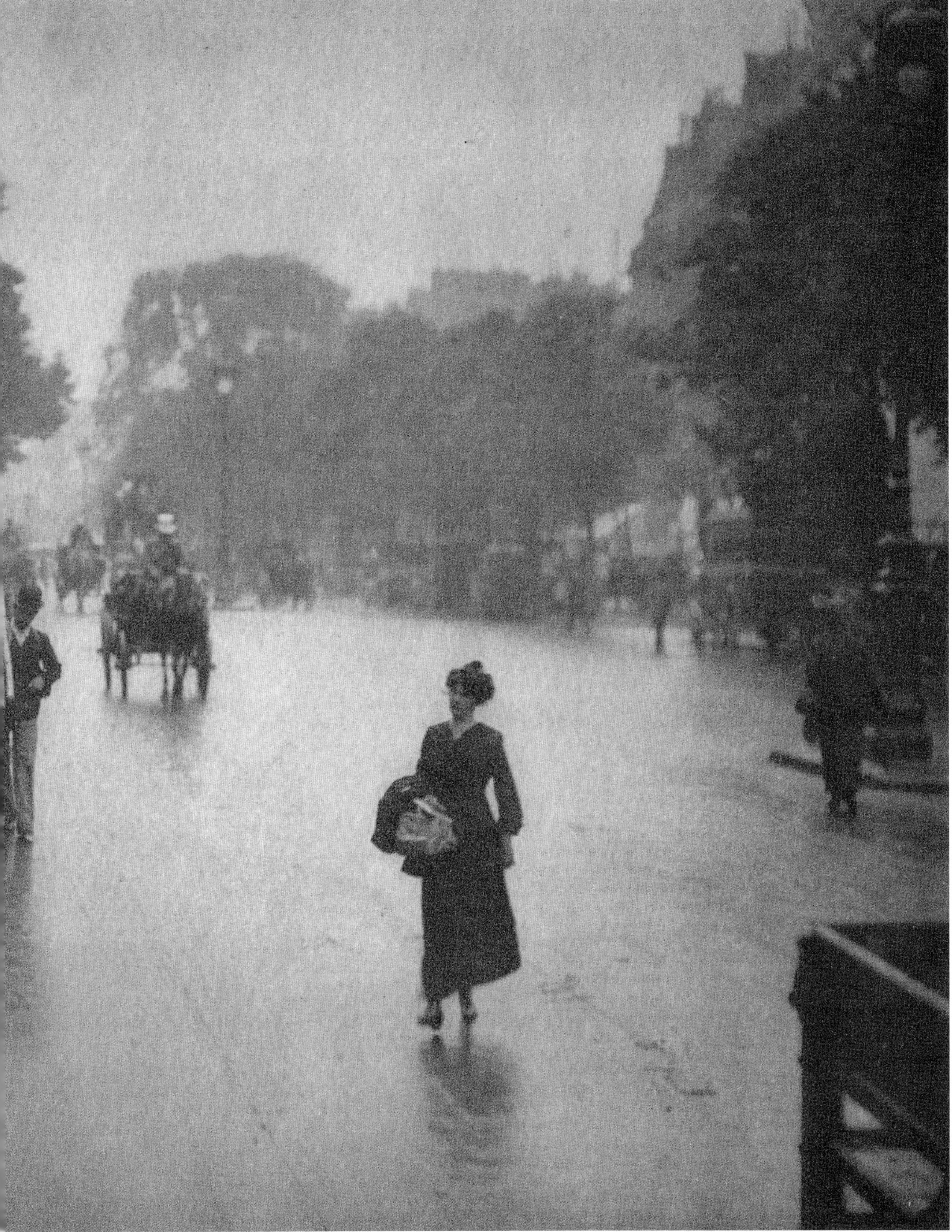

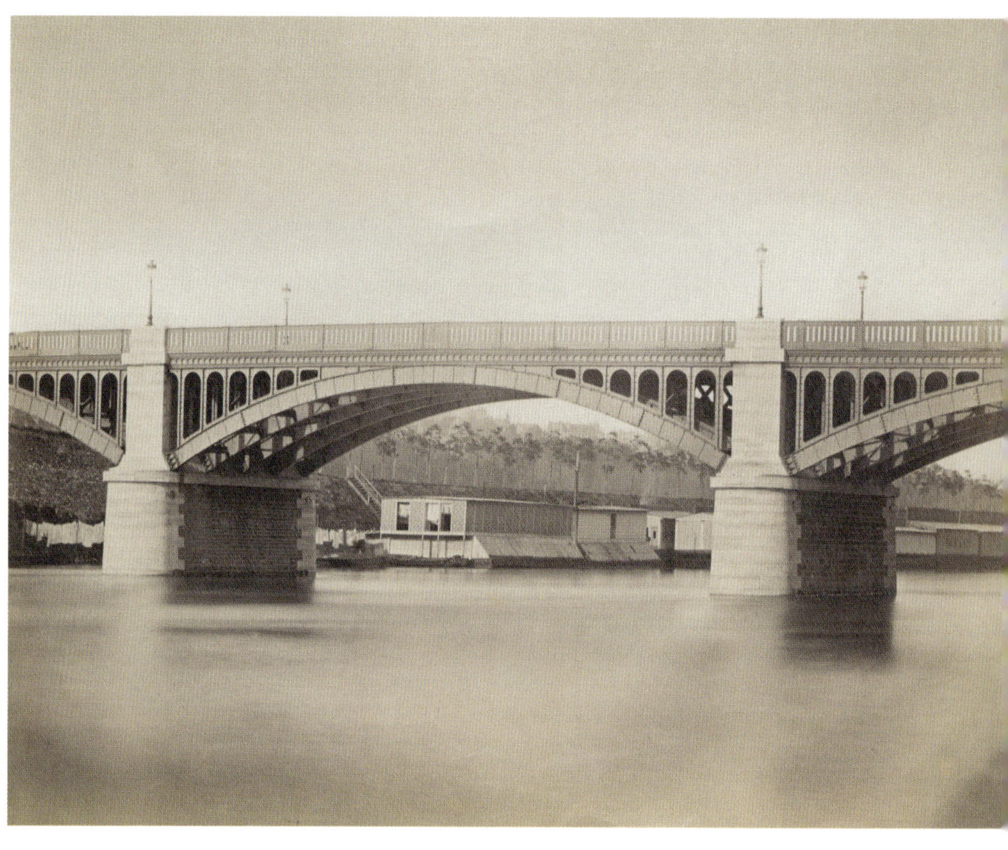

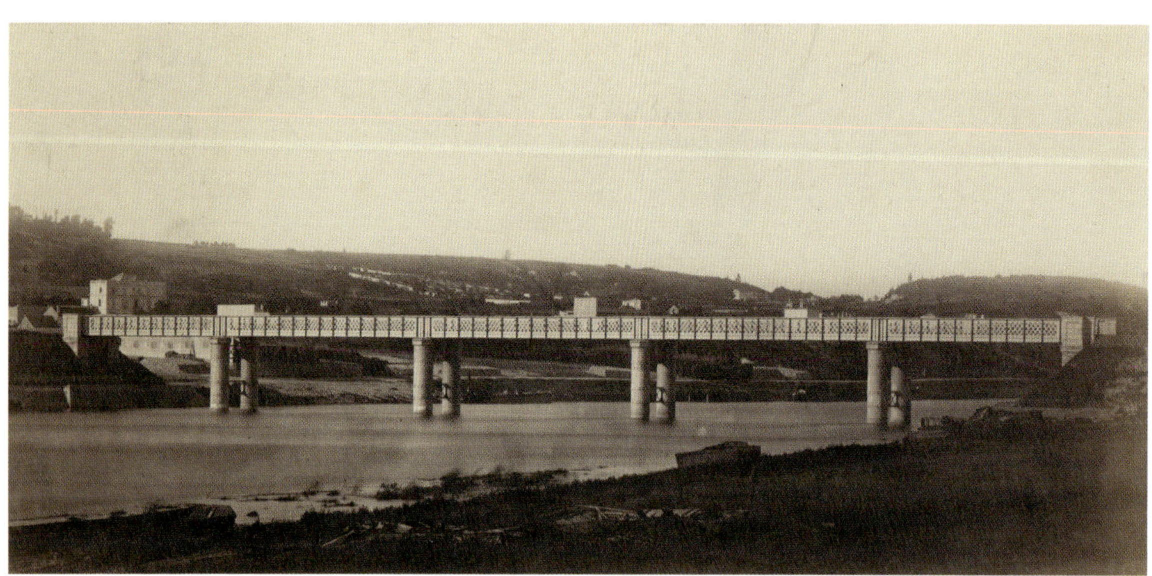

46 Augustin Hippolyte,
called Auguste Collard
*Path Beneath the Railway Bridge
at Auteuil,* 1865–66

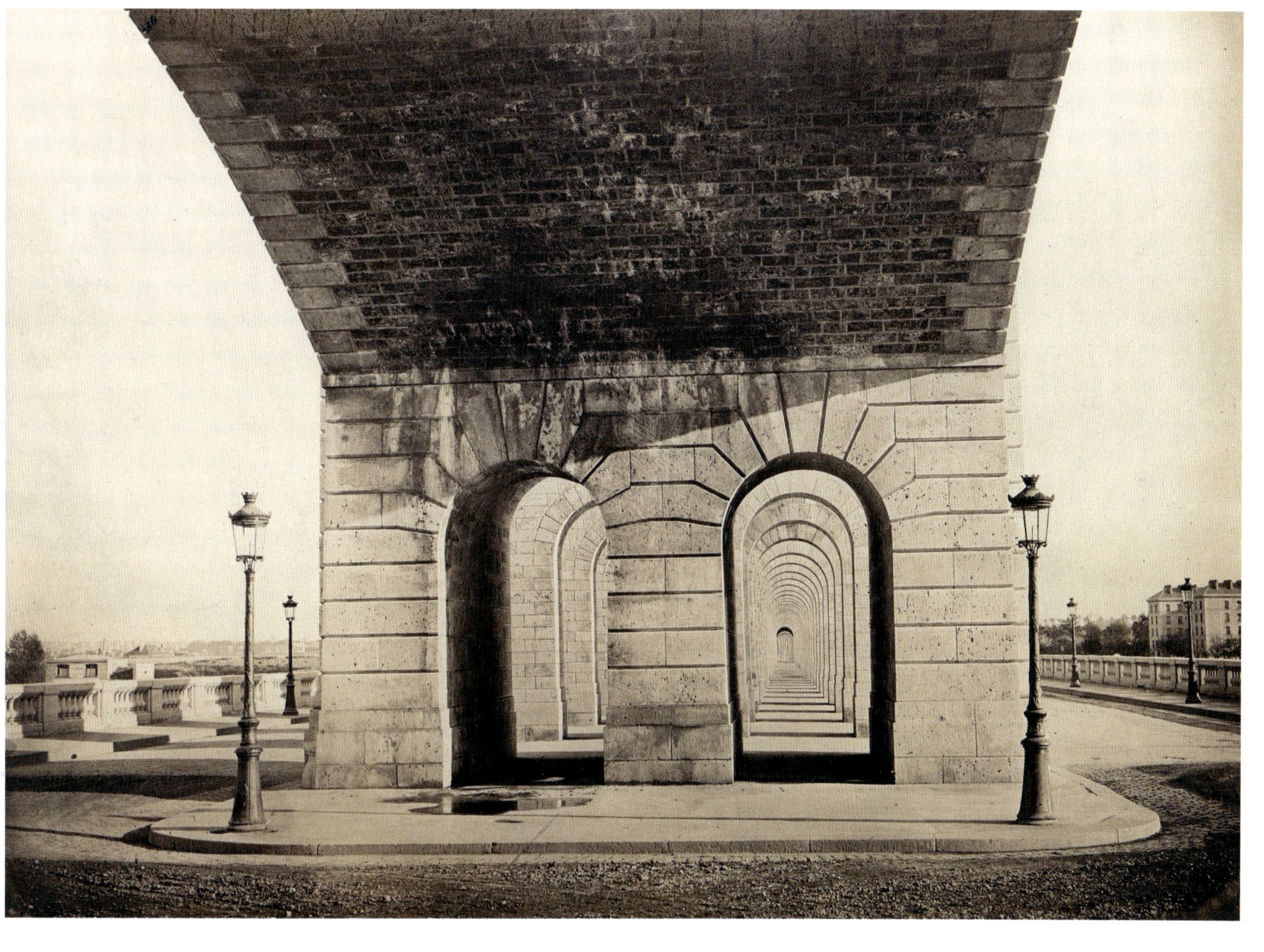

47 Augustin Hippolyte,
called Auguste Collard
Pont de Grenelle, Paris, ca. 1875–76

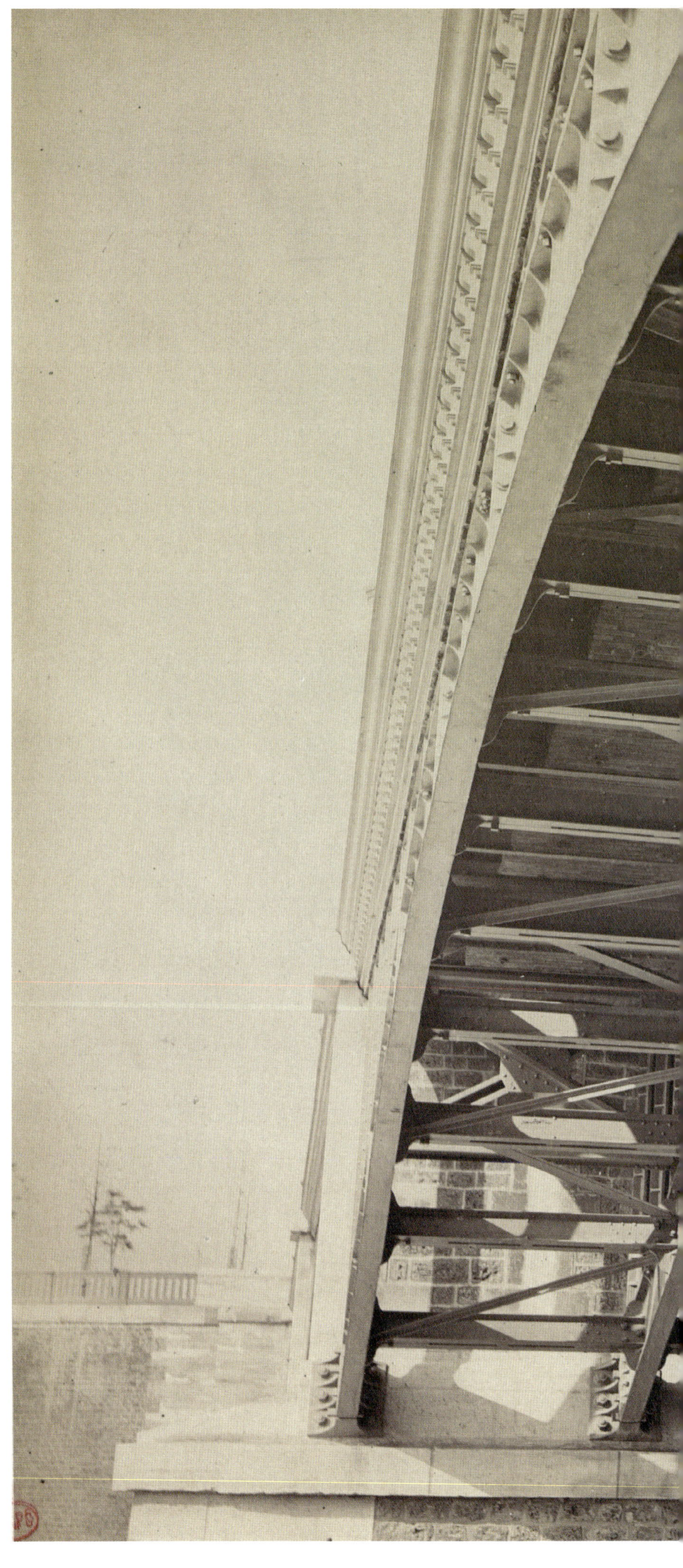

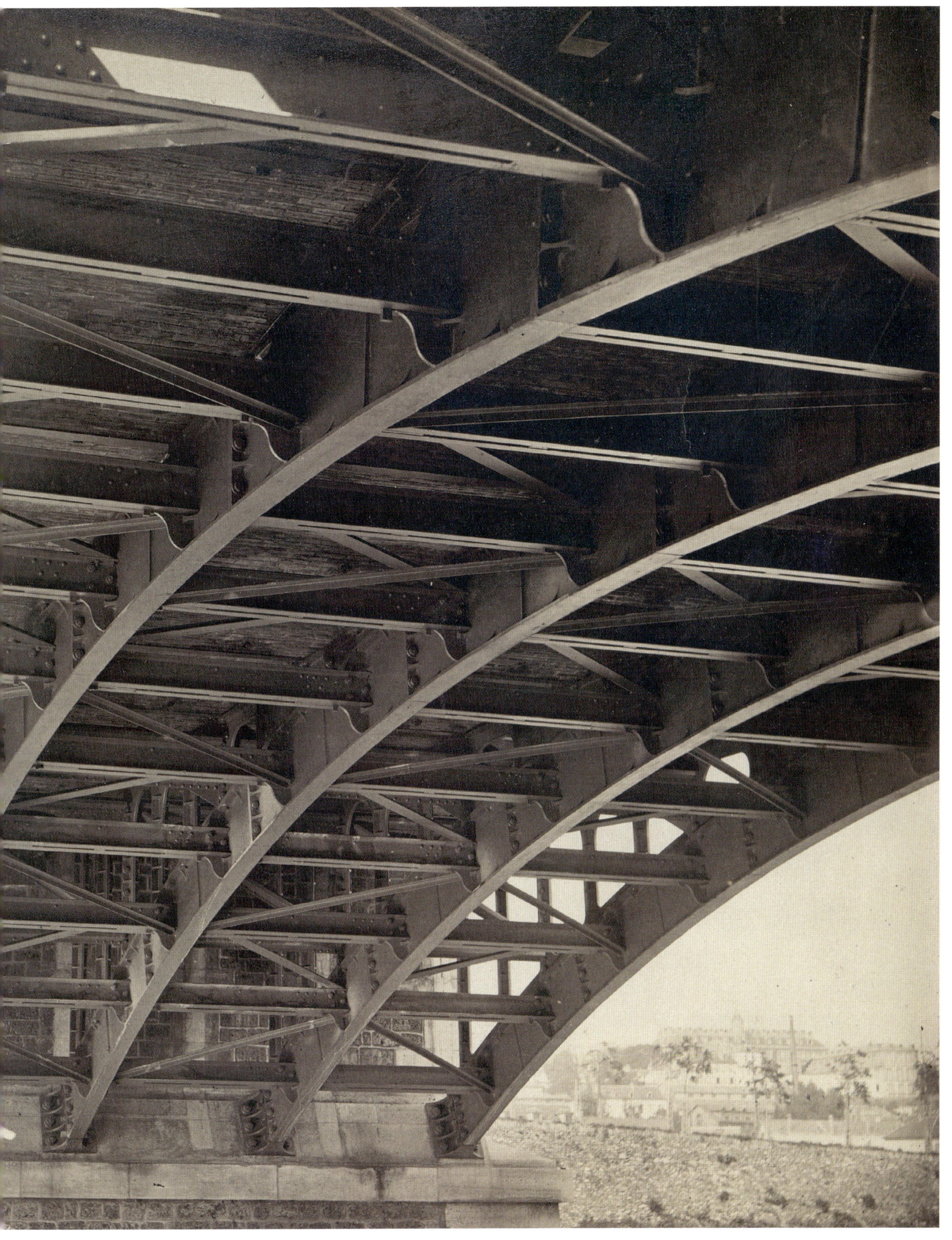

Daniel Zamani

Shadow and Light

Forest Scenes

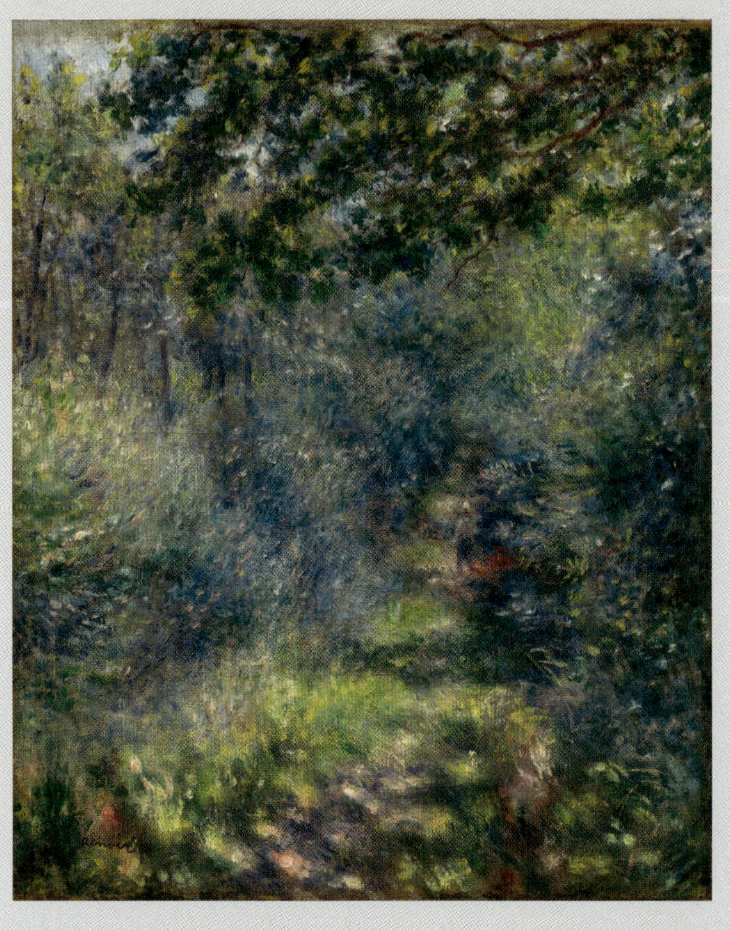

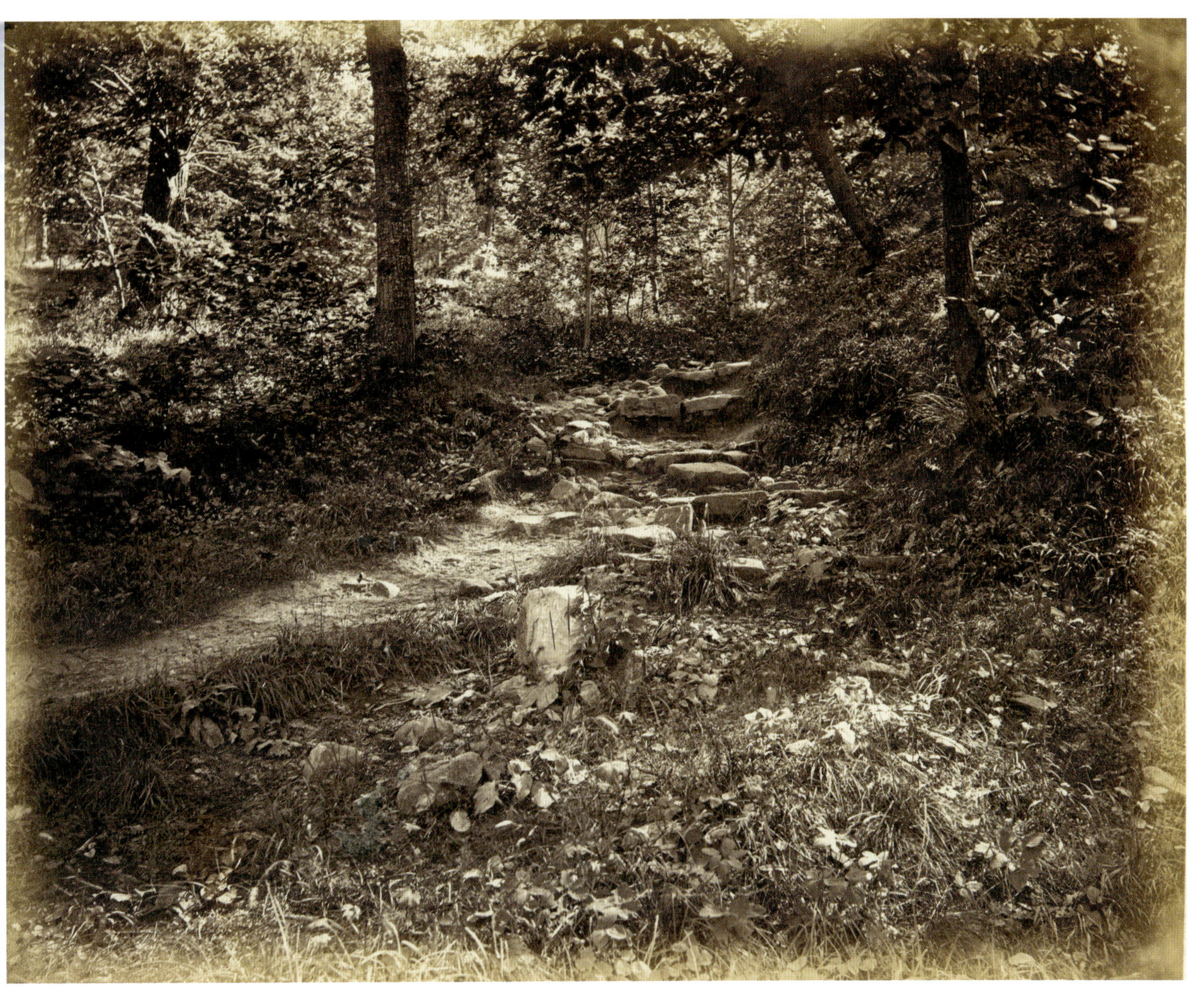

Pierre-Auguste Renoir
Path in the Forest, 1874–77
Oil on canvas
Hasso Plattner Collection

48 Georg Maria Eckert
*Middle Ground Study—Rocky Path
in the Forest, Heidelberg,* 1867–68

Landscape painting in France had undergone profound changes in the first half of the nineteenth century. Artists increasingly rejected the idealization of nature informed by the study of the Old Masters and instead pursued the realistic rendering of specific topographies, observing them on location and painting *en plein air.*[1]

This development was facilitated by the rapid expansion of the railway network from the 1840s on, which made it possible for painters from Paris to quickly travel to many different locations at comparatively little expense. An especially important region was the forest of Fontainebleau, a nature reserve about sixty kilometers south of Paris near the villages of Barbizon and Chailly. This 25,000-hectare area was known not only for its variety of species, but also for its abundance of tall trees, some of them centuries old. Numerous proponents of Realism regularly gathered here to paint in the open air. Their identification with the region was so strong that they became known as the Barbizon School, a group that included artists such as Camille Corot, Charles-François Daubigny, Jean-François Millet, and Théodore Rousseau. The style of the Barbizon painters, in particular their fresh colors and preference for loose, sketch-like brushwork, would later serve as an important source of inspiration for the Impressionists.[2]

Many early photographers also traveled to the forest of Fontainebleau in the mid-nineteenth century, where they frequently explored the same motifs as their painter colleagues.[3] Here the early interaction between the two media shows itself as if in a burning glass—a relationship marked from the beginning not only by rivalry, but also by collegial exchange and reciprocal influence. This close dialogue also arose from the fact that many pioneers of photography had been trained as painters—such as Gustave Le Gray, who made his first landscape photographs in the forest of Fontainebleau in 1849. Both the Barbizon painters and the Impressionists frequently depicted forest paths in their paintings, "paths into the image" intended to help viewers immerse themselves in the sensory experience of the landscape.[4] In *The Forest of Fontainebleau* (cat. 49), Le Gray used the same pictorial formula, enhancing the photograph with a decidedly painterly element through the multifaceted play of shadow and light. Like many of the later founding members of the Société française de photographie, established in Paris in 1854, Le Gray was an early advocate for the recognition of photography as an autonomous art form and argued that the medium ought to transcend the mechanical reproduction of nature.[5]

While many photographers presented the forest as an untouched natural idyll, others chose views that incorporated modern elements such as handcarts or paved streets, alluding to forestry and an expanding infrastructure (cats. 53, 54, 58). From 1849 on, the rail connection between Paris and Fontainebleau brought about an enormous increase in middle-class tourism. Travel guides and folding maps provided information on scenic tours that strategically combined historic buildings and picturesque views. In their search for motifs, painters and photographers could make use of such resources, which even offered special recommendations for artists. Works such as Constant Alexandre Famin's photograph of the area around the pond Mare aux Fées depict views that were widely recognized as stations along established hiking routes for tourists (cat. 63). With its focus on the broad surface of the water and the reflections of the surrounding vegetation, however, the image was also meant to evoke ephemeral impressions of nature—a quest for momentariness that united both painting and landscape photography in the mid-nineteenth century. The carefully placed hiker dressed in black sets a striking accent that extends to his reflection in the sunlit pond. Furthermore, the inclusion of the diminutive-seeming figure also serves to dramatize the majestic size of the imposing oaks for which the forest was famous.

While many painters and photographers made only shorter summer trips to Barbizon as a part of seasonal tourism, the life and work of Eugène Cuvelier were inseparably connected to the region. Like Le Gray, Cuvelier trained as both a painter and a photographer and was acquainted with many of the leading proponents of Realism. The most important gathering place for these artists was the Auberge Ganne, an inn in Barbizon. In 1859 Cuvelier married the innkeeper's daughter, Louise, in a ceremony whose attendees included Corot, Millet, and Rousseau—a telling indication of the friendships and social connections that bound painters and photographers.[6] Although Cuvelier had joined the Société française de photographie in 1855, he participated in only three of their exhibitions, and never ran a commercial atelier. As an enthusiastic amateur photographer, he created an extensive oeuvre of forest scenes that bear witness to his artistic ambitions (cats. 54, 56, 62, 64, 85). His technical ability is evident in his views of landscapes covered in a thick blanket of snow (cats. 57, 58), an especially challenging subject due to the long exposure times. *Fontainebleau near the Porte de Rochefort* (cat. 58) derives its sense of depth from the triangular form of the forest path running toward the center of the picture. Brilliant white and deep black are strikingly juxtaposed, but even the lighter areas of the picture show subtle differentiation with the empty, transparent sky contrasting tonally with the deeper white of the reflective blanket of snow. Such fine modulations within monochromatic areas would soon become a trademark of Impressionist winter scenes, especially the numerous snowy landscapes of Claude Monet and Alfred Sisley.

Like their French colleagues, German photographers also frequently explored the aesthetic possibilities of forest, park, and garden scenes (cf. cats. 48, 65, 66). As a professor of photochemistry and spectral analysis at the Technische Hochschule in Berlin, Hermann Wilhelm Vogel was a well-known pioneer of scientific photography.[7] His best-known works include the *View near the Grosser Stern* (cat. 66), published in 1866 as part of his portfolio *Pictures from the Thiergarten*. The image combines sharply focused details with a dramatic chiaroscuro effect. In a scene without figures, Vogel alludes to human intervention in nature solely through his choice of view. Modern, cast-iron gas lanterns are visible next to two wooden fences, while numerous ruts from the wheels of carriages appear on the muddy path to the right. Dancing flecks of light draw the viewer's gaze back and forth between the ground and the thick foliage—a play with visual points of stimulation that recalls the contemporaneous forest scenes of Renoir and his fellow Impressionists.

Translated from German by Melissa M. Thorson

[1] Cf. David 2013, Callen 2015, and Giverny 2020.

[2] Cf. Adams 1994.

[3] Cf. Washington 2008.

[4] Linda Hacka, "Paths into the Picture: Forest and Clearing," in Potsdam 2017, 112–27.

[5] Kansas City 2013, 157–58; on Le Gray's photographs, see also Paris 2002.

[6] Kansas City 2013, 160; on Cuvelier and Fontainebleau, see also Gauss/Challe/Weidemann 1996.

[7] Cf. Cologne 2006, 178.

49 Gustave Le Gray
The Forest of
Fontainebleau, 1849–52

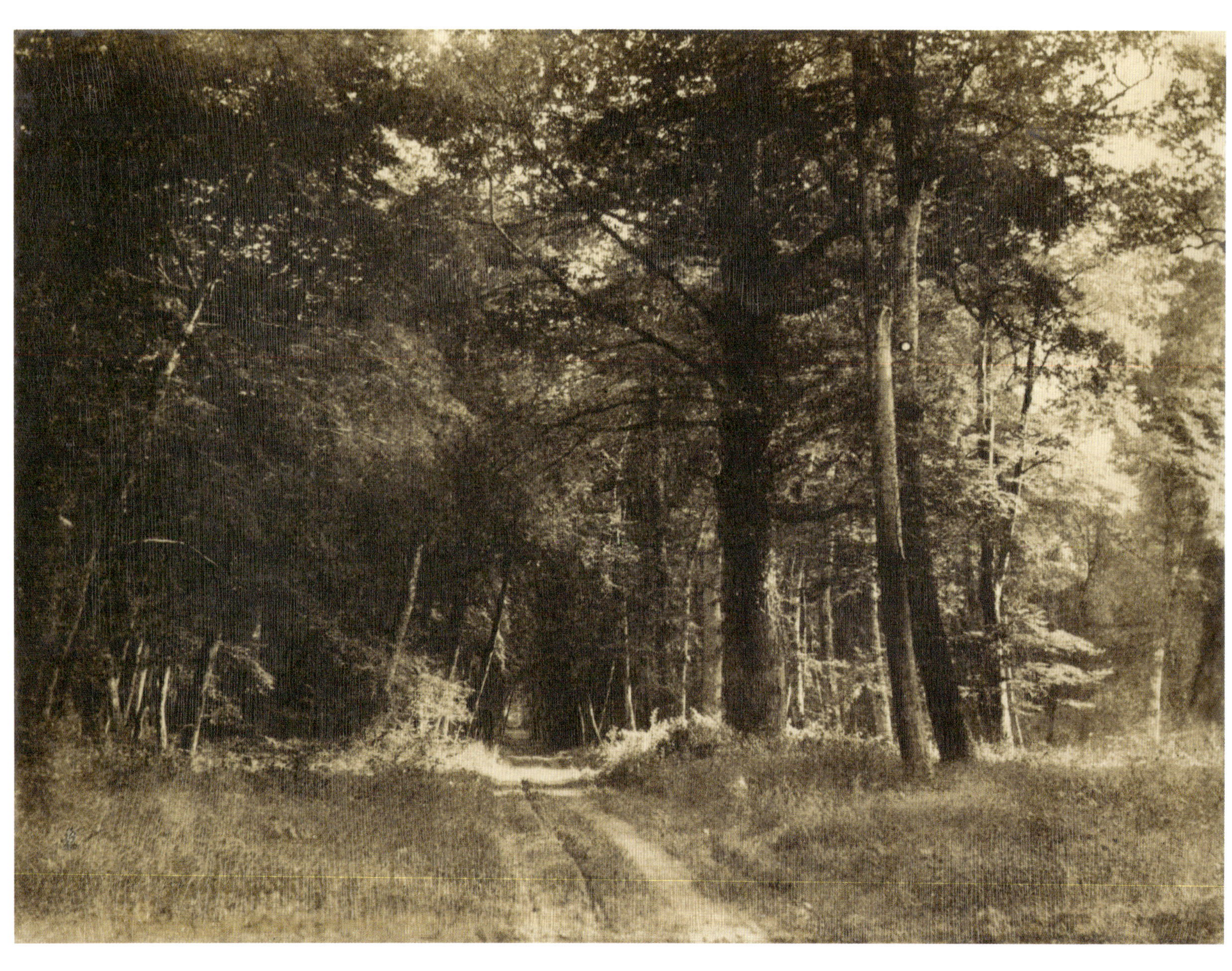

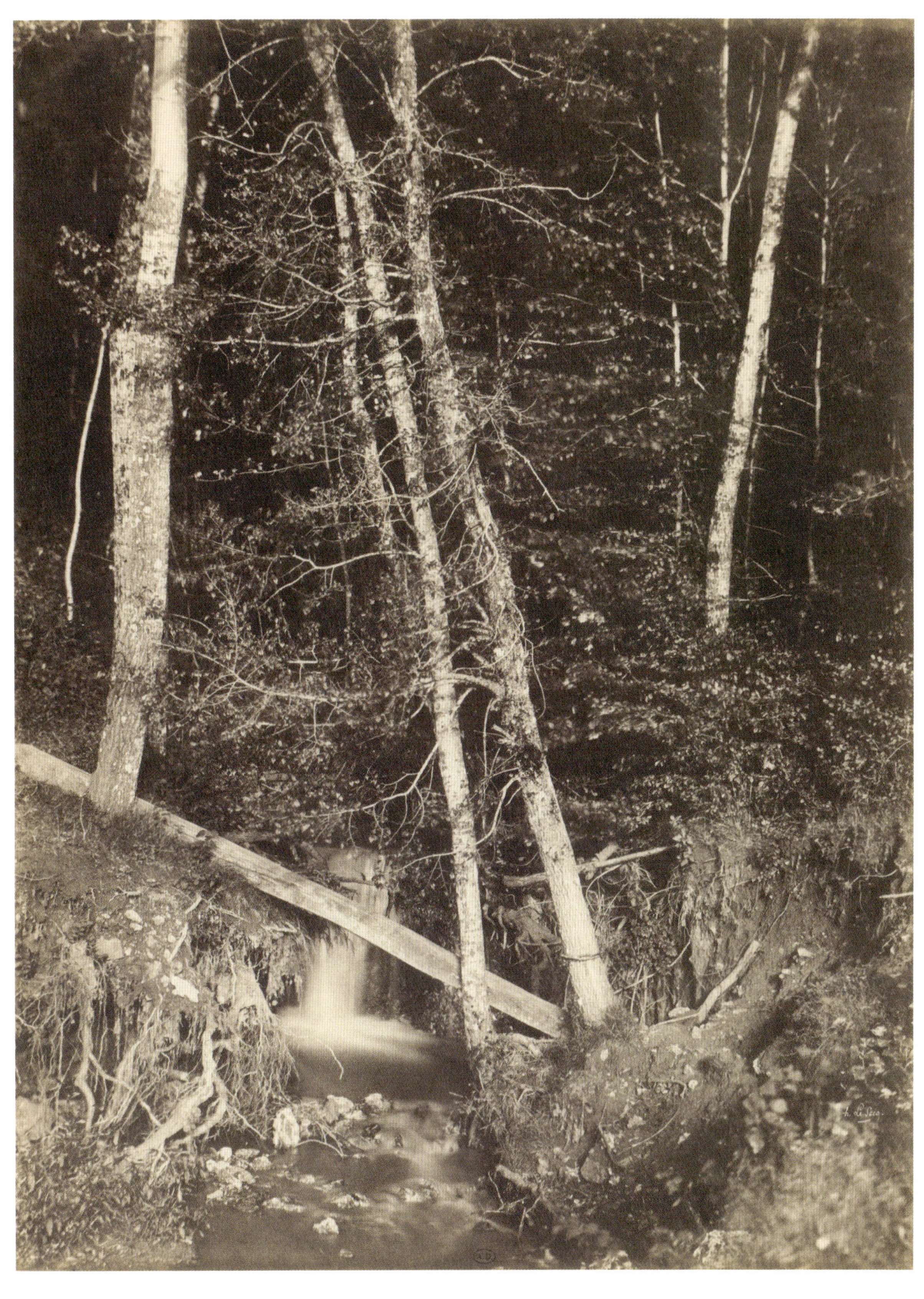

50 Henri Le Secq
Forest Brook, ca. 1852–53

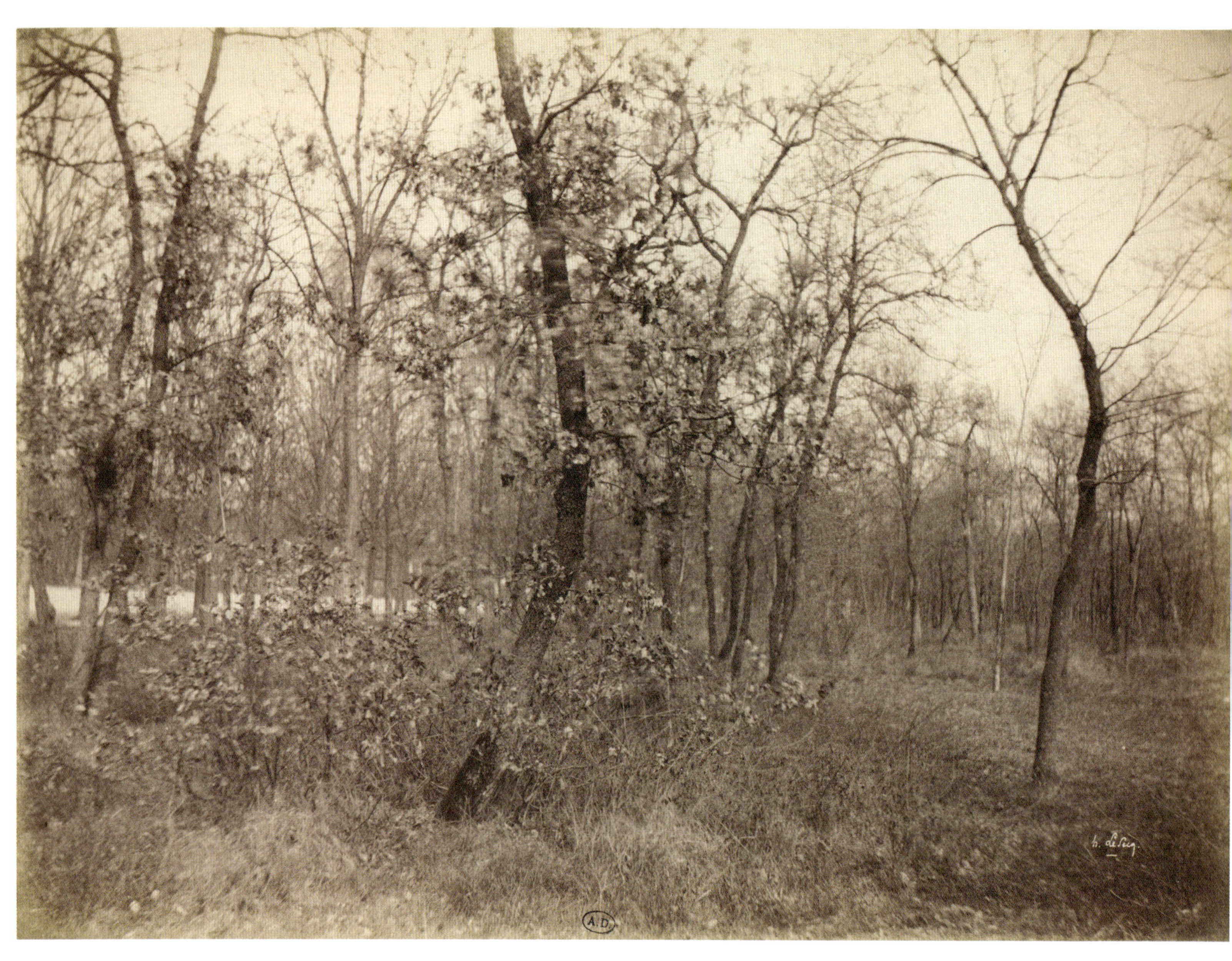

51 Henri Le Secq
High Forest, ca. 1852–53

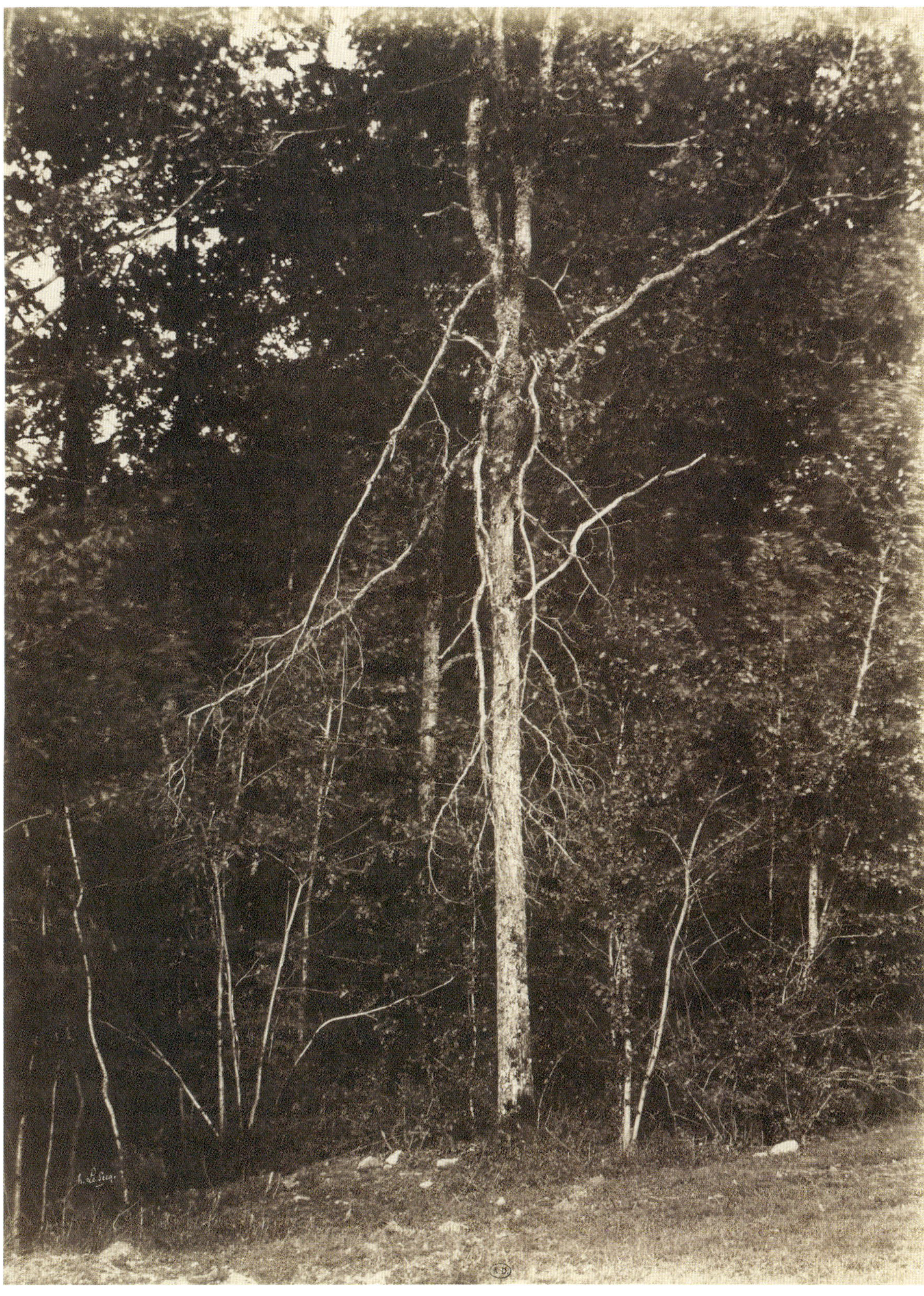

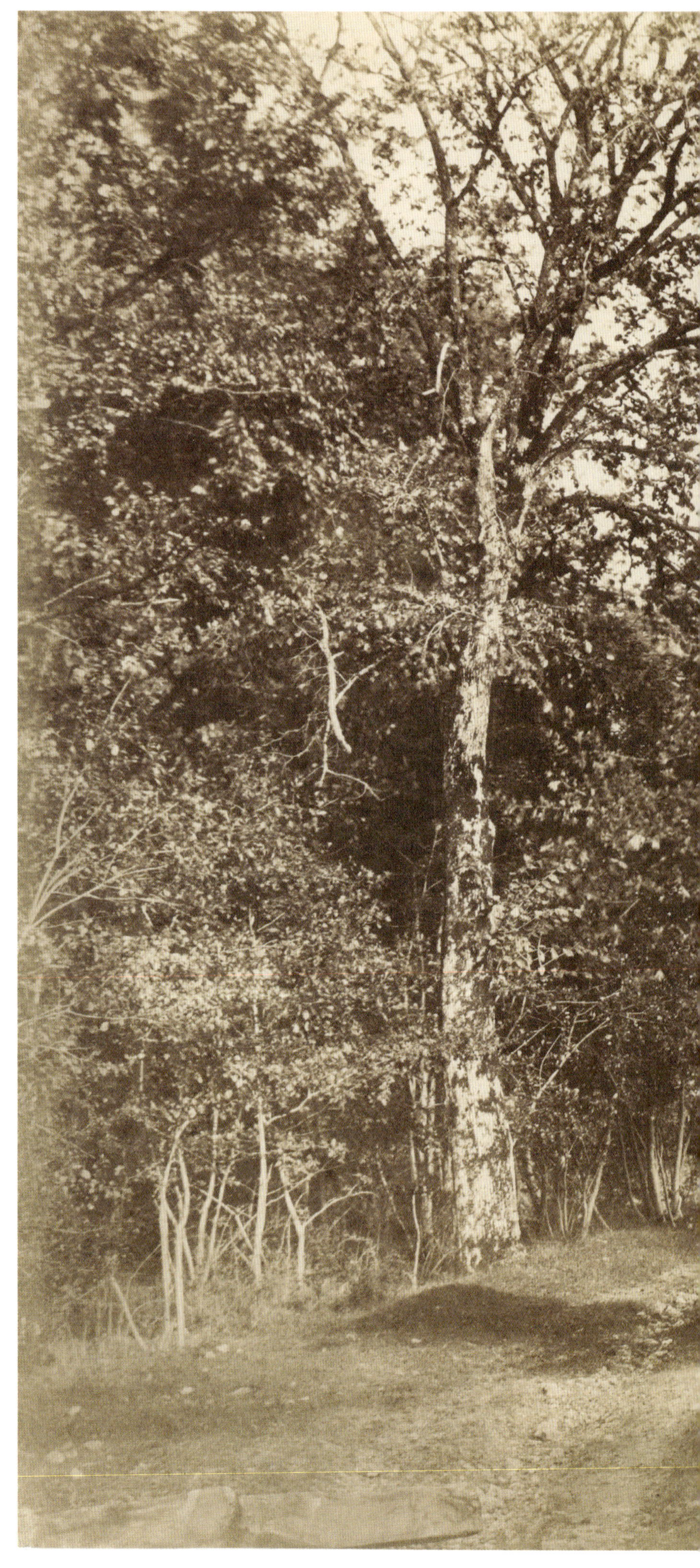

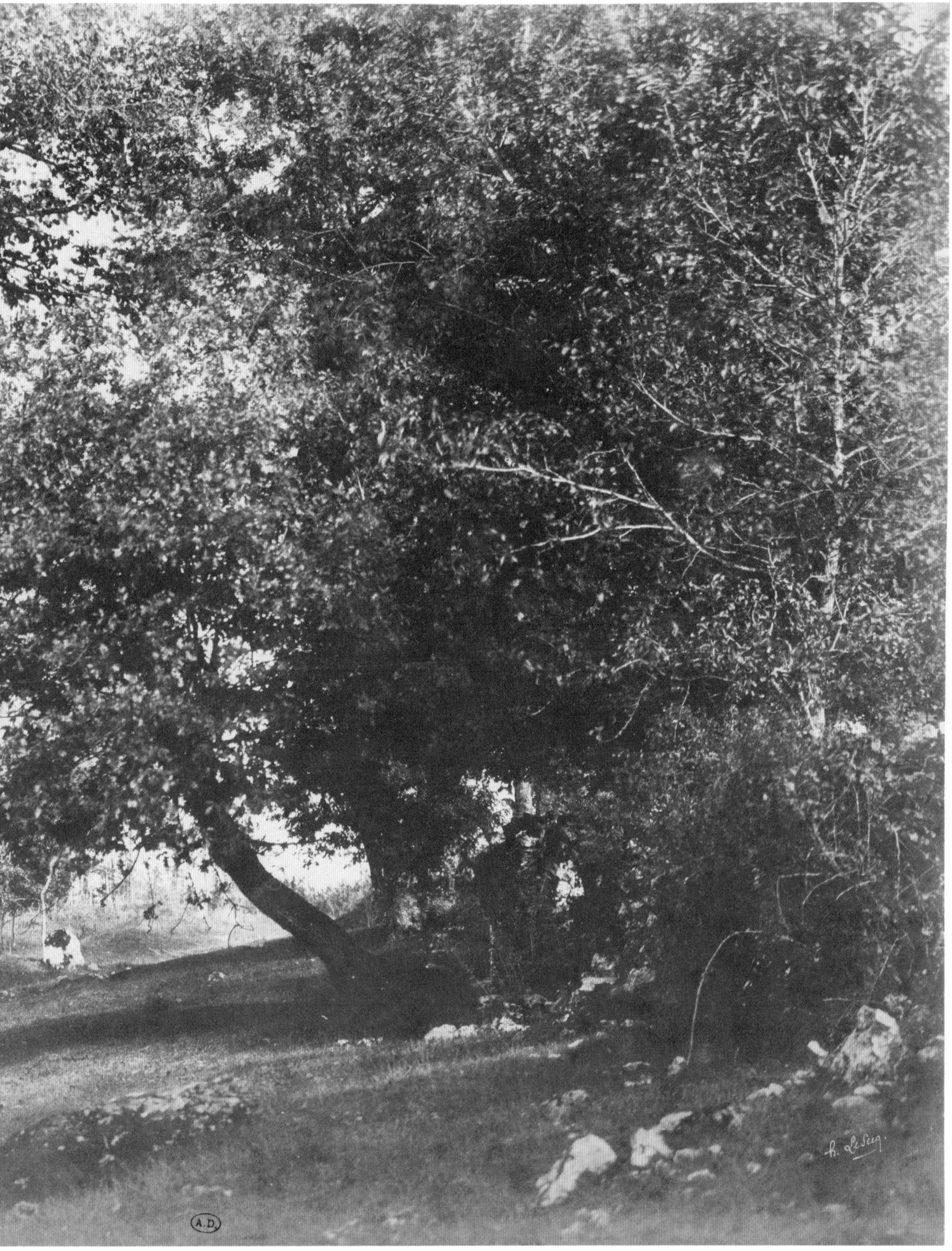

54 Eugène Cuvelier
*Cart on the Road,
with Squaring Grid,* 1862

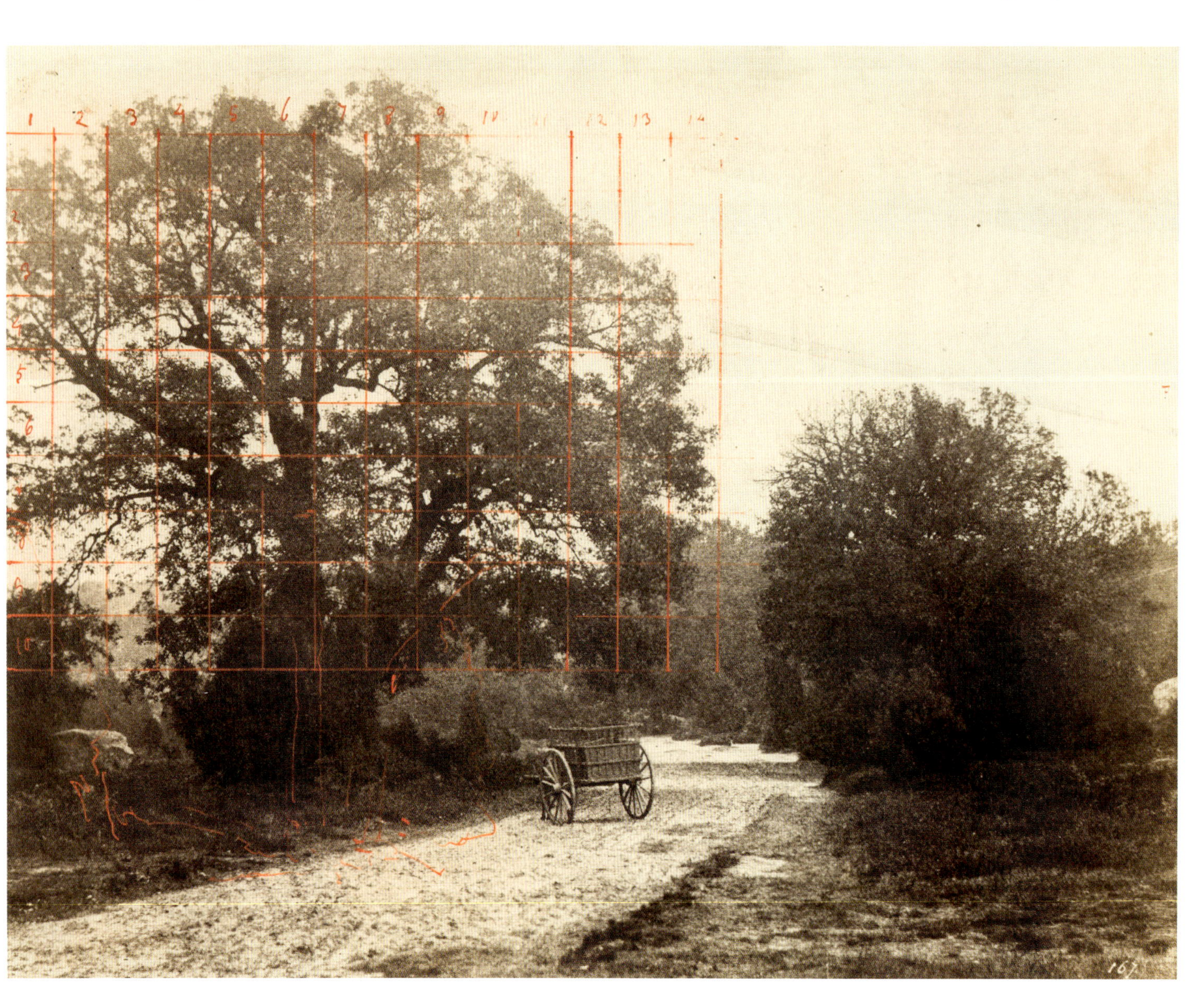

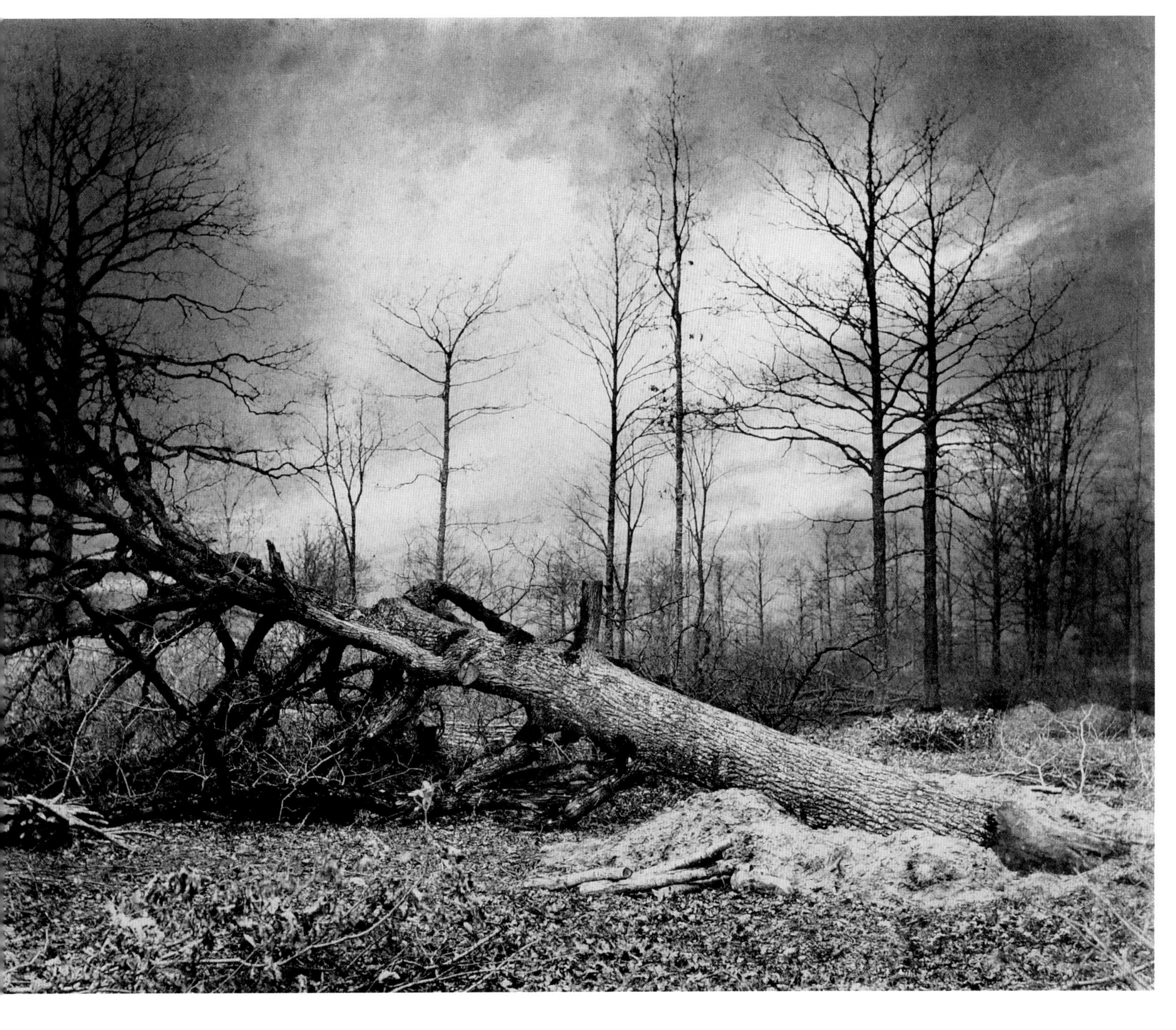

55 André Giroux
Felled Tree in a Forest in Winter,
ca. 1853

56 Eugène Cuvelier
Beneath the Overlook in the Field,
September 17, 1862, 1862

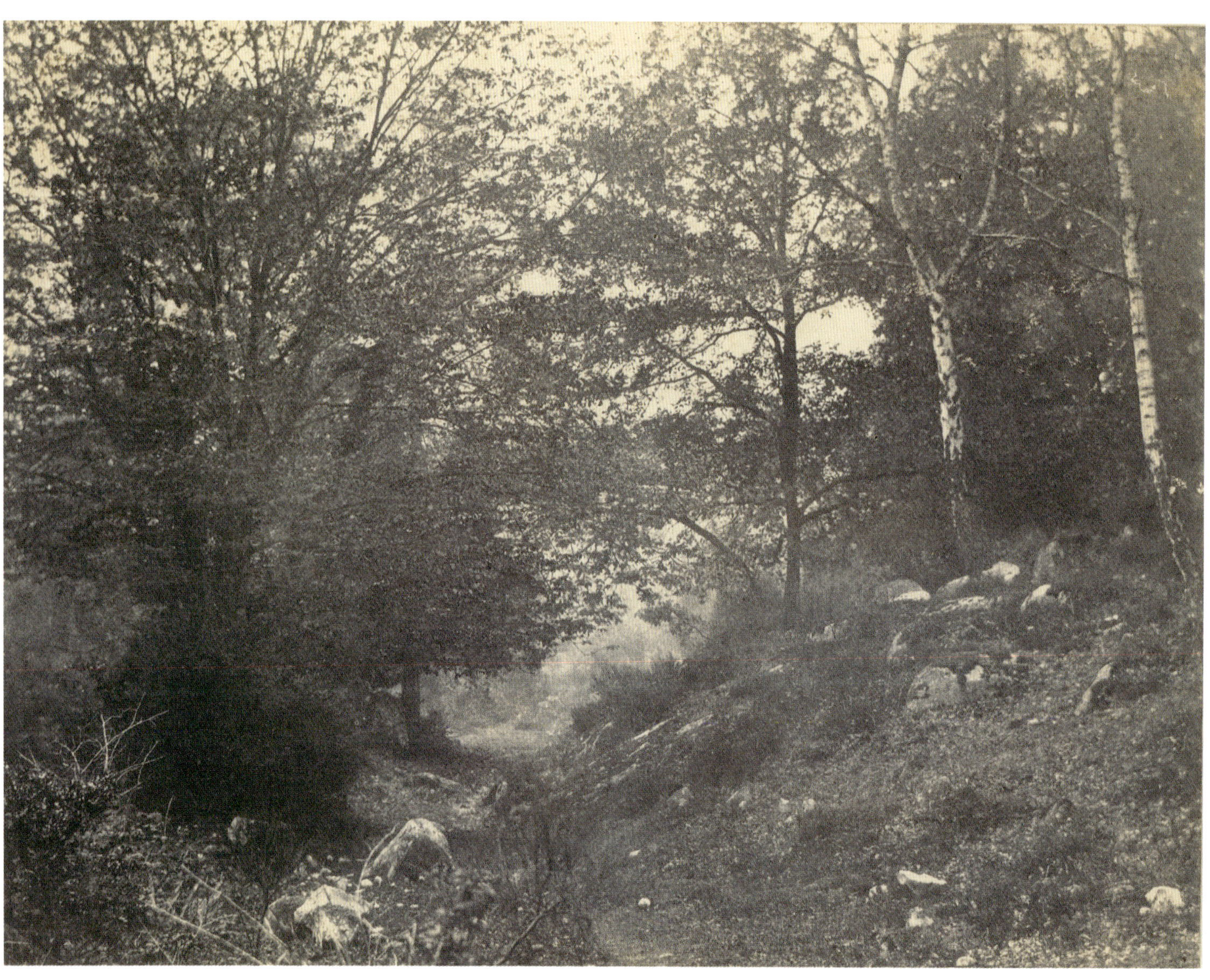

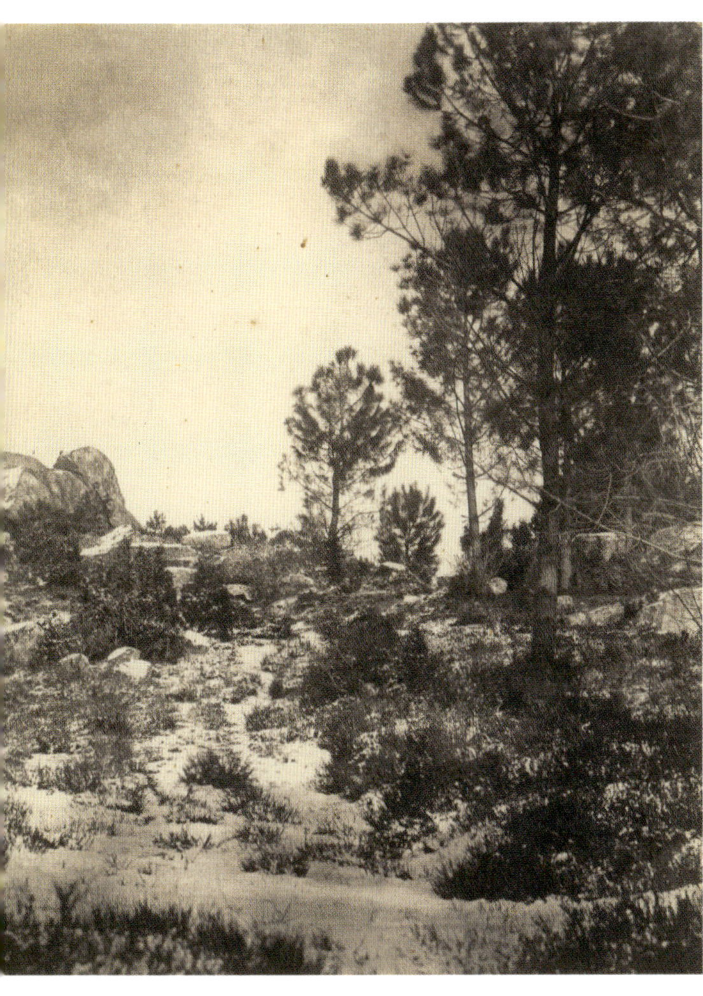

57 Eugène Cuvelier
Pines near Rochefort—Snow, 1862

58 Eugène Cuvelier
*Fontainebleau near the Porte de
Rochefort, ca. 1860*

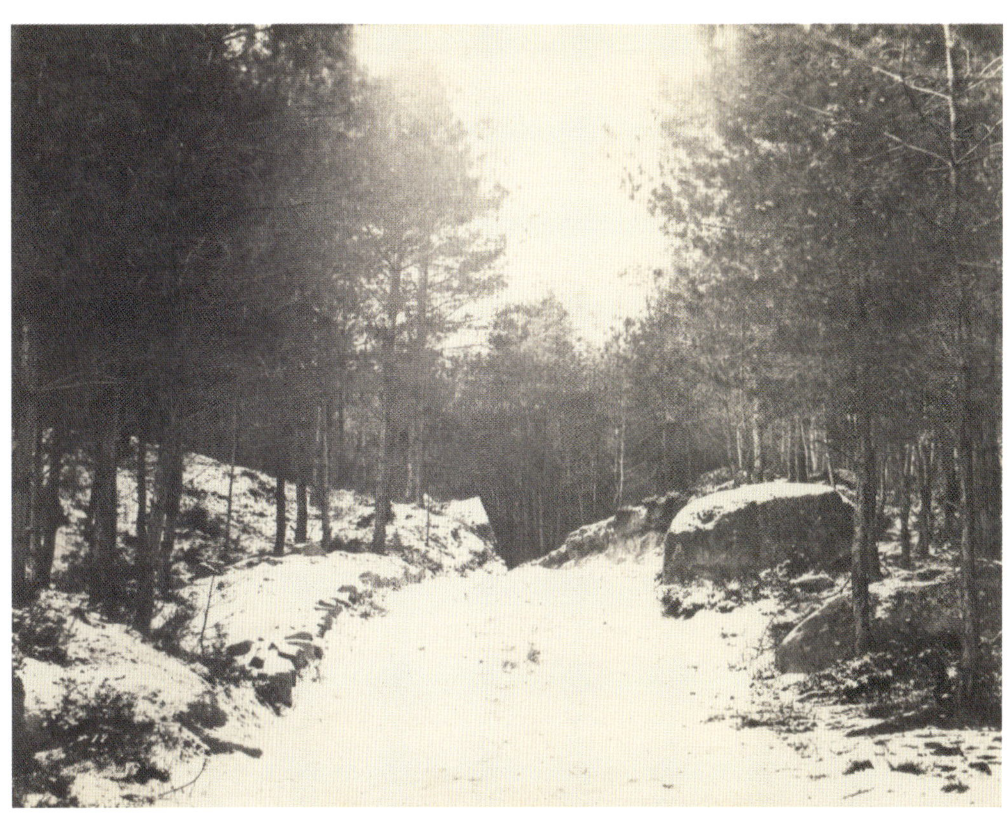

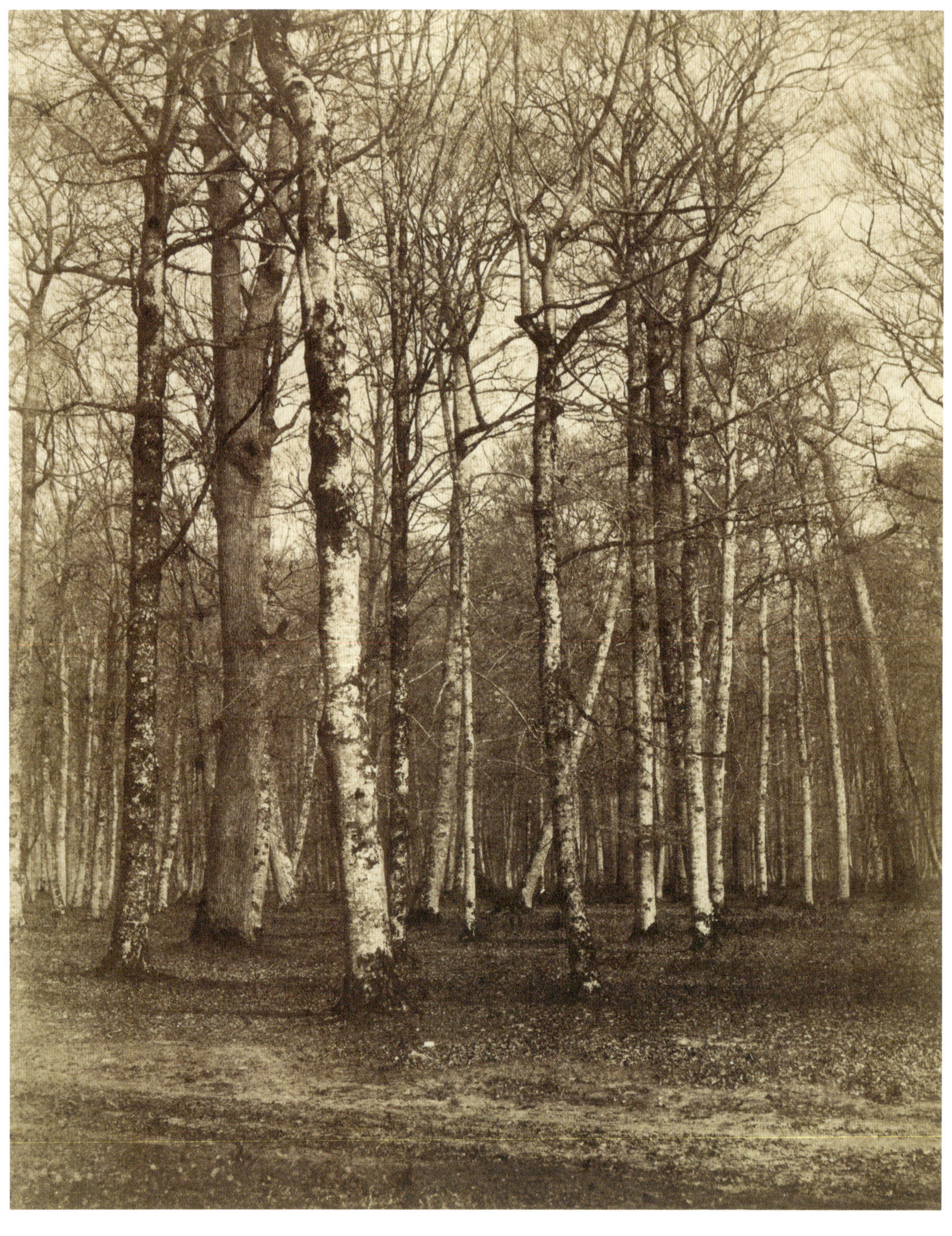

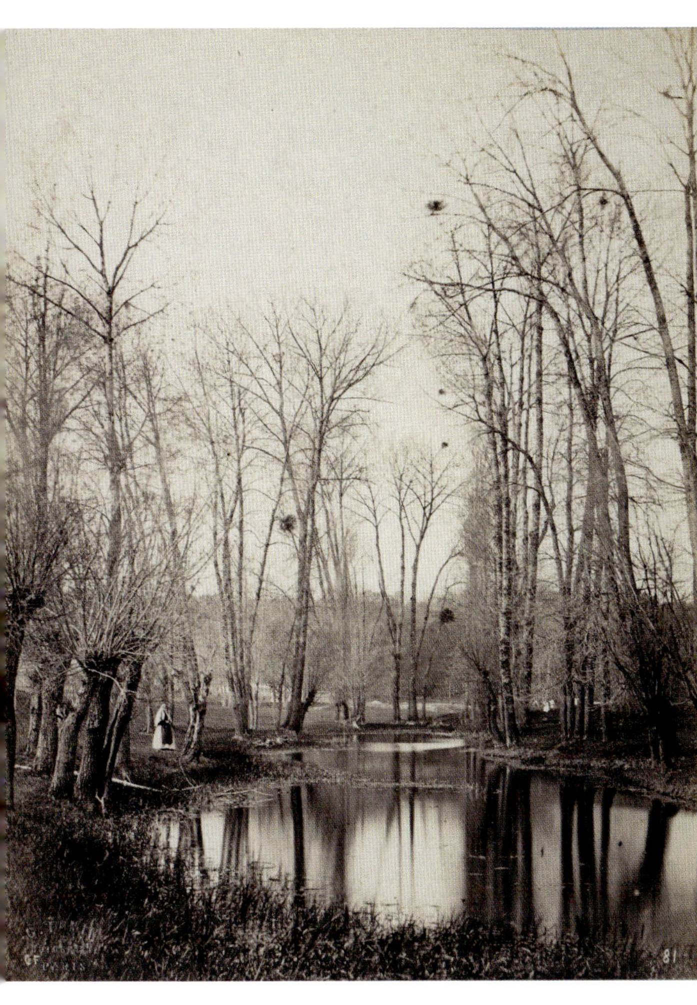

60 Constant Alexandre Famin
Landscape near Barbizon, 1862

61 Constant Alexandre Famin
Forest Path in Autumn, ca. 1865

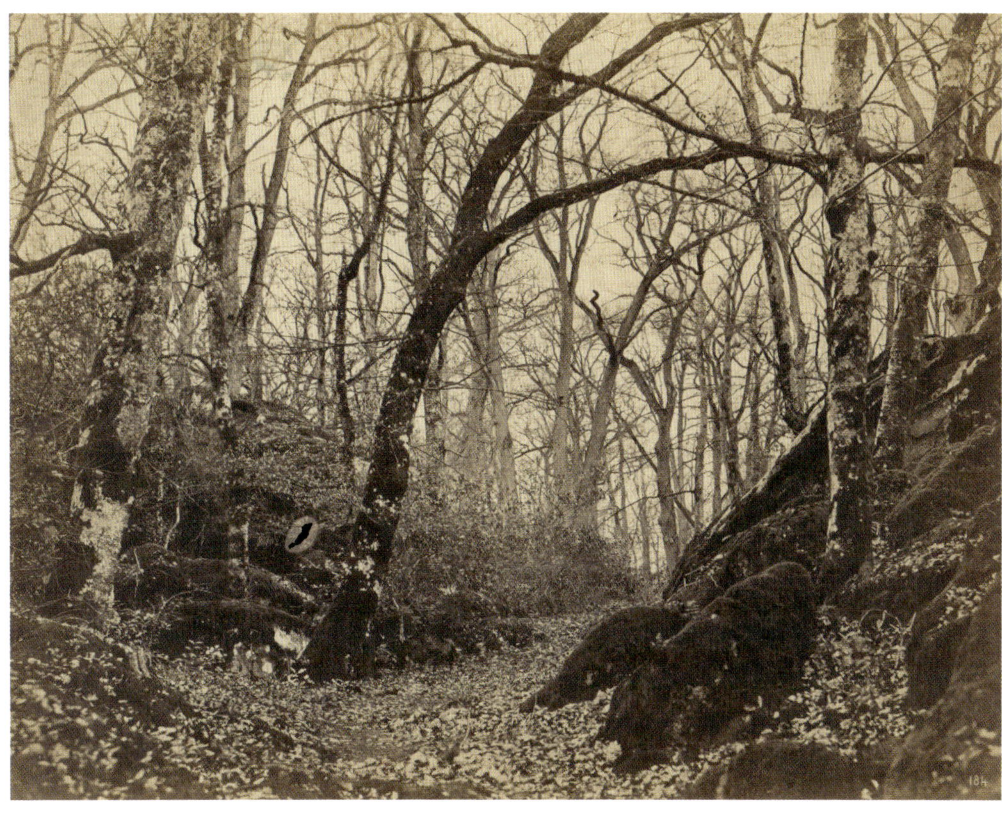

41

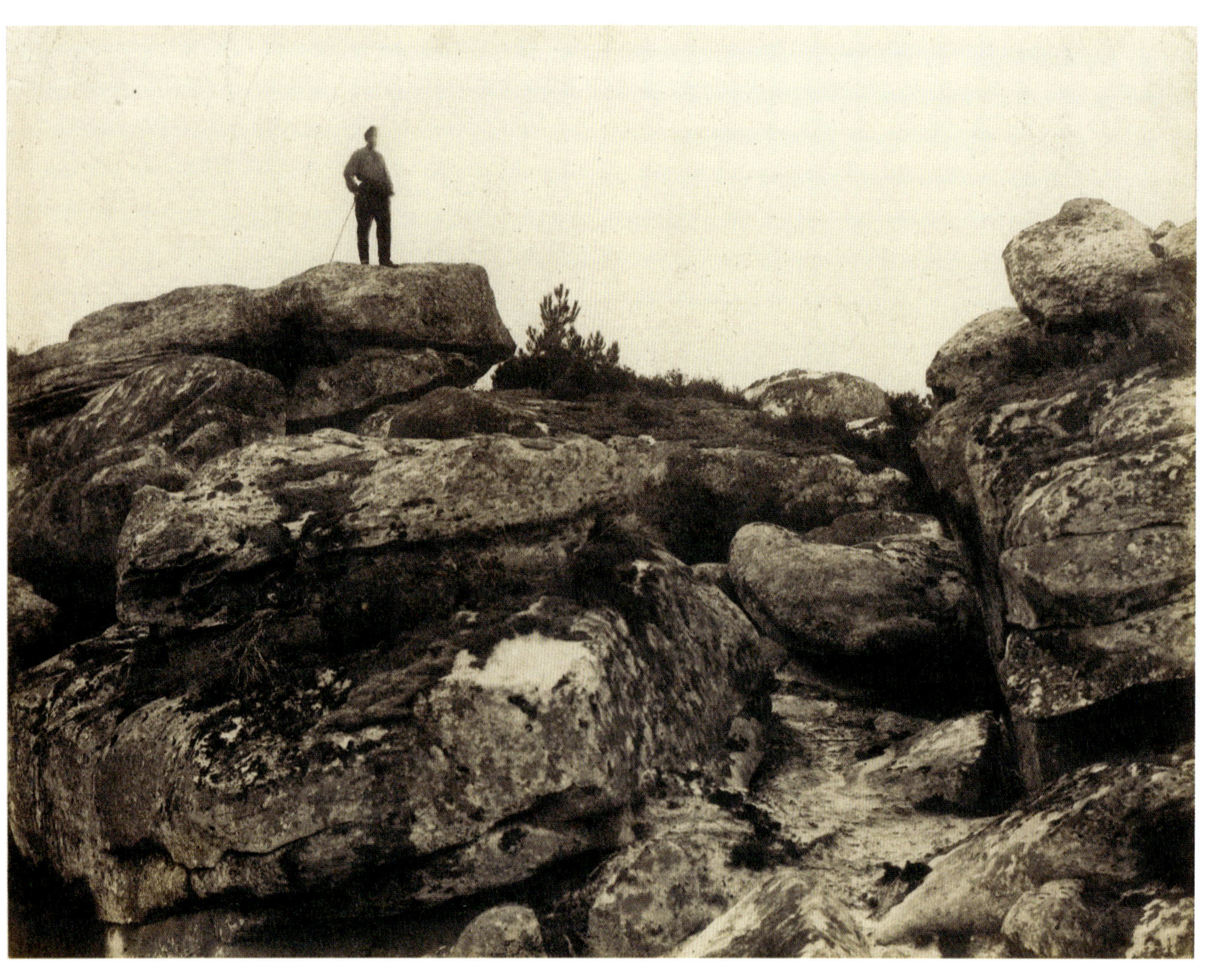

62 Eugène Cuvelier
Franchard, 1863

53 Constant Alexandre Famin
*Théophile Chauvel, near the Mare
aux Fées, 1865–70*

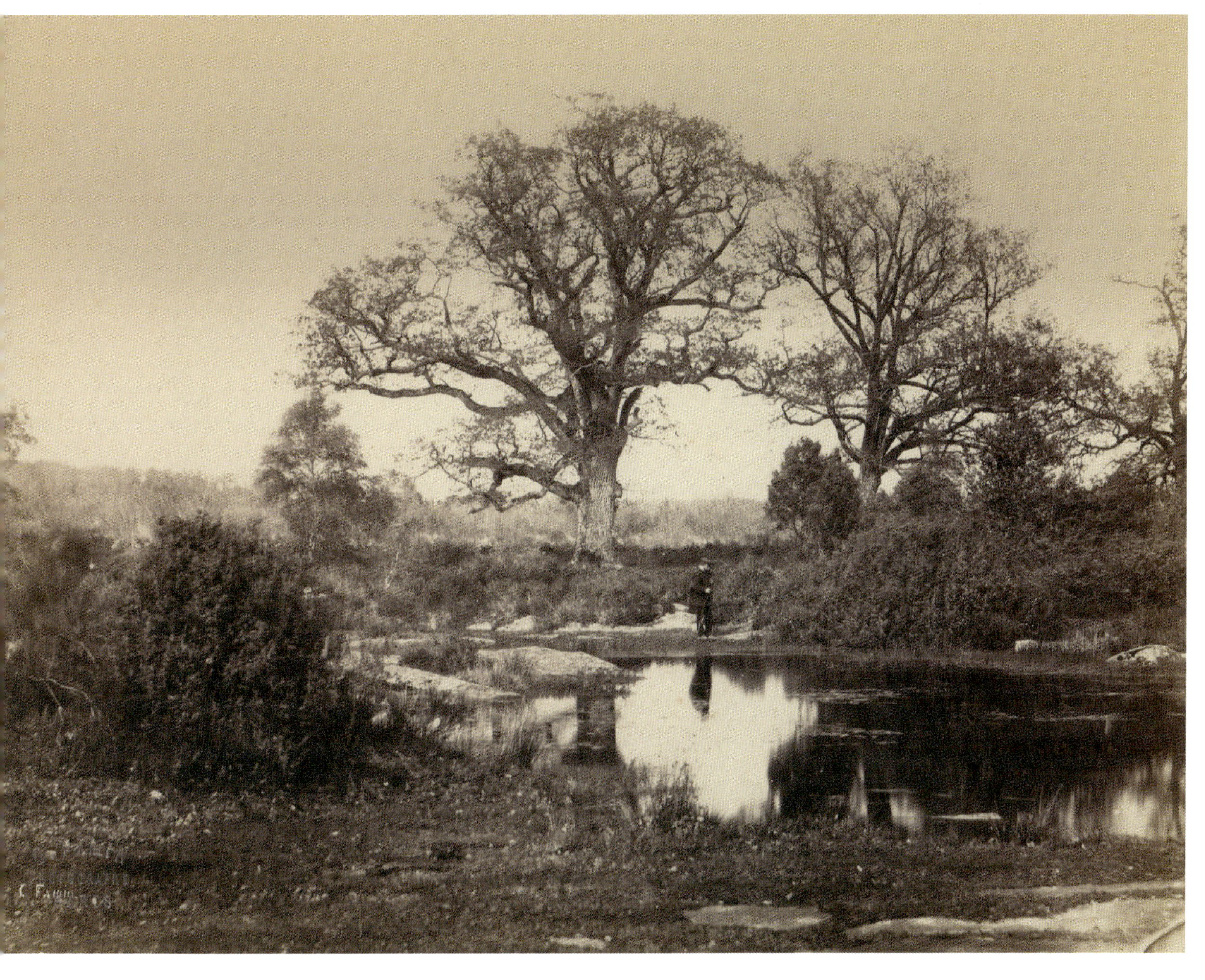

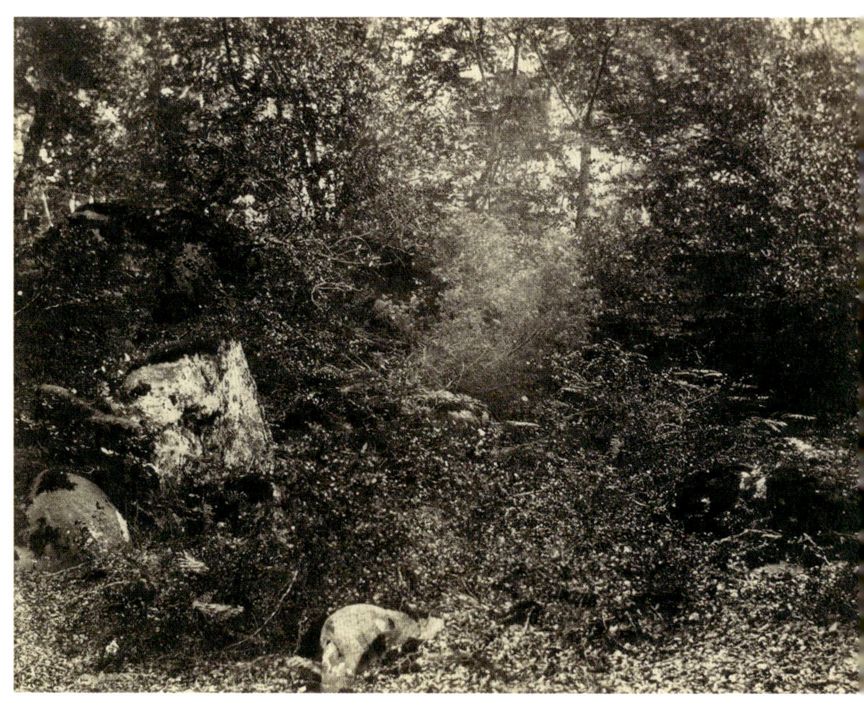

64 Eugène Cuvelier
Broussailles, Belle Croix, Forest of Fontainebleau, September 14, 1863, 1863

65 Georg Maria Eckert
Middle Ground Study: Well House Overgrown with Wild Vine, Heidelberg, 1866–68

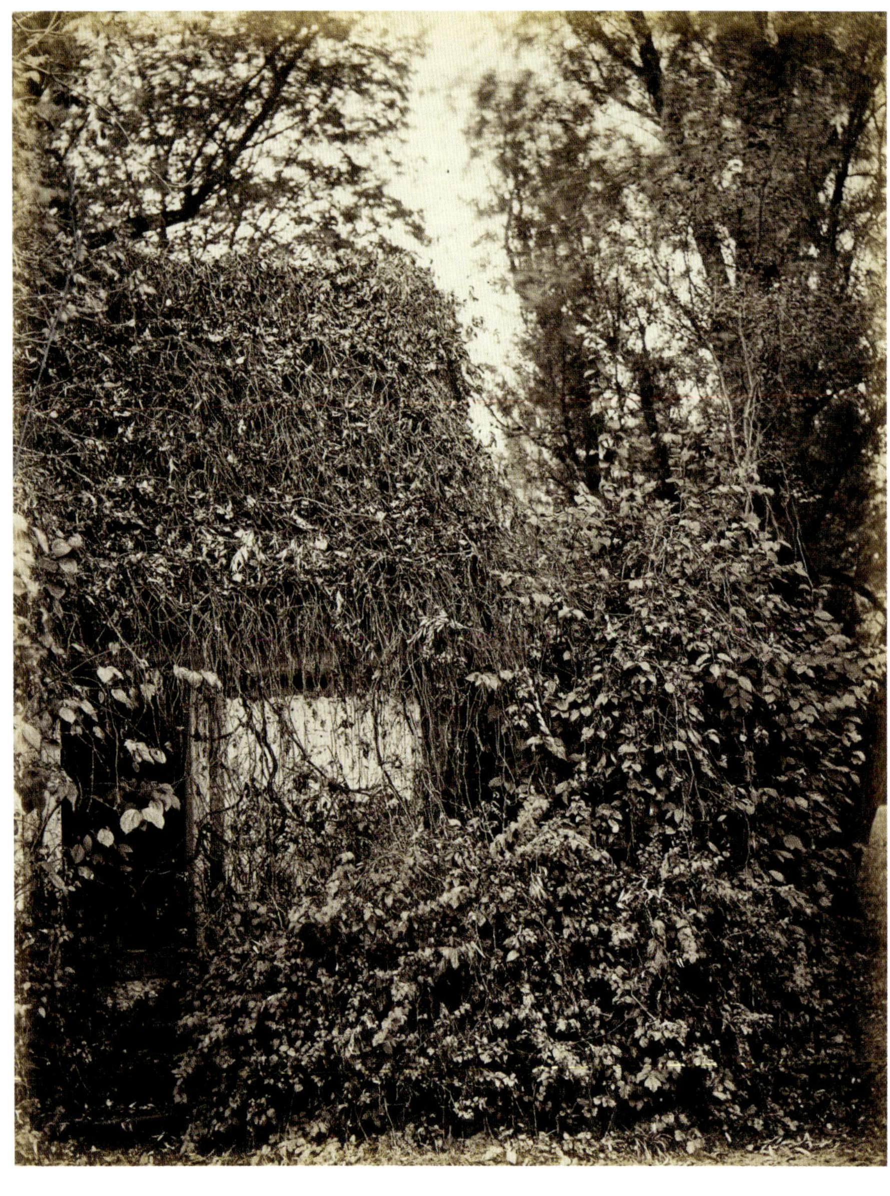

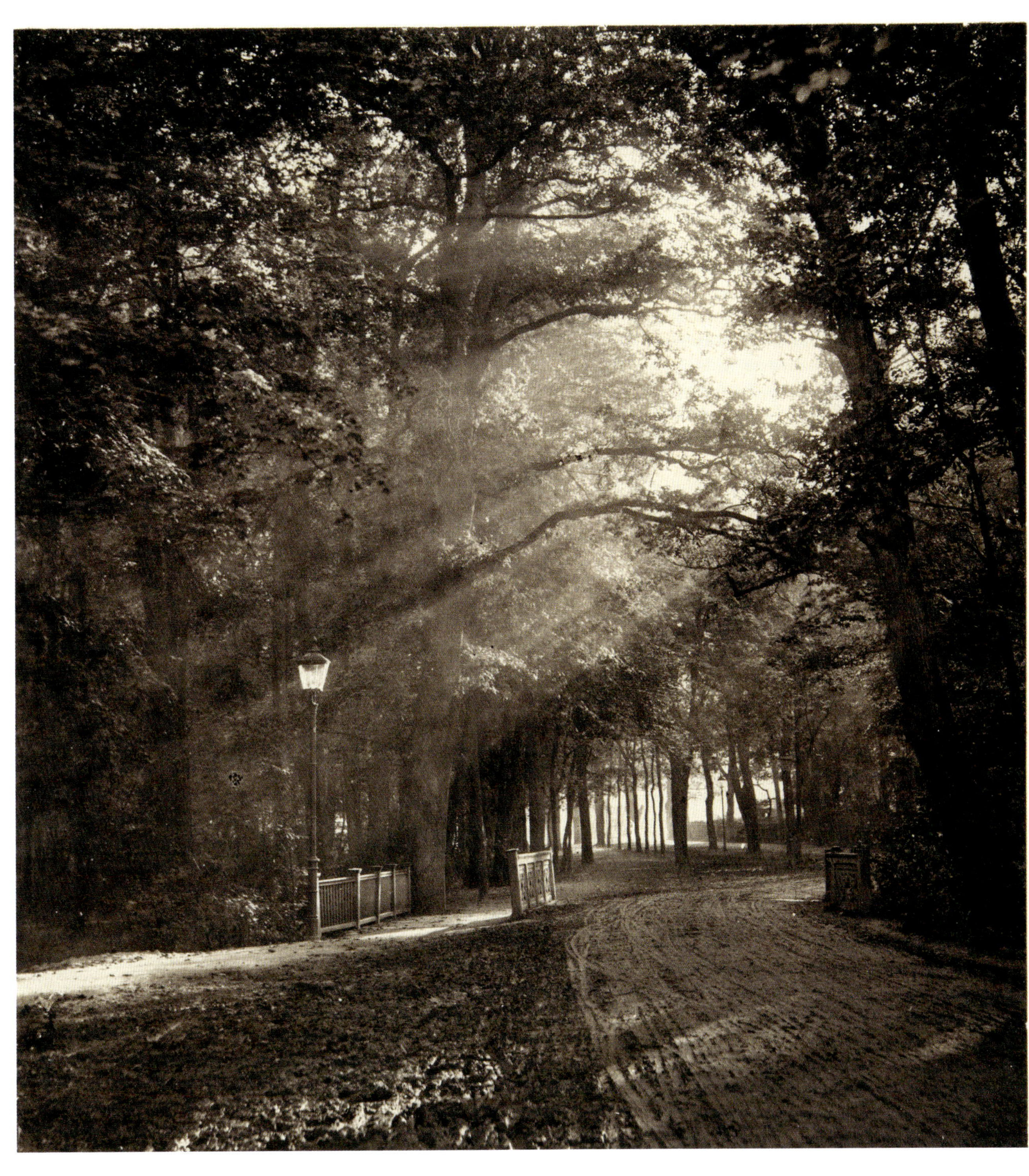

66 Hermann Wilhelm Vogel
View near the Grosser Stern,
from the album *Pictures from the
Thiergarten,* 1866

Daniel Zamani

Everyday Motifs

Countryside and River

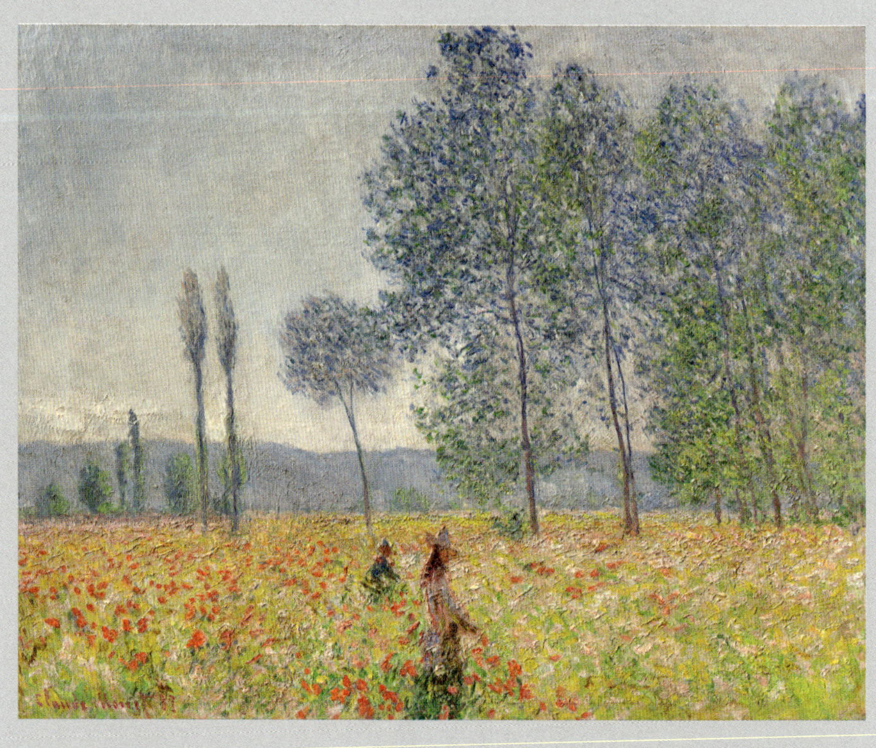

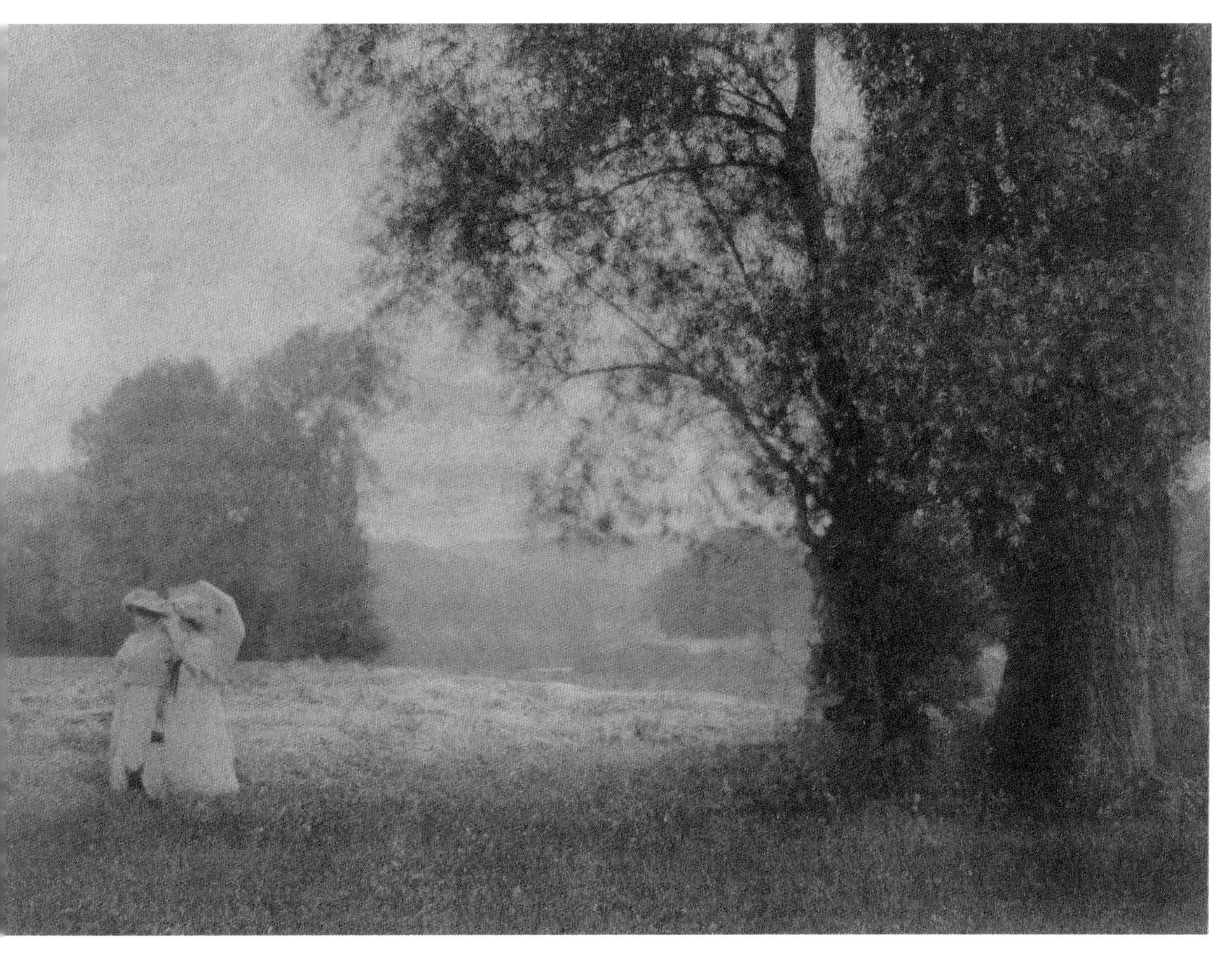

Claude Monet
Under the Poplars, 1887
Oil on canvas
Hasso Plattner Collection

67 Constant Puyo
Two Women in a Field, 1894–1926

One of the most important innovations of nineteenth-century painting was its embrace of the *paysage intime*—a term that refers to landscape images free of moralizing or anecdotal elements.[1] Painters of the Barbizon School such as Camille Corot or Charles-François Daubigny turned their attention to the country-side of their French homeland. In their works, often painted *en plein air,* they endowed simple motifs such as rocks, thickets, or riverbanks with pictorial dignity. Numerous photographers also explored the new genre of *paysage intime* in their images of countryside and rivers.

Like the Impressionists around Claude Monet, they sought out unspectacular landscapes and turned their attention with seeming nonchalance to such unassuming motifs as rivers, fields, or flowering meadows. The forms of landscape photography ranged from the purely documentary in support of an interest in local or regional identity to the artistically ambitious, decidedly "painterly" photographs of the Pictorialists. In painting as in photography, the motifs reflect a reassessment of rural life as a refuge from the hustle and bustle of the city—a development that should be viewed against the backdrop of rapidly expanding industrialization. Photographs such as André Giroux's depiction of a felled tree also functioned as emblems of the human threat to nature, particularly in view of the increasing deforestation of historic woodland areas (cf. cat. 55).

From the beginning, landscape images had played a decisive role in the elevation of photography as an autonomous art form. The Société française de photographie, founded in Paris in 1854, promoted landscape photography since it, unlike genres such as portraiture, was comparatively free from commercial interests. In addition, the landscape genre also afforded opportunity to explore motifs that were well received in contemporary Salons. Henry Peach Robinson's *The Painter* (cat. 78) is one of many late nineteenth-century photographs depicting artists at work *en plein air,* thus metaphorically reflecting the affinity between painting and photography (cf. cats. 137, 138). The subtle arrangement of the figure group is typical of Robinson, who modeled his photographs on English landscape painting and often imbued his compositions with a staged quality through careful scenographic preparation. Such orchestrations of nature as a *tableau* arranged by the artist's hand were rejected by many of Robinson's colleagues as unjustified manipulation. Among the advocates of a natural approach to the landscape was his British compatriot Peter Henry Emerson, who had come to the fore with the publication of his handbook *Naturalistic Photography* in 1889. There he called for as simple and direct a rendering of the motif as possible, with no element whatsoever of contrived mise-en-scène. His work *Gathering Water Lilies* (cat. 90) conveys this aesthetic of immediacy through the unusual perspective as well as the dynamic quality of the image, which seems snapshot-like and spontaneous.

Many photographers attempted to elevate the artistic value of their landscapes by emulating painting in both style and motif, a strategy in which the model of the Barbizon School as well as Impressionism acquired particular significance. Conversely, painters reacted to photography—which they often perceived as a threat—by experimenting with its cropped quality or focusing on the depiction of fleeting, ephemeral impressions of nature.[2] An important point of connection between the two media was provided by the reference photos that, from the 1850s on, increasingly served the traditional function of preliminary drawings and sketches and often found their way into the repertoire of the artist's studio as part of an extensive photo archive. Typical motifs for these studies, which were often produced specifically for use by painters, included natural phenomena such as billowing waves, cloud formations illuminated by the sun (cats. 20–23, 96) or sharply focused details of plants, animals, and rocks, whose almost mathematical precision elicited great admiration.[3] Many of these photographs were widely circulated in comprehensive collections of motifs; the publisher Imprimerie photographique, for example, marketed books such as *Études photographiques* and *Études de paysage* in large editions.[4]

One of the most successful commercial photographers of the nineteenth century was Adolphe Braun. His company Braun & Cie., founded in 1853, achieved international fame for its photographic reproductions of works of art and served the French national museums in an official capacity from 1885 on. Braun had originally worked as a textile designer, and in the late 1840s he recognized the potential of photography as an important means of disseminating sample patterns. His album *Fleurs photographiées,* published in 1854, contained three hundred large-format flower arrangements, intended to serve as a source of inspiration for textile designers; due to their tremendous aesthetic appeal, however, they also garnered recognition as independent works of art. The following year he exhibited two additional series of flower still lifes at the world's fair in Paris, with great success.[5] Braun's flourishing business soon covered a broad spectrum of motifs, including topographical views and images of young women in traditional costumes from many different regions of France. In the early 1860s he produced a number of animal photographs, probably influenced by models from the Barbizon School (cats. 69, 70). Unlike the "pure" representations of animals preferred by professional breeders, his photographs show oxen, horses, cows, and sheep in an agricultural context, surrounded by farmers, equipment, and stables. The broad spectrum of motifs covered by Braun in this series of works suggests that these photographs, too, were intended to function as models for landscape painters.[6]

Braun's flower pictures were a central source of inspiration for his younger colleague Charles Aubry. Like Braun, Aubry had originally worked as a textile designer and had spent over thirty years creating patterns for fabric and wallpaper production. In 1864 he opened a studio in Paris, where he began assembling a photographic archive of flower pictures, plant studies, and botanical still lifes. His over two hundred documented works are characterized by astonishing luminosity and often recall the Old Masters in their visual opulence (cf. cats. 74, 75).[7] Still lifes and plant studies also occur in the contemporary work of August Kotzsch, a pioneer of photography in Germany known above all for his landscape photographs.[8] But while the works of Braun and Aubry derive their appeal from opulent arrangements and wide-ranging textures, photographs such as Kotzsch's *Cut Melon* (cat. 76) or *Potatoes* (cat. 77) are marked by a reduction to essences that seems radically modern. With their cool, detached evocation of the sculptural concreteness of objects, his photographs anticipate the sober, reduced aesthetic of the Neue Sachlichkeit decades in advance.

Translated from German by Melissa M. Thorson

[1] Cf. Wuppertal 2007, 98.

[2] Steven Jacobs, "Landscape," in Hannavy 2008, vol. 2, 818–24, here 823.

[3] Pohlmann 2016a, 7.

[4] Ibid.

[5] Cf. Naomie Rosenblum, "Braun, Adolphe," in Hannavy 2008, vol. 1, 203–05, here 204.

[6] Ulrich Pohlmann, "Tierstudien im Elsass," in Munich 2017, 103–04, here 104.

[7] On Aubry's photographs, see Anne McCauley, "Photographs for Industry: The Career of Charles Aubry," in *The J. Paul Getty Museum Journal* 14 (1986), 157–72.

[8] On Kotzsch's contribution to the development of photography, see Dresden 1992.

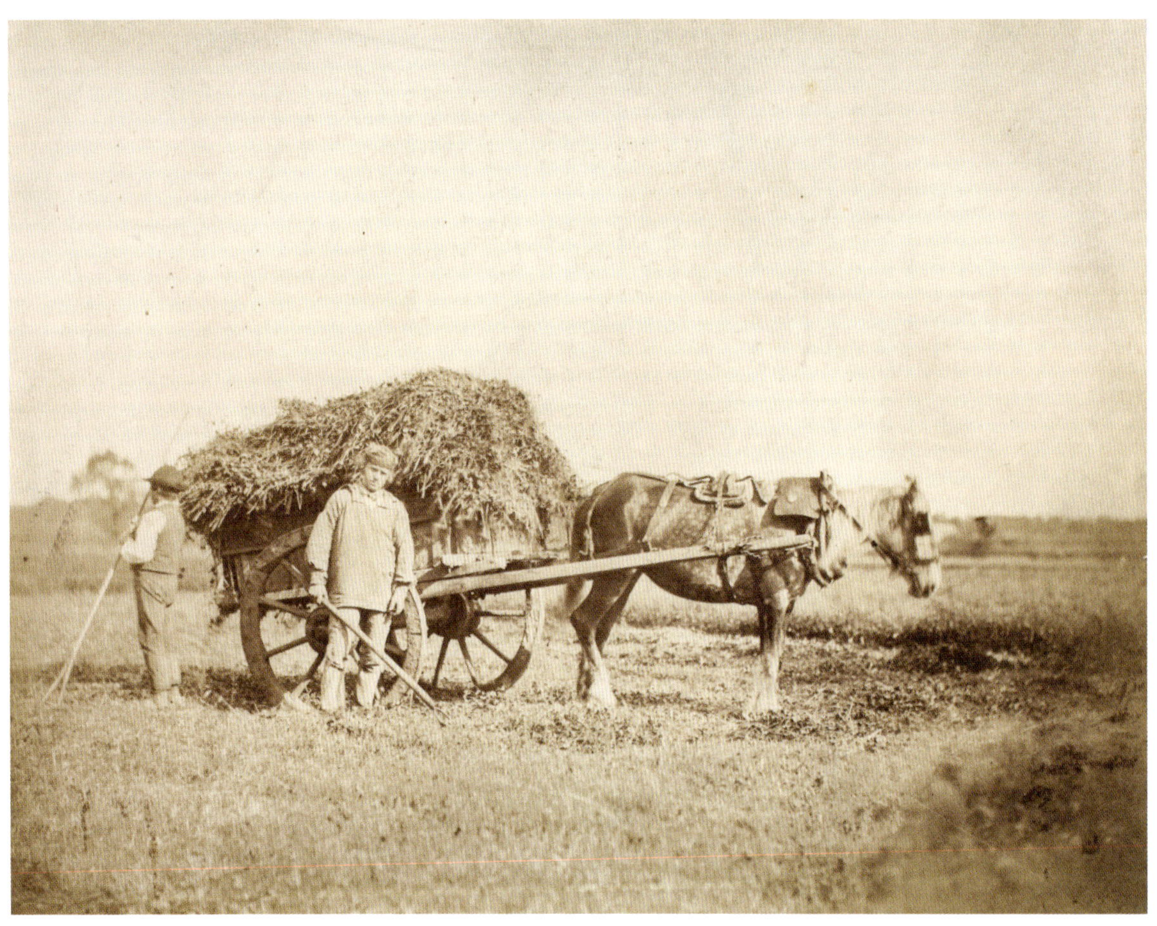

68 William Sherlock
Landscape, ca. 1852

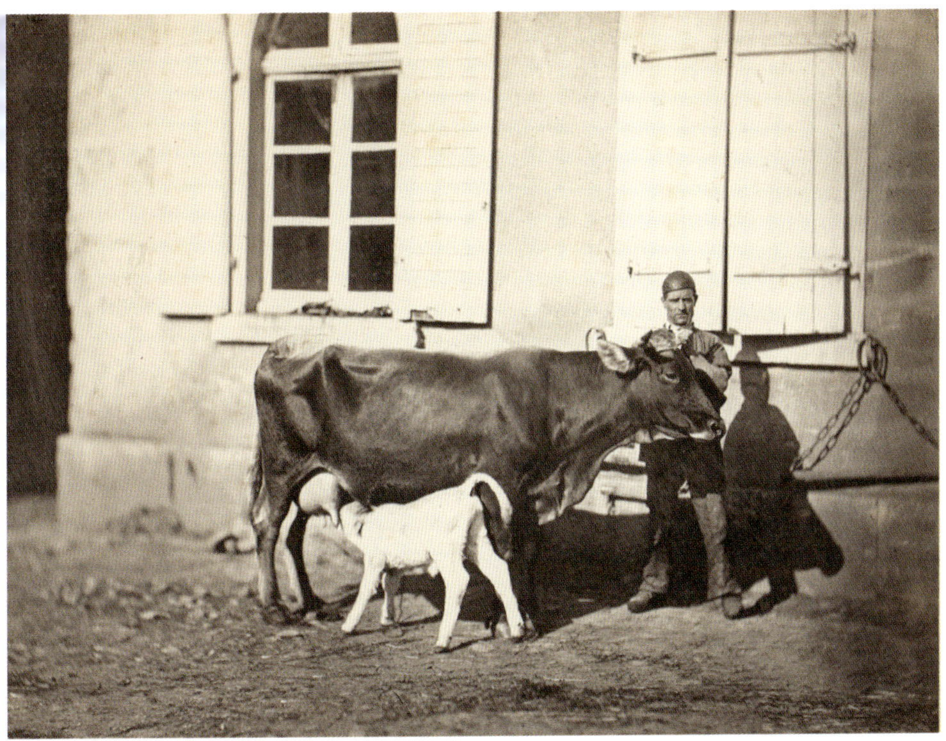

69 Adolphe Braun
Farmer with Cow and Calf, 1860–62

70 Adolphe Braun
*Teams of Horses and Oxen in
the Field,* 1860–62

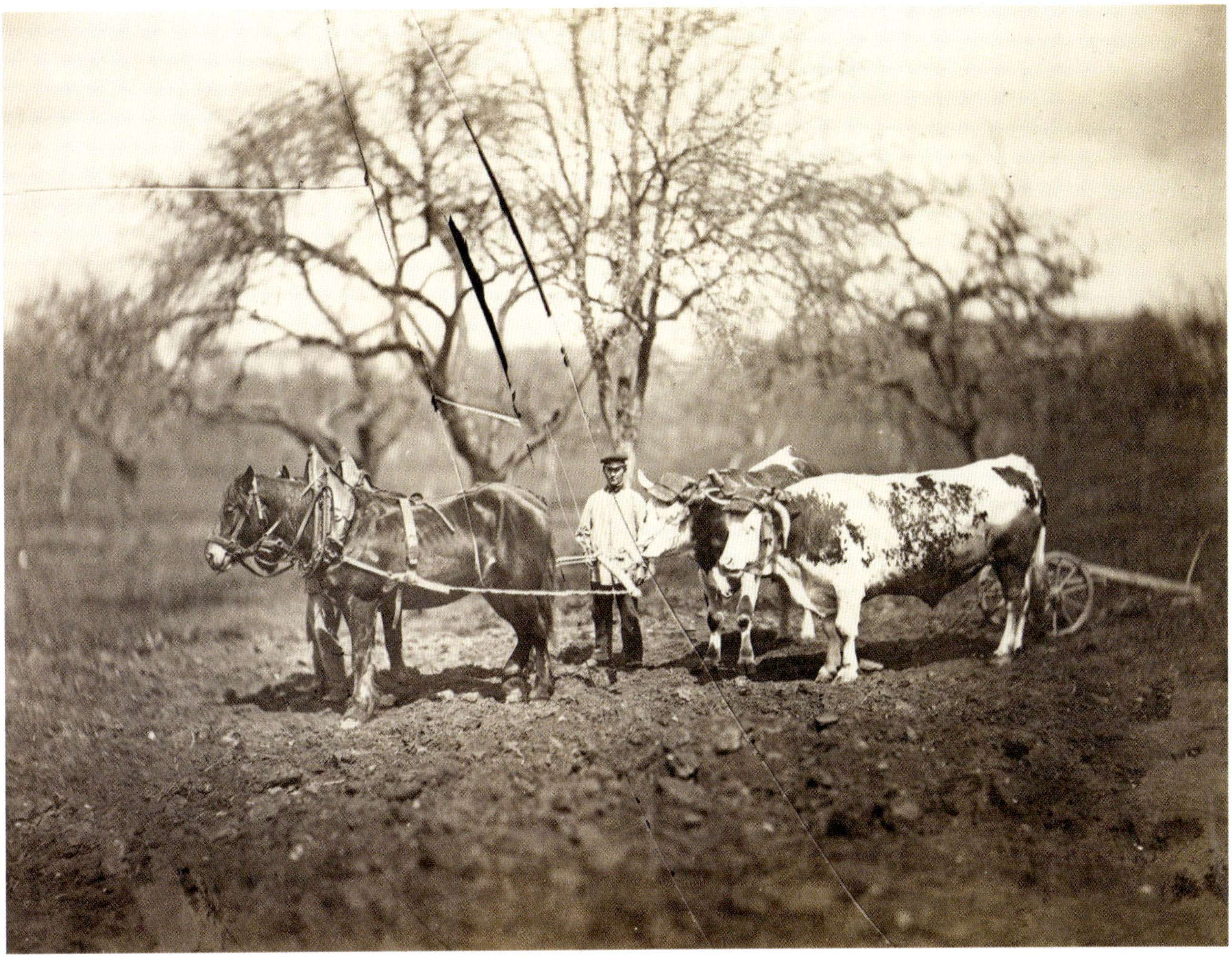

71 Louis Désiré Blanquart-Evrard
Women Making Cider, 1851–53

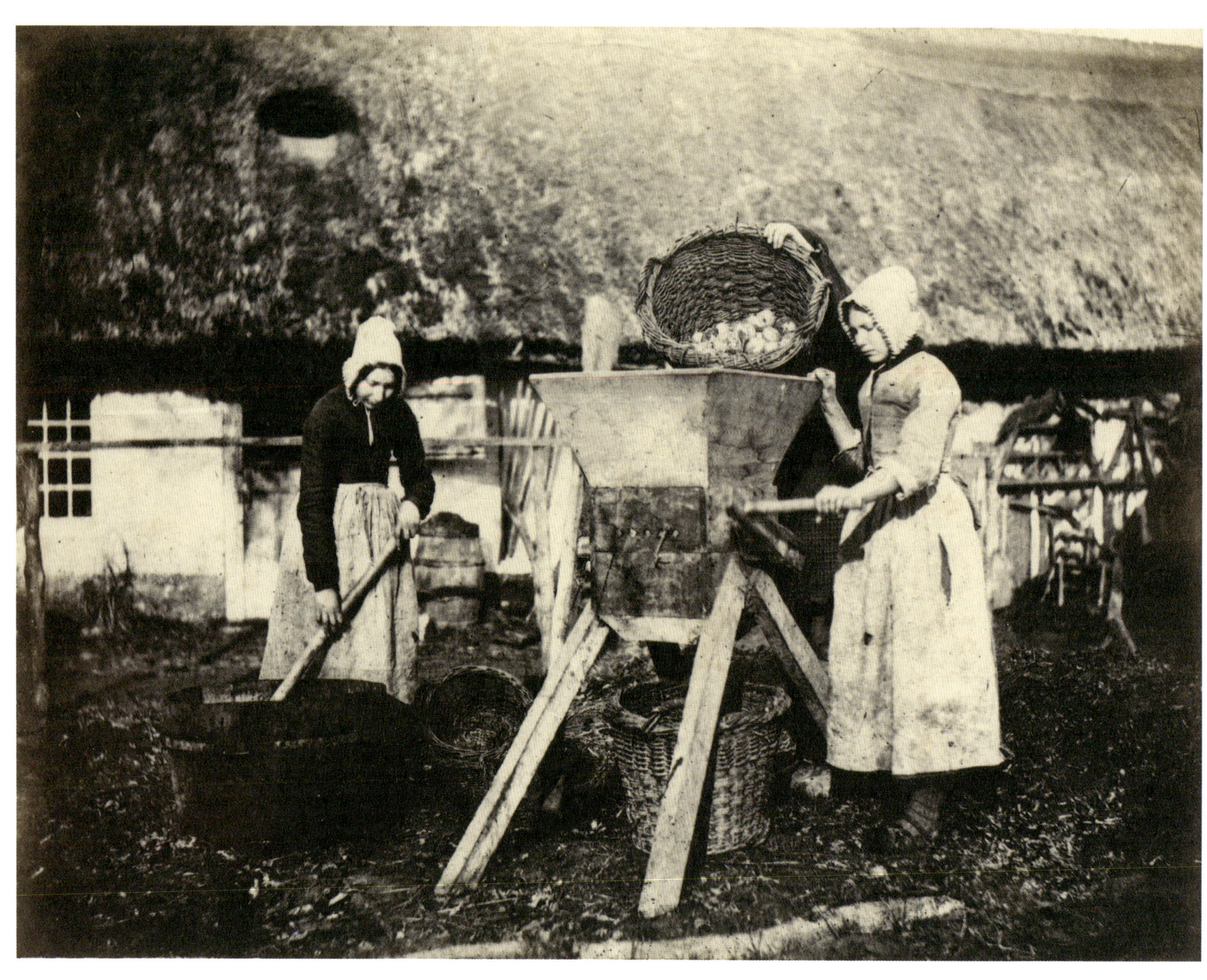

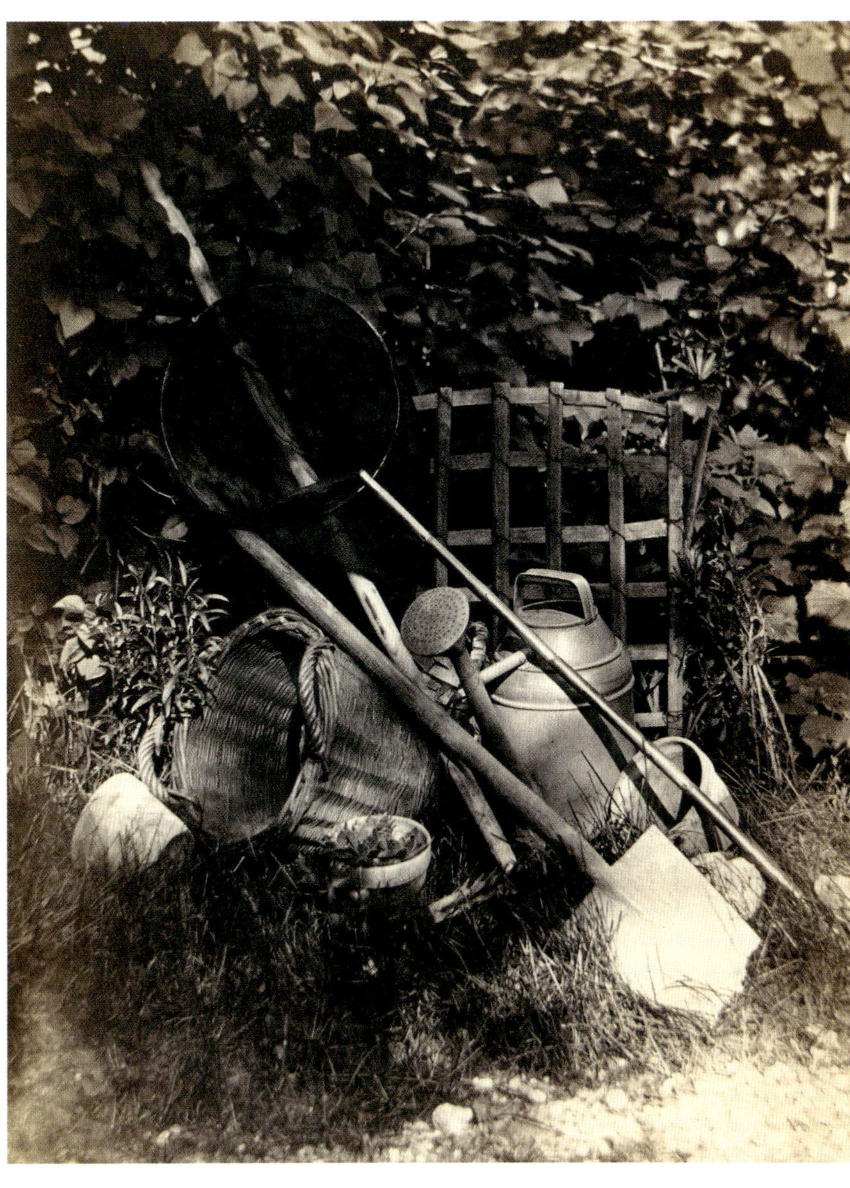

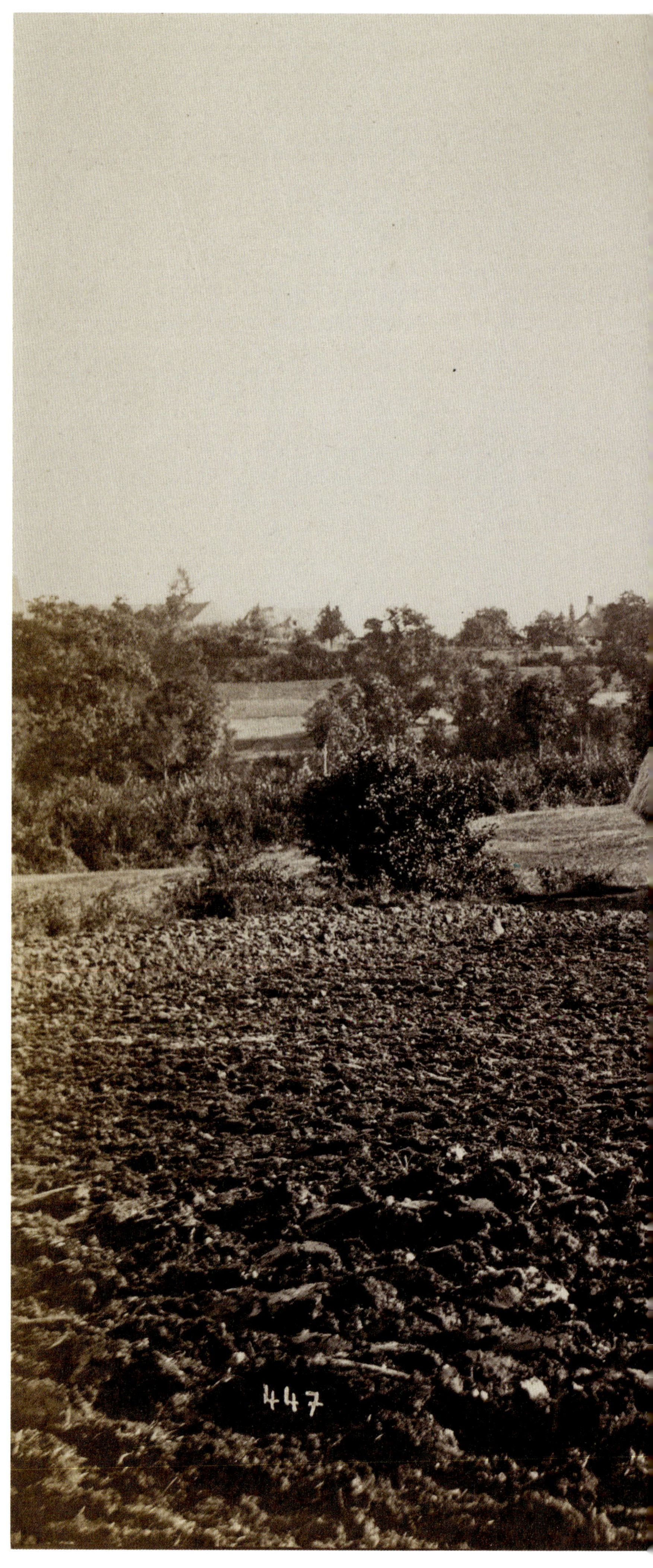

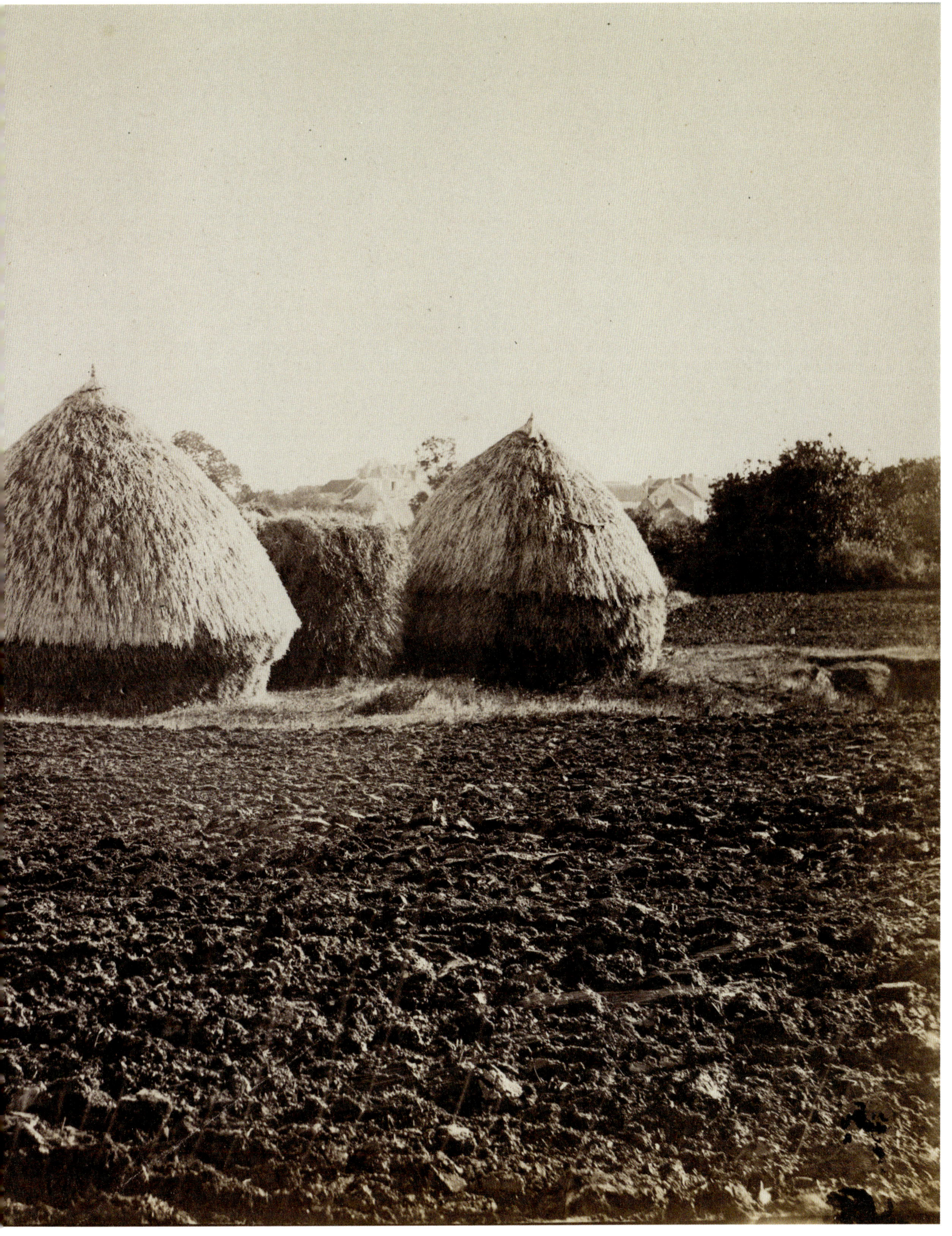

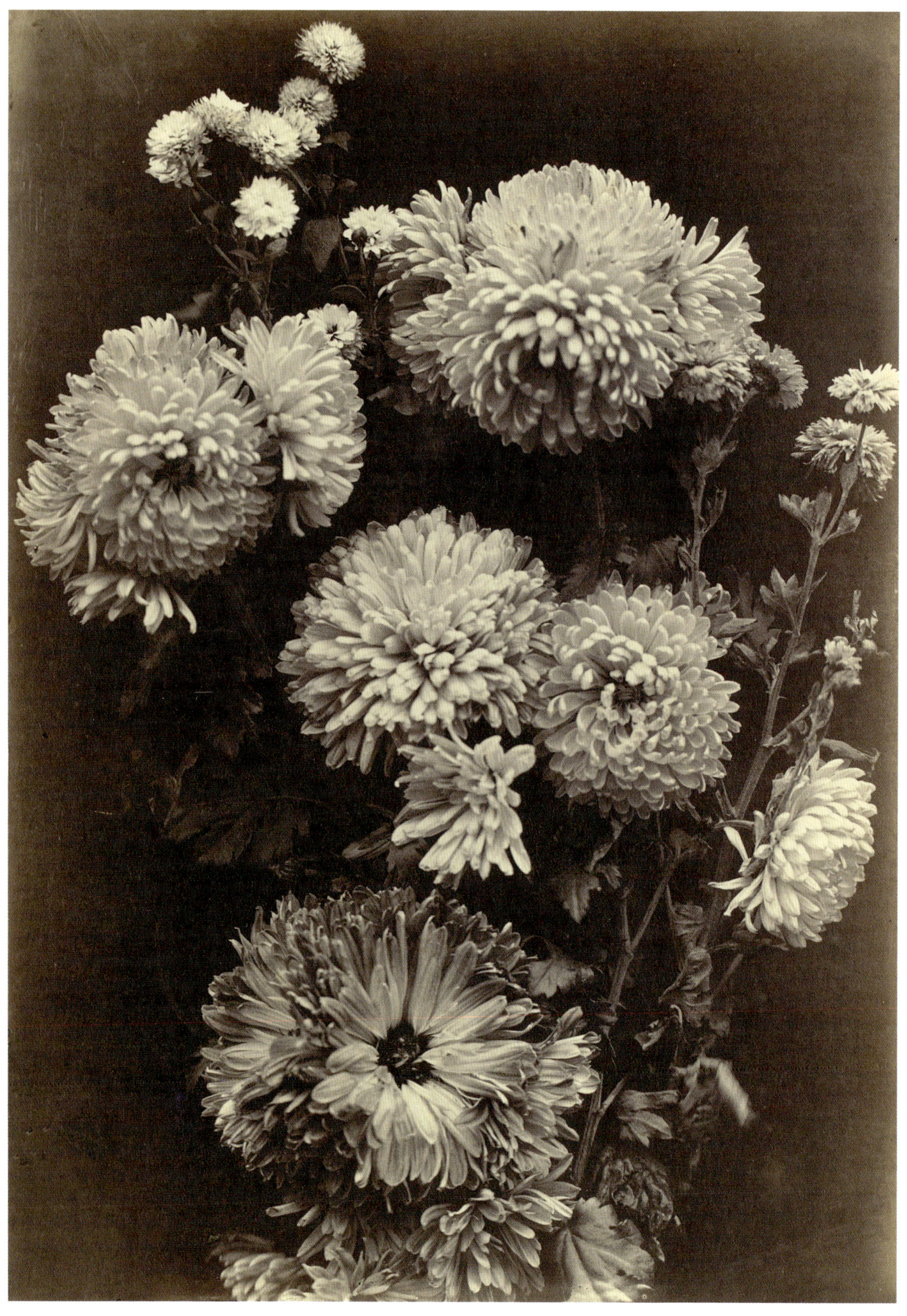

74 Charles Aubry
Garden Asters, ca. 1864

75 Charles Aubry
Still Life, ca. 1864

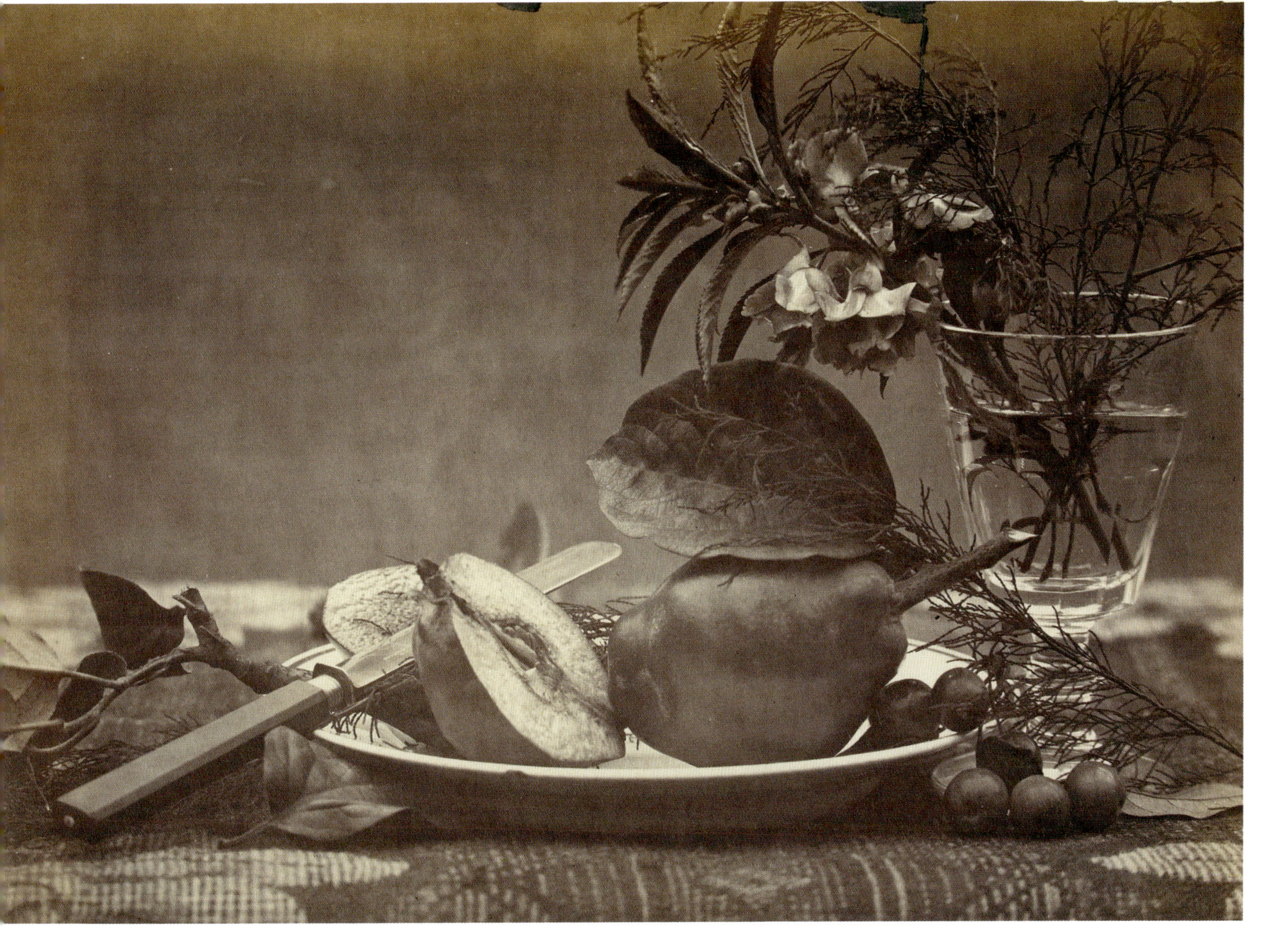

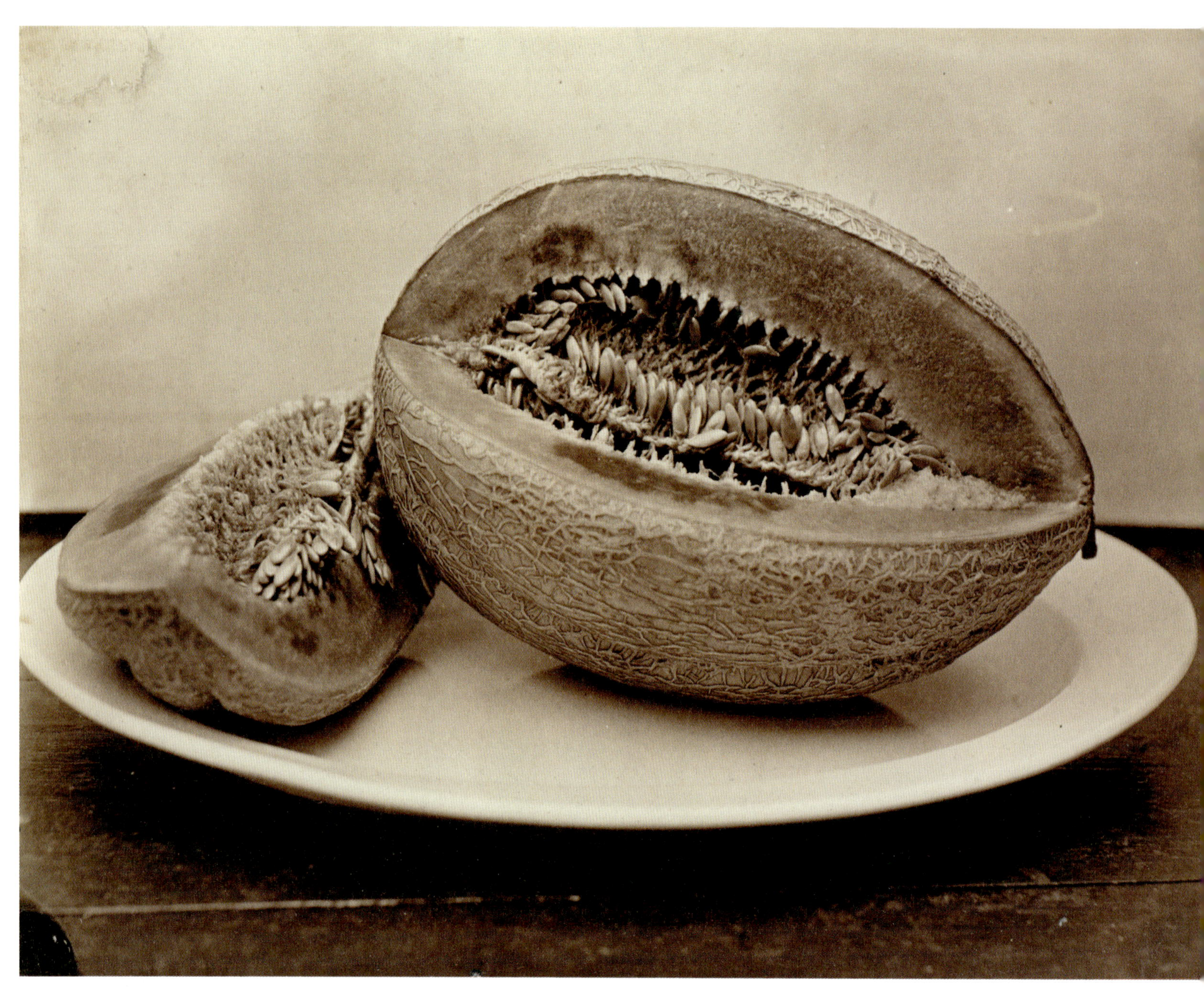

76 August Kotzsch
Cut Melon, ca. 1870

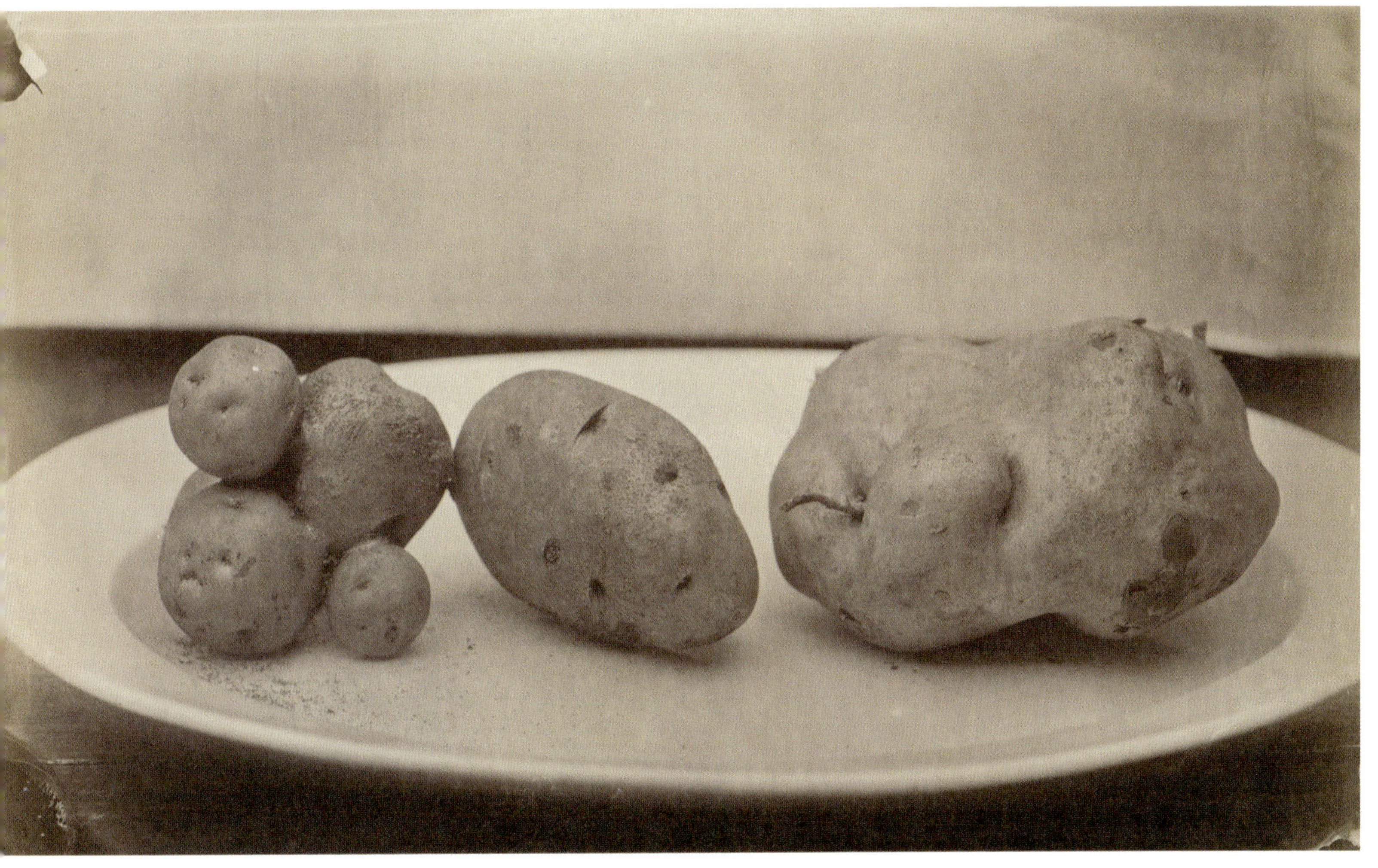

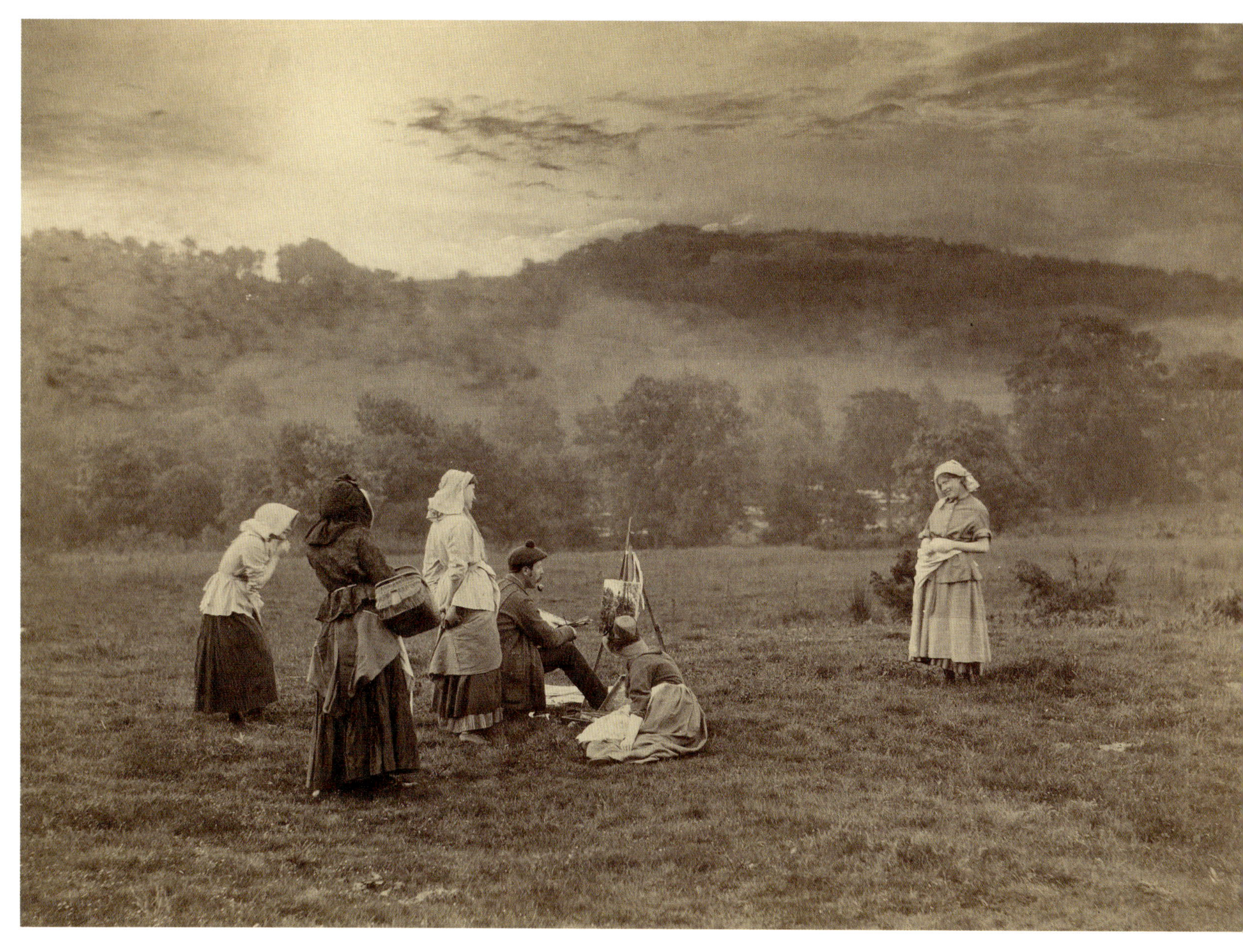

78 Henry Peach Robinson
The Painter, ca. 1890–1901

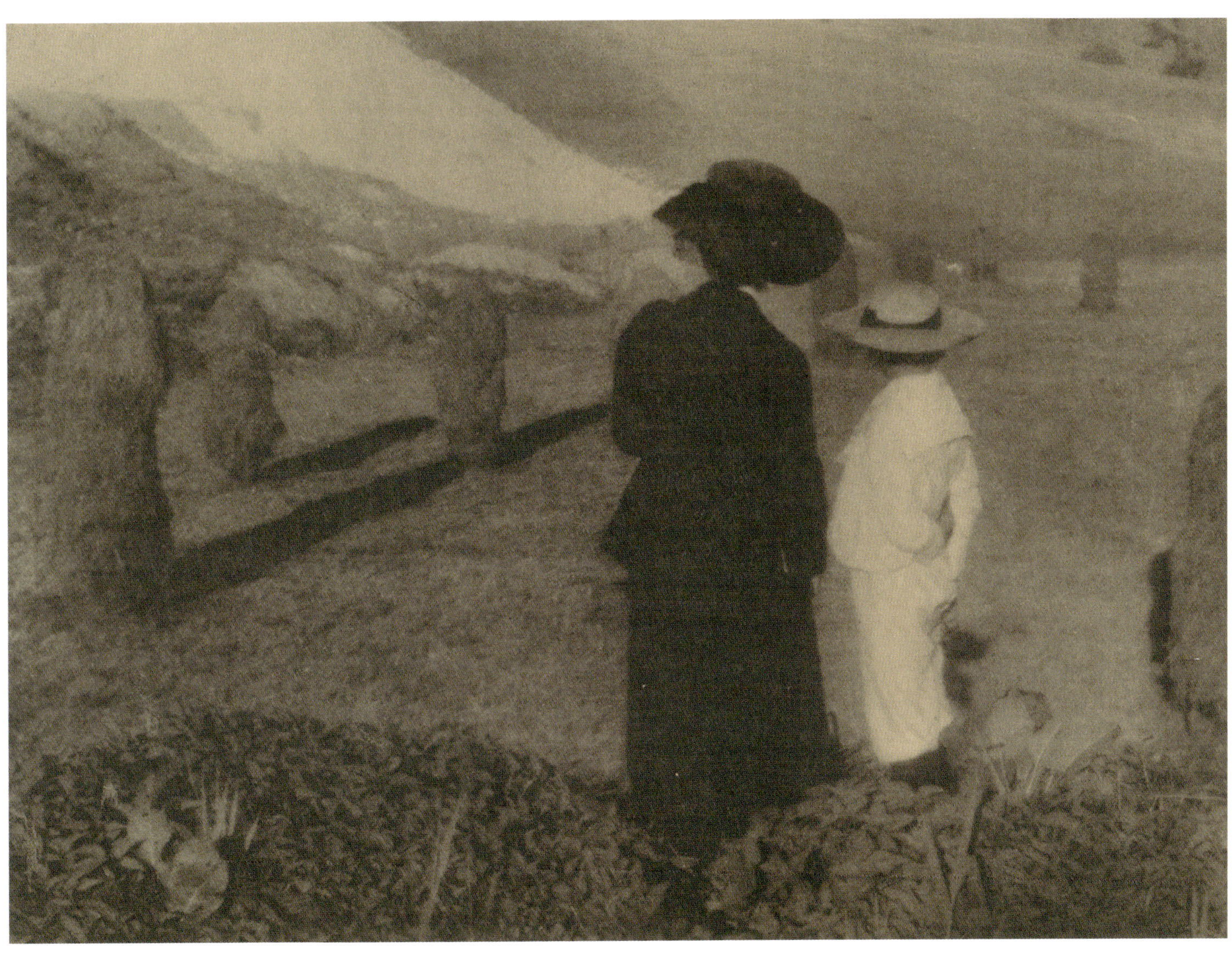

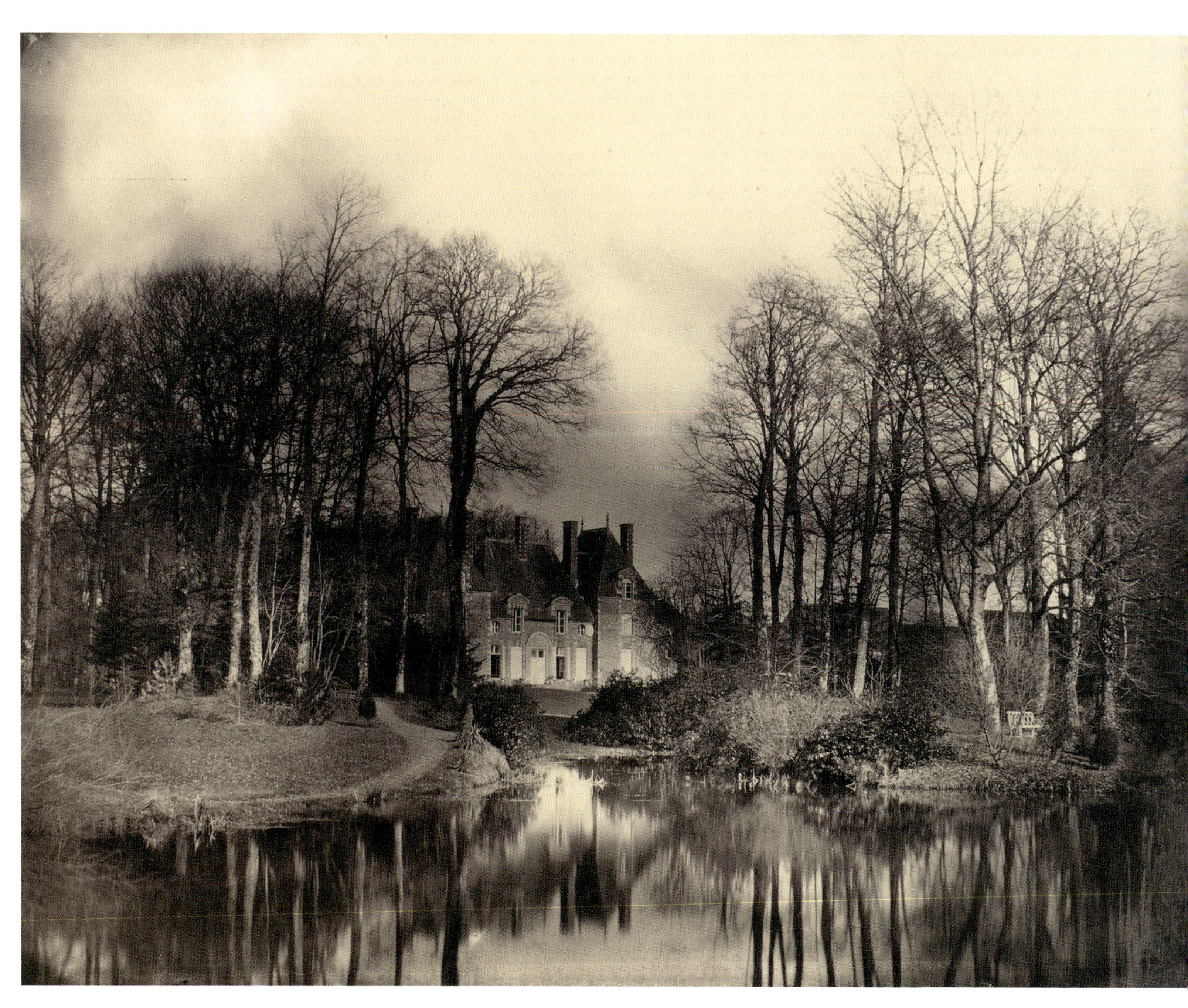

80 Stéphanie Breton
The Castle of Franqueville near Rouen, 1861

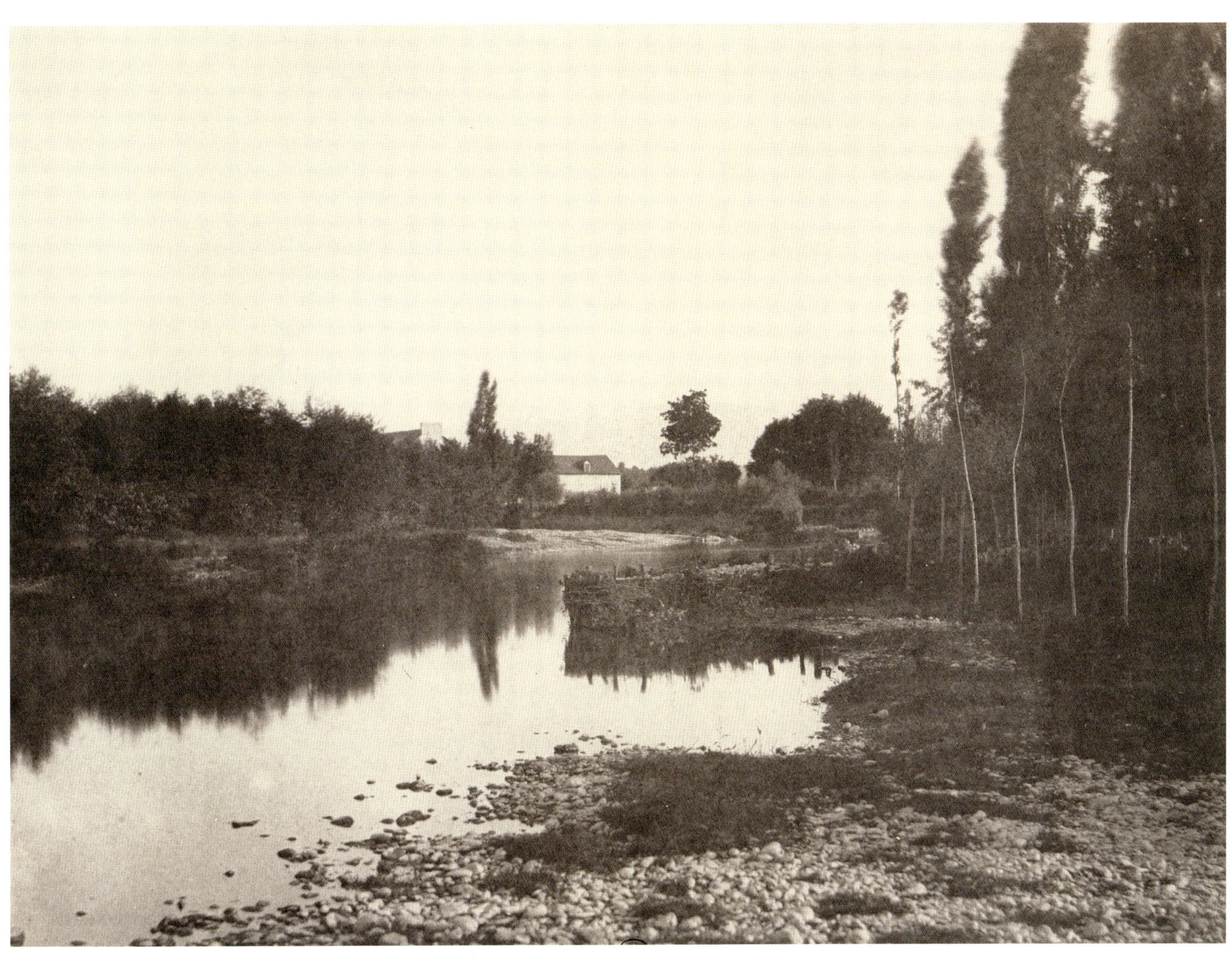

81 Joseph Vigier
*Landscape in Pau with View
of the Pyrénées,* 1853

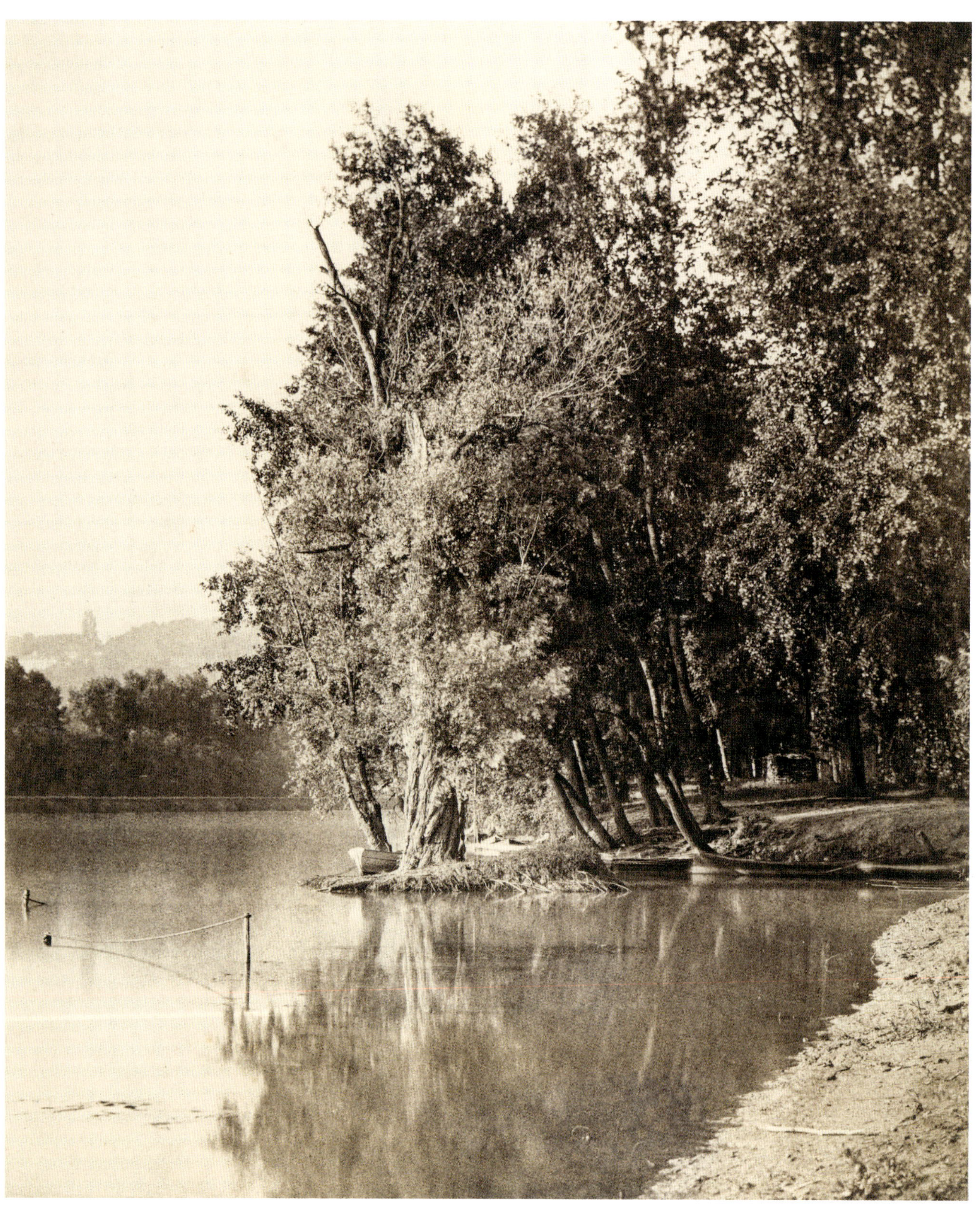

82 André Giroux
La Grenouillère,
Croissy, Bougival, ca. 1853

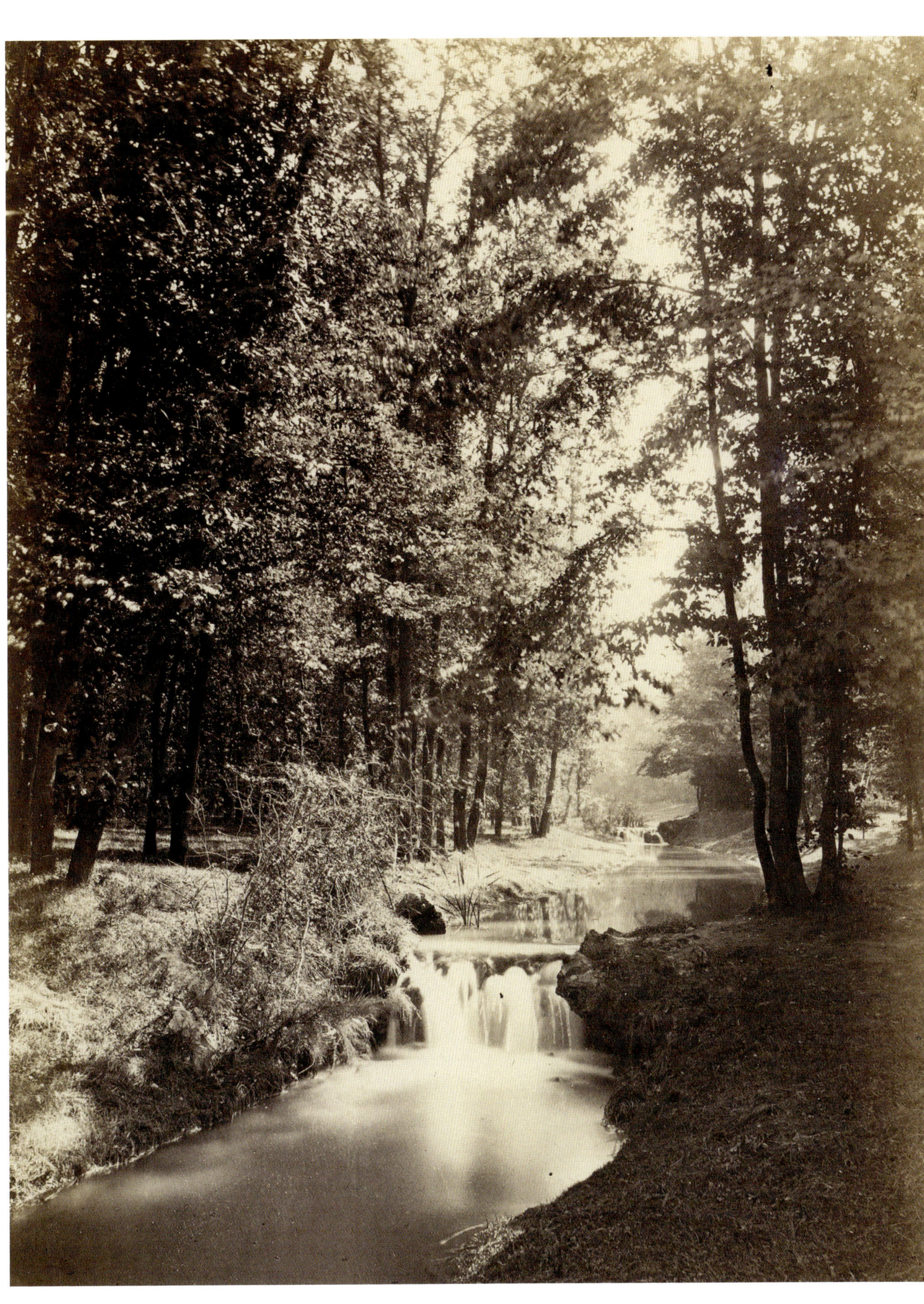

84 Olympe Aguado
*Banks of the Seine, Île des
Ravageurs, Meudon,* 1855

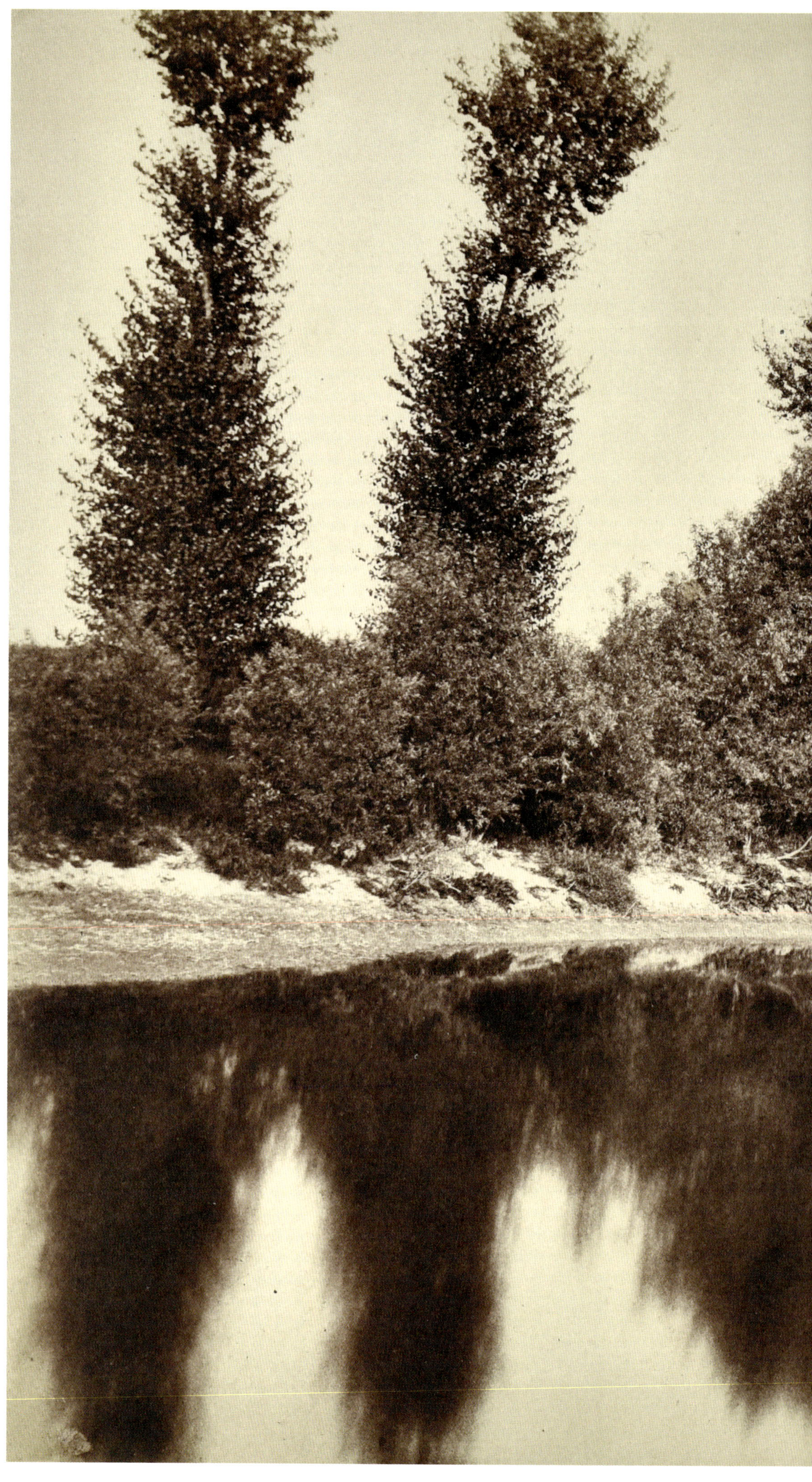

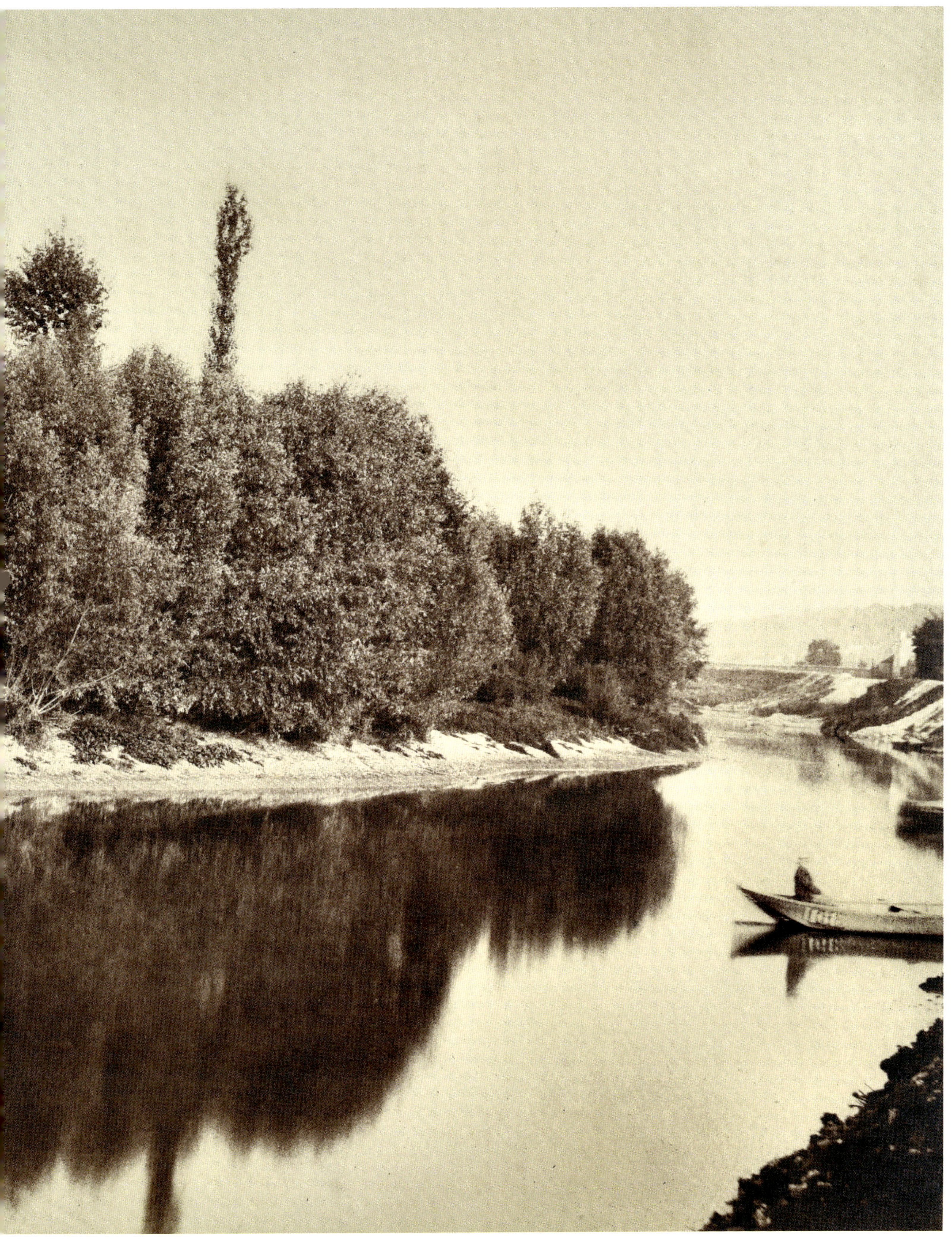

85 Eugène Cuvelier
Franchard, Mare aux Pigeons,
October 19, 1863, 1863

86 Victor Albert Prout
Mousley, ca. 1862

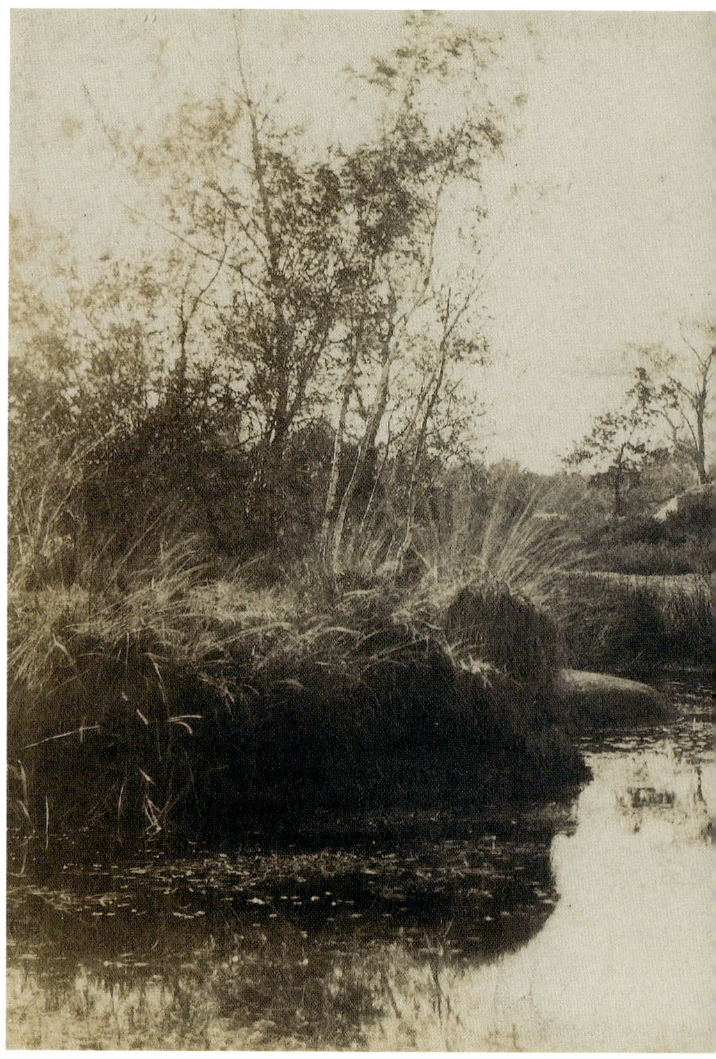

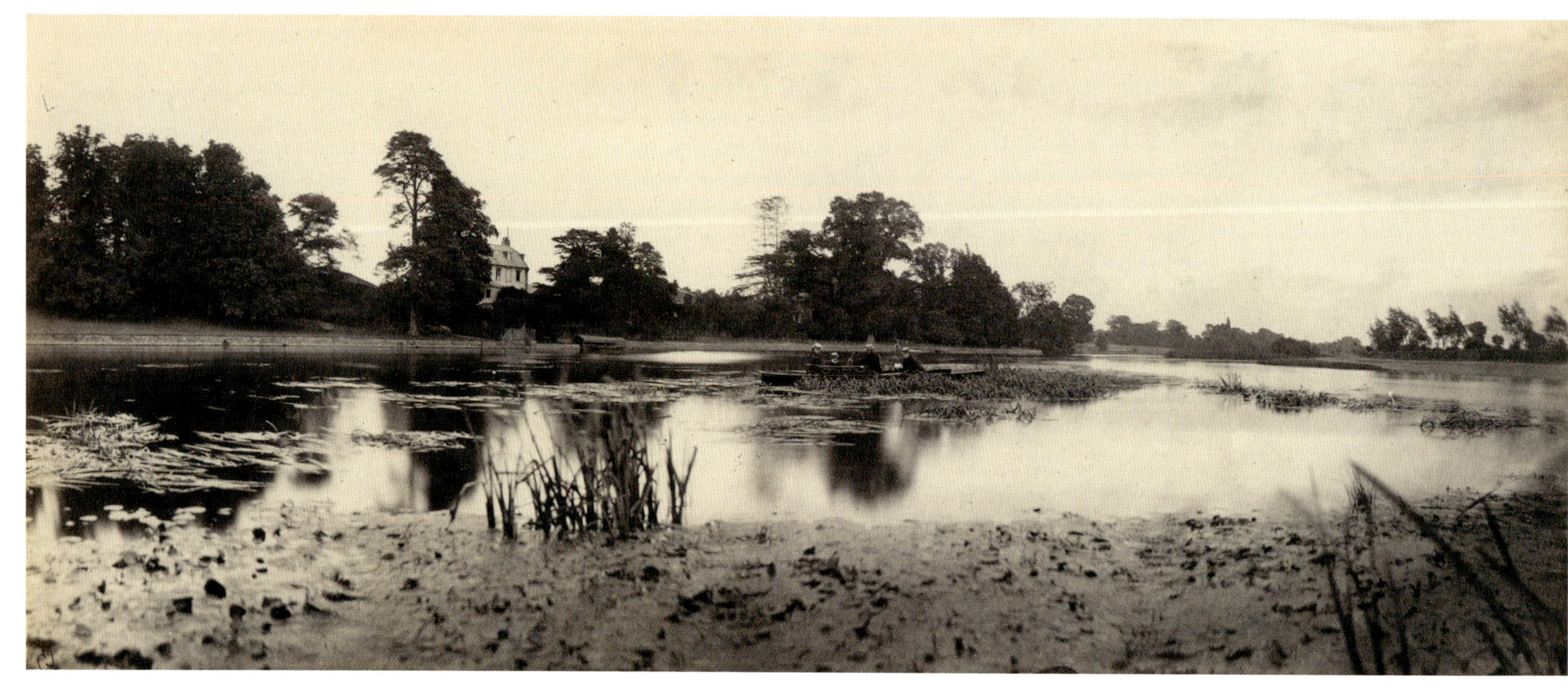

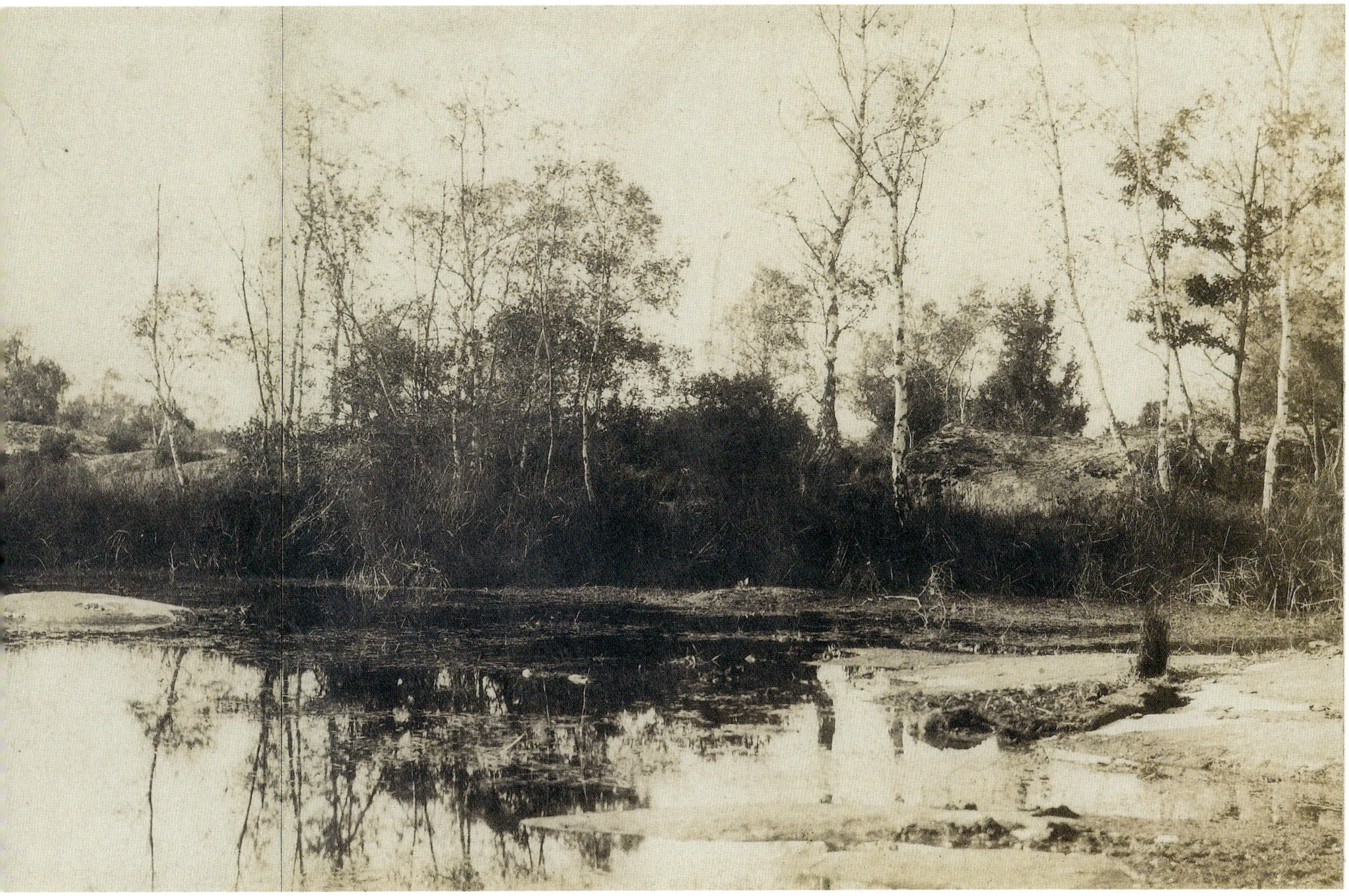

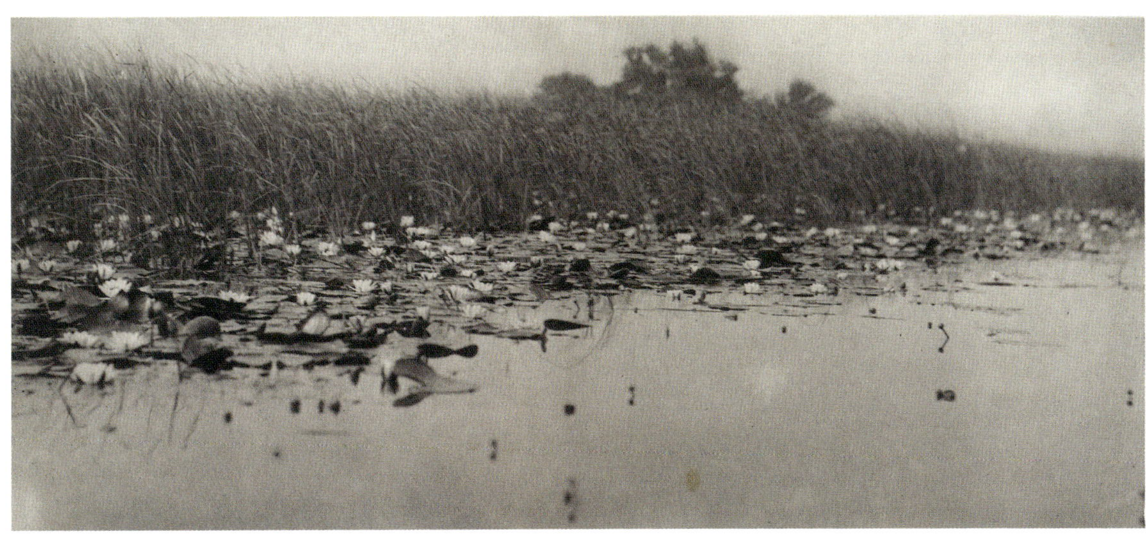

87 Peter Henry Emerson
Water Lilies, 1886

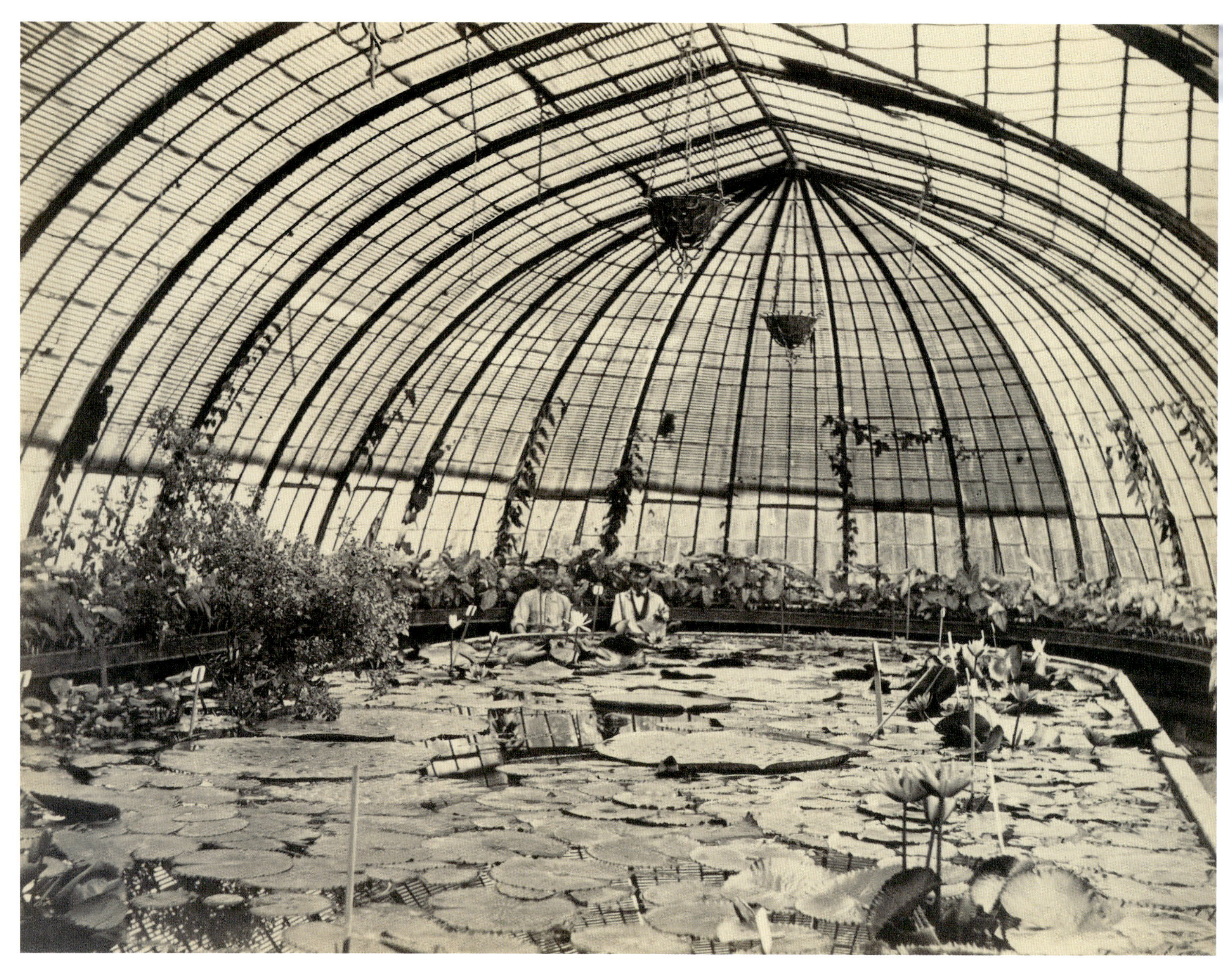

88 Pierre Petit
*Water-Lily Pond at the World's
Fair in Paris,* 1867

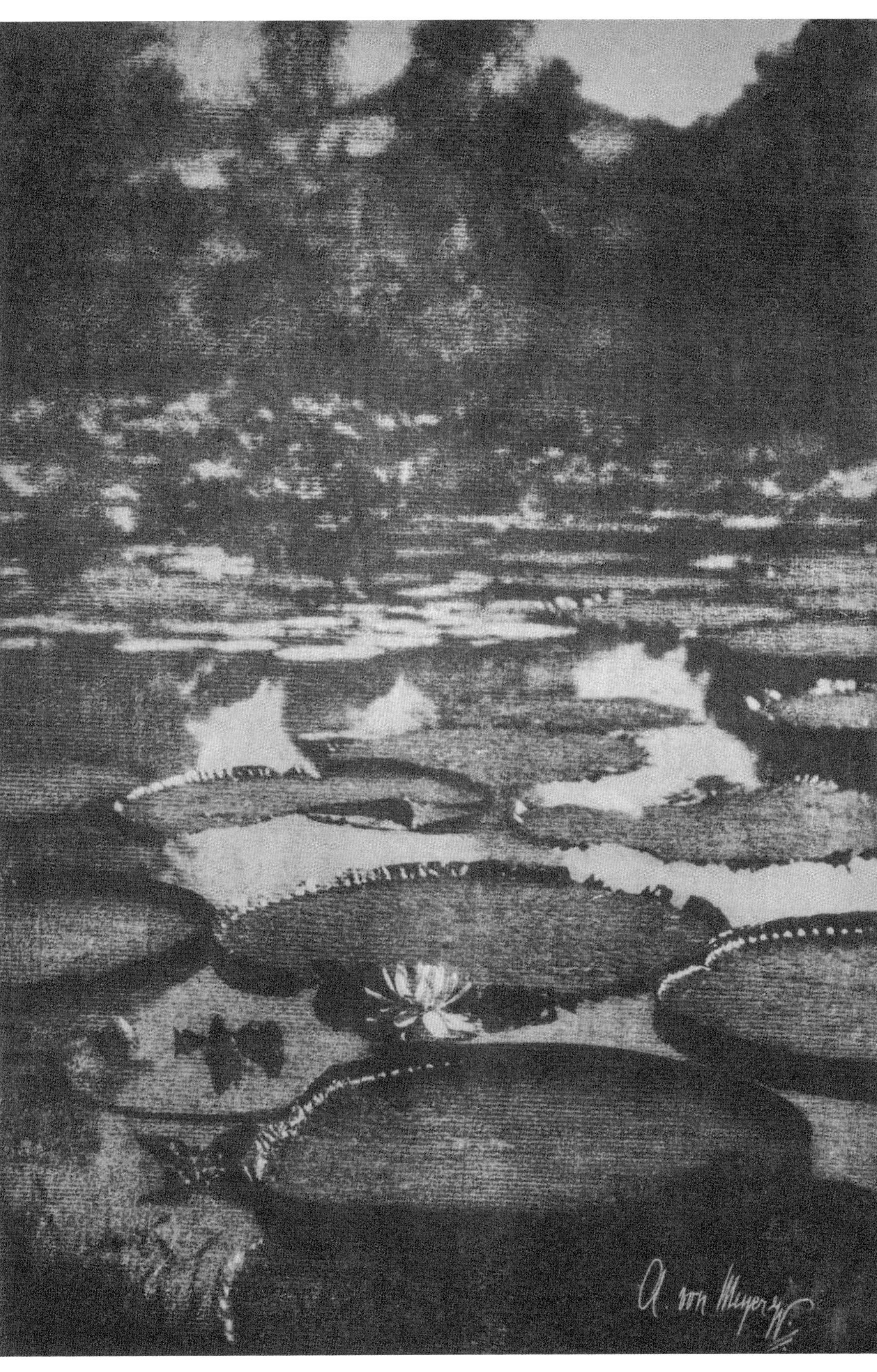

89 Adolphe De Meyer
Victoria regia, ca. 1899,
from the yearbook *Die Kunst in
der Photographie,* 1899

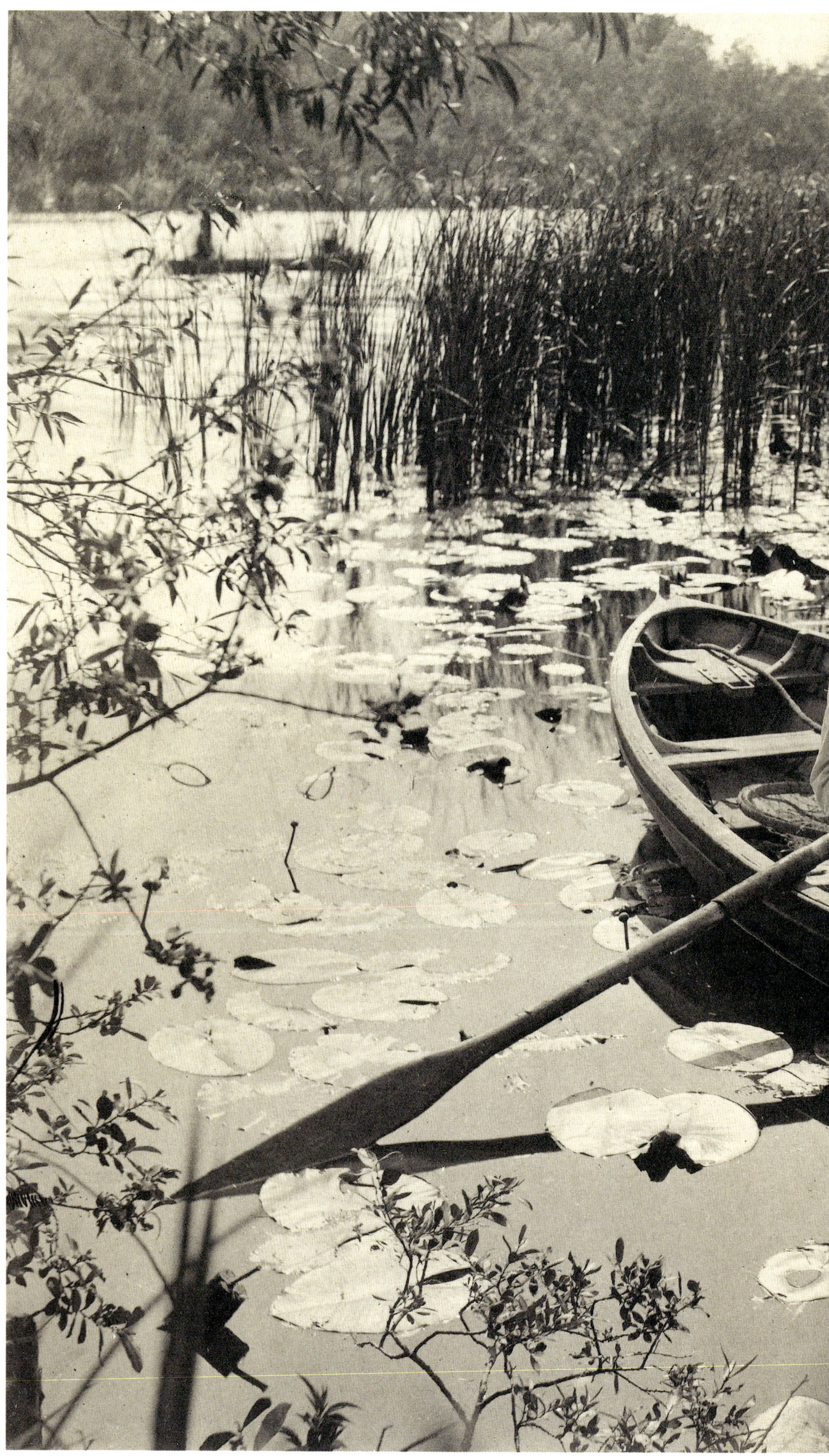

90 Peter Henry Emerson
Gathering Water Lilies, 1886

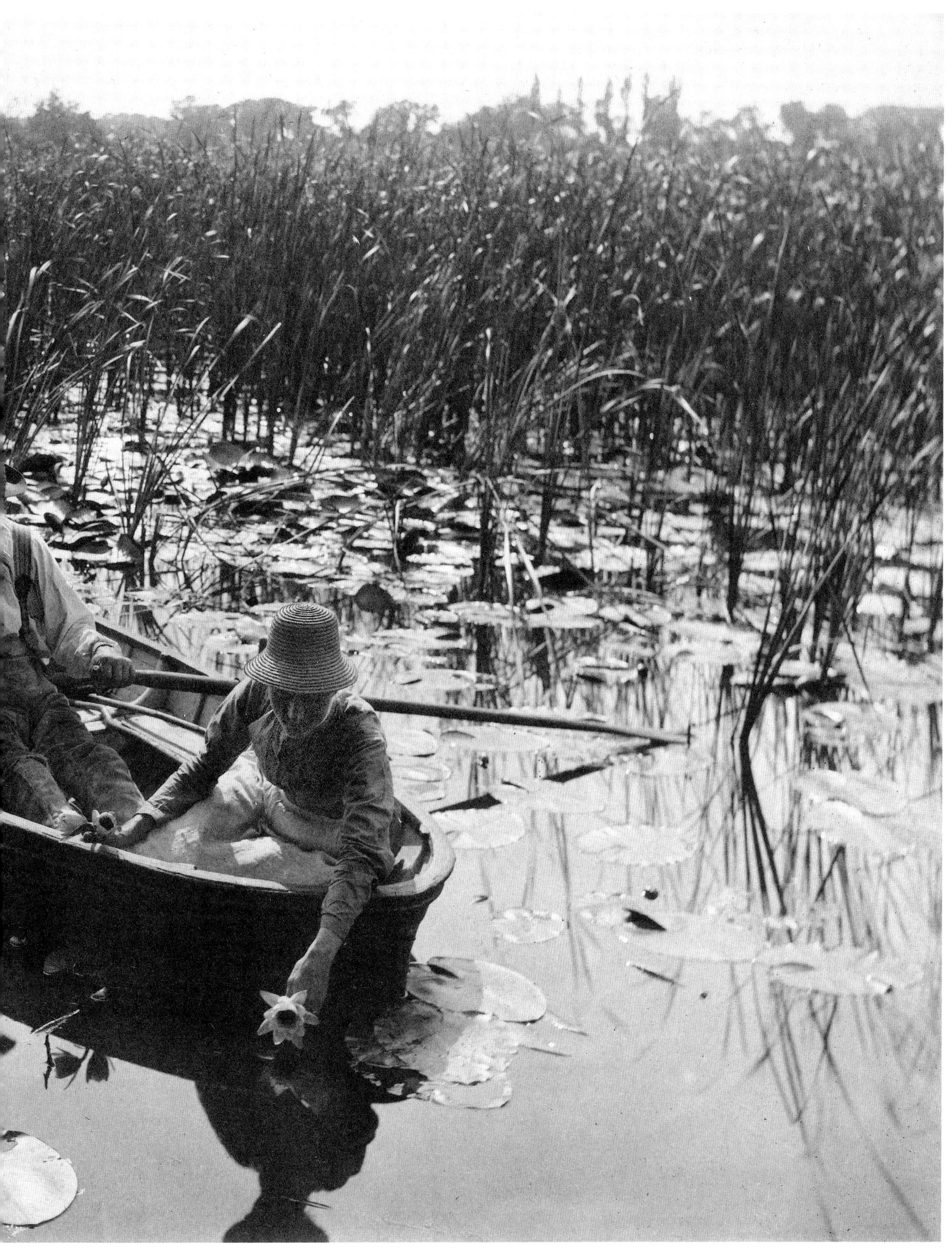

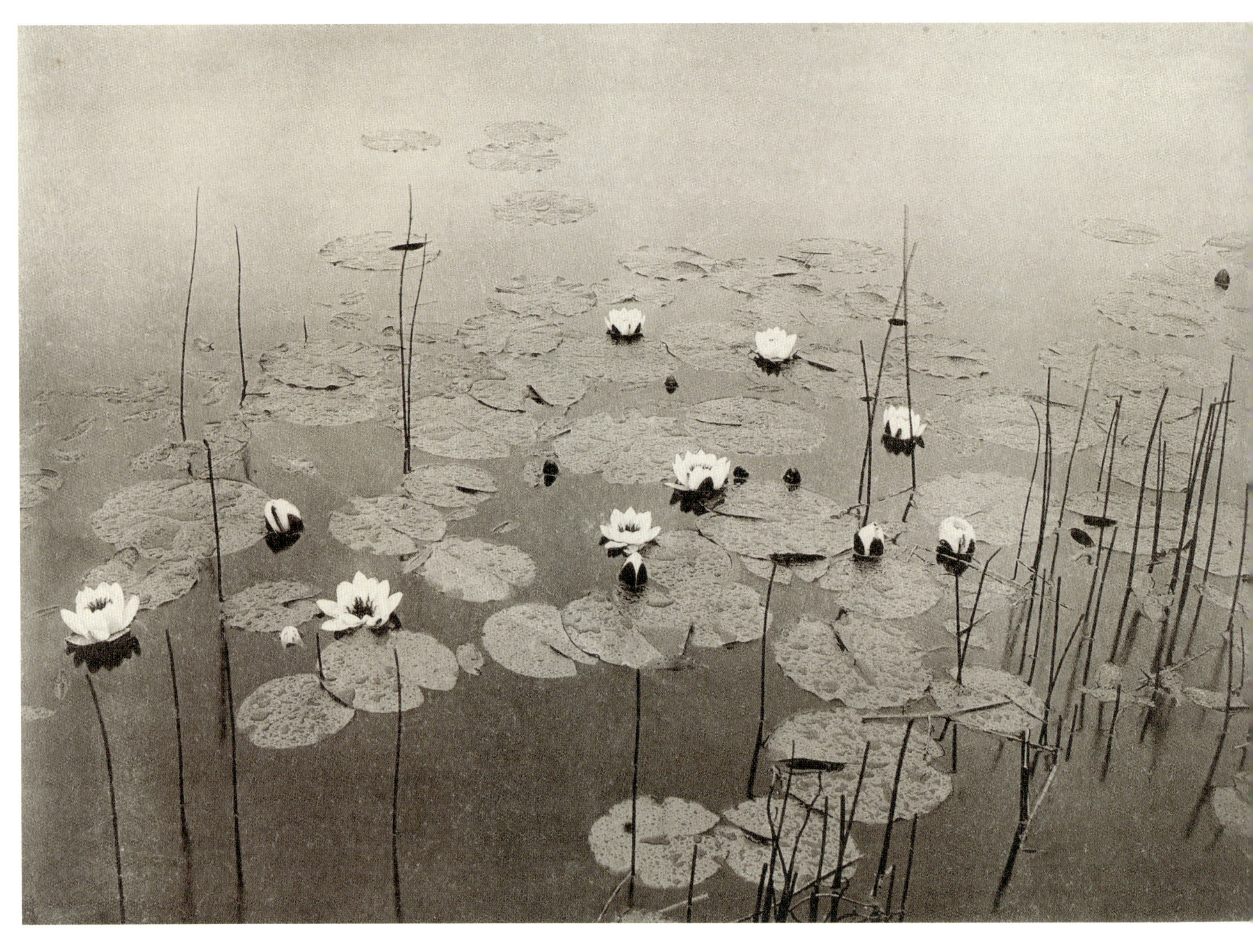

91 Robert Collett
Water Lilies in the Rain, from the
album *Norwegian Motifs,* 1897

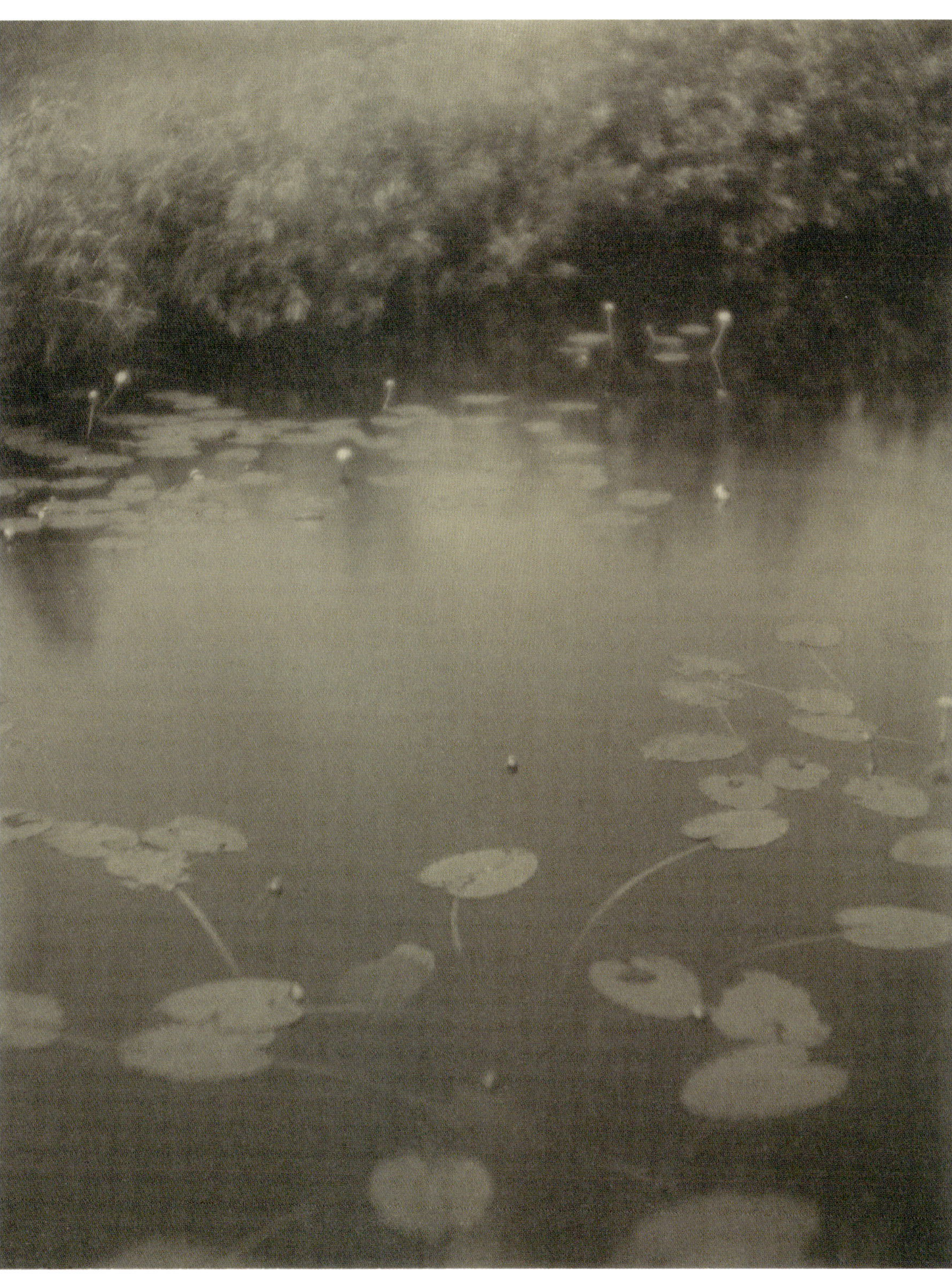

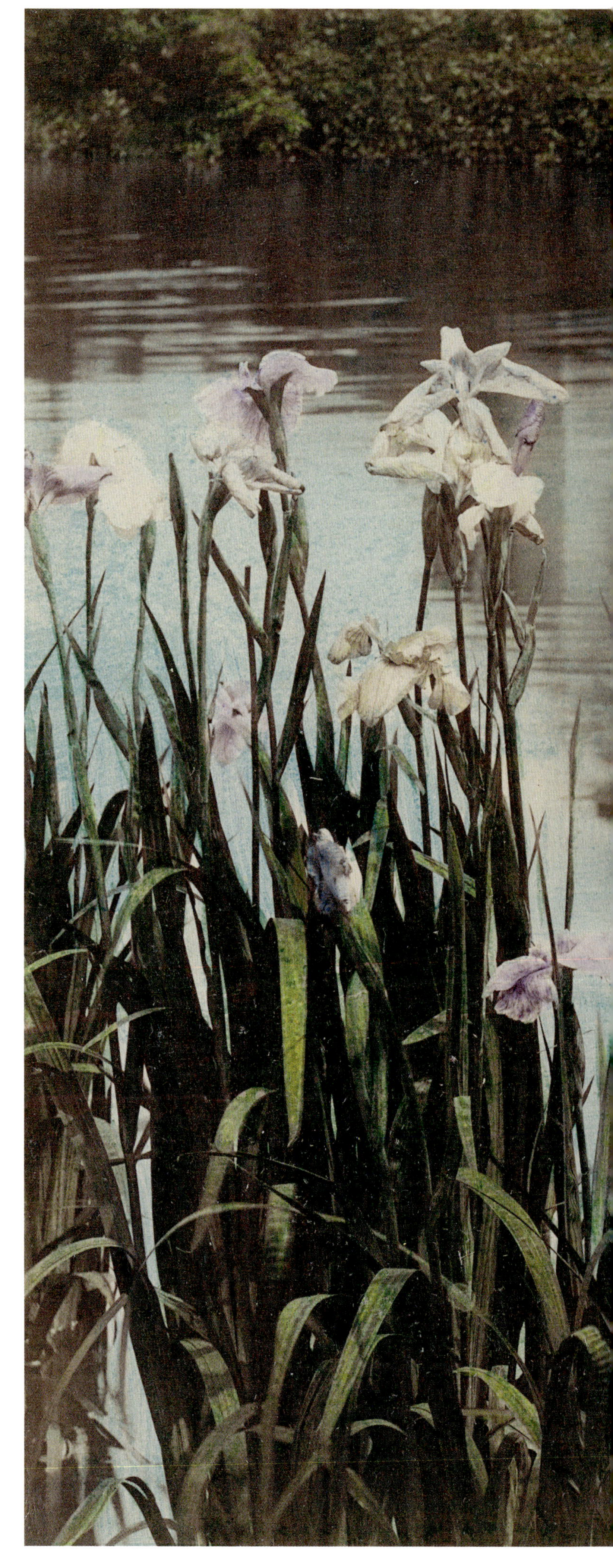

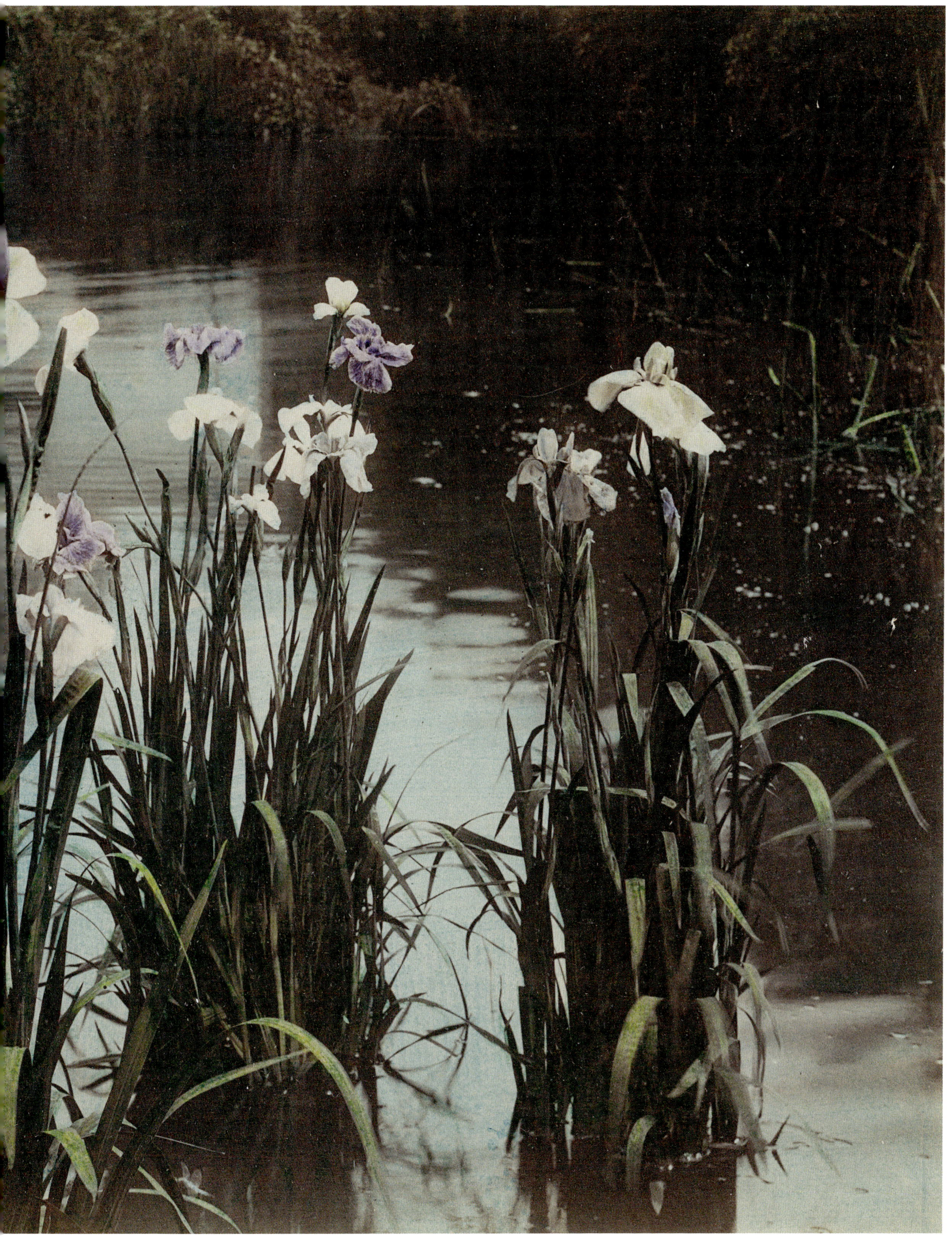

Painterly
Photographs
Pictorialism

Daniel Zamani

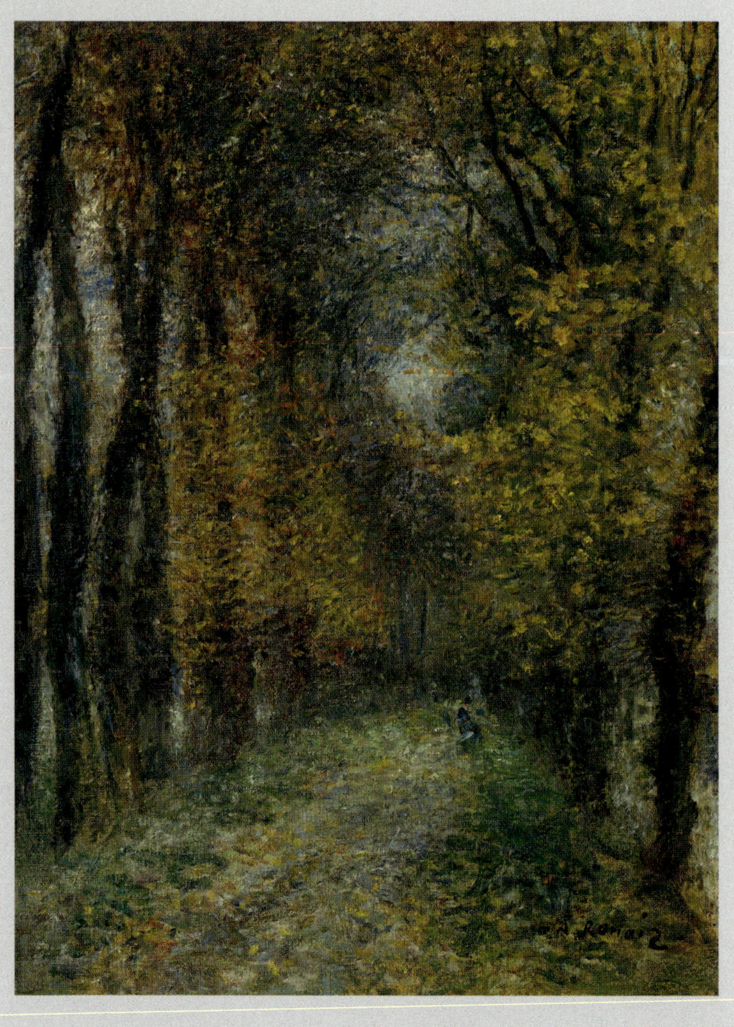

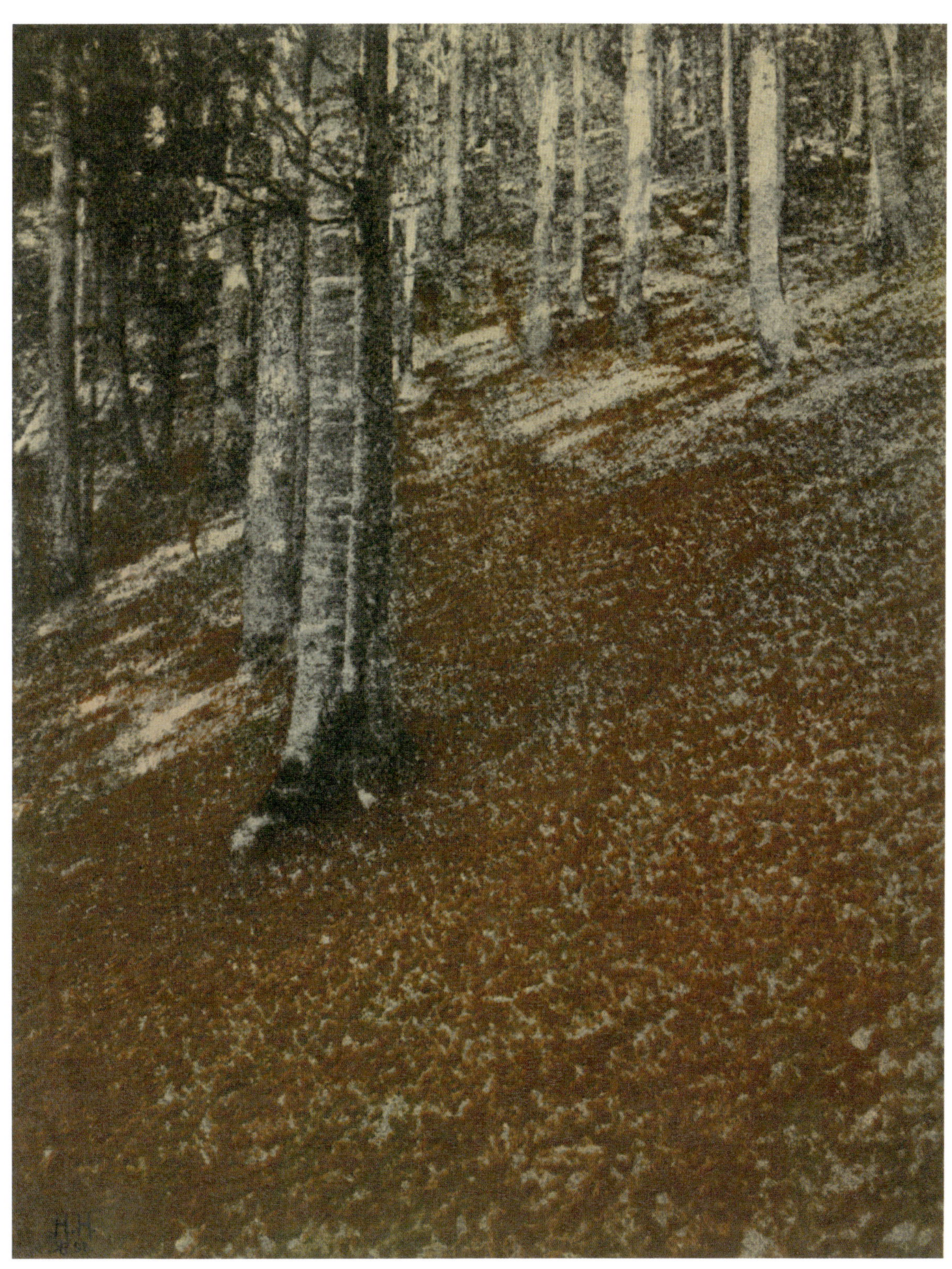

Pierre-Auguste Renoir
Shaded Path, 1872
Oil on canvas
Hasso Plattner Collection

94 Hugo Henneberg
Beech Forest in Autumn, 1898

In the late nineteenth century, the artistic value of photography remained a controversial subject. Many critics adopted a polemical position similar to that of the writer Charles Baudelaire, who had denounced the new medium as the antithesis of art and its "most mortal enemy."[1] While painting as a true art—as the common topos would have it—sought not only to imitate reality but also to convey expression, feeling, and individual temperament, the mechanical nature of photography allegedly made it nothing more than a purely material, lifeless reproduction.

The elevation of photography to a form of aesthetic expression equal to painting was the concern of Pictorialism, an international current of art photography that flourished from the latter decades of the nineteenth century to World War I.[2] The British photographer Henry Peach Robinson played a key role in this movement: in his book *Pictorial Effect in Photography,* published in 1869, Robinson presented photography as an extension of the fine arts and recommended eighteenth- and nineteenth-century paintings in particular as a source of inspiration for photographic compositions. Furthermore, he encouraged the artful placement of figures within landscape photographs—a theatrical component that also manifested itself in his own work (cf. cat. 78). Another important benchmark was Peter Henry Emerson's 1889 handbook *Naturalistic Photography for Students of the Art,* which addressed questions of light dispersion and the sharpness of contours. According to Emerson, photographs were of equal value with painting, and his work, like that of many of his contemporaries, drew particular inspiration from the model of Impressionism (cf. cat. 90).

Many Pictorialists were passionate amateur photographers who worked together to strategically develop an apparatus of institutional structures comparable to those of painting. In addition to the practice of photography itself, they achieved prominence through exhibitions, critical reviews, and art theoretical publications—or by intentionally seeking opportunities to show their works on equal footing alongside examples of contemporary painting. A number of new photography societies emerged in Europe and the United States, often formed by breaking away from previously established organizations; as the artistic avant-garde, they sought to distance themselves from the latter's concentration on technical and commercial questions. Such associations included the Photo-Club de Paris (founded in 1888), the Brotherhood of the Linked Ring in London (founded in 1892), the Vienna Camera-Club (founded in 1887), and the Photo-Secession in New York, founded in 1902 by Alfred Stieglitz, Frank Eugene, and Edward Steichen.

The Kodak camera, marketed from 1888 on under the fitting slogan "You press the button we do the rest," made photography affordable and accessible almost overnight to the broad mass of consumers. The Pictorialists distanced themselves from the new phenomenon of mass photography in a variety of ways. For their works, they preferred technically demanding fine-art printing processes, and often manipulated their prints in elaborate ways. For many art photographers, the negative was not the result, but only the starting point of the artistic process, and the modification of the print served to guarantee the artistic value of the photograph as a unique, non-reproducible entity. The often large formats, handmade materials, and expensive supports were likewise intended to elevate the new medium and many Pictorialists also preferred artfully fashioned frames for the presentation of their works.

In addition to technically ambitious and time-consuming processes of production, the approach to lighting and the handling of contours also played a role. Many art photographers attributed special significance to the "artistic blurring" propounded by Emerson—an effect that bears witness to the influence of the Impressionist aesthetic. While documentary photography was associated with clear contours and sharp detail, the Pictorialists preferred diffused light and a blurred rendering of forms. Accordingly, they chose motifs well-suited to such visual effects: bodies of water veiled in mist or fog, billowing clouds of steam, or colored shadows on snow-covered forest floors—subjects closely associated with the plein-air painting of the Impressionists (cats. 97–99, 122, 123) Photographic still lifes frequently included arrangements of glass objects, which refracted the light and produced a complex play of reflections as well as finely nuanced chiaroscuro effects (cats. 124–26).

One of the most influential spokesmen of Pictorialism was the French photographer Constant Puyo.[3] He contributed regularly to the journal of the Photo-Club de Paris, and in 1896 he published the book *Notes sur la photographie artistique,* devoted to the recognition of photography as an autonomous art form. For many of his photographs, Puyo used special soft-focus lenses to achieve a blurred, "impressionistic" effect. In his work *Two Women in a Field* (cat. 67), a group of trees in the shadows to the right serves as a repoussoir, while the strolling figures of two elegantly dressed women animate the landscape. With its formal integration of human figures into nature, the photograph recalls Monet's paintings of fields and meadows from Argenteuil and Giverny (cf. ill., p. 146). The diffused lighting lends the composition a dreamy mood that shows certain affinities to the pictorial inventions of Symbolism. Puyo's works were published by Alfred Stieglitz in the American photography magazine *Camera Work,* and in 1906 selected photographs were exhibited in Stieglitz's gallery 291 in New York, which he had founded the previous year together with Edward Steichen.

The gum bichromate process often used in Pictorialism lent the works a decidedly "painterly" effect, sheerly by virtue of their coloration. While the autochrome process involved the mechanical reproduction of natural colors, the tinting of gum bichromate prints was determined by the choice of pigments, which were added to an emulsion of gum arabic and chromate salts and hardened in the areas exposed to light. Heinrich Kühn, one of the most prominent members of the Vienna Camera-Club, often created extensive series of works based on a single motif in which he experimentally varied the tints. Viewed as an ensemble, the photographs evoke the impression of landscapes captured under differing conditions of light and weather, thus recalling the painted series of Claude Monet (cats. 111, 112, 116–19).[4] Like his fellow photographers Hugo Henneberg and Hans Watzek, Kühn often worked with gum bichromate in multiple layers, making possible the interplay of a wide range of tonal values (cf. cats. 94, 103, 110, 126). Although the free handling of color had long been considered the privilege of painters, the Pictorialists likewise sought to employ this expressive means in the service of the aesthetic goals of art photography.

Translated from German by Melissa M. Thorson

[1] For Baudelaire's attack on photography, see Raser 2015.

[2] The word *pictorial* carries the connotation of "picturesque," "painterly," or "resembling a painting." On Pictorialism, see Rennes 2005, Berlin 2008, Vancouver 2008, Constance 2011, and Chalon-sur-Saône 2018.

[3] On Puyo, see Brest 2008.

[4] On Kühn, see Vienna 2010.

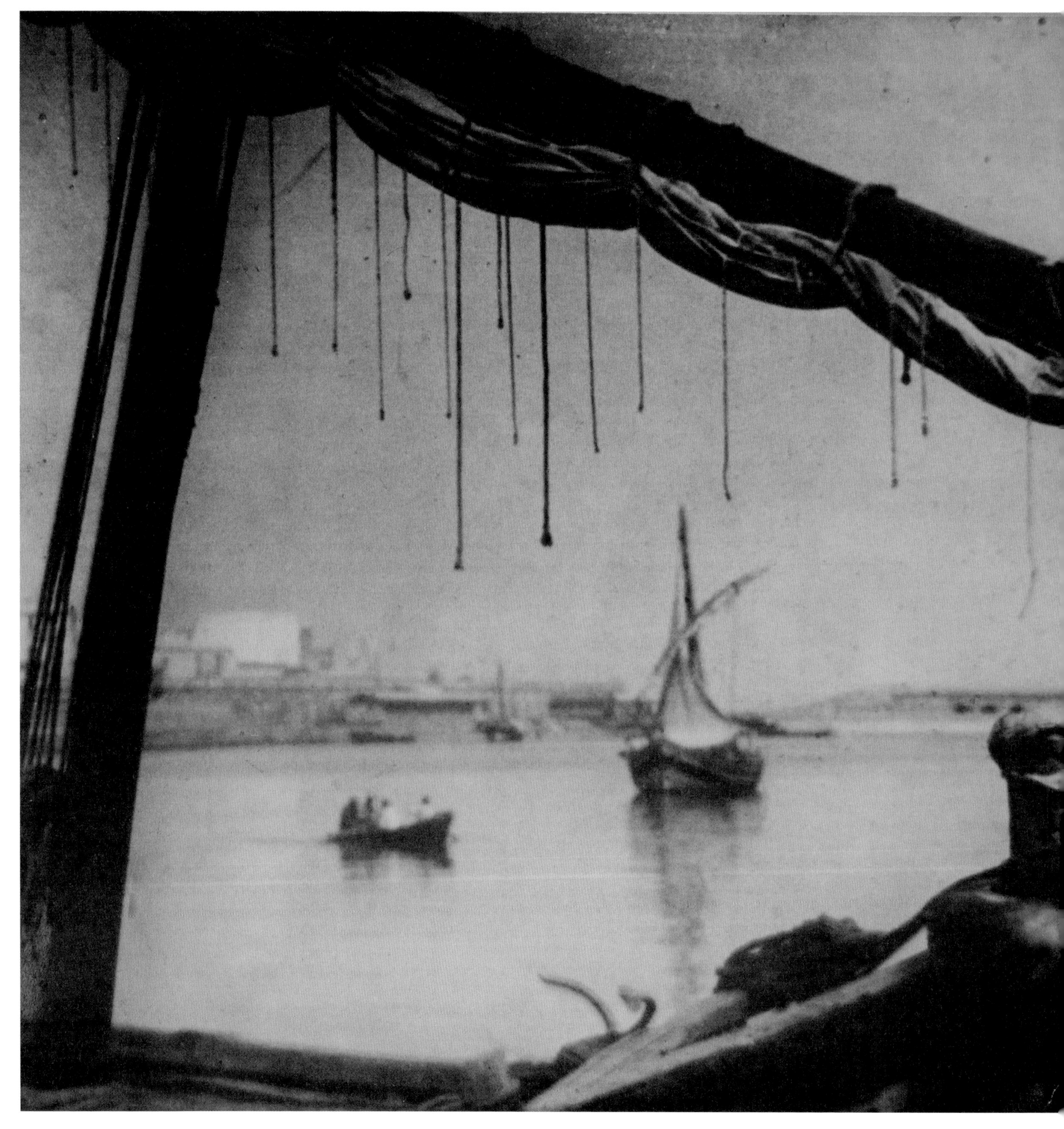

95 Alvin Langdon Coburn
Cadiz Harbor, 1906

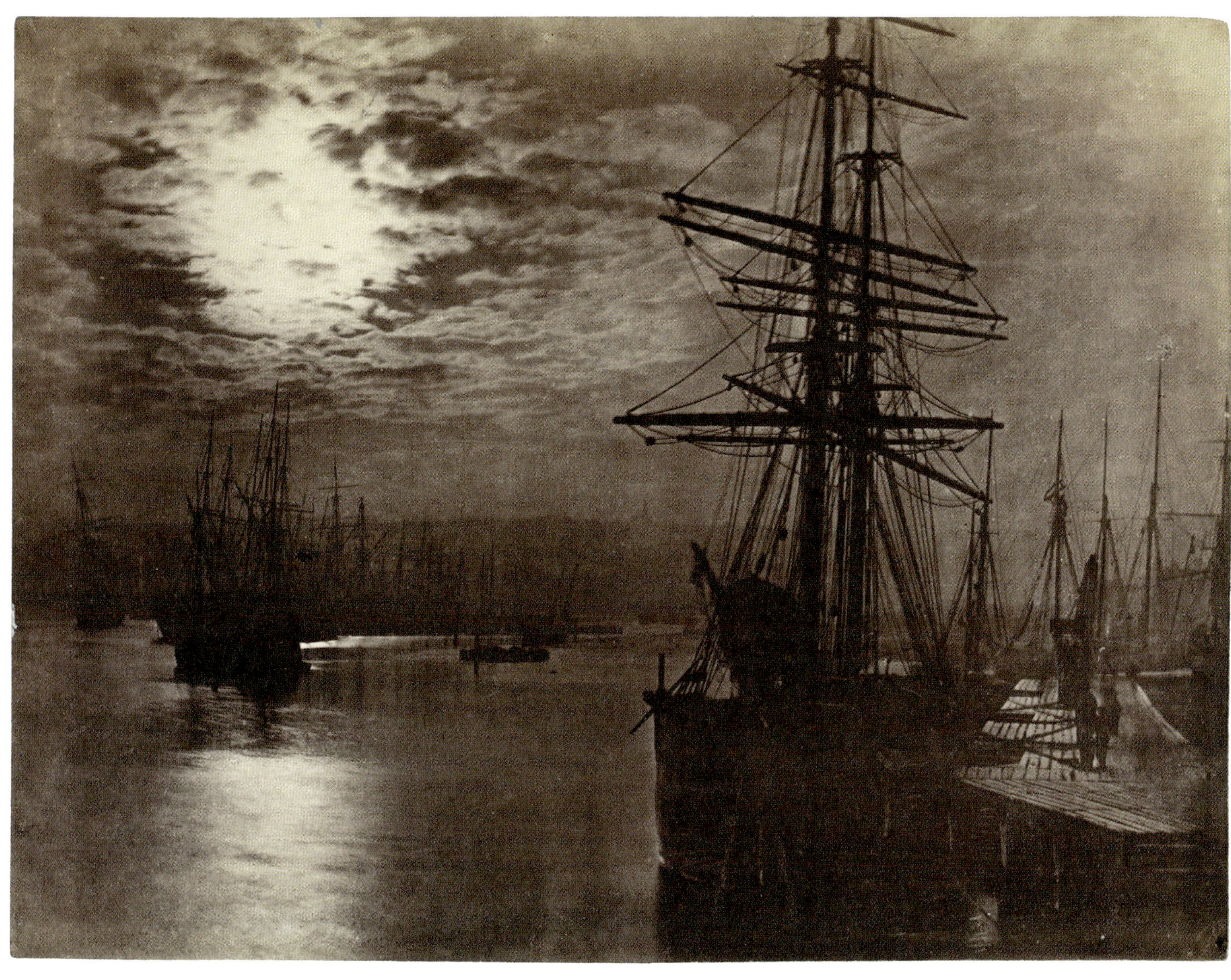

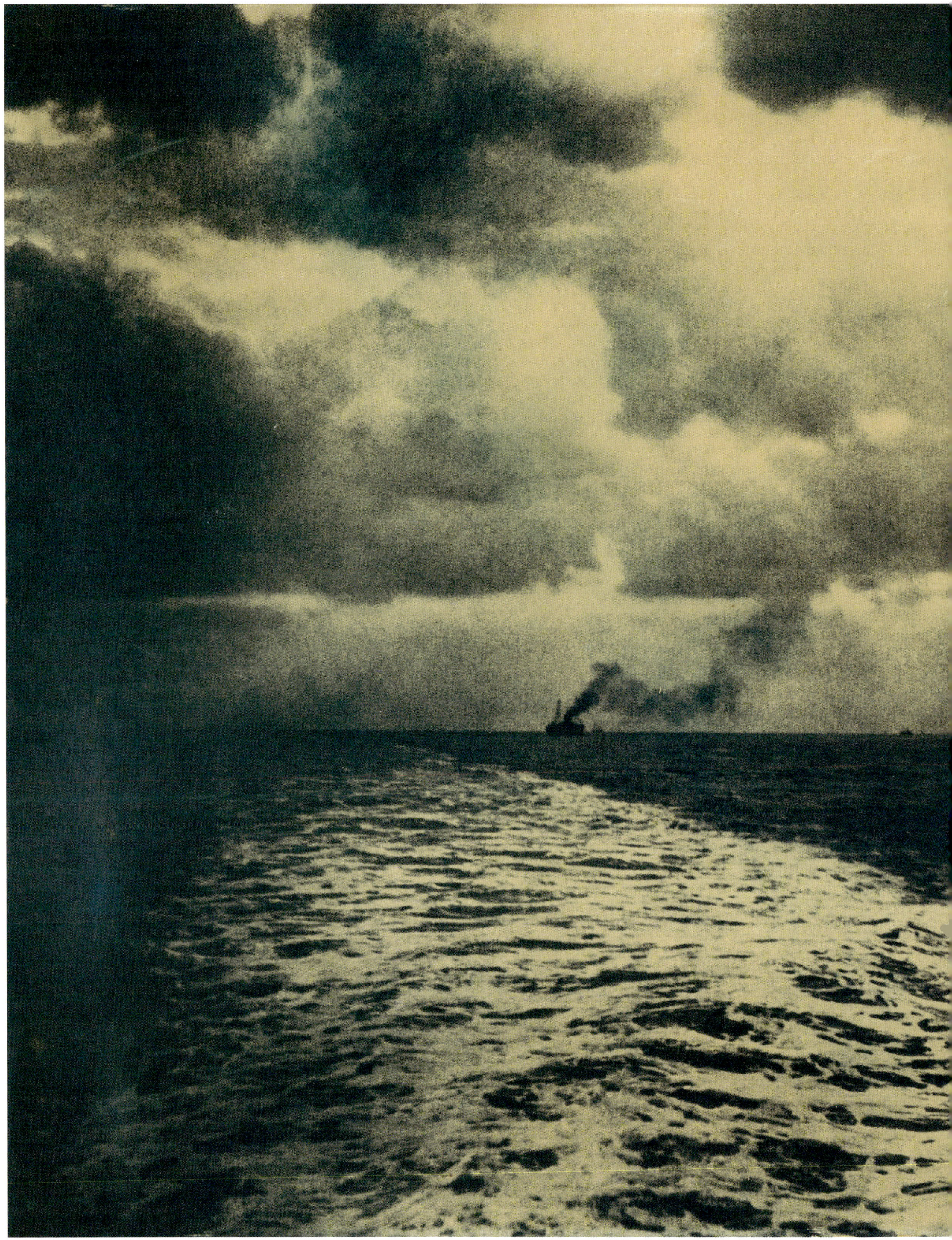

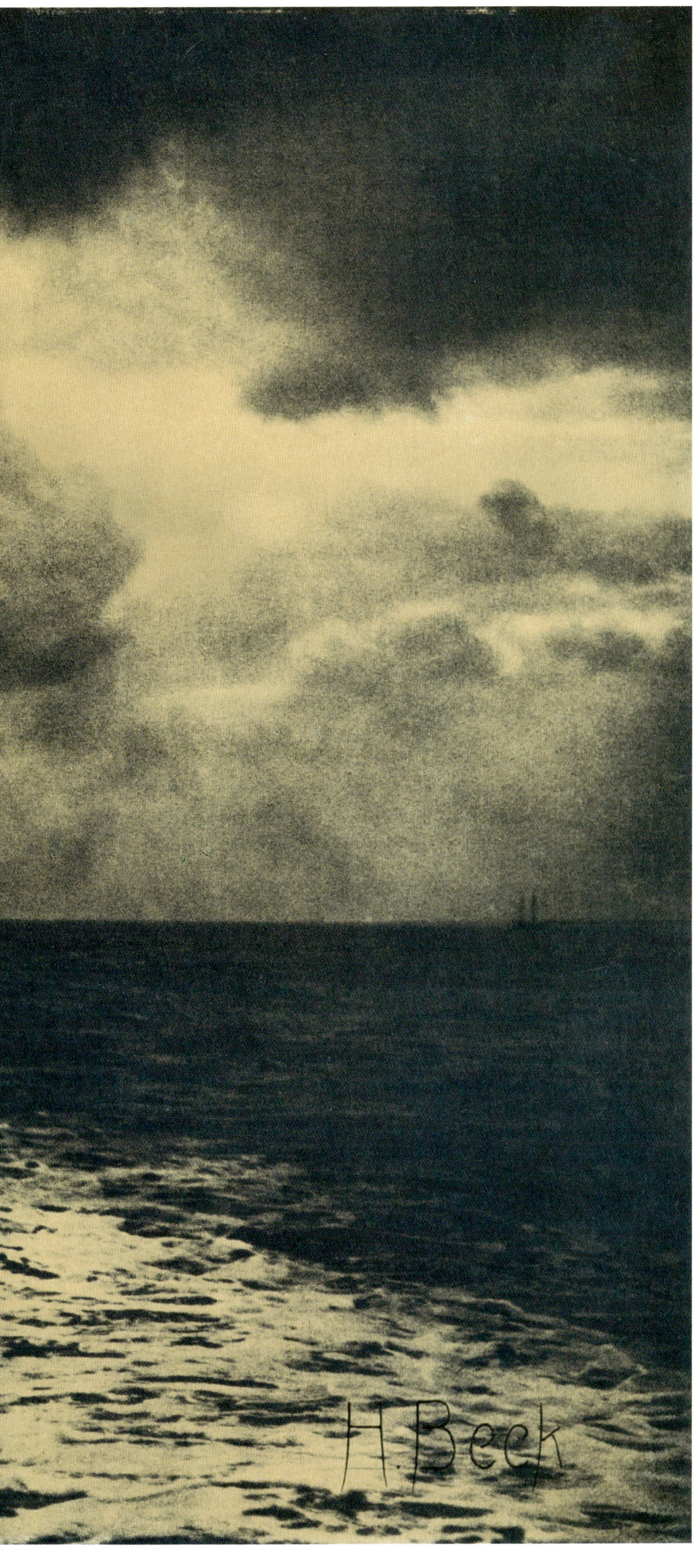

97 Heinrich Beck
Wake, 1903

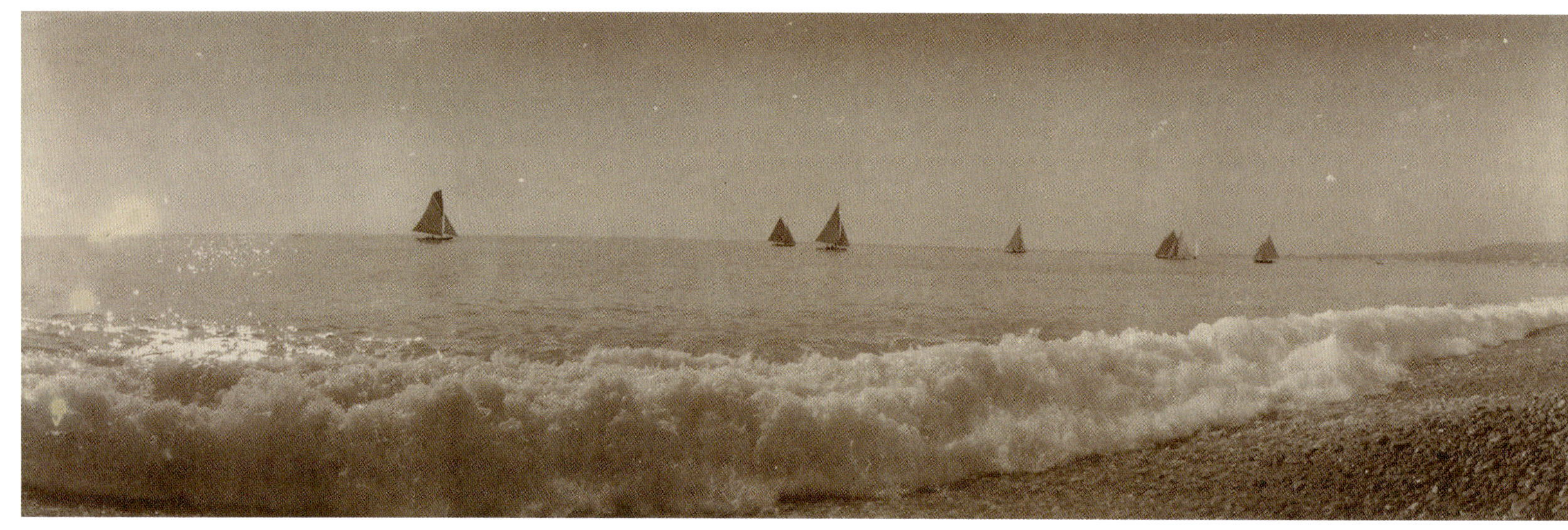

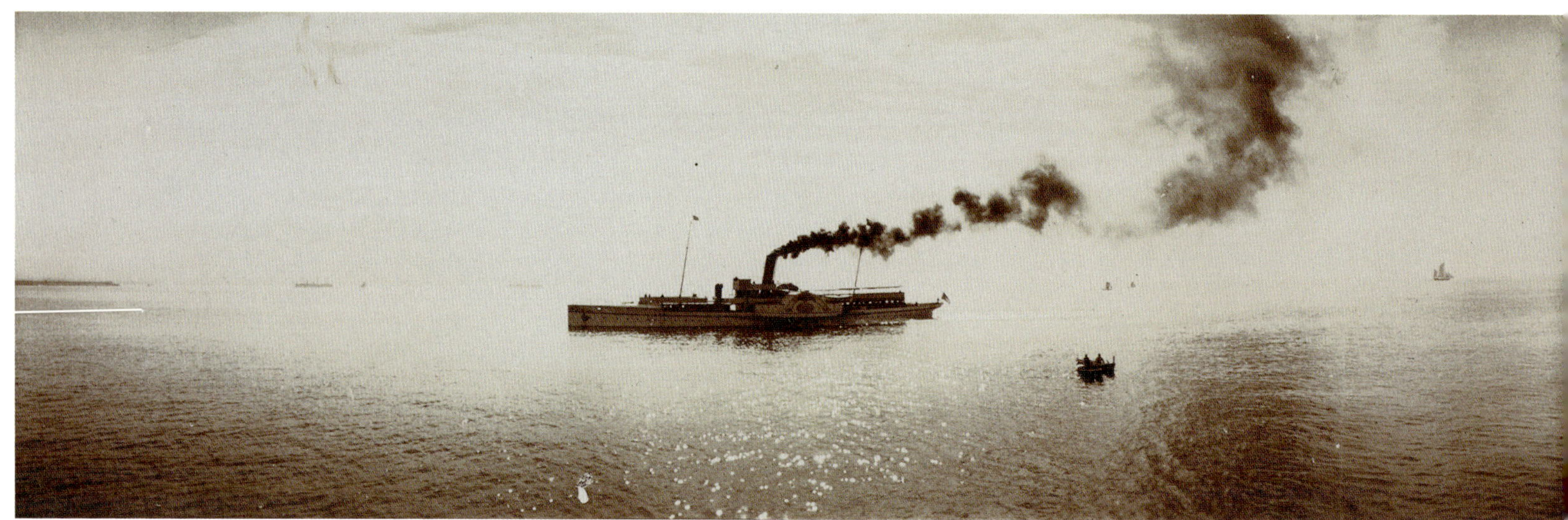

98 Constant Puyo
*Waves and Sailboats
on the Horizon at Penmarc'h in
Brittany*, ca. 1902–14

99 Constant Puyo
*Paddle Steamer in the Gulf of
Naples*, ca. 1903

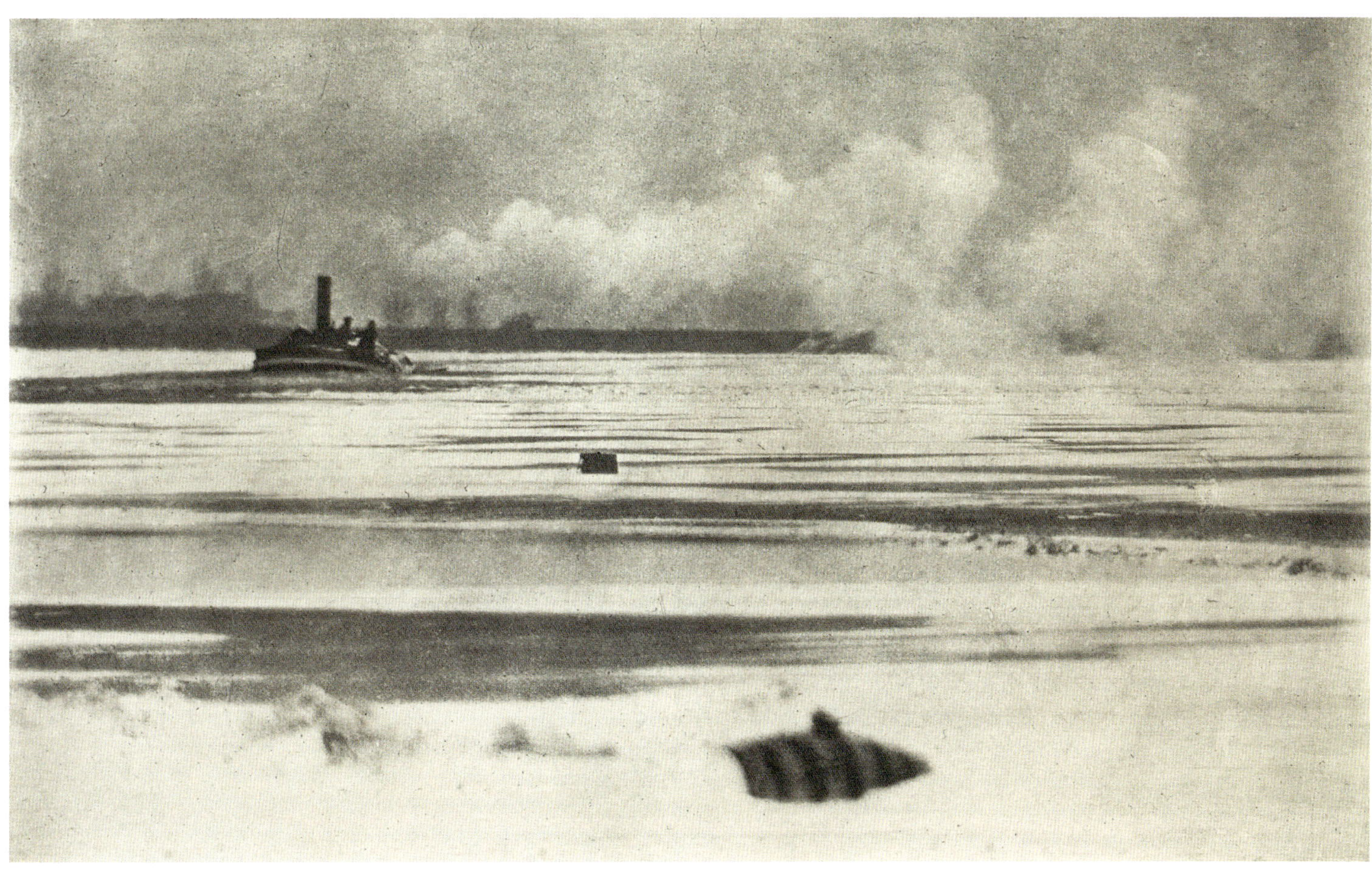

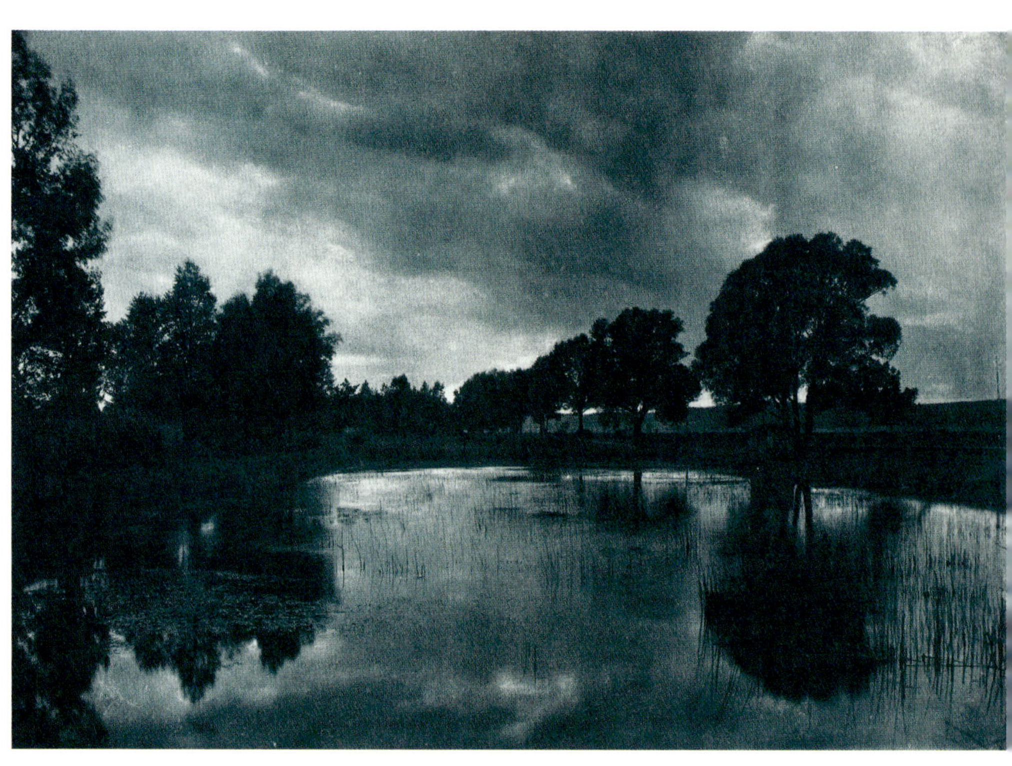

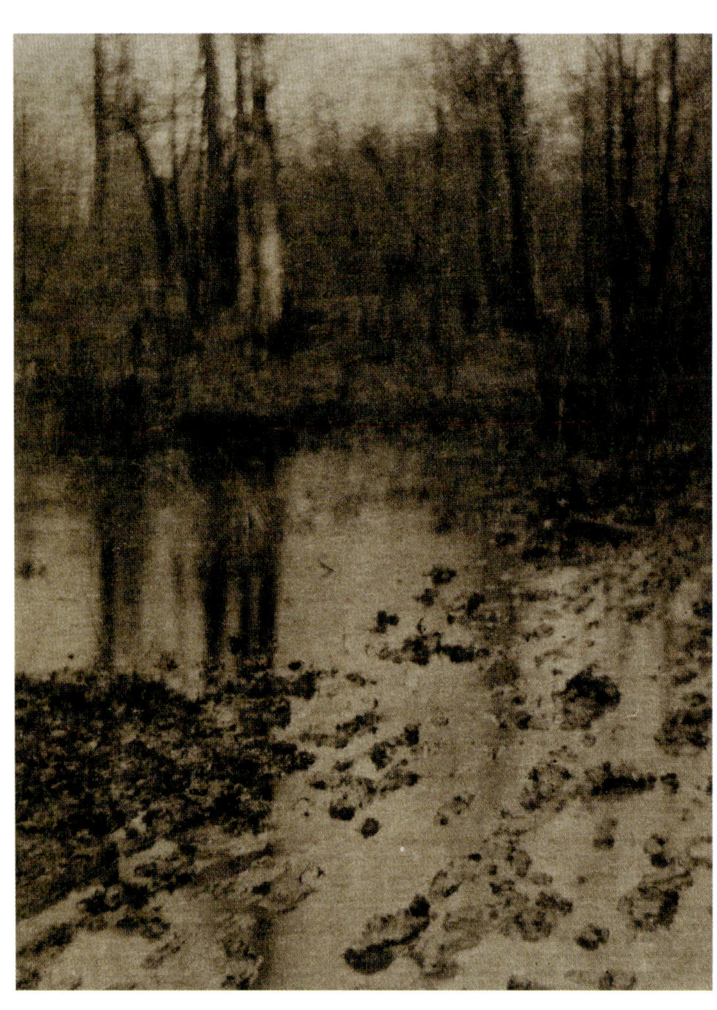

101 Viktor Knollmüller
Landscape with Pond, ca. 1904

102 Edward Steichen
The Pool—Evening,
Milwaukee, 1902

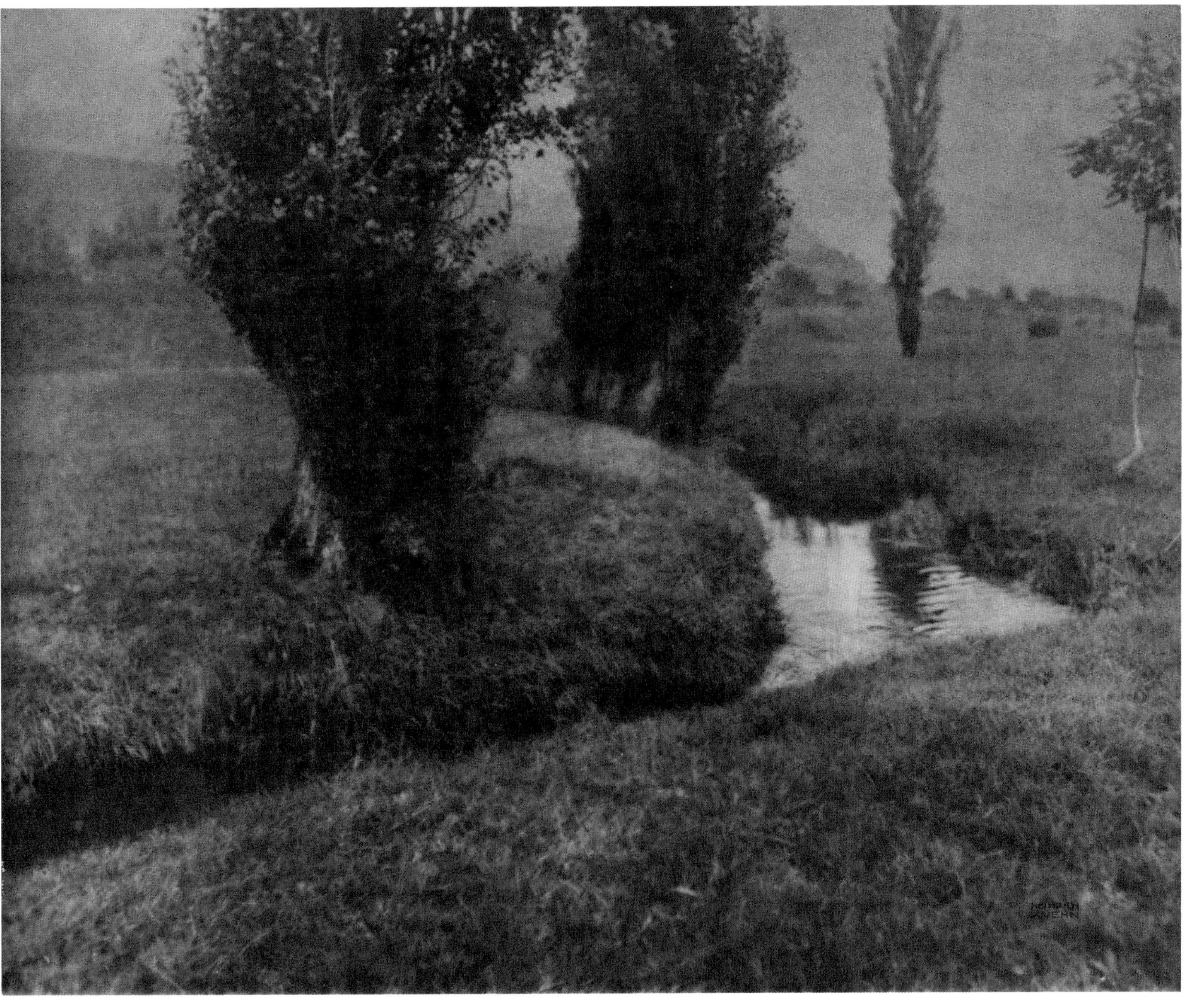

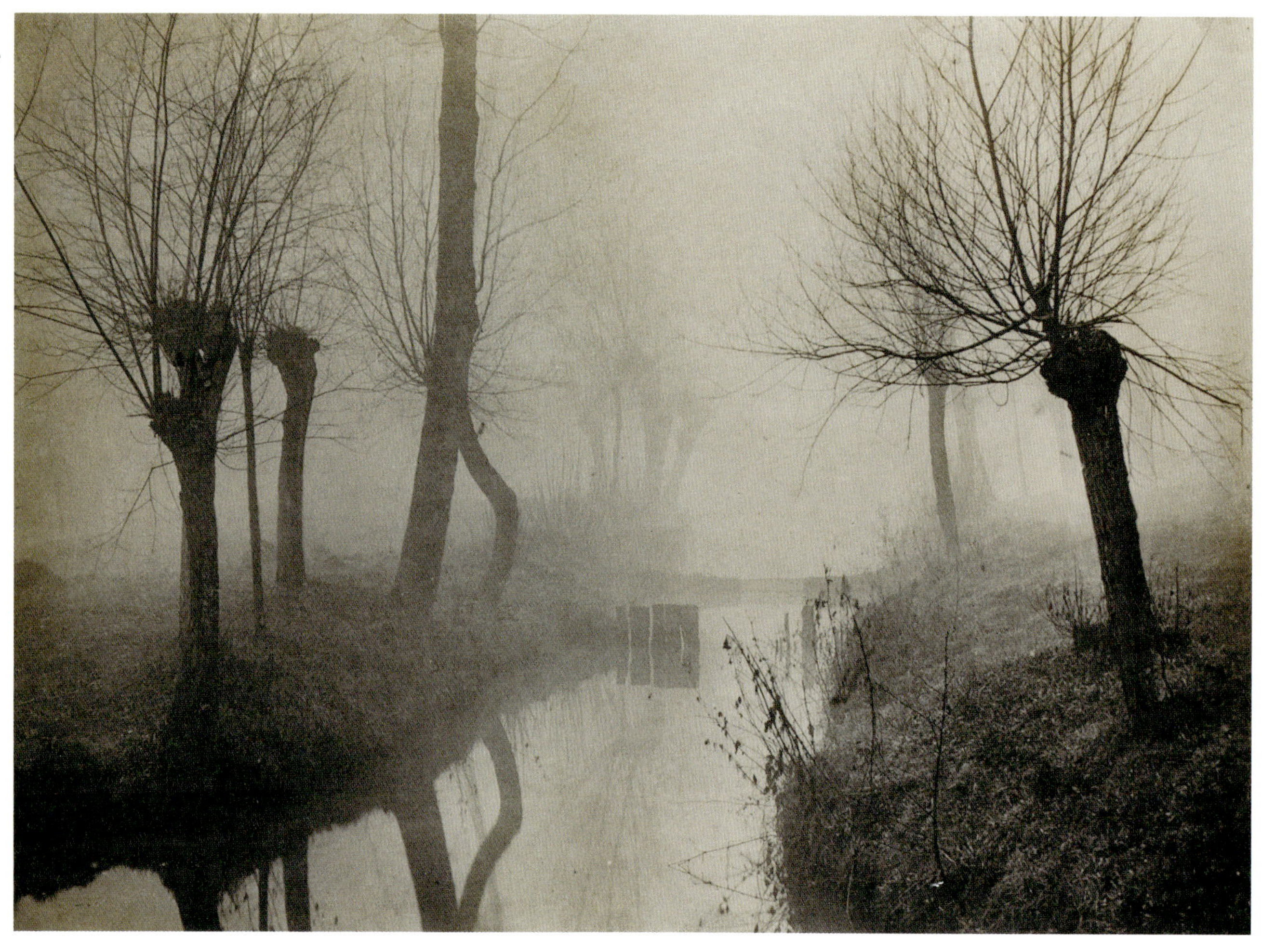

104 Marcel Vanderkindere
Winter Fog, 1897

After the Storm, 1896

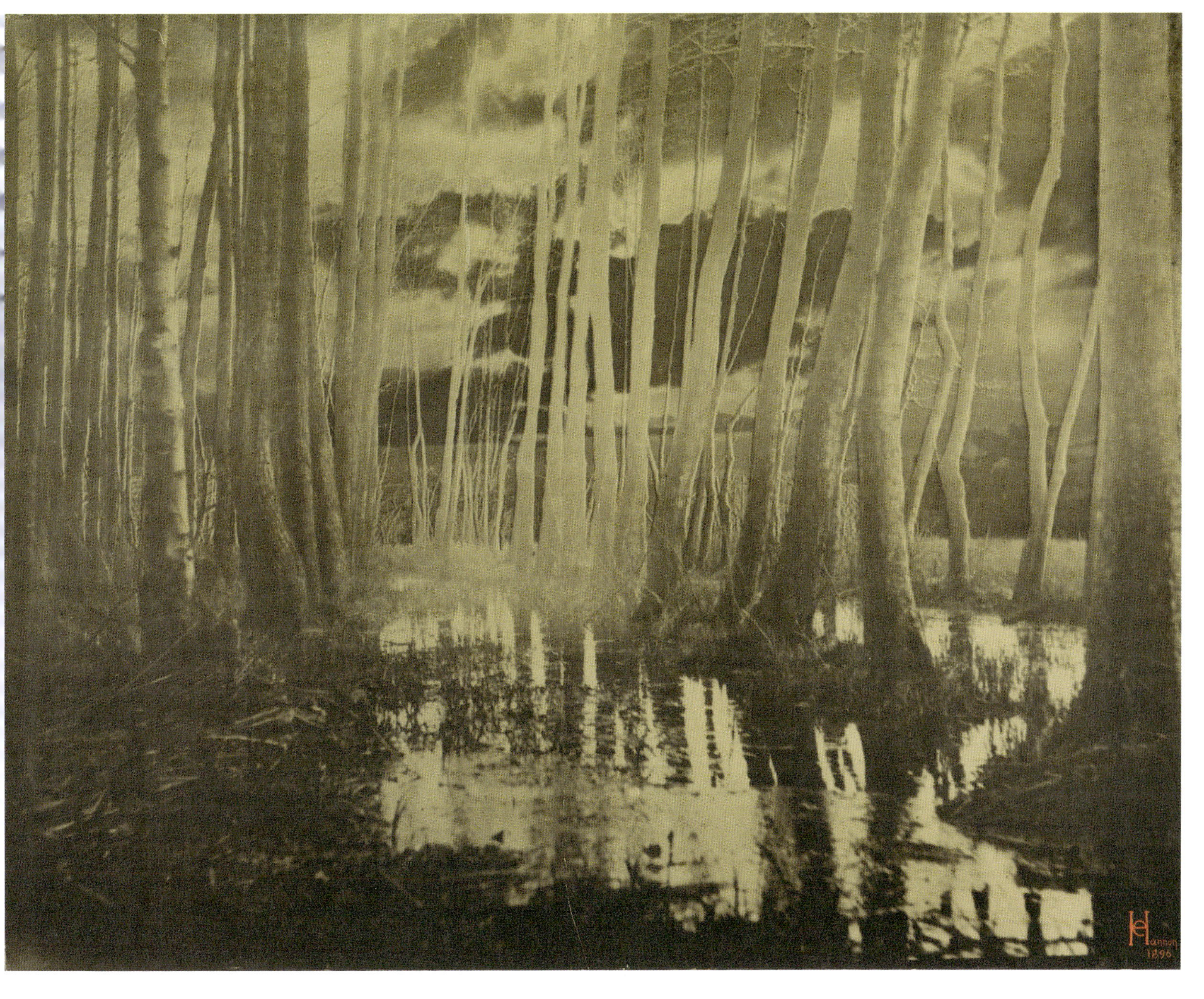

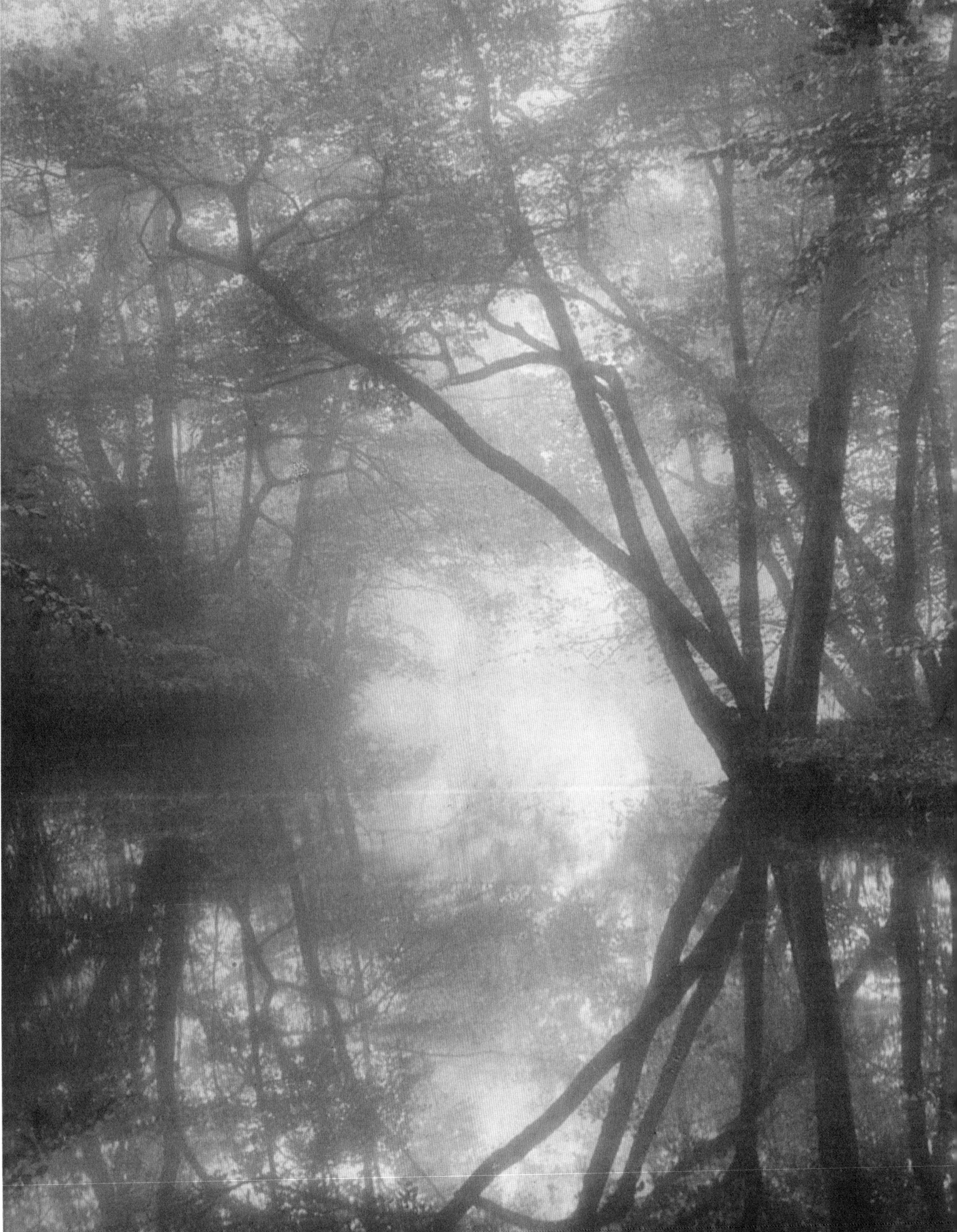

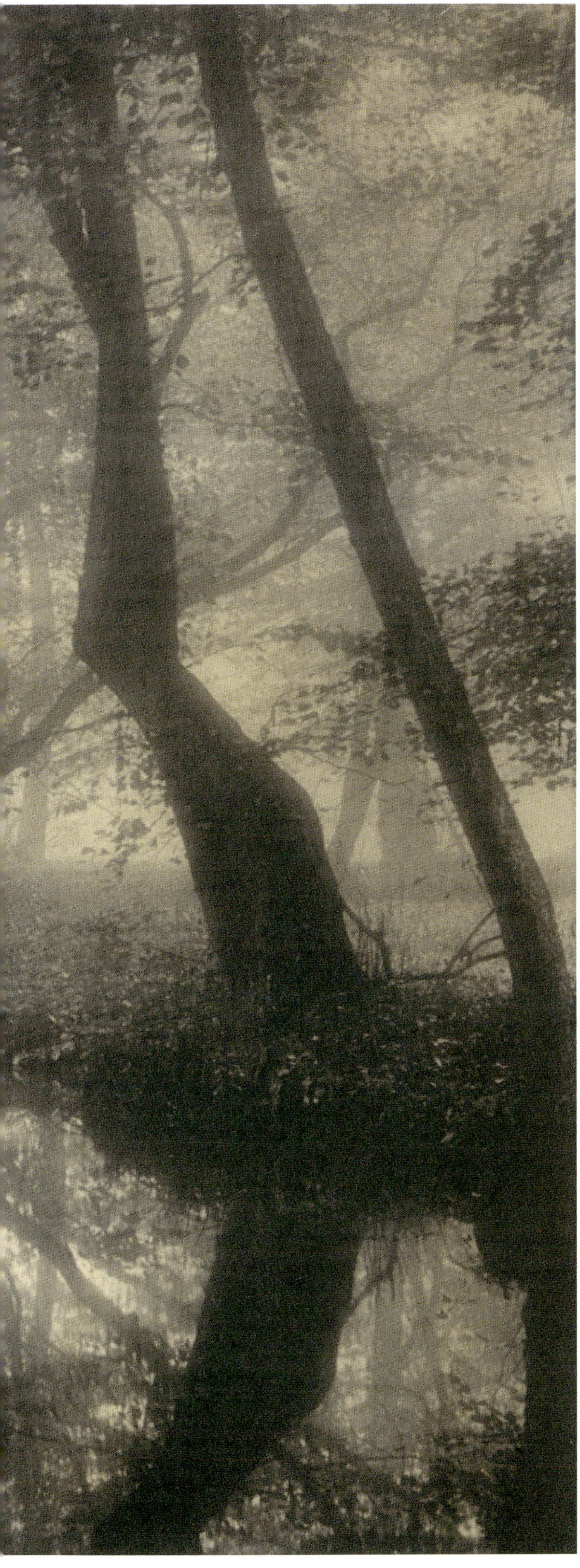

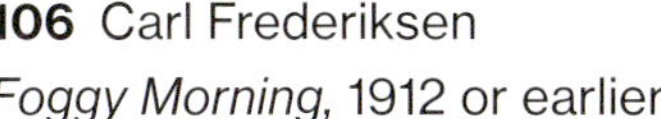

106 Carl Frederiksen
Foggy Morning, 1912 or earlier

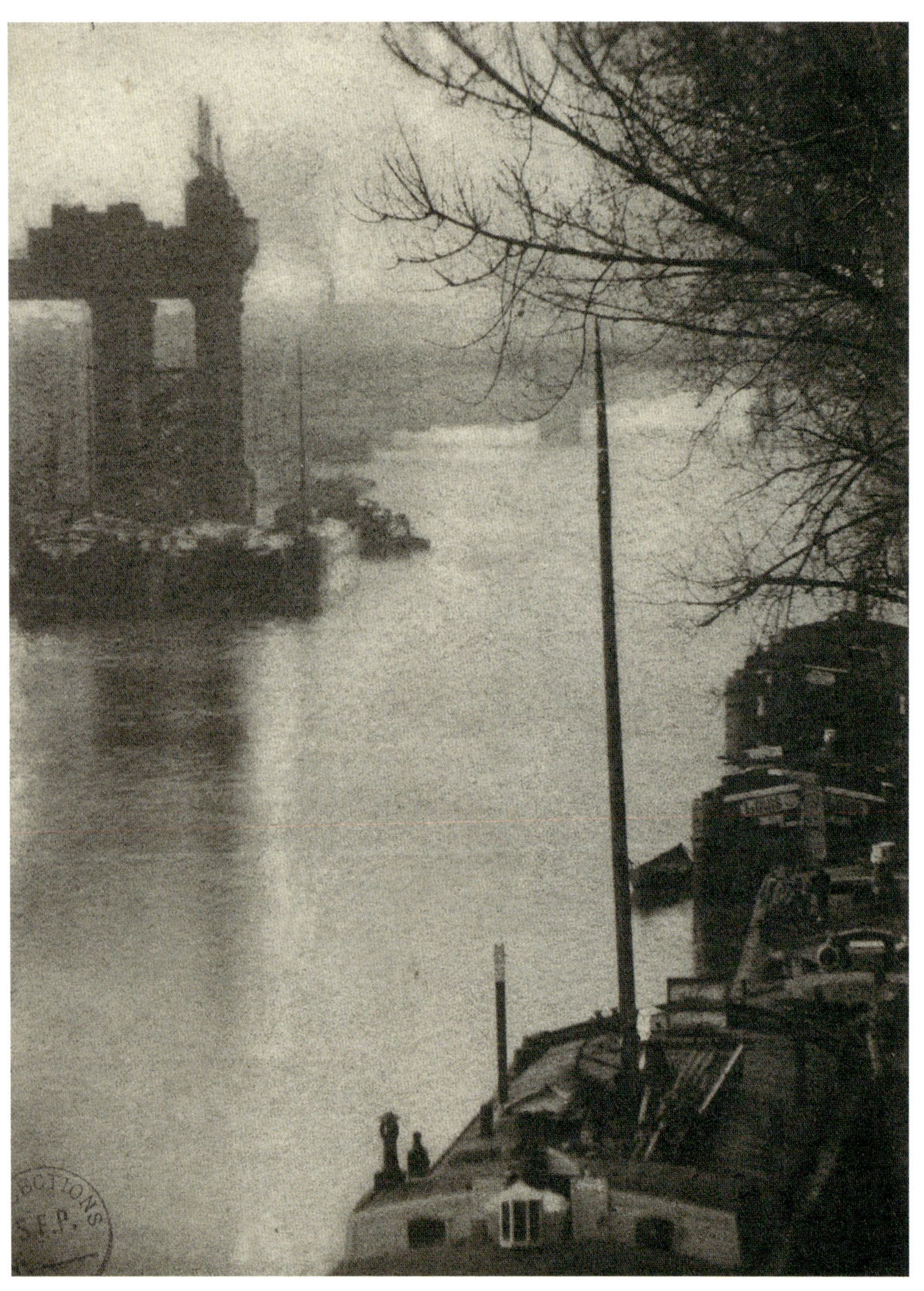

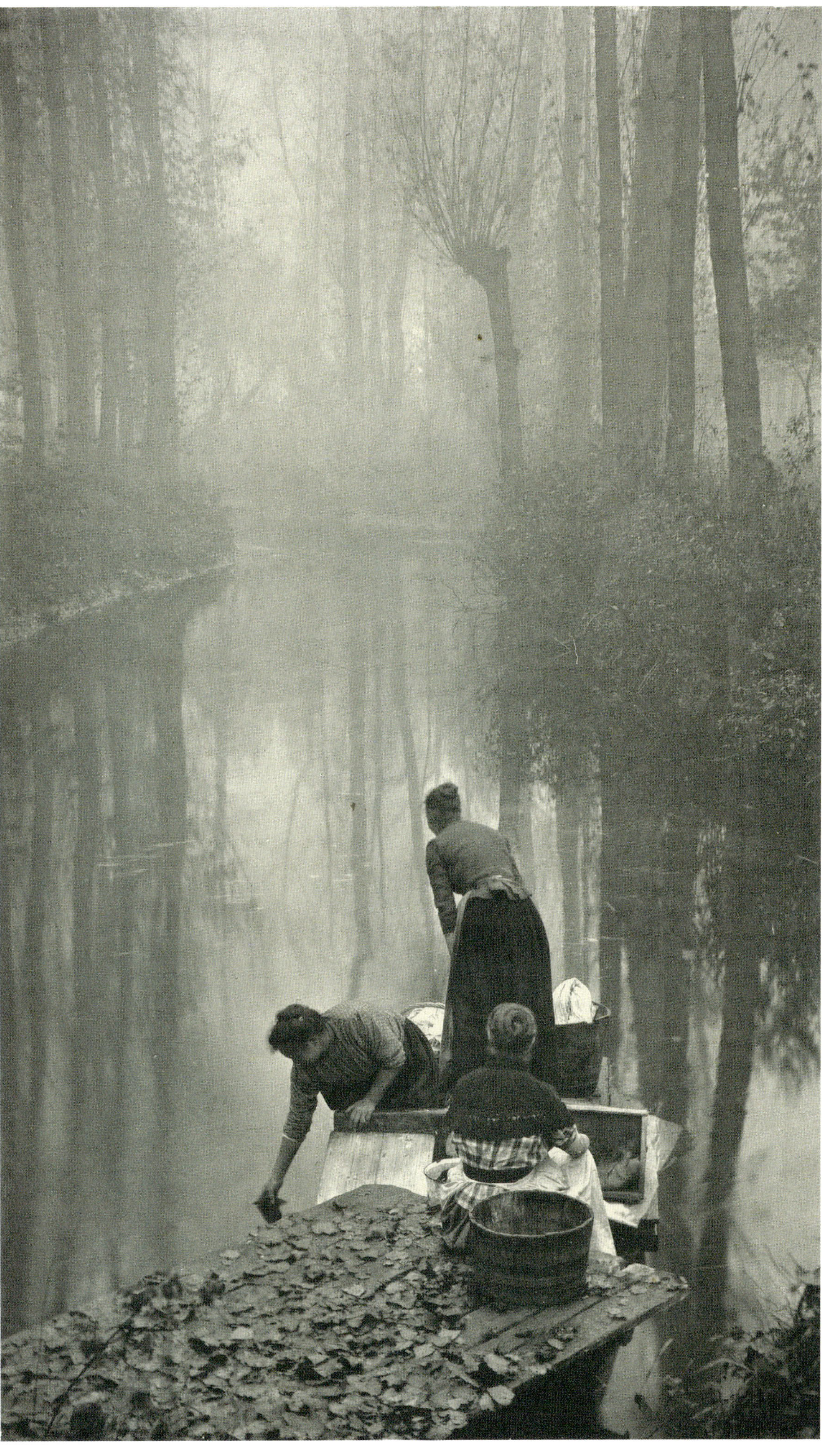

Banks of the Seine, ca. 1906

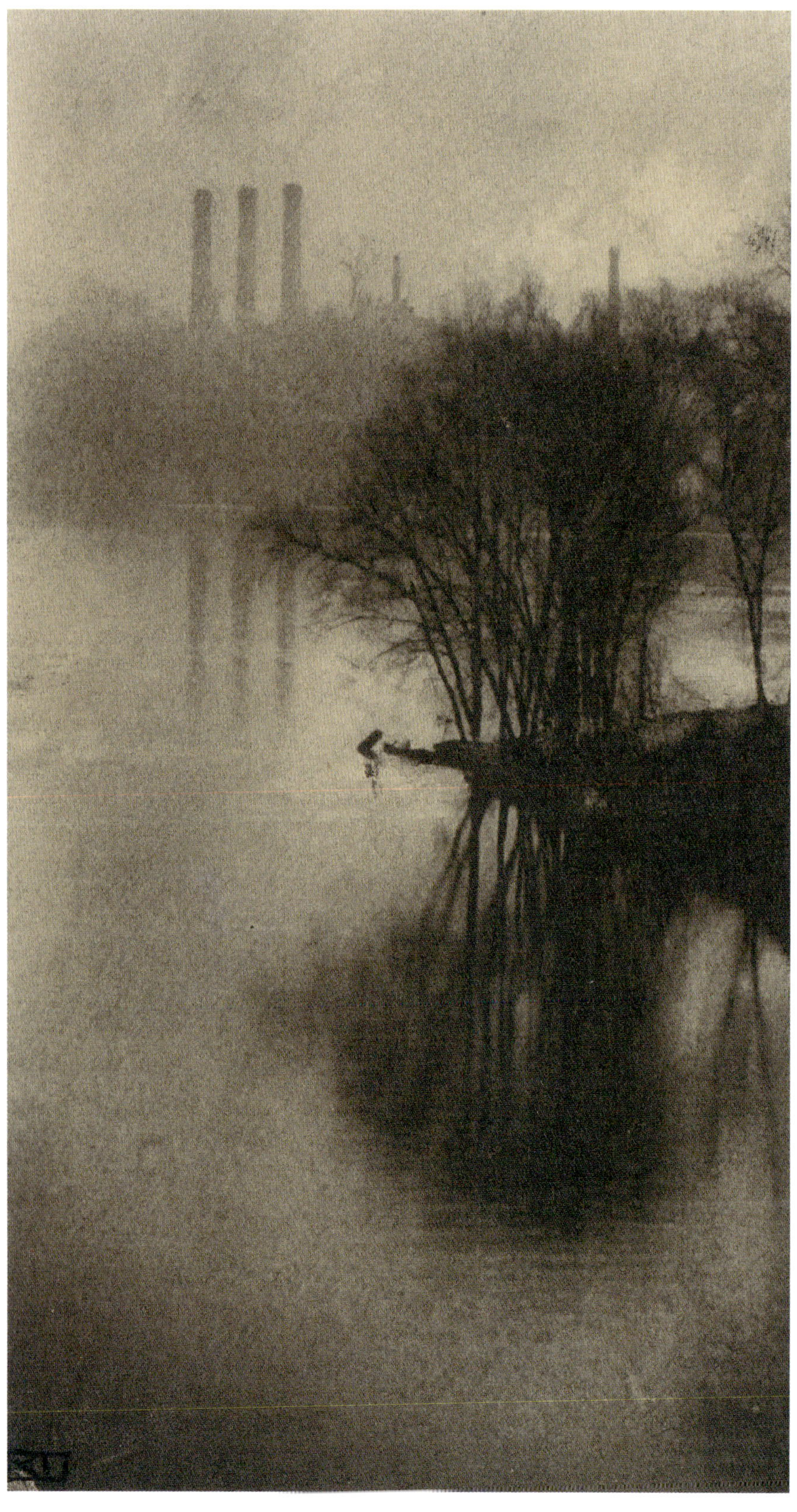

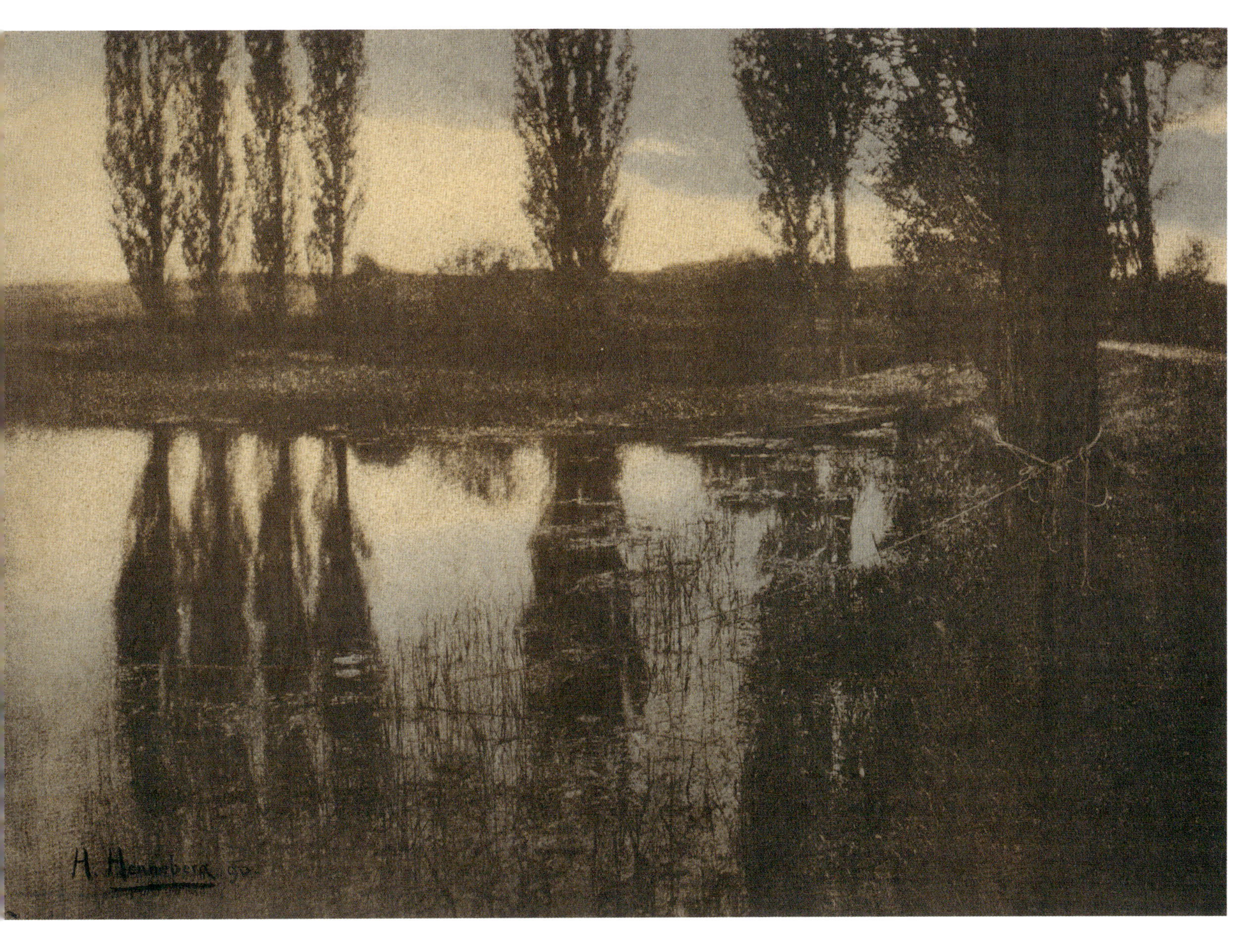

110 Hugo Henneberg
After Sunset, 1898 or earlier

111 Heinrich Kühn
Lindens in the Sunlight, ca. 1900

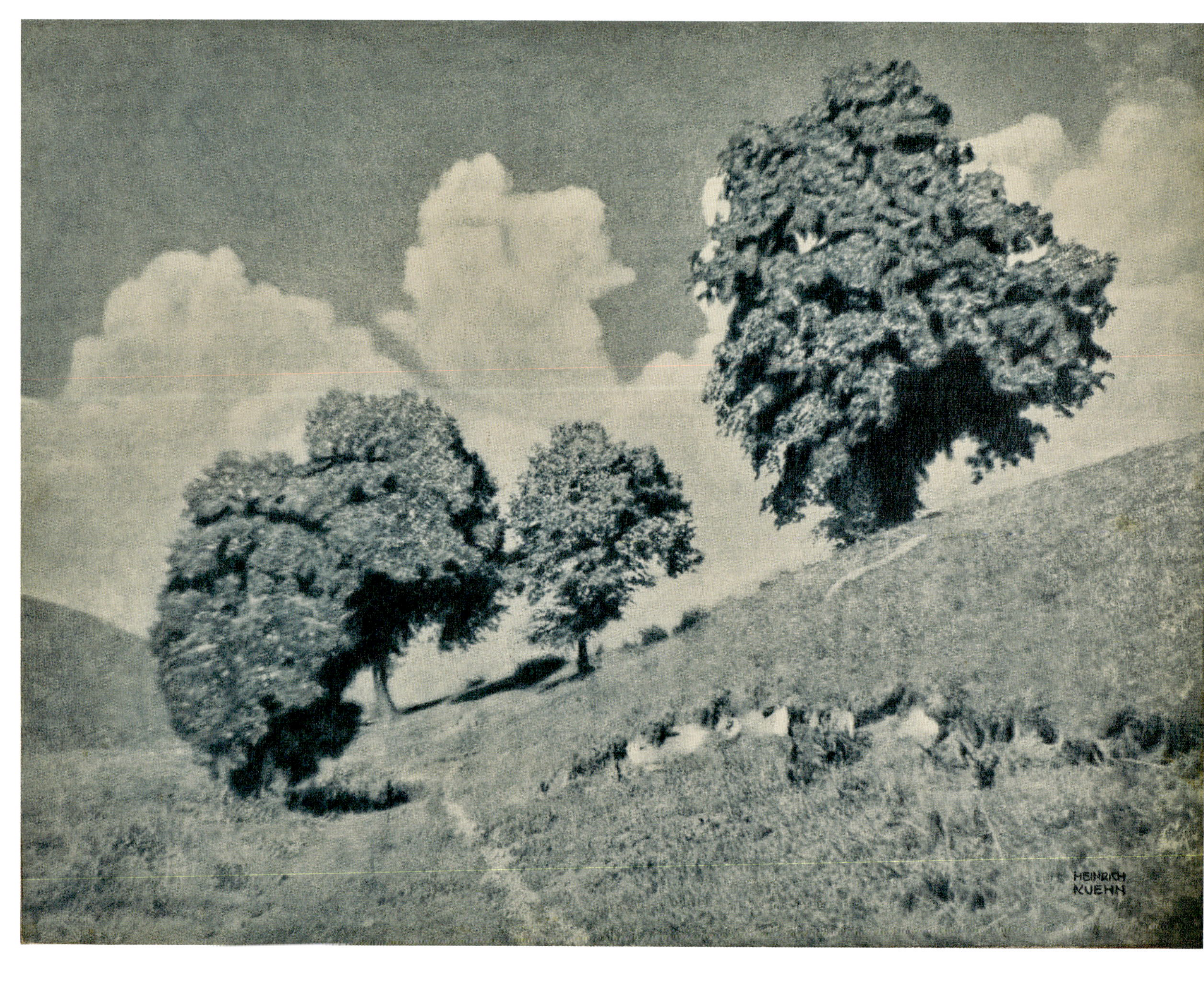

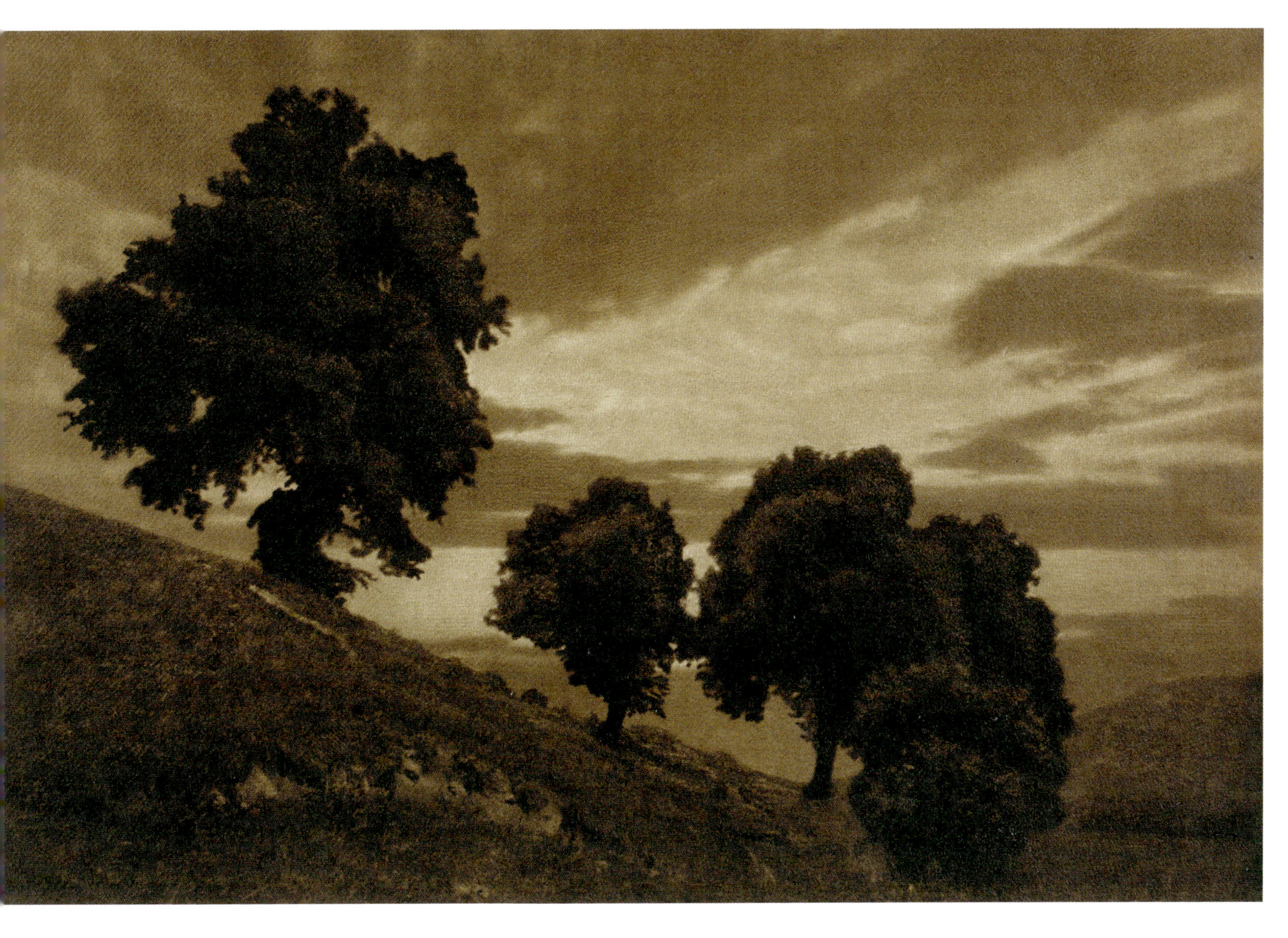

112 Heinrich Kühn
Landscape with Lindens, 1898

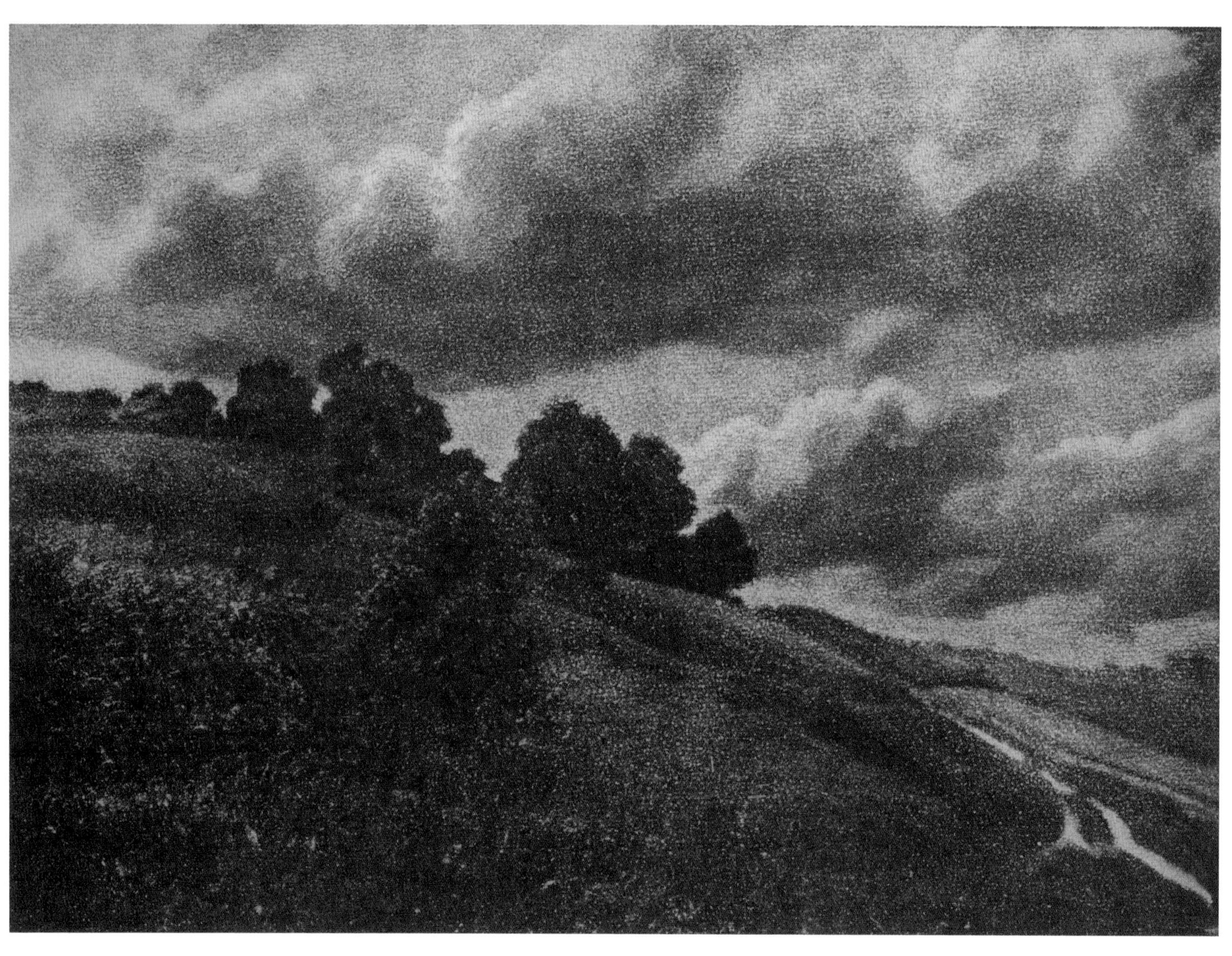

113 Heinrich Kühn
Landscape with Clouds, ca. 1899

114 Hugo Henneberg
Evening, 1899 or earlier

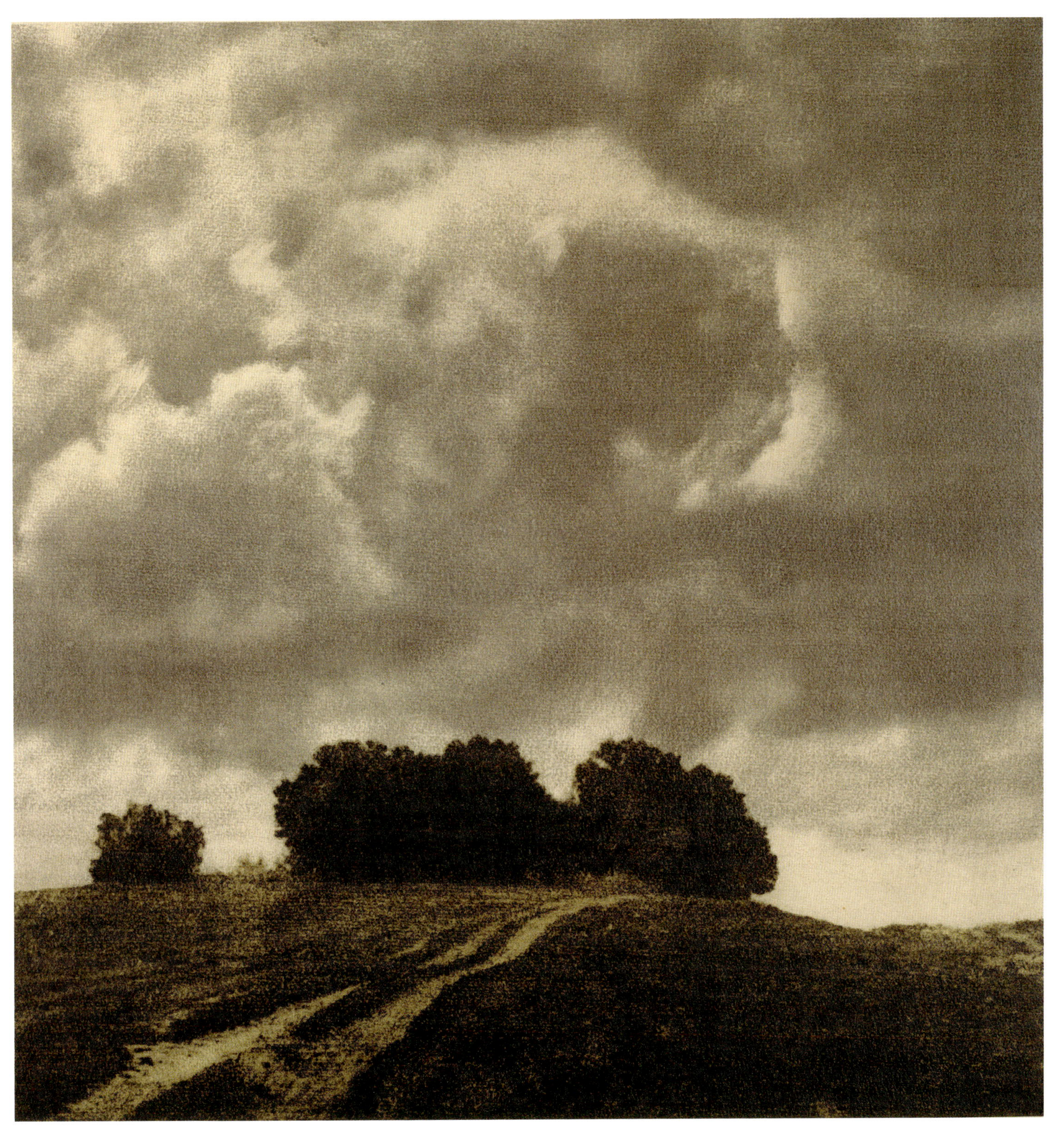

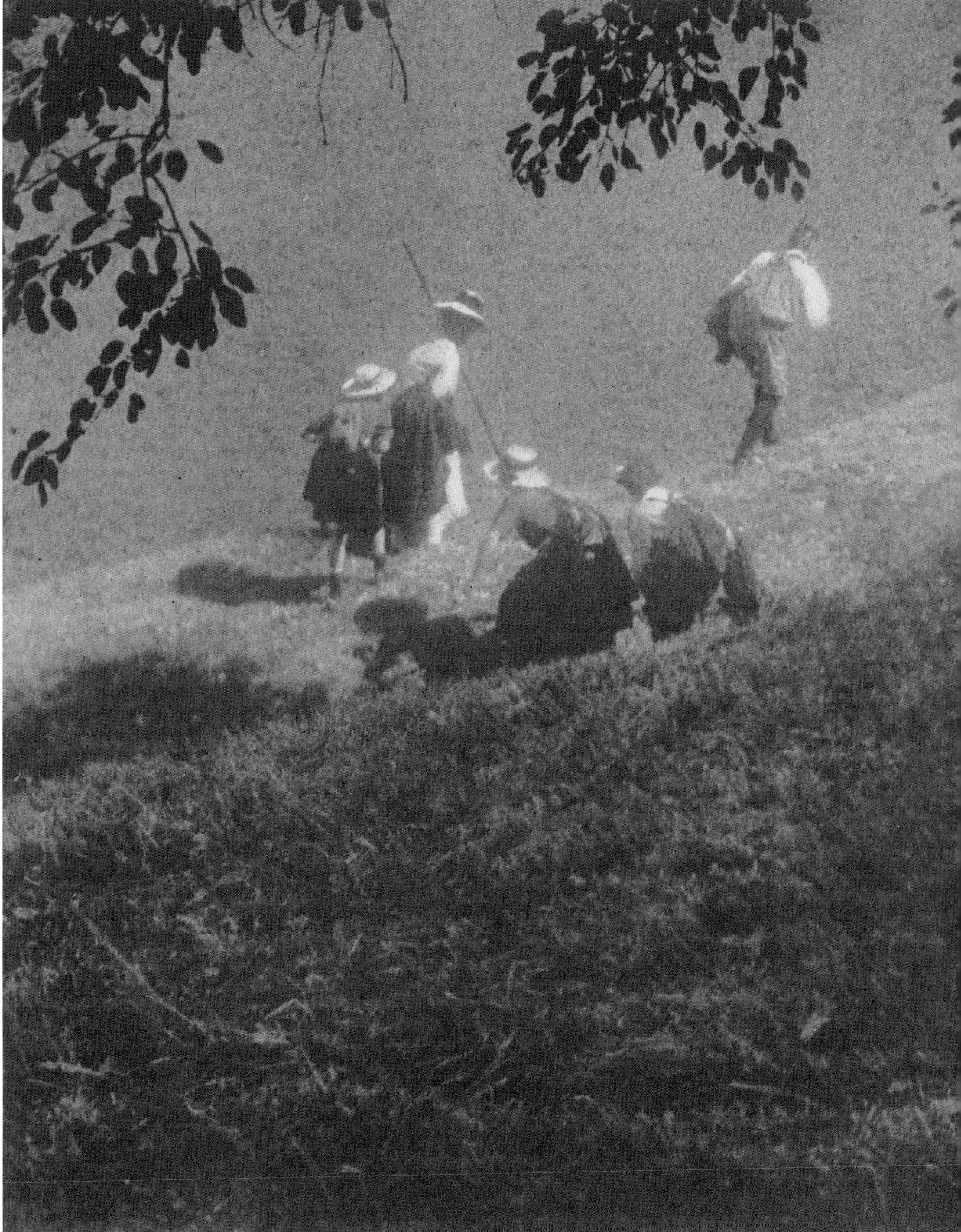

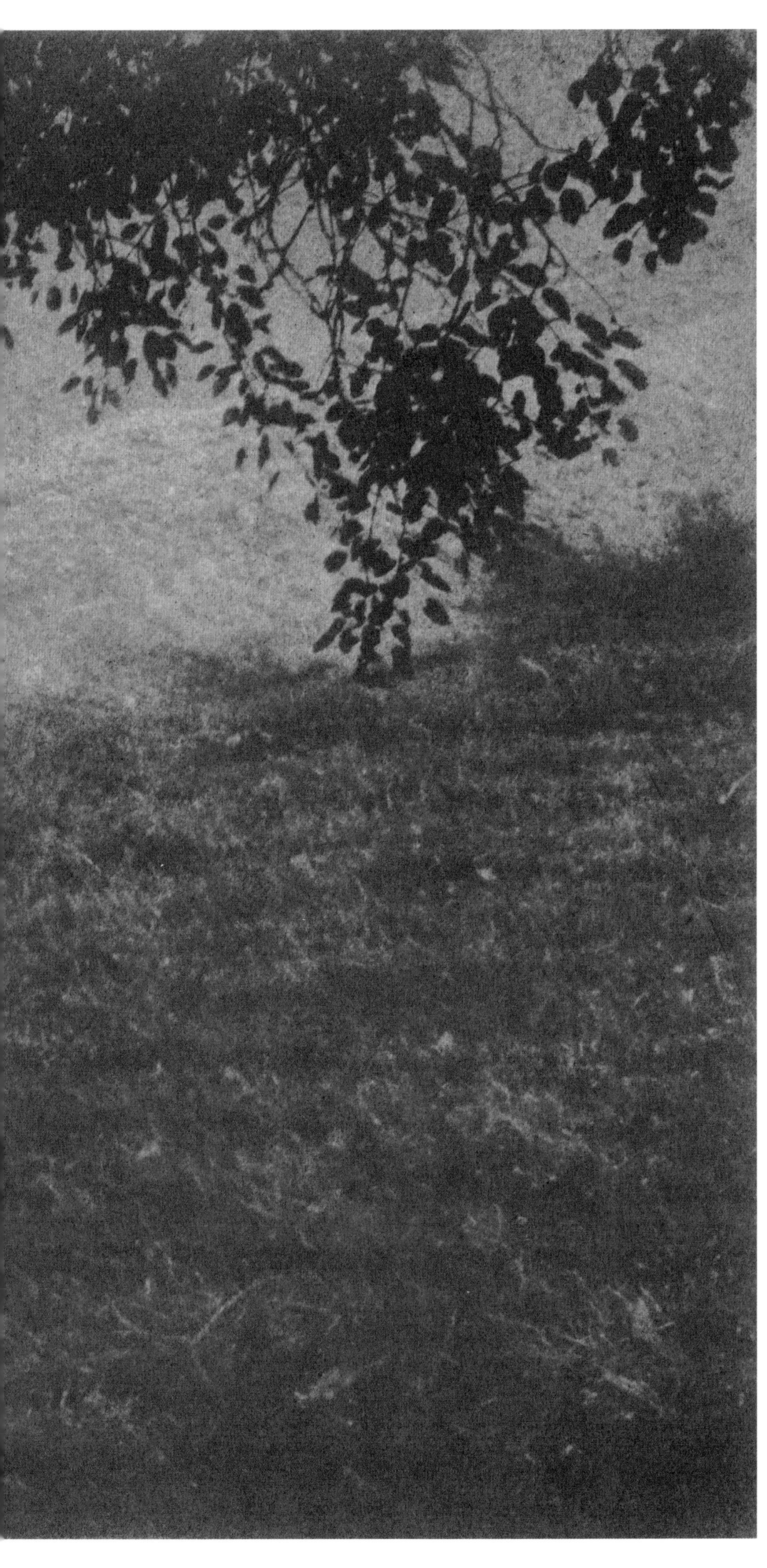

115 Heinrich Kühn
Hikers beneath Branches, ca. 1915

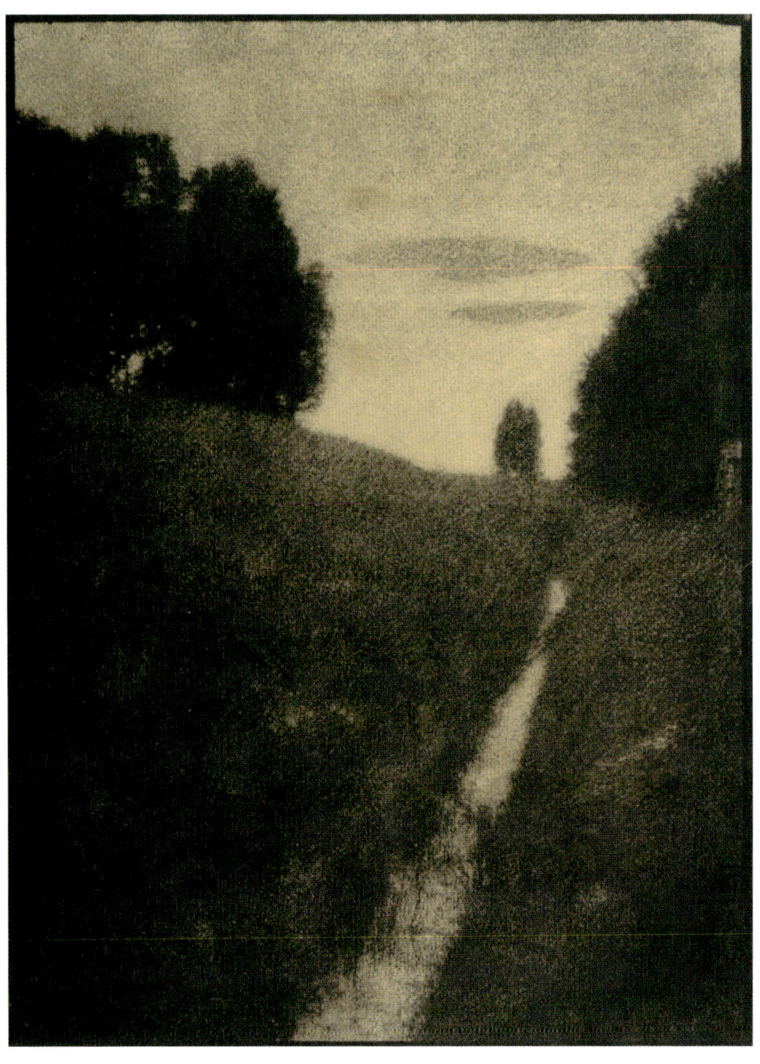

116 Heinrich Kühn
Twilight, 1897

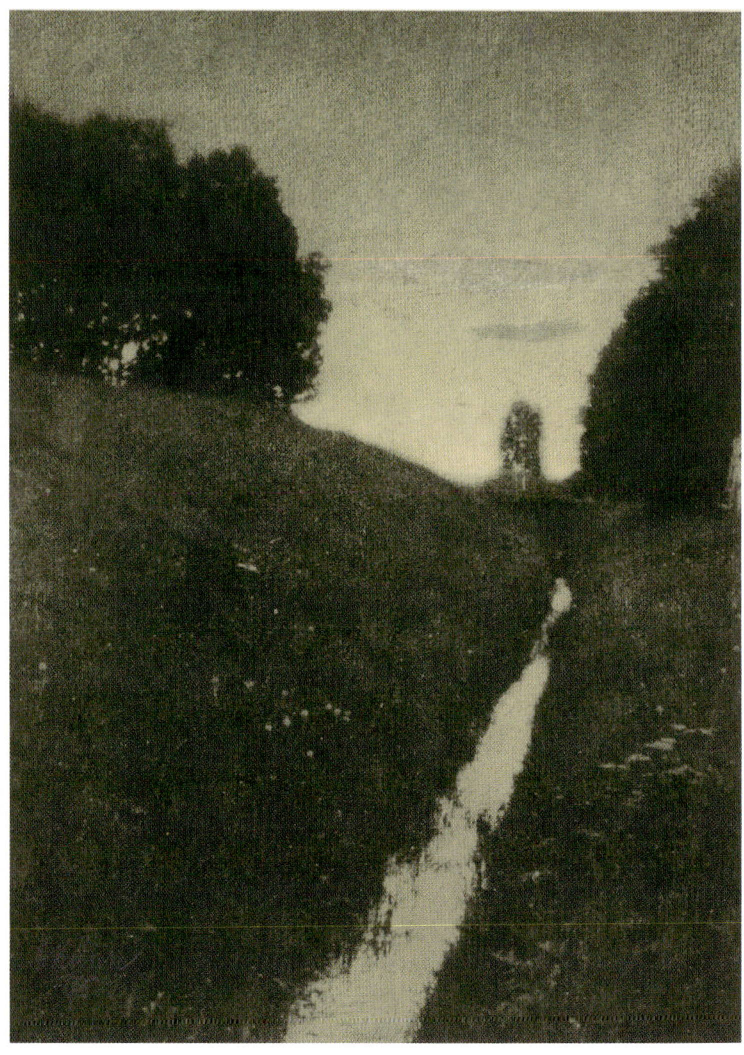

117 Heinrich Kühn
Twilight, 1896

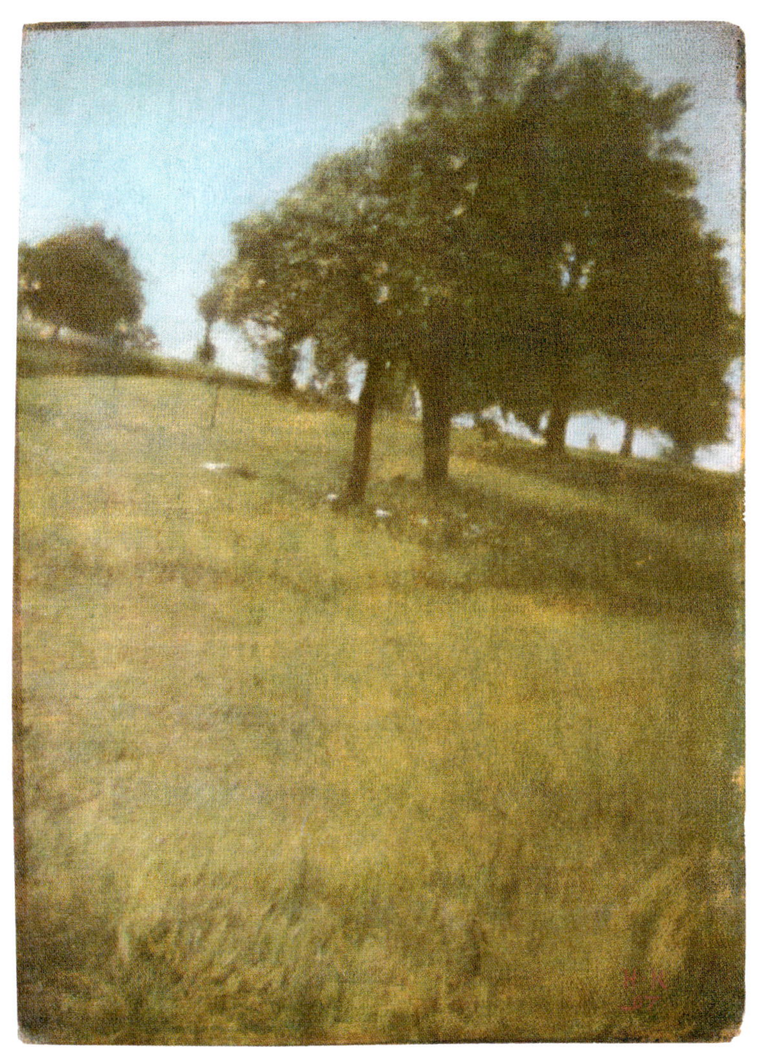

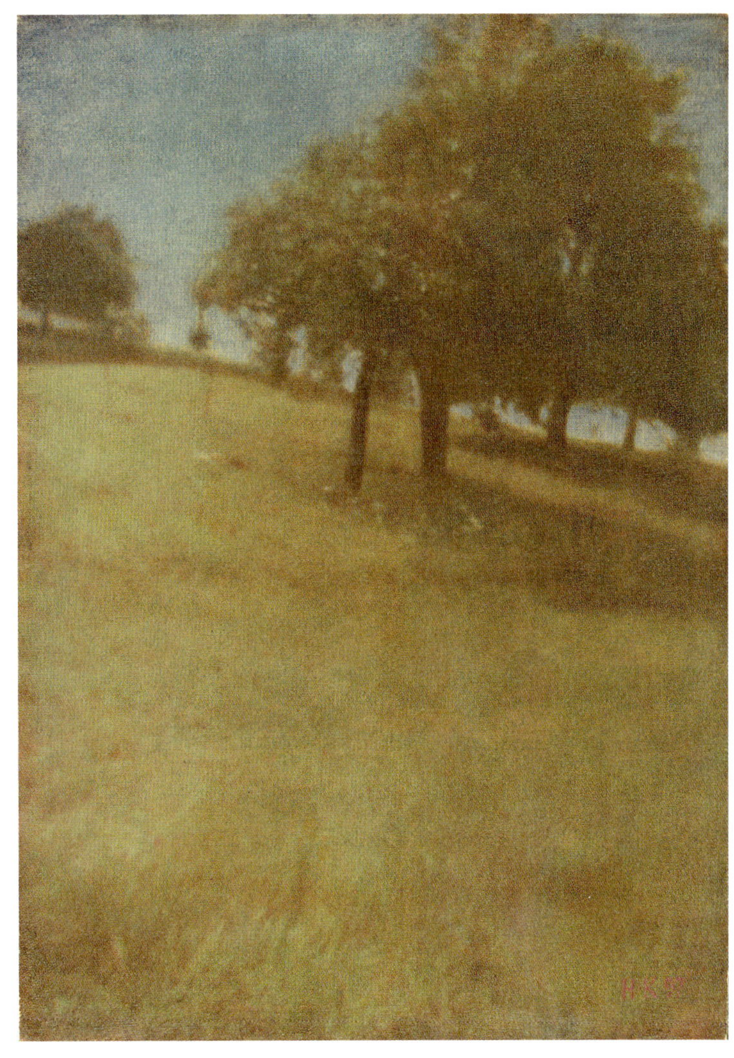

118 Heinrich Kühn
Meadow with Trees, 1897

119 Heinrich Kühn
Landscape, 1897

205

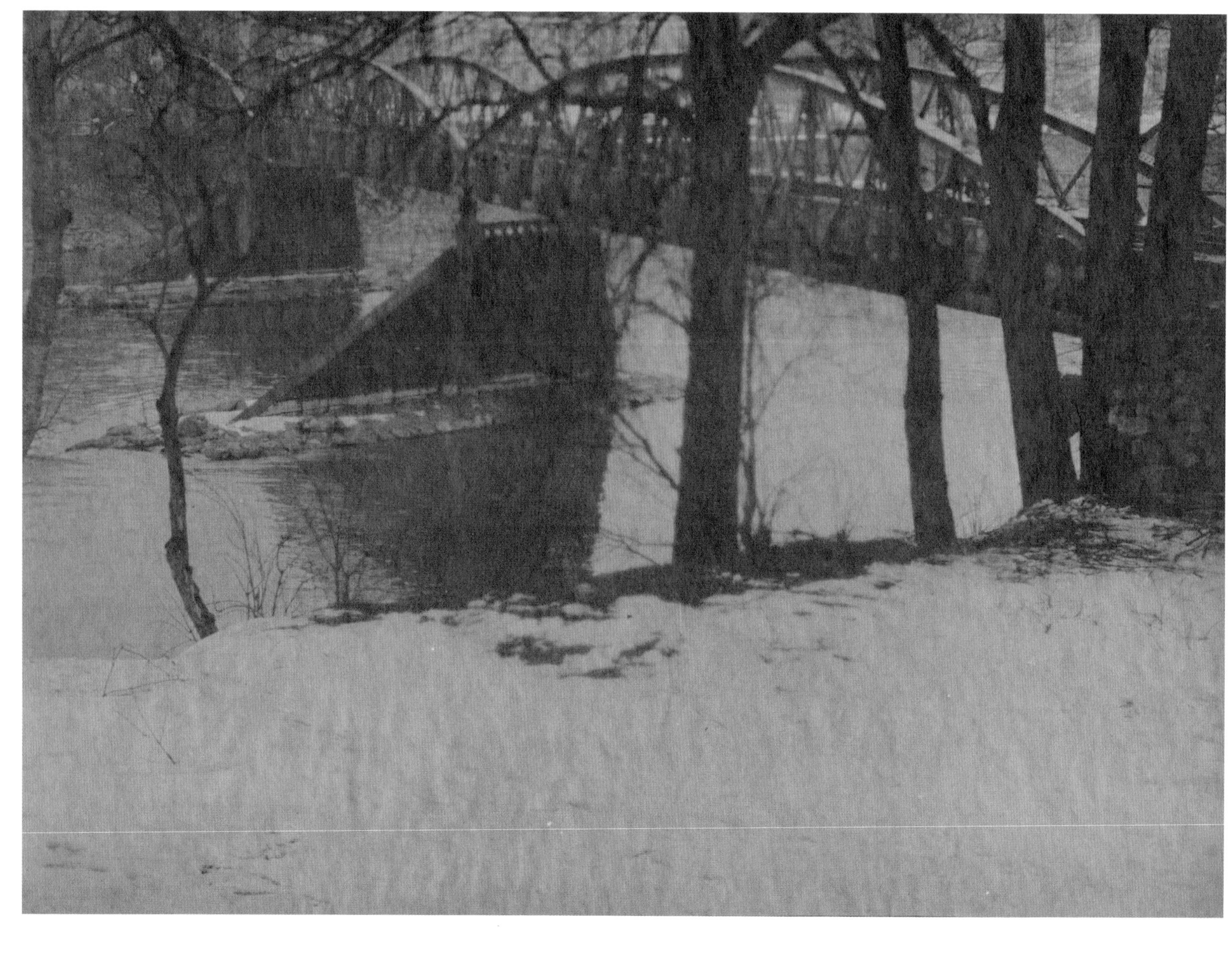

121 Robert Demachy
*The Jardin des Tuileries
in the Snow, Paris*, 1910

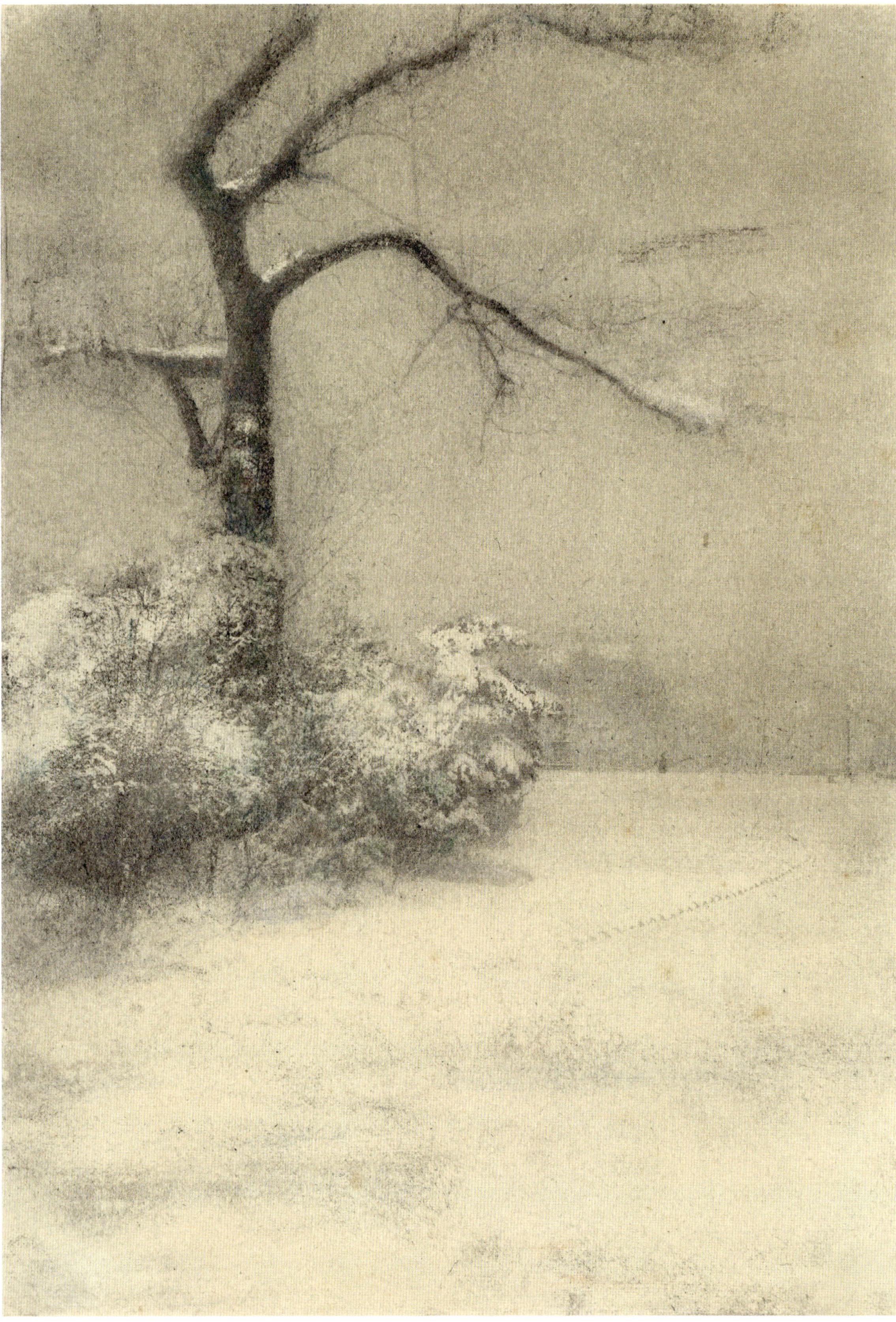

River in Winter, 1904 or earlier

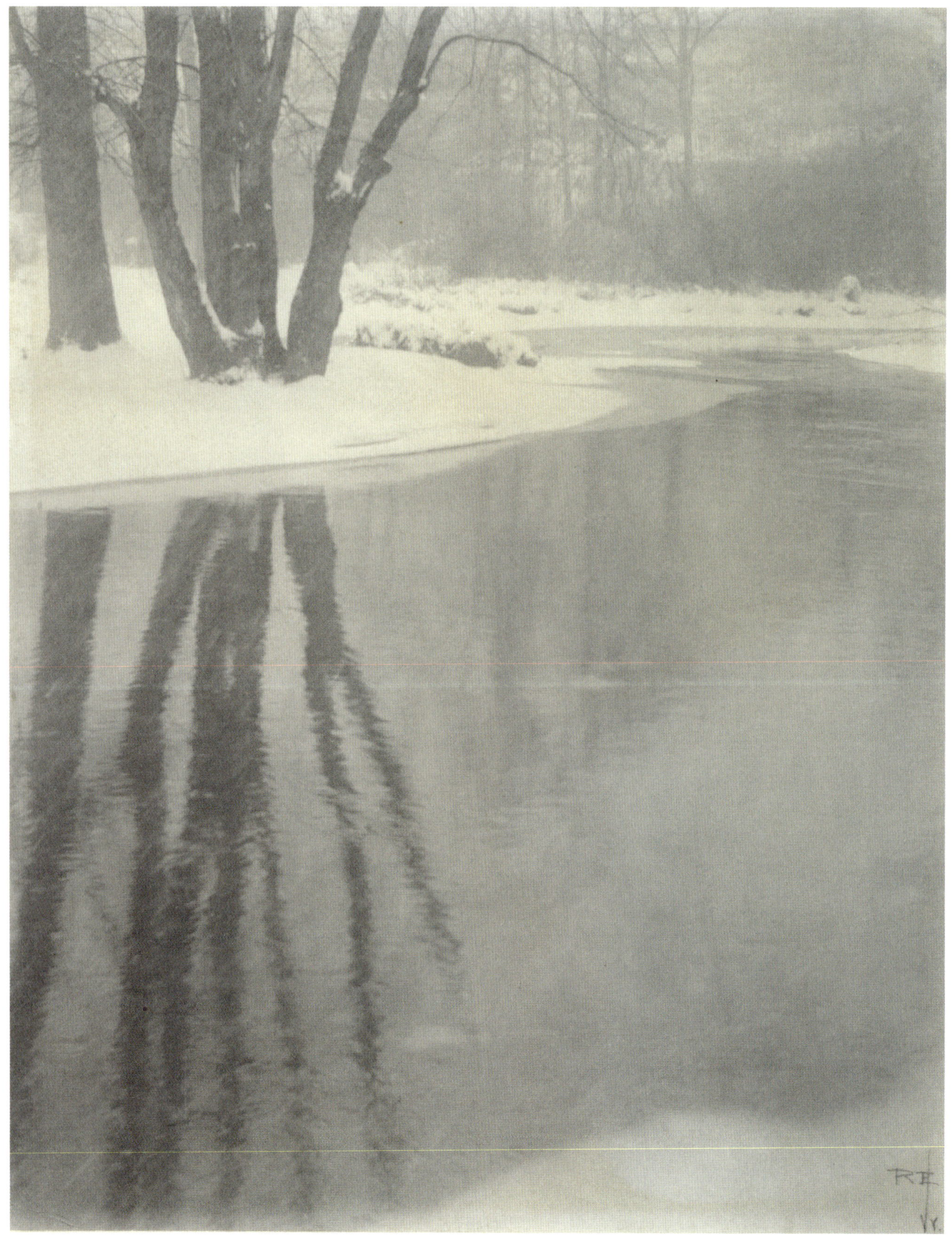

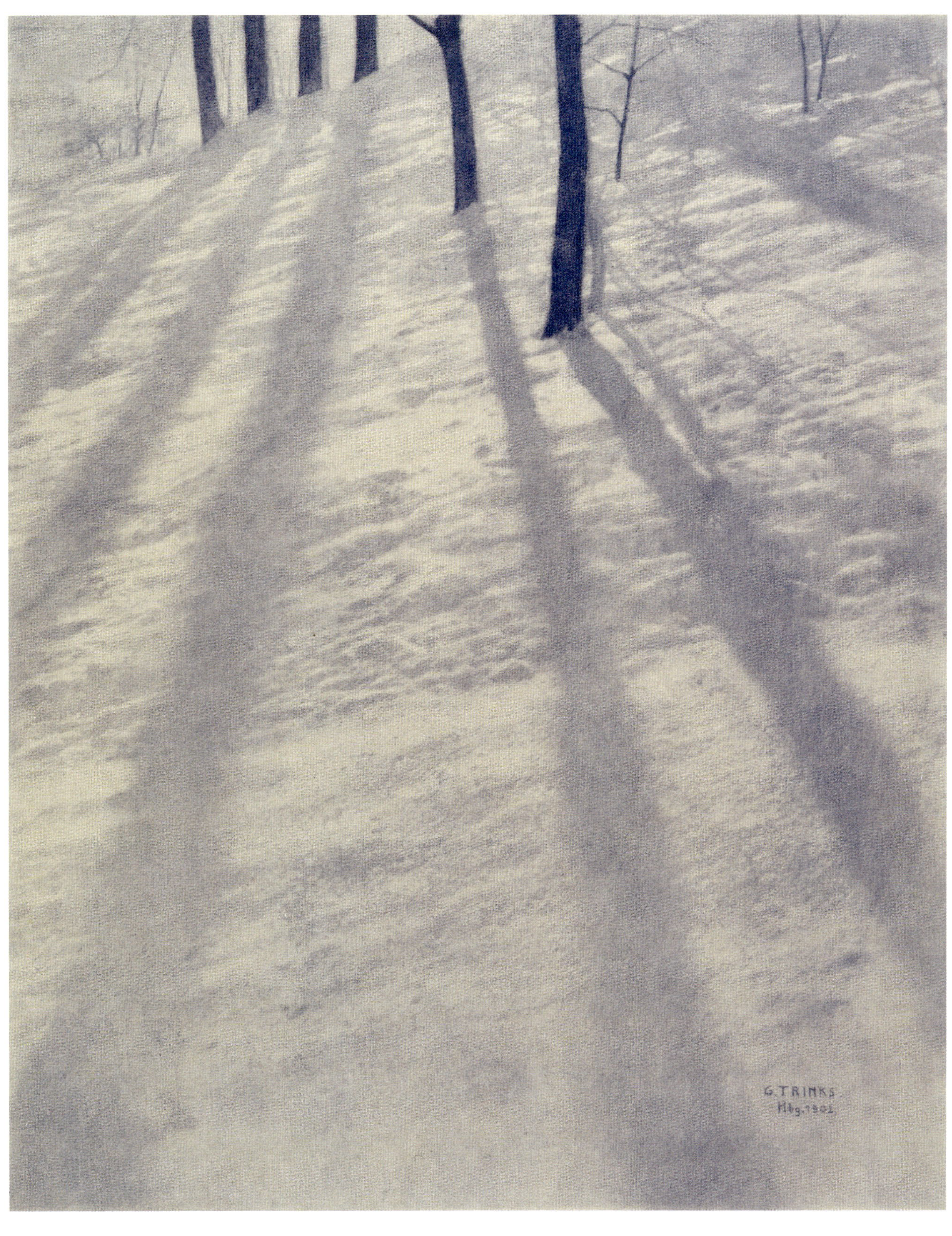

123 Gustav Eduard Bernhard Trinks
Colored Shadows, 1897

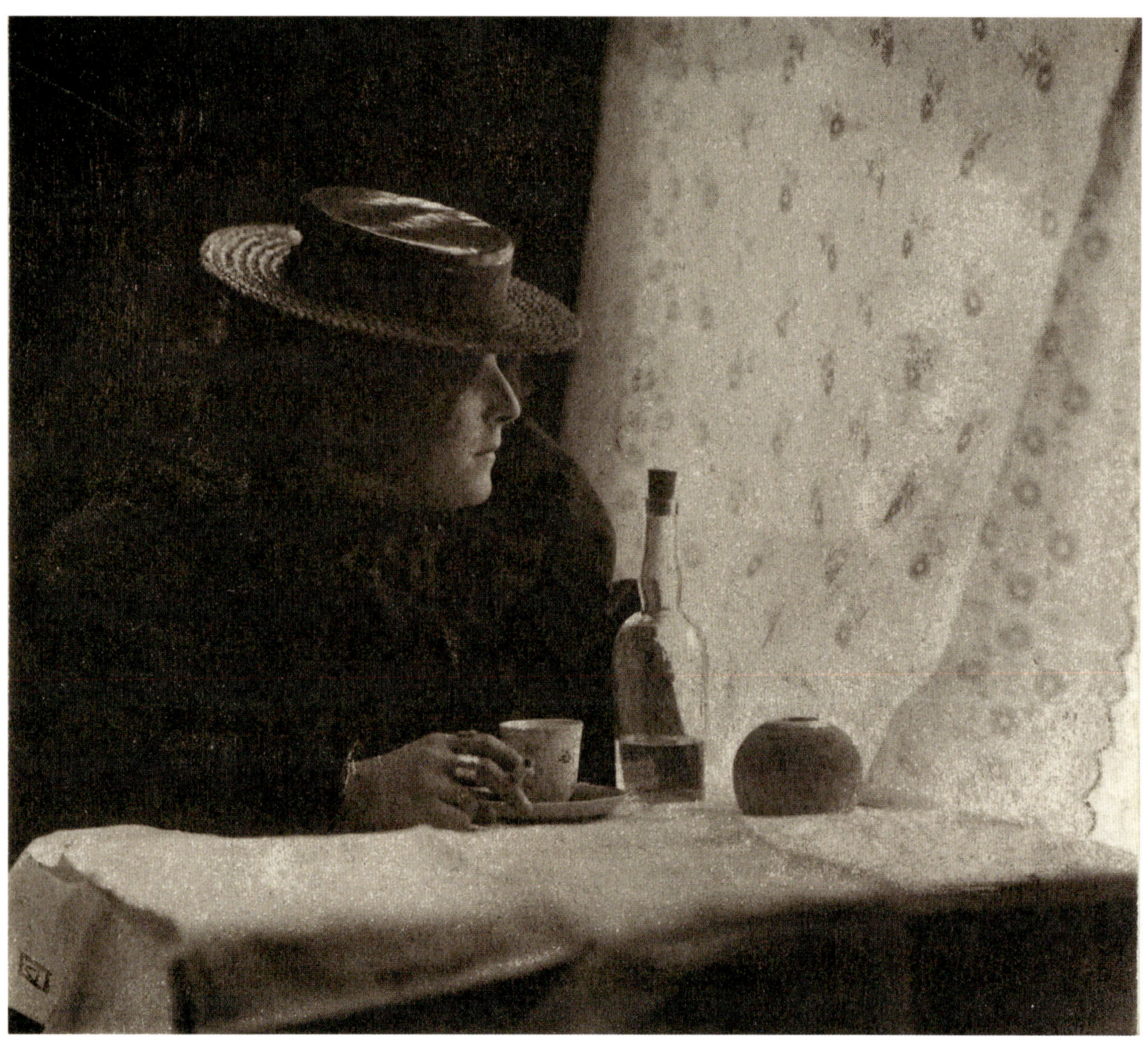

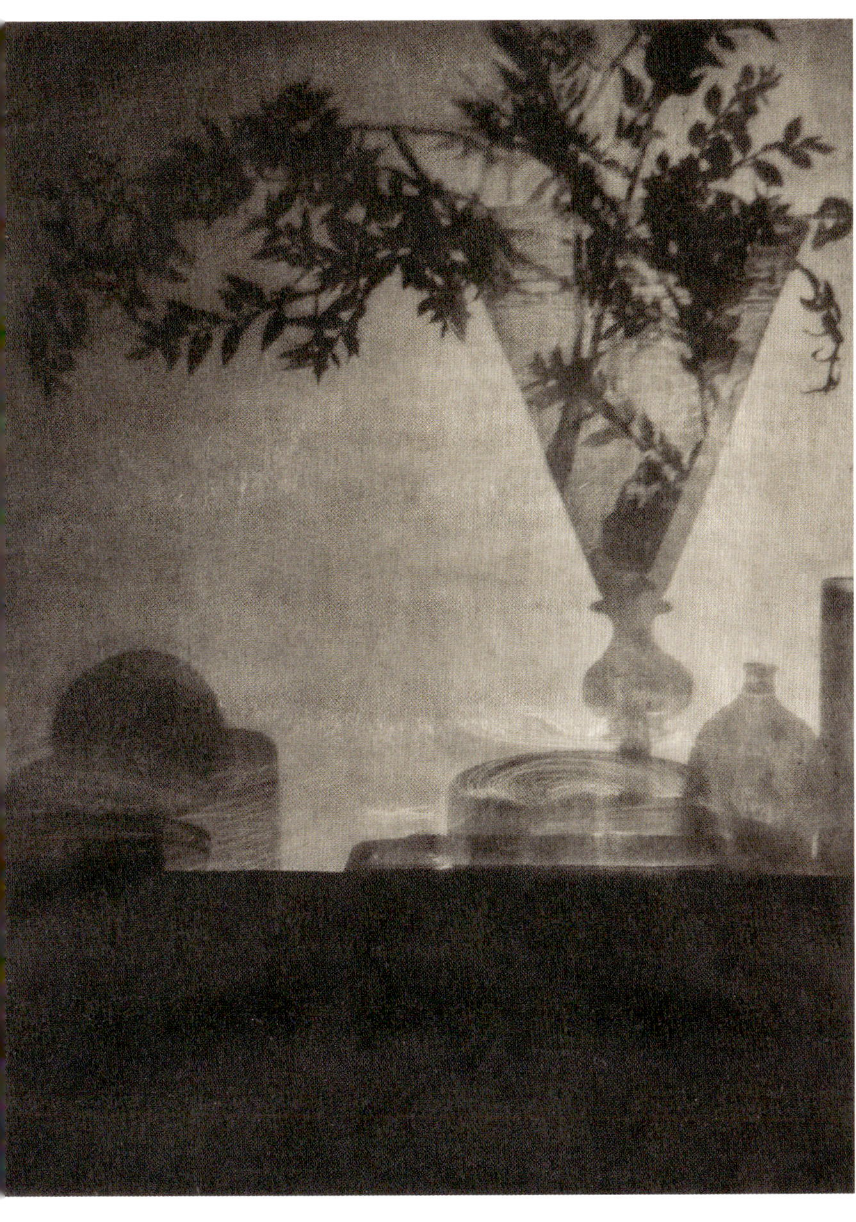

125 Adolphe De Meyer
Glass and Shadows, 1897

126 Heinrich Kühn
Carafe and Glass, ca. 1911

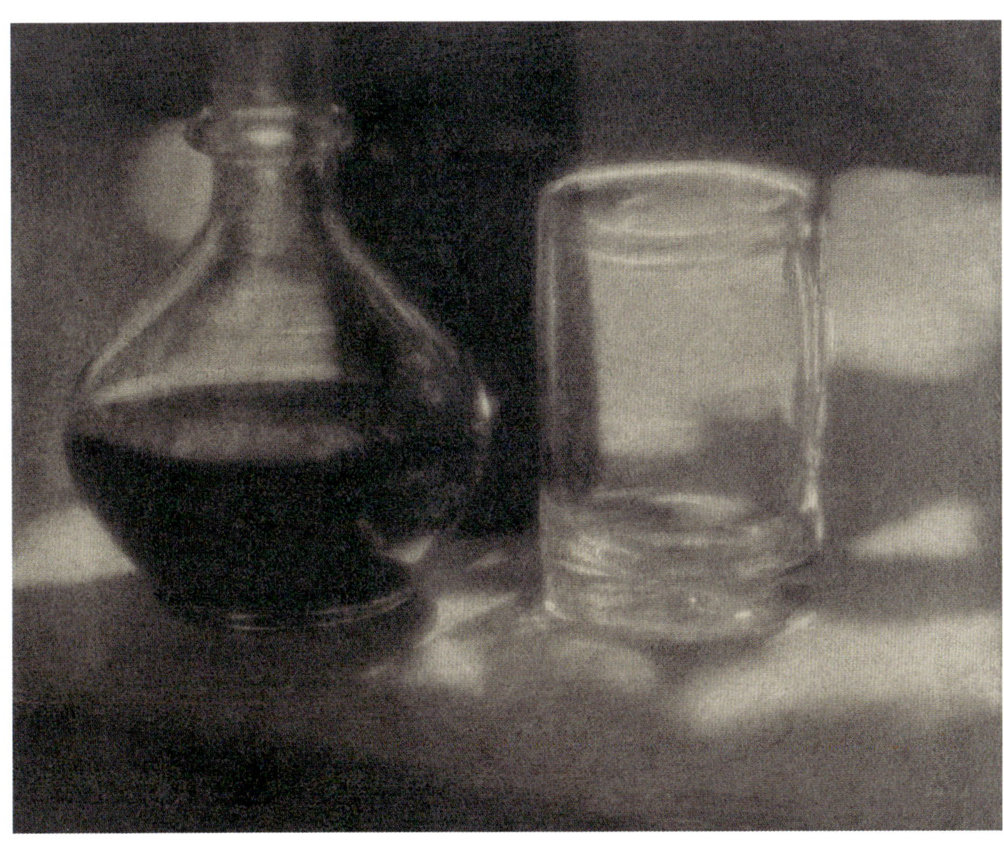

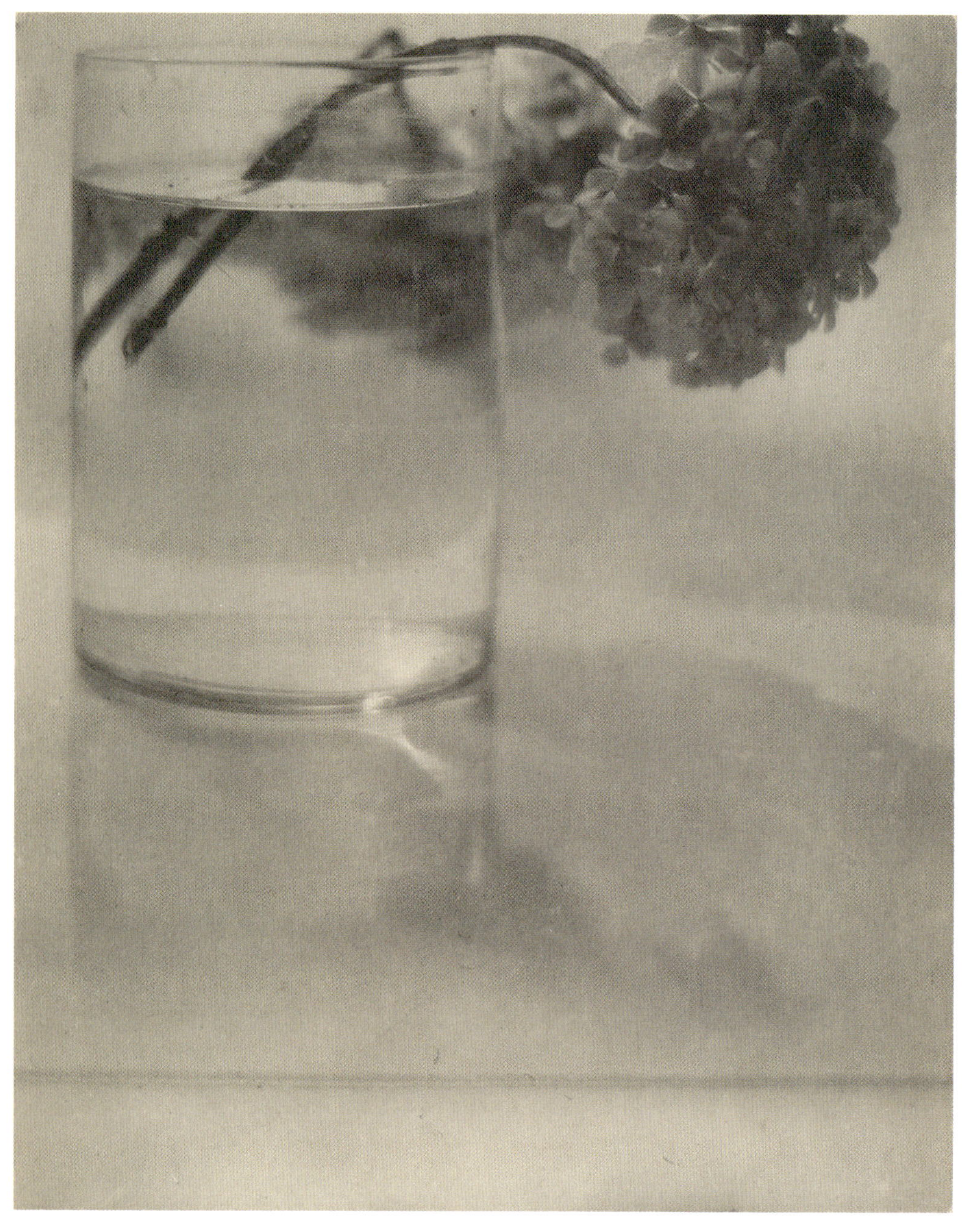

127 Adolphe De Meyer
Still Life, 1908

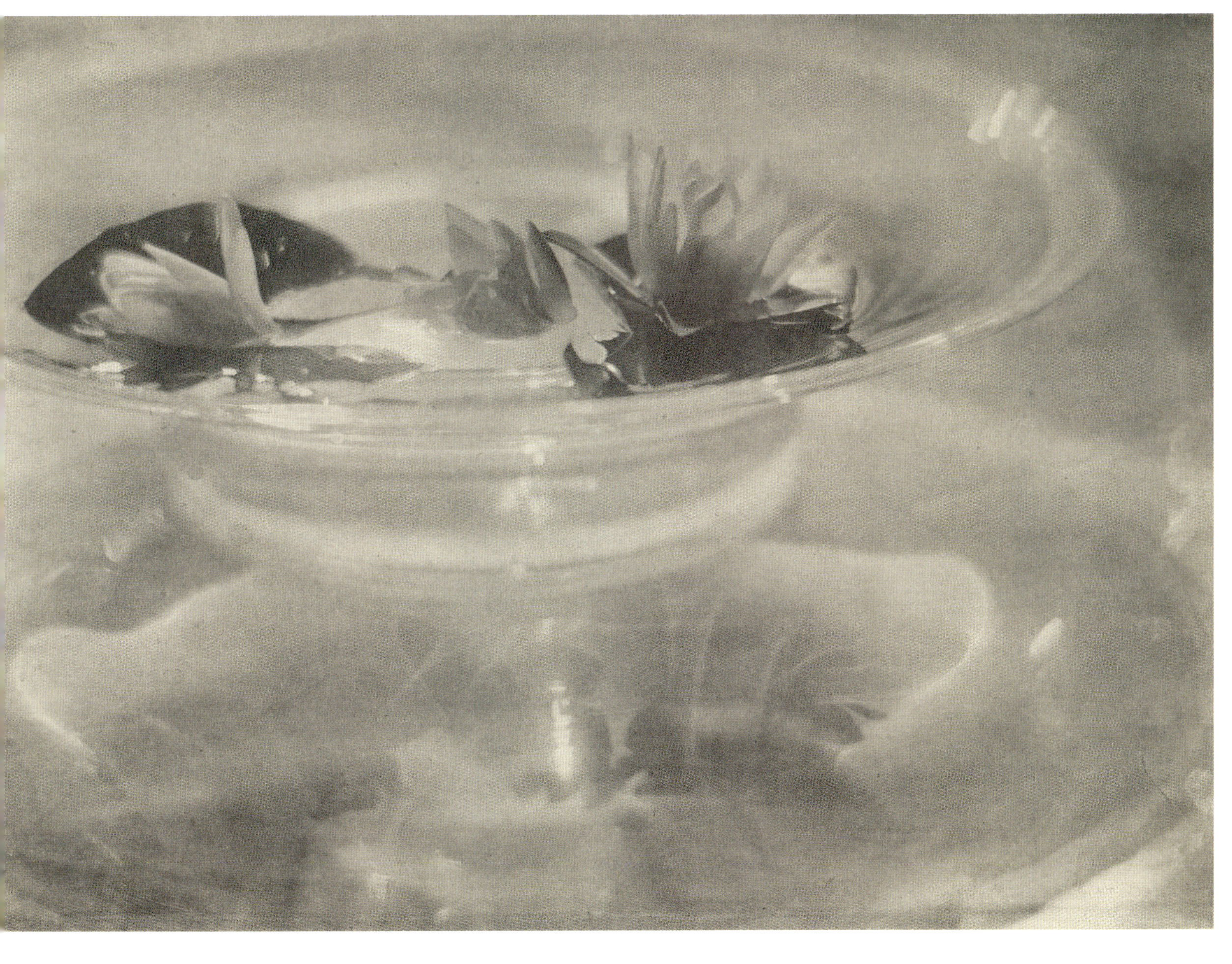

The World in Color
Autochromes

Daniel Zamani

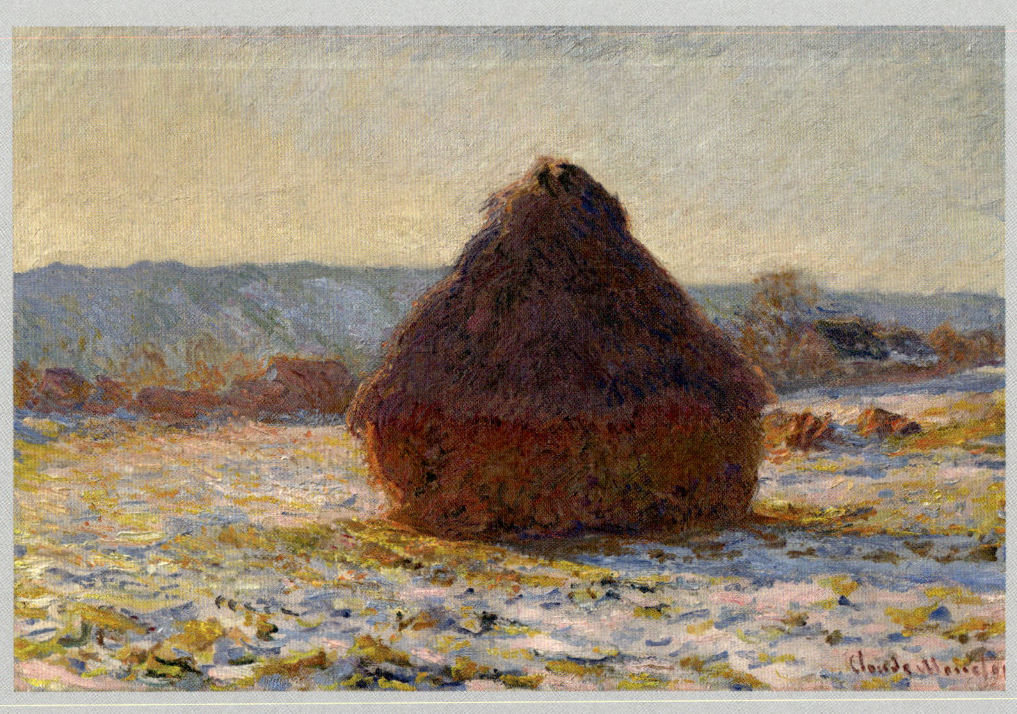

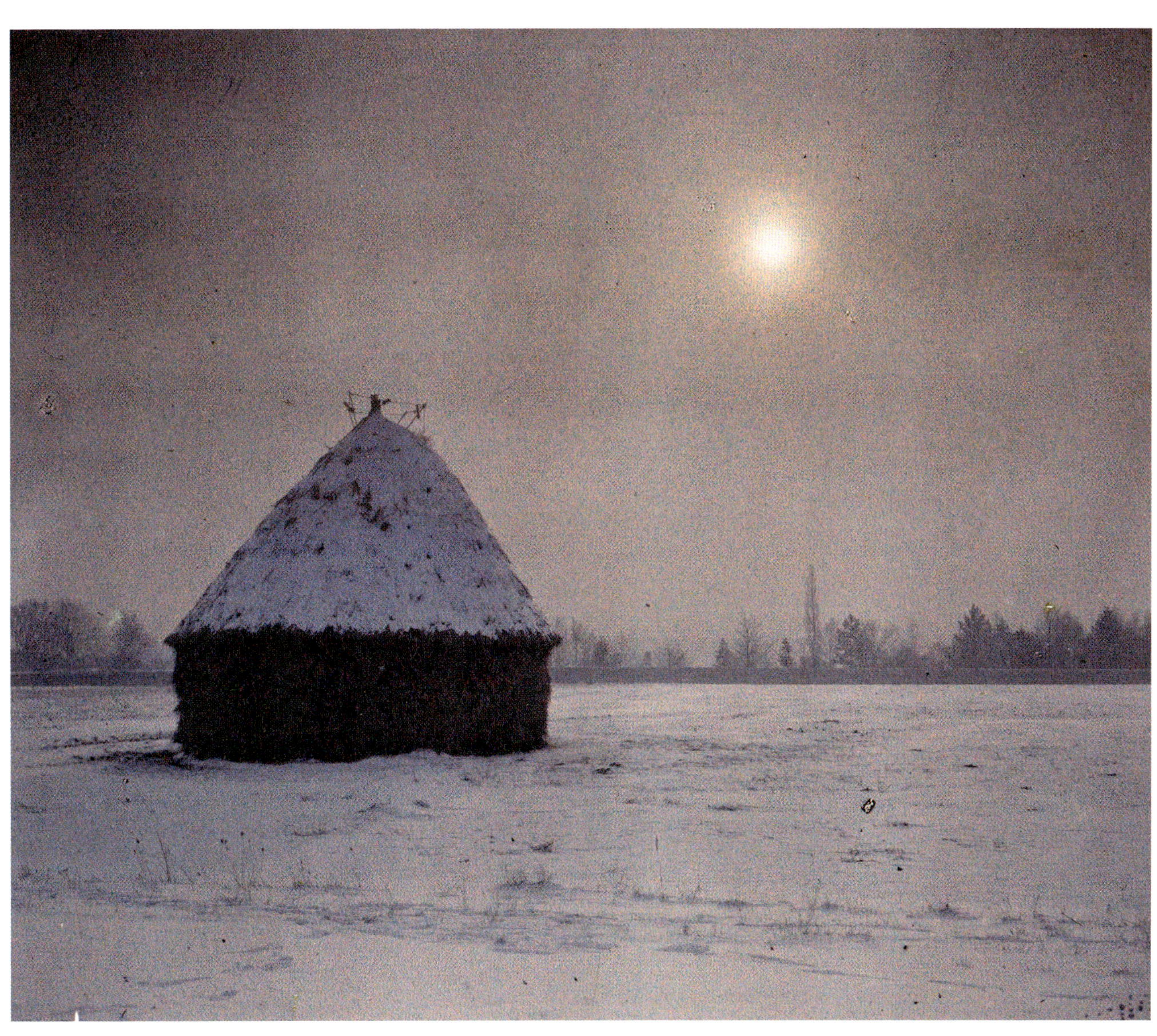

Claude Monet
*Grainstack in the Sunlight, Snow
Effect,* 1891
Oil on canvas
Hasso Plattner Collection

129 Antonin Personnaz
Sunrise with Snow, ca. 1907–14

The autochrome process, invented by the brothers Auguste and Louis Lumière at the beginning of the twentieth century, revolutionized the development of photography.[1] Their industrially manufactured color screen plates, marketed internationally from 1907 on, made it possible to produce color photographs with a single exposure for the first time.[2] Since the mosaic screen plate process was based on additive color mixing, the photographs sometimes showed a grainy effect reminiscent of the fine surface texture of Pointillism. The images were developed on glass plates, enabling them to be projected onto a screen at a considerable size.

Unlike the fine prints preferred by many art photographers, the autochrome did not lend itself to manual manipulation, and many Pictorialists viewed the automatic production process as unsuitable for elevating photography to the status of an autonomous art form.[3] Among amateur photographers, however, the autochrome enjoyed tremendous popularity, until it was superseded by the three-layer color films introduced by Agfa and Kodak in the 1930s.

One of the most zealous champions of the autochrome was the photographer Antonin Personnaz, who had made a name for himself as a collector of Impressionist paintings.[4] He served as secretary general of the Société française de photographie from 1911 to 1919 and came to prominence with publications on the artistic merits of the autochrome process. According to Personnaz, the autochrome was characterized by an inherently Impressionistic pictorial effect, which he sought to amplify through composition and choice of motif. His numerous river landscapes recall the pictorial strategies of Claude Monet and his circle in their evocation of fleeting natural phenomena, such as the play of light from the setting sun or reflections on the gently moving surface of the water (cats. 133, 134). A number of Personnaz's photographs depict landscape painters at work in the outdoors and constitute an avowal of the plein-air aesthetic of Impressionism (cats. 137, 138). One of them shows the artist Armand Guillaumin, a friend of Personnaz, painting his composition *Bathers near Crozant* (cat. 138) in the company of fashionably dressed city-dwellers relaxing on a riverbank. The leaves in the foreground, rustling in the wind, appear blurry, while the middle ground is enlivened by the shifting play of shadow and light. The arrangement of figures is reminiscent of Georges Seurat's painting *A Sunday Afternoon on the Island of La Grande Jatte* (p. 263, fig. 12), which was considered a visual manifesto of Pointillism at its first exhibition in 1886.

Personnaz's dialogue with Impressionist and Post-Impressionist painting also came to the fore in his images of grainstacks, an agricultural subject to which Claude Monet had devoted an entire series in 1890–91. Like his role model, Personnaz explored the motif serially and also methodically studied the imposing conical structures at various times of day and under differing lighting conditions (cats. 129–32). Personnaz preferred to show his autochromes using slide projection, which permitted the photographs to be enlarged to formats typical of painting. Another motif from Monet's art to be adopted by contemporary photographers was the dramatic rock formations of Normandy—including the stone arch known as the Porte d'Aval in Étretat, which Monet had painted a number of times in the 1880s (ill., p. 74). A photograph by Louise Deglane, who like

Personnaz was a member of the Société française de photographie, shows a view of the towering cliff across a beach crowded with boats. Here, as in many autochromes, the painterly impression is enhanced by the lack of focus, which gives a diffuse quality to the forms in the middle ground and background. The contrasting interplay of pink and green enlivens the composition, which is dominated by pale tones of white and gray.

Austrian art photographer Heinrich Kühn likewise made extensive use of the autochrome, producing several hundred photographs between 1907 and 1913.[5] For Kühn, the charm of the autochrome lay in its unnaturally vivid color, which according to him made it easy to achieve "picturesque results."[6] Like the Impressionists, Kühn attempted to give his compositions a sense of immediacy and spontaneity, although his photographs were scenographically orchestrated down to the smallest detail. Strategies that Kühn had used in his fine art prints—such as the interplay of focused and blurred forms and the varying juxtapositions of light and shadow—also underpinned the aesthetic of his autochrome photographs (cf. cats. 139, 142). In addition, the new technique also required a trained eye for the interaction of differing colors as well as the way in which they could influence the perception of space. Thus Kühn argued that blue tones intensified the sense of depth, while eye-catching red was suitable for the foreground.

Kühn's 1910 photograph *Miss Mary in a Blue Dress* (cat. 140) shows Mary Warner, his partner and frequent model. The young woman casually leans on the walking stick in her right hand and gazes confidently at the viewer. In the background, the soft purplish-blue of the sky and the vibrating greenish-brown of the grassy hill adjoin one another like layered bands, while the decorative silhouette of Mary's elegant dark-blue dress stands out against the sunlit backdrop. Kühn's skillful use of color as an element of design is also evident in the photograph *Landscape* (cat. 142), a work remarkable for its unusually high vantage point. The green of the meadow fills the entire background, while a stark cast shadow divides the image into approximately equal zones of light and dark. The diagonal line of the shadow lends the composition a dynamic element, echoed in the group of rambling figures moving in the opposite direction. The arched arrangement of the figures leads the viewer's gaze from the center of the picture toward the upper left, where the red dress of the young girl sets a powerful accent. The variety of gestures and poses make this carefully orchestrated composition seem like a casual snapshot. Despite the considerable distance, the hikers seen from the rear offer a point of identification for the viewer—a pictorial effect reflective of Kühn's conviction that a photograph should "present the slice of nature just as we saw it with emotional participation." Like the Impressionists, he too sought to imbue his images with the sense of an "inner perception" going beyond the mere reproduction of visible reality.[7]

Translated from German by Melissa M. Thorson

[1] On the history of the autochrome, see Boulouch 1999, Lavédrine/Gandolfo 2013, and Fuchs 2017.

[2] The color screen plates were sold under the slogan "autochrome—automatically colored" in sizes of 18 × 24, 13 × 18, and 9 × 12 centimeters and were about three times as expensive as black-and-white plates.

[3] Cf. Natalie Boulouch, "Les Pictorialistes et le procédé autochrome," in Paris 1993, 35–40.

[4] On Personnaz and Impressionism, see Rouen 2020.

[5] Cf. Schögl 2014 as well as Monika Faber's contribution, 54–65.

[6] Kühn 1921, 222.

[7] Heinrich Kühn, quoted in Schögl 2002, 118.

130 Antonin Personnaz
Field, Haystack, ca. 1907–14

131 Antonin Personnaz
Fields and Haystacks, Fog,
ca. 1907–14

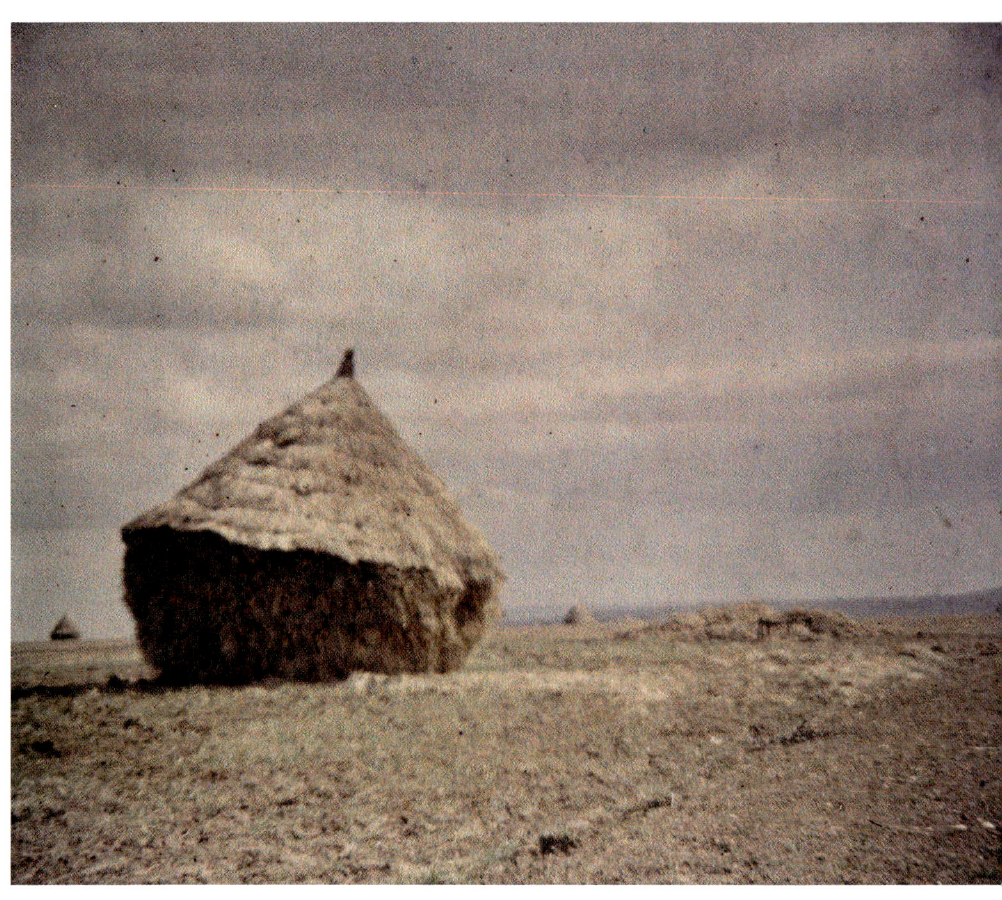

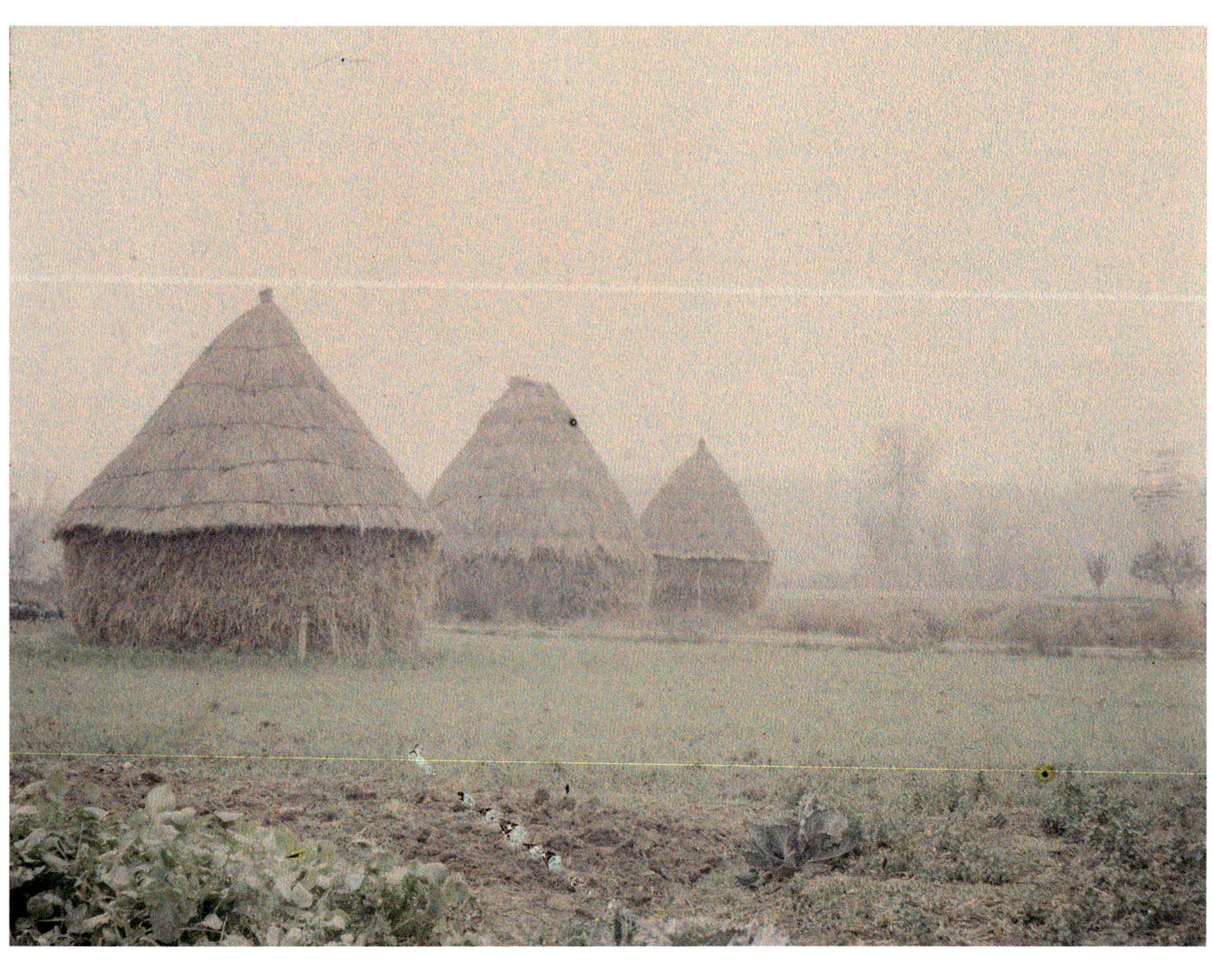

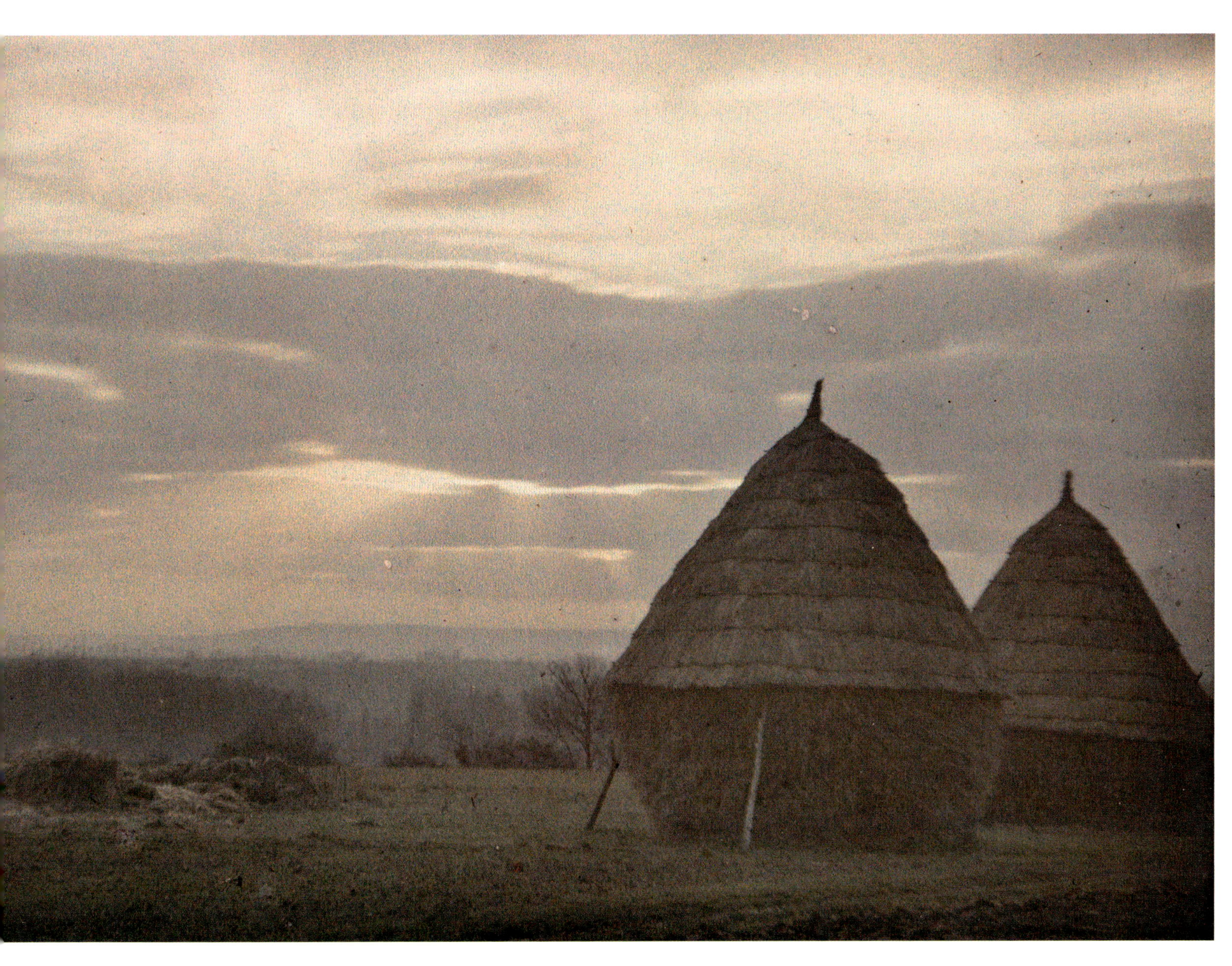

132 Antonin Personnaz
Field, Haystacks at Sunset,
ca. 1907–14

Barges, Boat, Crane, ca. 1907–14

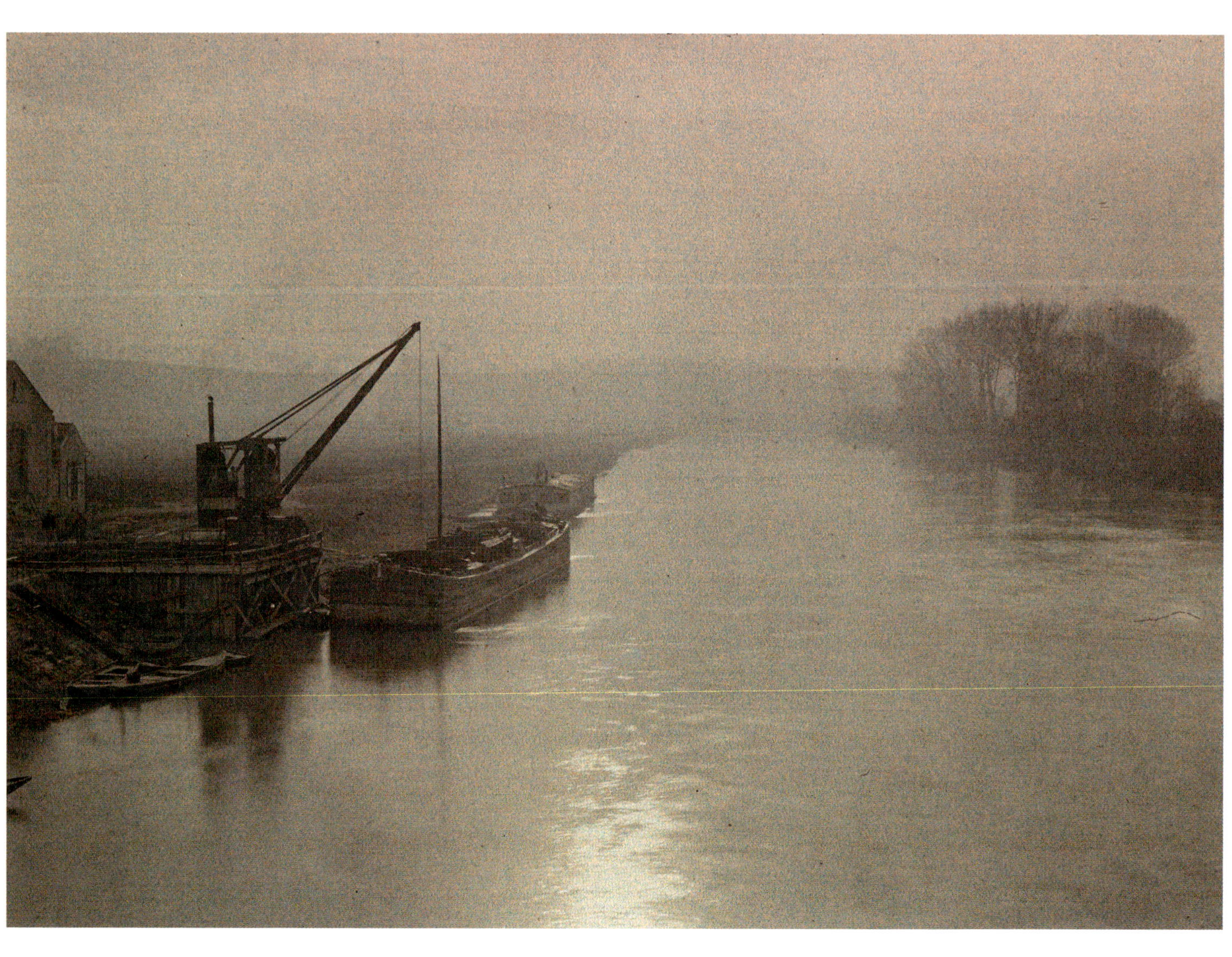

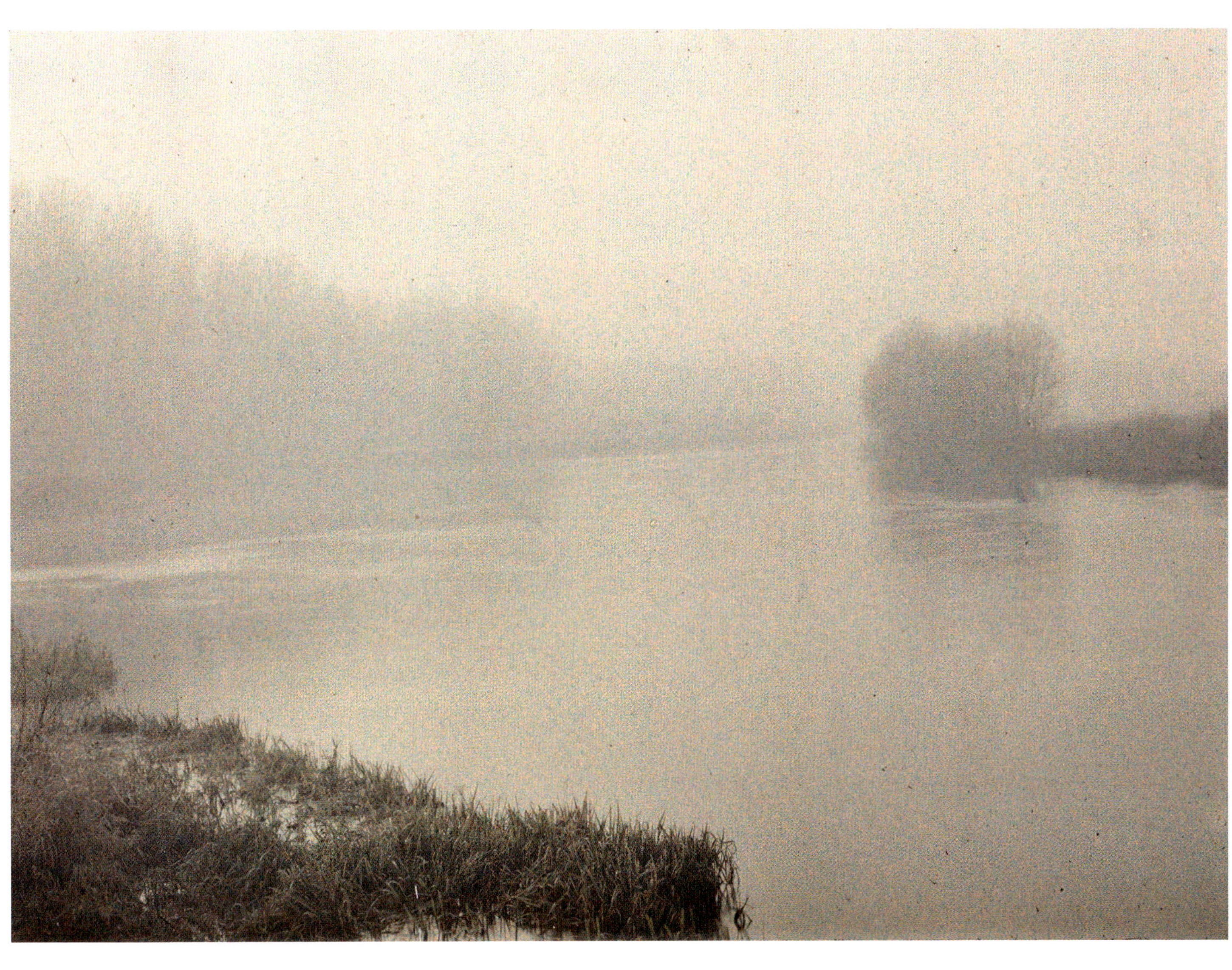

134 Antonin Personnaz
Fog over the Water, ca. 1907–14

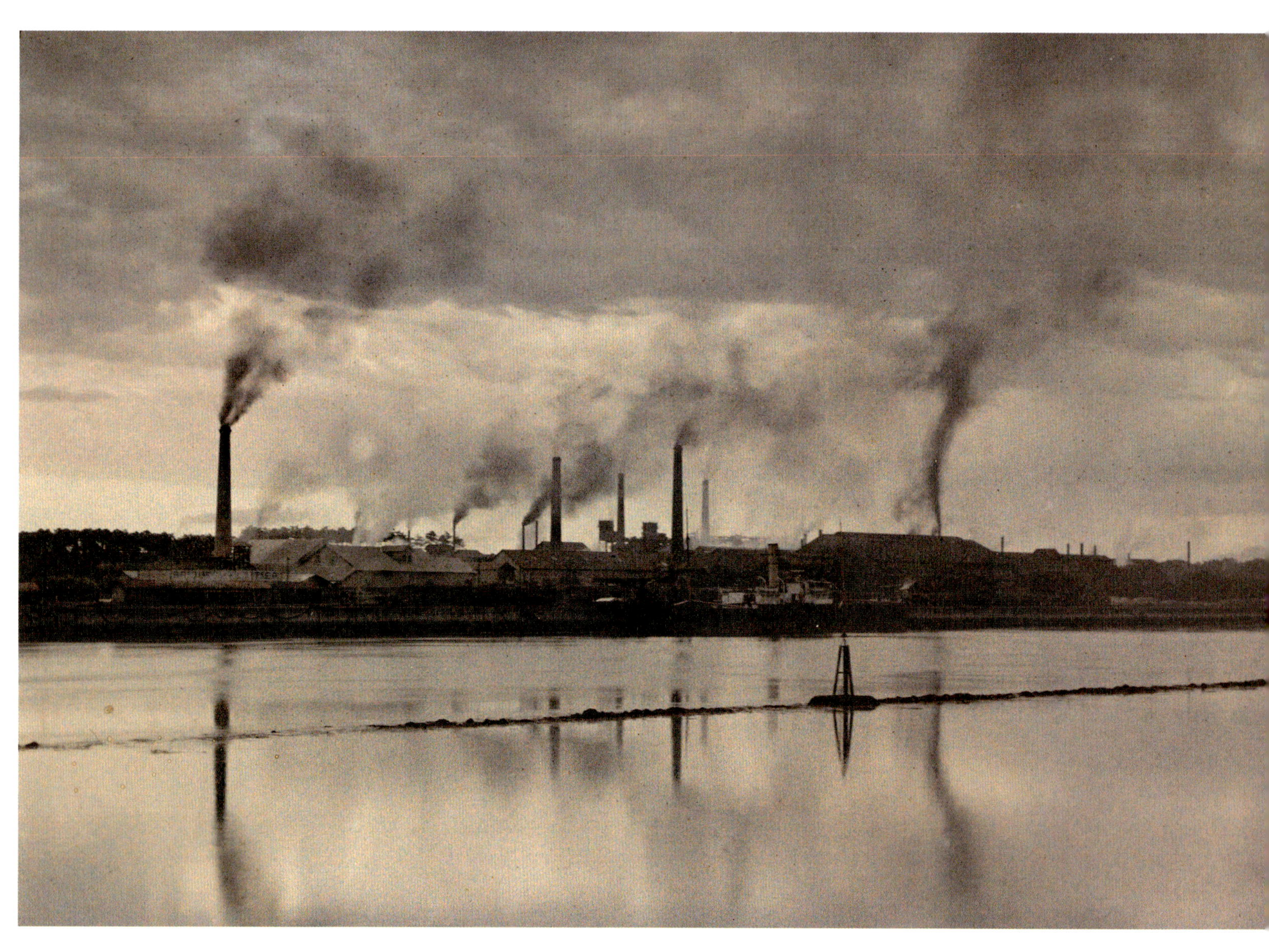

135 Antonin Personnaz
River, Factory, Smoke, ca. 1907–14

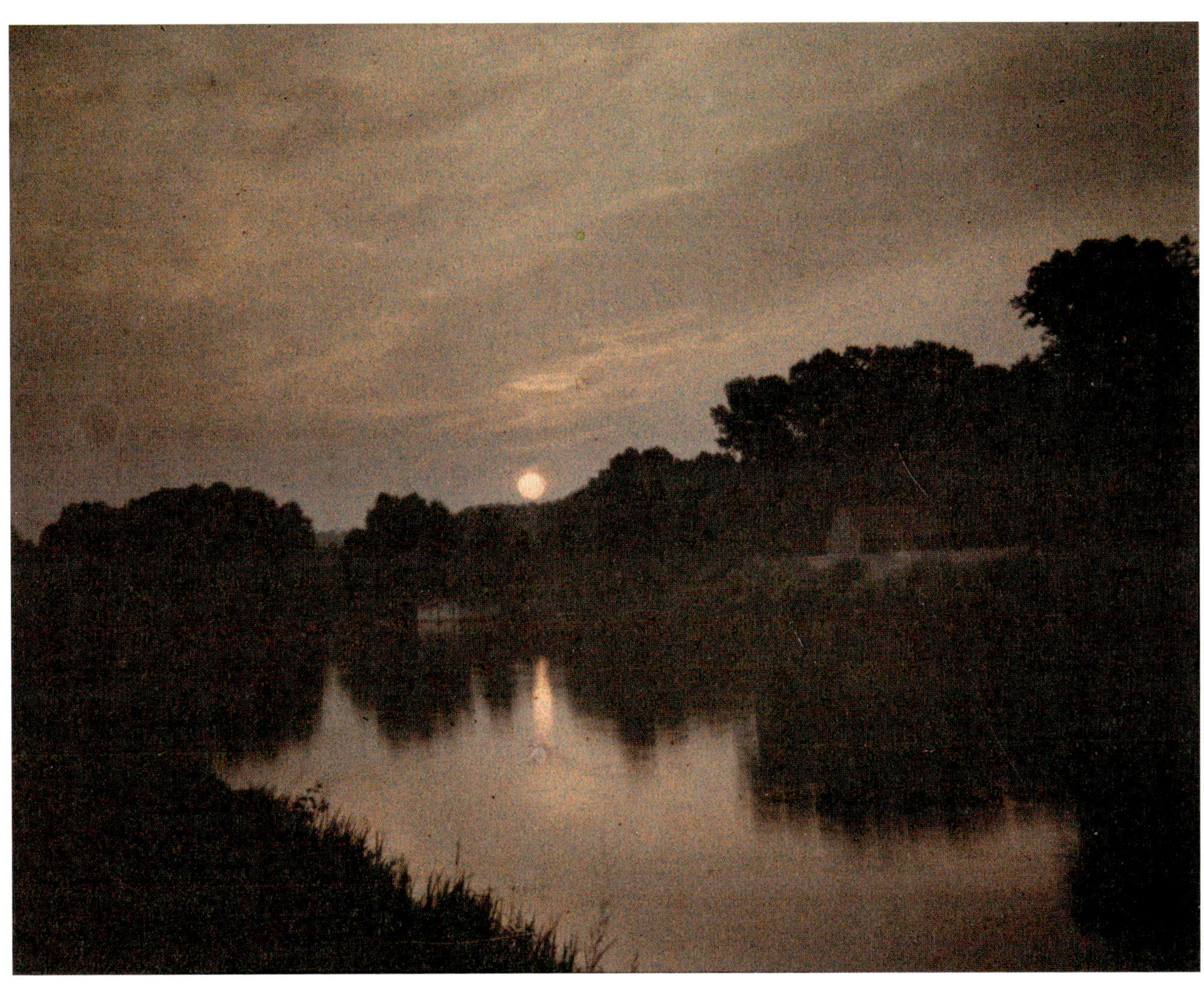

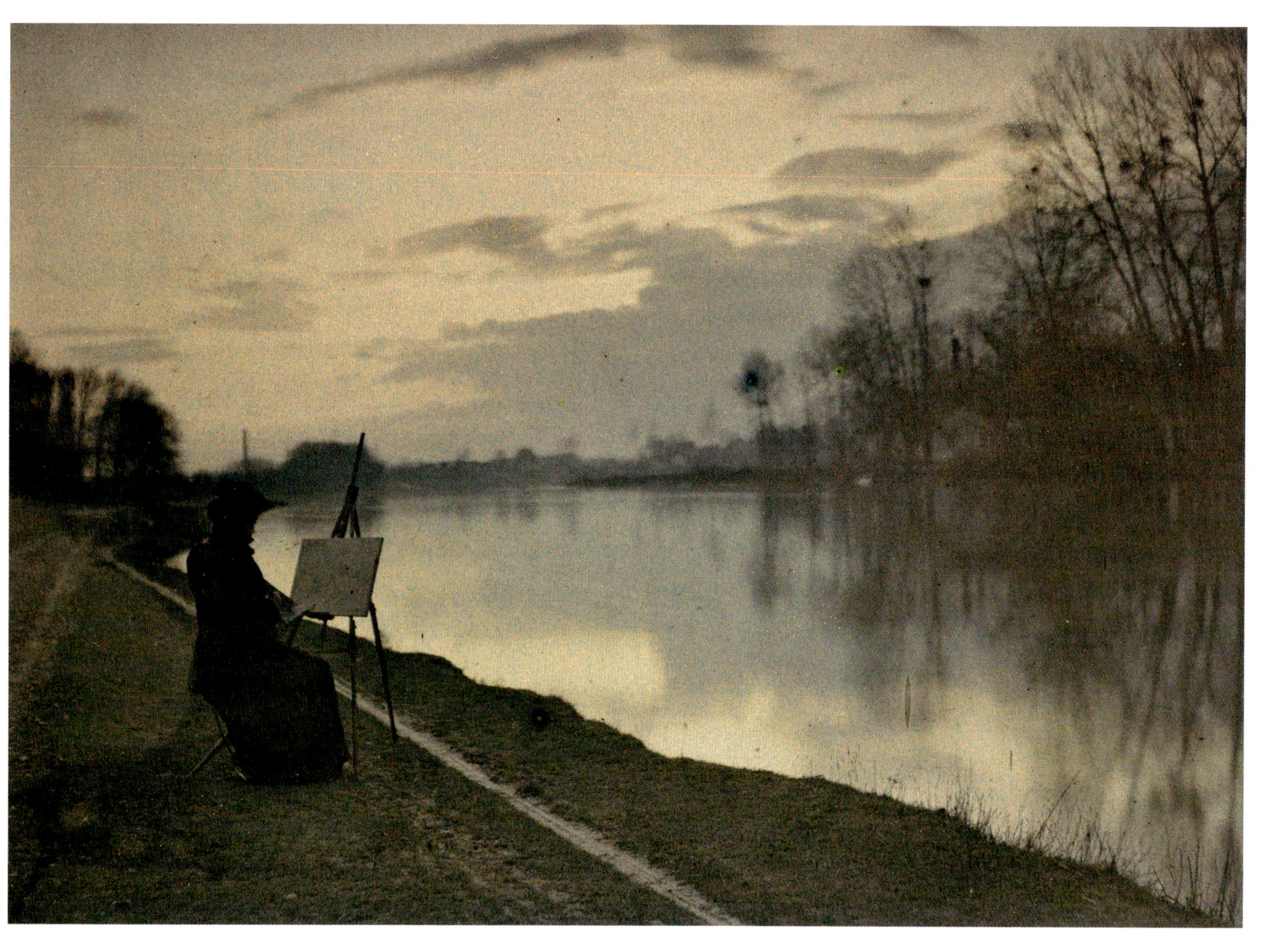

137 Antonin Personnaz
Woman Painting Before the Motif,
ca. 1907–14

138 Antonin Personnaz
*Armand Guillaumin Painting
"Bathers near Crozant,"* ca. 1907

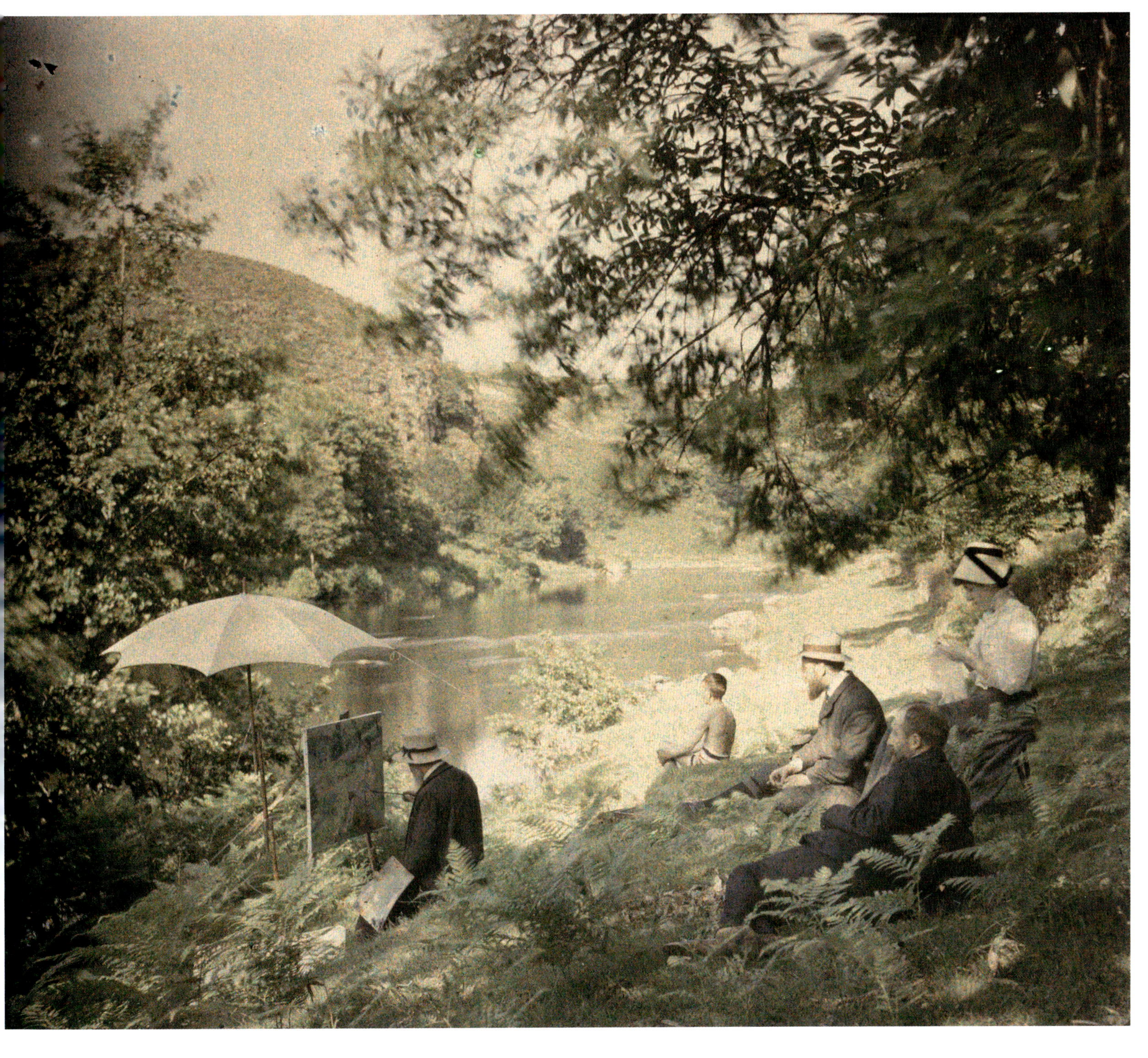

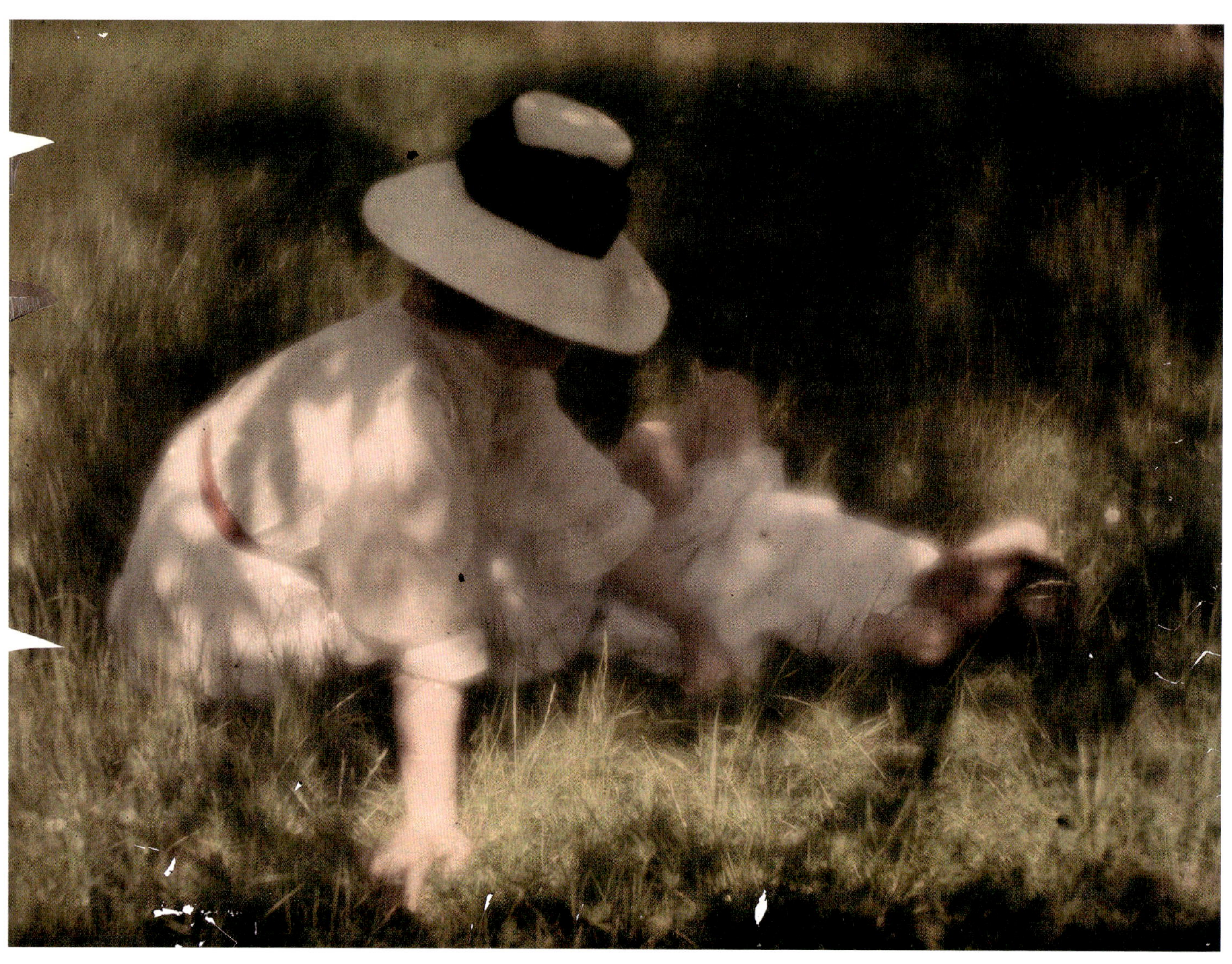

226

139 Heinrich Kühn
Miss Mary and Lotte, 1907

140 Heinrich Kühn
Miss Mary in a Blue Dress, 1910

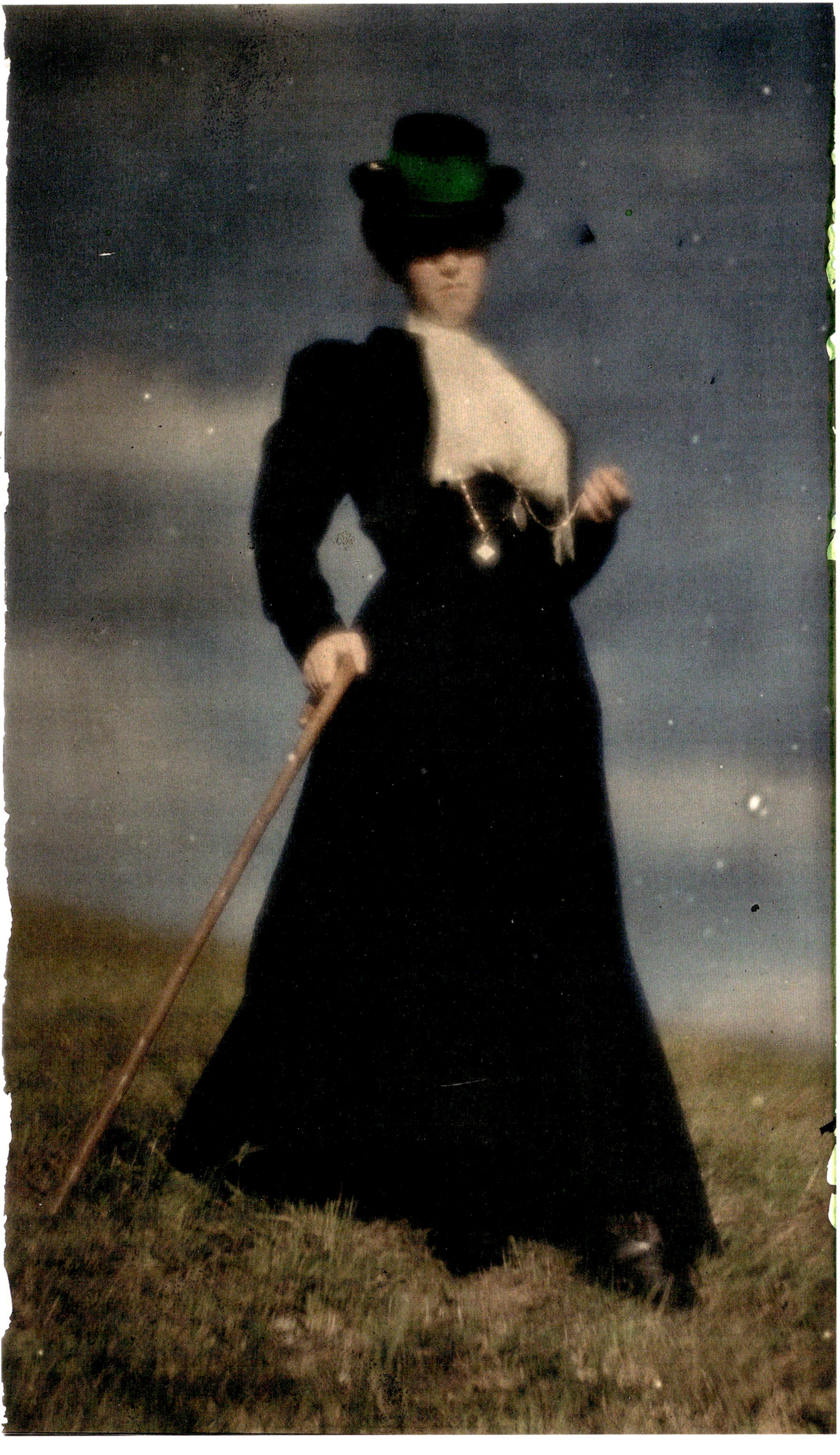

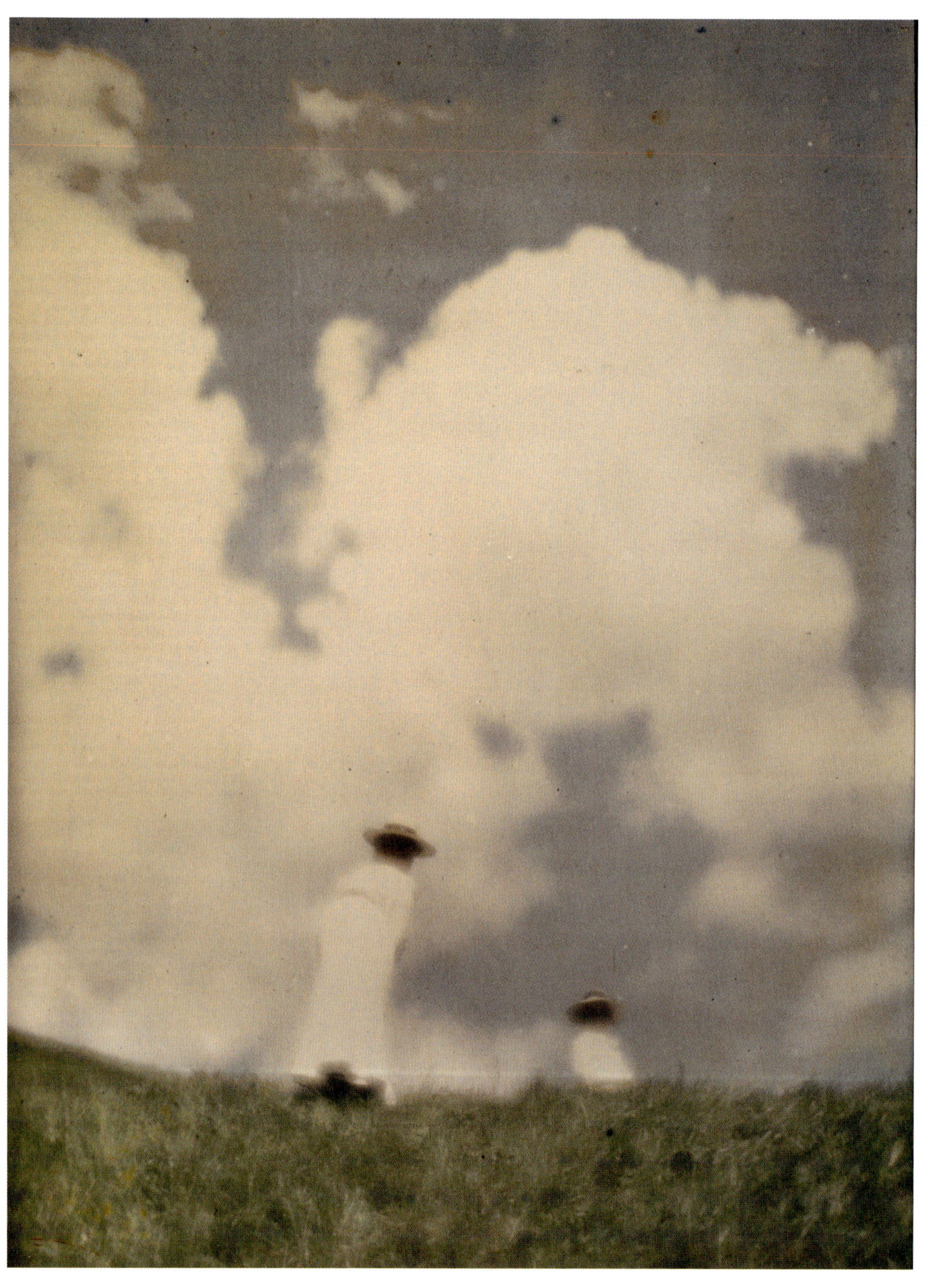

141 Heinrich Kühn
*Mary Warner and Edeltrude on
the Brow of a Hill,* ca. 1908

142 Heinrich Kühn
Landscape, ca. 1912–15

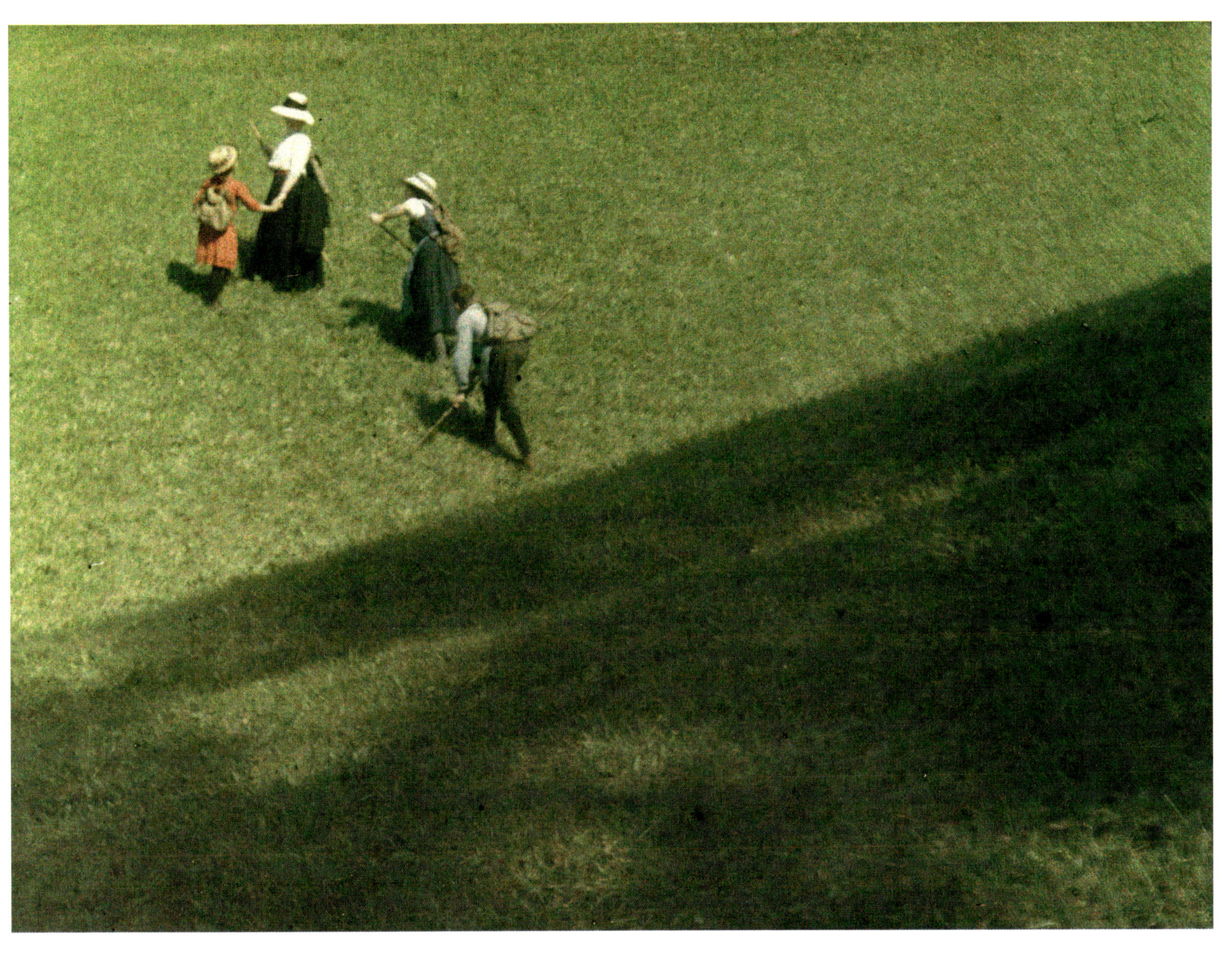

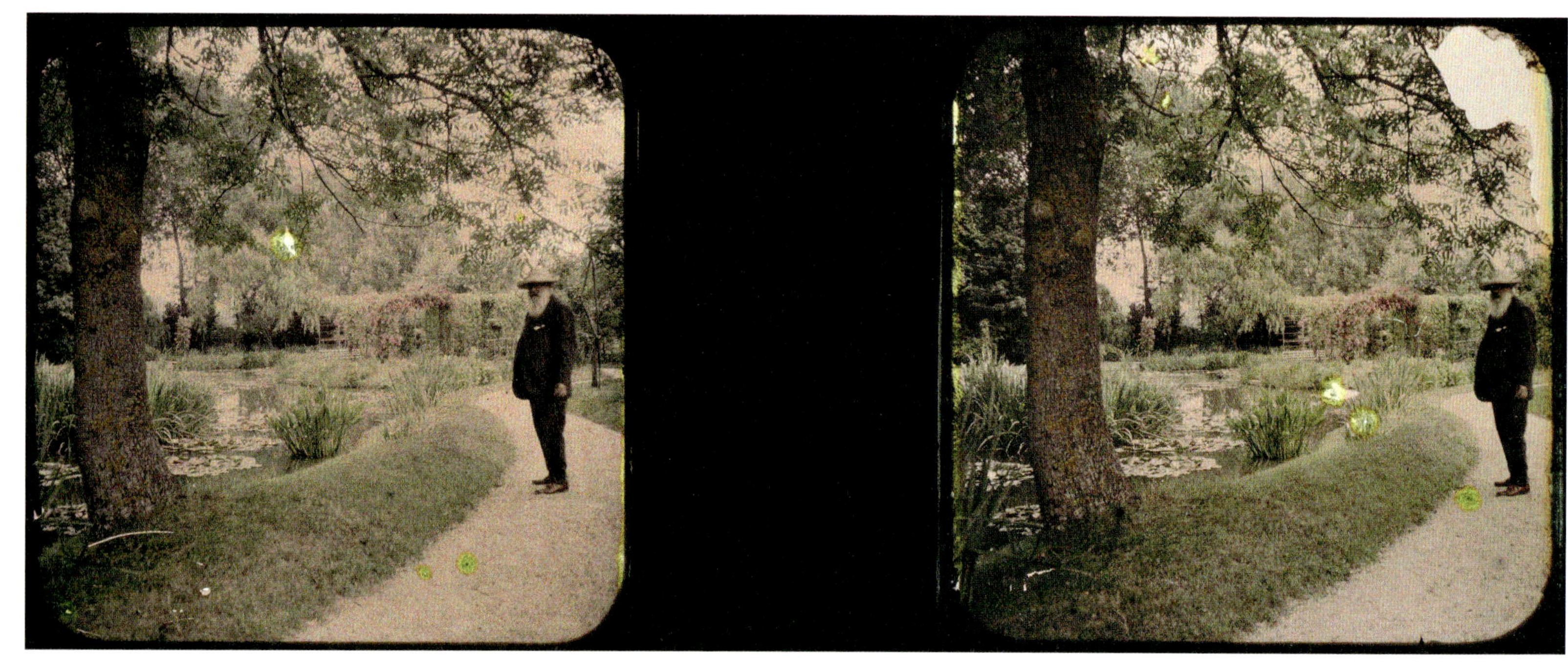

143 Étienne Clémentel
*Claude Monet Standing in Profile
before the Water Lilies in the
Garden at Giverny*, ca. 1920

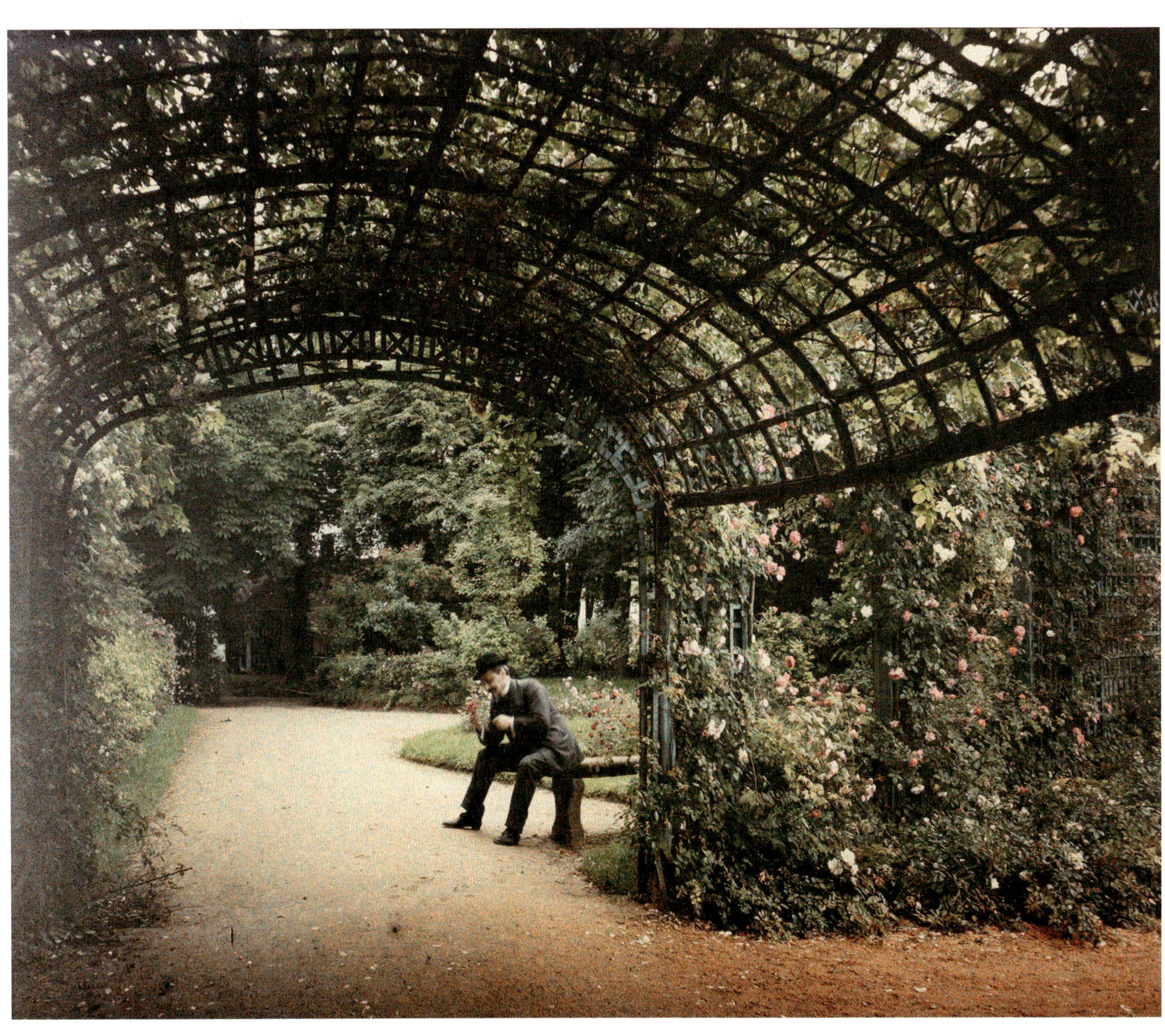

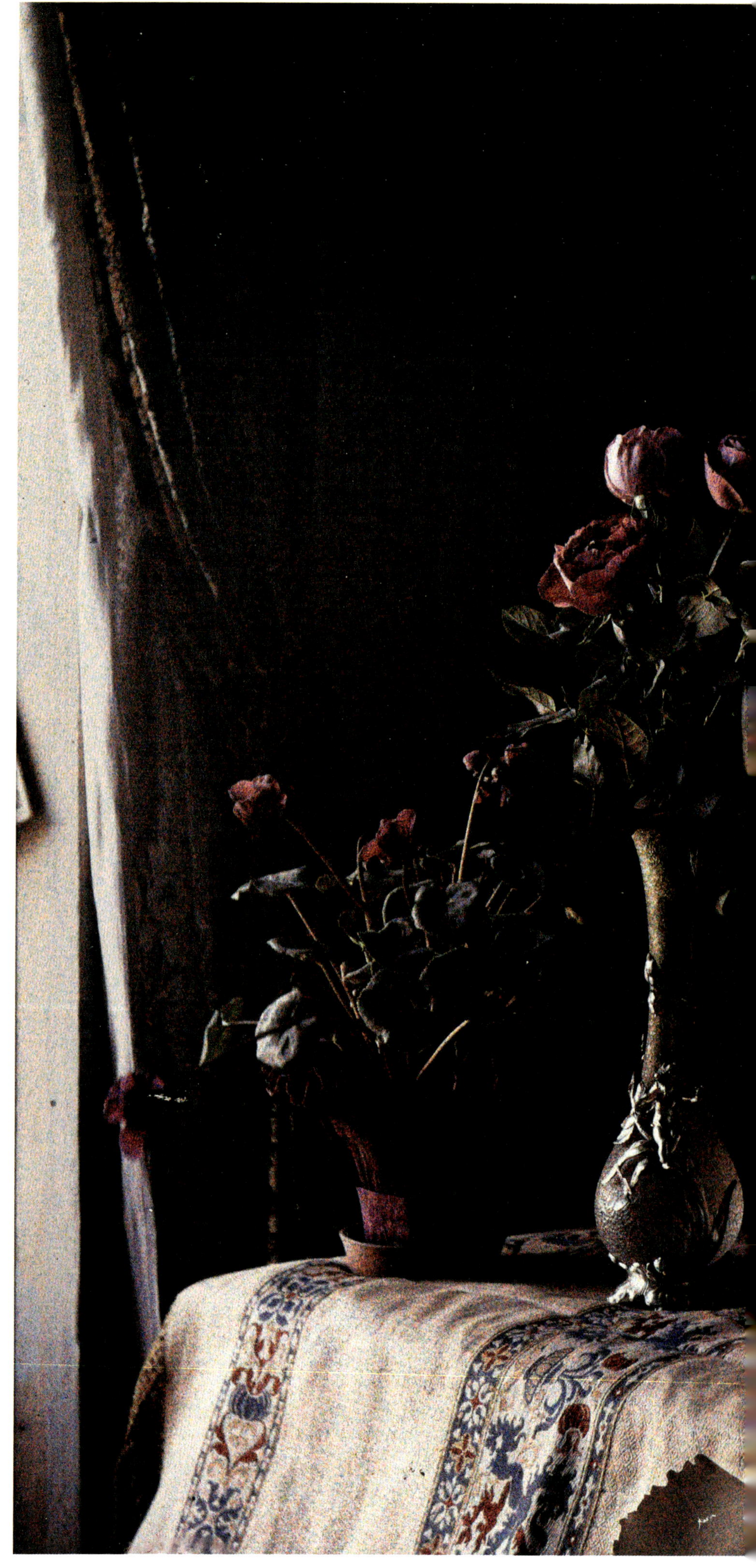

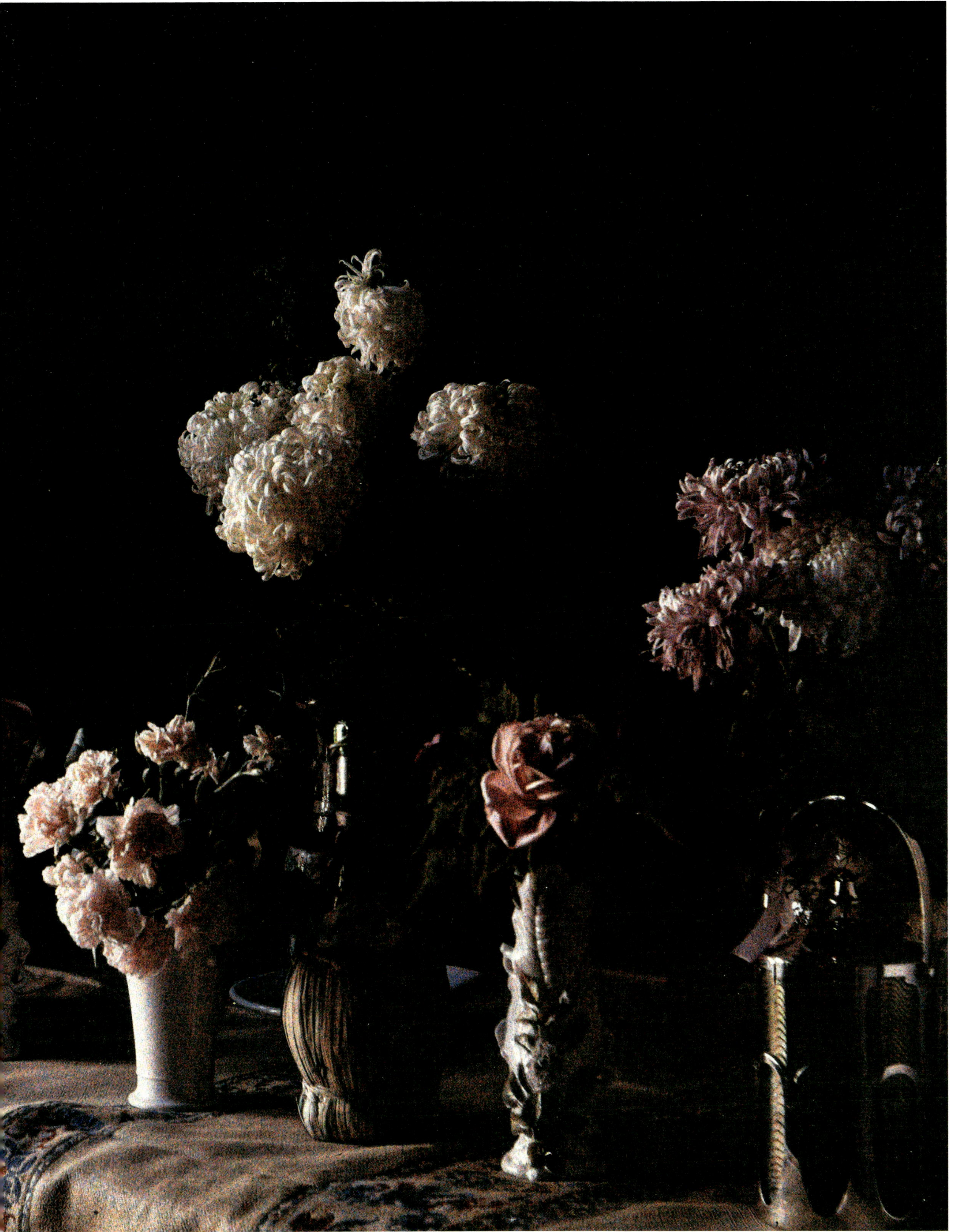

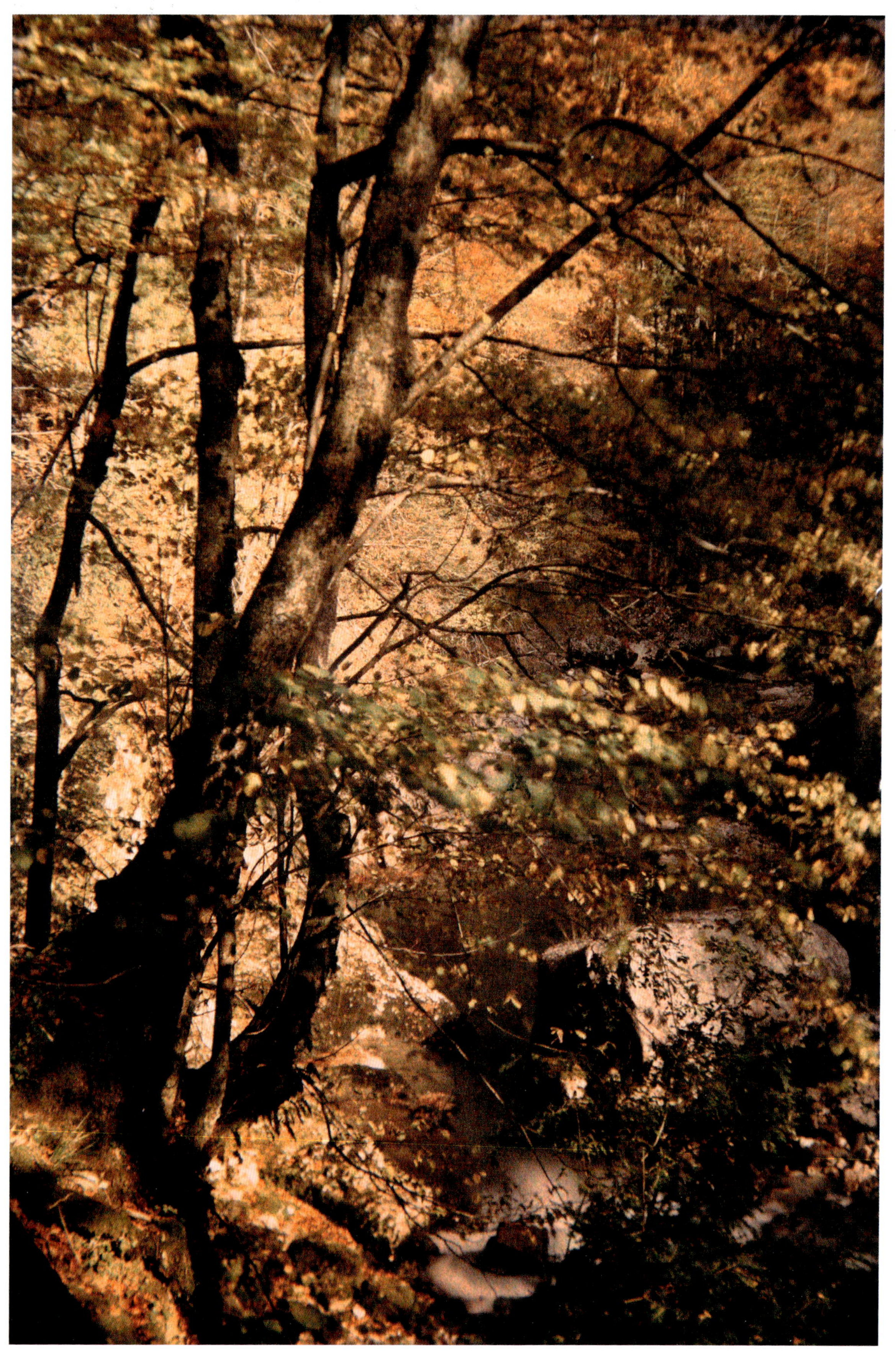

146 Auguste and Louis Lumière
Autumn Scene, 1907

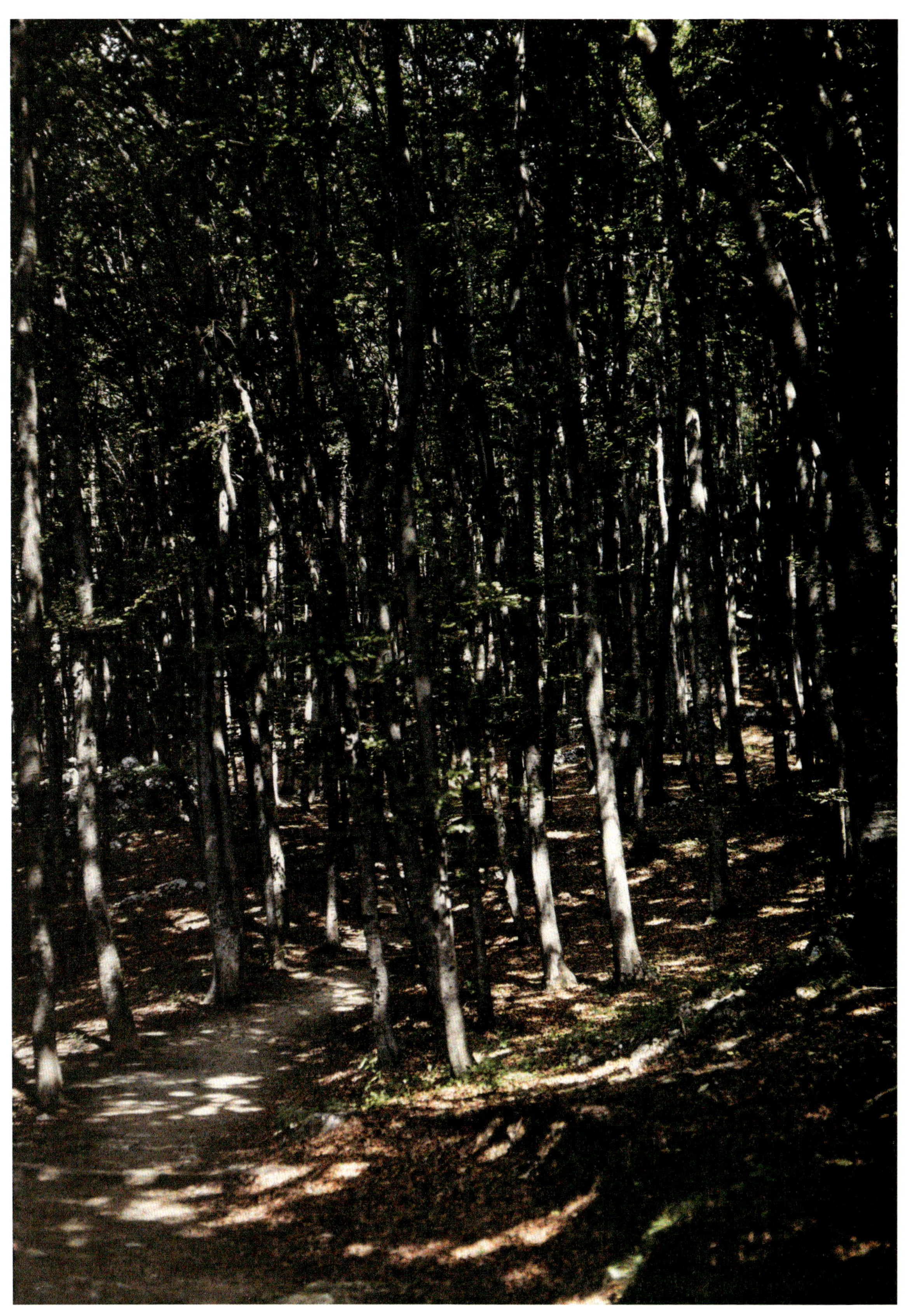

147 Hohmann
Deciduous Forest, ca. 1910

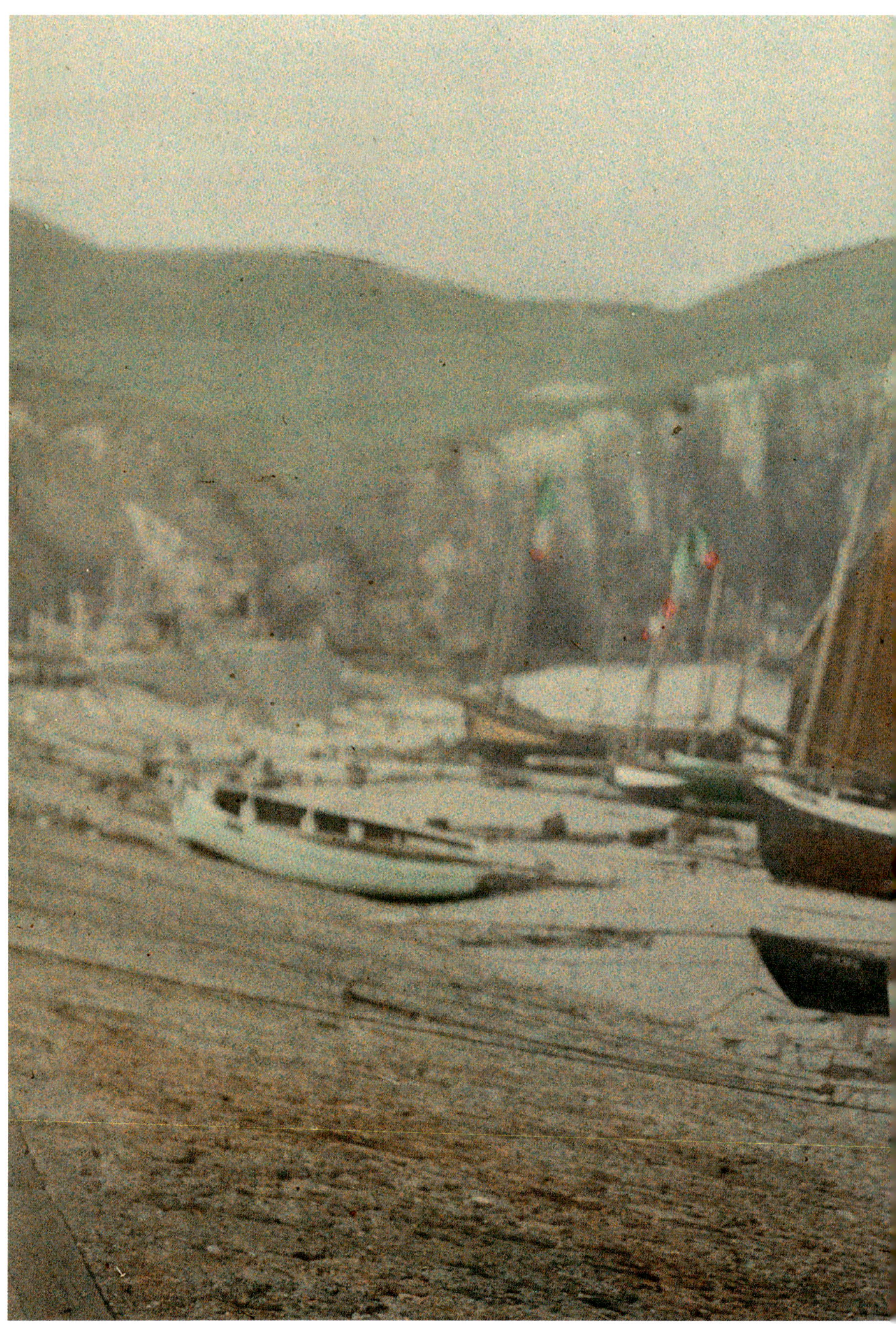

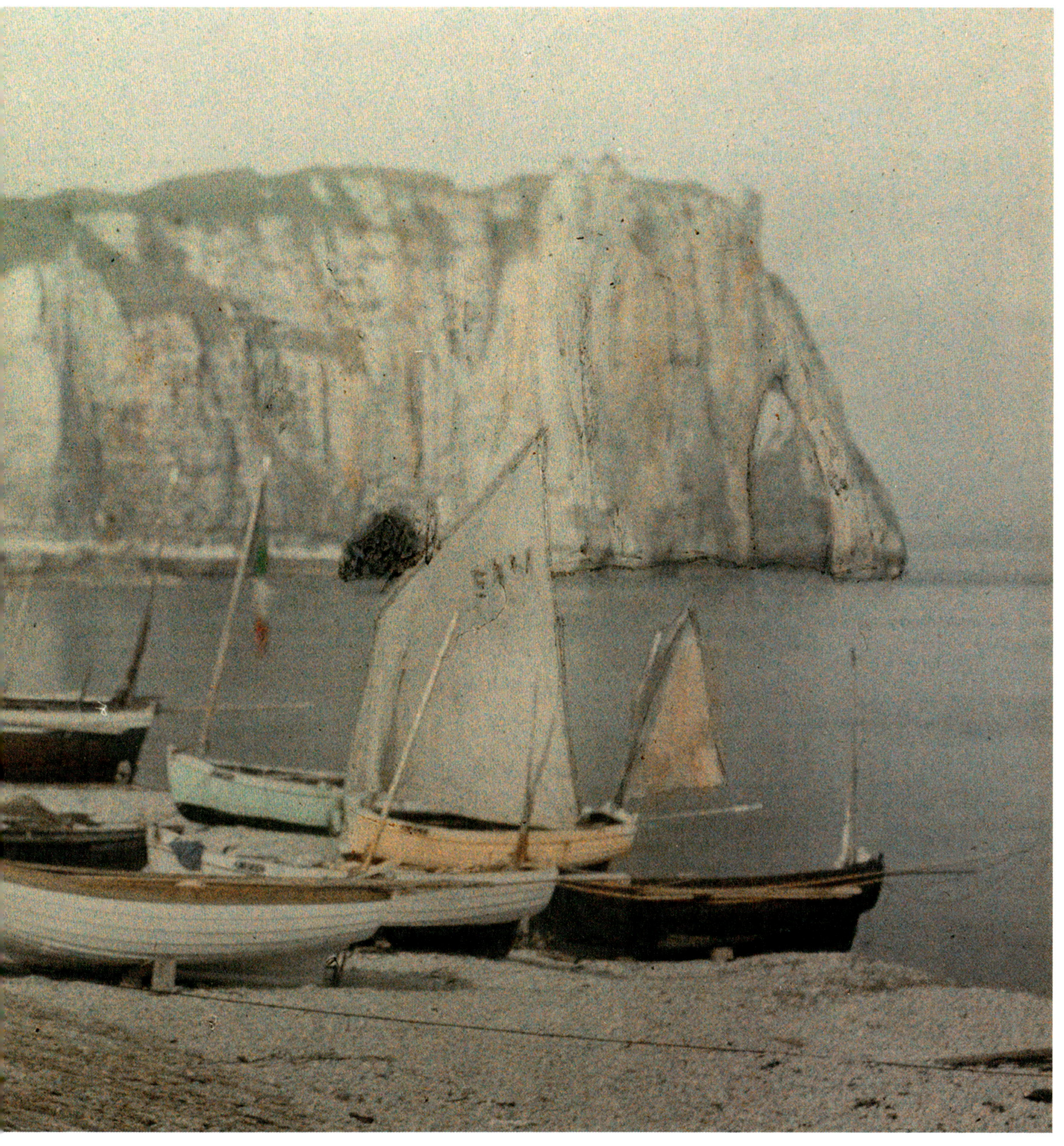

List of Exhibited Works

Majestic Expanses:
Sky and Sea

1 Louis Alphonse Davanne (1824–1912)
Étretat, Cliff to the Left, No. 2, 1864
Albumen print, 21.1 × 30.9 cm
Beaux-Arts de Paris
Inv. no. PH 234
(Potsdam only)

2 Louis Alphonse Davanne (1824–1912)
Étretat, ca. 1864
Albumen print, 21.2 × 30 cm
Société française de photographie, Paris
Inv. no. rSFP_0094im_EP_0087
(Potsdam and Wuppertal)

3 Anonymous
Étretat, from the album *Bretagne
Normandie,* 1889
Gelatin print, album 32 × 27 cm
Münchner Stadtmuseum, Munich,
Sammlung Fotografie
Inv. no. FM 97/236.1
(Potsdam and Wuppertal)

4 Arthur Da Cunha
(documented in the 1890s)
Étretat, 1895
Photogravure, 9 × 11.6 cm
Musée d'Orsay, Paris
Inv. no. PHO 1991 15 35
(Potsdam only)

5 Gustave Le Gray (1820–1884)
The Sun at Zenith, Normandy, 1856–57
Albumen print, 31.2 × 40.2 cm
Musée des Beaux-Arts de Troyes
Inv. no. MAH.D.46.19.574
(Potsdam only)

6 Gustave Le Gray (1820–1884)
Sunlight in the Clouds—Ocean, 1856
Albumen print, 31 × 38 cm
Céline, Aeneas, Heiner Bastian
(Potsdam only)

7 Gustave Le Gray (1820–1884)
Cloud Study, Clair-obscur, 1856–57
Albumen print, 31 × 41 cm
Céline, Aeneas, Heiner Bastian
(Potsdam only)

8 Henry Stuart Wortley (1832–1890)
*How Sweet the Moonlight Sleeps upon
the Wave,* ca. 1869
Albumen print, 29.4 × 35.3 cm
Céline, Aeneas, Heiner Bastian
(Potsdam only)

9 Gustave Le Gray (1820–1884)
Steam, 1856
Albumen print, 32 × 41 cm
Céline, Aeneas, Heiner Bastian
(Potsdam only)

10 Gustave Le Gray (1820–1884)
The Brig (*Brig in Moonlight*), 1856
Albumen print, 32 × 41 cm
Céline, Aeneas, Heiner Bastian
(Potsdam only)

11 Gustave Le Gray (1820–1884)
Salute of the French Fleet off Cherbourg,
1858
Albumen print, 21.8 × 28.3 cm
Musée des Beaux-Arts de Troyes
Inv. no. MAH.D.46.19.594
(Potsdam only)

12 Eugène Colliau (documented between
1859 and 1867, died 1884)
Seascape with Ship, ca. 1865
Albumen print, 17 × 24.1 cm
Dietmar Siegert Collection
(Potsdam only)

13 Auguste Autin (1809–1889)
Sunset, October 1861 at 5 p.m., 1861
Albumen print, 18.6 × 15 cm
Société française de photographie, Paris
Inv. no. frSFP_0018im_EP_0004
(Potsdam only)

14 Gustave Le Gray (1820–1884)
The Great Wave, Sète, 1857
Albumen print, 34 × 41 cm
Céline, Aeneas, Heiner Bastian
(Potsdam only)

15 Gustave Le Gray (1820–1884)
*The Brig, Seascape and Clouds
Photographed Simultaneously
(Mediterranean),* 1857
Albumen print, 41.7 × 32.9 cm
Société française de photographie, Paris
Inv. no. frSFP_0243im_EP_0032
(Potsdam only)

16 Charles Grassin (1828–1900)
Breaking Waves, ca. 1882–84
Albumen print, 19.4 × 25.4 cm
Société française de photographie, Paris
Inv. no. frSFP_0185im_EP_0001
(Potsdam and Wuppertal)

17 Henry Peach Robinson (1830–1901) and
Nelson King Cherrill (documented in the
1860s and 70s)
The Beached Margent of the Sea, 1870
Albumen print, 25.8 × 38 cm
Albertina, Vienna, on permanent loan
from the Höhere Graphische Bundes-
Lehr- und Versuchsanstalt
Inv. no. FotoGLV2000/11277
(Potsdam and Wuppertal)

18 Albert Londe (1858–1917)
The Wave, 1893 (printed 1992)
New print from original glass negative,
24 × 30 cm
Beaux-Arts de Paris
Inv. no. Ph 1684 P
(Potsdam only)

19 Robert Demachy (1859–1936)
Breaking Wave, 1900
Bromoil print, 27.3 × 36.1 cm
Société française de photographie, Paris
Inv. no. frSFP_0099im_EP_0117
(Potsdam and Wuppertal)

20 Carl Teufel (1845–1912)
Cloud Study, Bavaria, ca. 1890
Albumen print, 16.3 × 21.4 cm
Münchner Stadtmuseum, Munich,
Sammlung Fotografie
Inv. no. FM-89/74.111
(Potsdam and Wuppertal)

21 Carl Teufel (1845–1912)
Cloud Study, Bavaria, ca. 1890
Albumen print, 16.3 × 20.5 cm
Münchner Stadtmuseum, Munich
Sammlung Fotografie
Inv. no. FM-89/74.104
(Potsdam and Wuppertal)

22 Robert Scholz (1843–1926)
Cloud Study, ca. 1870
Albumen print, 19 × 25.9 cm
Inv. no. FM-2014/300.277
Münchner Stadtmuseum, Munich,
Sammlung Fotografie
(Potsdam and Wuppertal)

23 Léopold Louis Mercier (1866– after 1914)
Cloud Study, No. 2694, 1890
Albumen print, 21.8 × 28.6 cm
Münchner Stadtmuseum, Munich,
Sammlung Fotografie
Inv. no. FM-99/13.105
(Potsdam and Wuppertal)

24 Heinrich Kayser (1853–1940)
*Photograph of Lightning, Enlarged Six Times,
July 16, 1884,* 1884
Silver gelatin print, 14.1 × 10 cm
Albertina, Vienna, on permanent loan from
the Höhere Graphische Bundes-
Lehr- und Versuchsanstalt
Inv. no. FotoGLV2000/11628
(Potsdam and Wuppertal)

25 Emil Jacobsen (1836–1911)
Lightning, 1885
Albumen print, 23.5 × 27.6 cm
Albertina, Vienna, on permanent loan from
the Höhere Graphische Bundes-
Lehr- und Versuchsanstalt
Inv. no. FotoGLV2000/11608
(Potsdam and Wuppertal)

Center of Modernity:
Paris

26 Anonymous
Grand Boulevard, Paris, ca. 1875
Albumen print, 12.2 × 16 cm
Münchner Stadtmuseum, Munich,
Sammlung Fotografie
Inv. no. FM-90/939
(Potsdam and Wuppertal)

27 Charles Marville (1813–1879)
Paris, Rue de Rivoli, ca. 1877
Albumen print, 25.6 × 37 cm
Bibliothèque historique de la Ville de Paris
Inv. no. 1-EPR-00560
(Potsdam only)

28 Charles Marville (1813–1879)
Paris, Rue de Lisbonne, ca. 1877
Albumen print mounted on cardboard,
24.3 × 34.9 cm
Bibliothèque historique de la Ville de Paris
Inv. no. 1-EPR-00559
(Potsdam only)

29 Édouard Baldus (1813–1889)
*Paris, View of the Pont d'Arcole and the Hôtel
de Ville,* ca. 1860
Albumen print, 31.2 × 43.8 cm
Universität der Künste Berlin,
Universitätsarchiv
Inv. no. 300 d-V gr, 5 f
(Potsdam and Wuppertal)

30 Ferrier père, fils et Soulier (1811–1889,
1831–1912, 1830–1891)
The Seine and the Pont-Neuf in Paris, 1860
Stereograph, albumen slide on glass,
6.8 × 13.6 cm
Serge Kakou Collection, Paris
Inv. no. 07311
(Potsdam only)

31 Ferrier père, fils et Soulier (1811–1889,
1831–1912, 1830–1891)
Pont des Arts, 1860, 1860
Stereograph, albumen slide on glass,
6.7 × 13.4 cm
Serge Kakou Collection, Paris
Inv. no. 07302
(Potsdam only)

32 Ferrier père, fils et Soulier (1811–1889,
1831–1912, 1830–1891)
*Boulevard de Sébastopol (Looking East),
Paris,* 1860
Stereograph, albumen slide on glass,
8.4 × 17.1 cm
Serge Kakou Collection, Paris
Inv. no. 03292rued
(Potsdam only)

33 Ferrier père, fils et Soulier (1811–1889,
1831–1912, 1830–1891)
Boulevard de la Madeleine, No. 1, Paris, 1860
Stereograph, albumen slide on glass,
8.4 × 17.1 cm
Inv. no. 07290
Serge Kakou Collection, Paris
(Potsdam only)

34 Anonymous
Boulevard Saint-Martin, ca. 1870
Albumen print, 15.4 × 10.6 cm
Münchner Stadtmuseum, Munich,
Sammlung Fotografie
Inv. no. FM-88/601
(Potsdam and Wuppertal)

35 Hippolyte Jouvin (1825–1889)
Place de la Concorde, Paris, ca. 1870
Three stereograph cards, albumen prints,
8.3 × 17.2 cm each
Münchner Stadtmuseum, Munich,
Sammlung Fotografie
Inv. no. FM-65/134 a-c
(Potsdam and Wuppertal)

36 Attributed to Louis Antonin Neurdein
(1846–1914)
Avenue de l'Opéra and Place de la Concorde,
from the album *Paris et ses environs,*
ca. 1885
Albumen print, album 20.9 × 27.8 cm
Münchner Stadtmuseum, Munich,
Sammlung Fotografie
Inv. no. FM 76/3
(Potsdam and Wuppertal)

37 Anonymous
Park Scene, ca. 1890
Gelatin print, 12.2 × 16.8 cm
Münchner Stadtmuseum, Munich,
Sammlung Fotografie
Inv. no. FM-90/867
(Potsdam and Wuppertal)

38 Anonymous
*Street Scenes, Photographed with C. P.
Stirn's Secret Camera,* ca. 1885
Accordion-folded booklet, 17.3 × 138 × 0.7 cm,
Münchner Stadtmuseum, Sammlung
Fotografie
Inv. no. FM-88/371
(Potsdam and Wuppertal)

39 Anonymous
*The Pretty Passersby,
Parisian Women in Hats,* from the album
The Pretty Passersby, 1906–08
Albumen print, album 8 × 10.8 cm
Serge Kakou Collection, Paris
Inv. no. 025268
(Potsdam only)

40 Jacques Henri Lartigue (1894–1986)
Arlette Prevost, called Anna la Pradvina,
Avenue du Bois de Boulogne, January 15,
1911, 1911
Silver gelatin print, 16.9 × 24 cm
Dietmar Siegert Collection
(Potsdam only)

41 Louis Vert (1865–1924)
Clochard, Paris, ca. 1900
Bromide silver gelatin print, 16.5 × 16.5 cm
Serge Kakou Collection, Paris
Inv. no. 08820-20
(Potsdam only)

42 Robert Demachy (1859–1936)
Crowd, 1910
Bromoil print, 15.5 × 22.4 cm
Société française de photographie, Paris
Inv. no. frSFP_0099im_EP_0146
(Potsdam and Wuppertal)

43 Alfred Stieglitz (1864–1946)
A Snapshot, Paris, 1911
Photogravure, 13.7 × 17.4 cm
Museum Folkwang, Essen
Inv. no. 1378/87
(Potsdam and Wuppertal)

44 Augustin Hippolyte, called Auguste
Collard (1812–1893)
Pont de Grenelle, Paris, ca. 1875–76
Albumen print, 32 × 42 cm
Bibliothèque de l'École nationale des Ponts
et Chaussées, Marne-la-Vallée
Inv. no. PH126 P.2
(Potsdam only)

45 Anonymous
The Railway Bridge at Argenteuil, 1863
Albumen print, 23.5 × 51 cm
Bibliothèque de l'École nationale des Ponts
et Chaussées, Marne-la-Vallée
Inv. no. PH 49G
(Potsdam only)

46 Augustin Hippolyte, called Auguste
Collard (1812–1893)
Path Beneath the Railway Bridge at Auteuil,
1865–66
Albumen print, 25.5 × 35 cm
Bibliothèque de l'École nationale des Ponts
et Chaussées, Marne-la-Vallée
Inv. no. PH 521 A.12
(Potsdam only)

47 Augustin Hippolyte, called Auguste
Collard (1812–1893)
Pont de Grenelle, Paris, ca. 1875–76
Albumen print, 34 × 42.5 cm
Bibliothèque de l'École nationale des Ponts
et Chaussées, Marne-la-Vallée
Inv. no. PH 126.P.3
(Potsdam only)

Shadow and Light:
Forest Scenes

48 Georg Maria Eckert (1828–1901)
Middle Ground Study—Rocky Path in the
Forest, Heidelberg, 1867–68
Albumen print, 20.8 × 26.4 cm
Münchner Stadtmuseum, Munich,
Sammlung Fotografie
Inv. no. FM-2014/300.201.170
(Potsdam only)

49 Gustave Le Gray (1820–1884)
The Forest of Fontainebleau, 1849–52
Varnished salt print, 19.6 × 26.9 cm
Dietmar Siegert Collection
(Potsdam only)

50 Henri Le Secq (1818–1882)
Forest Brook, ca. 1852–53
Calotype, 50.7 × 37.7 cm
Musée des Arts Décoratifs, Paris
Inv. no. 466 T3
(Potsdam only)

51 Henri Le Secq (1818–1882)
High Forest, ca. 1852–53
Calotype on salt paper, 24.2 × 33.2 cm
Musée des Arts Décoratifs, Paris
Inv. no. 3/447
(Potsdam only)

52 Henri Le Secq (1818–1882)
Dead Tree in a Forest, ca. 1852–53
Calotype, 50.6 × 37.9 cm
Musée des Arts Décoratifs, Paris
Inv. no. 5/459
(Potsdam only)

53 Henri Le Secq (1818–1882)
Forest Path, ca. 1852–53
Calotype, 50.6 × 37.9 cm
Musée des Arts Décoratifs, Paris
Inv. no. 464 T2
(Potsdam only)

54 Eugène Cuvelier (1837–1900)
Cart on the Road, with Squaring Grid, 1862
Calotype, 20 × 25.7 cm
Universität der Künste Berlin,
Universitätsarchiv
Inv. no. 301-M III 10, 9 F
(Potsdam and Wuppertal)

55 André Giroux (1801–1879)
Felled Tree in a Forest in Winter, ca. 1853
Calotype, 25.6 × 31.5 cm
Serge Kakou Collection, Paris
Inv. no. 00995
(Potsdam only)

56 Eugène Cuvelier (1837–1900)
Beneath the Overlook in the Field,
September 17, 1862, 1862
Calotype, 19.8 × 25.7 cm
Mayer Collection, Stuttgart
(Potsdam and Wuppertal)

57 Eugène Cuvelier (1837–1900)
Pines near Rochefort—Snow, 1862
Calotype, 25.6 × 19.7 cm
Mayer Collection, Stuttgart
(Potsdam and Wuppertal)

58 Eugène Cuvelier (1837–1900)
Fontainebleau near the Porte de Rochefort,
ca. 1860
Calotype, 19.7 × 25.8 cm
Dietmar Siegert Collection
(Potsdam only)

59 Paul Gaillard (1832–1890)
Autumn Forest, ca. 1852
Calotype, 32.3 × 25.8 cm
Dietmar Siegert Collection
(Potsdam only)

60 Constant Alexandre Famin (1827–1888)
Landscape near Barbizon, 1862
Albumen print, 25.5 × 19.5 cm
Münchner Stadtmuseum, Munich,
Sammlung Fotografie
Inv. no. FM-96/142.2
(Potsdam and Wuppertal)

61 Constant Alexandre Famin (1827–1888)
Forest Path in Autumn, ca. 1865
Albumen print, 24.7 × 32.2 cm
Dietmar Siegert Collection
(Potsdam only)

62 Eugène Cuvelier (1837–1900)
Franchard, 1863
Calotype, 20 × 25.7 cm
Staatsgalerie Stuttgart, Graphische
Sammlung, acquired 1990 with lottery funds
Inv. no. F 1990/423
(Potsdam only)

63 Constant Alexandre Famin (1827–1888)
Théophile Chauvel, near the Mare aux Fées,
1865–70
Albumen print, 18.5 × 24.6 cm
Dietmar Siegert Collection
(Potsdam only)

64 Eugène Cuvelier (1837–1900)
Broussailles, Belle Croix, Forest of
Fontainebleau, September 14, 1863, 1863
Albumen print, 19.7 × 25.8 cm
Société française de photographie, Paris
Inv. no. rSFP_0090im_EP_0002
(Potsdam and Wuppertal)

65 Georg Maria Eckert (1828–1901)
*Middle Ground Study: Well House Overgrown
with Wild Vine, Heidelberg,* 1866–68
Albumen print, 26.3 × 20.8 cm
Münchner Stadtmuseum, Munich,
Sammlung Fotografie
Inv. no. FM-2014/300.201.46
(Potsdam only)

66 Hermann Wilhelm Vogel (1834–1898)
View near the Grosser Stern, from the album
Pictures from the Thiergarten, 1866
Albumen print, 19.3 × 18 cm
Münchner Stadtmuseum, Munich,
Sammlung Fotografie
Inv. no. FM-2014/300.709
(Potsdam and Wuppertal)

Everyday Motifs:
Countryside and River

67 Constant Puyo (1857–1933)
Two Women in a Field, 1894–1926
Bromoil print, 16.7 × 22.7 cm
Société française de photographie, Paris
Inv. no. frSFP_0526im_EP_0136
(Potsdam and Wuppertal)

68 William Sherlock (born 1813,
documented in the 1850s)
Landscape, ca. 1852
Calotype, 23.5 × 30.7 cm
Münchner Stadtmuseum, Munich,
Sammlung Fotografie
Inv. no. FM-89/437
(Potsdam only)

69 Adolphe Braun (1812–1877)
Farmer with Cow and Calf, 1860–62
Albumen print, 20.5 × 27 cm
Münchner Stadtmuseum, Munich,
Sammlung Fotografie
Inv. no. FM-88/434
(Potsdam only)

70 Adolphe Braun (1812–1877)
Teams of Horses and Oxen in the Field,
1860–62
Albumen print, 26.3 × 35.4 cm
Münchner Stadtmuseum, Munich,
Sammlung Fotografie
Inv. no. FM-92/446.3
(Potsdam only)

71 Louis Désiré Blanquart-Evrard
(1802–1872)
Women Making Cider, 1851–53
Calotype, 15.4 × 20.2 cm
Dietmar Siegert Collection
(Potsdam only)

72 Achille Louis Bonnuit (1833–1894)
Garden Still Life, ca. 1870
Albumen print, 15 × 11.5 cm
Musée d'Orsay, Paris
Inv. no. PHO 1984 70 71
(Potsdam and Wuppertal)

73 Alphonse Taupin (documented
between the 1860s and 1880s)
Haystacks, ca. 1870
Albumen print, 18.5 × 24 cm
Münchner Stadtmuseum, Munich,
Sammlung Fotografie
Inv. no. FM-94/642.3
(Potsdam and Wuppertal)

74 Charles Aubry (1811–1877)
Garden Asters, ca. 1864
Albumen print, 36 × 26 cm
Musée d'Orsay, Dépôt du Mobilier
national, Paris
Inv. no. DO 1979 50 / INV-981-050
(Potsdam only)

75 Charles Aubry (1811–1877)
Still Life, ca. 1864
Albumen print, 26 × 36 cm
Musée d'Orsay, Dépôt du Mobilier national,
Paris
Inv. no. DO 1979 7 / INV-981-018
(Potsdam only)

76 August Kotzsch (1836–1910)
Cut Melon, ca. 1870
Albumen print, 15 × 19 cm
Kupferstich-Kabinett,
Staatliche Kunstsammlungen Dresden
Inv. no. D 1929-11
(Potsdam only)

77 August Kotzsch (1836–1910)
Potatoes, ca. 1870
Albumen print, 12 × 19.7 cm
Dietmar Siegert Collection
(Potsdam only)

78 Henry Peach Robinson (1830–1901)
The Painter, ca. 1890–1901
Albumen print, 25.5 × 35.2 cm
Société française de photographie, Paris
Inv. no. frSFP_0361im_EP_0008
(Potsdam and Wuppertal)

79 Heinrich Kühn (1866–1944)
Mary Warner and Hans Kühn, 1907
(printed after 1911)
Gummigravüre (photogravure and gum
bichromate), 28.1 × 38.9 cm
Albertina, Vienna
Inv. no. Foto2004/16
(Potsdam and Wuppertal)

80 Stéphanie Breton (1809–1895)
The Castle of Franqueville near Rouen, 1861
Albumen print, 22.8 × 28.8 cm
Société française de photographie, Paris
Inv. no. frSFP_0049im_EP_0004
(Potsdam and Wuppertal)

81 Joseph Vigier (1821–1894)
Landscape in Pau with View of the Pyrénées,
1853
Calotype, 24.5 × 33 cm
Musée d'Orsay, Dépôt de la Fondation
Dosne-Thiers, Paris
Inv. no. DO 1983 18
(Potsdam only)

82 André Giroux (1801–1879)
La Grenouillère, Croissy, Bougival, ca. 1853
Calotype, 33.9 × 28.3 cm
Universität der Künste Berlin,
Universitätsarchiv
Inv. no. 301-M III 5, 4 F
(Potsdam and Wuppertal)

83 Ildefonse Rousset (1817–1878)
Rivière de la Pompadour, from *Le Bois de Vincennes,* Paris 1866 (novel illustrated with photos)
Albumen print, 30.8 × 24.5 cm
Münchner Stadtmuseum, Munich, Sammlung Fotografie
Inv. no. FM-98/149
(Potsdam and Wuppertal)

84 Olympe Aguado (1827–1894)
Banks of the Seine, Île des Ravageurs, Meudon, 1855
Calotype, 27.7 × 39.9 cm
Serge Kakou Collection, Paris
Inv. no. 22727
(Potsdam only)

85 Eugène Cuvelier (1837–1900)
Franchard, Mare aux Pigeons, October 19, 1863, 1863
Calotype, 20 × 47.6 cm
Staatsgalerie Stuttgart, Graphische Sammlung, acquired 1998 with lottery funds
Inv. no. F 1998/483
(Potsdam only)

86 Victor Albert Prout (1835–1877)
Mousley, ca. 1862
Albumen print, 11.6 × 27.9 cm
Dietmar Siegert Collection
(Potsdam only)

87 Peter Henry Emerson (1856–1936)
Water Lilies, 1886
Platinum print, 12.5 × 28.5 cm
Staatsgalerie Stuttgart, Graphische Sammlung, acquired 1989
Mayer Collection, Stuttgart
Inv. no. F 1989/25
(Potsdam and Wuppertal)

88 Pierre Petit (1831–1909)
Water-Lily Pond at the World's Fair in Paris, 1867
Albumen print, album 32.5 × 26.5 × 3 cm, opened 32.5 × 51 cm
Dietmar Siegert Collection
(Potsdam only)

89 Adolphe De Meyer (1868–1946)
Victoria regia, ca. 1899, from the yearbook *Die Kunst in der Photographie,* 1899
Book 34.5 × 27 cm
Universitätsbibliothek Marburg—Dr. Rolf H. Krauss-Forschungsbibliothek / Deutsches Dokumentationszentrum für Kunstgeschichte—Bildarchiv Foto Marburg
(Potsdam and Wuppertal)

90 Peter Henry Emerson (1856–1936)
Gathering Water Lilies, 1886
Platinum print, 19.5 × 29 cm
Staatsgalerie Stuttgart, Graphische Sammlung, acquired 1989
Mayer Collection, Stuttgart
Inv. no. F 1989/24
(Potsdam and Wuppertal)

91 Robert Collett (1842–1913)
Water Lilies in the Rain, from the album *Norwegian Motifs,* 1897
Collotype, 20 × 27.9 cm
Museum für Kunst und Gewerbe Hamburg, Sammlung Fotografie und neue Medien
Inv. no. P1976.346.4
(Potsdam and Wuppertal)

92 Dwight A. Davis (1852–1944)
A Still Pond, 1912 or earlier
Platinum print, 24.4 × 19.4 cm
Staatliche Museen zu Berlin, Kunstbibliothek
Inv. no. 1914, 268 / 1561007
(Potsdam only)

93 Anonymous
Water Irises, ca. 1890
Albumen print, 19.3 × 24.7 cm
Münchner Stadtmuseum, Munich, Sammlung Fotografie
Inv. no. FM-94/266.6
(Potsdam and Wuppertal)

Painterly Photographs: Pictorialism

94 Hugo Henneberg (1863–1918)
Beech Forest in Autumn, 1898
Gum bichromate, 44.1 × 34.2 cm
Staatliche Museen zu Berlin, Kunstbibliothek
Inv. no. 1914, 268 / 1439583
(Potsdam only)

95 Alvin Langdon Coburn (1882–1966)
Cadiz Harbor, 1906
Pigment print, 32.2 × 31.6 cm
Museum für Kunst und Gewerbe Hamburg, Sammlung Fotografie und neue Medien
Inv. no. AB1988.633
(Potsdam and Wuppertal)

96 Anonymous
Sky Study, Sunset, 1855
Albumen print, 15 × 19.9 cm
Serge Kakou Collection, Paris
Inv. no. 25308
(Potsdam only)

97 Heinrich Beck (1874–1960)
Wake, 1903
Gum bichromate in original frame, 44.1 × 60.5 cm
Museum für Kunst und Gewerbe Hamburg, Sammlung Fotografie und neue Medien
Inv. no. AB1988.776
(Potsdam and Wuppertal)

98 Constant Puyo (1857–1933)
Waves and Sailboats on the Horizon at Penmarc'h in Brittany, ca. 1902–14
Citrate print, 5.7 × 17.8 cm
Société française de photographie, Paris
Inv. no. frSFP_0526im_EP_0311
(Potsdam only)

99 Constant Puyo (1857–1933)
Paddle Steamer in the Gulf of Naples, ca. 1903
Citrate print, 5.7 × 17.8 cm
Société française de photographie, Paris
Inv. no. frSFP_0526im_EP_0312
(Potsdam only)

100 Peter Henry Emerson (1856–1936)
The Fetters of Winter in 1895, 1895
Photogravure, 11.2 × 18.7 cm
Musée d'Orsay, Paris
Inv. no. PHO 1979 67
(Potsdam and Wuppertal)

101 Viktor Knollmüller (1889–1971)
Landscape with Pond, ca. 1904
Pigment print and cyanotype, 32.4 × 47.8 cm
Münchner Stadtmuseum, Munich, Sammlung Fotografie
Inv. no. FM-95/147.11
(Potsdam and Wuppertal)

102 Edward Steichen (1879–1973)
The Pool—Evening, Milwaukee, 1902
Heliogravure, 20.5 × 15.4 cm
Museum für Kunst und Gewerbe Hamburg,
Sammlung Fotografie und neue Medien
Inv. no. P1988.H.133
(Potsdam and Wuppertal)

103 Heinrich Kühn (1866–1944)
Poplars along the Brook, ca. 1900
Gum bichromate, 49 × 60.3 cm
Museum Folkwang, Essen
Inv. no. 100/2/92
(Potsdam and Wuppertal)

104 Marcel Vanderkindere (1865–1941)
Winter Fog, 1897
Platinum print, 18.4 × 25.5 cm
Museum für Kunst und Gewerbe Hamburg,
Sammlung Fotografie und neue Medien
Inv. no. AB1988.93
(Potsdam and Wuppertal)

105 Édouard Hannon (1853–1931)
After the Storm, 1896
Gelatin silver print in original frame,
47.5 × 60 cm
Museum für Kunst und Gewerbe Hamburg,
Sammlung Fotografie und neue Medien
Inv. no. AB1988.625
(Potsdam and Wuppertal)

106 Carl Frederiksen (1892–1932)
Foggy Morning, 1912 or earlier
Platinum palladium print, 27.5 × 34.4 cm
Staatliche Museen zu Berlin, Kunstbibliothek
Inv. no. 1914, 268 / 1438203
(Potsdam only)

107 Robert Demachy (1859–1936)
The Seine at Clichy, ca. 1906
Bromoil print, 22.8 × 17 cm
Société française de photographie, Paris
Inv. no. frSFP_0099im_EP_0150
(Potsdam only)

108 Constant Puyo (1857–1933)
The Washerwomen, 1894–1926
Photogravure, 23.3 × 13.9 cm
Société française de photographie, Paris
Inv. no. frSFP_0526im_EP_0242
(Potsdam and Wuppertal)

109 Robert Demachy (1859–1936)
Banks of the Seine, ca. 1906
Gum bichromate, 20.2 × 11.2 cm
Société française de photographie, Paris
Inv. no. frSFP_0099im_EP_0083
(Potsdam and Wuppertal)

110 Hugo Henneberg (1863–1918)
After Sunset, 1898 or earlier
Gum bichromate, 36 × 51 cm
Photoinstitut Bonartes, Vienna
Inv. no. BON_1648
(Potsdam and Wuppertal)

111 Heinrich Kühn (1866–1944)
Lindens in the Sunlight, ca. 1900
Gum bichromate, 55.3 × 72.5 cm
Museum Folkwang, Essen
Inv. no. 100/2/98
(Potsdam and Wuppertal)

112 Heinrich Kühn (1866–1944)
Landscape with Lindens, 1898
Gum bichromate, 50.8 × 73.5 cm
Private collection
(Potsdam and Wuppertal)

113 Heinrich Kühn (1866–1944)
Landscape with Clouds, ca. 1899
Gum bichromate, 27.7 × 38.2 cm
Photoinstitut Bonartes, Vienna
Inv. no. HK_22
(Potsdam and Wuppertal)

114 Hugo Henneberg (1863–1918)
Evening, 1899 or earlier
Gum bichromate, 60.5 × 58.5 cm
Staatliche Museen zu Berlin, Kunstbibliothek
Inv. no. 1914, 268 / 1439666
(Potsdam only)

115 Heinrich Kühn (1866–1944)
Hikers beneath Branches, ca. 1915
Oil print, 21.2 × 29.4 cm
Photoinstitut Bonartes, Vienna
Inv. no. HK_69
(Potsdam and Wuppertal)

116 Heinrich Kühn (1866–1944)
Twilight, 1897
Gum bichromate in original frame,
38 × 28.3 cm
Museum für Kunst und Gewerbe Hamburg,
Sammlung Fotografie und neue Medien
Inv. no. AB1988.772
(Potsdam and Wuppertal)

117 Heinrich Kühn (1866–1944)
Twilight, 1896
Gum bichromate, 38 × 28 cm
Staatliche Museen zu Berlin, Kunstbibliothek
Inv. no. 1914, 268 / 1442555
(Potsdam only)

118 Heinrich Kühn (1866–1944)
Meadow with Trees, 1897
Gum bichromate, 37.9 × 27.8 cm
Photoinstitut Bonartes, Vienna
Inv. no. HK_26
(Potsdam and Wuppertal)

119 Heinrich Kühn (1866–1944)
Landscape, 1897
Gum bichromate in original frame,
36.3 × 25.5 cm
Museum für Kunst und Gewerbe Hamburg,
Sammlung Fotografie und neue Medien
Inv. no. AB1988.771
(Potsdam only)

120 Heinrich Kühn (1866–1944)
Winter Landscape, 1897
Platinum print, 20.8 × 28.5 cm
Photoinstitut Bonartes, Vienna
Inv. no. HK_36
(Potsdam and Wuppertal)

121 Robert Demachy (1859–1936)
The Jardin des Tuileries in the Snow, Paris,
1910
Bromoil print, 20.6 × 14.8 cm
Société française de photographie, Paris
Inv. no. frSFP_0099im_EP_0149
(Potsdam and Wuppertal)

122 Rudolf Eickemeyer (1862–1932)
River in Winter, 1904 or earlier
Platinum palladium print, 23.9 × 19 cm
Staatliche Museen zu Berlin, Kunstbibliothek
Inv. no. 1914, 268 / 1438170
(Potsdam only)

123 Gustav Eduard Bernhard Trinks
(1871–1967)
Colored Shadows, 1897
Heliogravure, 23.7 × 19.2
Museum für Kunst und Gewerbe Hamburg,
Sammlung Fotografie und neue Medien
Inv. no. P1988.H.643
(Potsdam and Wuppertal)

124 Robert Demachy (1859–1936)
Portrait of a Woman in a Straw Hat,
1894–1914
Gum bichromate, 14.3 × 16.3 cm
Société française de photographie, Paris
Inv. no. frSFP_0099im_EP_0111
(Potsdam and Wuppertal)

125 Adolphe De Meyer (1868–1946)
Glass and Shadows, 1897
Heliogravure, 22 × 16.5
Museum für Kunst und Gewerbe Hamburg,
Sammlung Fotografie und neue Medien
Inv. no. P1988.H.102
(Potsdam and Wuppertal)

126 Heinrich Kühn (1866–1944)
Carafe and Glass, ca. 1911
Platinum gum bichromate, 23.1 × 29.3 cm
Kicken Berlin
(Potsdam and Wuppertal)

127 Adolphe De Meyer (1868–1946)
Still Life, 1908
Photogravure, 19.2 × 15.5 cm
Dietmar Siegert Collection
(Potsdam only)

128 Adolphe De Meyer (1868–1946)
Water Lilies, ca. 1906
Platinum print, 16.4 × 22.4 cm
Dietmar Siegert Collection
(Potsdam only)

The World in Color:
Autochromes

129 Antonin Personnaz (1854–1936)
Sunrise with Snow, ca. 1907–14
Autochrome (exhibited in facsimile),
9 × 12 cm
Société française de photographie, Paris
Inv. no. FRSFP_0804im_A_0926
(Potsdam and Wuppertal)

130 Antonin Personnaz (1854–1936)
Field, Haystack, ca. 1907–14
Autochrome (exhibited in facsimile),
9 × 12 cm
Société française de photographie, Paris
Inv. no. FRSFP_0804im_A_0360
(Potsdam only)

131 Antonin Personnaz (1854–1936)
Fields and Haystacks, Fog, ca. 1907–14
Autochrome (exhibited in facsimile),
9 × 12 cm
Société française de photographie, Paris
Inv. no. FRSFP_0804im_A_0355
(Potsdam only)

132 Antonin Personnaz (1854–1936)
Field, Haystacks at Sunset, ca. 1907–14
Autochrome (exhibited in facsimile),
9 × 12 cm
Société française de photographie, Paris
Inv. no. FRSFP_0804im_A_0357
(Potsdam only)

133 Antonin Personnaz (1854–1936)
Barges, Boat, Crane, ca. 1907–14
Autochrome (exhibited in facsimile),
9 × 12 cm
Société française de photographie, Paris
Inv. no. FRSFP_0804im_A_0692
(Potsdam only)

134 Antonin Personnaz (1854–1936)
Fog over the Water, ca. 1907–14
Autochrome (exhibited in facsimile),
9 × 12 cm
Société française de photographie, Paris
Inv. no. FRSFP_0804im_A_0913
(Potsdam only)

135 Antonin Personnaz (1854–1936)
River, Factory, Smoke, ca. 1907–14
Autochrome (exhibited in facsimile),
9 × 12 cm
Société française de photographie, Paris
Inv. no. FRSFP_0804im_A_0872
(Potsdam only)

136 Antonin Personnaz (1854–1936)
Sunset, ca. 1907–14
Autochrome (exhibited in facsimile),
9 × 12 cm
Société française de photographie, Paris
Inv. no. FRSFP_0804im_A_0588
(Potsdam only)

137 Antonin Personnaz (1854–1936)
Woman Painting Before the Motif, ca. 1907–14
Autochrome (exhibited in facsimile),
9 × 12 cm
Société française de photographie, Paris
Inv. no. FRSFP_0804im_A_0121
(Potsdam and Wuppertal)

138 Antonin Personnaz (1854–1936)
Armand Guillaumin Painting "Bathers near Crozant," ca. 1907
Autochrome (exhibited in facsimile),
9 × 12 cm
Société française de photographie, Paris
Inv. no. FRSFP_0804im_A_0120
(Potsdam and Wuppertal)

139 Heinrich Kühn (1866–1944)
Miss Mary and Lotte, 1907
Autochrome (exhibited in facsimile),
18 × 24 cm
Österreichische Nationalbibliothek, Vienna
Inv. no. Pk 3900, 51 POR MAG
(Potsdam and Wuppertal)

140 Heinrich Kühn (1866–1944)
Miss Mary in a Blue Dress, 1910
Autochrome (exhibited in facsimile),
24 × 18 cm
Österreichische Nationalbibliothek, Vienna
Inv. no. Pk 3900, 89 POR MAG
(Potsdam and Wuppertal)

141 Heinrich Kühn (1866–1944)
Mary Warner and Edeltrude on the Brow of a Hill, ca. 1908
Autochrome (exhibited in facsimile),
23.8 × 17.8 cm
The Metropolitan Museum of Art, New York,
Gilman Collection, Purchase, Mrs. Walter Annenberg and The Annenberg Foundation Gift, 2005
Inv. no. 2005.100.370.
(Potsdam only)

142 Heinrich Kühn (1866–1944)
Landscape, ca. 1912–15
Autochrome (exhibited in facsimile),
9 × 12 cm
Musée d'Orsay, Paris
Inv. no. PHO 2010 1
(Potsdam only)

143 Étienne Clémentel (1864–1936)
*Claude Monet Standing in Profile before the
Water Lilies in the Garden at Giverny,*
ca. 1920
Stereo autochrome (exhibited in facsimile),
4.5 × 10.5 cm
Musée d'Orsay, Paris
Inv. no. PHO 1988 2 2
(Potsdam only)

144 Louise Deglane (1868–1936)
A Man in a Rose Garden, after 1907
Autochrome (exhibited in facsimile),
8.2 × 9.7 cm
Société française de photographie, Paris
Inv. no. frSFP_0808im_A_0106
(Potsdam only)

145 Hohmann
Flower Bouquets, ca. 1910
Autochrome (exhibited in facsimile),
9 × 12 cm
Münchner Stadtmuseum, Munich,
Sammlung Fotografie
Inv. no. FM-92/121.172
(Potsdam and Wuppertal)

146 Auguste Lumière (1862–1954)
and Louis Lumière (1864–1948)
Autumn Scene, 1907
Autochrome (exhibited in facsimile),
18 × 13 cm
Auer Photo Foundation, Hermance
Inv. no. 40270
(Potsdam and Wuppertal)

147 Hohmann
Deciduous Forest, ca. 1910
Autochrome (exhibited in facsimile),
12 × 9 cm
Münchner Stadtmuseum, Munich,
Sammlung Fotografie
Inv. no. FM-92/121.109
(Potsdam and Wuppertal)

148 Louise Deglane (1868–1936)
Beach with Boats (Étretat), 1907–36
Autochrome (exhibited in facsimile),
5.4 × 10.5 cm
Société française de photographie, Paris
Inv. no. frSFP_0808im_A_0132
(Potsdam and Wuppertal)

Not Included in the Catalog

149 Anonymous
Fontainebleau, La Gorge aux Loups, ca. 1865
Albumen print, 11.2 × 17 cm
Münchner Stadtmuseum, Munich, Sammlung
Fotografie
Inv. no. FM-2006/255
Not illustrated
(Potsdam and Wuppertal)

150 Anonymous
Two Peasant Women, before 1878
Albumen print, 15.4 × 11.6 cm
Musée d'Orsay, Paris
Inv. no. PHO 1984 88 144
p. 260, fig. 6
(Potsdam and Wuppertal)

151 Arthur Da Cunha (documented
in the 1890s)
Étretat, 1895
Photogravure, 9 × 11.6 cm
Musée d'Orsay, Paris
Inv.-Nr. PHO 1991 15 33
Not illustrated
(Wuppertal only)

152 Georg Maria Eckert (1828–1901)
Group of Lime Trees with Path, 1866–68
Albumen print, 26.4 × 21 cm
Münchner Stadtmuseum, Munich,
Sammlung Fotografie
Inv.-Nr. 2014/300.202.17
Not illustrated
(Wuppertal only)

153 Georg Maria Eckert (1828–1901)
*Foreground Study: Trunks—Poplar Trunk
with Ivy Roots,* 1867–68
Albumen paper, 26.2 × 20.9 cm
Münchner Stadtmuseum, Munich,
Sammlung Fotografie
Inv.-Nr. 2014/300.201.19
Not illustrated
(Wuppertal only)

154 Gustave Le Gray (1820–1884)
Mediterranean Sea, Sète, 1857
Albumen print, 31 × 40 cm
Céline, Aeneas, Heiner Bastian
Not illustrated
(Potsdam only)

155 Hippolyte Jouvin (1825–1889)
*Boulevard de la Madeleine and Boulevard des
Capucines, Paris,* ca. 1862
Stereograph, albumen print, 8.3 × 17.2 cm
Münchner Stadtmuseum, Munich,
Sammlung Fotografie
Inv. no. FM-2015/66
Not illustrated
(Potsdam and Wuppertal)

156 Heinrich Kühn (1866–1944)
Hikers on the Edge of the Shadows, ca. 1915
Oil print, 21.2 × 29.4 cm
Photoinstitut Bonartes, Vienna
Inv. no. HK_1
Not illustrated
(Potsdam and Wuppertal)

157 Henri Le Secq (1818–1882)
Forest Brook, ca. 1852–53
Calotype on salt paper, 37.8 × 50.8 cm
Musée des Arts Décoratifs, Paris
Inv. no. 467 T3
Not illustrated
(Potsdam only)

Miriam Leimer

Biographies

→ = Reference to the glossary
► = Reference to another biography

Olympe Aguado
(1827 Paris – 1894 Compiègne)

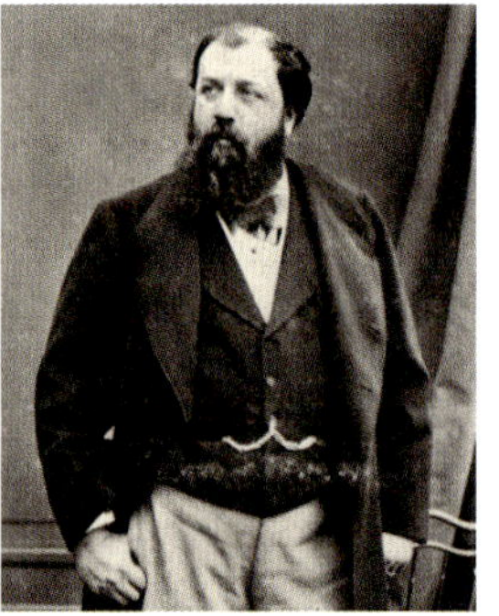

Aguado was an ambitious amateur photographer who focused on landscapes, interiors, portraits, and staged group photos. Coming from a wealthy background, he began to devote himself to photography in the late 1840s. In 1849, presumably thanks to Joseph Vigier, he received instruction from Gustave Le ► Gray in Paris. With Édouard Delessert he developed the idea of photographic *cartes de visite,* and he also took photographs in the forest of Fontainebleau. In 1851 Aguado was a founding member of the Société héliographique and in 1854 of the Société française de photographie. (Cat. 84)

Charles Aubry
(1811 Paris – 1877 Paris)

In their reduced aesthetic, Aubry's images of flowers and plants anticipated the New Vision style of the twentieth century. Aubry worked for a good thirty years designing textile patterns in the applied arts before founding a company to produce plaster casts and photographs in 1864. Inspired by the success of Adolphe ► Braun, he turned to photography and created about two hundred photographs of floral still lifes, draped fruits, and plant leaves, which he intended to sell to textile manufacturers and art schools for use as models. Commercial success, however, failed to materialize, and Aubry had to file for bankruptcy as early as 1865. (Cats. 74, 75)

Auguste Autin
(1809 Harfleur – 1889 Harfleur)

Autin was one of the first commercial photographers in Normandy. Beginning in 1844 he worked as a portrait photographer, first in Caen and later in Le Havre. He often made use of → daguerreotypes and was instrumental in the development of the → collodion process. His oeuvre also includes numerous seascapes and harbor scenes. Autin's photograph *Sunset, October 1861 at 5 p.m.* was displayed in 1863 at one of the exhibitions of the Société française de photographie. (Cat. 13)

Édouard Baldus
(1813 Grünebach –
1889 Arcueil-Cachan)

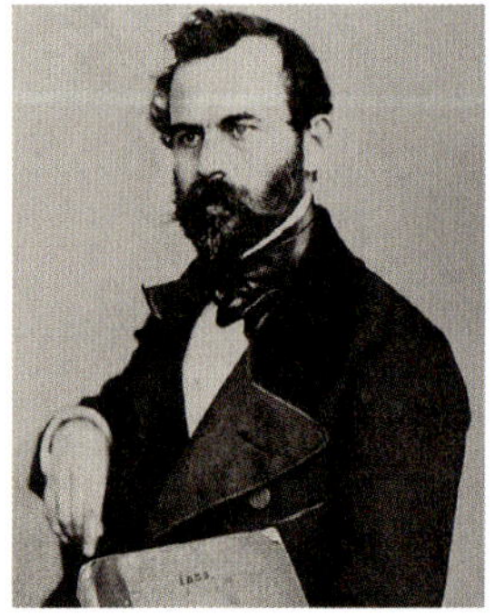

Baldus was a successful architectural photographer employed by the French administration. While serving with the Prussian Army in Cologne, the native Rhinelander was accused of counterfeiting and fled to France. In 1838 he moved to Paris, where he attempted to establish himself as a painter. Around 1850 he discovered photography, and in 1851 he, like Olympe ► Aguado, was a founding member of the Société héliographique. Starting in 1851, similar to Gustave Le ► Gray and Henri Le ► Secq, Baldus made numerous architectural photographs on behalf of the state Comité des monuments historiques (Commission on Historical Monuments), especially in the South of France. (Cat. 29)

Heinrich Beck
(1874 Dingelstädt – 1960 Lüneburg)

Beck was an amateur photographer in Hamburg in the early twentieth century. From 1903 he was the accountant of the Freie Vereinigung von Amateur-Photographen zu Hamburg (Free Association of Amateur Photographers in Hamburg), of which Gustav Eduard Bernhard ► Trinks was also a member. Beck was close to Pictorialism and worked with the → gum bichromate printing process. (Cat. 97)

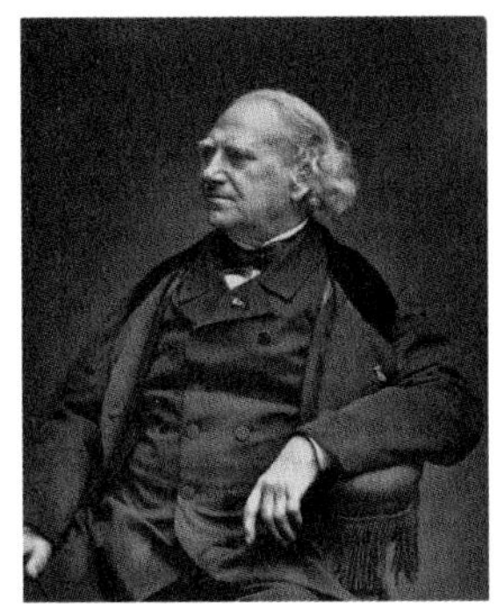

Louis Désiré Blanquart-Evrard
(1802 Lille – 1872 Lille)

Blanquart-Evrard was a photochemist and publisher who used innovative reproduction processes in his print shop. He worked in the textile industry and as a laboratory assistant before becoming involved with → daguerreotypes, which had only just been invented in 1839. In 1847 Blanquart-Evrard presented an improved procedure for → calotypes, in 1850 printing on → albumen paper, a process that he had developed himself. With a business partner, he founded a company near Lille that produced photographic prints on an industrial scale. Blanquart-Evrard published books and albums with the work of other photographers, including Charles ▸ Marville. (Cat. 71)

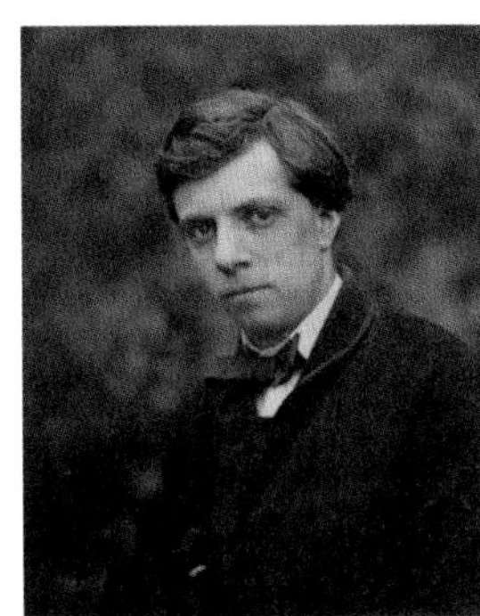

Achille Louis Bonnuit
(1833 Paris – 1894 Sèvres)

From 1858 to 1894 Bonnuit worked as a decorator for a porcelain factory in Sèvres. Many of his photographs were taken with his father-in-law, Gérard Derischweiler. Bonnuit's most frequent subjects include portraits of his family, still lifes, and group portraits from the factory's surroundings. (Cat. 72)

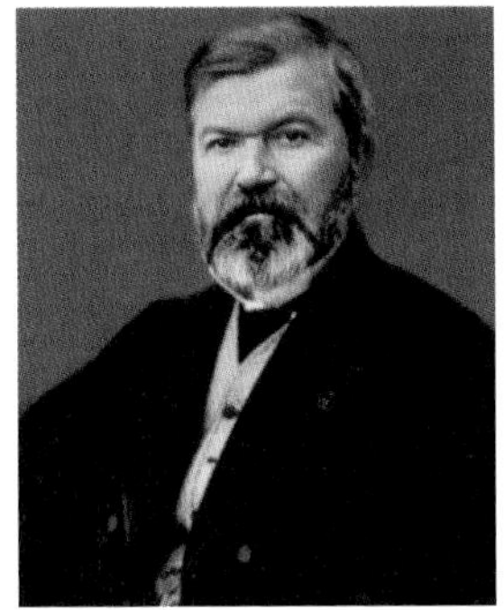

Adolphe Braun
(1812 Besançon – 1877 Dornach, Alsace-Lorraine)

As a photography entrepreneur, Braun enjoyed commercial success with series of landscape depictions and reproductions of works of art. His photographic still lifes received recognition from art critics at the 1855 world's fair in Paris. He first worked as a textile designer in Mulhouse, Alsace-Lorraine, and in Paris. His first publication with views of Alsace-Lorraine appeared in 1858, followed by numerous series of farm animals as well as cultural monuments, panoramas, and European mountain landscapes. In addition, Braun specialized in stereoscopes (→ stereo photography), for which he often commissioned fellow photographers. In 1870 Braun's company distributed more than seven thousand different motifs. (Cats. 69, 70; p. 50, fig. 9)

Stéphanie Breton
(1809 Vienna – 1895 Fontainebleau)

Breton is one of the few women in the history of early photography. Born in Vienna as Françoise Romaine Stéphanie Breton, she later called herself Madame Breton. From 1828 she lived as a painter in Rouen. In 1857 she was one of the first women to join the Société française de photographie. She participated in the 1867 world's fair in Paris with her photographs. Her photographs of the 1850s and 1860s were often taken in Rouen as well as while traveling, for example in the Pyrénées. Breton's photographic self-portrait is one of the earliest examples of its type. (Cat. 80)

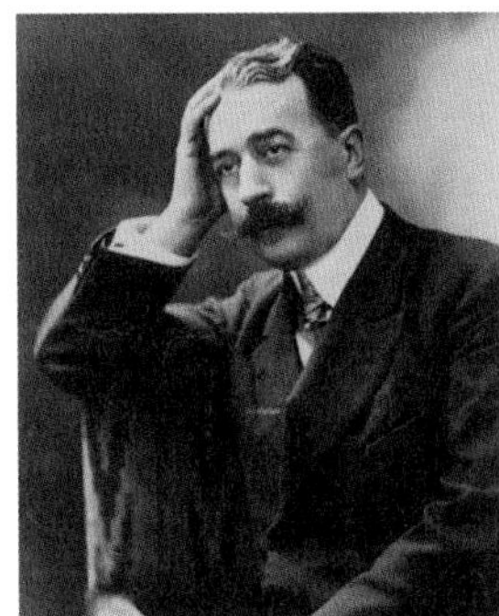

Étienne Clémentel
(1864 Clermont-Ferrand – 1936 Prompsat)

Clémentel, an art-loving politician, was also a painter and photographer. From 1900 to 1936 he was a member of the French parliament and held various ministerial posts. As an art collector, he championed Impressionism, and as a photographer he began to create stereoscopic (→ stereo photography) → autochromes in 1907. His subjects were family members, the city of Paris, and landscapes. Clémentel was friends with the sculptor Auguste Rodin, who made a portrait bust of the politician in 1916. In around 1920 Clémentel photographed the painter Claude Monet in the latter's garden at Giverny. (Cat. 143)

Alvin Langdon Coburn
(1882 Boston – 1966 Rhos-on-Sea, Wales)

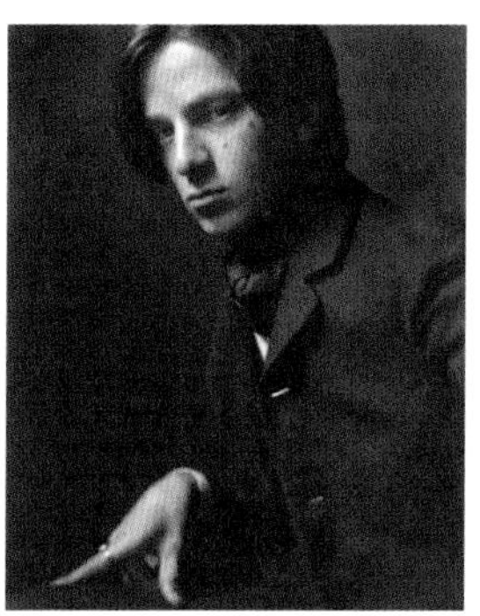

As an important proponent of art photography, Coburn left his mark on Pictorialism at the turn of the century, later becoming a pioneer of abstract photography. He became interested in photography as a teenager. In 1902 Coburn worked in the studio of the photographer Gertrude Käsebier in New York. That same year he was one of the founding members of the American Photo-Secession with Edward ▸ Steichen and Alfred ▸ Stieglitz. In 1904 Coburn went to England and picked up the technique of → photogravure. In 1917 he began to work with "Vortographs," in which prismatic effects were created using mirrors. (Cat. 95)

Auguste Hippolyte, called Auguste Collard
(1812 Valençay – 1893 Saint-Mandé)

Collard worked as a professional photographer on behalf of the French administration. His series of bridges testifies to the documentary character of his photographs as well as to his flair for unusual perspectives. After initially working as a gilder, Collard was engaged in photography from 1842 and founded his own studio in Paris in 1855. In 1857 he began to collaborate with the French authorities, documenting bridges, aqueducts, and railroad construction projects. (Cats. 44, 46, 47)

Robert Collett
(1842 Christiania [now Oslo] –
1913 Christiania)

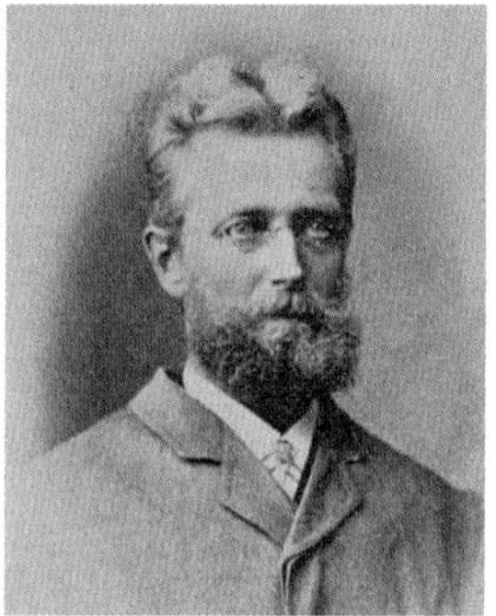

Collett worked as a curator at the Zoological Museum of the university in Christiania (now Oslo) before becoming its director in 1882. He photographed nature on his extensive expeditions in Norway. In 1861 Collett had initially taken up studies in law while at the same time furthering his education in animal and natural history. In 1871 he received his first position at the Zoological Museum and was made professor of zoology in 1885. (Cat. 91)

Eugène Colliau
(Documented in France between 1859 and
1867, died in 1884)

The financial officer and photographer, whose real name was Jean-Baptiste Émile, became known as Eugène Colliau. Like Olympe ▸ Aguado and Joseph ▸ Vigier, he was a student of Gustave Le ▸ Gray. Colliau worked with → calotypes and later with → waxed paper negatives and the wet plate → collodion process as well. He opened a shop for photographic prints in Montmartre in Paris. In addition to portraits and photographs of Parisian monuments, his subjects included rural scenes and seascapes, primarily in Normandy. Colliau showed his works between 1859 and 1861 at the exhibitions of the Société française de photographie. (Cat. 12)

Arthur Da Cunha
(Documented in France in the 1890s)

A photographer from the Portuguese aristocracy, Da Cunha's activity is documented in France in the 1890s. His landscape photographs are close to Pictorialism. Like Robert ▸ Demachy and Constant ▸ Puyo he was a member of the Photo-Club de Paris, which, in a split from the Société française de photographie, conceived of the young medium as an art form in its own right. Cunha's photograph of the chalk cliffs of Étretat in Normandy was shown at the second exhibition of the Photo-Club, held in Paris in 1895. (Cat. 4, 151)

Eugène Cuvelier
(1837 Arras – 1900 Thomery)

Similar to the painters of the Barbizon School, the photographer Eugène Cuvelier found his subjects in the forest of Fontainebleau. His father, Adalbert Cuvelier, had introduced him to photography. In 1856 he visited Barbizon and the adjacent forest south of Paris for the first time. In 1859 he married the daughter of an innkeeper, in whose establishment the plein-air painters of the forest met. Cuvelier was friends with the artists Camille Corot, Jean-François Millet, and Théodore Rousseau. His photographic work includes depictions of nature from the forest of Fontainebleau as well as still lifes with objects of peasant life. (Cats. 54, 56–58, 62, 64, 85)

Louis Alphonse Davanne
(1824 Paris – 1912 Saint-Cloud)

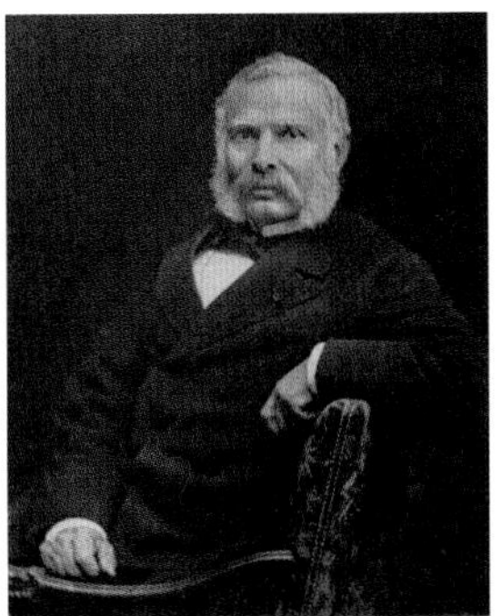

Davanne's interest lay in the scientific aspects of photography, and he researched new processes to give prints greater resistance to light. Davanne had studied under the chemist Aimé Girard. In 1852 he began to experiment with various processes such as → calotypes and the wet plate → collodion process. Later he created his own cameras. In 1854 he was one of the founding members of the Société française de photographie. In 1872 he taught first at the École nationale des ponts et chaussées, and later at the Sorbonne, where he used photography to teach classes. (Cats. 1, 2)

Dwight A. Davis
(1852–1944)

Little is known about Davis's origins or career. Primarily active in Massachusetts, he was a member of the Pictorial Photographers of America in Worcester. He showed his work in December 1904 at the First American Photographic Salon in New York, which marked a break with the American Pictorialists affiliated with the Photo-Secession and Alfred ▶ Stieglitz. (Cat. 92)

Louise Deglane
(1868 Paris – 1936 Marquay)

Deglane was one of the few female photographers of her time. She used the → autochrome process for her color photographs of landscapes and historic buildings. Born Louise Albertine Rosset, in 1893 she married the architect Henri Deglane, who was involved in the construction of the Grand Palais in Paris. Like Stéphanie ▶ Breton before her, she was a member of the Société française de photographie from 1914. (Cats. 144, 148)

Robert Demachy
(1859 Saint-Germain-en-Laye –
1936 Hennequeville)

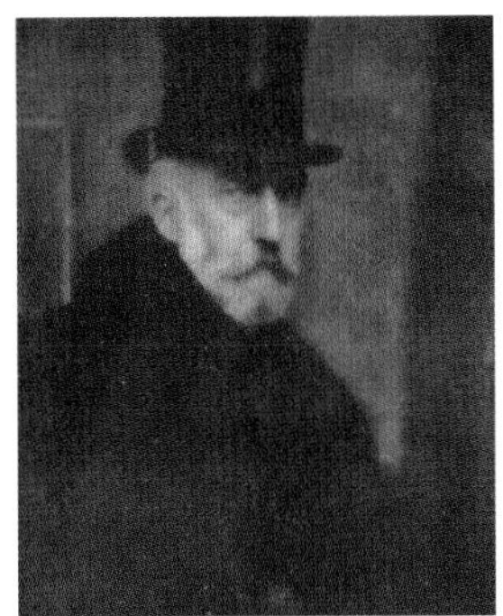

Demachy was an internationally important Pictorialist. From a wealthy banking family, he devoted himself to photography as an amateur from the 1870s on. He became a member of the Société française de photographie in 1882, and later a member of the Photo-Club de Paris, the Linked Ring in London, and the Photo-Secession in New York. Like his friend Constant ▶ Puyo, Demachy was interested in the → gum bichromate printing process, introducing it to Hugo ▶ Henneberg as well. In 1914 he gave up photography and returned to his profession as a banker. (Cats. 19, 42, 107, 109, 121, 124)

Georg Maria Eckert
(1828 Heidelberg – 1901 Karlsruhe)

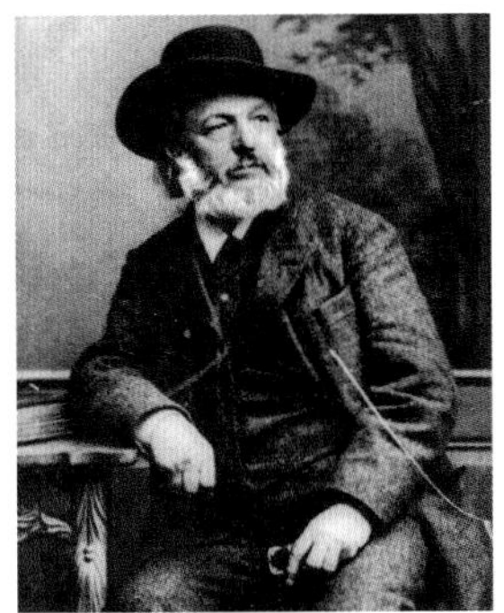

Eckert's Late-Romantic landscape paintings depict castles, palaces, and ruins in southern Germany—motifs that can also be found in his photography. Eckert began his studies at the Düsseldorf Art Academy in 1846. In 1856 he settled in his native city, where he worked as an art teacher and landscape painter. In the 1860s Eckert turned to photography. His photographs include landscapes and depictions of nature, which were to serve as models for artistic training. After financial difficulties, Eckert gave up photography in 1877 and moved to Karlsruhe, where he again devoted himself to landscape painting. (Cats. 48, 65, 152, 153)

Rudolf Eickemeyer
(1862 Yonkers, New York – 1932 Yonkers)

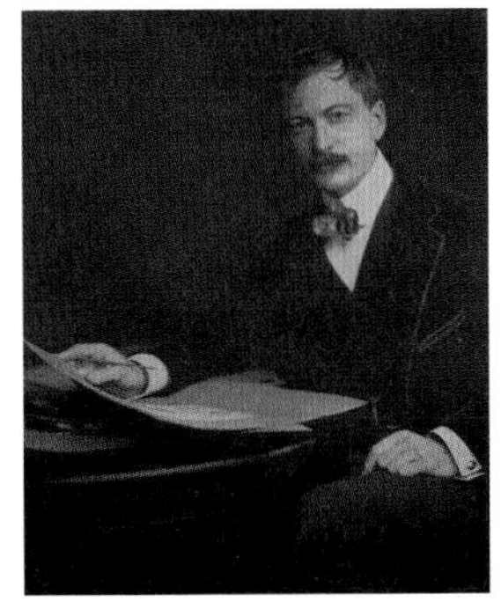

Eickemeyer was an American Pictorialist. He initially worked in his father's engineering company. In 1893 Eickemeyer began to teach himself photography. Two years later he was working as a professional photographer in New York. Eickemeyer specialized in portraits of women. His series of photographs of the actress Evelyn Nesbit became well known. He also produced landscape and genre photographs. Eickemeyer's commercial photographs similarly show his artistic aspirations. He was acquainted with Alfred ▶ Stieglitz, who published Eickemeyer's photographs in his quarterly journal *Camera Work*. (Cat. 122)

Peter Henry Emerson
(1856 La Palma, Cuba –
1936 Falmouth, England)

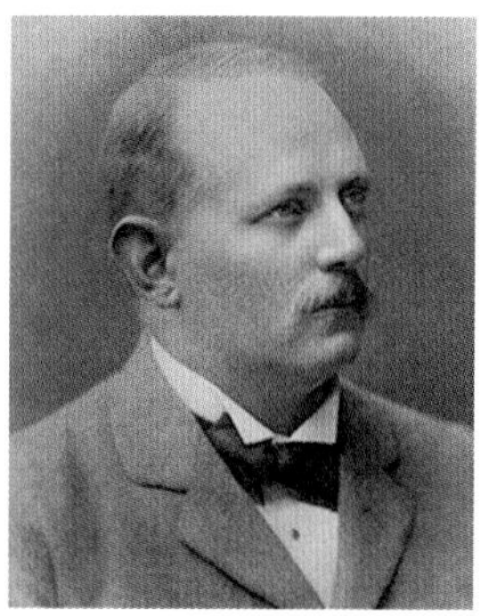

Emerson was one of the most controversial photo theorists in turn-of-the-century England. In 1869 he began studying medicine, but in 1881 turned his attention to photography. In 1883 he joined the Photographic Society of London, and two years later was a cofounder of the Camera Club there. In 1889 he published the first edition of his book *Naturalistic Photography for Students of the Art.* In his photographs, Emerson varied the sharpness of the individual subjects in order to mimic human perception. In the early 1890s he again distanced himself from his proclamations on art photography. (Cats. 87, 90, 100)

Constant Alexandre Famin
(1827 Paris – 1888 Paris)

Famin photographed genre scenes of country life, often in the surroundings of Paris. Little is known about his origins or early career. In 1858 he was working as a photographer with his own studio in Paris. He was one of the many photographers who, following Gustave Le ▸ Gray's example, found their subjects in the forest of Fontainebleau. In 1881 Famin published his series *Scène des champs* (Scene from the Fields), which was also used as a template for artists, with Adolphe ▸ Giraudon's publishing house. (Cats. 60, 61, 63)

Ferrier père, fils et Soulier
Claude-Marie Ferrier
(1811 Lyon – 1889 Passy)
Jacques Alexandre Ferrier
(1831 Lyon – 1912, location unknown)
Charles Soulier
(ca. 1830–after 1891, location unknown)

The company Ferrier père, fils et Soulier was specialized in stereoscopic (→ stereo photography) photographs of Paris. Claude Marie Ferrier began making the first stereoscopes in the 1850s. With his son, Jacques Alexandre, in 1859 he issued the first sales catalog with around two thousand stereoscopes, including shots by other photographers. That same year, they joined forces with the glass painter and photographer Charles Soulier. The latter brought another 1,200 negatives to the company, including his own photographs from Moscow and Saint Petersburg. Since 1969 the collection has been part of the holdings of the Roger-Viollet photo agency in Paris. (Cats. 30–33)

Carl Frederiksen
(1892–1932)

Few details of Frederiksen's biography could be determined to date. He was a Danish amateur photographer who experimented with color photography. Between 1905 and 1913 he participated in the exhibitions of the Association for Amateur Photography in Copenhagen. (Cat. 106)

Paul Gaillard
(1832 Hyères – 1890 Paris)

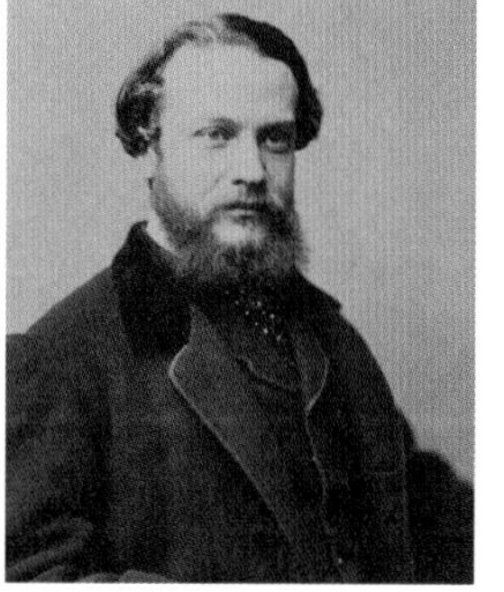

Little is known about Gaillard's origins or career. Like many other photographers, he followed the example of Gustave Le ▸ Gray and sought his subjects in the forest of Fontainebleau. In 1854 together with Olympe ▸ Aguado, Louis Alphonse ▸ Davanne, Le Gray, and Joseph ▸ Vigier he was a founding member of the Société française de photographie. His images, including views of Paris and portraits, were displayed at exhibitions in Brussels, Paris, and Marseille. (Cat. 59)

Adolphe Giraudon
(1849 Chârost – 1929 Chârost)

In 1877 Giraudon founded the Bibliothèque photographique, a precursor of today's image databases. This was an archive of shots by various photographers, which Giraudon made available to publishers and the specialist public for a fee. His publishing house also produced publications with photographs, for example by Constant Alexandre ▸ Famin. The focus of Giraudon's archive was on art reproductions. His collection, which also included his own works, comprised 115,000 photographs in 1900. (Cat. 150)

André Giroux
(1801 Paris – 1879 Paris)

Although Giroux's family was involved in the development and distribution of cameras for → daguerreotypes, as a landscape painter his interest in the potential of photography developed later. In 1821 he began studying at the École des beaux-arts in Paris. In 1825 he went to Rome, where he met Camille Corot. In 1830 Giroux returned to Paris, establishing himself as a landscape painter and working in his parents' business. Although he and his brother signed a contract with the inventors of the daguerreotype in 1839, it was not until the early 1850s that Giroux's own involvement with photography truly began. He often found his subjects in the forest of Fontainebleau. (Cats. 55, 82; p. 26, fig. 6)

Charles Grassin
(1828 Arras – 1900 Boulogne-sur-Mer)

Grassin's photographs show seascapes and harbor scenes, and often feature crashing waves. There is no information about Grassin's life or education. From the 1870s at the latest, he worked as a photographer in Boulogne-sur-Mer on the Atlantic coast in northern France. In 1882 Grassin became a member of the Société française de photographie. From 1891 he was president of the Union photographique du Pas-de-Calais, which he cofounded. (Cat. 16)

Gustave Le Gray
(1820 Villiers-le-Bel – 1884 Cairo)

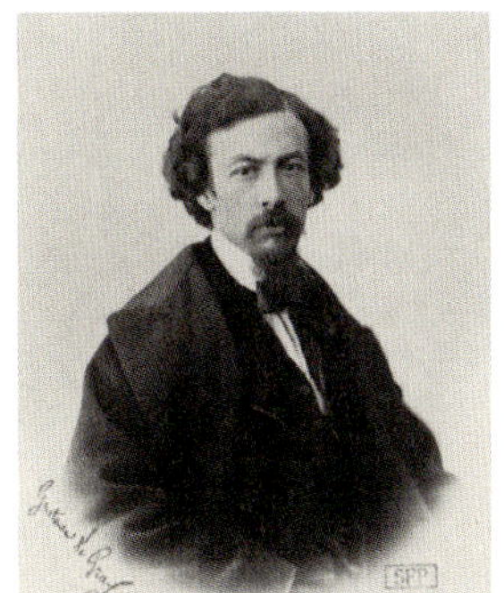

A photographer, inventor, and teacher, Le Gray was a driving force in the history of early photography. He began his career studying painting in Paris, where he got to know Henri Le ▸ Secq. Beginning in 1847 he concentrated on photography and developed a process for the use of → waxed paper negatives. From 1849 on Le Gray was one of the first to photograph regularly in the forest of Fontainebleau. Many photographers followed his example, including Olympe ▸ Aguado, who, like Eugène ▸ Colliau and Joseph ▸ Vigier, was a student of his. In 1851 he began taking numerous architectural photographs on behalf of the Comité des monuments historiques (Commission on Historical Monuments). That same year he was a founding member of the Société héliographique and in 1854 of the Société française de photographie. Despite recognition and public commissions, in 1860 Le Gray gave up his photography studio in Paris for financial reasons and settled in Egypt. (Cats. 5–7, 9–11, 14, 15, 154; p. 29, fig. 8)

Édouard Hannon
(1853 Brussels – 1931 Brussels)

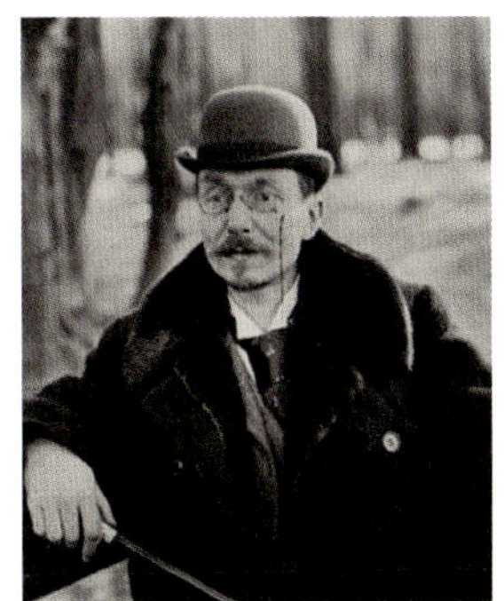

An engineer and amateur photographer, Hannon was one of the most important Pictorialists in Belgium. He often photographed atmospheric woodland scenes. As an engineering student Hannon was engaged in photography, and in 1874 was a cofounder of the Association belge de photographie, to which Marcel ▸ Vanderkindere later belonged as well. From 1876 he worked for the chemical company Solvay. On business trips to the United States and Russia, he photographed landscapes and scenes of everyday life. Hannon's former home in Brussels now houses a museum for contemporary photography. (Cat. 105)

Hugo Henneberg
(1863 Vienna – 1918 Vienna)

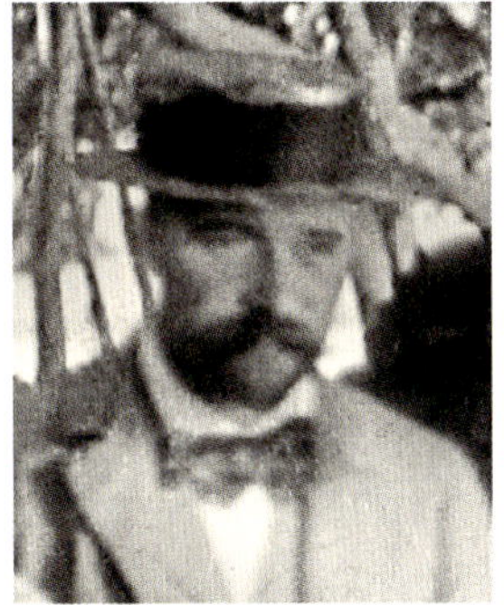

Henneberg was an important Pictorialist in Austria. Although he initially studied natural sciences, he began to focus on photography in 1887. In 1891 he became one of the first members of the Club of Amateur Photographers in Vienna, which gave birth to the Vienna Camera-Club in 1893. It was during that time that he got to know the photographers Heinrich ▸ Kühn and Hans Watzek, with whom he formed the artist's collective Trifolium. After 1895 Robert ▸ Demachy introduced them to the → gum bichromate printing process, which they developed further. In 1910 Henneberg gave up photography in favor of painting. (Cats. 94, 110, 114; p. 59, fig. 4)

Emil Jacobsen
(1836 Danzig – 1911 Berlin)

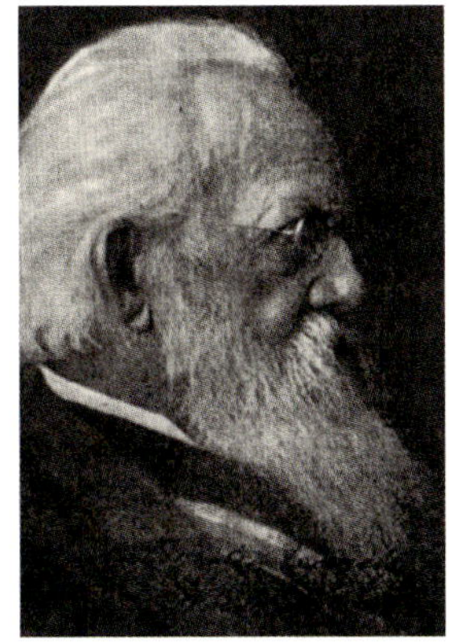

As a chemist, Jacobsen was concerned with the scientific aspects of photography and also took photographs himself. He began studying pharmacy and chemistry in Breslau in 1858. He was friends with the pharmacist Ernst Schering, in whose pharmaceutical company, Schering AG, he worked. Jacobsen was one of the first members of the Photographischer Verein zu Berlin (Photographic Association of Berlin), founded in 1864 by Hermann Wilhelm ▸ Vogel, where he gave lectures on subject such as the coloring of → albumen paper prints. (Cat. 25)

Hippolyte Jouvin
(1825 Mesnil-Clinchamps – 1889 Paris)

Little is known about Jouvin's origins or career. Like his brother Léon, Jouvin was active as a photographer, particularly in the 1860s and 1870s. Characteristic of his work are his stereoscopes (→ stereo photography), often printed on → albumen paper. He found his subjects in France as well as in neighboring countries, often photographing the streets and monuments of Paris. In 1871 Jouvin documented the barricades of the Paris Commune. (Cats. 35, 155)

Heinrich Kayser
(1853 Bingen – 1940 Bonn)

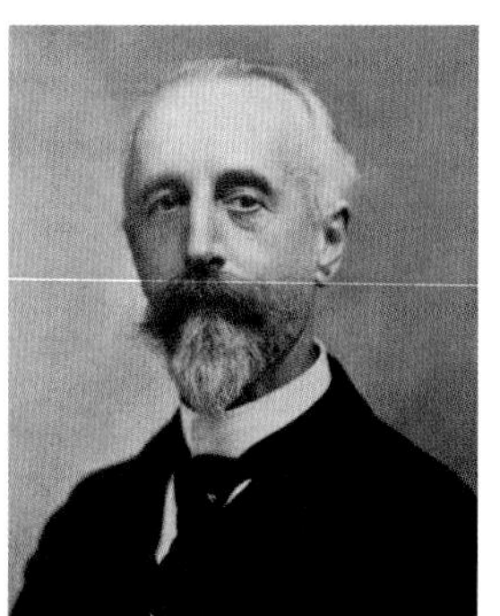

Kayser was a physicist who worked on spectroscopy. He studied physics and chemistry, first in Strasbourg and later in Berlin. In 1880 he attended a course in photography given by Hermann Wilhelm ▸ Vogel. In 1885 Kayser received a professorship at the Technical University in Hanover. From 1894 until his retirement in 1920, he taught in Bonn. Kayser's interests were not limited to physics or photography. After the death of his friend Carl Justi, he published some of the latter's writings on art history. (Cat. 24)

Viktor Knollmüller
(1889 München – 1971 Kempten)

Little is known about Knollmüller's origins or career. As a photographer in the Bavarian town of Kempten, he was well disposed to Pictorialism. With his daughter, he founded the Vereinigung der Amateurphotographen (Association of Amateur Photographers) in Kempten in 1910; he probably also had his own photographic studio business. (Cat. 101)

August Kotzsch
(1836 Loschwitz – 1910 Loschwitz)

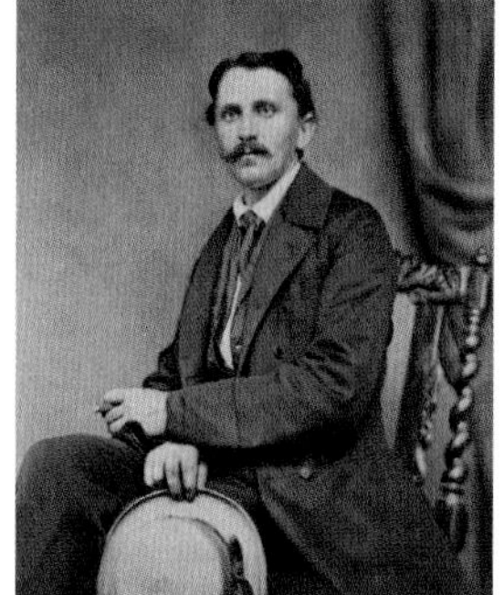

Kotzsch worked as a photographer in the area around Dresden, where he took nature photographs as well as austere still lifes with fruits and vegetables. Kotzsch, who came from a family of winegrowers, worked in his parents' business as a teenager. It was there that in 1852 he met the painter Ludwig Richter, who awakened his interest in art. After his first attempts at drawing, Kotzsch had to abandon his desire to study art due to financial reasons. From 1860 he was the assistant of the photographer August Niemann. After Niemann's death, Kotzsch took over his equipment and worked as a commercial photographer. (Cats. 76, 77)

Heinrich Kühn
(1866 Dresden – 1944 Birgitz, Austria))

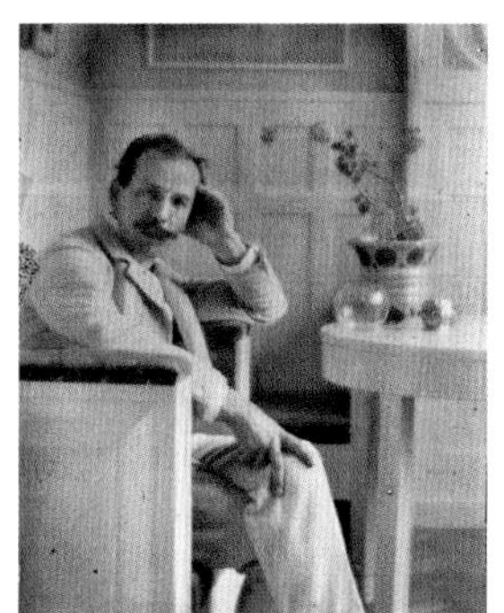

Kühn was one of the best-known proponents of Pictorialism. His works produced using the colored → gum bichromate printing process resemble Impressionism in their treatment of subject matter. After studying natural sciences and medicine, he became financially independent in 1890 and was able to devote himself to photography. In 1895 he became a member of the Vienna Camera-Club. There he met the photographers Hugo ▸ Henneberg and Hans Watzek, with whom he made up the artist's collective Trifolium. After 1895 Robert ▸ Demachy acquainted him with the gum bichromate printing process, which he in turn developed further. In 1904 Kühn met Alfred ▸ Stieglitz, with whom he developed a longstanding friendship. Together with Stieglitz and Edward ▸ Steichen, early on Kühn experimented with the → autochrome process. (Cats. 79, 103, 111–13, 115, 116–20, 126, 139–42, 156; p. 56, figs. 1–2; p. 59, figs. 5–6; p. 60, fig. 7; p. 63, figs. 9–11; p. 64, figs. 12–13)

Jacques Henri Lartigue
(1894 Courbevoie – 1986 Nice)

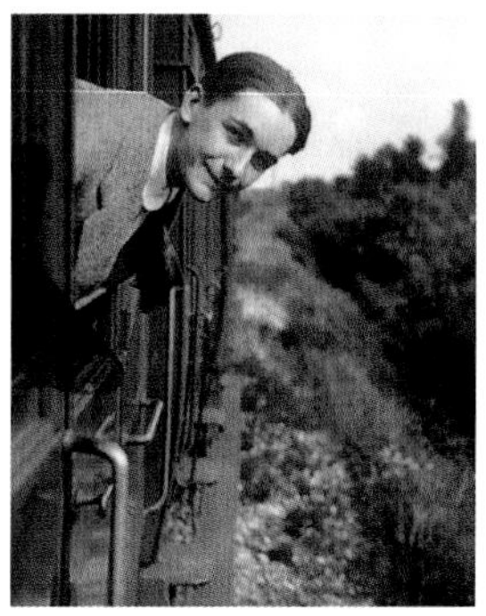

Lartigue's photographs are among the earliest snapshots of movement and speed. He received his first camera as a child. Self-taught, he photographed street scenes, sporting events, and car races. In 1915 he began studying painting in Paris and became acquainted with the artistic avant-garde. Financially independent at first, Lartigue devoted himself to the sophisticated life of French high society in the 1920s. After his divorce in 1931, he had to look for a job and supported himself by painting. It was not until the 1960s that his photographic work was received internationally. (Cat. 40)

Albert Londe
(1858 La Ciotat – 1917 Rueil-en-Brie)

Londe was a pioneer of scientific and medical photography. He became a member of the Société française de photographie in 1879. In 1882 Londe began working as a medical photographer at the Salpêtrière Clinic in Paris. His best-known photographs include images of female patients treated at the clinic for what was then known as "hysteria," a mental condition. In addition, Londe worked with X-rays and microphotography. He was also involved with the development of cameras for → chronophotography. Starting in the late 1880s he also took photographs of fireworks and wave movements. (Cat. 18)

Frères Lumière
Auguste Lumière
(1862 Besançon – 1954 Lyon)
Louis Lumière
(1864 Besançon – 1948 Bandol)

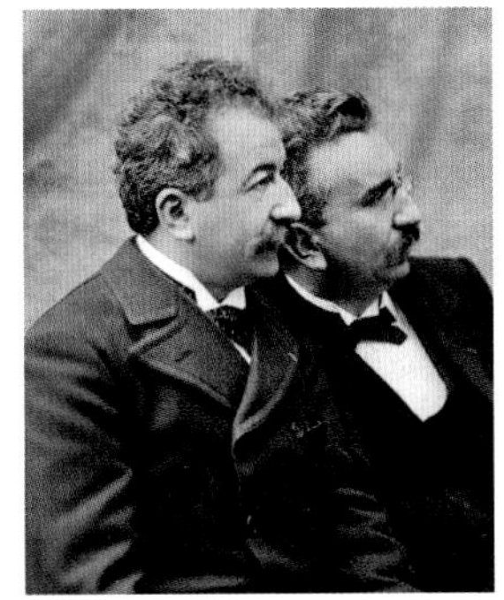

The Lumière brothers are known for their innovations in the field of moving images. They also invented an early process for producing color photographs. Auguste and Louis's father ran a photography studio in Lyon. As a teenager, Louis developed a photographic plate that was highly sensitive to light, establishing the financial success of the family business. In 1894 the brothers saw a demonstration of Thomas Edison's kinetoscope in Paris, which inspired them to experiment with the possibilities of the moving image. In February 1895 they received a patent for the Cinématographe, an apparatus that could record a short film and project it onto a screen. Louis's first film, which shows workers—mostly women—leaving the Lumière works, was created in 1895. In 1903 the Lumière brothers invented the → autochrome process for color photography, which was distributed successfully from 1907. (Cat. 146)

Charles Marville
(1813 Paris – 1879 Paris)

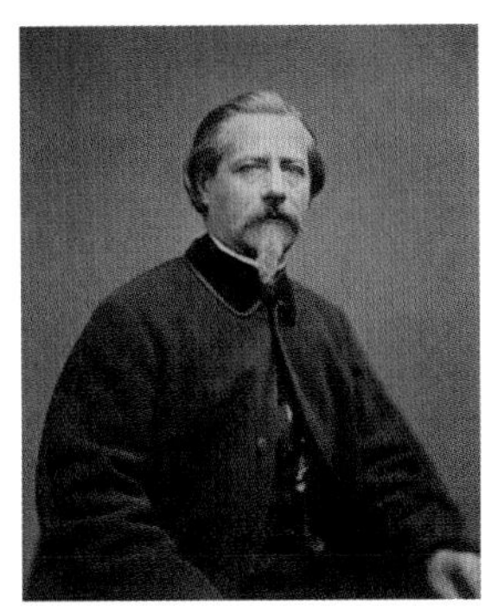

Marville photographed the old Paris on behalf of the city authorities. From 1870 he also took pictures of the metropolis following its fundamental transformation by Georges-Eugène Haussmann. Following training as an artist, he changed his name from Bossu to Marville around 1831 and worked as an illustrator. In 1850 he began to devote himself to photography. His early photographs were often published by Louis-Désiré ▸ Blanquart-Evrard's publishing house. Occasionally, like many of his colleagues, he photographed in the forest of Fontainebleau. Beginning in 1858 Marville worked as an official photographer for the city of Paris, documenting the old neighborhoods before they were demolished. In the 1870s he took pictures of the new boulevards, magnificent buildings, and Neoclassical residential buildings. (Cats. 27, 28; p. 35, fig. 1)

Adolphe De Meyer
(1868 Paris – 1946 Los Angeles)

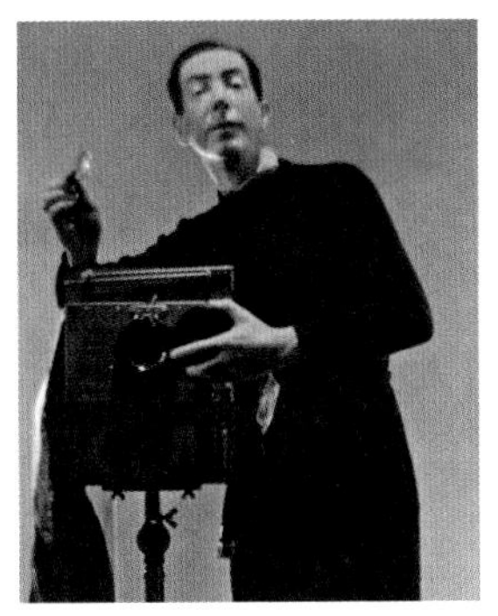

De Meyer is considered a pioneer of fashion photography. His early works show the influence of Pictorialism. Meyer, who also called himself Meyer-Watson after his mother's maiden name, spent his childhood in France and Germany. He received his first artistic lessons from Claude Monet. In 1895 he moved to London, taking up photography at the turn of the century. In 1906 he became a member of the Linked Ring association. In 1914 he immigrated to the United States. In addition to portraits of important cultural and society figures, his fashion photographs helped shape the genre. (Cats. 89, 125, 127, 128)

Léopold Louis Mercier
(1866 Angers – after 1914 Cabourg)

Mercier was successful as a publisher of photographic images. His own photographs of the 1889 world's fair in Paris and the 1895 photograph of a derailed train in the Gare Montparnasse gained recognition. In around 1891 Mercier opened his photography studio and publishing house in Paris. He specialized in publishing photographic art reproductions and acquired works by other photographers for publication in albums and books. In 1914 he sold his business. The collection of his negatives, consisting of about thirty thousand glass plates, has been in the possession of the Roger-Viollet photo agency in Paris since 1938. (Cat. 23)

Louis Antonin Neurdein
(1846 Paris – 1914 Paris)

Neurdein and his brother, Étienne, were the owners of Neurdein frères, founded in Paris after 1863, which in addition to commercial portrait photography published postcards of landscape images. Their father was also a photographer. While Étienne ran the studio, Louis-Antonin traveled extensively, finding the subjects for the postcards and other publications. (Cat. 36)

Antonin Personnaz
(1854 Bayonne – 1936 Bayonne)

Personnaz was an art collector and amateur photographer from a wealthy family of cloth merchants in Bayonne. In 1878 he went to Paris, where he worked in the family business. He was friends with Camille Pissarro and purchased works by Edgar Degas, Claude Monet, and Pierre-Auguste Renoir. He also became interested in photography and from 1896 was a member of the Société française de photographie. In 1907 Personnaz began to produce → autochromes, in which he explored Impressionist motifs and showed the artists at work. (Cats. 129–38)

Pierre Petit
(1831 Aups – 1909 Paris)

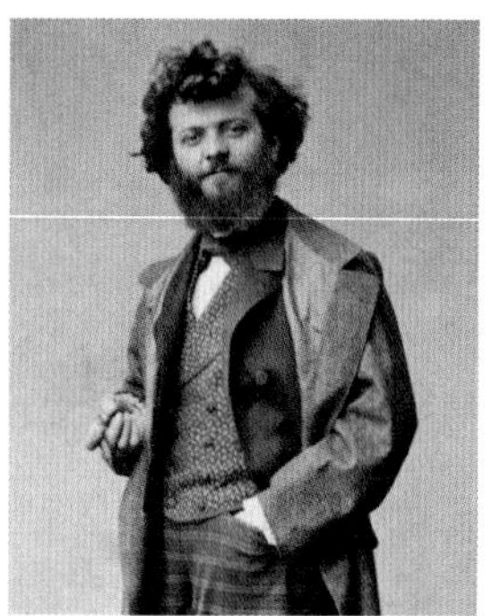

The versatile photographer Pierre Petit received his training in the studio of André Adolphe Eugène Disdéri in Paris. There, with his colleague André René Trinquart, he opened his own studio in 1859. As a successful portraitist, Petit photographed prominent personalities of his time, including the composer Hector Berlioz and the painter Eugène Delacroix, as well as 25,000 clergymen throughout France. In 1867 Petit was an official photographer at the world's fair in Paris. Between 1871 and 1886 he traveled to New York several times on behalf of the government to document the construction of the Statue of Liberty. In Paris he photographed the building of the Eiffel Tower. From 1875 onward Petit also worked as a photographer for the medical faculty in Paris, and that same year he became a member of the Société française de photographie. (Cat. 88)

Victor Albert Prout
(1835 Bristol – 1877 Sussex)

Prout was active in England in the 1860s creating photographs in → panorama format. No details regarding his career are known. Around 1860 he photographed the river landscape of the Thames between London and Oxford. Prout immigrated to Australia, where he ran a photography studio in Sydney. After returning to England, he died at Sussex Asylum Hospital. (Cat. 86)

Constant Puyo
(1857 Morlaix – 1933 Paris)

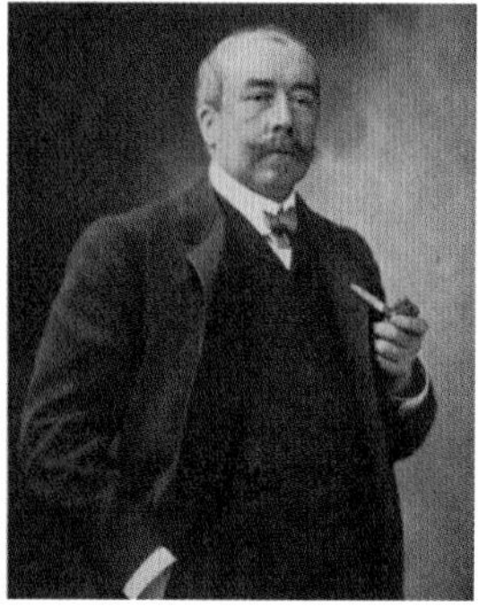

Puyo was one of the most important proponents of Pictorialism in France. While still a career member of the French military he became a dedicated amateur photographer in 1887. In 1894 he joined the Photo-Club de Paris, and later he also belonged to the Linked Ring in London. In 1902 Puyo left the army and opened a photography studio in Paris. Like his friend Robert ▸ Demachy he experimented with → gum bichromate printing. He was also involved in the development of a soft-focus lens. Among his favorite motifs were atmospheric landscapes with female figures. (Cats. 67, 98, 99, 108)

Henry Peach Robinson
(1830 Ludlow – 1901 Tunbridge Wells)

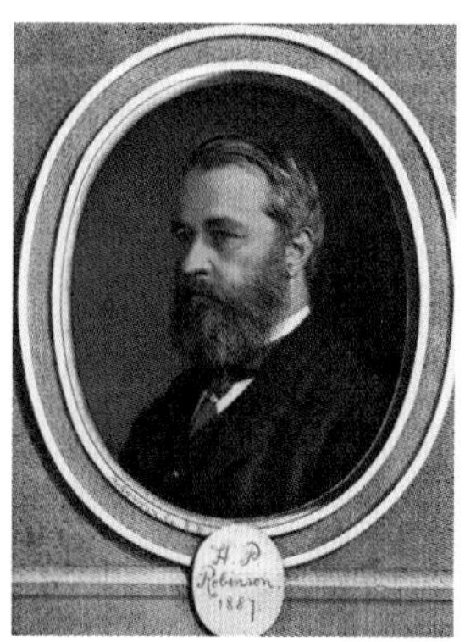

Robinson was an English Pictorialist and an important photo theorist. Beginning his career as a bookseller, from 1852 he dedicated himself to photography and opened his first photographic studio in 1857 in Leamington. His principal theoretical work *Pictorial Effect in Photography: Being Hints on Composition and Chiaroscuro for Photographers* (1869) had a great influence on his contemporaries and was published in German in 1886. Robinson used composition photography, for which he arranged several negatives into a subject and then exposed them. His subjects, often scenes from mythology or poetry, are reminiscent of Pre-Raphaelite painting. In 1891 he was one of the founders of the Linked Ring in London. In the 1870s Robinson began to collaborate with Nelson King Cherill, with whom he photographed seascapes. (Cats. 17, 78)

Ildefonse Rousset
(1817 Paris – 1878 Maisons-Alfort)

Rousset was a republican-minded journalist who founded several magazines, including *Le Spectateur républicain* (1848). He also worked as a photographer and joined the Société française de photographie. In 1865, with the journalist and writer Émile de La Bédollière, he published the book *Le Tour de Marne,* including his own photographs of the river landscape. One year later his book *Le Bois de Vincennes,* featuring images from the municipal forest of Paris, was published. (Cat. 83)

Robert Scholz
(1843 Bunzlau, now Bolesławiec –
1926 Görlitz)

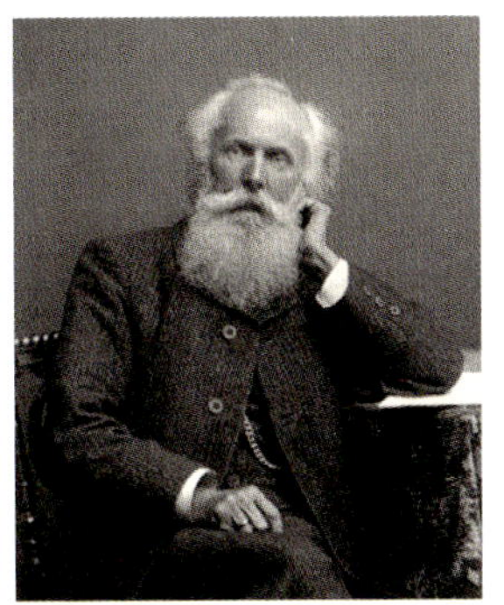

Scholz worked as a photographer in Görlitz and its environs. After an apprenticeship in his father's store as a porcelain painter working with photography, Scholz completed further training in photography studios in Hamburg and Nordhausen between 1861 and 1863. In 1867 he founded his own studio in Görlitz, offering architectural photographs as well as individual and group portraits. He also photographed landscape and cloud motifs that were to serve as models for artists. He participated with his photographs in the 1876 world's fair in Philadelphia. After Scholz's death, his children took over the business. His estate of around four thousand exposed glass plates is now in the Görlitz city archive. (Cat. 22)

Henri Le Secq
(1818 Paris – 1882 Paris)

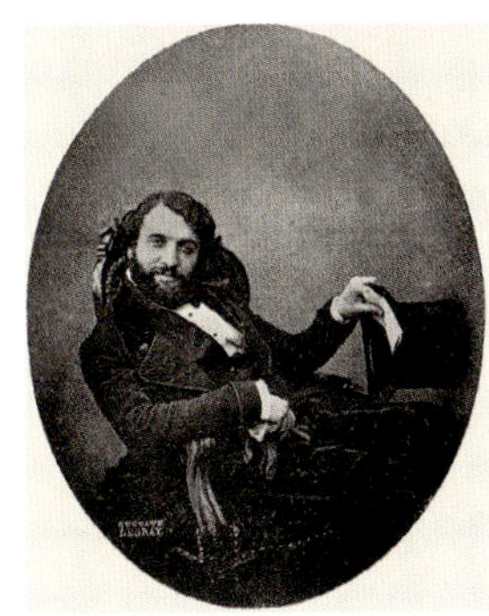

Le Secq is considered one of the most important architectural photographers of the nineteenth century. In addition to historical monuments, he also photographed landscapes. Beginning in 1835 he studied painting in Paris. It was there that he got to know Gustave Le ▸ Gray, who taught him photography in 1848. At first Le Secq concentrated on the → calotype before moving on to → waxed paper negatives. Like Édouard ▸ Baldus and Le Gray, from 1851 he produced architectural photographs on behalf of the Comité des monuments historiques (Commission on Historical Monuments). That same year he became a cofounder of the first photographic association in France, the Société héliographique. (Cats. 50–53, 157)

William Sherlock
(1813 Lambeth, documented in England
in the 1850s)

Sherlock, who was a lawyer, came to photography in 1843 after reading an article on → daguerreotypes and William Henry Fox Talbot's → calotype. He planned to open a portrait studio in London, but to do so he required a license from Talbot. After these negotiations failed, Sherlock turned to landscape photography. In the 1850s he produced photographs of rural life, and later cloud studies that were used as models for artists. Celebrated by his contemporaries, Sherlock later fell into oblivion, probably due to his work long being attributed to the photographer John Whistler. (Cat. 68)

Edward Steichen
(1879 Bivingen, Luxemburg –
1973 West Redding, Connecticut)

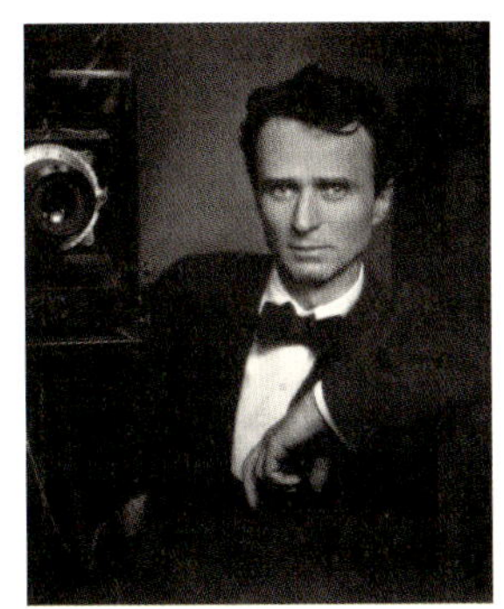

Steichen is one of the most important protagonists in the history of photography in the United States. His style ranged from Pictorialism to straight photography. After immigrating to the US with his family as a child, he trained as a lithographer in 1894 and then studied painting. At the same time, Steichen became a self-taught photographer. In 1902, with Alvin Langdon ▸ Coburn and Alfred ▸ Stieglitz, he founded the Photo-Secession in New York. From 1911 Steichen worked as a fashion photographer. In World War I he was stationed in France as a war photographer; thereafter his style changed. From 1947 to 1962 he was the director of the photography department at the Museum of Modern Art in New York. (Cat. 102; p. 17, fig. 12)

Alfred Stieglitz
(1864 Hoboken, New Jersey –
1946 New York)

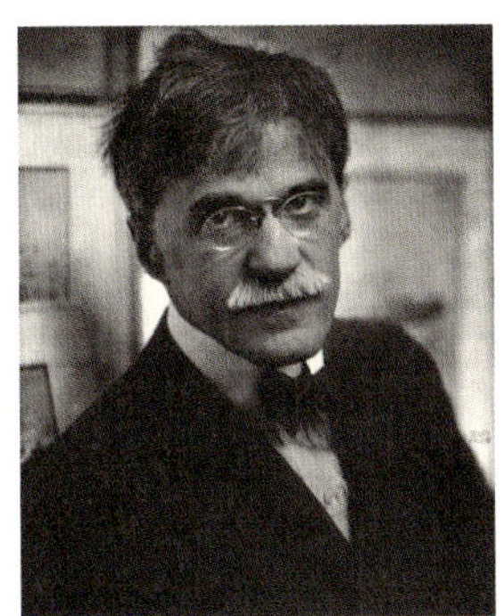

As a photographer, gallery owner, and publisher, Stieglitz was instrumental in establishing photography as part of the art canon in the United States. Beginning in 1882 he studied engineering and photochemistry with Hermann Wilhelm ▸ Vogel in Berlin. In 1890 Stieglitz returned to New York, producing photographs influenced by Pictorialism. In 1902, together with Alvin Langdon ▸ Coburn and Edward ▸ Steichen, he founded the Photo-Secession. From 1903 to 1917 he published the quarterly journal *Camera Work*. At his gallery he sold paintings and sculptures by artists of the European avant-garde as well as photographs. In 1924 Stieglitz married the painter Georgia O'Keeffe. (Cat. 43)

Carl P. Stirn
(Documented in New York in the 1880s
and 1890s)

Stirn, a German immigrant, was a toy manufacturer in New York in the late nineteenth century.
In 1886 he acquired the rights from inventor Robert D. Gray for a handheld → secret camera,
which Carl's brother Rudolph had manufactured in Berlin. This camera was marketed in
Germany as C. P. Stirn's Secret Camera and in North American as C. P. Stirn's Concealed
Vest Camera. Stirn's secret camera, with its characteristic round glass plates, was sold
thousands of times over before the invention of roll film in 1884. (Cat. 38)

Henry Stuart Wortley
(1832 Wortley – 1890 London)

Colonel Stuart Wortley worked as a photographer after his military career. His series of
moonlit seascapes with poetic titles were famous. Wortley joined the British Army in 1848
and began photographing while stationed in Africa in 1853. In 1855, during the Crimean War,
he took a number of photographs with Roger Fenton. After the end of his active military
career and a brief stint as a British parliamentarian, he devoted himself primarily to
photography in the 1860s. In 1862 Wortley joined the Photographic Society of London. In 1861
and 1862 he documented the eruption of Mount Vesuvius in snapshots, which earned him
particular esteem. (Cat. 8)

Alphonse Taupin
(Documented in France between the
1860s and 1880s)

Little is known about Taupin's origins or career. He was a French photographer who worked
between 1860 and the 1880s. Like Olympe ► Aguado, Eugène ► Cuvelier, Constant Alexandre
► Famin, Paul ► Gaillard, André ► Giroux, and Gustave Le ► Gray, he took photographs in the
forest of Fontainebleau. (Cat. 73)

Carl Teufel
(1845 Bayreuth – 1912 Munich)

Teufel was a photographer at the Bavarian court who worked primarily in Munich. His
photographs of artists' studios were taken there in 1889–90. He also photographed
numerous works of art and decorative art objects. In addition, he produced photographs
depicting nature, which were to serve as models for artists. In 1911 Teufel's glass plates
were sold to the Munich publishing house Riehn & Tietze; today they are part of the
Bildarchiv Foto Marburg. (Cats. 20, 21)

Gustav Eduard Bernhard Trinks
(1871 Joinville, Brazil – 1967 Joinville)

Trinks's family was from Brazil. In 1880 Trinks moved from Brazil to Hamburg, where he later
worked as a merchant. He was co-owner of the Gebrüder Trinks company, established in
1896, which specialized in exports to Brazil. Like Heinrich ► Beck he was a member of the
Freie Vereinigung von Amateur-Photographen zu Hamburg (Free Association of Amateur
Photographers in Hamburg), which was close to Pictorialism. In 1948 he returned to the town
where he was born, which had been founded by his grandfather. (Cat. 123)

Marcel Vanderkindere
(1865 Ukkel – 1941 Brussels)

Vanderkindere was a lawyer and amateur photographer close to Pictorialism. His images,
most of which are landscapes, were exhibited internationally. From 1895 to 1911
Vanderkindere served as the secretary of the Association belge de photographie, which was
founded in Brussels in 1874 by Édouard ► Hannon and existed until 1940. Vanderkindere was
in contact with the Freie Vereinigung von Amateur-Photographen zu Hamburg (Free
Association of Amateur Photographers in Hamburg), which had Heinrich ► Beck and Gustav
Eduard Bernhard ► Trinks among its members. This association had split off from the
Hamburger Gesellschaft zur Förderung der Amateur-Photographie (Hamburg Society for the
Promotion of Amateur Photography) in 1898. (Cat. 104)

Louis Vert
(1865 Paris – 1924 Épluches)

Like Eugène Atget, the amateur photographer Vert devoted himself to life on the streets of
Paris. He often chose market stalls, street vendors, and clochards as his subjects. His father,
a trained typographer, ran a print shop in Paris where Vert also worked. Inspired by his
uncle, a passionate amateur photographer, Vert took up photography before the turn of the
century. In 1904 he became a member of the Société d'excursions des amateurs de
photographie. He sporadically published his photographs in local magazines. From 1911 he
lived in the countryside near Saint-Ouen-l'Aumône, outside of Paris. (Cat. 41)

Joseph Vigier
(1821 Savigny-sur-Orge – 1894 Paris)

Around 1848 Vigier took up photography under Gustav Le ▶ Gray. Of noble descent, he photographed the British royal family in 1852. In 1853, on a trip to Spain, he took numerous photographs of the Pyrenées that were published as an album by Alexandre La Chevardière. Vigier was one of the founding members of the Société héliographique in 1851 and the Société française de photographie in 1854. Nevertheless, he gave up photography in the 1860s. La Chevardière came from a publishing family and maintained one of the largest printing houses in Paris. He founded several magazines and edited publications that contained photographs, such as the album of Vigier's photographs. One of the few female printers of the era, Adèle Élisabeth Hubert de Fonteny, was probably responsible for printing the photographic originals. (Cat. 81)

Hermann Wilhelm Vogel
(1834 Dobrilugk – 1898 Berlin)

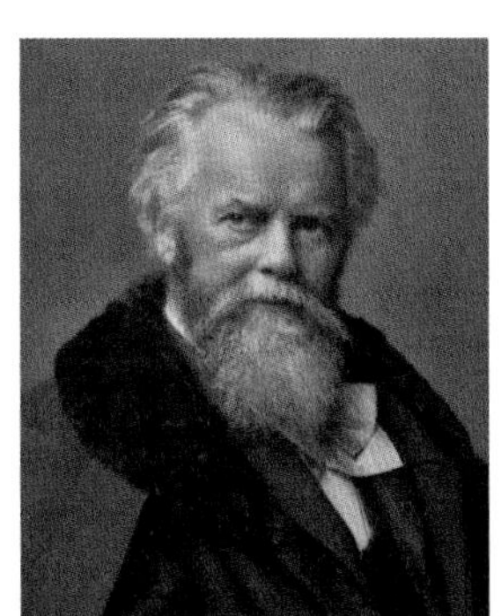

Vogel was a photochemist who also worked as a teacher. From 1854 he studied chemistry, physics, and mineralogy in Berlin. His 1863 dissertation is considered one of the first scientific studies on photography. In 1864 Vogel founded a photographic society in Berlin, which in turn gave birth to the Verein zur Förderung der Photographie (Society for the Promotion of Photography). That same year he established the professorship for photography at the Royal Trade Institute in Berlin. His students included Heinrich ▶ Kayser and Alfred ▶ Stieglitz. In 1866 Vogel's portfolio *Bilder aus dem Thiergarten* (Photographs from the Tiergarten) was published in Berlin. (Cat. 66)

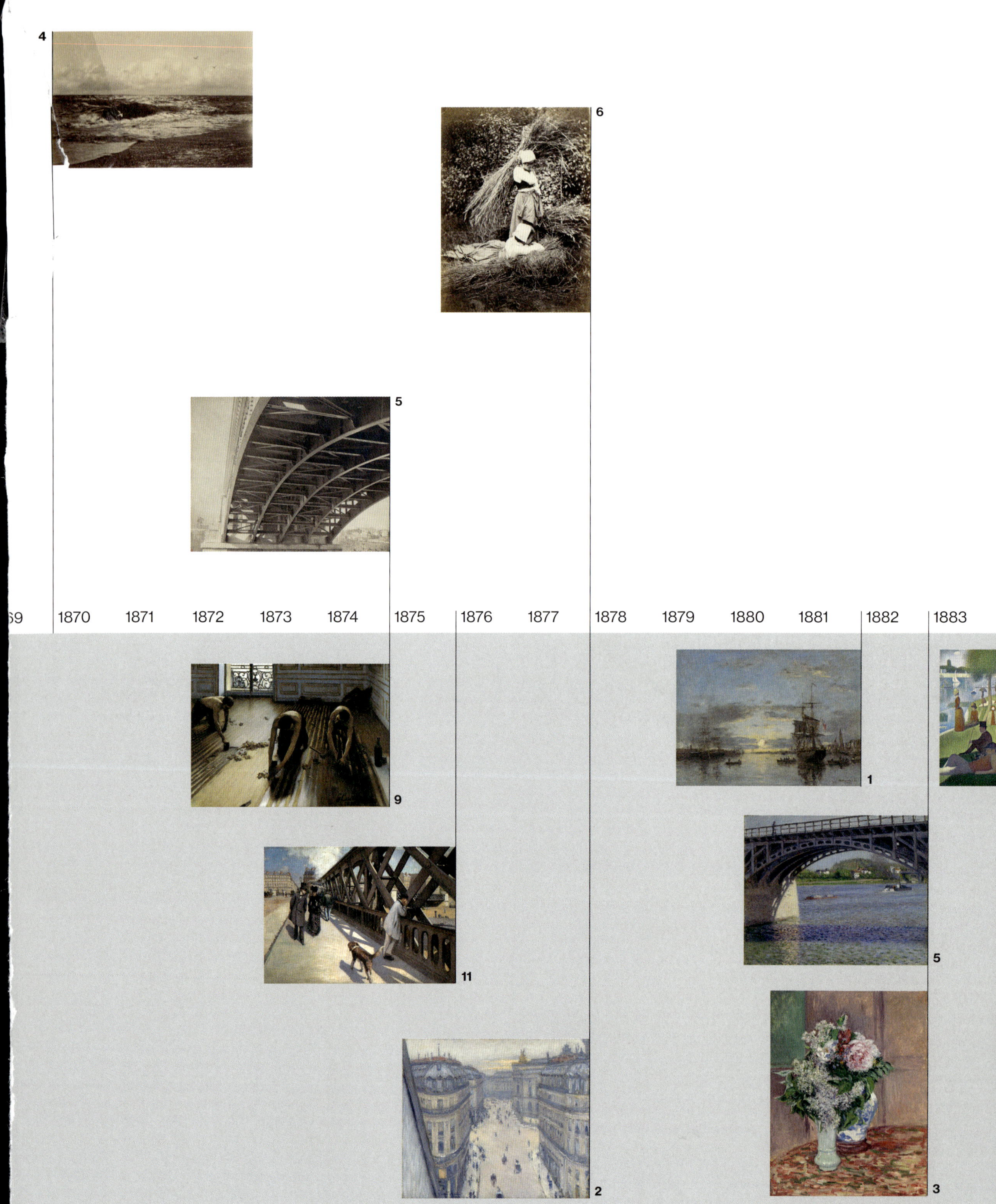

4
6
5
69 1870 1871 1872 1873 1874 1875 1876 1877 1878 1879 1880 1881 1882 1883
9
1
11
5
2
3

In the nineteenth century numerous
photographers chose the same motifs as
the Impressionist painters: the forest
of Fontainebleau, the cliffs of Étretat, or
the modern metropolis of Paris. They
too studied the changing light situations,
the seasons, and weather conditions.
Until World War I the dialogue between
photography and painting was characterized
by both competition and influence.
The overview shows these interactions in
selected examples.

<h1>Dialogue</h1>

Photographs

1 Anonymous
Sky Study, Sunset, 1855
cat. 96

2 Ferrier père, fils et Soulier
*Boulevard de Sébastopol (Looking East),
Paris,* 1860
cat. 32

3 Charles Aubry
Garden Asters, ca. 1864
cat. 74

4 Henry Peach Robinson
and Nelson King Cherrill
The Beached Margent of the Sea, 1870
cat. 17

5 Augustin Hippolyte, called Auguste Collard
Pont de Grenelle, Paris, ca. 1875–76
cat. 47

6 Anonymous
Two Peasant Women, before 1878
cat. 150

7 Peter Henry Emerson
Gathering Water Lilies, 1886
cat. 90

8 Robert Collett
Water Lilies in the Rain, 1897
cat. 91

9 Eugène Atget
Asphalting, Paris, ca. 1900
Bibliothèque historique de la Ville de Paris

10 Rudolf Eickemeyer
River in Winter, 1904 or earlier
cat. 122

11 Anonymous
*The Pretty Passersby, Parisian Women
in Hats,* 1906–08
cat. 39

12 Antonin Personnaz
*Armand Guillaumin Painting
"Bathers near Crozant,"* ca. 1907
cat. 138

13 Heinrich Kühn
Miss Mary in a Blue Dress, 1910
cat. 140

14 Antonin Personnaz
Sunrise with Snow, ca. 1907–14
cat. 129

15 Antonin Personnaz
River, Factory, Smoke, ca. 1907–14
cat. 135

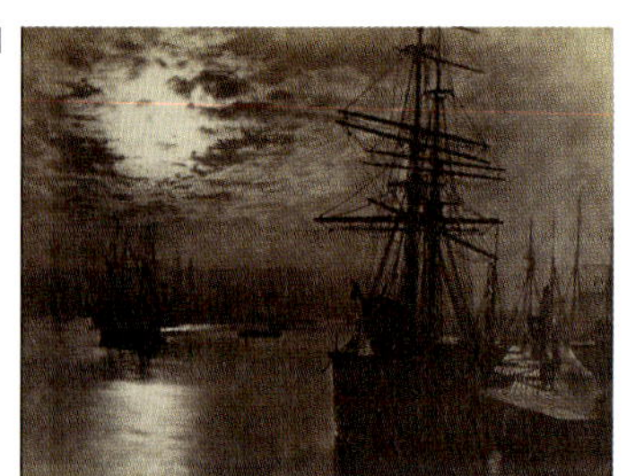

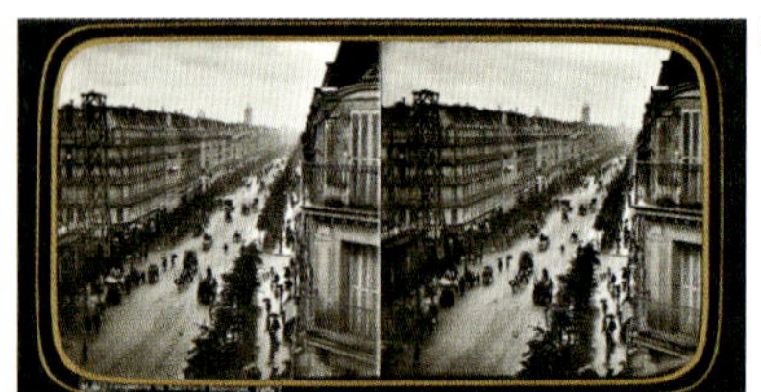

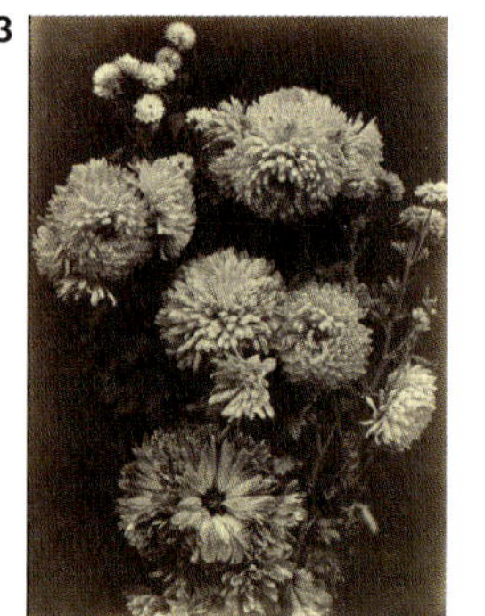

1855   1856   1857   1858   1859   1860   1861   1862   1863   1864   1865   1866   1867   1868   18

Photography and Painting, 1860–1914

Paintings

1 Eugène Boudin
Le Havre: The Outer Harbor at Sunset, 1882
Oil on canvas
Hasso Plattner Collection

2 Gustave Caillebotte
Rue Halévy, View from the Sixth Floor, 1878
Oil on canvas
Hasso Plattner Collection

3 Gustave Caillebotte
Lilacs and Peonies in Two Vases, 1883
Oil on canvas
Hasso Plattner Collection

4 Claude Monet
View of the Sea, 1888
Oil on canvas
Von der Heydt-Museum, Wuppertal

5 Gustave Caillebotte
The Argenteuil Bridge and the Seine, ca. 1883
Oil on canvas
Hasso Plattner Collection

6 Camille Pissarro
Hoar-Frost, Peasant Girl Making a Fire, 1888
Oil on canvas
Hasso Plattner Collection

7 Mary Cassatt
Summertime, 1894
Oil on canvas
Hammer Museum, Los Angeles

8 Claude Monet
Water Lilies, 1914–17
Oil on canvas
Hasso Plattner Collection

9 Gustave Caillebotte
The Floor Planers, 1875
Oil on canvas
Musée d'Orsay, Paris

10 Claude Monet
Floes at Bennecourt, 1893
Oil on canvas
Hasso Plattner Collection

11 Gustave Caillebotte
Le Pont de l'Europe, Paris, 1876
Oil on canvas
Association des Amis du Petit Palais, Geneva

12 Georges Seurat
A Sunday Afternoon on the Island of La Grande Jatte, 1884–86
Oil on canvas
The Art Institute of Chicago

13 Claude Monet
Woman with a Parasol, Facing Left, 1886
Oil on canvas
Musée d'Orsay, Paris

14 Claude Monet
Grainstack in the Sunlight, Snow Effect, 1891
Oil on canvas
Hasso Plattner Collection

15 Gustave Loiseau
Hoarfrost at Pontoise, 1906
Oil on canvas
Hasso Plattner Collection

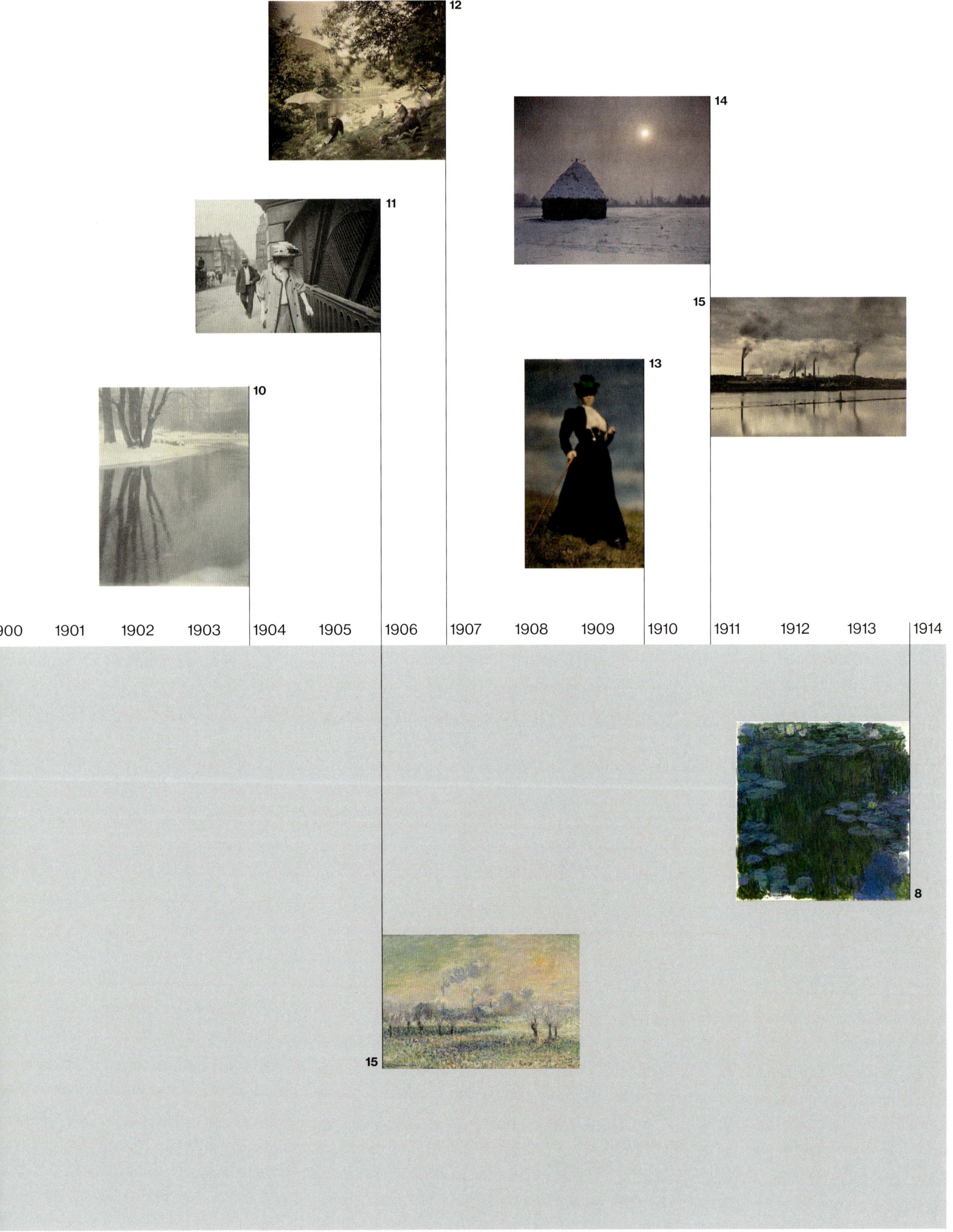

12
14
11
15
13
10
8
15
900 1901 1902 1903 1904 1905 1906 1907 1908 1909 1910 1911 1912 1913 1914

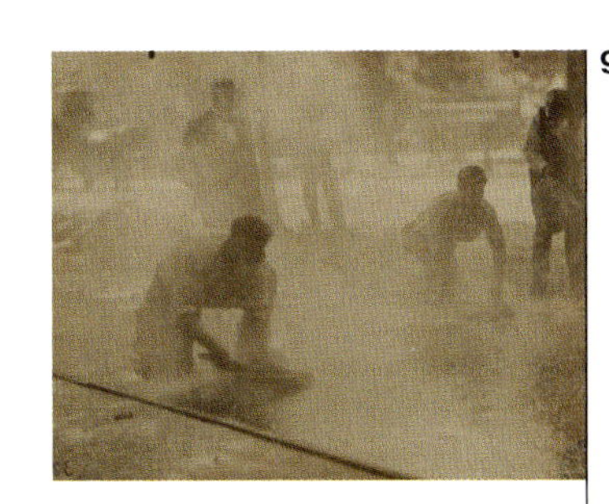

9

7

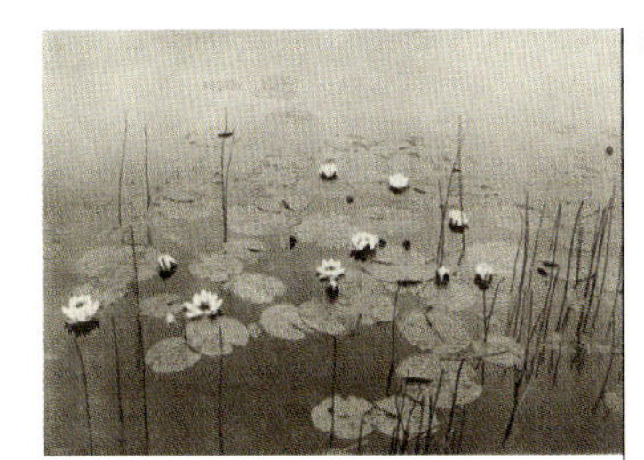

8

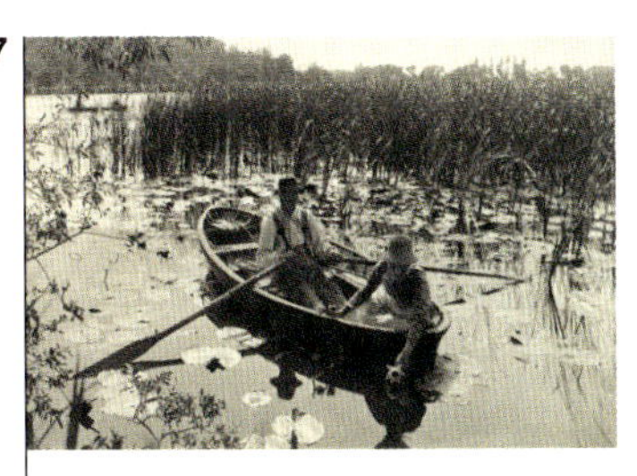

12

4

7

13

6

10

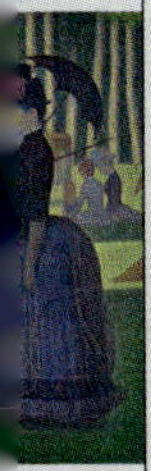

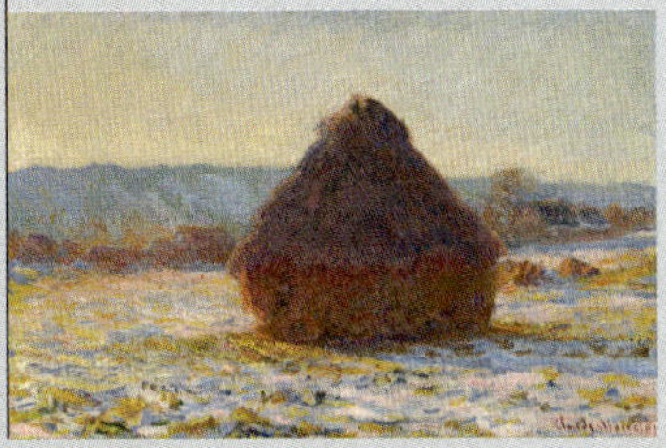

14

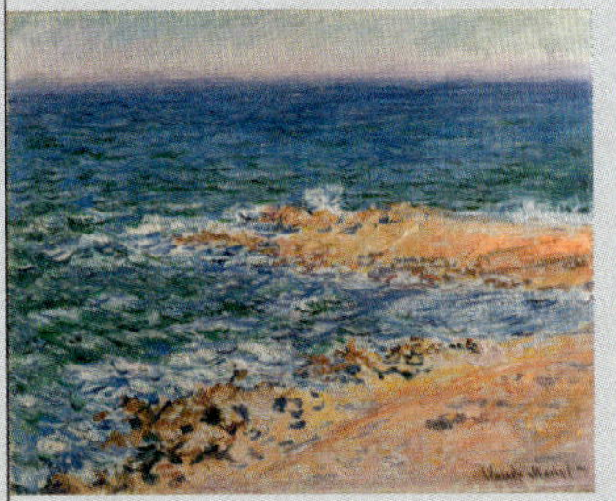

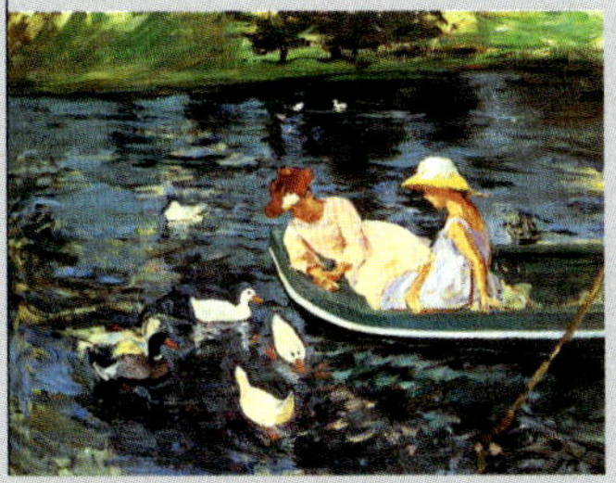

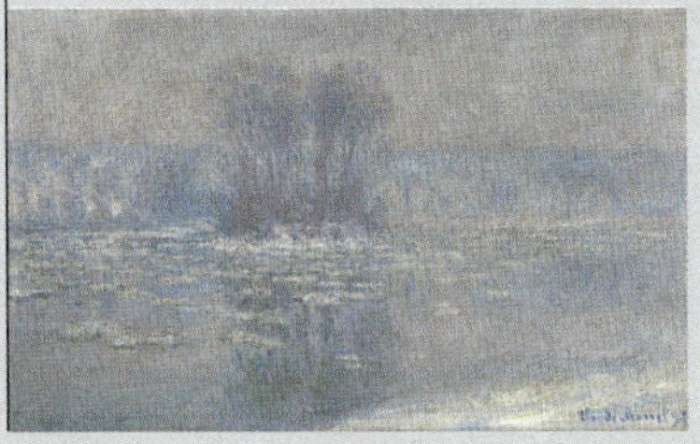

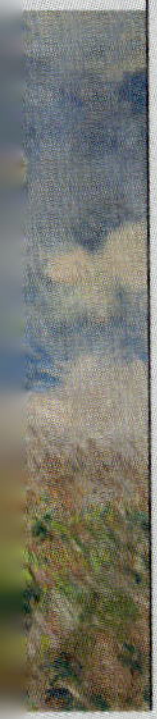

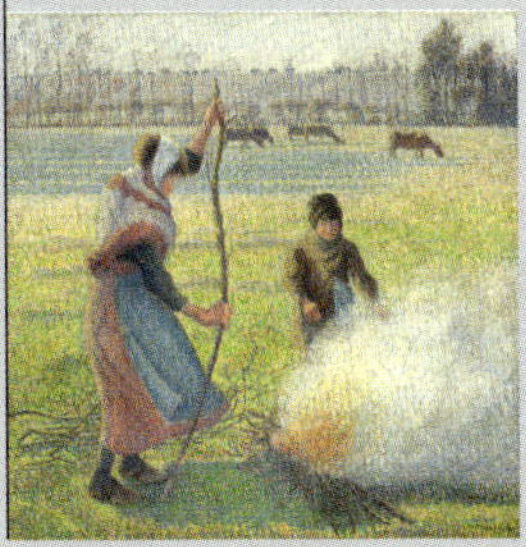

Glossary

Christine Rottmeier-Keß

► = see biography
→ = see glossary entry

Albumen paper (1850s–1920s)

Albumen paper was the most widely used black-and-white photography paper in the nineteenth century. It permitted the production of positive prints from a negative through exposure alone, without chemical development. It was introduced by Louis Désiré ► Blanquart-Evrard in 1850. Albumen is a protein obtained from egg whites. It served as a binder for the image-producing silver salts and increased the sharpness of the picture. It also yielded a slightly glossy surface, which substantially improved the image contrast. For the manufacture of albumen paper, a thin sheet of paper was coated in a solution of egg white and ammonium chloride, dried, and then dipped in a silver nitrate solution to render it light sensitive. Dried once again, the paper served as the picture support.

After exposure together with a negative (→ contact printing) the paper was washed, toned, and fixed. Additional gold toning baths were a standard part of the process and gave the albumen prints greater depth. Due to the thinness of the paper, prints were usually mounted on cardboard in a variety of formats, from *carte de visite* to → panorama. In the late 1850s industrially manufactured albumen papers were available on the market, but still had to be sensitized with silver nitrate before use. After 1870 presensitized albumen paper with a monthslong shelf life began to be produced. The center of production for albumen paper was Dresden; the work was performed by women, who cracked and separated eggs in assembly-line fashion. From the 1880s on albumen paper was increasingly replaced by other → printing-out papers, until it disappeared from the market entirely in the 1920s.

Autochrome (1907–1930s)

In 1903 the brothers Auguste und Louis ► Lumière developed one of the first methods for producing color photographs in the form of slides: the autochrome process. The invention of color photography was based on the development of panchromatic photo emulsions (1906), which are sensitive to all colors of the spectrum. Autochrome plates were manufactured by applying a very thin layer of potato starch grains, dyed orange-red, green, and purple, to a glass plate; the spaces between the grains were filled with soot to block white light. The color screen was coated first with a protective waterproof varnish, then with a layer of panchromatic silver halide. Since each grain filters only the light of its own color, during exposure the incident light is broken down into these three colors, which then register on the light-sensitive layer behind. Dark colors allow only a little light to penetrate, while lighter colors allow more; subsequent reversal processing produces a color-correct slide. The viewer perceives the color when the picture is seen at a sufficient distance; psychologically, the impression of color arises from the additive juxtaposition of dots of differing hues. The finished plate was covered with protective varnish and a cover glass and sealed with black paper tape. Due to the relative simplicity of the process and the naturalistic rendering of color, autochrome plates were popular with professional photographers as well as amateurs and artists. The disadvantages of the technique were its very long → exposure times and the difficulty of duplicating or printing the one-off images. Autochromes were viewed through a *laterna magica* or with special viewing devices in which a mirror reflected light through the autochrome plate.

Calotype (1845–60)

Calotype—a name invented by its developer, William Henry Fox Talbot, to mean "beautiful image," also known as the talbotype—is a process for creating paper negatives. Its invention in 1840 was a decisive turning point in the history of photography, for it allowed the production of unlimited prints from a single negative. Talbot had already successfully produced negative contact prints ("photogenic drawings") of objects such as textiles or plants on silver chloride-coated paper in 1834. With the calotype process, which he patented in 1841, writing paper was sensitized to light using silver nitrate, acetic acid, and gallic acid. When dry, it was exposed in the → camera obscura, with an exposure time ranging from a few seconds to several minutes. The latent image created in this way became visible through additional treatment with silver nitrate and gallic acid. The negative was then fixed with sodium thiosulfate, washed, dried, and used to print positive images on → salt paper. The positives created from the paper negative were called calotypes. Calotypes were always fairly coarsely grained, since the texture of the paper negative was transferred to the positive during printing. While this effect could be seen as a disadvantage compared to the highly detailed → daguerreotype, it could also be viewed more positively as "picturesque."

Camera obscura

The principle of the camera obscura can be traced back to antiquity. Originally it consisted of a closed room with a hole in one wall; light entering the hole projected an inverted image of the external world onto the opposite wall. In order to see the image, one had to enter the chamber. In the sixteenth century, the image was sharpened by means of a lens in the opening; only at this point did the camera obscura become an optical instrument. The seventeenth century saw the development of a portable device with a lens and a tilted mirror inside. The image produced by the lens on the ground glass was thus visible outside the box. In later models, the ground glass was located on the top, and a mirror mounted at a forty-five-degree angle corrected the orientation of the image. The artist could thus lay a piece of paper on the ground glass and trace the picture. This device was widely used in the early nineteenth century and served as both a scientific instrument and a drawing aid for travelers. The optical knowledge gained in this way facilitated the invention of photography.

Carbon printing / pigment printing (1862–1940)

The term carbon printing comes from the original use of finely ground charcoal or lampblack as pigments for the image-producing material in the photograph; thus carbon prints were also called pigment prints. The carbon printing technique was based on the light sensitivity of dichromate salts, which were dissolved in pigmented gelatin. Exposure through a negative hardened the layer of gelatin to varying degrees—more in areas of shadow and less in lighter areas, where it remained soft and water-soluble. "Development" in warm water produced a reversed pigment image as a relief, which regained its original orientation through transfer to temporary support and from there to hardened → gelatin paper. Pigment prints can be produced in a variety of colors depending on the choice of pigment. Tones of black, dark brown, and violet-brown were most widely used and resembled prints made on → albumen paper. The process could also be used on surfaces such as porcelain and glass. Pigment prints are generally very well preserved, since the image-producing charcoal and pigments are lightfast and therefore quite stable.

Chronophotography

The technique of chronophotography was used primarily in a scientific context for the analysis of movement. It made it possible to capture sequences of motion in individual frames, rendering them visible to the human eye. The prerequisite for chronophotography was the invention of highly sensitive → gelatin dry plates and faster camera shutters, which first made it possible to take snapshots.

Chronophotographs were produced using a variety of techniques. The first series was created by the astronomer Jules Janssen in 1874: for his photographs of Venus passing in front of the sun, he used a "photographic revolver" in which a glass plate turned at brief intervals during the exposure. In 1878 Eadweard Muybridge was commissioned to photograph the precise sequence of motion of galloping horses. He set up a row of twelve cameras that were triggered in rapid succession by contact with the horses. In this way, he was able to photographically capture the brief instant when all four legs of a galloping horse lift off the ground. Muybridge then combined the individual image sequences into a tableau.

The physician Étienne-Jules Marey used chronophotography for systematic research in the area of physiology. For his "chronograph" of 1883, he took multiple exposures on a single plate at precise intervals of time. The body parts whose sequences of motion were to be captured were marked in white, and the photographs were taken against a black background. The photographer Albert ▸ Londe also used chronophotography for medical purposes.

Contact printing / printing-out paper (1840–1920)

In contact printing, a positive print from a negative is created merely by exposing it to sunlight or diffuse daylight, without chemical development. The positive paper (printing-out paper) is placed in a printing frame along with the negative and exposed to light until the image is completely visible; then the exposed paper is washed, fixed, and washed again. Toning baths, primarily with gold but later with platinum and palladium as well, were a standard part of the process and were used to obtain various brownish hues and to improve stability. An unlimited number of positive prints can be produced from a single negative; the positive is the same size as the negative. The color tone of a photograph results from the absorption and reflection of light by the variously sized particles of silver with which the printing-out papers are coated. Exposure in the printing frame results in small, round silver particles, known as photolytic silver, which gives printing-out papers their characteristic reddish-brown tone. Printing-out papers include → salt paper, → albumen paper, and aristotype paper.

Daguerreotype (1839–ca. 1860)

The announcement of the daguerreotype on August 19, 1839, in Paris marked the birth of photography. The daguerreotype was the first commercially viable photographic process and bears the name of the French painter Louis Daguerre, who developed it in collaboration with Joseph Nicéphore Niépce and the latter's son, Isidore. The daguerreotype process is based on the light-sensitive properties of silver halides. A metal plate, usually a sheet of copper plated with silver, was polished to a mirror finish and sensitized to light using iodine vapors. After exposure to light through the lens of a camera, the "latent image" was developed with mercury fumes and fixed with a concentrated salt solution. The use of highly toxic mercury, as well as later sodium thiosulfate and potassium cyanide, resulted in the early demise of many daguerreotypists. Until 1841 daguerreotype images were upside down and reversed, a situation that was remedied by the development of a prism in front of the lens by the optician Charles Chevalier. Ongoing improvements reduced the initial exposure from between fifteen and thirty minutes to a few seconds, making it possible to photograph people. As a result, portrait studios sprang up throughout the world, and viewers were enthralled by the sharply focused, highly detailed images. In order to protect the sensitive surface of the images against oxidation and physical damage, daguerreotypes were covered with glass and hermetically sealed. They were displayed either in leather-covered, velvet-lined wooden cases or frames with decorative mats. Unlike the negative-positive process that permits unlimited prints to be made from a single negative, each daguerreotype is a unique image.

Development paper (1850–present)

Techniques for producing black-and-white prints from negatives using chemical development were available since the 1840s. In the nineteenth century, however, this method was little used, since at first it was difficult to achieve the desired degree of contrast and the black-and-white aesthetic was at odds with contemporary taste. Only in the early twentieth century did development papers supersede → printing-out papers, which were exposed in the printing frame without chemical development. Professional photographers appreciated the shorter processing time and the reduction in cost, since toning with precious metal was no longer necessary. Development papers can be exposed through contact with a negative or in an enlarger, resulting in a "latent image" that is then chemically developed. During the development process, silver ions are converted into visible silver particles in a redox reaction. The subsequent fixing with sodium thiosulfate removes the unexposed silver salts, followed by washing to remove chemical residue from the paper. The photographs show neutral black-and-white tones and are less susceptible to chemical damage from the environment than are printing-out papers.

Exposure

Exposure is the length of time during which a light-sensitive material is exposed to light in order to record a motif. In the early days of photography, exposures were determined above all by external factors such as the time of day or year, the conditions of weather, or the nature of the motif. Throughout the first decades of photography, the development of fast lenses and more light-sensitive materials served to considerably reduce exposure times: while the → daguerreotype required an exposure of thirty minutes, the → calotype required only three minutes, the → wet collodion process ten seconds, and the → gelatin dry plate one thousandth of a second. During the exposure of a negative in a printing frame (→ contact printing), the photographer could visually monitor the entire process and discontinue the exposure at exactly the right moment. Inside the camera, however, exposure was initially guided by empirical values. Published exposure tables offered at best a point of reference and included no specifications for aperture, since the smallest aperture was always used to achieve optimal depth of field. In order to define a constant between the intensity of incident light, the light-sensitivity of the plate, exposure time, and development, various aids for measuring exposure were developed, such as the Photometer invented by Jules Decoudun (1888) or the Expometer by Watson (1890). These devices ended the purely empirical determination of exposure time.

Gelatin dry plate (1879–2000)

In 1871 amateur photographer Richard Leach Maddox was the first to successfully produce a gelatin dry plate for use as a negative. The process was based on the light sensitivity of silver halides, which were suspended in gelatin and applied to a glass plate. The process was used to produce both negatives and slides. Improvements in the production of gelatin emulsions led to increased light sensitivity, mechanical coating of the glass plates (1880), and finally to the sensitization of pigments, which extended light sensitivity beyond the blue light spectrum to green light (commercially in 1882) and then to the entire visible spectrum (1906). The much greater light sensitivity of gelatin emulsion compared to the → wet collodion process made snapshots possible for the first time. Gelatin dry plates were produced by exclusively industrial means. Negative material was sold ready to use and had a shelf life of several months. In contrast to the wet collodion process, the negatives did not have to be processed immediately after exposure. Portable darkrooms were no longer necessary, making photography simpler and more practicable for amateurs. Thus began the history of the modern photo industry. Due to their capacity for high resolution, gelatin dry plates were used for spectroscopic and astronomical photography until the introduction of digital photography in the late twentieth century.

Gelatin paper / Silver gelatin process (1884–present)	Gelatin paper was introduced to the market in 1884 and became the preferred development paper for black-and-white photography in the early twentieth century. Its high degree of light sensitivity made it possible to enlarge prints from a negative. The process is based on the light sensitivity of silver salts (silver bromide or silver chloride) suspended in a gelatin emulsion. Beneath the emulsion is a baryta layer, which covers the fibers of the heavy paper that forms the substrate. In 1970 PE paper also came into use; the designation PE refers to the polyethylene coating on the front and back of the paper. Such papers are produced	exclusively by industrial manufacture and are available in many variants, depending on the desired surface and gradation. Different colors (such as white, chamois, and ivory) and surface textures are achieved through additives such as starch or the mechanical manipulation of the baryta layer. Alternatively, the photographer can use toning to alter the neutral black-and-white color; selenium, sulfur, or gold chloride are used to obtain sepia, brown, and violet-brown tones. This additional treatment also increases the stability of the prints.
Gum bichromate (1894–1920s)	The gum bichromate technique makes it possible to print a negative on paper in a single step or in multiple layers. A simple print yields black-and-white images with minimal tonal gradations, while multiple layers create a broad spectrum of tonal values. Later, colored images were also produced. The emulsion for gum bichromate prints consisted of a solution of gum arabic, dichromate salts, and colored pigments in water. This mixture was applied to heavy paper with a brush. When dry, the paper was exposed through contact with a negative. The exposure to light hardened the pigmented gum arabic, rendering it insoluble in water. Areas of shadow that received the strongest exposure hardened completely, while	the emulsion in lighter areas remained soft and soluble and was washed away during the "development" in warm water. To some extent, the photographer could also work the emulsion after the fact with a brush to lighten individual areas. Because the middle tonal values tended to lose density during washing, photographers transitioned to gum bichromate prints with multiple layers. In order to achieve greater contrast, the first print, when dry, was painted over again with a light-sensitive emulsion and briefly exposed a second time. The process was typically repeated two to three times, but could involve up to ten separate layers.
Heliogravure / photogravure (1880–present)	Heliogravure is a photomechanical process for reproducing black-and-white photography that combines aquatint and photography. A copper plate is coated with a thin layer of rosin or bitumen dust and heated so that the particles fuse with the plate, creating an irregular grain for rendering halftones. Then a layer of gelatin is applied and sensitized to light with potassium and ammonium dichromate. When exposed together with a slide, the gelatin hardens in proportion to exposure to the light, and the unhardened areas are washed away in warm water during the "development." The resulting gelatin relief protects the layer	of bitumen during the subsequent etching process. Etching with ferric chloride creates different levels of depressions in the plate, depending on the thickness of the gelatin. After removal of the gelatin layer, the plate is warmed for printing, spread with copperplate etching ink, and wiped clean, so that the ink remains only in the depressions. During the printing process with a copperplate printing press, the ink is transferred to dampened rotogravure paper. The fine, irregular grain of the aquatint yields a precise gradation of tones. Even today, art photographers still use heliogravure for small editions.
Oil printing / bromoil printing (1904–1940s)	Oil printing is a photochemical method for producing a printing block for the reproduction of motifs on paper. The principle resembles that of → carbon printing, though here the pigments are applied to the colloidal layer rather than embedded in it. In oil printing, gelatin combined with chromium salts is hardened through exposure to light, thus losing its ability to swell in water. The unexposed areas of the gelatin layer swell in the water and resist the oil pigment. The paper, prepared with chromium salts and gelatin, is	exposed with a negative and washed, allowing the unhardened gelatin to swell, after which oil-based pigment is applied. The colored image created in this way is printed onto normal paper in the copperplate printing press, resulting in an oil print (also known as a bromoil print). This process can be repeated in multiple layers, on different pieces of paper, and with various colors. Because the image layer consists of pigmented color, the pictures are very stable and do not deteriorate.

Panorama (1839–present)

Panoramas showing landscapes and city views are known from the earliest days of photography. Even before the advent of special cameras, individual photos were carefully pieced together to create panoramic views. The camera would be mounted on a tripod on which it could be rotated. After the first shot, the photographer would mark the motifs on the extreme right edge of the ground glass and move the camera until these same motifs appeared at the left edge of the picture; the second photograph would then be taken, and so on. With special panoramic cameras, pictures with a very wide field of view could be produced. In some of them, the lens rotated on an axis; in others, the film moved behind the lens. In 1845 the photographer Friedrich von Martens (also known as Frédéric Martens) introduced the "megascope"

designed for cylindrically curved → daguerreotypes. During exposure, the lens moved along the daguerreotype plate and could thus achieve a 150-degree field of view. Since the curved daguerreotype was very difficult to work with, this technique was little used. The painter and photographer Ludwig Schuller modified Martens's camera and replaced the curved plate with a flat glass plate whose movement followed the lens. In 1858 the photographer Thomas Sutton patented a special panoramic lens capable of capturing a ninety-degree field of view. The later invention of flexible negative material made possible the development of the panoramic camera by Kodak (1900). With a revolving lens and sliding focal plane shutter, it could take snapshots with a wide field of view.

Platinum printing / platinotype (1873–1937)

The platinum printing technique, which produces an effect reminiscent of pencil and ink drawings, was popular with the Pictorialists and was used especially between 1880 and 1914. Although the scientist John Herschel had discovered the light sensitivity of platinum salts as early as 1832, only in 1873 did the inventor William Willis develop a patented method for creating black-and-white platinum prints, which was ready for factory production six years later. The paper was sensitized using potassium platinum chloride and iron oxalate; after exposure with a negative, it was developed with potassium and ammonium oxalate. Since the platinum solution was applied directly to the paper, platinotypes have a matte surface. The aesthetic quality of the platinotype arises from its fine value gradations, and the technique enjoyed

increasing popularity with professional photographers and artists. By around 1890 platinotype paper was produced by numerous manufacturers of photographic papers and was available in a variety of surface textures, paper thicknesses, and color nuances, with image tones ranging from neutral black to warm brown. The image tone could also be manipulated through additives and by raising the temperature of the developer. Due to increasing demand for platinum for nonphotographic purposes during World War I, prices rose and the metal grew rare. Platinotype papers were manufactured less and less frequently and were partially replaced by palladium papers. The image material of platinotypes is very stable, though the paper can be damaged by residue from the acid developer.

Salt paper (1839–60)

Salt paper is a variety of black-and-white → printing-out paper. It was used to produce positive prints through exposure with a negative, without chemical development. The salt paper process was first invented by William Henry Fox Talbot (→ calotype) in 1834–35 and was published in 1839; in 1855, salt paper was superseded by → albumen paper. In the first phase of the process, the paper was bathed in a salt solution. When dry, it was coated with silver nitrate, either in a bath or with a brush, and the paper was exposed to sunlight in contact with the negative. Until John Herschel's 1841 discovery of the fixing bath with sodium thiosulfate, Talbot stabilized the prints with a saturated salt solution, without removing the unexposed silver salts. Better

stability and variations in image tone were achieved by subsequent toning with gold chloride or sulfur. The brownish salt papers have a matte surface; the visual information is in the paper fibers. In order to achieve a greater sense of depth as well as a glossy surface and clarity of detail in salt paper prints, they were sometimes varnished with wax, shellac, copal, or dammar. The advantage of salt paper over the → daguerreotype was that neither hazardous chemicals nor special devices were needed for processing. In addition, unlimited positives could be printed from a negative, while each daguerreotype was a one-off image that could not be easily reproduced.

Secret camera (1880s)

The invention of the → gelatin dry plate opened up new possibilities for the manufacture of cameras, as the increased light sensitivity allowed for handheld cameras with no tripod. The earliest models were leather-covered wooden box cameras used for law enforcement, as introduced to the Photographic Society of London by Thomas Bolas in 1880. A large number of secret cameras came onto the market in the 1880s, capable of taking snapshots quickly and surreptitiously. Compact and inconspicuous, they resembled everyday objects such as a gun, book, opera glass, or pocket watch. A popular model was the Stirn "concealed vest

camera" designed by Robert D. Gray in 1885. A year later, the rights were acquired by Carl P. ► Stirn, and the camera was manufactured by his brother Rudolph in Berlin. It allowed six photographs to be taken in succession without changing the plate: pulling a string triggered the exposure and at the same time turned the plate for the next shot. The negative was a disk-shaped gelatin dry plate 150 millimeters in diameter. The camera was worn on a strap around the photographer's neck and could be hidden under his clothing, with the lens resembling a button and pointing outward through a buttonhole.

Stereoscopy / stereophotography (1849–ca. 1910)

Stereophotography uses the principle of binocular vision: due to their slightly different positions, our two eyes register different images, which the brain then combines into a spatial whole. Initially, two photographs of the same object were taken from slightly different angles, creating a spatial effect when the two images were viewed in a binocular stereoscope. Since the photographs were not taken at the same time, motifs in motion had the potential to change the image between shots. Beginning in 1849, physicist David Brewster and photographer Jules Duboscq constructed and produced a "double-eyed" camera that could record both images at the same time. Due to the small format of the individual picture and the short focal length of the lens, even moving motifs could be captured in a fraction of a second. This technique created the impression of spatial depth for the viewer. Stereoscopy was quickly embraced for numerous purposes, including scenic views, genre pictures, nudes, and documentary photography. Stereophotographs were created using every photographic process available between 1850 and 1870, and all stereo images had a more or less standard format. Some companies began to specialize in the mass production and worldwide marketing of stereophotography. The images were viewed using binocular stereoscopes, which were manufactured in a number of versions and were a standard item in every middle-class household.

Wax paper negative (1841–55)

The wax paper negative is a modification of the → calotype, invented to make paper negatives more transparent and capable of producing more detailed prints. In the method published by Gustave Le ► Gray in 1847, the paper was coated in liquid beeswax either before or after sensitization. When the paper had fully absorbed the wax, the excess was removed with blotting paper or a hot iron. The wax served to seal the pores between the paper fibers so that the light was less refracted; in addition, it strengthened the paper and protected it from physical damage. Thus even very thin papers could be used. At the same time, the wax layer ensured a consistent action of the sensitizing solution and developing liquid and prevented chemical reactions. The prepared paper was dry when inserted into the camera, so that exposure and development could occur a number of weeks apart—an advantage for travel photographers, who no longer had to develop their photographs immediately. By the mid-1850s, numerous readymade wax paper negatives were available on the market.

Wet collodion process (1851–ca. 1885)

The wet collodion process, developed by Frederick Scott Archer and published in 1851, played a key role in the decades that followed and significantly expanded the aesthetic possibilities of photography. It served for the production of black-and-white glass plate negatives, using collodion as a binder for the light-sensitive silver salts. Unlike paper negatives, glass negatives offered the advantage of greater sensitivity to light. Collodion consists of cellulose nitrate dissolved in alcohol and ether. This syrupy, fast-drying liquid was applied to a glass plate and sensitized to light with iodide salts and silver nitrate. While still wet, it was exposed in the camera, developed with ferrous sulfate or gallic acid, and fixed. All steps in the process had to be performed while the layer was still wet, hence the name wet collodion process. After washing and drying, the negatives were coated with varnish to protect the collodion layer. Exposure times varied from a single second to several minutes, depending on the intensity of the light. The wet collodion process was the first to produce completely transparent, fine-grained negatives. When printed on → albumen paper, which emerged at around the same time, the result was detailed, high-contrast positive images whose quality remained unsurpassed by any other method for three decades. The need to complete the process while wet made it difficult to photograph outside the studio; thus mobile, portable darkrooms were invented to facilitate outdoor photography. In contrast to the coarse-grained → calotype, the wet collodion process was praised by contemporaries for its precise reproduction of the motif.

Selected Bibliography

Abbott 1963
Berenice Abbott, *Eugène Atget,* Prague 1963.

Abrell 2003
Joachim Abrell, *Der Photograph Henry Peach Robinson,* Berlin 2003.

Adams 1994
Steven Adams, *The Barbizon School and the Origins of Impressionism,* London 1994.

Addleman-Frankel 2018
Kate Addleman-Frankel, *After Photography? The Photogravures of Édouard Baldus Reconsidered,* Amsterdam 2018.

Amsterdam 2017
Le Nouveau Paris: Charles Marville Photographs the City Transformation, exh. cat., Rijksmuseum, Amsterdam 2017.

Ang 2014
Tom Ang, *Photography: The Definitive Visual History,* New York 2014.

Ann Arbor 2008
The Lens of Impressionism: Photography and Painting along the Normandy Coast, 1850–1874, exh. cat., University of Michigan Museum of Art, Ann Arbor 2008.

Aubenas 1998
Sylvie Aubenas, "Un album de photographies d'Eugène Delacroix," in *Delacroix, le trait romantique,* exh. cat., Bibliothèque nationale de France, Paris 1998, 51–55.

Aubenas 2018
Sylvie Aubenas, "Précisions biographiques sur Adalbert et Eugène Cuvelier," in *Du texte à l'image,* ed. Laurent Baridon and Pierre Vaisse, Lyon 2018, 48–56.

Augsburg 2014
Edward Steichen: Portraits d'Artistes / Die Künstlerporträts, exh. cat., Kunstsammlungen und Museen Augsburg, H2—Zentrum für Gegenwartskunst im Glaspalast, Augsburg 2014.

Baier 1980
Wolfgang Baier, *Geschichte der Fotografie,* Munich 1980.

Bajac 2017
Quentin Bajac, "'The Black Clothing of Things': French Photography under the Second Empire," in *Photography at MoMA, 1840–1920,* ed. Quentin Bajac, New York 2017, 56–97.

Barbizon 1998
Photographies: Barbizon d'hier et d'aujourd'hui; La Collection du peintre Théophile Chauvel au Musée d'Orsay, exh. cat., Musée municipale de l'École de Barbizon, 1998.

Barger/White 2000
M. Susan Barger und William B. White, *The Daguerreotype: Nineteenth-Century Technology and Modern Science,* Baltimore 2000.

Barreswil/Davanne 1854
Charles Louis Barreswil and Alphonse Davanne, *Handbuch des Photographen: Anweisung zur Erzeugung von Lichtbildern auf Metall, Papier und Glas nach den neuesten Methoden,* Leipzig 1854.

Barreswil/Davanne 1866
Charles Louis Barreswil and Alphonse Davanne, *Handbuch der praktischen Photographie-Chemie: Enthaltend die Elemente der Chemie durch Beispiele an der photographischen Praxis erläutert,* Leipzig 1866.

Barrett 2003
Laura Barrett, "Ekphrastic Photographs: A Study in Time and Timelessness," in *Literary Texts and the Arts: Interdisciplinary Perspectives,* ed. Corrado Federici and Esther Raventós-Pons, New York et al. 2003, 81–92.

Barthes 1981
Roland Barthes, *Camera Lucida: Reflections on Photography* [1980], New York 1981.

Bastian 2006
Fragmente zur Melancholie: Bilder aus dem ersten Jahrhundert der Fotografie, ed. Heiner Bastian, Ostfildern 2006.

Beck 1913
Heinrich Beck, *Lehrbuch der Photographie,* Leipzig 1913.

Beck 1938
Heinrich Beck, *Das große Agfa Labor-Handbuch,* Berlin 1938.

Bedburg-Hau 2016
Natur als Kunst: Landschaft im 19. Jahrhundert in Malerei und Fotografie, aus den Sammlungen der Christoph Heilmann Stiftung am Lenbachhaus München und des Münchner Stadtmuseums, exh. cat., Museum Schloss Moyland, Bedburg-Hau 2016.

Benjamin 1974
Walter Benjamin, "Das Kunstwerk im Zeitalter seiner technischen Reproduzierbarkeit [1939]," in Walter Benjamin, *Gesammelte Schriften,* ed. Rolf Tiedemann and Hermann Schweppenhäuser, vol. 1: *Abhandlungen,* Frankfurt am Main 1974, 431–508.

Berlin 1998
Eugène Atget: Frühe Fotografien, exh. cat., Staatliche Museen zu Berlin, Kunstbibliothek, 1998.

Berlin 2003
Kunstfotografie um 1900: Die Sammlung Fritz Matthies-Masuren, 1873–1938, exh. cat., Staatliche Museen zu Berlin, Kunstbibliothek, 2003.

Berlin 2008
Pictorialism: Hidden Modernism; Photography 1896–1916, exh. cat., Galerie Kicken, Berlin 2008.

Berson 1996
Ruth Berson, *The New Painting: Impressionism, 1874–1886,* 2 vols., San Francisco 1996.

Blanquart-Évrard/Harrad/Sutton 1864
Louis Désiré Blanquart-Évrard, Alfred Harrad, and Thomas Sutton, *On the Intervention of Art in Photography,* London 1864.

Blanquart-Évrard 1869
Louis Désiré Blanquart-Évrard, *La Photographie: Ses origines, ses progrès, ses transformations,* Lille 1869.

Bochner 2005
Jay Bochner, *An American Lens: Scenes From Alfred Stieglitz's New York Secession,* Cambridge, MA 2005.

Bonn 1978
Eugène Atget: Das alte Paris, exh. cat., Rheinisches Landesmuseum, Bonn 1978.

Bottrop 2021
Patrick Faigenbaum: Fotografien 1974–2020, exh. cat., Josef Albers Museum Quadrat, Bottrop 2021.

Boulouch 1999
Nathalie Boulouch, *Les Autochromes Lumière, la couleur inventée: Photographies couleur, collection privée de la famille Lumière, Lyon 1903,* Lyon 1999.

Bradford 2006
The Old Order and the New: P. H. Emerson and Photography, 1885–1895, exh. cat., National Museum of Photography, Film and Television, Bradford 2006.

von Brauchitsch 2020a
Boris von Brauchitsch, "Alfred Stieglitz: Unter den Wolken Amerikas," in Kaufbeuren 2020, 34–45.

von Brauchitsch 2020b
Boris von Brauchitsch, "Adolphe de Meyer: 'Der beste Fotograf der Welt,'" in Kaufbeuren 2020, 62–85.

Brennan 2001
Marcia Brennan, *Painting Gender, Constructing Theory: The Alfred Stieglitz Circle and American Formalist Aesthetics,* Cambridge, MA 2001.

Brest 2008
Constant Puyo (1857–1933): Entre volonté d'art et intuition photographique, exh. cat., Centre atlantique de la photographie de Brest, 2008.

Brettel 1984
Richard R. Brettel, *Paper and Light: The Calotype in Britain and France, 1839–1870,* London 1984.

Buddemeier 1970
Heinz Buddemeier, *Panorama, Diorama, Photographie: Entstehung und Wirkung neuer Medien im 19. Jahrhundert,* Munich 1970.

Buddemeier 1981
Heinz Buddemeier, *Das Foto: Geschichte und Theorie der Fotografie als Grundlage eines neuen Urteils,* Reinbek 1981.

Burns 2009
Sarah Burns, "Advice for Women Photographers," in Sarah Burns and Johan Davis, *American Art to 1900: A Documentary History,* Berkeley 2009, 844–48.

Busch 1995
Bernd Busch, *Belichtete Welt: Eine Wahrnehmungsgeschichte der Fotografie,* Frankfurt am Main 1995.

Callen 2015
Anthea Callen, *The Work of Art: Plein-air Painting and Artistic Identity in Nineteenth-Century France,* London 2015.

Campany 2003
David Campany, *Art and Photography,* Berlin 2003.

Chalon-sur-Saône 2018
Vision d'artistes: Photographies pictorialistes, 1890–1960, exh. cat., Musée Nicéphore Niépce, Chalon-sur-Saône 2018.

Chantilly 2018
Primitifs de la photographie du XIXe siècle: De Baldus à Le Gray, exh. cat., Musée Condé, Chantilly 2018.

Chardère 1995
Bernard Chardère, *Les Images des Lumière,* Paris 1995.

Chicago 1987
The Photography of Gustave Le Gray, exh. cat., The Art Institute of Chicago, 1987.

Cincinnati 2018
Old Paris and Changing New York: Photographs by Eugène Atget and Berenice Abbott, exh. cat., Taft Museum of Art, Cincinnati 2018.

Crary 1996
Jonathan Crary, *Techniques of the Observer: On Vision and Modernity in the Nineteenth Century,* Cambridge, MA 1990.

Dahlberg 2005
Laurie Dahlberg, *Victor Regnault and the Advance of Photography: The Art of Avoiding Errors,* Princeton 2005.

David 2013
Frédéric David, *Peindre en plein air: L'Endurance au travail au XIXe siècle,* Rouen 2013.

Demachy 1909
Robert Demachy, *L'Interprétation en photographie,* Paris 1909.

Demachy/Puyo 1906
Robert Demachy and Émile Joachim Constant Puyo, *Les Procédés d'art en photographie,* Paris 1906.

Denton 2002
Margaret Denton, "Francis Wey and the Discourse of Photography as Art in France in the Early 1850s: 'Rien n'est beau que le vrai; mais il faut le choisir,'" in *Art History* 25,5 (November 2002), 622–48.

Didi-Huberman 2007
Georges Didi-Huberman, *Bilder trotz allem,* Paderborn et al. 2007.

van Dijke 2013
Frouke van Dijke, *A Dutch Daubigny: Charles-François Daubigny (1817–1878) in Holland,* Utrecht 2013.

Dresden 1992
August Kotzsch 1836–1910: Pionier der deutschen Photographie, exh. cat., Staatliche Kunstsammlungen Dresden, Kupferstich-Kabinett, 1992.

Dresden 2010
Von Loschwitz nach Amerika: Fotografien von August Kotzsch (1836–1910), exh. cat., Stadtmuseum Dresden, 2010.

Dumesnil 1875
Henri Dumesnil, *Corot: Souvenirs intimes,* Paris 1875.

Eberle 2006
Sandra Eberle, "Georg Maria Eckert: Ein badischer Fotograf im Dienst der Kunst," in *Historische Ansichten— Glanzvolle Aussichten: Die Bruchsaler Prunkräume vor der Zerstörung,* exh. cat., Schloß Bruchsal, 2006, 52–59.

Essen 1965
Die Kalotypie in Frankreich: Beispiele der Landschafts-, Architektur- und Reisedokumentationsfotografie, exh. cat., Museum Folkwang, Essen 1965.

Essen 1978
Heinrich Kühn 1866–1944: 110 Bilder aus der Fotografischen Sammlung, exh. cat., Museum Folkwang, Essen 1978.

Essen 1999
Die Brüder Bisson: Aufstieg und Fall eines Fotografenunternehmens im 19. Jahrhundert, exh. cat., Museum Folkwang, Essen 1999.

Essen 2010
Edward Steichen: Celebrity Design, exh. cat., Museum Folkwang, Essen 2010.

Faber 2018
Monika Faber, "Hugo Henneberg: Meister des fotografischen Stimmungsbilds," in Halle an der Saale 2018, 177–95.

Fanelli/Mazza 2014
Giovanni Fanelli and Barbara Mazza, *Paris animé: Paris instantané; Photographie stéréoscopiques 1850–1900,* Lille and Rennes 2014.

Farwell 1977
Beatrice Farwell, *The Cult of Images: Baudelaire and the 19th-Century Media Explosion,* Santa Barbara 1977.

Ferrier père, fils & Soulier 1860
Ferrier père, fils & Soulier, *Excursion sur le théâtre de la guerre d'Italie, photographiée pour l'usage du stéréoscope,* Paris 1860.

Fidell-Beaufort/Bailly-Herzberg 1975
Daubigny, ed. Madeleine Fidell-Beaufort and Janine Bailly-Herzberg, Paris 1975.

Figuier 1860
Louis Figuier, *La Photographie au Salon de 1859,* Paris 1860.

de Font-Réaulx 1997
Dominique de Font-Réaulx, "Courbet et la photographie: L'Exemple d'un peintre réaliste, entre vérité et réalité," in *L'Art du nu au XIXe siècle: Le Photographe et son modèle,* exh. cat., Bibliothèque nationale de France, Paris 1997, 84–91.

de Font-Réaulx 2006
Dominique de Font-Réaulx, "Parallel Lines: Gustave Courbet's *Paysages de Mer* and Gustave Le Gray's *Seascapes,* 1856–70," in *Looking at the Landscapes: Courbet and Modernism,* ed. Mary Morton, Los Angeles 2006, 35–45.

de Font-Réaulx 2012
Dominique de Font-Réaulx, *Painting and Photography, 1839–1914,* Paris 2012.

Forberg 1975
Gabriele Forberg, *Lichtbilder: Eugène Atget,* Munich 1975.

Fosca 1958
François Fosca, *Corot: Sa vie et son œuvre,* Brussels 1958.

Foucault 1999
Michel Foucault, "Photogenic Painting" [1975], in *Photogenic Painting: Gilles Deleuze, Michel Foucault, Gérard Fromanger,* ed. Sarah Wilson, London 1999, 81–104.

Frankfurt am Main 1993
Pioniere der Landschaftsphotographie: Beispiele aus der Sammlung des J. Paul Getty Museums, Malibu, exh. cat., Städtische Galerie, Frankfurt am Main 1993.

Frankfurt am Main 2012a
Gustave Caillebotte: Ein Impressionist und die Fotografie, exh. cat., Schirn Kunsthalle, Frankfurt am Main 2012.

Frankfurt am Main 2012b
Malerei in Fotografie: Strategien der Aneignung, exh. cat., Städel Museum, Frankfurt am Main 2012.

Frizot 1998
Michel Frizot, *Neue Geschichte der Fotografie,* Cologne 1998.

Fuchs 2017
Caroline Fuchs, *Das Autochrom in Großbritannien: Revolution der Farbfotografie,* Berlin 2017.

Ganz 2008
James A. Ganz, *Édouard Baldus at the Château de La Faloise,* Clark Art Institute, Williamstown 2008.

Garb 1986
Tamar Garb, *Women Impressionists,* Oxford 1986.

Garnier-Pelle 2001
Nicole Garnier-Pelle, *19th-Century Photography at Chantilly: Masterpieces of the Condé Museum,* Chantilly 2001.

Gauss/Challe/Weidemann 1996
Eugène Cuvelier, ed. Ulrike Gauss, Daniel Challe, and Henning Weidemann, Stuttgart 1996.

Gautrand 1999
Jean-Claude Gautrand, *Blanquart-Évrard,* Douchy-les-Mines 1999.

Geiger 2004
Annette Geiger, *Urbild und fotografischer Blick: Diderot, Chardin und die Vorgeschichte der Fotografie in der Malerei des 18. Jahrhunderts,* Munich 2004.

Geimer 2002
Ordnungen der Sichtbarkeit: Fotografie in Wissenschaft, Kunst und Technologie, ed. Peter Geimer, Frankfurt am Main 2002.

Geimer 2009
Peter Geimer, *Theorien der Fotografie zur Einführung,* Hamburg 2009.

Geissmann 2009
Tobias Geissmann, *Zwischen Zeichnung und Photographie: Die graphische Technik Cliché-verre im Werk der französischen Künstler Corot und Daubigny,* Munich 2009.

Gernsheim/Gernsheim 1969
Helmut Gernsheim and Alison Gernsheim, *The History of Photography from the Camera Obscura to the Beginning of the Modern Era,* London 1969.

Giverny 2020
Plein air: De Corot à Monet, exh. cat., Musée des impressionnismes Giverny, 2020.

Le Gray 1851
Gustave Le Gray, *Photographie: Traité nouveau théorique et pratique des procédés et manipulations sur paper sec, humide, et sur verre au collodion, à l'albumine,* Paris 1851.

Le Gray 2015
Gustave Le Gray: Seestücke; Mit einem Text von Hubertus Amelunxen, Munich 2015.

Gruber 1964
Leo Fritz Gruber, *Große Photographen unseres Jahrhunderts,* Düsseldorf et al. 1964.

von Grüningen 1964
Berchtold von Grüningen, *Vom Impressionismus zum Tachismus: Malerei, Lithographie, Photographie, angewandte Graphik,* Basel et al. 1964.

Hacking/Lukitsh 2020
Juliet Hacking and Joanne Lukitsh, *Photography and the Arts: Essays on Nineteenth-Century Practices and Debates,* London 2020.

Halle an der Saale 2018
Gustav Klimt und Hugo Henneberg: Zwei Künstler der Wiener Secession, exh. cat., Kunstmuseum Moritzburg, Halle an der Saale 2018.

Halwani 2012
Miriam Halwani, *Geschichte der Fotogeschichte, 1839–1939,* Berlin 2012.

Hambourg 1980
Maria Morris Hambourg, *Eugène Atget, 1857–1927: The Structure of the Work,* New York 1980.

Hamburg 2011
Eyes on Paris: Paris im Fotobuch, 1890 bis heute, exh. cat., Deichtorhallen, Hamburg 2011.

Hamburg 2012
New York Photography 1890–1950: Von Stieglitz bis Man Ray, exh. cat., Bucerius Kunst Forum, Hamburg 2012.

Hamburg 2015
Über Wasser: Malerei und Photographie von William Turner bis Olafur Eliasson, exh. cat., Bucerius Kunst Forum, Hamburg 2015.

Hamburg 2019
Welt im Umbruch: Kunst der 20er Jahre, exh. cat., Bucerius Kunst Forum, Hamburg 2019.

Hämmerle 1996
Patricia Anne Hämmerle, *Schattenriss der Zeit: Fotografie und Wirklichkeit,* Zurich 1996.

Hammond 1991
Anne Hammond, "Impressionist Theory and the Autochrome," in *History of Photography* 15,2 (1991), 96–100.

Hannavy 2008
John Hannavy, *Encyclopedia of Nineteenth-Century Photography,* 2 vols., New York 2008.

Harker 1988
Margaret F. Harker, *Henry Peach Robinson: Master of Photographic Art, 1830–1901,* Oxford 1988.

Hauswald 2016
Cathrin Hauswald, "(K)eine 'Kunstgeschichte machen': Von der Kunstreproduktion zum fotografischen Objekt," in *ReVision: Fotografie im Museum für Kunst und Gewerbe Hamburg,* exh. cat., Museum für Kunst und Gewerbe Hamburg, 2016, 96–123.

Hauswald 2018
Cathrin Hauswald, *Alvin Langdon Coburn: Photographie zwischen Piktorialismus und Moderne,* Bielefeld 2018.

Hauswald/Stiegler 2015
Cathrin Hauswald and Bernd Stiegler, *Auf der Suche nach der Schönheit: Schriften zur Photographie,* Paderborn 2015.

Haworth-Booth 1992
Mark Haworth-Booth, *Camille Silvy: River Scene, France,* Malibu 1992.

Hedgecoe 1979
John Hedgecoe, *Die Kunst der Farbfotografie,* Munich 1979.

Heilbrun 1995
Françoise Heilbrun, "Nadar and the Art of Portrait Photography," in *Nadar,* exh. cat., The Metropolitan Museum of Art, New York 1995, 35–58.

Heilbrun 2009
Françoise Heilbrun, "Impressionism and Photography," in *History of Photography* 33,1 (2009), 18–25.

Hersbruck 1989
Das Porträt im 19. Jahrhundert: Fotografie und Malerei, exh. cat., Deutsches Hirtenmuseum Hersbruck, 1989.

Hirsch 2000
Robert Hirsch, *Seizing the Light: A History of Photography,* Boston 2000.

Hirsch/Griebel/Herre 1986
August Kotzsch 1836–1910: Photograph in Loschwitz bei Dresden, ed. Ernst Hirsch, Matthias Griebel, and Volkmar Herre, Dresden 1986.

Hoffman 2011
Katherine Hoffman, *Alfred Stieglitz: A Legacy of Light,* New Haven 2011.

Hofmann-Johnson 2018
Barbara Hofmann-Johnson, "Perspektivwechsel: Die Stadt in den Bildern der Kamera," in *Der Flaneur: Vom Impressionismus bis zur Gegenwart,* exh. cat., Kunstmuseum Bonn, 2018, 133–54.

Holme 1905
Art in Photography with Selected Examples of European and American Work, ed. Charles Holme, London et al. 1905.

Holme 1908
Colour Photography and Other Recent Developments of the Art of the Camera, ed. Charles Holme, London et al. 1908.

Humphrey 1858
Samuel D. Humphrey, *American Hand Book of the Daguerreotype,* New York 1858.

Hütt 1963
Wolfgang Hütt, *Landschaftsfotografie: Ein Beitrag zu ihrer Geschichte und ihrer Theorie,* Halle an der Saale 1963.

Jacobson 2001
Ken Jacobson, *The Lovely Sea-View: A Study of the Marine Photographs Published by Gustave Le Gray, 1856–1858,* Petches Bridge 2001.

Jacobson/Jacobson 1996
Ken Jacobson and Jenny Jacobson, *Étude d'après nature: Nineteenth-Century Photographs in Relation to Art,* Essex 1996.

Jay 1974
Bill Jay, *Robert Demachy, 1859–1936: Photographs and Essays,* London 1974.

James 1994
Anne Clark James, "Antonin Personnaz: Art Collector and Autochrome Pioneer," in *History of Photography* 18,2 (1994), 147–50.

Jammes 1981
Isabelle Jammes, *Blanquart-Evrard et les origines de l'édition photographique française: Catalogue raisonné des albums photographiques édités 1851–1855,* Geneva 1981.

Jammes/Parry 1983
André Jammes and Eugenia Parry, *The Art of French Calotype: With a Critical Dictionary of Photographers, 1845–1870,* Princeton 1983.

Juhl 2012
Ernst Juhl, "Eduard J. Steichen" [1902], in Stiegler 2012a, 77–90.

Kansas City 2013
Impressionist France: Visions of Nation from Le Gray to Monet, exh. cat., The Nelson-Atkins Museum of Art, Kansas City 2013.

Kaufbeuren 2020
Strike a Pose: Intuition und Inszenierung; Die Kunstfotografie der 1890er bis 1920er Jahre, exh. cat., Kunsthaus Kaufbeuren, 2020.

Kaufhold 1986
Enno Kaufhold, *Bilder des Übergangs: Zur Mediengeschichte von Fotografie und Malerei in Deutschland um 1900,* Marburg 1986.

Kaufhold 1988
Enno Kaufhold, *Heinrich Kühn und die Kunstfotografie um 1900,* Berlin 1988.

Keller 1984
Ulrich Keller, "The Myth of Art Photography: A Sociological Analysis," in *History of Photography* 8,4 (1984), 249–75.

Keller 2016
Corey Keller, "Die Ästhetik der Objektivität: Fotografie, Wissenschaft und Kunst," in *ReVision: Fotografie im Museum für Kunst und Gewerbe Hamburg,* exh. cat., Museum für Kunst und Gewerbe, Hamburg 2016, 44–69.

Kemp 2006
Wolfgang Kemp, *Foto-Essays zur Geschichte und Theorie der Fotografie,* Munich 2006.

Kemp 2011
Wolfgang Kemp, *Geschichte der Fotografie von Daguerre bis Gursky,* Munich 2011.

Kemp/von Amelunxen 2006
Theorie der Fotografie I–IV: 1839–1995, ed. Wolfgang Kemp and Hubertus von Amelunxen, Munich 2006.

Kennel 2008
Sarah Kennel, "An Infinite Museum: Photography in the Forest of Fontainebleau," in *In the Forest of Fontainebleau: Painters and Photographers from Corot to Monet,* exh. cat., National Gallery of Art, Washington, DC 2008, 152–167.

Kennel 2015
Sarah Kennel, "Photography and the Painter's Eye," in Washington, DC 2015, 109–22.

Kicken 2007
Annette Kicken, *Points of View: Masterpieces of Photography and their Stories,* Göttingen 2007.

Cologne 1989
Silber und Salz: Zur Frühzeit der Photographie im deutschen Sprachraum (1839–1860), exh. cat., Josef-Haubrich-Kunsthalle, Cologne 1989.

Cologne 1998
Alvin Langdon Coburn: Fotografien 1900–1924, exh. cat., Römisch-Germanisches Museum, Cologne 1998.

Cologne 2006
Tatsachen: Fotografien des 19. und 20. Jahrhunderts; Die Sammlung Agfa im Museum Ludwig, exh. cat., Museum Ludwig, Cologne 2006.

Konstanz 2011
Lichtmaler: Kunst-Photographie um 1900; Bilder einer Privatsammlung, exh. cat., Städtische Wessenberg-Galerie, Konstanz 2011.

König 1912
Ernst König, *Die Autochrom-Photographie,* Berlin 1912.

Koschatzky 1984
Walter Koschatzky, *Die Kunst der Photographie: Technik, Geschichte, Meisterwerke,* Salzburg et al. 1984.

Krauss 1978
Rolf H. Krauss, *Die Fotografie in der Karikatur,* Seebruck am Chiemsee 1978.

Krauss 1990
Rosalind Krauss, *Le Photographique: Pour une théorie des écarts,* trans. Marc Bloch and Jean Kampf, Paris 1990.

Krüger 2007
Matthias Krüger, *Das Relief der Farbe: Pastose Malerei in der französischen Kunstkritik 1850–1890,* Munich and Berlin 2007.

Kubnick 1938
Henri Kubnick, *Les Frères Lumière,* Paris 1938.

Kühn 1921
Heinrich Kühn, *Technik der Lichtbildnerei,* Halle an der Saale 1921.

Lacan 1853
Ernest Lacan, "Publications photographiques de M. Blanquart-Evrard," in *La Lumière* (April 9, 1853), 57.

Lammert 2008
Angela Lammert, *Albert Londe und die Moderne,* Berlin 2008.

Lammert 2016
Angela Lammert, "Fotografischer Blick: Albert Londe," in *Bildung und Bildlichkeit von Notation: Von der frühen Wissenschaftsfotografie zu den Künsten des 20. Jahrhunderts,* ed. Angela Lammert, Munich 2016, 70–114.

Langer 2002
Freddy Langer, *Fotografie! Das 19. Jahrhundert,* Munich 2002.

Lavédrine/Gandolfo 2013
Bertrand Lavédrine and Jean-Paul Gandolfo, *The Lumière Autochrome: History, Technology, and Preservation,* Los Angeles 2013.

Leblanc 2016
Charlotte Leblanc, "La Bibliothèque nationale en chantier: Les Photographies de Louis-Émile Durandelle," in *Revue de la Bibliothèque nationale de France* 53,2 (2016), 167.

Lerebours 1852
Noël Marie Paymal Lerebours, "Plaque, Papier, ou Verre?," in *La Lumière* (May 1, 1852), 75.

Lichtwark 1991
Alfred Lichtwark, *Erziehung des Auges: Ausgewählte Schriften,* ed. Eckhard Schaar, Frankfurt am Main 1991.

Lisbon 1998
Waterproof: Water in Photography since 1852, exh. cat., Centro Cultural de Belém, Lisbon 1998.

Londe 1896
Albert Londe, *Photographie moderne,* Paris 1896.

London 2000
Painting Quickly in France, 1860–1890, exh. cat., The National Gallery, London 2000.

London 2010
Camille Silvy: Photographer of Modern Life, exh. cat., National Portrait Gallery, London 2010.

London 2015
Salt and Silver: Early Photography 1840–1860, exh. cat., Tate Britain, London 2015.

Los Angeles 1999
Ghost in the Shell: Photography and the Human Soul, 1850–2000, exh. cat., Los Angeles County Museum of Art, 1999.

Los Angeles 2016
Real—Ideal: Photography in Mid-Nineteenth-Century France, exh. cat., The J. Paul Getty Museum, Los Angeles 2016.

Lux 2020
Sebastian Lux, "Edward Steichen: Intuition und Konzept," in Kaufbeuren 2020, 46–61.

Madrid 2019
The Impressionists and Photography, exh. cat., Museo Nacional Thyssen-Bornemisza, Madrid 2019.

Marien 1997
Mary Warner Marien, *Photography and Its Critics: A Cultural History, 1839–1900,* Cambridge 1997.

Maskell/Demachy 1897
Alfred Maskell and Robert Demachy, *Photo-Aquatint or the Gum-Bichromate Process: A Practical Treatise on a New Process of Printing in Pigment Especially Suitable for Pictorial Workers,* London 1897.

Massen 2012
Ernst Massen, *Londe—Paris: Drei Beiträge zur Fotogeschichte,* Cologne 2012.

Matthies-Masuren 1903
Fritz Matthies-Masuren, *Gummidrucke von Hugo Henneberg, Wien, Heinrich Kühn, Innsbruck, und Hans Watzek, Wien,* Halle an der Saale 1903.

Matthies-Masuren 1907
Fritz Matthies-Masuren, *Künstlerische Photographie: Entwicklung und Einfluss in Deutschland,* Berlin 1907.

McAuliffe 2020
Mary Sperling McAuliffe, *Paris, City of Dreams: Napoleon III, Baron Haussmann, and the Creation of Paris,* Lanham 2020.

McCauley 1994
Elizabeth Anne McCauley, *Industrial Madness: Commercial Photography in Paris, 1848–1871,* New Haven 1994.

McCauley 1997
Elizabeth Anne McCauley, "Les Frères Aguado, photographes amateurs à la cour du Second Empire," in *Olympe Aguado (1827–1894): Photographe,* exh. cat., Musées de Strasbourg, 1997, 51–88.

McElhone 2020
John McElhone, "The Evolution of Salted Paper Printing during the 1850s: Published Recipes," in *Journal of the American Institute for Conservation* 59,34 (October 1, 2020), 211–17.

Mebes 1911
Albert Mebes, *Farbenphotographie mit Farbrasterplatten: Theorie und Praxis der Autochrom-, Thames-, Omnicolore-, Aurora-, Dioptichrom-Platte und des deutschen Farbenfilms,* Bunzlau 1911.

Meier 2017
Auf der Suche nach dem fotografischen Unikat: Zwischen analoger und digitaler Reproduktion, ed. Marco Meier, Zurich 2017.

Mellot 1993
Philippe Mellot, *Paris, sens dessus-dessous: Marville et Nadar photographies 1852–1870,* Paris 1993.

Minneapolis 2008
Peter Henry Emerson and American Naturalistic Photography, exh. cat., Minneapolis Institute of Art, 2008.

Moholy-Nagy 1927
László Moholy-Nagy, *Malerei, Fotografie, Film,* Munich 1927.

Molderings 2007
Herbert Molderings, *Die Moderne der Fotografie: Aufsätze und Essays,* Hamburg 2007.

de Mondenard 2002
Anne de Mondenard, *La Mission héliographique: Cinq photographes parcourent la France en 1851,* Paris 2002.

Munich 1996
Corot, Courbet und die Schule von Barbizon, exh. cat., Haus der Kunst, Munich 1996.

Munich 2004
Eine neue Kunst? Eine andere Natur! Fotografie und Malerei im 19. Jahrhundert, exh. cat., Kunsthalle der Hypo-Kulturstiftung, Munich 2004.

Munich 2011
IndustrieZEIT: Fotografien 1845–2010, exh. cat., Münchner Stadtmuseum, Munich 2011.

Munich 2017
Adolphe Braun: Ein europäisches Photographie-Unternehmen und die Bildkünste im 19. Jahrhundert, exh. cat., Münchner Stadtmuseum, Munich 2017.

Munich 2020
Vorbilder/Nachbilder: Die fotografische Lehrsammlung der Universität der Künste Berlin 1850–1930, exh. cat., Münchner Stadtmuseum, Munich 2020.

Nadar 2015
Félix Nadar, *When I Was a Photographer* [1900], trans. Eduardo Cadava and Liana Theodoratou, Cambridge, MA 2015.

Nesbit 1992
Molly Nesbit, *Atget's Seven Albums,* New Haven 1992.

Newhall/Doty 1962
Beaumont Newhall and Robert Doty, "The Value of Photography to the Artist, 1839," in *Image* 11,6 (1962), 25–28.

Newhall 1988
Beaumont Newhall, *The History of Photography,* New York 1988 [1937].

Newhall 1975
Nancy Wynne Newhall, *P. H. Emerson: The Fight for Photography as Fine Art,* Millerton, NY 1975.

New York 1937
Photography 1839–1937, exh. cat., The Metropolitan Museum of Art, New York 1937.

New York 1963
The Photographs of Jacques Henri Lartigue, exh. cat., The Museum of Modern Art, New York 1963.

New York 1994
The Photographs of Édouard Baldus: Landscapes and Monuments of France, exh. cat., The Metropolitan Museum of Art, New York 1994.

New York 1996
Eugène Cuvelier: Photographer in the Circle of Corot, exh. cat., The Metropolitan Museum of Art, New York 1996.

New York 2007
An Important Collection of Photographs by Eugène and Adalbert Cuvelier, auction catalog, Sotheby's, New York 2007.

New York 2012
Heinrich Kuehn and His American Circle: Alfred Stieglitz and Edward Steichen, exh. cat., Neue Galerie, New York 2012.

Nuremberg 2018
Licht und Leinwand: Fotografie und Malerei im 19. Jahrhundert, exh. cat., Germanisches Nationalmuseum, Nuremberg 2018.

Osmond 2013
Joan Osmond, *Victor Albert Prout: A Mid-Victorian Photographer (1835–1877),* London 2013.

Paris 1955
Un siècle de vision nouvelle, exh. cat., Bibliothèque nationale de France, Paris 1955.

Paris 1984
Atget, Géniaux, Vert: Petits metiers et types parisiens vers 1900, exh. cat., Musée Carnavalet, Paris 1984.

Paris 1986a
Henri Le Secq, Photographe de 1850 à 1860: Catalogue raisonné de la collection de la Bibliothèque des Arts Décoratifs, exh. cat., Musée des arts décoratifs, Paris 1986.

Paris 1986b
Les Paysages des impressionnistes, XIXe siècle, exh. cat., Musée d'Orsay, Paris 1986.

Paris 1991a
Les Chefs-d'œuvre de la photographie dans les collections de l'École des beaux-arts, exh. cat., École nationale supérieure des beaux-arts, Paris 1991.

Paris 1991b
Les Photographes de Barbizon: La Forêt de Fontainebleau, exh. cat., Bibliothèque nationale de France, Paris 1991.

Paris 1991c
Paris—Haussmann: "Le Pari d'Haussmann," exh. cat., Pavillon de l'Arsenal, Paris 1991.

Paris 1993
Le Salon de Photographie: Les Écoles pictorialistes en Europe et aux États-Unis, exh. cat., Musée Rodin, Paris 1993.

Paris 1994
Photographier l'architecture, 1851–1920, exh. cat., Musée national des monuments français, Paris 1994.

Paris 1997
L'Art du nu au XIXe siècle: Le Photographe et son modèle, exh. cat., Bibliothèque nationale de France, Paris 1997.

Paris 2002
Gustave Le Gray, Photographe (1820–1884), exh. cat., Bibliothèque nationale de France, Paris 2002.

Paris 2007a
Eugène Atget: Retrospektive, exh. cat., Bibliothèque nationale de France, Paris 2007.

Paris 2007b
Edward Steichen: Ein Leben für die Fotografie, exh. cat., Jeu de Paume, Paris 2007.

Paris 2008
Delacroix et la photographie, exh. cat., Musée national Eugène-Delacroix, Paris 2008.

Paris 2011
Dans l'intimité des frères: Caillebotte, peintre et photographe, exh. cat., Musée Jacquemart-André, Paris 2011.

Paris 2012
Modernisme ou Modernité: Les Photographes du Cercle Gustave Le Gray (1850–1860), exh. cat., Petit Palais, Paris 2012.

Paris 2015
Who's Afraid of Women Photographers? 1839–1919, exh. cat., Musée de l'Orangerie, Paris 2015.

Paulsen 2016
Svenja Paulsen, "Studien des Ephemeren: Wolken und Wellen," in Bedburg-Hau 2016, 46–53.

Paun 2002
Christopher Paun, *Die Annäherung der Fotografie an die Malerei im Piktoralismus* [sic] *als Strategie zur Anerkennung der Fotografie als Kunst,* PhD diss., Europa-Universität Viadrana, Frankfurt an der Oder 2002, www.paun.de/archiv /piktoralismus.pdf.

Le Pelley Fonteny 2005
Monique Le Pelley Fonteny, *Adolphe et Georges Giraudon: Une bibliothèque photographique,* Paris 2005.

Pessiot 2020
Guy Pessiot, "Découvertes sur Mme Breton, la première femme française photographe," in *Études normandes* 16 (December 2020), 74–78.

Peters 1979
Ursula Peters, *Stilgeschichte der Fotografie in Deutschland, 1839–1900,* Cologne 1979.

Philadelphia 2005
Looking at Atget, exh. cat., Philadelphia Museum of Art, 2005.

Plumpe 1990
Gerhard Plumpe, *Der tote Blick: Zum Diskurs der Photographie in der Zeit des Realismus,* Munich 1990.

Pohlmann 1995
Ulrich Pohlmann, "Der Traum von Schönheit—das Wahre ist schön, das Schöne wahr: Fotografie und Symbolismus 1890–1914," in *Fotogeschichte* 15,58 (1995), 3–26.

Pohlmann 1996
Ulrich Pohlmann, "Barbizon und die Photographie," in Munich 1996, 403–16.

Pohlmann 2012
Ulrich Pohlmann, "Alles wie durch einen Zauberschlag gebannt": Die Darstellung des Straßenlebens in Fotografien des 19. Jahrhunderts," in Frankfurt am Main 2012a, 138–51.

Pohlmann 2016a
Ulrich Pohlmann, "Eine andere Natur oder Arsenale der Erinnerung: Die fotografische Künstlerstudie im 19. Jahrhundert," in Bedburg-Hau 2016, 6–13.

Pohlmann 2016b
Ulrich Pohlmann, "Fotografische Exkursionen im Wald von Fontainebleau," in Bedburg-Hau 2016, 14–45.

Pohlmann 2019
Ulrich Pohlmann, "Glühendes Eis: Malerei und Fotografie der 20er Jahre im künstlerischen Dialog," in Hamburg 2019, 10–21.

Poivert 1992
Michel Poivert, *Le Pictorialisme en France,* Paris 1992.

Pollack 1962
Peter Pollack, *Die Welt der Photographie: Von den Anfängen bis zur Gegenwart,* Berlin 1962.

Pomèrade/Grishin/Canguilhem 2005
André Giroux, ed. Vincent Pomèrade, Alexander Grishin, and Denis Canguilhem, London 2005.

Potsdam 2017
Impressionism: The Art of Landscape, exh. cat., Museum Barberini, Potsdam 2017.

Princeton 1994
Pictorial Effect, Naturalistic Vision: The Photographs and Theories of Henry Peach Robinson and Peter Henry Emerson, exh. cat., Princeton University Art Museum, 1994.

Providence 2000
Image and Enterprise: The Photographs of Adolphe Braun, exh. cat., RISD Museum, Rhode Island School of Design, Providence 2000.

Raser 2015
Timothy Bell Raser, *Baudelaire and Photography: Finding the Painter of Modern Life,* Cambridge 2015.

Raupp 1889
Karl Raupp, "Die Photographie in der modernen Kunst," in *Die Kunst für Alle: Malerei, Plastik, Graphik, Architektur* 21 (August 21, 1889), 326.

Rennes 2005
Impressionist Camera: Pictorial Photography in Europe, 1888–1918, exh. cat., Musée des beaux-arts, Rennes 2005.

Rice 1997
Shelley Rice, *Parisian Views,* Cambridge, MA 1997.

Rittaud-Hutinet 1985
Jacques Rittaud-Hutinet, *Le Cinéma des origins: Les Frères Lumière et leurs opérateurs,* Seyssel 1985.

Rivière 2011
Henri Rivière, *Paysages bretons, études de vagues,* Paris 2011.

Robinson 1886
Henry P. Robinson, *Der malerische Effect in der Photographie als Anleitung zur Composition und Behandlung des Lichtes in Photographien,* Halle an der Saale 1886.

Roth 2001
The Book of 101 Books: Seminal Photographic Books of the Twentieth Century, ed. Andrew Roth, New York 2001.

Rouen 2013
Éblouissants reflets: Cent chefs-d'œuvre impressionistes, exh. cat., Musée des beaux-arts de Rouen, 2013.

Rouen 2020
Antonin Personnaz, photographe impressioniste, exh. cat., Musée des beaux-arts de Rouen, 2020.

Rouillé 1989
André Rouillé, *La Photographie en France: Textes et controverses; Une anthologie, 1816–1871,* Paris 1989.

Rubin 2008
James H. Rubin, *Impressionism and the Modern Landscape: Productivity, Technology and Urbanization from Manet to Van Gogh,* Berkeley 2008.

Rüter 2014
Ulrich Rüter, "'Die denkbar größte Freiheit der Bildgestaltung': Der Fotograf Heinrich Kühn," in *Von Liebermann bis Nolde: Impressionismus in Deutschland auf Papier,* exh. cat., Altes Rathaus, Ingelheim 2014, 180–93.

Saalman 1971
Howard Saalman, *Haussmann: Paris Transformed,* New York 1971.

Sachsse 2003
Rolf Sachsse, *Fotografie: Vom technischen Bildmittel zur Krise der Repräsentation,* Cologne 2003.

Sagner 2012
Karin Sagner, "Gustave Caillebotte: Ein Impressionist und die Fotografie," in Frankfurt am Main 2012a, 16–33.

San Diego 2000
The Model Wife: Photography by Baron Adolph De Meyer, Alfred Stieglitz, Edward Weston, Harry Callahan, Emmet Gowin, Lee Friedlander, Masahisa Fukase, Seiichi Furuya, Nicholas Nixon, exh. cat., Museum of Photographic Arts, San Diego 2000.

San Francisco 1999
The Artist and the Camera: Degas to Picasso, exh. cat., San Francisco Museum of Art 1999.

Scharf 1968
Aaron Scharf, *Art and Photography,* London 1968.

Scharf 1976
Aaron Scharf, *Pioneers of Photography: An Album of Pictures and Words,* New York 1976.

Schasler 1865
Max Schasler, "Die Photographie in ihrer Beziehung zu den bildenden Künsten," in *Die Dioskuren: Deutsche Kunst-Zeitung* 10,26 (1865), 221–23; 10,27 (1865), 229–30.

Scheutle 2016
Rudolf Scheutle, "Stereofotografien von Adolphe Braun," in Bedburg-Hau 2016, 76–79.

Schnelle-Schneider 1990
Marlene Schnelle-Schneider, *Photographie und Wahrnehmung am Beispiel der Bewegungsdarstellung im 19. Jahrhundert,* Marburg 1990.

Schögl 2002
Uwe Schögl, "Heinrich Kühn und die Farbfotografie," in *Im Blickpunkt: Die Fotosammlung der Österreichischen Nationalbibliothek,* exh. cat., Österreichische Nationalbibliothek, Vienna 2002, 114–35.

Schögl 2014
Uwe Schögl, "Heinrich Kühn und die Erfindung der künstlerischen Farbfotografie," in Tirol 2014, 18–37.

Schwarz 2006
Heinrich Schwarz, *Techniken des Sehens—vor und nach der Fotografie: Ausgewählte Schriften 1929–1966,* ed. Anselm Wagner, Salzburg 2006.

Smith 1999
Joel Smith, *Edward Steichen: The Early Years,* Princeton 1999.

Smith 2010
Graham Smith, "The Lens of Impressionism: Painting and Photography on the Normandy Coast," in *History of Photography* 32,2 (2010), 193–99.

Sontag 1977
Susan Sontag, *On Photography,* London 1977.

Sramek 2013
Peter Sramek, *Piercing Time: Paris after Marville and Atget,* Bristol 2013.

Stiegler 2001
Bernd Stiegler, *Philologie des Auges: Die photographische Entdeckung der Welt im 19. Jahrhundert,* Munich 2001.

Stiegler 2006a
Bernd Stiegler, *Theoriegeschichte der Photographie,* Munich 2006.

Stiegler 2006b
Bernd Stiegler, *Bilder der Photographie: Ein Album photographischer Metaphern,* Frankfurt am Main 2006.

Stiegler 2012a
Das subjektive Bild: Texte zur Kunstphotographie um 1900, ed. Bernd Stiegler, Paderborn et al. 2012.

Stiegler 2012b
Robert Demachy, "Die künstlerische Photographie in Frankreich," in Stiegler 2012a, 91–108.

Stiegler 2020a
Bernd Stiegler, "Nach der Natur: Die Études d'après nature," in Munich 2020, 68–125.

Stiegler 2020b
Bernd Stiegler, "Überall Bilder sehen: Das Wiener Trifolium Heinrich Kühn, Hugo Henneberg und Hans Watzek," in Kaufbeuren 2020, 130–49.

Stieglitz 1997
Alfred Stieglitz, *Camera Work: The Complete Illustrations 1903–1917,* Cologne 1997.

Strasbourg 1997
Olympe Aguado (1827–1894): Photographe, exh. cat., Musées de Strasbourg, 1997.

Stuttgart 1989
Photo-Kunst: Arbeiten aus 150 Jahren; Du XXième au XIXième siècle, aller et retour, exh. cat., Staatsgalerie Stuttgart, 1989.

Stuttgart 1997
Eugène Cuvelier, exh. cat., Staatsgalerie Stuttgart, 1997.

Thürlemann/Stiegler 2011a
Felix Thürlemann and Bernd Stiegler, "H. P. Robinson vs. P. H. Emerson: Grenzen und Möglichkeiten der Photographie als Kunst," in Konstanz 2011, 7–16.

Thürlemann/Stiegler 2011b
Felix Thürlemann and Bernd Stiegler, "August Kotzsch: Vom Einfangen des Lebensraumes," in Konstanz 2011, 17–28.

Tirol 2014
Das bedrohte Paradies: Heinrich Kühn fotografiert in Farbe, exh. cat., Landesmuseum Schloss Tirol, Tirol 2014.

Vancouver 2008
Truth Beauty: Pictorialism and the Photograph as Art, 1845–1945, exh. cat., Vancouver Art Gallery, 2008.

Varnedoe 1980
Kirk Varnedoe, "The Artifice of Candor: Impressionism and Photography Reconsidered," in *Art in America* 68 (January 1980), 66–78.

Vienna 2003
The Eye and the Camera: The Albertina Collection of Photographs, exh. cat., Albertina, Vienna 2003.

Vienna 2006
Inkunabeln einer neuen Zeit: Pioniere der Daguerreotypie in Österreich, 1839–1850, exh. cat., Albertina, Vienna 2006.

Vienna 2010
Heinrich Kühn: Die vollkommene Fotografie, exh. cat., Albertina, Vienna 2010.

Vienna 2016
Inspiration Fotografie: Von Makart bis Klimt; Eine Materiliensammlung, exh. cat., Orangerie des Belvedere, Vienna 2016.

Vogel 1878
Hermann Wilhelm Vogel, *Lehrbuch der Photographie,* Berlin 1878.

Vogel 1883
Hermann Wilhelm Vogel, *Die chemische Wirkung des Lichts und die Photographie,* Leipzig 1883.

Vogel 1885
Hermann Wilhelm Vogel, *Die Photographie farbiger Gegenstände in den richtigen Tonverhältnissen,* Berlin 1885.

Wagner 1996
Monika Wagner, "Bewegte Bilder und mobile Blicke: Darstellungsstrategien in der Malerei des neunzehnten Jahrhunderts," in *Die Mobilisierung des Sehens: Zur Vor- und Frühgeschichte des Films in der Literatur und Kunst,* ed. Harro Segeberg, Munich 1996, 169–88.

Warstat 1913
Willi Warstat, *Die künstlerische Photographie: Ihre Entwicklung, ihre Probleme, ihre Bedeutung,* Leipzig 1913.

Washington 2000
Modern Art and America: Alfred Stieglitz and His New York Galleries, exh. cat., National Gallery of Art, Washington, DC 2000.

Washington 2008
In the Forest of Fontainebleau: Painters and Photographers from Corot to Monet, exh. cat., National Gallery of Art, Washington, DC 2008.

Washington 2013
Charles Marville: Photographer of Paris, exh. cat., National Gallery of Art, Washington, DC 2013.

Washington 2015
Gustave Caillebotte: The Painter's Eye, exh. cat., National Gallery of Art, Washington, DC 2015.

Weaver 1986
Mike Weaver, *Alvin Langdon Coburn, Symbolist Photographer, 1882–1966: Beyond the Craft,* New York 1986.

Wey 1851
Francis Wey, "De l'influence de l'héliographie sur les beaux-arts," in *La Lumière* (February 9, 1851), 2–3.

Wood 1993
John Wood, *The Art of the Autochrome: The Birth of Color Photography,* Iowa City 1993.

Wuppertal 2007
Abenteuer Barbizon: Von Corot bis Monet; Landschaft, Malerei und Fotografie, exh. cat., Von der Heydt-Museum, Wuppertal 2007.

Zurich 1963
Pioniere der Photographie: Edward Steichen, Charles Nègre, exh. cat., Kunstgewerbemuseum Zürich 1963.

Zurich 1977
Malerei und Photographie im Dialog: Von 1840 bis heute, exh. cat., Kunsthaus Zürich 1977.

Image Credits

© For works by Heinrich Beck:
Estate Heinrich Beck

© For works by Alvin Langdon Coburn:
The Universal Order

© For works by Viktor Knollmüller:
Estate Viktor Knollmüller

© For works by Jacques Henri Lartigue:
Ministère de la Culture (France),
MAP-AAJHL

© For works by Edward Steichen:
VG Bild-Kunst, Bonn 2022

© For works by Gustav Eduard Bernhard
Trinks: Estate Gustav Eduard Bernhard
Trinks

akg-images, Berlin: p. 13, fig. 6 (De Agostini/
Biblioteca Ambrosiana); p. 29, fig. 8
(Liszt Collection); p. 35, fig. 2; p. 39, fig. 6
(Science Source); p. 39, fig. 7 (British
Library/Science Photo Library); p. 49, fig.
5 (Erich Lessing); p. 50, fig. 8; p. 260, fig. 11
(Heritage Images/Fine Art Images)

© Céline, Aeneas, Heiner Bastian, Berlin:
cats. 6–10, 14

bpk, Berlin: p. 13, figs. 4, 5 (adoc-photos);
p. 17, figs. 12 (Los Angeles Museum of
Art/Art Resource, NY/Edward Steichen);
p. 22, fig. 1 (The Trustees of the British
Museum); p. 22, fig. 2 (Victoria and Albert
Museum, London); p. 25, fig. 3, p. 36, fig. 3,
p. 49, fig. 7 (RMN—Grand Palais/Hervé
Lewandowski); p. 25, fig. 4 (RMN—Grand
Palais/Charles Desavary); p. 26, fig. 5
(De Agostini/New Picture Library); p. 26,
fig. 6 (Victoria and Albert Museum, London/
André Giroux); p. 29, fig. 7 (RMN—Grand
Palais/Gérard Blot); p. 30, fig. 10 (The
Metropolitan Museum of Art); p. 35, fig. 1
(Coll. Ph. Doublet/adoc-photos); p. 45,
fig. 1, p. 46, fig. 4, p. 49, fig. 6, p. 260, fig. 9
(RMN—Grand Palais/Patrice Schmidt);
p. 56, fig. 2, cat. 141 (The Metropolitan
Museum of Art/Heinrich Kühn); p. 59, fig. 4
(Kunstbibliothek, SMB/Hugo Henneberg);
p. 69, fig. 3 (Hamburger Kunsthalle);
p. 261, fig. 12 (The Art Institute of Chicago/
Art Resource, NY); p. 261, fig. 13 (RMN—
Grand Palais/Stéphane Maréchalle); cat. 1
(RMN—Grand Palais/Louis Alphonse
Davanne); cat. 4 (RMN—Grand Palais,
Patrice Schmidt/Arthur Da Cunha);
cat. 18 (RMN—Grand Palais/Albert
Londe); cats. 62, 85 (Staatsgalerie
Stuttgart/Eugène Cuvelier); cat. 72
(RMN—Grand Palais, Patrice Schmidt/
Achille Louis Bonnuit); cats. 74, 75

(RMN—Grand Palais/Charles Aubry); cat.
81 (RMN—Grand Palais/Vicomte Joseph
de Vigier); cats. 87, 90 (Staatsgalerie
Stuttgart/Peter Henry Emerson); cat. 100
(RMN—Grand Palais, Alexis Brandt/
Peter Henry Emerson); cat. 142 (bpk/
RMN—Grand Palais, Hervé Lewandowski/
Heinrich Kühn); cat. 143 (RMN—Grand
Palais/Étienne Clémentel)

Bridgeman Images, Berlin: p. 69, fig. 2

© Kicken Berlin: cat. 126

Staatliche Museen zu Berlin, Kunstbibliothek
(© Photo: Dietmar Katz): cats. 92, 94, 106,
114, 117, 122

Universitat der Kunste Berlin (© Photo:
Markus Hilbich): cats. 29, 54, 82

Overbeck-Museum, Bremen: p. 71, fig. 4

Kupferstich-Kabinett, Staatliche Kunstsammlungen Dresden (© Photo: Herbert
Boswank): cat. 76

© Museum Folkwang, Essen/ARTOTHEK:
cats. 43, 103, 111

© Museum für Kunst und Gewerbe Hamburg,
Sammlung Fotografie und neue Medien:
p. 70, figs. 5, 6; cats. 91, 95, 97, 102, 104,
105, 116, 119, 123, 125

© Auer Photo Foundation, Hermance: cat.
146

Rheinisches Bildarchiv, Cologne: p. 17, fig. 10
(© rba c021024)

© Universitätsbibliothek Marburg—Dr. Rolf
H. Krauss-Forschungsbibliothek /
Deutsches Dokumentationszentrum
für Kunstgeschichte—Bildarchiv Foto
Marburg: cat. 89

Collections de la Bibliothèque de l'École
nationale des Ponts et Chaussées,
Marne-la-Vallée (© École nationale des
Ponts et Chaussées): cats. 44–47

Münchner Stadtmuseum, Munich (© Münchner
Stadtmuseum, Sammlung Fotografie):
p. 10, figs. 1–3; p. 14, figs. 7–9; p. 14, fig. 10;
p. 17, fig. 11; cats. 3, 20–23, 26, 34–38, 48,
60, 65, 66, 68–70, 73, 83, 93, 101, 145, 147

© Dietmar Siegert Collection, Photo:
Christian Schmieder: cats. 12, 40, 49, 58,
59, 61, 63, 71, 77, 86, 88, 127, 128

Nasjonalmuseet, Oslo: p. 36, fig. 5

© Bibliothèque historique de la Ville de Paris:
p. 258, fig. 8; cats. 27, 28

© Collection Serge Kakou, Paris:
cats. 30–33, 39, 41, 55, 84, 96

© Musée des Arts Décoratifs, Paris:
cats. 50–53

© Société française de photographie, Paris:
p. 50, fig. 9; cats. 2, 13, 15, 16, 19, 42, 64,
67, 78, 80, 98, 99, 107–09, 121, 124, 129–
38, 144, 148

© Mayer Collection, Stuttgart: cats. 56, 57

Musée de Beaux-Arts de Troyes (© Carole
Bell, Ville de Troyes): cats. 5, 11

Albertina, Vienna: cat. 17 (© Inv. Foto
GLV2000/11277); cat. 24 (© Inv. Foto
GLV2000/11628); cat. 25 (© Inv. Foto
GLV2000/11608); cat. 79 (© Albertina
Wien, Inv. Foto GLV2004/16),

© Photoinstitut Bonartes, Vienna: p. 56, fig. 1;
p. 59, fig. 6; p. 60, fig. 8; cats. 110, 113, 115,
118, 120

Private collection, Ingelheim: cat. 112
(© Grisebach GmbH)

Österreichische Nationalbibliothek, Vienna:
p. 59, fig. 5; p. 60, fig. 7; p. 63, figs. 9–11;
p. 64, fig. 12; p. 64, fig. 13; cats. 139, 140
(© ÖNB/Kühn)

Von der Heydt-Museum, Wuppertal: p. 56,
fig. 3; p. 261, fig. 4

Wikimedia Commons Public Domain: p. 30,
fig. 9 (Murauchi Art Museum); p. 39, fig. 8;
p. 46, fig. 3; p. 50, fig. 10; p. 261, fig. 7

Portrait photographs in the artist biographies
were provided by:

akg-images, Berlin: Aguado (Coll. B. Garrett);
Kayser (Universal Images Group);
Lumière, Stieglitz (© Edward Steichen/VG
Bild-Kunst)

Alamy: Coburn

bpk-images, Berlin: Bonnuit (RMN—Grand
Palais/Patrice Schmidt); Steichen
(Berlon/The Art Institute of Chicago/Art
Resource, NY/Edward Steichen)

Wikimedia Commons Public Domain:
Baldus, Blanquart-Evrard, Braun,
Clémentel, Eckert, Eickemeyer, Emerson,
Hannon, Jacobsen, Kotzsch, Marville,
De Meyer, Scholz, Le Secq, Vogel

The Art of the Photogravure, Mark Katzman:
Davanne

Société française de photographie, Paris:
Demachy, Gaillard, Le Gray, Puyo

Österreichische Nationalbibliothek, Vienna:
Kühn

Münchner Stadtmuseum: Prout, Wortley

Albertina, Vienna: Robinson

Jacques Henri Lartigue, *L'album d'une vie /
A Life's Diary,* exh. cat., Centre Pompidou,
Paris 2003, back cover: Lartigue

One illustration was taken from the following
publication: Arsène Houssaye, *Voyage à
ma fenêtre,* Paris 1851, n.p.; p. 36, fig. 4

Detail photos have been used on the following pages: p. 45, fig. 2; p. 50, fig. 9

Every effort has been made to trace the
copyright holders and obtain permission
to reproduce material. Please contact us
with any enquiries or any information
relating to images or copyright holders.

The assertion of claims according to § 60h
UrhG for the reproduction of pictures of
the exhibitions/existing works has been
carried out by VG Bild-Kunst.

Authors

Monika Faber, art historian, director of the Photoinstitut Bonartes in Vienna since 2011; previously chief curator of photography at the Albertina in Vienna; curator at mumok—Museum moderner Kunst Stiftung Ludwig in Vienna from 1979 to 1999; author and editor of numerous publications on the history of photography including *Das Innere der Sicht: Surrealistische Fotografie der 30er und 40er Jahre* (1989); *Die Frau, wie Du sie willst: Glamour, Kult und korrigierte Körper* (1998); *The Eye and the Camera: The Albertina Collection of Photographs* (2003); *Portraits of an Age: Photography in Germany and Austria, 1900–1938* (2005); *Heinrich Kuehn and His American Circle* (2012); and *Photo, Politics, Austria* (2018).

Dominique de Font-Réaulx, general curator at the Musée du Louvre, director of mediation and cultural programs at the Louvre since 2018; editor-in-chief of the journal *Histoire de l'art,* chair of the art center Le Point du Jour in Cherbourg, teaching activity at the Institut d'études politiques de Paris; director of the Musée national Eugène-Delacroix in Paris from 2013 to 2018, previously curator of the photography collection at the Musée d'Orsay; curator of numerous exhibitions including *Le Daguerreotype français, un objet photographique* (2003) and *Jean-Léon Gerôme* (2010); numerous publications on photography and painting including *Painting and Photography 1839–1914* (2012; 2nd ed. 2020).

Matthias Krüger, art historian, lecturer at the Ludwig-Maximilians-Universität (LMU) in Munich since 2019, previously interim professor at the Universität Hamburg, the Goethe-Universität Frankfurt am Main, and the LMU, as well as visiting professor at the Università Ca' Foscari in Venice and the Universität Graz; PhD in 2004 with dissertation on impasto painting as seen in French art criticism between 1850 and 1890 (2007); habilitation in 2019 at the LMU with postdoctoral thesis on local color in regionalist and exoticist painting of the nineteenth and twentieth centuries; numerous publications on artistic techniques, materials, and tools as well as art theory and criticism; editor of *Die Biologie der Kreativität: Ein produktionsästhetisches Denkmodell in der Moderne* (2013) and *Pro domo: Kunstgeschichte in eigener Sache* (with Léa Kuhn and Ulrich Pfisterer, 2021).

Miriam Leimer (née Häßler), art historian in Zurich; studied art history and history in Münster and Hamburg; assistant curator at the Bucerius Kunst Forum in Hamburg from 2012 to 2014, where she collaborated on the exhibitions *Rodchenko: A New Era* (2013) and *Mondrian: Colour* (2014); research assistant at the Museum für Kunst und Gewerbe in Hamburg from 2014 to 2016 and the Kunsthalle in Hamburg from 2016 to 2017; research fellowships at the Saint Petersburg State University in 2015 and 2016; publications on nineteenth- and twentieth-century Russian art and classic modernism, including contributions to the exhibition catalogs *From Hopper to Rothko: America's Road to Modern Art* (2017) and *Max Beckmann: The World as a Stage* (2018) at the Museum Barberini in Potsdam; currently completing her dissertation on the artistic consequences and political implications of the *Erste Russische Kunstausstellung* in Berlin in 1922.

Ulrich Pohlmann, art historian, director of the photography collection at the Münchner Stadtmuseum in Munich since 1991; numerous publications on the history of photography collections and the reciprocal relationship between photography and painting in the nineteenth century; curator of numerous exhibitions on photography, most recently *Adolphe Braun: Ein europäisches Photographie-Unternehmen und die Bildkünste im 19. Jahrhundert* (2017); *Paragons / Afterimages: Photographs from the Berlin University of the Arts, 1850–1930* (2020); *Modern Times: Industrial Themes in Painting and Photography* (2021); international activity as guest curator, including at the Musée d'Orsay in Paris, the Musée des beaux-arts de Montréal, and the Kunstmuseum Den Haag in The Hague.

Christine Rottmeier-Keß, conservator at the Münchner Stadtmuseum in Munich since 1993, is also an independent photography conservator.

Esther Ruelfs, art historian, director of the photography and new media collection at the Museum für Kunst und Gewerbe in Hamburg, where she curated the recent exhibitions *ReVision: Photography at the Museum für Kunst und Gewerbe* (2017); *Make Me Beautiful, Madame d'Ora! Dora Kallmus: Photographer in Vienna and Paris, 1907–1957* (2018); *Amateur Photography: From Bauhaus to Instagram* (2019); previously independent curator, including at the Biennale für aktuelle Fotografie in Mannheim, the Museum Folkwang in Essen, and the Museum der Moderne in Salzburg; PhD in 2009 with dissertation on the photographer Herbert List.

Helene von Saldern, assistant curator at the Museum Barberini in Potsdam since 2021; studied art history and history in Munich and London from 2015 to 2020, with a focus on modern art; master's degree in 2020 with the thesis *The Artist's Presence: Bourgeois Expectations and Pictorial Boundaries in Monet and Caillebotte* on the relationship of masculinity to the bourgeois interior; practical experience at national and international museums including the Peggy Guggenheim Collection in Venice (2019) and auction houses such as Sotheby's in London (2018); as curatorial assistant at the Museum Barberini she is involved in preparations for exhibitions on Edvard Munch and Amedeo Modigliani.

Bernd Stiegler, professor of modern German literature and media at the Universität Konstanz; PhD in 1992, habilitation in 2000; program director for scholarly publications at Suhrkamp Verlag until 2007; research on nineteenth- and twentieth-century German and French literature as well as the theory and history of photography; numerous publications on photography including *Philologie des Auges: Die photographische Entdeckung der Welt im 19. Jahrhundert* (2001); *Theoriegeschichte der Photographie* (2006); *Konstruierte Wirklichkeiten: Die fotografische Montage 1830–1900* (with Felix Thürlemann, 2019); *Der montierte Mensch: Eine Figur der Moderne* (2016); *Nadar: Bilder der Moderne* (2019); and *Meisterwerke der Fotografie* (with Felix Thürlemann, 2011; 2nd expanded ed. 2020).

Daniel Zamani, curator at the Museum Barberini in Potsdam since 2018; PhD in 2017 with dissertation on the interplay of occult and medieval themes in the work of André Breton; coeditor of *Surrealism, Occultism, and Politics: In Search of the Marvellous* (2017) and *Visions of Enchantment: Occultism, Magic and Visual Culture* (2019); served as assistant curator and subsequently as research assistant at the Städel Museum in Frankfurt am Main from 2015 to 2017, where he curated the exhibition *Matisse—Bonnard: Long Live Painting!* (with Felix Krämer, 2017); curated the exhibitions *Color and Light: The Neoimpressionist Henri-Edmond Cross* (2018) and *Monet: Places* (with Ortrud Westheider, 2020) at the Museum Barberini; currently preparing the exhibitions *The Shape of Freedom: International Abstraction after 1945* and *Surrealism and Magic: Enchanted Modernity.*

Colophon

This catalog is published
in conjunction with the exhibition

**A New Art:
Photography and Impressionism**

Museum Barberini, Potsdam
February 12 to May 8, 2022

Von der Heydt-Museum, Wuppertal
October 2, 2022, to January 8, 2023

Editors:
Ortrud Westheider, Michael Philipp, and
Daniel Zamani

Exhibition and Catalog:
Ulrich Pohlmann and Helene von Saldern

Curator, Wuppertal:
Anna Baumberger

Catalog Editing:
Michael Philipp, Marie-Louise Monrad Møller,
and Helene von Saldern

Image Editing:
Anne Barz, Matthias Heitbrink, Marie-Louise
Monrad Møller, and Anna Nolte

Museum Barberini, Potsdam

Director: Ortrud Westheider
Personal Assistant to the Director:
Theresa Büning
Director Finance and Administration:
Claudia Thurow
Personal Assistant to the Director
Finance and Administration: Nadine Müller
Chief Curator: Michael Philipp
Curator: Daniel Zamani
Research Associate (Publications):
Marie-Louise Monrad Møller
Research Associate (Provenance):
Linda Hacka
Research Associate: Julia Nagel
Assistant Curator: Helene von Saldern
Registrars: Anne Barz, Matthias Heitbrink
Press and Communications: Achim Klapp,
Marte Kräher, Esther Knuth, Carolin Stranz
Digitalization and Information Security:
Remigiusz Plath, Stefan Scholze
IT Administrator: Sebastian Semmler
Educational Service: Dorothee Entrup,
Andrea Schmidt
Events: Marie-Christin Hupp, Julia Teller,
Ines Wenzel-Hirschfeld
Guest Management: Jutta Bockhacker,
Frauke Herlyn, Karl Wegmann, Angela Winkler
Accounting and Ticketing: Yvonne Benesch
Office Manager: Sandra Spudy
Head of Building Services: Carsten Loeper
Building Services: Frank Altmann,
Dennis Kokert

In collaboration with:

Conservation: Felicitas Klein, Berlin
Friederike Beseler, Berlin
Exhibition Design: Gunther Maria Kolck,
Hamburg
BrücknerAping, Büro für Gestaltung, Bremen
Museum Shop: Museum Barberini. Der Shop,
Jörg Klambt

Von der Heydt-Museum, Wuppertal

Director: Roland Mönig
Assistant to the Director:
Stefanie Masberg-Falk
Deputy Director: Antje Birthälmer
Curators: Anna Baumberger, Anika Bruns,
Beate Eickhoff, Anna Storm
Assistant Curator: Kateryna Kostiuchenko
Digitalization: Tatjana König
Press and Communications, Marketing:
Marion Meyer
Education: Julia Dürbeck, Karolina Bürger,
Henrike Stein
Registrar/Reproduction and Image Rights:
Sarah Breuer, Bettina Klecha
Conservation: Andreas Iglhaut
Department of Prints and Drawings:
Stefanie Wachmann
Bookbinding: Sindy Brödno
Library: Anne Kessler
Assistant Press and Communications:
Mechthild Küster
Head of Museum Administration and
Service: Nicole Schey
Head of Accounting, Von der Heydt-Museum
gGmbH: Katja Friedmann
Administration and Service:
Yvonne Heunatzki, Monika Ahlbrecht
Guest Management: Jean Oehm
Shipping Department: Zdenka Hardi
Technical Services: Marcel Körn,
Meinhard Mach, Ulrich Schultz
Switchboard: Barbara Drebing, Claudia Heer,
Carsten Hinz
Shift Coordination: Annette Lang,
Rita Potschaski
Front Desk: Annemarie Dämmer
Security Service: Erisen Demirel,
Dina Gradecak, Elke Martini,
Gundula Pellegrini

The exhibition in the
Von der Heydt-Museum is funded by:

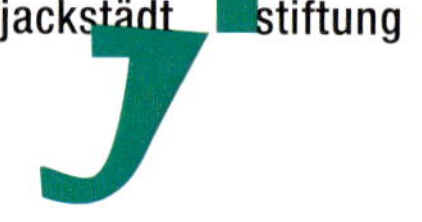

Catalog

© 2022 Barberini. Museen der Hasso
Plattner Foundation gGmbH, Potsdam;
Von der Heydt-Museum, Wuppertal;
authors; and Prestel Verlag,
Munich · London · New York,
a member of Penguin Random House
Verlagsgruppe GmbH
Neumarkter Straße 28
81673 Munich

Editorial Direction, Prestel: Markus Eisen
Graphic Design and Typesetting:
BrücknerAping, Büro für Gestaltung, Bremen
Copyediting: Tas Skorupa, Berlin
Translations: Alexander Booth, Berlin;
Melissa M. Thorson, Jackson
Production Management: Cilly Klotz
Color Separations: Reproline Genceller,
Munich
Printing and Binding: Printer Trento, Trento
Typeface: Neue Haas Grotesk, Lexicon No2 A
Paper: Garda Matt Ultra, 150 g/m^2

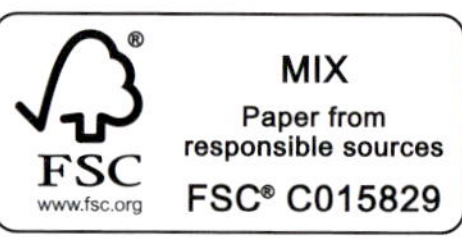

Penguin Random House Verlagsgruppe
FSC® N001967

Printed in Italy

With respect to links in the book, Penguin
Random House Verlagsgruppe expressly
notes that no illegal content was discernible
on the linked sites at the time the links were
created. The publisher has no influence
at all over the current and future design,
content, or authorship of the linked sites.
For this reason the Penguin Random House
Verlagsgruppe expressly disassociates
itself from all content on linked sites that has
been altered since the link was created and
assumes no liability for such content.

Library of Congress Control
Number:
2022930016

A CIP catalog record for this book is
available from the British Library.

ISBN 978-3-7913-7939-5
(German trade edition)
ISBN 978-3-7913-9079-6
(German museum edition)
ISBN 978-3-7913-7940-1
(English trade edition)
ISBN 978-3-7913-9080-2
(English museum edition)

www.prestel.de
www.prestel.com